Barcelona

The Complete **Residents'** Guide

Passionately Publishing...

EXPLORER

Barcelona Explorer 1st Edition   ISBN 13 - 978-9948-03-380-6   ISBN 10 - 9948-03-380-9

Copyright: Explorer Group Ltd 2007
All rights reserved.

Front Cover Photograph: Casa Batlló – Victor Romero

Printed and bound by Emirates Printing Press, Dubai, United Arab Emirates.

Explorer Publishing & Distribution
PO Box 34275, Dubai
United Arab Emirates
Email   info@explorerpublishing.com
Web   www.explorerpublishing.com

Welcome...

Your life in Barcelona has just become a lot simpler. This book is going to help you get to know the city, its people, their customs and more. Becoming a fully fledged resident of Catalonia has never been more enjoyable.

Over the following pages you'll find everything you need to know to make the most of your life in Barcelona, and settle in to one of Europe's most captivating cities. From backstreet markets to finding your dream home, we'll tell you how and where to do it.

Firstly, the **General Information** (p.2) chapter will bring you up to speed with Barcelona's history, geography and customs, and offer suggestions for places to stay and how to get around.

The **Residents** (p.45) chapter is the one for life admin. It will help you decide where to live, with an area by area run down on where is best for families, bohemians or young professionals.

There is also essential information on visas, schools, health care, and all the formalities involved in the big move.

Next comes **Exploring** (p.137), which takes you through Barcelona's varied neighbourhoods, highlighting the beautiful architecture, places of interest, parks, tours and beaches.

Turn to the **Activities** (p.197) section when you are feeling frivolous or you have more time on your hands. These pages tell you the best spas and beauty salons for a good pampering, and where to indulge in hobbies as diverse as castells, flower arranging and sky diving.

For most, the **Shopping** (p.273) chapter will prove invaluable when kitting out your new life. This section will tell you where to go for all you shopping needs, no matter how large or small.

Then, to celebrate all your achievements, turn to the **Going Out** (p.315) chapter for a run down of Barcelona's premier places for eating, drinking and dancing until early morning.

To help you navigate your new home town, we've included a chunky **Maps** (p.373) chapter at the back. You'll notice coloured icons dotted throughout the book; these refer to this chapter, and should help you find the bar, beach, shop or association you're looking for. Turn to the inside back cover for our map of the metro system.

And if you think we have missed something, whether it's somewhere to drink, or a spectacularly talented basket weaving tutor, please let us know.

Go to www.explorerpublishing.com, fill in the Reader Response form, and share the knowledge with your fellow explorers.

The Explorer Team

Explorer's Barcelona

This glorious, cacophonous, rebellious city is one of the most enviable places to live on earth. It can also be a little dazzling. Here are a few things we wouldn't want to miss. Gaudi's flights of fancy at Casa Batlló (p.166), La Pedrera (p.166) Park Güell (p.179) and the Sagrada Familia (p.169) could convince the most detrmined philistine that the built environment can also be art. Then, you can take in the city's natural blessings at Montjuïc (p.159) or from Tibidabo Amusement Park (p.180), the waters at Nova Mar Bella (p.178) or down the coast in Sitges (p.191). Or, for a complete escape, head to the Pyrenees (p.192). But this city really comes alive at night, in the revellery of the Ciutat Vella (try the cocktails at Gimlet on p.352), the swank of Eixample (try Omm Session, p.366) or the alternative scene of Gràcia (head to the Daliesque La Fira, p.354).

Alice Ross Alice moved to Barcelona to learn some Spanish and soak up the city for a couple of months. Three years on, she's finding ever-more obscure corners and writing on all things BCN for local and overseas publications. **Favourite restaurant**: Els Pescadors' terrace on a summer evening (p.335).

Cass Chapman Cass moved from London to Barcelona in 2006 to work as a freelance food and travel writer. She fell in love with the city's eclectic restaurant scene, tiny cobbled alleyways and delightful locals, and continues to write about this glistening city by the sea. **Favourite daytrip:** hiking to the peak of Montserrat mountain from its monastery (p.207).

Emma Buckle Emma was born in South Africa and has been on the move ever since. She settled in Barcelona in 2006, motivated by her passion for foreign languages, different cultures and tapas. When she's not losing herself in the Ciutat Vella, you'll find her doing something active. **Best Barcelona memory**: hiking in La Mola and Aigüestortes National Park (p.218).

Hannah Pennell Hannah moved to Barcelona seven years ago, one of the many benefits of a Catalan boyfriend. She started freelancing for the city's main English-language magazine, *Barcelona Metropolitan*, in 2003, and is now its editor. **Best shop**: the farmers market next to the Boqueria (p.310).

Jennifer Baljko It was castells, the crazy Catalan human tower tradition, which lured Jennifer here. Freelance writing supports her travel habit, and her work has appeared in *Islands, Travelers ' Tales*, the *Christian Science Monitor* and other publications. **Best cultural experience**: speaking Catalan with the locals, and watching their reaction.

Jethro Soutar Jethro got his first taste of Barcelona aged 13, on a school exchange. He returned for the Olympics, then later as a student and finally settled in the city to work on a biography; *Ronaldinho: Football's Flamboyant Maestro*. **Best view**: Turó de la Rovira. City-wide panorama from an abandoned Civil War lookout.

*Having trouble navigating your way around Barcelona? Look no further than the **Barcelona Mini Map**, an indispensable, pocket-sized aid to getting to grips with the city's roads, areas and attractions.*

Julius Purcell With two children and numerous articles on Spanish social and cultural issues to his name, Julius has put his knowledge of the intricacies of the Catalan health and education systems to good use in the Residents section. He also writes regularly for the *Financial Times*. **One Barcelona must-do**: See a correfoc (p.173).

Paul Cannon Having tried just about every barrio in the city, Paul now lives in La Ribera, where he writes short stories and travel articles. He also works for Spanish TV. When the city gets too much, he likes to get lost in the Pyrenees or camp on a clifftop. **Worst thing about Barcelona**: Children with mullets.

*Once settled in Barcelona, you may find waves of family and friends visiting. While you're at work, send them out with the **Barcelona Mini Explorer**, a fantastic visitors' guide.*

Susanna Jacobs Susanna made the move from Nottingham to Barcelona five years ago and has been working as a freelance writer for three. She's a regular contributor to magazines in the city and on the Costa Brava and also writes the occasional book review. **Favourite Catalan dish**: Espinacs a la Catalana (spinach with pine nuts and sultanas).

Thanks...

As well as our star team of authors, whose expert advice and research have been invaluable, many others have contributed to this book. Special thanks go to: María Luisa Albacar-Fracanzani of Turisme de Barcelona; Francesca Hector at *Barcelona Connect*; Grace Carnay for the fact checking, eagle eyes and general diligence; Tracy Fitzgerald for the cutting, writing and creative input; Jo Holden MacDonald and Kaye Holland for the proofing; Katie Drynan for the ad-hoc translation; Joe Evans for the close-up of a beer bottle; Jayde Fernandes for staying awake; Moulin d'Or for the manakish and Anna for the buns.

Where are we exploring next?

- Abu Dhabi
- Amsterdam
- Bahrain
- Barcelona
- Beijing*
- Berlin*
- Boston*
- Brussels*

- Cape Town*
- Dubai
- Dublin
- Geneva
- Hong Kong
- Kuala Lumpur*
- Kuwait
- London

- Los Angeles*
- Moscow*
- New York
- New Zealand
- Oman
- Paris
- Qatar
- San Francisco*

- Shanghai
- Singapore
- Sydney
- Tokyo*
- Vancouver*
- Washington DC*

* Available 2008

Where do you live?

Is your home city missing from our list? If you'd love to see a residents' guide for a location not currently on Explorer's horizon, please email editorial@explorerpublishing.com.

Advertise with Explorer...

If you're interested in advertising with us, please contact sales@explorerpublishing.com.

Make Explorer your very own...

We offer a number of customization options for bulk sales. For more information and discount rates, please contact corporatesales@explorerpublishing.com.

Contract Publishing

Have an idea for a publication or need to revamp your company's marketing material? Contact designlab@explorerpublishing to see how our expert contract publishing team can help.

www.explorerpublishing.com

Life can move pretty fast, so to make sure you can stay up to date with all the latest goings on where you are, we've revamped our website to further enhance your time there, whether long or short.

Keep in the know…

Our Complete Residents' Guides and Mini Visitors' series continue to expand, covering destinations from Amsterdam to New Zealand and beyond. Keep up to date with our latest travels and hot tips by signing up to our monthly newsletter, or browse our products section for info on our current and forthcoming titles.

Make friends and influence people…

…by joining our Communities section. Meet fellow residents in your city, recommend your favourite restaurants, bars, childcare agencies or dentists, and find answers to your questions on daily life, from long-term residents.

Discover new experiences…

Ever thought about living in a different city, or wondered where the locals really go to eat, drink and be merry? Check out our regular features section, or submit your own feature for publication.

Want to find a badminton club, the number for your bank, or maybe just a restaurant for a hot first date?

Check out city info on various destinations around the world in our residents' section – from finding a Pilates class to contact details for international schools in your area, or the best place to buy everything from a spanner set to a Spandau Ballet album, we've got it all covered.

Let us know what you think!

All our information comes from residents; which means you! If we missed out your favourite bar or market stall, or you know of any changes in the law, infrastructure, cost of living or entertainment scene, let us know by using our Feedback form.

CROSS BORDERS
WITHOUT BARRIERS.

Whether you're connecting with family and friends or sending goods for business, you'll find all the help you need to cross borders without barriers at one of our many offices around the world.

www.dhl.com

AMOUAGE

Gold

EAU DE TOILETTE

The most valuable perfume in the world

The world has much to offer.
It's just knowing where to find it.

If you're an American Express® Cardmember, simply visit
americanexpress.com/selects or visit your local homepage, and click on
'offers'. You'll find great offers wherever you are today, all in one place.

selects

THE WORLD OFFERS. WE SELECT. YOU ENJOY.

Contents

Contents

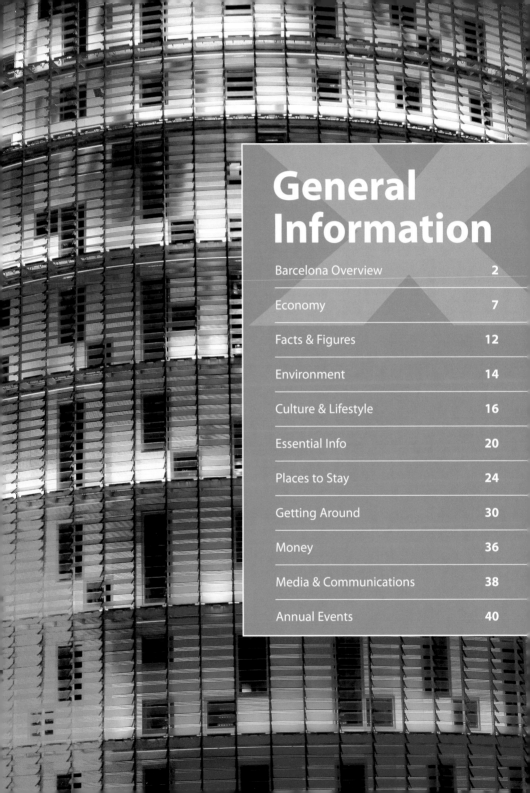

General Information

General Information

Geography

Catalonia is in the north-eastern corner of the Iberian peninsula. It borders France to the north, with the Pyrenees tumbling either side of the national boundary. This impressive mountain range also marks Catalonia's western limits, while the Mediterranean is to the east and the Ebro Delta to the south.

Its capital, Barcelona, is spread across a five kilometre wide plateau by the sea. Two rivers form natural boundaries to its north and south-west; the Besòs and the Llobregat respectively. To the immediate west of the city is the Collserola mountain ridge, whose peak, Tibidabo, is 150m high. Immediately to the city's north are the municipalities of Santa Coloma de Gramanet and Sant Adrià de Besòs, while to the south are L'Hospitalet de Llobregat and Esplugues de Llobregat. In the north-west lie Montcada i Reixac and Sant Cugat del Vallès.

Overall, the city of Barcelona has ten administrative districts; Ciutat Vella, Eixample, Les Corts, Sants-Montjuïc, Horta-Guinardó, Sarrià-Sant Gervasi, Gràcia, Sant Martí, Nou Barris and Sant Andreu. Ciutat Vella, the city's historical centre, envelopes Barri Gòtic, La Ribera, El Raval, La Rambla, Passeig de Gràcia and Rambla de Catalunya. Its nucleus is the well-connected transport hub of Plaça de Catalunya. The upper reaches of Avinguida Diagonal are where the main commercial part of the city can be found.

Barcelona's skyline today is as much about skyscrapers as the spires of medieval basilicas or art deco ballustrades. The glass-panneled Torre Mapfre and Hotel Arts buildings (both 154 metres) rate as the city's tallest, standing side by side on the Vila Olímpica seafront. Dense urban jungle though it is, Barcelona has 68 parks. Lining the streets and squares are more than 150,000 trees, from 140 different species. The most common of these is the Spanish plane tree, which you'll see giving shade to passers-by on La Rambla. At the western limits of the city, along the Collserola ridge, there is a green belt with pine forests, walking and biking trails and spectacular views.

Several smaller hills, such as Putxet (181m), Carmel (267m) and Rovira (261m), are found within the city itself. To the south-east, lying between the old city and the Llobregat delta is another major natural feature; Montjuïc (173m), which has great views of the harbour.

Barcelona also has four and a half kilometres of sand beaches. Lying between Port Vell and Port Olímpic are the two most popular; La Barceloneta and San Sebastia, both more than one kilometre long. North of Port Olìmpic are the cleaner (though only slightly less crowded) beaches of Nova Icària, Bogatell, Mar Bella and Nova Mar Bella (ranging from 400 to 640 metres long), which owe their existence to a big-clean up in preparation for the 1992 Olympic Games.

Factbox

Co-ordinates: 41° 23' North, 2° 9' East
Bordering areas: Santa Coloma de Gramanet; Sant Adrià de Besòs; L'Hospitalet de Llobregat; Esplugues de Llobregat; Montcada i Reixac; Sant Cugat del Vallès
Total land area: 100sqkm
Total coastline: 4.5kms
Highest point: 150m

History

Foundation of the City

Although tribes such as the Laetani originally inhabited the area, the general consensus is that the sea-faring Carthaginians founded Barcelona in around 230 BC.

Romans & Visigoths

When the Romans defeated the Carthaginians, they made a military camp of Mons Taber, today a maze of backstreets between Plaça Sant Jaume and Carrer Ample. Although overshadowed by nearby Tarracon (Tarragona), the capital of the province, the Roman city of Barcino flourished as a market town, eventually establishing its own harbour and coin mint. In the fifth century, Rome crumbled under repeated onslaughts by Barbarian tribes and Barcelona was left to the mercy of the Visigoths, who crossed over the Pyrenees from Gaul. Under Theodoric the Great, the Visigoths (West Goths) united with the Ostrogoths (East Goths) and in 511 ruled most of the peninsula, with Barcelona as their capital.

Short-Lived Moorish Rule

In the early 700s the peninsula was invaded by the Moors. An Islamic dynasty, the Umayadds, took over from the Visigoths. Barcelona was occupied, but not for long enough to have absorbed any lasting impression of Moorish culture. It was liberated in 801 by Louis of Aquitaine and then used as a buffer zone to protect France.

Medieval Prosperity & the Catalan Empire

Despite occasional attacks by Arab pirates and a sacking by al-Mansur in 985, Barcelona's star was on the rise. In 878, independence from Frankish influence was achieved. Guifre El Pelòs, aka Wilfred the Hairy, was the first Barcelonin count to rule an independent Catalonia (878-897). Under Ramon Berenguer III (1082-1131), Catalonia expanded as far north as Nice in France, and Ibiza and Mallorca were captured from the Moors. Catalonia now had an empire, and Barcelona was its capital. Catalonia became united with neighbouring Aragon in 1137, though each region controlled its own affairs. Under Jaume I (1213-76), Valencia was captured. Sardinia, Corsica, Naples, the Roussillon region of south east France, and even Athens were soon added. Trade flourished. Catalan merchants had exclusive rights to gold from the Sudan, and Barcelona was a port to rival Venice and Genoa. During this period, steps were taken to lay the foundations of future democracy. An early system of law, the Usatges de Barcelona, and a city council, the Consell de Cent, were founded. The origins of today's Generalitat can be traced back to a parliament formed in 1282. It was around this time that some of the major

Museu d'Història de Catalunya (p.162)

Rambling On

La Rambla, Las Ramblas or Les Rambles? The pedestrian walkway that runs from Plaça de Catalunya to the Monument a Colom can be a touch confusing. The street commonly known as La Rambla should more accurately be described as Las Ramblas (Les Rambles in Catalan), because its name changes every few hundred feet. At the top is Rambla de Canaletes, while down by Drassanes station is Rambla de Santa Monica. However, for simplicity's sake, we refer to this whole strip simply as La Rambla. Similar walkways in other areas take their full name, such as Rambla del Raval, Rambla del Poblenou and Rambla de Catalunya (the strip that runs up from Plaça de Catalunya to Diagonal).

landmarks of today's Barri Gòtic sprang up, many of them joining old Roman remains. The Palau del Bisbe is one example; you can look at Gothic stained glass windows while strolling through a Roman arcade. La Ribera's Palacio Berenguer d'Aguilar is another, and now houses the Picasso Museum (p.165).

Decline of the Empire

It was in the 14th Century that Barcelona's economy began to falter. The rising naval power of the Ottoman empire left the city bankrupt in 1391. Meanwhile, neigbouring Castile was making astute alliances and growing rich on its wool and corn trade. Following the 1469 alliance with Aragon, Castile granted all overseas trade to Seville and Cadiz. Castile was entering its golden age, while Catalonia was in decline. In an effort to challenge Castilian dominance, in 1640, Catalonia signed the Pact of Ceret with the French. This made it a free republic under the protection of the French king, Louis XIII. In 1659, however, Barcelona was taken by Castilian troops under King John Joseph of Austria. Rosellò, Conflent, Vallespir and part of Cerdanya were annexed to the French.

During the Spanish War of Succession, Catalonia backed the wrong horse; supporting a British-Austrian alliance against the French Bourbon pretender, Felipe. The Austrian Habsburg claim duly dissolved, leaving Catalonia all on its own against Felipe. He triumphed and, installed as the Spanish king, in 1714, set about punishing a defenceless Barcelona.

Once he had sacked the city, Felipe outlawed the Catalan language (by now largely spoken only by the peasantry), declared Catalonia a province of Spain and built a huge fortress, the Cuitadella, to watch over it. Today it is the site of one of Barcelona's loveliest green areas, el Parc de la Ciutadella (p.178).

By the end of the 18th century, Barcelona was leaving feudalism behind and its attentions were turned towards industry and trade with Spain and the 'new world' across the Atlantic. One of the world's first textile-dyeing factories was inaugurated in 1783, and provided 75,000 jobs for Barcelonin workers.

Casa Figueras, on La Rambla (p.146)

The Expansion

Thanks to its cotton industry, 19th century Barcelona enjoyed a revival and became the seat of an autonomous Catalan government. Between 1890 and 1915, the bourgeoisie, growing rich on a tide of industrial production and keen to maximise influence within Spain, financed an adventurous plan of urban growth beyond the old city walls. Called L'Eixample (The Expansion), it was much-needed, as the old city was over-populated and suffering from unhealthy living conditions. Eixample became the playground for a generation of unusually gifted architects who pioneered the *modernista* movement. They included Lluís Domènech i Muntaner, Josep Puig i Cadafalch, Josep Maria Jujol and Antoni Gaudí. Barcelona's *renaixenca*, or renaissance, also saw the resurrection of the Catalan language and the emergence of poets such as Jacint Verdaguer. Enric de Prat de la Riba, meanwhile, became the first president of the Commonwealth of Catalonia, comprising the four provinces of Barcelona, Girona, Tarragona and Lleida.

The International Brigades

During the Civil War (1936-39), 32,000 men from as many as 53 different countries arrived in Barcelona hoping to fight on the Republic's side against Franco's fascists. These new arrivals were banded into international brigades. They were notoriously disorganised, but had many notable recruits, among them left-wing intellectuals and the British writer George Orwell, whose *Homage to Catalonia*, is an engaging account of the struggle.

The General Strike

Through the early 20th century, Barcelona endured similar troubles to those affecting other industrialising nations. Growing disparity in wealth and the competing philosophies of the political left and right began to create social rifts. These were exacerbated by Spain's economic problems during the Great War (1914 - 1918), which caused factories to close and mass unemployment. The capitalist classes feared a Russian-style revolution and so leaned heavily on workers' unions such as the CNT (Confederación Nacional de Trabajo) – many of whose members were blacklisted or even assassinated. Anarchist unionist activity grew as a result, leading to the general strike of 1917, which ended in bitter riots and 33 deaths in Barcelona. Another general strike followed in 1919, when a local hydroelectric plant reduced workers' wages. The Primo de Rivera dictatorship (1923 - 30) banned all organisations and literature related to anarchism, which resulted in anarchists resorting to ever more violent methods. Primo de Rivera, a monarchist, abolished the Catalan commonwealth in 1925. Curiously enough, he was a Catalan himself by birth.

Civil War & Franco

In 1931, Catalonia was again given control over its regional affairs. During the Civil War (1936-1939) Barcelona became the principle seat of Spain's Republican government, the Popular Front. Militarily, government forces were hampered by internecine fighting between socialist, communist and anarchist factions, and disagreements between the different unions these were aligned to. Warfare ravaged the city, with eventual defeat for the Republicans at the hands of General Francisco Franco's right-wing falangists, who were bolstered by German military support. The President of the Generalitat, Lluís Companys, a supporter of the failed Republic, fled to France. When France was invaded by Germany, the Gestapo delivered him back to Spain and he was executed. His last words, spoken in front of the firing squad, were '*visca* (long live) *Catalunya*.'

Installed as dictator, Franco set about 'reincorporating' Catalonia into Spain. This involved public burnings of Catalan literature, the outlawing of Catalan street-names and the prohibition of the language's use in television, radio, the press and the classroom. Outbreaks of violence followed; in 1944, there was an attempted coup by local communists, and throughout the 40s anarchists were responsible for a series of bombings, shootings and assassinations. But these achieved little, and opponents of the regime turned to peaceful public protests instead.

The Olympic Games

On 17 October 1986, Barcelona was granted the 1992 Olympic Games. Ambitious building projects were approved, including the Arata Isozaki-designed Palau Sant Jordi, Roy Lichtenstein's Barcelona Head sculpture at Port Vell and the Juan Carlos I hotel at Les Corts. Barcelona's makeover also included the replenishment of disused areas of what is now Vila Olímpica and its beachfront. The games themselves turned out to be one of the most successful ever. As well as the economic boost created by tourism (£29 million taken during 1992 alone) they provided an injection of civic pride and morale that has sustained Barcelona ever since. Ever since the flame was lit, there's been no looking back.

5

After Franco

On 20 November 1975, General Francisco Franco died. Under the democratically elected government of Adolfo Suarez that followed, Catalonia was granted autonomy, in 1977. The Catalan language was re-introduced to classrooms the following year. The Catalan Parliament held its first elections in 1980, and Jordi Pujol was elected as President of the Generalitat, holding office until 2003. During this time, as Catalonia modernised and opened itself to foreign markets, its economy, culture and language all flourished.

Barcelona Today

Barcelona is a model cosmopolitan city, attracting foreign investment and immigration from other EU countries. Its redevelopment schemes are the envy of Europe and studied worldwide. Its tourism industry is thriving and the city is a hot-bed of industrial design. History has attempted many times to subvert the nature of this amazing city but in the end its character shines through. Barcelona, two millennia old, is in the middle of yet another *renaixenca*.

Barcelona Timeline

230BC	Carthaginians settle in the area
100BC	Roman camp of Mons Taber established
AD400-500	Visigoths invade
711	Barcelona occupied by Moors
801	Louis of Aquitaine and his Frankish forces liberate Barcelona
1162	Catalonia united with Aragon under Alfonso II
1213	Jaume I (The Conqueror) proclaimed King
1220s	Birth of Catalan Gothic style in Barcelona
1298	Construction of the Gothic cathedral begins
1385	Addition of the cloister of Santa Eulalia to the cathedral
1479	Marriage of the Catholic monarchs, Isabella and Fenando, unites Aragon and Castile
1783	Barcelona's population reaches 860,000
1847	Construction of Liceu Theatre begins
1852	Birth of the architect Antoni Gaudi
1873	Abdication of King Amadeo I and declaration of first Spanish Republic
1874	Restoration of Bourbon monarchy with Alfonso XII as king
1893	Birth of surrealist painter and sculptor Joan Miro
1899	Barcelona Football Club is founded by Joan Gamper
1904	Birth of surrealist painter Salvador Dali
1923	A Catalan, Primo de Rivera, becomes Spain's dictator
1929	Universal Exhibition comes to Barcelona. Poble Espanyol is built to host it.
1929	Second Republic of Spain
1930	Catalonia declares autonomy
1936	Spanish Civil War begins
1939	Republican Barcelona falls. End of Spanish Civil War. General Franco takes power
1953	Spain joins the United Nations
1975	Franco dies. Power passes to King Juan Carlos I.
1977	Adolfo Suarez is elected President and grants Catalonia autonomy.
1980	Jordi Puyol elected President of Barcelona's Generalitat.
1992	FC Barcelona win their first European Champions Cup. Barcelona hosts the Olympic Games
1997	Joan Clos becomes Mayor
2003	Pascal Maragall replaces Jordi Pujol as President of the Generalitat
2004	Torre Agbar unveiled in Glòries as part of Poble Nou development
2006	FC Barcelona win their second European Cup. Jordi Hereu becomes mayor. José Montilla Aguilera is voted president

Spain Overview

Spain has the ninth largest economy in the world, according to 2006 figures. On joining the European Union in January 1986, Spain reformed its legislation and was helped to modernise its economy with grants from the European Regional Development Fund. This led to steady GDP growth and a significant reduction in unemployment and inflation. In the early '90s, the economy felt a backlash from the late 80s recession, but recovered during the Aznar administration (1996-2000), thanks to increased private consumption and consumer confidence. The potentially problematic transition from the peseta to the euro, in January 2002, was counterbalanced by increased trade with other European nations.

Spain is currently one of the most prosperous economies within the EU. It has performed consistently well by OECD (Organisation for Economic Co-operation and Development) measures over the last decade. Another encouraging sign is the improvement of Spain's credit rating from AA to AA+, just one lower than European top dog Germany. There are growing concerns, however, that Spain's current consumer boom is unsustainable. The addition of ten new EU members will challenge the economy, as EU funds become more widely distributed. Other worries include how to reduce unemployment, which stood at 8.6% in 2006, and Europe's highest rate of inflation, estimated at 3.8% and rising due to a 150% increase in house prices.

Spanish GDP
GDP ranking: 9th globally
GDP (at PPP): €976 billion
GDP growth: 3.6%
GDP per capita (at PPP): €27,200
GDP by sector: agriculture 3.9%, industry 29.4%, services 66.7%

But, Spain also has the world's second largest tourism industry, which is its main source of income. If part of Spain's tourist appeal lies in its sunny weather, its thriving agriculture is equally attributable to the Mediterranean climate. No country in the world produces more olive oil and only two nations press more wine. Its best known regions are Penedès, La Rioja and Jerez. Spain also tops all other European countries in the farming of lemons and oranges, which is only natural, for it was in the groves of Andalusia that the Moors first introduced the fruits to Europe. Overall, agriculture contributes 3.9% of the country's GDP.

The other primary industries in Spain include textiles, chemicals, metals and metal manufacture, shipbuilding, automobiles and machine tools. Internationally, France, Germany and Portugal are the main purchasers of Spanish goods, while Germany, France and Italy are the main importers of goods to Spain. The main imports include petroleum, iron and steel, transport equipment and consumer goods. But Spain's trade deficit continues to rise; to €8.49 billion at the last count. Only the US has a higher figure.

Leading Industries

Some 64.4% of Spanish workers are in services, 30.1% in industry and 5.3% in agriculture. Telefonica, with more than 550 million customers, is the sixth largest telecommunications company in the world. It has more than 95,000 workers, although cutbacks were forecast and its services are the subject of fierce criticism by European industry watchdogs. Enormous investment in scientific research and development has led to biotechnology becoming a leading industry, growing at the phenomenal rate of 350% between 1998 and 2003, and currently employing more than 151,000 workers. Nationwide, wages range from an average yearly salary of €11,842 for an employee in the services sector, to €49,292 for a company director. A job as a manual labourer in construction or agriculture is likely to earn around €13,474. Wages in Catalonia are typically 5-10% higher.

7

Barcelona Overview

Jordi Pujol, the ex-President of the Generalitat, once likened Catalonia to a locomotive pulling the Spanish economy along without ever controlling its driver. Despite playing second fiddle to Madrid politically, Barcelona does play a vital role in Spain's economy, contributing 14.29% of its overall GDP. It has a large tertiary sector (tourism, services) contributing to more than half of its local economy. There is a reliance on heavy industry (iron, steel, copper), and it is accumulating high technology parks, such as the Barcelona Biomedical Research Park in Vila Olímpica. Another growth sector is the automobile industry; Volkswagen-owned Seat's opening of a new plant in the suburb of Martorell provided 12,000 local jobs. A total of 450,000 cars are manufactured there every year.

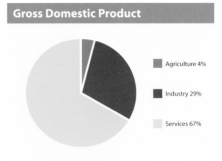

Gross Domestic Product

- Agriculture 4%
- Industry 29%
- Services 67%

Source: Idescat (Catalan Institute of Statistics)

New Developments

Once a dilapidated industrial ghost-town, the district of Poble Nou is getting the kind of make-over its neighbour Vila Olímpica received for the Olympics. This ambitious scheme of regeneration is referred to as 22@Barcelona (www.22barcelona.com). It aims to provide new housing, business and technical facilities to lure innovative companies and foreign investment. Its showpiece, the Jean Nouvel-designed Torre Agbar tower (often known locally as *el supositori*, see picture below left) was finished in 2004, but there is still a lot left to do in the rest of district. Since the project was approved in 2000, 300 firms have been drawn in and many more are expected to follow. It is hoped the development will eventually create over 130,000 jobs and increase Poble Nou's current 4% share in economic production to over 15%. It sounds rather optimistic, but then, so did plans for the Olympics.

Torre Agbar in Sant Martí (p.157)

Fira de Barcelona

Continuing the commercial traditions of its golden age as a medieval port, the Catalan capital is a popular business location for the international market, attracting more foreign investment than any other Spanish city. The impressive Fira de Barcelona congress centre in Plaça d'Espanya hosts five of the eleven top trade events in Europe, including the 3GSM mobile phone convention and Bread and Butter, one of the world's top fashion fairs. The centre's facilities are being extended in the Gran Via M2 development.

Tourism

Tourism accounts for a great deal of Barcelona's rapidly rising economy. In 1990, 1.7 million tourists visited the city, by 2000, this figure was above 3.1 million and by 2005, it had passed five million. Catalonia's capital is especially popular for short stays, and was winner of the 2006 British Travel award for top short break destination. New ferry terminals have also become popular for cruise liners. This has brought an enormous number of tourists, stopping to do some guerrilla-style sightseeing and shopping. An extraordinary total of nine UNESCO World Heritage sites adds to the popular appeal. The Gaudí trail alone has seven, including La Sagrada Familia (p.169), the incredible unfinished church designed by Gaudí. Barcelona's museums are popular, with the recently revamped Museu Picasso (p.165) and the innovative CosmoCaixa science museum (p.171) among the most visited. Tourisme de Barcelona reckons that the city's 'places of interest' receive more than 17 million visitors a year.

The vibrant, chaotic nightlife attracts Europe's young and trendy (along with drunken stags and hens). And the buzzing and highly-regarded Catalonian gastronomic scene lures in the gourmet crowd.

Beyond the purely hedonistic, Barcelona is also the world's third most visited congress destination, with several historic locations for receptions and gala events. The newly unveiled CCIB international convention centre, south-east Europe's biggest, is capable of hosting up to 15,000 people. Business trips, conventions and fairs account for 53.5% of visitors. Imaginative plans to increase tourism however, are still constantly being hatched. The Barcelona Science 2007 programme (www.bcn.cat/ciencia2007) saw exhibitions and workshops in 80 different research centres, institutes, colleges and other sites. To allow for the ever-swelling tourist ranks, the number of hotels is rising rapidly, from 187 in 2000, to 268 in 2005 and counting. By 2008 there should be some 30,000 hotel rooms available.

International Relations

Following the Franco years (p.5), Spain has improved its diplomatic relations with the west, joining NATO in 1982, and the European Community (now European Union) in 1986. The establishment of ambassadorial level relations with North Korea in 2001, shows that Spain is certainly filling her diplomatic address book.

Spain's relationships with other EU countries are excellent. On global affairs her stance is generally aligned with Europe's. The only sore spot is the ongoing dialogue with Britain over Gibraltar's sovereignty, which has been an issue since the Treaty of Utrecht in 1713. A fledgling allegiance with the United States cooled off when Prime Minister Zapatero withdrew Spanish troops from Iraq. Particularly solid for the moment is the understanding with Latin America's socialist countries. Relations with Venezuela, sour during the Aznar administration, are improving under Zapatero, who in 2006 also became the first European premier to receive a visit from Bolivia's Evo Morales.

Spread across the city are consulates for the United Kingdom, the United States, Australia and Canada (p.21). Barcelona has many sister cities, including Boston (USA), Glasgow (Scotland), Dublin (Ireland), Montreal (Canada), Rio de Janeiro (Brazil), Tel Aviv (Israel) and Montpellier (France).

Marauding Moroccans

Of traditional importance is Spain's diplomatic relationship with North Africa. Particularly with Morocco, in which, on the northern coast, the Spanish enclaves of Melilla and Ceuta can be found. They are the only two European territories in mainland Africa. The border of Melilla is marked by a six metre high fence with tear gas dispensers to keep out illegal immigrants. A mini-crisis arose as recently as 2002, when a dozen Moroccans tried to occupy Isla Perejil, a deserted island half the size of a football pitch 200m off the coast of Africa, but ostensibly belonging to Spain. Spanish soldiers forcibly removed them within a week, without firing a shot.

Government & Politics

Spain & the National Government

Spain is a constitutional monarchy ruled by King Juan Carlos I and governed by a democratically elected General Court comprising of two chambers; the Congress of Deputies and the Senate (the upper house). Once elected these chambers serve for a four year term. Election is by proportional representation. The most recent election, in 2004, saw

9

José Luis Rodríguez Zapatero and his socialist PSOE (Partido Socialista Obrero Español) beat José Maria Aznar's centre-right PP (Partido Popular), winning 43.3 % of the overall vote.

Catalonia & the Generalitat

Of the 17 autonomous regions within Spain, only Navarra and the Basque Country have more self-government than Catalonia. The Catalan Generalitat consists of a parliament, a president and an executive council. In 2006, Jose Montilla Aguilera of the socialist PSC (Partit Socialista de Catalunya) was elected as its 128th president, defeating the centre-right CiU (Convergència I Unió), which had enjoyed 26 years of continuous power with Jordi Puyol (1980-2003) then Pascal Maragall (2003-2006) at the helm. The seat of the Generalitat is found in Plaça Jaume, opposite the Ajuntament (town hall, see below). Local governments are divided into *comarques* (counties) and smaller municipalities. While shared jurisdiction with the Spanish government is common, in certain matters of commerce, culture and transport, local authorities are granted autonomy. The justice system is an exception, run by national judicial institutions. One major drawback of being an autonomous community within the Spanish state – and one that rankles – is that Catalonia has no official international status.

Moves for Independence

'Catalonia is not Spain' – you may see this statement unfurled on a giant banner at a Barcelona football game. This plea for recognition is somewhat more complex than the desire for a total break with Spain. The situation is similar to that of devolution in the United Kingdom; like the Scottish or Welsh, most Catalans are proud of their culture, language and history, but would vote against outright independence. Catalonia's nationalist parties would like to see the region as one of four nations on equal footing within the state of Spain, the others being Galicia, the Basque Country and Castilian Spain (i.e. the rest). The latest Catalan Estatut (statute) therefore, which was approved by all the mainstream Catalan parties, demanded increased fiscal autonomy and recognition of Catalonia's national identity – in a declaratory, if not legal sense. It was accepted by the Spanish government in July 2006, effectively making a federal community of Catalonia.

Barcelona & the Ajuntament

While the Generalitat and its president control regional affairs, the Ajuntamient and its mayor are responsible for the city of Barcelona. In May 2007, Jordi Hereu, also of the PSC, was re-elected as Mayor of Barcelona, having replaced Joan Clos in 2006. In terms of administration, Barcelona is divided into ten districts. Each of these has an elected council and city councillor. At election time, voters don't select a specific candidate. Instead, they rate each candidate in order of preference. Once a party gets enough votes for four seats, those seats are taken by its four candidates with the most votes. The winning party's top candidate then becomes mayor. So, on election day, if you find yourself in one of the city's ajuntaments (town halls), remember; don't just tick one box. Once elected, the 41-man council can veto government decisions and has a say in local matters such as city traffic, road safety and telecommunications. A worrying concern in Barcelona is a growing level of absenteeism at the ballots. In the 2007 local elections, only 52% of Barcelona's electorate voted.

Parlament de Catalunya, Parc de la Ciutadella (p.178)

When you're lost what will you find in your pocket?

Item 71. The half-eaten chewing gum

When you reach into your pocket make sure you have one of these minature marvels to hand – far more use than a half-eaten stick of chewing gum when you're lost.

London Mini Map
Fit the city in your pocket

Population

Barcelona is Spain's second most inhabited city. In 1979, the population stood at a peak of 1,906,998 inhabitants. By 2000, it had slimmed down to 1,496,266 after an exodus to nearby towns. In 2006, according to city council statistics, the population had risen again, to 1,605,602. This increase is attributed to the return of young people from the suburbs, reflected by the fact that there are more 30-34 year-olds (146,847) than any other age group. By 2015, the population is expected to fall to around 1,590,700. On the gender front, single men can celebrate, with just 761,870 male residents, compared to 843,372 women. Average life expectancy has never been higher, with men expected to live to 77.5 years old and women to 84.3. This is an increase of four and 2.5 years respectively, over the past decade.

National Flag

The Spanish flag has three vertical stripes, one yellow and two red, with an off-centre coat of arms. The coat of arms is a shield flanked by the Pillars of Hercules, bearing the Latin inscription *Plus Ultra* ('further' in English) and topped by a crown. The shield represents the four kingdoms that merged to form a unified Spain in the 15th century. Castile, in the form of a castle, León in the form of a lion, Navarra represented by linked chains, and Aragon, a gold shield with four red bars (also the flag of Catalonia). Three central fleur de lys represent the ruling House of Bourbon and a lower pomegranate shows the flower of Granada.

This flag is not seen much around Barcelona, as for many Catalans it is synonymous with the oppression of the Franco years. However, the flag of Catalonia can be seen all around the city, especially on saint's days such as San Jordi's (23 April) and is always present over the town hall and parliament buildings. The four red bars represent a Catalan legend from the 10th century; that King Charles the Bald dipped his fingers in the wounds of Wilfred the Hairy (Count of Barcelona), and drew them over the dying Count's shield.

Need Some Direction?

The *Explorer Mini Maps* pack a whole city into your pocket and once unfolded are excellent navigational tools for exploring. Not only are they handy in size, with detailed information on the sights and sounds of the city, but their fabulously affordable price means they won't make a dent in your holiday fund. Wherever your travels take you, from the Middle East to Europe and beyond, grab a mini map and you'll never have to ask for directions.

Barcelona Population Age Breakdown

(chart showing age groups 0-9 through 90+ on vertical axis, percentage 0% to 20% on horizontal axis)

Population by Principal Language

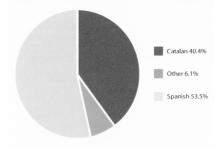

- Catalan 40.4%
- Other 6.1%
- Spanish 53.5%

Education Levels

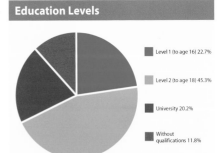

- Level 1 (to age 16) 22.7%
- Level 2 (to age 18) 45.3%
- University 20.2%
- Without qualifications 11.8%

Source: Idescat (Catalan Institute of Statistics)

Time Zones

Adelaide	+9.5 hrs
Amsterdam	CET
Athens	+1 hr
Berlin	CET
Bern	CET
Bogota	-6 hrs
Brasilia	-4 hrs
Brussels	CET
Buenos Aires	-4 hrs
Casablanca	-1 hr
Darwin	+9.5 hrs
Dublin	-1 hr
Edinburgh	-1 hr
Harare	+1 hr
Helsinki	+1 hr
India	+5.5 hrs
Istanbul	+1 hr
Jerusalem	+1 hr
Kuwait	+2 hrs
Lima	-6 hrs
Lisbon	-1 hr
London	-1 hr
Los Angeles	-9 hrs
Madrid	CET
Mexico City	-7 hrs
Moscow	+2 hrs
Nairobi	+2 hrs
New York	-6 hrs
Oslo	CET
Paris	CET
Reykjavik	-1 hr
Riyadh	+2 hrs
Rome	CET
Saskatchewan	-7 hrs
Stockholm	CET
Vienna	CET

Local Time

Spain is on CET (Central European Time), one hour ahead of Universal Coordinated Time, or UCT (formerly known as GMT). Clocks go forward by one hour on the last Sunday of March to save on daylight hours. On the last Sunday of October they go back one hour again. The period in between this is known as Spain Time. On both days the time changes at 01:00. The table shows differences between CET and the time in cities around the world, not incorporating daylight saving.

Social & Business Hours

The Spanish are known internationally for their tendency to procrastinate. The stereotype suggests that nothing will be done that can be put off until *mañana* (tomorrow, or literally, 'the morning'). And while an element of the myth remains true (particularly for those dealing with builders or the public sector) it is less prevalent in Catalonia than other parts of the country. Spain's famed siesta (a two to four hour lunch break to allow time for a midday snooze) lives on here, but its popularity is dwindling. At best, businesses offer a two hour lunch break and a 19:00 finish.

The biggest jolt to the body clock of new residents is likely to be social. Nights out in Barcelona begin late. Eat out before 22:00 and the only other diners you're likely to see will be confused tourists wondering where everyone is. Bars don't get going till midnight, and clubs until 02:00.

Opening Hours

Most industries require 40 hours per week, from Monday to Friday. Working hours tend to be between 09:00 and 19:00 with a one or two hour lunch break between 14:00 and 16:00. You should receive 22 days paid annual leave, as well as around 15 days for public holidays. Shops generally open at 10:00 and close for a siesta between 14:00 and 17:00, although many of the big chain stores stay open all afternoon. On Sunday, smaller places will tend not to open at all. Many family run businesses will close down for the whole of the month of August. Many museums close on Mondays, and market stalls normally open from 07:00 to 14:00.

Public Holidays

Sometimes it can seem like you've only just finished one public holiday before the next one begins. Some holidays have spawned lavish celebrations, such as the Festa de La Mercé (p.41), an explosion of tradition and popular culture in the name of The Merciful Virgin. The city's Barri Gòtic sees most of the action, hosting carnivals, dancing and live music. Particularly worth catching is the correfoc midnight procession featuring fire-breathing dragons, devils and wild mythological creatures. Check holiday dates on the www.barcelona-turisme.com website.

Photography

In general, taking pictures is fine and causes no offence. It's polite to ask before photographing individuals, but local people are extremely unlikely to demand money. Photography is only restricted in some galleries, museums and near military bases. The various police may get a little antsy if you snap them too.

Public Holidays

New Year's Day	Jan 1
Reyes (Epiphany)	Jan 6
Easter Friday	Lunar
Easter Monday	Lunar
Festa del Treball (Labour Day)	May 1
Sant Joan (summer solstice)	Jun 24
Assumpció (Assumption)	Aug 15
Diada de Catalunya 'national' holiday	Sep 11
La Mercè (Our Merciful Virgin)	Sep 24
Dia de la Hispanitat (Columbus Day)	Oct 12
Tots Sants (All Saints)	Nov 01
Dia de la Constitució (Constitution Day)	Dec 6
Inmaculada Concepció (Immaculate Conception)	Dec 8
Christmas Day	Dec 25
Sant Esteve (Boxing Day)	Dec 26

13

Temperature & Humidity

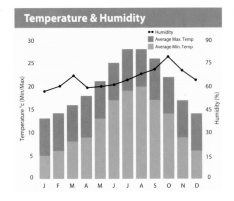

Rainfall

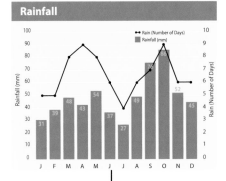

Climate

With cool, clement winters, hot summers and year-round sun, few climates are more agreeable. January and February are the coldest months, with an average temperature of 10°C. Snowfall and freezing temperatures are very rare but Barcelona apartments – the ones with tiled floors and no central heating – tend to become refrigerated at this time of year, so it is worth getting an electric heater. A decent electric fan is definitely in order during summer, as August temperatures average 25°C. It has been known to hit the high thirties, which can be unbearable. Locals often pack their bags in August and move down the coast to seaside resorts like Sitges. Some even take to sleeping on their balcony. Generally though, the climate is very benign. October is the wettest month, receiving an average of 8.6 centimetres of rainfall. Fortunately, Barcelona has a growing army of umbrella salesmen, who seem to come out of the shadows as soon as you are caught in a shower.

Flora & Fauna

From the snowy peaks of the Pyrenees to the wild shoreline of Cap de Creus and the marshy flats of the Delta del Ebre, Catalonia is blessed with exciting flora and fauna.

Flora

Barcelona's 60 parks are home to 140 different kinds of trees, including common Mediterranean species such as figs, cedars and cypresses. To see real diversity though, you must head for the mountains. With beechwood and evergreen oak forests, extraordinary rock formations, glacial lakes and thousands of plant species, the Catalan Pyrenees are one of Europe's greatest natural wonders. The range goes back 80,000 years to the Hercynian Orogeny, when mountains covered central Europe. In spring, its alpine meadows display trumpet gentians and pheasant's eye narcissi, with shimmering beds of maroon fritillaries, wild jasmine and Pyrenean hyacinths. In September and October there are the spectacular autumnal shades of the Montpellier maples and downy oaks, while on the ground, crocuses and purple merendera come to the fore. After Christmas, giant orchids emerge, as well as irises and tree spurge. Great places to enjoy the full range of Pyrenean flora are Vall d'Aran, where meadows and hillsides burst with colour all year round, and Aigües Tortes, home to the beautifully clear, glacial lake of Sant Maurici and forests of Scots pine and silver fir.

Fauna

Catalonia has a greater diversity of wildlife than any other region of Spain. On a hike in the Pyrenees you could hear the high-pitched whistle of the marmot (a large rodent), see the dainty legs of an isard (a goat-like chamois) darting between the trees, or a wild boar snorting out truffles. Other creatures to spot are ibex, badgers, genets, otters and beech martens. Much rarer, indeed almost non-existent, are sightings of the Iberian lynx, or (recently reintroduced) bears and wolves, which were once very populous. The rocky habitats of the mountains provide cover for reptiles such as the oscillated lizard, the Pyrenean brook salamander and the painted frog, as well as viperine snakes and asps. In spring and early summer, river banks and meadows teem with golden ring dragonflies and butterflies with fantastical names; Zapater's ringlet, Zellet's skipper, Spanish festoon and Oberthur's anomalous blue. And in the evening your campfire might just attract a giant peacock moth, Europe's largest. The biggest critters you're likely to come across in the city are the common garden spider or wolf spider (they're big but harmless, and will only deliver an itch-inducing bite if provoked). Scorpion encounters are virtually unheard of.

Birds
Wallcreepers clinging to cliff faces, black woodpeckers tapping away at the trees, a golden eagle soaring over the peaks; there's a lot for spotters to see in mountainous areas. The flat plains of Delta de l'Ebre are equally rewarding, with fan-tailed warblers, red-crested pochards and flamingos. Closer to Barcelona, Delta de Lllobregat is the place to catch migrating species; around 350 varieties pass through each year, although that number is said to be decreasing due to contamination of the water.

Marine Life
Medusas (jellyfish) are a common sight on Barcelona's beaches, but are also much-needed, as they filter the water. Further afield, the reef of Illes Medes teems with shoals of sardines and anchovies, as well as the barricuda, bass and bonito that prey on them.

Water ◀
The water lapping Barcelona's beaches can be pretty filthy. Try not to swallow any, and always take a freshwater shower after a dip. Drinking tap water is inadvisable; it's not as clean as in the rest of western Europe.

Environmental Issues
Pollution and waste are taking a heavy toll on the environment. Sadly, Catalonia is hardly at the vanguard of environmental awareness. Since 1992, there has been a 40% rise in carbon dioxide emissions, while old nuclear power stations provide 60% of the region's electricity.

Recycling
The Ajuntament has been known to use innovative methods to spread awareness, with colour-coded recycling kits distributed throughout the city. Particularly imaginative were recent efforts to keep public areas tidy, including the employment of street theatre groups to embarrass people into cleaning up after themselves. Across the city, an army of street cleaners gets to work each night, often just as the city's socialising begins to get into full flow.

Conservation
It's not all doom and gloom. In 2002, a 10 year plan was adopted, which aims to save energy and reduce the city's environmental impact by using more renewable energy. Currently, 41% of newly-constructed buildings are made to include solar panels. It is forecast that by 2010 greenhouse gas emissions will have been reduced by 20% and energy consumption by 4%.

Pollution & Environmental Impact
The election in 2004 of a coalition government including the ecosocialist ICV party (Iniciativa per Catalunya Verds) has not brought much change. Since then, the Department for the Environment has cleared the establishment of an incinerator to burn 90,000 metric tonnes of waste in the highly-populated valley of Sant Pere de Torelló. It has also rubber-stamped the development of the Bracons tunnel, running through an attractive bit of countryside near Olot. Plans for the routing of Spain's new high-speed AVE train through the city centre, which would create tremendous environmental and urban impact, are further evidence that ICV are doing little to live up to their name.

Guiris

Northern Europeans, Americans and other western visitors are known locally as guiris, *a term of mild disdain similar to the* Latin American gringo, *and not meant to cause offence.*

Culture

Catalans are befriended slowly. They have a reputation within Spain for being a little closed off and surly, but this is a tad unfair. Those who make an effort will find the natives opening up, and keen to demonstrate their warmth. They also have a reputation for being frugal (some may say tightfisted) but the only way foreigners will notice this is in the low level of tipping. Around 2-3% is considered perfectly reasonable.

A desire to protect and nurture everything Franco's Spain sought to repress has been a preoccupation for the past 30 years. This is seen in the fervent celebration of Catalan saints and festivals, in the worship of Barcelona FC and the support for traditional dance and activities like castelling (p.252).

It is also a politically charged city. During the Civil War, Barcelona saw communists fighting fascists, republicans fighting monarchists, and anarchists fighting capitalists. It is a city that retains an 'alternative', vaguely leftist feel, particularly in comparison to the more conservative, devout Spain to the south. But today, that alternative energy is more likely to be expressed through the arts than street protests.

Barcelona's cultural confidence derives from medieval times, when it was a sea-faring, mercantile power, and has developed through an interaction with its conquerors. The Romans and Visigoths left a political and artistic mark before the city fell under the rule of the Spanish and French, which is more evident today. Barcelona has a largely secular and progressive society. It is becoming increasingly cosmopolitan as flocks of Europeans, Africans and Latin Americans move here, attracted by the easy-going, multicultural lifestyle.

La Rambla performers

Attitudes Towards Immigrants

Throughout Spain certain medieval attitudes linger. Barcelona is no different. With North Africans, and Moroccans in particular, there is some cultural baggage. You can find its origins in the ideological and territorial disputes of the Spanish Reconquest, and more recently, as a result of an influx of illegal North African immigrants. Fortunately, any bitter sentiments seldom spill over into violence, meaning that even multicultural neighborhoods such as Raval and La Ribera don't have an ominous atmosphere. The worst that western immigrants (and those from within Spain) can expect is initial coldness or surliness on meeting Catalans. Some immigrants like to think Catalans would rather have the city to themselves, but Catalans actually take great pride and satisfaction in the appeal that their city has. Those who show an interest in Barcelona's culture and language find themselves welcomed with open arms and great enthusiasm.

Basic Spanish & Catalan

General	Spanish	Catalan
Yes	Si	Si
No	No	No
Please	Por favor	Si us plau
Thank you	Gracias	Graciès
Welcome	Bienvenido	Benvinguts
Bad	Malo	Malament
Good	Bueno	Bé
Monday	Lunes	Dilluns
Tuesday	Martes	Dimarts
Wednesday	Miercoles	Dimecres
Thursday	Jueves	Dijous
Friday	Viernes	Divendres
Saturday	Sabado	Dissabte
Sunday	Domingo	Diumenge
Greetings		
Good morning/hello	Buenos dias	Bon dia
Goodbye	Adios	Adeu
How are you?	Qué tal?	Qué tal?
Fine, thank you	Muy bien, gracias	Molt bé, graciès
Introduction		
My name is…	Me llamo…	El meu nom és…
What's your name?	Come te llamas?	Quin és el teu nom?
Where are you from?	De donde eres?	D'on ets?
I am from…	Yo soy de…	Jo soc de…
Questions		
How much?	Cuanto es?	Cuant és?
When?	Cuando?	Cuan?
How?	Como?	Com?
What	Que	Qué
Who	Quien	Qui
Why?	Por que?	Per que?
Where is?	Donde esta?	On es?
What time is it?	Que hora es?	Que hora és?
Taxi & Car Related		
Is this road to	Este es el camino a	És quest el camí a
Stop	Parada	Parar
Right	Derecha	Dreta
Left	Izquierda	Esquerra
Straight ahead	Todo recto	Tot recte

North	Norte	Nord
South	Sur	Sud
East	Éste	Est
West	Oueste	Oest
First	Primera	Primer
Second	Segundo	Segon
Road	Carretera	Carretera
Street	Caller	Carrer
Roundabout	Ronda	Ronda
Trafiic light	Semaforo	Semàfor
Near	Cerca	A prop
Petrol station	Gasolinera	Benzinera
Airport	Aeropuerto	Aeroport
Hotel	Hotel	Hotel
Restaurant	Restaurante	Restaurant
Slow down	Reducir	Reduir
Numbers		
One	Uno(a)	Un(a)
Two	Dos	Dos (dues)
Three	Tres	Tres
Four	Cuatro	Cuatre
Five	Cinco	Cinc
Six	Seis	Sis
Seven	Siete	Set
Eight	Ocho	Vuit
Nine	Nueve	Nou
Ten	Dies	Deu
Eleven	Once	Onze
Twelve	Doce	Dotze
Thirteen	Trece	Tretze
Accidents		
Police	Policia	Policia
Licence	Licencia	Llicencia
Accident	Accidente	Accident
Papers	Papeles	Papers
Insurance	Seguro	Assegurança
Sorry	Lo siento	Ho sento
Hospital	Hospital	Hospital
Doctor	Doctor	Metge
Ambulance	Ambulancia	Ambulància

Slang ◀

*An enjoyable
afternoon can be spent
on Barcelona's streets
listening to slang.
Young Catalans like to
call each other* nen
(babe) or tio *(uncle).
When surprised they
might exclaim,* hostia!
*(literally, 'communion
wafer'), not to be
confused with* la
hostia, *which is the
wafer of all wafers, or
the best.*

Language

Other options **Language Schools** p.223, **Learning Catalan** p.128

Barcelona is a bilingual city. A survey by the Generalitat, in 2003, claimed equal usage of Catalan and Spanish in everyday situations. A 2001 Linguistic Census established that 94.5% of the Catalonian population could understand Catalan, while 74.5% could speak it and 49.8% could write it. Barcelona itself has the lowest statistics, with 93.8% of its citizens understanding Catalan. Street signs are in Catalan and businesses are also obliged to display information in Catalan or receive heavy fines. Business is conducted in both languages, although contracts are often written in Spanish. Public education is in Catalan and only partly in Spanish. Because of this, 10-29 year olds are the most Catalan-literate of all age groups. Many fear that this is creating a minor cultural rift between parents and their more nationalist children.

Immigrants are also encouraged to learn Catalan, with free courses offered by the city council. Restaurant menus tend to be in both Spanish and Catalan, unless they're near La Rambla, where English, French and German translations can be found. Barcelona's growing immigrant population means that in the Raval you're just as likely to hear Urdu as Catalan, whilst Chinese is omnipresent between Plaça Urquinaona and Berber. Dialects of Arabic are commonplace in the squares of La Ribera.

Religion

Nationally, 94% of the population claims to be Roman Catholic. However, the majority of Barcelona's young, Catalan-born population, neglect church. In fact, church-going is generally the domain of the older generations and those from Latin America. There are 208 churches representing the Catholic faith, 71 for Evangelists and 21 for Jehovah's Witnesses. Catalonia's large North African and Pakistani population provide a sizable Muslim community,

Places of Worship		
Basílica de Santa Maria del Mar	Plaça Santa Maria	93 310 23 90
Centro Islámico Camino de la Paz	Carrer Arc del Teatre	93 317 71 23
Eglèsia Evangèlica de la Barceloneta	Carrer Ginebra	93 319 26 98
Fundació Casa del Tibet	Carrer Roselló	93 207 59 66
International church of Barcelona	Carrer Urgell	93 894 80 84

and there are many Islamic centres. There are also 13 places of worship for Buddhists. Other than Christmas, Easter Sunday and Saint's Week, important events in the calendar include Saint George's Day (Sant Jordi, the Patron Saint of Catalonia), on 23 April, Saint John's Day (Sant Joan) 23 June and Three Kings (Los Reyes) on 5 January, which is traditionally when Christmas presents are given. Many of Barcelona's Pakistani and North African inhabitants observe the Muslim rite of Ramadan and fast for one month each year. Some Muslim-owned shops and restaurants (mostly in Raval) may alter their hours during this time. For more churches and other places of worship, try Paginas Amarillas; www.paginasamarillas.es.

Nuestra Señora de Guadalupe

National Dress

Perhaps the closest thing to a Catalonian national costume is the uniform worn by castellers. Castells is a tradition of human tower building, with teams in most towns. The most important meeting of the castellers is in Valls on St Ursula's Day. The uniform consists of a pair of loose white trousers, a sash and varying coloured shirts, depending on the town represented. For castelling as a spectator sport, see p.252. If you fancy a go yourself, see p.205.

Lunching Out
At weekends and festivals, when the sun is shining, locals love to find a shaded terrace and enjoy a long, late lunch, washed down with some good wine. And there's no rush by the way, Catalans like to savour every moment of mealtime.

Food & Drink

Other options **Eating Out** p.316

Barcelona has a fine Mediterranean cuisine, with markets full of enticing cured meats (*embotits/embutidos*) and wonderful fresh seafood. Dining out is more expensive here than in other regions of Spain. A typical bar in Granada, Seville or Madrid will most likely offer free tapas with your beer, whereas here there is no such generosity. A medium-sized tapa will usually cost around €4 - €5 euros. If on a tight budget, a *menu del dia* generally provides the best value, costing as little as €7. This includes a starter, main course and a dessert, as well as wine, water and bread. A typical menu will often feature Spanish staples such as gazpacho (cold soup with tomato, garlic and peppers), tortilla (omelette) and albóndigas/mandonguilles (meatballs), as well as local specialties. A tasty starter is escalivada; aubergine, red peppers and onions marinated in olive oil and spices. Paella, a rice dish spiced with saffron and turmeric, is always a good introduction to Spanish cuisine. Fideua tastes like paella but is made with noodles instead of rice, and comes with a serving of all-i-olli (oil and garlic sauce) on the side. An exceedingly popular springtime dish is calçots; onions shaped like leeks, dipped in romesco sauce. Fricandó is a veal dish cooked with plums and rovellòn mushrooms. Barcelona's location by the sea means there is a wealth of seafood cuisine, including calamars a la romana (fried squid rings), sèpia (octopus) and exqueixada de bacallá (marinated raw cod with peppers, tomatoes and olives). Bread is particularly important at the dining table. Instead of buttering their bread, Catalans like to crush tomato into the dough and dribble olive oil and salt over it. This is known as pa amb tomaquet and is a local institution. Fillings for a traditional bocata (baguette) include botifarra blanc (white pork sausage), choriço (chorizo sausage), or the traditional Spanish jamon serrano (cured serrano ham).

Christmas treats include roast suckling pig, lobster and bacallá (cod) as well as dozens of sweet fancies such as turron, marzipan and polvoron (powder cake). In Catalonia there are ten wine producing regions. Penedés, Costers del Segre, Pla El Bages and Alella are known for their white wines, Conca de Barbara, Empordà and Costa Brava for their rosés, while Tarragona produces sweet wines. More general produce is associated with the regions of Piorat and Terra Alta. Sitting on one of the terraces of El Born to savour a glass of Catalonia's locally produced wine is a must. During festivals and at family get-togethers, wine is traditionally enjoyed from a peaked jar called a porròn.

19

In Emergency

If you are robbed, go to a police station immediately. Waiting in a *comisaria* (police station) filling out forms is time consuming but worth doing if you have insurance, as your insurance company will need a police report. Fortunately, most stations now have translators. Details of the city's numerous police forces, what they look like and what they do, are on p.23.

Medical Attention

A European Health Card (EHC) will guarantee free or reduced-cost treatment in the Spanish public health system for EU citizens. You will need to get one from your home country. The old E111 form issued in the UK is no longer valid for use in Spain. Reciprocal healthcare agreements also exist with some Latin American countries. See www.gencat.net for details.
Non EU nationals will have to pay to use the public health system (Servei Català de la Salut). But, it may be quicker to visit a private hospital or clinic. See p.109.

Ooops
For more on driving, go to p.53 of the Residents chapter. And, if you want a lawyer, go to p.67.

Car Accidents

In the event of a minor collision, matters are often settled immediately between the two drivers, with an exchange of licence numbers, names and insurance details. If the other driver refuses to play along you should take a note of their licence number and any other details possible. You will have a maximum period of seven days to report the incident to the insurance company. If you are the victim of a car accident and the other driver is at fault you are entitled to compensation and can begin a criminal procedure up to six months after the incident.

Emergency Services	
Guardia Urbana (City Police)	092
Mossos de Esquadra (Catalan Police)	088
Policía Nacional (State Police)	091
General Emergencies	112
Medical Emergencies	061
24 Hour Pharmacy Information	93 481 00 60
Hospital Clínic i Provincial	93 227 54 00
Hospital General de la Mare de Deu del Mar 'Hospital del Mar'	93 248 30 00
Hospital de Bellvitge	93 335 90 11
Bomberos (Fire Services)	080

Health Requirements

No health certificates are required for entry to Spain. No vaccinations are required either, although being up to date on your anti-tetanus jabs is recommended if you plan to visit the countryside. In extremely rare circumstances, Spanish authorities can demand that you undergo medical examination to make sure you're not carrying any illness requiring quarantine. EU citizens are advised to bring a European Health Card (EHC), so they can receive free or reduced-cost treatment in the Spanish public health system.

Women

Try not to walk alone late at night in the back streets of Ciutat Vella, where handbag theft is very common. Getting public transport alone is not a cause for concern, although be more vigilant when taking the *nitbus* (nightbus). Ignore those who try to force conversation, there are some notoriously relentless sweet talkers out there. When mildly irritated, try not to get angry, and mention a (real or imaginary) boyfriend (*novio*). When unduly harassed, don't hesitate to attract the attention of other people.

Embassies & Consulates

Name	Phone
Australia	93 490 90 13
Austria	91 556 53 15
Belgium	93 467 70 80
Brazil	93 488 22 88
Canada	93 412 72 36
China	93 254 11 96
Denmark	93 488 02 22
France	93 317 81 50
Germany	93 292 10 00
Greece	93 321 28 28
Holland	93 363 54 20
Hungary	93 405 19 50
India	90 290 10 10
Ireland	93 491 50 21
Italy	93 467 73 05
Japan	93 280 34 33
Mexico	93 201 18 22
New Zealand	93 209 03 99
Norway	93 218 49 83
Poland	93 322 72 34
Portugal	93 318 81 50
Russian Federation	93 204 02 46
South Africa	91 436 37 80
Sweden	93 488 25 01
Switzerland	93 409 06 50
United Kingdom	93 366 62 00
United States	93 280 22 27

Bus Access
Transport on buses has been made easier with most now featuring adapted facilities. You can tell which buses have these by the presence of the international wheelchair sign. Multistorey car parks feature special blue badge areas designated for drivers with disabilities.

In terms of what you wear, Barcelona is a very liberal city. Short of wandering around completely naked there are no real restrictions. It is entirely down to what you find comfortable, but bear in mind that less clothes usually equals more attention, and in Barcelona there's no shortage of potential courtiers.

Children

Barcelona has endless options to entertain children. There are play areas in parks and squares, amusement parks, safe beaches and lots of outdoor activities. Great places to take kids include the Magic Mountain funfair on top of Mount Tibidabo (p.180), Barcelona Zoo (p.181), Barcelona Aquarium (p.181) and the FC Barcelona Football Museum (p.172). If you need someone to take care of your children, there are a babysitters (*canguros*) throughout the city. Tender Loving Canguros (www.tlcanguros.com) is a reliable agency with thoroughly referenced babysitters and nannies. See p.97 for more. Higher range hotels offer kid's clubs, while shopping malls sometimes have special play areas. Changing areas can be found in the L´Illa (p.312), and Maremagnum (p.312) shopping centres. Restaurants are child friendly, but high-chairs, special menus and colouring sheets are usually lacking.

People With Disabilities

The Municipal Institute of People with Disabilities (IMD, www.bcn.es) is the body established by the Ajuntament to promote the cause of people with disabilities. The airport and tourist attractions are well provisioned, although Parc Güell can be difficult to get around, due to its steep slopes. Restaurants generally have easy access toilets. Barcelona's metro, unfortunately, is not very well catered for. Only Line 2, the purple line, has lifts in all its stations, although there are plans to improve this situation. Street navigation is considerably easier, with lots of ramps, and parking areas have spaces for drivers with disabilities.

Dress

There are few rules when it comes to dress code. Barcelona's sense of the avant garde lets many outrageous dressers off the fashion hook. People walking down the road in pyjamas or fancy dress suffer nothing more than a raised eyebrow in places like Ciutat Vella or Gràcia. Things are a little more conservative in Eixample and the suburbs. During winter evenings you will probably find yourself colder than expected, so a warm coat, a jumper and a scarf are a good idea. In summer, temperatures get very high, so light, airy materials are advisable. In cinemas, banks, shopping malls and restaurants the air conditioning can be surprisingly cool compared with outside in the street, so it's a good idea to have something warm to wrap yourself in.

Dos & Don'ts

Each bar, restaurant and public space has its own policy on smoking. Drinking alcohol on the street is prohibited, although this doesn't stop people from doing it. If you are caught you will be asked to throw away your can or bottle. However, arrest is unlikely.

Queuing is more orderly than many may first think. The custom is to ask who is last (*Que es l'últim?*) When whoever answered has had their go, it's over to you. When you are last, simply reply *yo* (me) when a new arrival asks the same question.

21

In bars and clubs however, it is often every man for himself. Getting on the metro or bus in rush hour is problematic too. There can be a bit of barging in such situations, but there is no malice meant. Just give as good as you get.

Don't expect people to open doors for you or express gratitude when you do so for them. Unlike the perpetual apologising and excusing in some other European countries, Spaniards are not known for standing on ceremony.

It is normal when men and women meet to exchange a kiss on each cheek, even for a first meeting and in formal situations. The same is true when two women meet. Men tend to just offer a handshake.

ID

In theory, you can be arrested for lack of identification, so it's worth carrying some form of ID; a photocopy of your passport should do.

Crime & Safety

Other options **In Emergency** p.20

Barcelona's overall crime rate hasn't risen for a number of years. That said, bag-snatching and pick-pocketing are major concerns. In crowded streets and bars you should be especially vigilant. An increasing number of bars and restaurants are even hiring private security firms. On the streets, the area around La Rambla is particularly notorious. If someone comes up to you offering to show you one of Ronaldinho's football moves and attempts to stick his leg between yours you can be pretty sure his hand will be creeping around into your back pocket for your wallet, so maintain a healthy distance. Crime in the city is in general petty and does not involve violence, although muggings are known to happen on the more deserted streets late at night. Never leave handbags or valuables lying around on tables or on the floor as, sooner or later, they will disappear. Keep your camera close to you, don't leave valuables in the outer pockets of your bag or coat and keep your eyes open when withdrawing money from an ATM.

More than 50% of 2006's summer-time robberies occurred on beaches, whilst 33% took place on the city's metro and rail network. The Mossos d'Esquadra, Catalonia's police force, reported that there were 687 bag snatches. The Barcelona districts in which most crime was reported over the summer months of 2006 were: Ciutat Vella (13,339), Eixample (9,554) and Sants (5,091).

Victims of Crime

If you're the victim of a crime and there's no one around to help, phone the general emergencies number, 112. Whatever the crime, it's worth filling out a report and bringing it to the attention of the authorities. A crackdown on petty crimes is much needed in Barcelona. The Guardia Urbana (local police) are on 080.

Getting Arrested in Barcelona

In the unlikely event of being arrested, you will be allowed to contact your consulate. The consulate cannot pay for legal advice or bail, or secure a release. They will however, ensure fair and equal treatment and advise you on finding a solicitor. If you cannot afford one a court appointed attorney will be provided. The constitution and law prohibits arbitrary arrests and the detention of suspects must be with probable cause or a warrant based on sufficient evidence, determined by a judge. With certain exceptions, police may not hold a suspect for more than 72 hours without a hearing. There is a bail system in place. Those who jump bail and get caught, are imprisoned immediately. See Getting Arrested, p.67, for more.

Prison Time

Spanish prisons have a reasonable reputation. The system is modern and rehabilitative. The 2007 opening of the Can Brians 2 complex in Baix Llobregat managed to cause uproar. With cells for one or two people, en-suite bathrooms and excellent sporting facilities, it was deemed to be too much like a leisure resort. Prisoners are usually allowed one 30-45 minute visit per week, decided upon by the prison board. Parole may be granted to prisoners after serving three-quarters of their sentence. The death penalty is no longer permitted.

Traffic Accidents & Violations
Car accidents are common. One person dies in a road accident every 13 days in Spain. One main cause is drinking and driving. Spanish laws on drinking and driving are the following; the legal limit is 0.5 milligrams of alcohol per millilitre of blood, stricter than some other places in Europe. If the amount of alcohol exceeds this limit, the driver can be heavily fined. There is a points system in place; a driver starts with 12. Drink driving or speeding is charged with six points. Upon the loss of all points the driving licence is revoked. Traffic fines are strictly enforced and you can be charged up to €300 on the spot. See Fines and Offences for more, on p.133.

Police
Four police forces operate in Barcelona; the Guardia Urbana (city police), the Mossos D'Esquadra (Catalan police), the Policía Nacional and the Guardia Civil (both state police). All of them are armed. There are also the Policia Portuaria, who are limited to the ports. The Guardia Urbana wear sky blue shirts and navy blue trousers. Though armed with batons they are generally quite sympathetic, primarily responsible for controlling traffic and keeping order. They drive white and fluorescent yellow vehicles. The Mossos d'Esquadra also carry batons; they wear blue and red uniforms and berets. Their main function is to keep public order. The military Guardia Civil is less omnipresent, and is being faded out for the Mossos. Their uniform is green, topped with a black, three-cornered hat. The Policía Nacional are predominantly an anti-crime force who wear blue combat gear. Plainclothes police are known as *paisanos*. Although Barcelona's police can be helpful and approachable, 144 cases of police brutality were recorded last year, the highest figure in Spain.

Tourist Information

Tourist Information		
Barcelona Airport Tourist Office	El Prat Airport	93 478 47 04
Barcelona Tourist Office – Cultural Events	La Rambla	93 316 10 00
Plaça de Catalunya Tourist Information	Plaça Catalunya	93 285 38 34

Lost/Stolen Property
It's a long shot, but missing valuables might turn up in Portal de l'Angel's Oficina de Troballes (Plaça Carles Pi i Sunyer, 8-10 or call 010), the municipal lost property office. If you lose your passport you can apply for a temporary one at your consulate or embassy (p.21). Consulates are also expected to provide assistance should you lose all your money and bank cards.

Tourist Information
There are five main tourist offices in the city. The biggest is underground in Plaça de Catalunya on the El Corte Ingles side of the square, look for the big red signs. Multilingual staff are available from 09:00 to 21:00 every day. The Columbus monument tourist office, also open from 09:00 to 21:00 daily, offers information on the city's cultural attractions, but cannot help with hotel bookings. There is tourist information outside terminals A and B of Barcelona El Prat Airport, and Sants Station has an information centre, with maps and leaflets. Alternatively, visit www.barcelona-turisme.com.

Barcelona Tourism Offices Overseas		
Australia	Melbourne	+61 39 650 7377
Canada	Toronto	+141 69 61 3131
UK	London	+44 207 486 8077
USA	New York	+1 212 265 8822

23

Camping

If camping is your thing, you'll have to head out of the city. The season runs from March to November, and most places will give you the option to pitch a tent or rent a bungalow. For more information, go to the Associació de Càmping website, www.campings barcelona.com. Otherwise, see Weekend Breaks (p.192) or Camping (p.203).

Places to Stay

Since the 1992 Olympics, tourism has swelled, bringing a surge in accommodation options. The city has more than 400 lodging alternatives, serving all kinds of visitors and budgets. New construction and building renovation work promise even greater variety. The biggest concentration of youth hostels, *pensions* and hotels is around the bustling city centre.

Hotels

Other options **Main Hotels** p.26, **Weekend Break Hotels** p.195

The star ranking system is widely used, and signs indicating quality and service level are posted in the main entrance of most hotels. A high number of stars will indicate accommodation of high quality and usually a corresponding price.

Prices are competitive, but often depend on location, season, and increasingly, on which business conferences or cultural events are on the calendar. For a double room at a four or five star hotel, prices start around €200 and can rise to €2,500 per night. Moderate two and three star hotels and two star hostels, sometimes called *hostales* (not to be confused with youth hostels) cost between €50 and €200 per night. For youth hostel dorm beds, budget about €20 to €25. It's worth asking for a better rate as there may be promotional or seasonal discounts. And, if you're coming during peak travel season, it's wise to book ahead. The Barcelona Hotel Association (www.barcelonahotels.es) and Turisme de Barcelona (www.barcelonaturisme.com) can help cut down your search.

Budget Hotels

If you want a hotel in the heart of the action, head over to Carrer de Pelai (map XXX), near to Plaça de Catalunya, nestled between the big shopping outlets. A good one on this stretch is Hotel Jazz (93 552 96 96, Pelai 3) a smart, cosmopolitan spot with a rooftop pool and terrace. Closer to the waterfront is Hotel del Mar (93 319 30 47, Plaça Palau 19) housed in a historic building and decorated with maritime theme motifs. You can bring your dog, change money onsite and stroll 10 minutes to the beach.

Hotels

Main Hotels	Phone	Website
Abba Sants Hotel	93 600 31 00	www.abbasantshotel.com
AC Miramar	93 281 16 00	www.otelacmiramar.com
Barceló Hotel Atenea Mar	93 531 60 40	www.bchoteles.com/atenea_in.htm
Ciutat Barcelona Hotel	93 269 74 75	www.ciutathotels.com/EN/ciutathotels.htm
Gran Hotel La Florida	93 259 30 00	www.hotellaflorida.com
H10 Universitat	93 342 78 50	www.h10hotels.com
Hostal Gat Xino	93 324 88 33	www.gataccommodation.com
Hotel 1898	93 552 95 52	www.nnhotels.com
Hotel Alexandra	93 467 71 66	www.hotel-alexandra.com
Hotel Arts Barcelona	93 221 10 00	www.ritzcarlton.com
Hotel Avenida Palace	93 301 96 00	www.avenidapalace.com
Hotel Claris	93 487 62 62	www.slh.com/claris
Hotel Colón	93 301 14 04	www.hotelcolon.es
Hotel Majestic	93 488 17 17	www.hotelmajestic.es
Prestige Paseo de Gracia	93 272 41 80	www.prestigepaseodegracia.com
Three & Four Star		
Hotel del Mar	93 319 33 02	www.gargallo-hotels.com
Hotel Jazz	93 552 96 96	www.nnhotels.com
Hotel Nouvel	93 301 82 74	www.hotelnouvel.com
Hotel Torre Catalunya	93 600 69 99	www.expogrupo.com
Two Star		
Hostal d'Uxelles	93 265 25 60	www.hotelduxelles.com

Modernist interiors

Main Hotels

Abba Sants Hotel

C/ de Numància, 32
Sants
🚇 *Sants Estació*
Map p.392 A2 **1**

93 600 31 00 | *www.abbasantshotel.com*
Don't let the exterior's functional look fool you. Inside you'll uncover comfortable business class accommodation with Wi-Fi, massage services and satellite TV. It's a short walk to Sants train station and the Fira de Barcelona conference halls.

AC Miramar

Pl de Carlos
Ibáñez, 3
Montjuïc
🚇 *Paral·lel*
Map p.407 E2 **2**

93 281 16 00
While the building has ties to the 1929 World Fair, the 75 room five star Gran Luxe is a newcomer on the high-end hotel scene, having only opened in October 2006. Its Montjuïc location is a hike to get to, but the stunning sea, city and garden views make it a notable urban retreat.

Barceló Hotel Atenea Mar

Pg de García
Faria, 37-47
Poblenou
🚇 *Selva de Mar*
Map p.412 C3 **3**

93 531 60 40 | *www.bchoteles.com*
This 191 room hotel sits at the edge of the city, in the hot redevelopment zone surrounding the Forum Barcelona site. Although it's a long way from downtown and the area's identity is still taking shape, the La Nova Mar Bella beach and the Diagonal Mar shopping centre are within easy reach.

Ciutat Barcelona Hotel

C/ de la
Princesa, 33-35
Barri Gòtic
🚇 *Jaume I*
Map p.403 F4 **4**

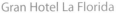

93 269 74 75 | *www.ciutathotels.com*
Bathrobes, piped music and a fresh, albeit basic, decor gives this mid-range hotel an upscale ambiance. The multilingual staff, central location and free bottled water push up the charm factor.

Gran Hotel La Florida

Cta Vallvidrera al
Tibidabo, 83-93
Tibidabo

93 259 30 00 | *www.hotellaflorida.com*
Far from the noise, 300 metres up on a hill, this is the place where the stars once stayed and the local elite holidayed. Inaugurated in 1925, the original La Florida hosted the likes of Ernest Hemingway, James Stewart, Rock Hudson and the King of Belgium. Closed in 1979, it reopened in 2003, after a major renovation.

H10 Universitat

Rda de la Universitat, 21
Eixample
Universitat
Map p.393 E4 6

93 342 78 50 | *www.h10hotels.com*
Although having street traffic below, the soft coloured tones, natural lighting and double-glazed windows make for a pleasant stay. There's no pool, but air conditioning will keep you cool in the sizzling summer months.

Hostal Gat Xino

C/ de l'Hospital, 115
Raval
Sant Antoni
Map p.402 A2 7

93 324 88 33 | *www.gataccommodation.com*
If you want a taste of Barcelona's ethnic diversity, stay in the multicultural, rough-around-the-edges, Raval neighbourhood. Accommodation is small and basic, but the blinding lime green curtains and graffiti decorated light shades give it a funky, fresh look.

Hotel 1898

La Rambla, 109
Raval
Liceu
Map p.402 C2 8

93 552 95 52 | *www.nnhotels.com*
The 19th Century building, designed by Catalan architect Josep Oriol Mestres, was once headquarters of the Compañía de Tabacos de Filipinas. Colonial touches and an elegant use of brick and wood create a nostalgic feel. An outdoor pool, spa facilities and plasma TVs help you to relax after busy sight-seeing days.

Hotel Alexandra

C/ de Mallorca, 251
Eixample
Diagonal
Map p.393 E3 9

93 467 71 66 | *www.hotel-alexandra.com*
Near Rambla de Catalunya, one of the city's main shopping districts, the hotel has a business-class air to it, and offers services to match: Wi-Fi, fax and a business centre. Friendly staff, car hire and garage services are also available.

Hotel Arts Barcelona

C/ de la Marina, 19-21
Port Olímpic
Ciutadella / Vila Olímpica
Map p.411 D3 10

93 221 10 00 | *www.ritzcarlton.com*
This is part of the Ritz-Carlton chain and one of the two high rise towers over Port Olímpic. The Arts is all about luxury. With terraced gardens, a collection of contemporary Spanish art, deluxe spa facilities and endless sea views, it is an excellent relaxation spot.

Hotel Avenida Palace

93 301 96 00 | www.avenidapalace.com

This four star hotel's claim to fame is that The Beatles stayed in the master suite when they performed in Barcelona in 1965. These days, it's wrapping up a renovation project that included modernising the restaurant, redesigning the beauty salon and updating all the rooms.

Hotel Claris

93 487 62 62 | www.slh.com

Housed in the recently renovated 19th Century Verduna Palace, the five-star GL hotel is one block from Passeig de Gràcia. It has 124 stylishly decorated rooms, some of which have a loft set up. Extras include a rooftop pool and a sizable collection of Egyptian artefacts.

Hotel Colón

93 301 14 04 | www.hotelcolon.es

You can't get much closer to Barcelona's Cathedral than this four-star hotel. Many of the rooms have views to the Gothic church, and Mercat de Santa Caterina is a few streets away. Rooms are bright and cheery.

Hotel Majestic

93 488 17 17 | www.hotelmajestic.es

As the name implies, the Majestic exudes Barcelona's old world glory days. The neoclassical facade, dating back to 1918, blends in with its Gaudí-influenced neighbours lining the upscale Passeig de Gràcia. It boasts a Michelin one-star rated restaurant and a panoramic terrace with a swimming pool.

Prestige Paseo de Gracia

93 272 41 80 | www.prestigepaseodegracia.com

An avant-garde, minimalist design with the right dose of oriental flair, make this boutique hotel stand out among the new generation of trendy accommodations. Spacious interior patios, Bang & Olufsen TVs and good use of natural lighting add to the sophistication.

Hotel Apartments

Barcelona has an excellent range of apartments available on short or long lets. These are a really useful first stop for new residents. Fully furnished and self-catering facilities are sometimes ranked by suns instead of stars. Amenities, such as parking, 24-hour security, fitness centres and cleaning services vary widely and may cost extra. Stays can be daily (usually with a two or three-day minimum), weekly, monthly or longer, to accommodate studies or business assignments. For shorter stays, prices are comparable to hotels, and discounts are typically available on long-term contracts.

Often, agencies manage apartments and handle reservations, and there's plenty of competition. To get started, the Associació d'Apartaments Turístics de Barcelona (Barcelona Association of Tourist

Hotel Apartments		
Desigbarcelona	93 467 67 74	www.desigbarcelona.com
Lofts & Apartments	93 268 33 88	www.lofts-apartments.com
MH Apartments Managers SL	93 323 87 90	www.mhapartments.com
Qualitur Consulting	93 485 04 24	www.feelathomeinbarcelona.com
Urban Flats	93 215 01 96	www.urban-flats.com

Apartments, www.apartur.com) and Turisme de Barcelona (www.barcelonaturisme.com) list companies, and the Barcelona Hotel Association (www.barcelonahotels.es) has an online reservation system.

Guest Houses

Phrases like guesthouses, bed & breakfasts, inns and *pensions* are sometimes interchanged, and the traditional distinctions are more grey here than in other places. Even apartments and boats call themselves B&Bs, further blurring the picture.

While they tend to have fewer amenities than their hotel counterparts, these places are cosier, more personal and may be part of a flat or take up an entire floor in a building. Like other rooms, prices and quality vary. The International Bed & Breakfast Pages

Guest Houses		
Ana's Guest House	93 459 18 43	www.anasguesthouse.com
Nisia Bed & Breakfast	93 415 39 60	www.nisiabcn.com
Willowmoon	93 484 23 65	www.willowmoon.uk.com

(www.ibbp.com) and BnB Finder (www.bnbfinder.com) may help you find an appropriate place.

Motels

If you're travelling outside of Barcelona and need a place to sleep en route, you'll find basic, no-frills accommodation along most major roadways. Blue *area de servicio* signs, which list gas stations, restaurants and rest stops, will indicate whether accommodation is available at certain exits, and will be marked with a bed symbol. Alternatively, pull into the roadside towns and look for motels, hotels or *pensions* there.

Hostels

Barcelona is a hot-spot among backpackers, student travellers and young people, so there's no shortage of hostels (*albergues*). Although they attract the younger crowd, couples, families and older travellers shouldn't feel out of place, and some hostels have allocated rooms accordingly. Keep in mind, however, that budget hotels may be better value for more than two people. While a number of hostels are affiliated with Hostelling International (www.hihostels.com), membership cards are not always required. Xarxa Nacional d'Albergs Socials de Catalunya (www.xanascat.net) provides descriptions, in Catalan, of regional hostels. The photos should help as well.

Hostels		
Ideal Youth Hostel	93 342 61 77	www.idealhostel.com
Pere Tarrés	93 410 23 09	www.peretarres.org/alberg
Sea Point Youth Hostel	93 231 20 45	www.seapointhostel.com

Getting Around
Other options **Exploring** p.137

Barcelona is an easy city to navigate, with a decent public transport network and plenty of ways to get around. Bicycles, scooters or motorcycles are very popular, and the old town can easily be covered on foot. Kids hop on skateboards, visitors jump onto tourist buses and fitness enthusiasts run, rollerblade or power walk through the parks and along the waterfront.

Since it's a big city with a growing population, traffic can be a problem and gets worse on long weekends and holidays. There's a web of major thoroughfares that criss-cross the city; Diagonal, Gran Via, Aragó, Meridiana and Balmes. Ronda de Dalt and Ronda Litoral, provide circular borders to the city's north and south. All of these are best avoided during morning and evening commute times, even if you're not behind the wheel. The noise and honking can dampen even the best of spirits.

For many, public transport or two wheels are better alternatives. Cars are often not worth the trouble, because of the difficulty in finding parking, and the fees you have to pay once you do get a spot.

The public transportation network, coordinated by the Authoritat del Transport Metropolità (ATM; www.atm-transmet.org), offers efficient, reliable and well connected local and regional bus, metro, train and tram services. In 2006, more than 910 million individual trips were taken on the integrated transportation network, up 2.7% from the previous year. Big development projects are underway, including the construction of a track for a high-speed train that will link Barcelona with Madrid and France. It should be a significant improvement to Spain's often frustrating cross country rail network. On the metro, the development of the massive Line 9 is expected to stretch more than 46 kilometres when it eventually opens.

Depending on where you're heading, your own two feet may be faster than the bus or metro. The city is flat and easy to walk and many streets have ample pedestrian pavements.

An extra bonus of walking is that Barcelona is an open-air museum, and the vibrant street scenes, everyday routines and curvy modernist facades are best experienced by lacing up your walking shoes and hitting the pavement. If you have the time, which may be tricky in the blur of first arriving, it's the best way to get a feel for your new home.

Scooting About
Many feel they aren't truly native until they have a scooter. These ubiquitous, buzzing runabouts may still be considered a little nerdy in the English-speaking world, but Barcelonins manage to make them look very cool. You're as likely to see suited business folk on one as modish media types or canoodling teenagers. This is primarily because they make getting around the city so easy, and can even navigate the tiny alleys of the Ciutat Vella. And they really do look very cool. See Motorbike & Scooter Hire, p.34.

Air
Barcelona International Airport (www.aena.es), known as El Prat, is 12 kilometres from the city. The recent addition of a third runway and the eventual completion of another terminal (expected before 2009) will open more air travel options to and from the city. Shuttles to Madrid depart nearly every half hour on most days, and there are frequent connections to other domestic destinations. Direct flights are available to many worldwide cities on major airlines, but Madrid is a slightly larger hub and you may have to connect through there. Low-cost airlines are making their presence felt too, and are putting more flights on their schedules. There are smaller airports in Girona and Reus, both about 90 kilometres from Barcelona.

Iberia and Spanair are the Spanish airlines and, as members of worldwide alliance programmes, have some global reach. Iberia's reputation took a hit in July 2006, when the company's baggage claim workers declared an illegal strike on a busy

Estació de França

Trams in Poblenou

The quaint trams of Tibidabo

Torre Agbar and Glòries Metro

La Rambla

summer day and shut down Barcelona airport, forcing hundreds of flight cancellations and leaving hundreds of thousands of passengers stranded. Outraged city officials and consumer advocate groups moved swiftly and called for airport management policy changes to prevent future problems. Claims, retributions, political finger-pointing and criminal and civil court cases will be settled well into 2007.

Airlines

Aer Lingus	93 342 88 90	www.aerlingus.com
Air France	90 220 70 90	www.airfrance.com
British Airways	90 211 13 33	www.ba.com
Continental Airlines	90 096 12 66	www.continental.com
Delta Airlines	93 478 23 00	www.delta.com
easyJet	80 707 00 70	www.easyjet.com
Iberia	90 240 05 00	www.iberia.es
KLM Royal Dutch Airlines	90 222 27 47	www.klm.com
Lufthansa	90 222 01 01	www.lufthansa.com
Singpore Airlines	93 297 13 08	www.singaporeair.com
Spanair	93 298 33 62	www.spanair.com
Vueling Airlines	90 233 39 33	www.vueling.com

Lost Luggage

Aeropuertos Españoles y Navegación Aérea (Aena) manages most of Spain's airports, including Barcelona's. For general information, 24 hours a day, call 90 240 47 04. There are a handful of lost luggage counters, and airport staff will be able to direct you to the correct one. Air France is on 90 219 09 47; Flightcare, 93 298 33 30; Groundforce, 93 298 48 49; Iberia 93 401 31 29 and Newco Spanair, 93 298 34 39. For emergencies, call the airport police on 93 297 12 19.

Luggage Lunacy
Make sure you go to the correct luggage collection point. Signs are not always clear, and it's easy to find yourself in the terminal B luggage bay after arriving at terminal A.

Airport Information

Despite the occasional glitch, the airport is clean, easy to get in and out of, and is well-signed in multiple languages. It has plenty of amenities including duty-free shops, Wi-Fi, lounges, banking services, cafes, a children's play area and an increasing number of electronic check-in facilities.

During peak travel times (Easter, July, August, the first week in December and the Christmas-New Year break) allow extra time to check-in and get through security. Queues can be very long, and, with international security regulations always in flux, it's hard to predict waiting times. Call your airline for specific requirements.

There are three terminals. Terminals A and B serve international and domestic flights and Terminal C is dedicated to regional flights and the shuttle service to Madrid.

Airport Transfer

Ground transport is readily available, and you have your pick of taxis, buses and trains. Aerobus (www.sarfa.com, 93 415 60 20) has the most frequent service, running, on average, every 10 minutes. Tickets, purchased on the bus, cost €3.90 one-way and stops at key points between Plaça d'Espanya and Plaça de Catalunya.

Public bus number 46 and night bus N17 (www.emt-amb.com, 010 or 93 318 70 74) also go into the city. Line 46 starts and ends at Plaça d'Espanya, where you can pick up the metro. The N17 stops near Plaça de Catalunya. Both cost €1.25 and tickets, purchased on the bus can be used for zone one public transport transfers within 60 minutes. The Renfe Cercanías Line 10 train (www.renfe.es, 90 224 02 02) links the airport with the Sants and França railway stations and stops at Passeig de Gràcia. Tickets, which can also be used for zone one transfers, cost €1.25 and can be bought at the electronic kiosk prior to boarding.

Boat

Boat travel takes a few different shapes, from cruise ships to ferries to the nearby Balearic Islands or tours of the city's shoreline and port area.

Barcelona has become a popular Mediterranean port for the cruising industry and most well-known companies pass through regularly.

If you're hankering for a bit of island life, Acciona Trasmediterrània (www.trasmediterranea.es, 93 295 91 00) and Iscomar (www.iscomar.com, 90 211 91 28) have ferries and catamarans sailing from Barcelona to Mallorca, Menorca and Ibiza. Trasmediterránea also sail to Rome.

There are a number of tour operators docked near Moll d'Espanya and Port Vell that will take you out on the sea for a few hours and tell you about Barcelona's coastal history and its expansive port project. See p.182 for more on these tours.

Bus

A complex but reliable bus network covers the city, connecting to all other transport modes. Buses run frequently during the day and are widely used by locals. There is a weekend and night service, albeit with less regularity. If you're not sure where to get off, ask the driver. They'll let you know when your stop is approaching.

Bus lines, maps and schedules are posted at nearly all bus stops. Since many buses use the same stop, it's best to flag down the one you want. Depending on the day and time, drivers may slow down but not always stop.

Entitat Metropolitana del Transport (www.emt-amb.com, 93 223 51 51) has schedules for buses serving Barcelona and surrounding cities. Transports Metropolitans de Barcelona (www.tmb.net) has online trip-planning tools and a service called TMB iBus that tells you when the next bus will arrive. You can access the info from the internet or have it sent to your mobile phone.

For paper timetables, go to the TMB booths at the Universitat, Diagonal, Sagrada Famíília and Sants Estació metro stops.

Single-trip tickets are €1.25, but if you'll be travelling on buses and the metro frequently, the T-10 is better value, at €6.90. Tickets need to be validated when you get on board and can be used for transfers for same-zone trains, metros and trams. Although signs do state that the exact change is required, most drivers will be able to provide change for small denominations. For general information about Barcelona public transportation dial the free number 010.

Car

Other options **Transportation** p.129

Like any other big city, Barcelona has its share of congestion, traffic jams and parking nightmares. It gets worse around holidays. Nonetheless, a grid system through much of the city will give you some orientation, and main avenues pull traffic to the bigger highways, which helps to ease the pain.

People drive on the right, and if you ask for directions, locals may use a different set of directional compass points to guide you, Girona (north), Mar (east), Tarragona (south) and Tibidabo (west), which make sense once you understand the city's layout. The main northbound street that cuts the city is Gran Via de les Corts Catalanes, the parallel southbound equivalent is Carrer d'Aragó. Avinguda Diagonal is just that, a diagonal east-west road that links the northeast corner near the sea with the far opposite south-west.

Circling the city is the Ronda Litoral, which runs along the waterfront, and feeds into the N-II and B-10 highways. Up near Tibidabo, there's Ronda de Dalt, also called the B-20, and it connects to a number of other highways and toll roads.

There are all sorts of arteries on Barcelona's outskirts, ranging from two and four-lane secondary motorways to fast-moving

Travel Cards

Multiple journey tickets are the best value for getting around. These *targetes* allow travel on the metro, trains, buses and FGC. One 'trip' covers an hour and 15 minutes across all forms of transport. Prices below are for Zone 1.

T-Dia (€5.25): valid for one day
T-10 (€6.90): valid for ten trips
T-50 (€28.60): valid for 50 trips over 30 days
T-Mes (€44.35): unlimited travel for 30 days
T-Trimestre (€122): unlimited travel for 90 days

Tickets can be bought from electronic kiosks with multi-lingual displays in stations, and you can pay with cash or credit card.

Car Rental Agencies

Anecar	90 228 76 00	www.anecar.com
Avis	93 298 36 00	www.avis.es
Barcelona Limousine Service	93 247 06 99	www.spain-bcnlimo.com
BCN Rent a Car	93 490 19 30	www.bcnrentacar.com
Blai Limousines	93 303 43 34	www.blailimousines.com
EasyCar	90 629 28 27	www.easycar.com
Europcar IB	93 491 48 22	www.europcar.com
The Golden Wheels	93 364 44 33	www.thegoldenwheels.com
Hertz	93 298 33 00	www.hertz.com
Limousines Miramar	90 250 08 40	www.miramar.net

tolls roads, called *autopistas*. Not too long ago, many roads were renamed to correspond with European standards, so expect some overlap. Signs get confusing when roads are merging or forking off, and there is a host of different letters and colours indicating which roads are which. Generally speaking, you'll have to pay to use the roads with blue signs and the letters A or AP; they'll also be marked *peatge* or toll. Some others, like those with blue signs and the letter C, have stretches where you'll have to pay. Tolls will be either fixed for certain portions, or will be based on the distance travelled (this is calculated when you come off the toll road). It's best to pick up a map from the local tourist office or a rental car company and take a look at the key for toll roads, secondary roads and the numbering systems. Speeds vary, depending on where you are. In some residential areas of Barcelona, 30 kilometres per hour may be the maximum. On autopistas, it can be up to 120kph.

Hiring a Car

Rent-a-car companies are scattered throughout the town, with most at the airport, near the port or by train and bus stations. Your hotel may also help, and you can see the table here for more. Choices normally range from small compact cars to luxury 4WDs, and you'll also find limos, campers and convertibles at some places. Base day rates vary widely, depending on the season, demand and car type. It's worth shopping around online to get the best deal.

Cycling

Bicycles are an increasingly common way of getting around. There are more than 60 kilometres of dedicated bike lanes, and the city plans to raise this to 200 kilometres in the near future. Helmet use is recommended, but not mandatory. And, you'll need a lock, or two, to ward off potential thieves.

Visitors can hire bicycles from any number of places, including Budget Bikes (93 304 18 85, Carrer del Marquès de Barberà 15, www.budgetbikes.eu) and Barna Bike (93 269 02 04, Pas Sota la Muralla 3, www.barnabike.com). The Barcelona tourism office (www.barcelona turisme.com, 93 285 38 32) has a list of bike rental companies, recommended sight-seeing routes and information about their affiliated Barcelona Bici organisation.

For residents, a new bike-sharing program, bicing (www.bicing.com, 902315531), was launched in March 2007. Annual membership is €24 a year, and you have access to 1,500 bicycles parked at 100 stations around the city. You can use the bikes for a maximum of two hours; the first half-hour is free and then you're billed 30 euro cents per half hour. For maps, safety regulations and general information, go to the Barcelona Ajuntament site (www.bcn.cat/bicicleta/en) or call the Comissió Cívia de la Bicicleta at 93 402 75 04.

Motorcycles

Motorbikes and, in particular scooters, are very popular ways to get about. Car drivers are used to having them buzz past, and so remain alert, though they don't always leave much space. Dawdling pedestrians are just as likely to provide a hazard as cars. Bikes and scooters are useful for nipping through traffic and can be used in areas of the Ciutat Vella that cars would never reach.

Motorbike & Scooter Hire

BarcelonaMoto.com	600 370 343
Motissimo	93 490 84 01
Quads & Mopeds to Rent	97 234 13 10
Vanguard	93 439 38 80

Nabbing Cabs
Given the number of one-way streets, it's best to pick an intersection facing the direction you're heading in. It will save a few unnecessary turns and a couple of cents on the tab.

Taxi

Black and yellow taxis, independently operated but regulated by local authorities, are reasonably affordable alternatives, particularly after midnight, when public transport is limited. Drivers are usually friendly and honest, but as English proficiency varies, you may want to write down the address of your destination or point to a map.

Taxi Companies	
Barcelona Taxi Van	670 531 619
Fonotaxi	93 300 11 00
Radio Taxi 033	93 303 30 33
Servitaxi	93 330 03 00
Taxi Amic	93 420 80 88

Taxis with a green light and a *lliure* or *libre* sign will stop if waved down on the street, unless they're within 50 metres of a taxi stand. You can also phone to order one (see table). Fares are set, and not negotiable. During week days from 07:00 to 21:00, meters start at €1.75 and charge 78 cents per kilometre thereafter. Night fares, weekends and holidays start at €1.85 and go to €1 per kilometre. For airport rides, expect to pay between €20 and €25 to Ciutat Vella. There are supplements for airport and port drop-offs and suitcases. For lost items, call 90 210 15 64 or e-mail objper-taxi@amb.cat.

Train

Renfe (www.renfe.es, 90 224 02 02) runs several regional and national trains. There are also sleeper trains to France and the far away reaches of Spain. You can check schedules online or at the Sants, Plaça de Catalunya, or França train stations. Standards of reliability, comfort and speed are generally lower than in the rest of western Europe. Ferrocarrils de la Generalitat de Catalunya, or FGC (www.fgc.es, 93 205 15 15), operates trains for the metropolitan area, linking Barcelona with its surrounding suburbs. Timetables and other information are available at the Plaça de Catalunya, Plaça d'Espanya and Provença stations.

Tram

Trams (www.trambcn.com, 90 219 32 75) are a recent addition to the integrated public transport network, with three lines running along parts of Diagonal and near Parc de la Ciutadella. Single-fare tickets are €1.25 and can be bought at vending machines at tram stops. They need to be validated onboard and can be used as bus and metro transfers.

Metro

Barcelona's colour coded and well signed metro (www.tmb.net, 93 318 70 74) provides a frequent service between the city's neighbourhoods and bus and train lines. Single fares are €1.25, but the multi trip *targetes* are better value; the T-10 (10-trip ticket) costs €6.90. They can also be used with any of the city's ATM – Autoritat del Transport Metropolità (www.atm.cat) – integrated transport services. Trains runs about every five minutes. The service is available from Sundays to Thursdays from 05:00 to midnight, and on Fridays and Saturdays from 05:00 until 02:00 the following morning. The city has been testing 24 hour service on Saturdays, with the trial period ending in autumn 2007. As this book went to print, there was no decision on continuing beyond this point.

Walking

Other options **Hiking** p.218

Barcelona is a walking town. Pavements on even the narrowest streets are adequate. Even better, many of the main boulevards are designed with leisurely strolls in mind and there are ample, tree-lined paths. Much of the city is flat, but if you want the extra challenge of hills, you'll get a dose around parks Güell, Montjuïc and Tibidabo. Most places are safe to walk in, although at night you may want to take extra care. The local tourist offices can provide suggestions for walking routes and maps.

35

Who Do You Think You Are?
Barcelona shop owners are fairly diligent in asking for a driving licence or passport before sliding your card through, so make sure you carry picture ID with you.

Money

Cash and major credits cards are the most common forms of payment. If your debit card bears a Visa or MasterCard logo, you may also be able to use that in shops, restaurants or hotels. Only euros are accepted, except in large hotels, which may accept major foreign currencies. But don't count on it.

Local Currency

Spain, an EU-member state, replaced the peseta with the euro in 2002, making it the official currency. Its economy initially suffered a little, along with other countries adopting the new currency. Primarily this was down to vendors, whether small *tabacs* or large industries, rounding up their prices.

Lately though, the euro has gained strength against many international currencies, including the US Dollar and Japanese Yen.

There are five, 10, 20, 50, 100, 200 and 500 euro banknotes, with each denomination a different size and colour. One and two euros come in coin form, as do one, two, five, 10, 20 and 50 euro cents. Occasionally, big ticket items like cars and expensive consumer goods still carry an approximate peseta equivalent.

Banks

You'll find a bank on almost every street in the main tourist areas. There are local, regional, national and international financial institutions, with a heavy concentration of money changing branches centred around Plaça de Catalunya. Some major local and national companies are La Caixa, Caixa Catalunya, BBVA and Santander, and international banks include Barclays, Citibank, Deustche and ING.

Banks are generally open from 08:30 to 14:00, Monday to Friday. Some have Saturday and evening hours, and many change schedules during the summer. A currency exchange sign, posted in several languages in the doorway, indicates which branches provide this service. Also, the degree of English proficiency varies, so be patient and remember, there's always smiling and pointing. For more information, see the Banks section in the Residence chapter (p.64).

Exchange Rates		
Currency	Currency buys	€ buys
AED	€0.19	5.33
ARS	€0.23	4.37
AUD	€0.61	1.64
CAD	€0.69	1.45
CHF	€0.60	1.66
CNY	€0.10	10.49
GBP	€1.47	0.68
HKD	€0.09	10.86
INR	€0.02	55.55
JPY	€0.01	162.26
MXN	€0.07	15.32
NZD	€0.54	1.85
RUB	€0.03	35.14
USD	€0.74	1.35
ZAR	€0.10	9.87

ATMs

Like banks, ATMs are everywhere. Look near banks first, but you'll also find them at train stations, airports and big shopping centres.

The ATM networks are compatible with most international systems, such as Cirrus, American Express, Visa, MasterCard and Plus. The most widely-used local networks are Telebanco and ServiRed.

Call your bank before you arrive and let them know you may make international withdrawals. This will avoid having your account flagged for potential fraud and save countless long-distance calls to straighten out problems. Also, ask about fees. Banks may charge more for ATM use abroad or sometimes even charge a percentage of the amount withdrawn.

Be careful too, when yanking out cards and money in public places. Pickpockets are not uncommon, so assume there are other eyes on you besides the bank's security camera.

Heads Up
When you get a one or two euro coin, try to figure out where it came from. Every EU country using the euro has it's own national image on the 'heads' side. Spanish coins have a sketch of the current king, Juan Carlos de Borbon y Borbon.

Money Exchanges

There are plenty of money exchanges throughout the city, namely along La Rambla, and at key transportation hubs, such as at the airport, bus and train stations. If you have time, shop around for the best deal.

Money Exchange Centers		
Chequepoint	La Rambla, 132	90 035 45 38
Inter Change	La Rambla, 74	93 481 49 15
Maccorp Exact Change	La Rambla, 130	93 342 51 60
Money Exchange	Carrer de Mata, 1	93 324 82 59

While the exchange rates are not likely to fluctuate much, commissions can take a chunk of change from your pocket.

Credit Cards

Most hotels, restaurants, retailers, supermarkets and tourist sites take Visa, MasterCard, American Express and Diner's Club. A sign in the shop window will indicate which cards are accepted.

Smaller shops and neighbourhood markets, like La Boqueria and Santa Caterina are normally cash-only businesses. Individual shop owners don't charge transactional fees on top of the stated prices, but your bank probably will, sometimes 1% to 2% of the amount charged.

Call your credit card company before you leave home and tell them you will be travelling internationally. If you don't do this, the company may ring you to confirm purchases or freeze your account until they can verify that you are in possession of your card. Jot down your credit company's international phone number and pack away a copy of your account information. It will come in handy if you have to report a lost or stolen card.

Tipping

Since bar, cafe and restaurant staff are paid decent salaries, tips are appreciated, but not expected. If they tip at all, locals leave small change or round up to the nearest note. Even if this comes to just 2%, you won't be considered tight. In classier joints, tips run higher, but often still less than 10% of the bill. If you feel that service has been spectacular, always tip in cash, as any extra added to a credit card is normally pooled, or may even be snaffled by management.

If you do want to tip taxi drivers and hotel crew, a euro or two is enough to register your appreciation. If you get a good haircut, you can normally drop a few euros in a tip jar near the cash register.

Plaça d'Espanya

Newspapers & Magazines

Local and international newspapers and magazines are not difficult to find in Barcelona, and there's a good cross-section of titles.

Being a bilingual city, the local daily newspapers come either in Spanish or Catalan, or sometimes both. *Avui* (www.avui.cat) and *El Punt* (www.vilaweb.cat) are Catalan papers, and broadly nationalist. *El Mundo* (www.elmundo.com, broadly centrist) and *El Pais* (www.elpais.com, left-leaning with good foreign coverage) are in Spanish. *La Vangaurdia* (www.lavanguardia.es, conservative, and Spain's best-seller) and *El Periódico* (www.elperiodico.cat, more serious than the bright layout suggests) are printed in both languages. They cost €1 on weekdays and €2 for the weekend editions. These papers all have a political slant, so it's important to understand what you're reading. They also tend to be quite serious and offer proper commentary and analysis. It is an endearing idiosyncrasy that they are sold next to gossip mags and prominently displayed pornography. The main sports dailies are *Marca* (www.marca.com) and *AS* (www.as.com). Both are quite tabloid in style.

During the morning commute, you'll see people reading *ADN*, *Metro* and *20 Minutos*, the free dailies distributed around newspaper kiosks, bakeries, cafes and main train, subway and bus stops. Stories run side-by-side in Catalan and Spanish, and just to confuse you further, some front-page headlines and summaries start in one language and continue on the jump page in the other. Every neighbourhood has free weekly papers highlighting the goings-on in the *barri*.

International papers line the racks of most newspaper kiosks and shops. You'll have better luck finding publications like the *Financial Times, Guardian, International Herald Tribune, Irish Times, New York Times, Telegraph, USA Today* and *Wall Street Journal*, in areas that get more tourist foot traffic, but, increasingly, they are becoming common in residential areas as well. Expect to pay €2 to €3 during the week for foreign papers. If you don't want to cough up the extra, head over to the library; many branches have a decent stack of regional and international broadsheets.

There are a couple of local English language titles worth noting. *Catalonia Today* (www.cataloniatoday.cat) is a weekly newspaper (€2) highlighting key city and regional news and events. It is published by the same people as *El Punt*, and aims to give a Catalan perspective to English speakers. *Barcelona Metropolitan* (www.barcelona-metropolitan.com) is a free, A4 sized monthly magazine targeting expats. Its classified section is a handy resource for finding English-speaking accountants, chiropractors, dentists, translators and what have you. *Barcelona Connect* (www.barcelonaconnect.com) is another freebie (A5), with detailed listings.

On the magazine side, besides finding dozens of locally-published glossies, you'll see familiar titles translated into Spanish. In stores like FNAC (p.306) or at train stations or airports, you'll find some original-language versions of the leading US and UK news, business, travel and fashion magazines.

Books

Barcelona has inspired some classic literature. Given its importance to Spanish-Catalan history and politics and the modernist art movement, this is not surprising. You can deepen your appreciation of the city with *Barcelona and Modernity: Picasso, Gaudí, Miró, Dalí*, a hefty hardcover tracking the city's progressive art and architectural development, or lick your lips as you browse *Catalan Cooking* by Coleman Andrews. If you're ready to dive into history and politics, grab a copy of the classic *Homage to Catalonia*, George Orwell's personal account of the Spanish civil war, or Colm Tóibín's *Homage to Barcelona*, which eloquently ties together the city's rich history with its democratic transition after the Franco dictatorship. *Barcelona* is an opinionated stroll through the city's violent history by Aussie scribe and art critic Robert Hughes.

Additionally, Carlos Ruiz Zafón's Barcelona based thriller *Shadow of the Wind* hit several international best-sellers lists, and Ildefonso Falcones' *The Cathedral of the Sea*, soon to be translated into English, has been hugely popular among locals.

Websites

Barcelona is well served for informative websites. Many, including most government sites, have very good English versions. For others, you'll need to have your Spanish or Catalan dictionary handy.

To get a general overview of city sights, services and the lay of the land, click around the Barcelona Ajuntament (www.bcn.cat), and Turisme de Barcelona (www.turismedebarcelona.com) pages. Both are very informative.

Blogs

Though not as popular as in other cities, blogs still have their place in Barcelona, especially in the football community. FC Barcelona Blog (www.fcbarcelonablog.com) and FC Barcelona English Speaking Supporters (www.fcbes.com) are a couple that track the local team. Lately, though, you'll see a more sophisticated use of slick and stylish multi-media snippets that mix text, video and audio to give you a slice of Barcelona life and a place to post messages or clips. Some of the better ones include Barcelona Visió (www.bvisio.com) and Scanner BCN (www.bcn.cat/scannerbcn/?idioma=2).

Walki-Talki
One other website worth a look is www.walki-talki.com. It has downloadable mp3 guides that talk you round Barcelona and other European cities, with a printable map to follow too.

Websites

City Information	
www.atm.cat	Transport links
www.bcn.cat	City government services and loads of useful information
www.bcn.cat/guia/welcomec.htm	Excellent interactive city map
www.euroave.com	Online maps
www.maps.google.es	Online maps
www.meteocat.com	Local weather
www.tmb.net	City transport network
www.turismedebarcelona.com	Tourism department
Business & Industry	
www.barcelonahotels.es	Hotels and reservations
www.cidem.com	Local business group, offers support to entrepreneurs
Entertainment & Culture	
www.barceloca.com	Clubs, bars, museums
www.barcelonareview.com	Reviews of contemporary fiction
www.guiadelociobcn.es	'What's on' guide
News & Media	
www.barcelonaconnect.com	Online version of the free monthly magazine
www.barcelona-metropolitan.com	Online version of the free montly magazine
www.barcelonareporter.com	Online Catalan news in English
www.bcnweek.com	Online version of the 'alternative' weekly
www.elperiodico.cat	Local newspaper in Spanish and Catalan
www.lecool.com	Weekly listings email
www.typicallyspanish.com	National news in English
Directories	
www.barcelona.angloinfo.com	Services listing in English
www.barcelona-online.com	Services listing in English
www.loquo.com	Community listings, similar to Craig's List
www.paginasamarillas.es	Yellow Pages
Others	
www.downloadalanguage.com	Useful Catalan and Spanish phrases
www.expatica.com	Expat advice
www.gencat.net	Catalan government
www.spainexpat.com	Expat information

Spain Annual Events 2007

The locals love a good fiesta (or *festa* in Catalan) and the year is littered with excuses to spill into the street for drink, dance and song. Liberal, republican, left-leaning Barcelona does not offer the same adoration of the Catholic church that can be witnessed in other parts of Spain, but the religious element of Christmas and Easter remains important, and these become times for families rather than raucous revelry (thought there's a bit of that too). The big events tend to be celebrations of (Catalan) national pride, rather than faith. La Mercè (patron saint of Barcelona) is celebrated with

A poster for one of Barcelona's last corridas (p.252)

particular vigour – a three day carnival of food, drink and music. The city also has a number of music festivals that are getting attention from across Europe. And then, far too numerous to mention here, are the *festas* to be found in each barrio. Often running within bigger events (and sometimes run of their own accord) each neighborhood will celebrate its own few streets at least once a year. Keep an eye of your free local paper for details.

Barcelona International Jazz Festival

Various locations
October – December

www.theproject.es

For almost four decades, the city's jazz festival has lured international performers. It kicks off at the end of October and runs for several weeks, with concerts scattered around the city.

Barcelona Marathon

L'Hospitalet de Llobregat
First Sunday in March

www.barcelonamarato.es

Thousands of runners hit the pavement for the annual marathon (the 2008 race is scheduled for 2 March). The mostly flat course passes Barcelona's main sights, and finishes at the Fira Exhibition area, just below MNAC.

Carnaval

Various locations
February

www.bcn.es/carnaval

Before the Christian calendar marks the Lenten period of fasting, there's Carnaval, the celebration of decadence and excess. Locals deck out in costumes and join the parade of bands marching randomly through different neighbourhoods. The bigger Carnaval celebrations take place in the nearby beach town of Sitges.

Public Holidays

January 1 New Year's Day
January 6 Epiphany
Good Friday changes annually
Easter Monday changes annually
May 1 Labour Day
Pentecost changes annually
August 15 Assumption
September 11 National Day of Catalonia
September 24 La Mercè
October 12 Columbus Day
November 1 All Saints' Day
December 6 Constitution Day
December 8 Day of the Immaculate Conception
December 25 Christmas Day
December 26 Saint Stephen's Day/Boxing Day

Annual Events

Various locations
5 January

Cavalcada dels Reis Mags d'Orient
www.barcelonaturisme.com

The Epiphany, the day in Christian folklore when three kings visited baby Jesus, is officially January 6, but the festivities kick-off with a bang the night before. Kings Melchior, Caspar and Balthasar are greeted with a huge fanfare, as the grand-scale parade winds its way from the downtown area to near Plaça d' Espanya. Streets are packed with families, and kids scramble to collect sweets thrown from those hitching a ride on the elaborately-decorated floats.

Various locations
First week in June

Corpus Christi and L'Ou Com Balla (The Dancing Egg)
www.catedralbcn.org

With origins dating back to 1637, the dancing egg is one Barcelona's quirkiest customs. Event organisers make eggs dance on top of water spouts shooting out of the fountains in the cathedral's cloister, patio and garden areas. Eggs aren't the only things dancing. Locals cut a rug with the customary sardana circle dance and *gegants* and *bestiari* (giants and beasts) shake their booties around the Ajuntamanet building in Plaça de Sant Jaume.

Various locations
23 April

Diada de Sant Jordi
www.bcn.es

This is the city's equivalent to Valentine's Day, but better. Catalonia's patron saint, Sant Jordi, or St. George, is said to have saved a princess by slaying a dragon. Legend has it that on the spot where the dragon's blood fell, a rose bloomed. Coincidentally, writers Miguel de Cervantes and William Shakespeare died on the same day, in 1616, tying in the book angle. Book and rose stalls line the main streets downtown, namely La Rambla and Rambla de Catalunya, and it's customary for men to give women a single long-stem rose, while women give men a book.

Various locations
Last two weeks in May

DiBa (Digital Barcelona Film Festival)
www.dibafestival.com

Although digital film-production is becoming more mainstream, DiBa, usually held during the last two weeks of May, continues to showcase how the technology is being used in short and feature-length films, videos and animation. Aspiring filmmakers are invited to submit their own clips, which must be based on the topic announced by event organisers and produced during the three-day event.

Various locations
Third week in September

Festa de La Mercè
www.bcn.cat

Barcelona ends the summer with a big party for its patron saint, La Mercè. It's the festival of the year, with hundreds of events, music concerts, castells exhibitions, parades of fire-breathing dragons and devils, sardana dances and an air show. The official holiday is September 24, and the festival runs for several days before or after that date, usually corresponding with the closest weekend. After experiencing it once, you'll be delighted that you live here.

Various locations
Gràcia
Second week in August

Festa Major de Gràcia
www.festamajordegracia.cat

Every neighbourhood has its special feast day, and Gràcia hosts one of the main *festa majors* on Barcelona's calendar. Music performances, *correfocs* (costumed devils that run around with fire and sparklers) and a host of other activities fill the garland-covered streets.

Festival de Música Creativa i Jazz de Citutat Vella

Various locations
June

93 301 77 75

This month-long event supports innovations in creative music and jazz. Concerts featuring local and international musicians are held at several venues and bars, and you can pick up the schedule at tourist offices.

Festival Guitarra Barcelona

Various locations
March – June

www.theproject.es

The annual guitar festival, running for almost two decades, showcases local and international musicians. Usually on from late March to early June, concerts are staged at various locations, with some shows scheduled at the Palau de la Musica (p.371), a Modernist building well worth visiting with or without an accompanying performance.

Fira de la Santa Llúcia

Various locations
December

www.bcn.cat

To ring in the holidays, head over to the cathedral area for the Santa Llúcia market during the first few weeks in December. Hundreds of stalls lining the plaza and pedestrian alleyways are stocked with Nativity figures, mistletoe, Christmas trees and miscellaneous arts and crafts. And what's up with that log-thing, you ask? The one with the *barratina* cap and goofy smile, hoisted up on two sticks? Well, that's Caga Tió, and a strange part of the Catalan Christmas tradition. There's no polite explanation, but the short story is: at Christmas, children sing a song and beat the log with a stick. Then, the log 'poops' sweets, nuts and turrons (a nougat-based bar also very popular during Christmas time) for them to snaffle up.

Grec Festival

Various locations
June – August

www.barcelonafestival.com

One of the city's beloved festivals, the Grec's dance, music and theatre programme has been a summer highlight for more than three decades. Performances are held throughout the city, and there are a number of kid-friendly events. It's usually held from mid-June through to the beginning of August, and the tourist office will have the updated schedule from around the end of May.

Independent Film Festivals

Various locations
Throughout the year

http://alternativa.cccb.org

Barcelona has a thriving independent film community, and a good number of events celebrating the indy scene. A notable one is L'Alternativa's Independent Film Festival of Barcelona, which runs during the second and third weeks of November and showcases a spectrum of genres and styles from local and international filmmakers. Other film festivals are scheduled throughout the year, check the sites for dates: Barcelona Asian Film Festival (www.baff-bcn.org); Jewish Film Festival (www.fcjbarcelona.org), and the Barcelona International Women's Film Festival (http://mostra.dracmagic.com).

La Revetlla de Sant Joan (Summer Solstice Celebration)

Various locations
23 June

www.santjoan.org

The summer solstice takes on a special meaning in Barcelona. On the eve of Sant Joan's day (24 June), locals pop the cork on a bottle of cava (locally-produced sparkling wine), chow down on the traditional cake filled with custard and pine nuts, and then go crazy with fireworks and bonfires. The parties start in the neighbourhoods soon after sundown and continue on the beach until sunrise.

LOOP Festival

Various locations
Last two weeks of May

www.loop-barcelona.com

A relatively new festival on the Barcelona agenda, LOOP promotes video art work and encourages young artists to explore the format. Work from 800 artists was displayed in 106 venues around the city during the 12 day event in 2007.

Primavera Sound

Parc del Forum
Sant Martí
Last week in May/
First week in June

www.primaverasound.com

One of the city's bigger music festivals, with more than 100 bands on the three-day line-up, Primavera Sound kicks off the summer season and has brought in the likes of Sonic Youth and The Smashing Pumpkins. Lately, it's been held at the Forum's seaside venue, but check out the website for upcoming dates and locations.

Santa Eulàlia Festival

Various locations
12 Februrary

www.barcelonaturisme.com

While Mercè now claims the title of Barcelona's patron saint, people still honour Santa Eulàlia, the former patroness, with a winter festival that lasts about a week. Activities staged throughout the city include an exhibition of *gegants* and *bestiary* (giants that resemble kings, queens, country folk and crazy beasts) combined with song and dance performances. The festival will be held around the 12 February feast day, but exact dates will change annually, so check with the tourist office for the most updated schedule.

Sónar

Various locations
Second week in June

www.sonar.es

In a city known for it edgy art scene, this increasingly popular three-day international music and multimedia festival brings together music, new media and audiovisual elements. Conferences, panel discussions and concerts, with past headliners like Devo and the Beastie Boys, are held across town.

Summercase Rock Festival

Fòrum
Poblenou
Mid-July
🚇 *El Maresme/*
Fòrum

www.summercase.com

With the Mediterranean Sea in the background, the days sizzle with the Summercase Rock Festival. Tag-teaming with similar concerts in Madrid, nearly 50 bands play Barcelona's Forum during the Friday and Saturday event.

Sunrise over Plaça d'Espanya

Residents

Overview

It's hard not to fall in love with a city like Barcelona, with its high quality of life, good weather, progressive attitude and thriving nightlife, arts and culture. And it is redefining itself, from a regional capital to a global city. You can't walk far without seeing a construction site, and whole neighbourhoods, such Poblenou and the Forum area, are getting complete makeovers. New waves of immigration from Africa, Asia, the Americas and other parts of Europe are also reshaping the city's demographics and influencing the job, consumer goods, services and housing markets. This expansion does bring some negatives (like rising rents), but it's an exciting time to live here. Whether you're still toying with the idea of making the leap, have just shipped your last boxes over, or have been here a while, this chapter is designed to steer you through all aspects of making this great city feel like home.

Urban Myths

Bullfighting? Flamenco? In Barcelona? Not really. These Spanish traditions are not a big part of life here. Tour operators may plug skirt-swirling, feet-tapping flamenco nights at restaurants or clubs, but for the real thing you'll have better luck elsewhere in Spain. Same with bullfighting. Not only did the city council vote to become an 'anti-bullfighting city' in 2004, one of its bullrings is being converted into a shopping centre and rumour has it that the fate of the other one, which still stages occasional bullfights (mostly for Andalusian immigrants), is on shaky ground. See p.252 for more.

Considering Spain

While many first-timers may come with the perception that Barcelona is a city of long siestas and beach lounging, the truth is a little different once you are a resident. The city's economic expansion during the last 15 years, along with the increased mobility of European Union residents and Spain's 2002 transition to the euro, have increased competition for jobs and apartments, put a greater emphasis on productivity, and meant longer working days and higher prices. Salaries, though, have held steady, and are generally lower than in other parts of Europe.

As the city has developed, construction and service jobs have boomed. Also, the local administration has backed several projects aimed at attracting the IT, bio-chemical, trade and commerce sectors, creating all sorts of opportunities for newcomers and

View from Montjuïc

entrepreneurs. But, you will probably need to demonstrate proficiency in either Spanish or Catalan before landing those gigs. The fallback for many native English speakers is teaching at one of the many language schools. Besides a modest pay cheque, the schools can help cut through the red tape of residency.

From a cost of living standpoint, Barcelona is not as cheap as it used to be. It's still cheaper than London or New York, but prices are always creeping up, blindsiding even the long-time residents. It's common, too, to hear people complain about the lack of affordable housing, and that young people must often share an apartment with two or three roommates to make ends meet.

But, if you build up a financial cushion before you come, and do pre-trip research on job, housing and visa requirements, you'll be able to make a good life in this dynamic city.

Before You Arrive

The ease with which you get the necessary work and residency permits for Barcelona will depend on your nationality. Residents of the European Union and the European Economic Area face much less bureaucracy.

Non-EU residents will typically have to provide more detailed explanations about the purpose of their stay, and the pile of paperwork will have to be routed through the Spanish consulate in their home country. Things should be easier if you get a job beforehand, as your company may be able to help with a visa application.

It's advisable to check with your local Spanish consulate or embassy (www.mae.es/en/WebEmbajadasConsulados) about the latest requirements, as laws are constantly changing. The Catalalan government also has a useful welcome guide with an overview of what is needed (www.gencat.net/benestar/immigracio/web_ac). And, you'll need all your essential documents; passport, birth and marriage certificates, driving licence and, if applicable, identity card. You will need to present these at almost every step.

You'll also need to sort your affairs at home; settle existing rental contracts; shut off water, electricity and phone services; organise shipping or storage; inform banks and financial institutions that you are moving aboard, and look into tax and pension implications.

Perhaps most importantly, take Spanish lessons. English will only get you so far, and you'll need to communicate with locals as soon as you get off the plane.

Browse the rest of this chapter for information about lining up work, a place to live and enrolling children at school.

Traducción ◄

For a list of officially approved translators (traductores), see the table on p.53 of this chapter. For many documents, you will need to carry your original, and a version in Spanish.

When You Arrive

Your first few weeks may be a little overwhelming. While enjoying the social distractions of your new city, there are a few 'life admin' basics that will ensure things run smoothly.

Social Security – EU and EEA residents (and non-EU residents with work permits) should enroll in the social security system. Most employers will do this, but if you're self-employed, go to www.seg-social.es. See more in the Work section, p.58.

Foreign Identity Card – Your NIE (Numero de Identidad de Extranjero) will be needed for any dealings with officialdom. You can apply for this at the Oficina de Extranjeros (www.extranjeros.mtas.es/en/index.html) or at your local police station. See p.23.

Open a bank account – Utility companies will debit monthly payments straight from your bank account. See Banks on p.36.

Turn on your new life – For info about connecting water, electricity, phone and internet services, see p.100. For a list of social groups and business organisations, see p.240.

Transfer you driving licence – See p.53 for how.

Register at your embassy – It's worth letting your embassy know that you're here. See p.21 for contact numbers.

Charm the locals – While you may have some Spanish under your belt, it's worth knowing Catalan too. It's the language on the street, and speaking it will help you integrate faster. Corsorci per a La Normalització Lingüística (www.cpnl.cat) can hook you up with free courses. See p.128 for more.

And most importantly, approach the whole process with a smile and a sense of humour.

Essential Documents

It may help to put together a packet of essential documents, such as:
- Passport, valid for at least one year (and an EU national identity card, where applicable)
- Passport or ID photocopies
- Passport photos
- Educational or professional certifications (attested in your home country)
- Resume and references
- Copies of bank, income or tax statements, or other proof you can support yourself
- Proof of health insurance (or a European Health Insurance Card; see p.107)
- Original birth and marriage certificates plus photocopies
- Employment contract, or for the self-employed, a business proposal
- Rental or housing agreements

Many of these documents must be translated into Spanish by a certified translator (see p.53), and some will need attestation by a notary public in your home country (this is sometimes known as an apostille seal). Start as early as you can on this. It's a lengthy (and costly) process and you may have to go to several different offices to get all the correct approvals. Check out the Ministerio de Trabajo y Asuntos Sociales website (www.mtas.es) for updated information.

When You Leave

Just as when you arrived, you'll want give yourself some time to wind down. Before you go, make sure you:
- Settle your contract with your landlord or flatmates, or decide what do with the property you bought here. See housing p.68.
- Decide what to take with you and what can stay behind. For shipping and moving services, see p.94. If you're looking to get rid of anything, find out when your neighbourhood's *trastos* day is. Every *barri* has one day in which you can leave sofas, beds and other household items at the street dumpster.
- Disconnect utilities (see p.100) and pay final bills. Make sure you give providers a forwarding address or way of contacting you for refunds or returned deposits.

Documents

Immigration Lawyers
While the information in this section covers all the rules and procedures you'll need to go through, it shouldn't replace your own due diligence or professional advice from a lawyer or other expert. See p.67 for listings.

Barcelona, along with the rest of Catalonia and Spain, is experiencing an immigration surge. Foreigners now account for 15.7% of the city's 1.59 million residents. With that comes a pile of legislation, red tape and long queues (that often just lead to longer queues elsewhere). How well you cut through the bureaucracy will depend on your nationality, the duration of your stay, the reasons you want to live here and your proficiency in Spanish. There are different rules for nationals of different countries, and therefore, different document, visa and work permit requirements. Since visas are not issued in Spain, you'll have to coordinate with the Spanish consulate in your country of origin well in advance. Although your own country's consulate or embassy in Spain will play no part in issuing visas and work permits, it's worth checking out their website, as they sometimes post useful advice. Keep the faith, and know that the city has set up a number of resources to help you through the process, many of which will be discussed in this section.

Entry Visa

The main visas are divided into short-term stay (transits and 90-day visits) and long-term stay (student, residency and combined labour and residency visas). EU residents do not need an entry visa, and neither do residents of the US, Canada, Australia or New Zealand who plan to spend up to 90 days in the country on holiday (so no work or study). Residents of countries signed up to the Schengen Agreement (that's the EU minus the UK and Ireland but including Norway and Iceland) do not even need a passport to enter, and can swan through on a national ID card.

Visa Runs

For non EU citizens, visa runs can be something of a pain. Your short stay visa only entitles you to 90 days in the Schengen area in a six month period. At the end of this 90 days, you don't just need to leave Spain for the rest of the six months, but the whole of the Schengen area. The nearest non-Schengen spots are the UK and Ireland, north Africa, Switzerland (though it is expected to join), and the countries that used to form Yugoslavia.

Short Stay Visa

If your country has an agreement with Spain, you may enter without a visa for up to 90 days in any six-month period. Residents of Australia, Canada, Japan, New Zealand, Singapore, the United States and many South American countries, for instance, do not need entry visas, but must present a valid passport. The length of passport validity required varies.

Residents of other countries (or visitors who want to extend their stay) must submit a visa application at the Spanish diplomatic mission or consulate's office in their home country. Besides the application, you'll present a valid passport; passport photos; the original of your previous short-stay visa (if any); the reason for your visit or extension; proof that you have the financial means to support yourself without work; valid medical insurance, and a guarantee to leave the country when your extension expires.

Depending on where you hail from, you may also need a transit visa, valid for less than five days, while you move through Spanish territories and international airports.

As mentioned above, Spain is a Schengen Agreement signatory. In essence, this means you can visit any other Schengen country on your 90 day Spanish visa. However, you are limited to a total of 90 days in any Schengen country, and the countdown does not begin again until you leave the Schengen area completely.

Resources
For fee information and forms to download, go to the Ministro de Asuntos Exteriores y de Cooperación site (www.maec.es) and follow the links to your home country's consulate and visa section. If you're in Barcelona and wondering if your documents are in order, or want advice on obtaining visas for friends planning a visit, head over to the Oficina de Extranjeros (Oficina d' Estrangers in Catalan, 93 520 14 10, Avinguda Marquès de l'Argentera 4, www.map.es) or to Servei Atenció Immigrants Estrangers i Refugiats (SAIER 93 423 7828, Avinguda del Paral·lel 202). La Conselleria de Benestar Social has also set up a free phone service to answer immigration-related questions; dial 012 and ask for an English-speaking representative.

Spanish Embassies
For a quick view of Spanish embassies around the world, go to www.spanish-living.com/info_embassies.htm.

Residence Visa

EU residents and those covered by the European Economic Agreement (Norway and Iceland) don't need residence visas. But, if you intend to stay in Spain for an extended period, you will need a Foreign Identity Number (Número de Identidad de Extranjero, or NIE) and may also need a Residence Card (Tarjeta de Residencia). You can apply through the Oficina de Extranjeros/Oficina d'Estrangers (http://extranjeros.mtas.es, available in English, French and Spanish). Once you have settled in, you'll want to head over to your local city hall (Ajuntament) and add your name to the Padró Municipal d'Habitants, the residency registry which entitles you to other benefits. See the ID card section on p.52 for more.

Non-EU Citizens

Everyone else, roll up your sleeves. This is where the cat and mouse game begins and the rubber-stamp collecting can get complicated.

First, you'll need to decide on the most appropriate visa for you. The broad categories include student, residency and a combined work and residency visa. There are also visas for family members, family reunification, retired persons, self-employment and investors. In all cases, though, you'll want to coordinate with the local Spanish consulate in your home country, which will act as the middleman for all visa-related matters. Other things to keep in mind:

• Confirm that what's listed on the consulate's website is the most up to date set of requirements. Rules change, so call and ask for specific lists of necessary forms, essential documents and certifications.
• Cross-check requirements with the Ministerio de Trabajo y Asuntos Sociales' Secretaría de Estado de Inmigración y Emigración (http://extranjeros.mtas.es), as there may be other forms you need once you get here.
• Verify if visas will be issued for a certain period of time and if they can renewed. Some are issued for 180 days and no more, while others may be initially offered for a year with renewals extending for two years.
• Build in extra time for getting documents translated.
• Clarify what tasks employers will organise and what burden falls back to you.
• Schedule time in Barcelona to get authorisations from proper agencies.
• Expect the process to be costly and take several months to complete.

Residence Visa

There are a few types of residence visa that allow you to live in Spain, but not to work or conduct 'lucrative activities' here. These visas include:

Retired resident: For this, you'll need medical and criminal record certificates, documents showing financial status and a passport valid for at least one year. Plus, you may need to prove family ties to someone already living in Spain.

Family residency: If you've been resident in Spain for one year and have your residency renewed for another 12 months you can make moves to 'sponsor' family members. Visa applications can be submitted for a spouse, unmarried children under 18 and parents (either the resident's or the spouse's) if they are dependants or their stay can be otherwise justified. The foreigner 'sponsoring' the family members must get approval from the Delegación or Subdelegación del Gobierno (www.map.es). Copies of this authorisation and the sponsoring resident's passport, along with certified birth and marriage certificates and proof of funds, may also be needed.

Labour & Residence Visa

There a handful of different live-work visas, issued for fixed periods of time or certain kinds of jobs, but you may have to trudge through several layers of bureaucracy to get all the right papers together.

Employee visa: Starting your life in Barcelona with a job contract will make the visa process much easier, but given the competitive market and increasing number of foreigners scrapping for these jobs, getting hired from abroad can be tricky. For more on work and the kinds of jobs you may find here, see p.60. In many cases, your employer will guide you through the process or submit documentation on your behalf. But, in order to complete your visa application at the consulate's office in your country of origin, you may need a letter from the Immigration Office in Spain (Oficina de Extranjero/Oficina d'Estrangers; Avinguda Marquès de l'Argentera 4, www.map.es, 93 520 14 10) granting you and your company work permit authorisation.

Reunite with an EU citizen: Spouses, children and parents of Spanish or EU citizens may apply for this visa and be granted the same work privileges as an EU citizen. You'll need to prove family ties and will also need a copy of the sponsoring Spanish or EU citizen's passport and Empadronamiento, the piece of paper that lists their residency in the Ajuntament's books.

Student Visa

If you're coming to Barcelona for studies, training or research, you can apply for a student visa. You can simultaneously request visas for your spouse or any children under 18 for the duration of your studies. Among the standard stack of documents, expect to show your admission or pre-registration letter from a recognised educational institution, a clean criminal record certificate, and, if you're below 18, notarised authorisation from your parents or legal guardian to study abroad.

Plaça d'Espanya

Other Useful Information

Once you clear the hurdles and walk away with a visa fixed to your passport, you'll have a month to apply for your Foreign Identity Number (Número de Identidad de Extranjero, or NIE) and possibly a Foreign Residence Card (Tarjeta de Identificación de Extranjero, or TIE). You can apply in person at the Oficina de Extranjeros/Oficina d'Estrangers (http://extranjeros.mtas.es, available in English, French and Spanish) or at the Police Department. Some visas will also require you to enrol in the Social Security system (National Social Security Institute, INSS, www.seg-social.es).

Labour Card

Spain doesn't have a labour card as such, but if you are a non-EU citizen you do need work permits to join the labour pool. For more on these see Residence Visa, p.50. EU and non-EU citizens must obtain a Foreign Identity Number (Número de Identidad de Extranjero, or NIE), which serves as your main identification here, and possibly a Foreign Residence Card (Tarjeta de Identificación de Extranjero, or TIE). See below for more.

ID Card

Gran Hermano
In theory, you can be arrested for not carrying officially recognised ID with you, although this is very rarely enforced. See Legal Issues, p.66 for more on local law.

Spanish law requires that you carry ID with you at all times. This can be a passport or picture driving licence, but for the administration that will be necessary in your first few months, you'll also need an ID number (NIE).

Número de Identidad de Extranjero (NIE)

Your main form of Spanish identification is your Foreign Identity Number (Número de Identidad de Extranjero, or NIE). It's a compulsory ID number and you'll need it for nearly all business, professional or personal activities. Often, you'll need to present both your NIE and passport when filling out government paperwork. You'll need to apply for both the NIE and TIE through the Oficina de Extranjeros/Oficina d'Estrangers (http://extranjeros.mtas.es, available in English, French and Spanish).

Tarjeta de Residencia (TIE)

There's also a Foreign Residence Card, sometimes called Tarjeta de Residencia, Tarjeta de Identificación de Extranjero, or TIE, and you may be asked to show this. It's the size of a credit card and easier to fit in your wallet than your passport. This card was required for all non-Spanish citizens living in the country, until 2003. Now, it is unclear how much use they are, particularly for EU citizens.

Based on new regulations approved in March 2007, all EU citizens planning to live in Spain for more than three months will need to register in person at the Oficina de Extranjeros or at police stations. Under this change, certificates stating the resident's name, address, nationality, identity number and date of registration will replace the previously issued cards.

Note that the certificate serves as confirmation that you've registered, but local authorities do not recognise it as a valid form of identification. So, you'll still have to carry either your passport or another type of photo ID. Non-EU residents should ask for confirmation as well, as laws are always changing.

Padró Municipal d'Habitants

After you've settled in and can prove residence in the form of housing contracts and utility bills, go to your neighbourhood's Ajuntament office and register for the Padró Municipal d'Habitants. This is the official record the city uses to count who's living here, and once you're on the list, you'll have access to other benefits, such as the national healthcare system.

Driving Licence

Other options **Transportation** p.129

You must be 18 years old to drive a car or motorcycle, and 16 to drive a scooter or moped. Depending on your country of origin, and any reciprocal agreements with Spain, you may or may not have to change your driving licence. Licences from most of the western world can be exchanged for a Spanish one, but in other cases, you'll have to start from scratch and take both a theory and practical exam.

You must have your licence, vehicle registration and motor insurance certificate with you at all times while operating a car or motorcycle, or risk being fined. Spot checks of licences tend to coincide with roadblocks looking for drunk drivers.

In Barcelona, all licences and applications are handled by the Dirección General de Tráfico office (Gran Vía de les Corts Catalanes 184, www.dgt.es, 93 298 65 39).

Translators		
Brenda Oldham Hulse	93 200 44 27	falcontraining@yahoo.com
Calbet Rebollo (C)	93 419 05 58	Pilarcalbet@terra.es
Froya Silvana Ek Florit	93 412 41 40	ek_idiomas@yahoo.com
Luís Pérez Vidal	93 217 16 09	LluisP9@netscape.net
Marisa Martínez Viñuales	93 454 41 77	mmv.interpret@retemail.es
Mercè Camp Alemany	617 503 078	mercecamp@yahoo.es
Sergio Pawlowsky Glahn (C)	93 486 42 80	spg@celerpawlowsky.com

These translators are all officially recognised. Those with a (C) can also translate Catalan.

Driving as a Resident

EU residents, or those covered by the European Economic Agreement, can use their licences, but will have to register with the traffic authorities within six months of moving to Spain. There is no obligation to exchange your licence.

If you are a non-EU citizen, and your country's licence is covered by a reciprocal agreement, your foreign licence will remain valid for six months, after which you will need to swap it for a Spanish one. If your country's licence is not covered by a reciprocal agreement with Spain, you will have to take the full driving test. This involves theory and practical exams. Driving schools, while a costly option, can be of immense value and eliminate many of the obstacles. You must have legal residence or a work permit to receive a Spanish licence, and in some cases you will need to be a resident for one year before applying.

You'll need an application form (Gran Vía de les Corts Catalanes 184, www.dgt.es, 93 298 65 39), your NIE, your passport (original and photocopies) and passport size photos. You may also need a medical certificate showing mental and physical health. Conveniently, in Barcelona, there are dozens of offices near the Dirección General de Tráfico building where you can get these pieces of paper. The local authorities may issue a temporary licence while they verify your identity and driving status in your home country.

Driving as a Visitor

EU-issued licences are valid for driving in Spain. For non-EU visitors, you may need an international driving licence, and sometimes an accompanying, valid licence from your home country. Alternatively, you may only have to present a valid licence with an official Spanish translation. The exact regulations vary from country to country, but car rental agencies or the DGT website can fill you in.

Driving Test

The driving test is divided into two sections, theory (written) and practical (on the road). The theory part consists of 40 questions testing your knowledge about road rules and safety. The study guides and tests are now available in English. The practical

53

Driving Schools

Atenea	93 329 69 24	www.ateneautoes.com
Bel-Air	93 425 06 58	www.belairautoescuelas.com
Canyelles	93 427 61 25	www.autoescolacanyelles.com
Corsa	93 204 29 52	www.autoescolescorsa.com
Cota	93 302 11 40	www.cota.es
Gràcia	93 454 99 27	www.autoescolagracia.com
Marte	93 458 93 83	www.aemarte.com
Mendi	93 357 93 48	www.autoescuelamendi.com
Santamaria	93 347 91 38	www.autoescolasantamaria.com
Zona F	93 331 86 12	www.autoescolazonaf.com

test will be conducted in Spanish. You must pass both parts to obtain a licence, and you have the opportunity to take them again if you fail.

Driving schools may be the best way to tackle the test. They provide lessons and study materials and help schedule the test. It's not cheap, though. There are registration fees, test fees and per hour rates for each lesson. The number of lessons will depend on your experience, but, more likely than not, will be conducted in Spanish. There are plenty of driving schools (*autoescuelas/autoescoles*) in Barcelona. See the table for details. A good place to research schools is at Federació d' Autoescoles de Barcelona (www.autoescoles-fab.net/cat).

Motorcycle Licences

There are two motorcycle licences. The A1 type is for mopeds and scooters, with a lower age limit of 16. The A type licence is for motorcycles, and applicants must be at least 18 years old. For an A1 vehicle, a car driving licence is sufficient, but for a motorcycle, a driving test is required. Both can be obtained from the Dirección General de Tráfico office (Gran Vía de les Corts Catalanes 184, www.dgt.es, 93 298 65 39).

Birth Certificate & Registration

When you have a baby, you are legally obliged to register the child's birth with the Registre Civil in the town where it was born. Once the baby has been alive for 24 hours, you have eight days to make the registration, or 20 days if there are extenuating circumstances.

If the baby was born in a hospital, you should receive a maternity report stating the name of the delivery doctor or medical professional, the location of the birth and the baby's statistics (name, date and time of birth, gender).

If the parents are married, the mother, the father or an authorised person representing the parents can make the registration. If the parents are not married, the mother and father may go together, each providing their personal data, or the mother can go alone. You will need to provide the documents from the hospital, forms provided by the Registre Civil, your identification (NIE, passport), proof of your relationship to the child and the baby's name, place and time of birth and sex. The birth is also to be entered in to the Family Book (Llibre de Família), which is also presented to couples when they get married.

After the registration is made, the baby's name will also be automatically added to the Padró Municipal d'Habitants. You can request a more formal birth certificate when you register the birth.

A baby born to foreign parents does not immediately have Spanish nationality. The baby must have residency for one year before nationality can be claimed. The Registre Civil, Oficina de Extranjeros (Oficina d'Estrangers), your country's consulate or the Spanish consulate in your country of origin will have more details about passports and visa procedures.

You should also register the birth at your country's consulate in Spain. Doing so establishes an official record of the child's claim to citizenship of your home country. Generalitat de Catalunya has more detailed information, predominantly in Catalan, about the birth certificate and registry process and other important life events; (www.cat365.net/Inici/FetsVitals).

Same-Sex Marriages
Same-sex marriages
were legalised by the
Spanish Parliament in
2005. The law also
allows same-sex
couples to receive
inheritances and
adopt children. See the
Gay and Lesbian
section of Going Out
(p.362) for info on the
city's vibrant gay scene.

Marriage Certificate & Registration

Barcelona offers a beautiful backdrop for a wedding. You have the sea, the sun, the architecture and frolicking romantics around each corner. Reflecting Barcelona's diversity, wedding ceremonies and receptions vary according to individual tastes. There are religious ceremonies and civil ones, big weddings and small ones. There are celebrations with all the trimmings, the fancy clothes, fancy dinner, fancy flowers, fancy photographer and hundreds of guests. Then, there the more intimate affairs, where small groups of family and friends toast the bride and groom at restaurants or at the family's home. There's also a whole business around weddings, with dress shops, florists, reception halls and caterers all offering to make the big day even more perfect. For a list of wedding services, see p.303.

Paperwork

Getting married in Barcelona is not necessarily difficult, but it does take time and patience to sort the paperwork. Give yourself two to four months before your wedding date, to get everything translated, certified, filed and approved.

Any citizen has the right to get married, as long as they are over 18 years old, are not already legally married and are not marrying a close family relative. Ceremonies can be performed by a justice of the peace, the mayor, a representative designated by the mayor, or a priest. They can be held at the Ajuntament, at the Registre Civil or in a public place, like a restaurant, garden or even a private home, as long as authorisation has been given for such events.

The first step is to go to the Registre Civil. You'll have to fill out forms and present your passport, DNI (for Spanish citizens), or Número de Identidad de Extranjero (NIE), or Foreign Residence Card (TIE, p.52 for both) in the case of foreigners, along with photocopies. You'll also need your original birth certificate translated into Spanish. Bring your Padró Municipal d'Habitants certificate (p.52) or other legal documents showing your last two years of residence. If you are a widow or widower, your previous marriage certificate and your spouse's death certificate are required, and if you're divorced or your marriage was annulled, relevant certificates must be presented. And, don't forget to bring a third-party witness who can vouch for your status.

Your country's consulate or embassy may wish to verify your identity and civil status. If so, you will have to submit similar forms and documentation there, too. While you're at the consulate's office, you may want to confirm that the marriage will be recognised in your home country and how to validate it there. Every country, including EU member states, has different regulations, so do your homework. The Registre Civil will provide you with some guidance as they see these situations all the time. Once the Registre Civil receives and reviews this information, it will give a stamp of approval. You'll then have to fill out more paperwork about the place, time and date of the wedding and to schedule an 'appointment' with the justice of the peace or other civil servant performing the ceremony.

After the ceremony, the official who conducted it will return the statements to the Registre Civil and confirm that the marriage has occurred. The Registre Civil will return to you a document known as

Adoption

Adoption is becoming more common in Spain, and same-sex couples are legally allowed to adopt as well.

Like everywhere else, though, it's a complicated process that could take several months, if not years, to complete. Abogado Servicios Jurídicos SL (www.spainlawyer.com) has overview information about adoption procedures for Spanish residents.

If you're thinking about adopting, the Federació d' Assocacions per a l'Adopció (www.federacioadopcio.org, 93 488 34 45) provides a comprehensive list of worldwide adoption organisations and services.

55

the Family Book (Llibre de Família). This is proof that the marriage is valid, and is the place where subsequent births, a spouse's death or a divorce or separation are recorded. Changing your name after marriage is not a common practice in Spain, but, if you do, you'll want to update all your ID, bank details and inform the social security office, as changes in martial status effect your financial and tax obligations.

Death Certificate & Registration

If a friend or relative dies in Barcelona or Spain, there are a few immediate steps to take. If the person dies at home or there are indications of violence, call 112, the local emergency number, for assistance.

Registering a Death

A medical examiner, doctor or authorised hospital official will provide a certificate listing the deceased's name, and the cause, date, time and place of death. This document will also contain the name and accreditation of the doctor who pronounced death. This document must be provided to the Registre Civil in the city where the death occurred, within 24 hours. The registry will also need the names of the deceased's parents, their civil status, nationality, date and place of birth, last known address and the place of the funeral. The office provides around-the-clock service for these kinds of matters, and without this information, the funeral cannot proceed.

While family members can register a death, it may be best to leave it to a funeral director. The funeral director can process all the necessary paperwork, secure a burial licence, arrange a cremation or return the deceased's remains to a country of origin. Often, your country's consulate can provide a list of funeral homes in Barcelona. A death certificate request can be made at the Registre Civil office where the death was registered, up to 15 days later. If you register the death with your country of origin's consulate, they may also issue something along the lines of Consular Report of a Death Abroad.

Organ Donation

Organ and tissue donation provide the gift of life to others in need of transplants. If you would like to become a donor, you can download a donor card from the Organització Catalana de Trasplantaments website (www10.gencat.net/catsalut/ocatt/ca/htm). Catalonia has one of the highest organ donation rates in the world, with liver and kidneys being the most commonly donated organs.

Returning Decreased to Country of Origin

When a foreign resident dies aboard, family members may decide to repatriate the deceased to their country of origin. This requires customs clearance certificates and meeting air travel regulations. Funeral directors can make these arrangements, but you should ensure that you choose one that has experience with these procedures. Also, given the high price of funerals, you may want to determine if the deceased had travel or life insurance that covers such costs. If they did, it could still take several months before the insurance claim will be paid, so discuss payment options with the funeral director in advance.

Investigation & Autopsy

Under certain circumstances, the police or the medical examiner may investigate a death, and an autopsy may be performed if the cause is unclear or suspicious. When the investigation is complete, a judicial permit will be issued and the body released for burial. Police records, unlike in other countries, are thought to be court property and are not often released. You may need to hire legal assistance if you wish to see those documents.

Are you always taking the wrong turn?

Whether you're a map person or not, these pocket-sized marvels will help you get to know the city – and its limits.

Explorer Mini Maps
Fit the city in your pocket

Working in Barcelona

Salaries may be lower than other EU countries, but a better work-life balance and bouyant social scene remain big draws for international workers. Working hours usually extend beyond 17:00, but this is often just to accommodate a proper lunch break (sometimes two hours long).

Residents have a healthy attitude about leaving work at the office. They try to squeeze more from life, whether that means hanging out with friends at outdoor cafes, going to concerts or museums, or jogging along the beach. Oddly enough, the way people balance their time has become such an important topic that Barcelona's city government has created a department for Nous Usos Socials del Temps (NUST), or New Social Uses of Time. It's charged with evaluating how citizens organise their work, family, leisure and private time, and developing a plan for how city services can be adjusted to fit residents' needs.

The influx of tourists and commercial activities keep Catalonia's unemployment rate low and the need for workers high. The fields of construction, public works and general business and consultancy are particularly buoyant. There's a continuing need for people with technical qualifications too, such as architects and engineers, and business admin and management experience.

But, even with strong economic growth, finding work in Barcelona can be overwhelming for newcomers. There's government bureaucracy, language barriers, challenges in transferring professional certificates and, at times, complicated labour laws and employee rights to contend with. Also, with the expansion of the EU, competition is tough, and despite the bevy of job-hunting resources, your best bet may come from your professional network and personal contacts. The Barcelona job market still very much relies on word-of-mouth recommendations.

For many English-speaking expats, the way to get started is to teach English and land a job at one of the many language schools. Finding seasonal work in the tourism industry or at restaurants and bars may also open doors. The city has a number of English language call centre operations; although for each one attached to a big corporation, another is a dodgy boiler room, running phone scams.

Of course, how smoothly the process goes depends on where you come from. EU and EEA residents have an advantage, in that their rights to live and work in the country are already protected. Therefore, they don't need special visas. For non-EU and non-EEA residents, if you want to work in Barcelona, you'll need permits which will be tied to your residence visa. These will need to be routed through the Spanish consulate in your country of origin. See p.50 for more on visas.

The top of La Rambla

Work

Qualifications

To obtain a professional or technical position, you may have to show accreditations, qualifications or other certificates attesting to your skills. This can be complicated, because not all documents, diplomas or citations, even from other parts of the EU, will be recognised. Also, you may need official stamps or sign-off by a notary public to make your documents legal internationally.

A list of professions that are regulated in Spain and require qualifications can be found at the Ministry of Education and Science website, though only in Spanish; Ministerio de Educación y Ciencia (wwwn.mec.es/educa/formacion-profesional). The Education Inspectorate in Barcelona (93 520 96 03, Carrer Bergara 12) can clarify qualification requirements, and so can the Generalitat's Department of Education (www.gencat.net/educacio) or any of the Education Offices at the Spanish consulate in your country of origin.

Learning The Lingo
For a few basic words of Catalan and Spanish, go to the table on p.17 of General Information. To learn Catalan, see p.128. For Language Schools, see p.223

Languages

If you want to work in Barcelona for an extended period of time, you will need to try and learn Spanish and, eventually, Catalan. Businesses tend to operate in both languages and for some civil service and education sector jobs you may need to prove proficiency in both. Spanish and Catalan courses are provided by private and public organisations. The Instituto Cervantes (www.cervantes.es) offers Spanish courses at its centres and organises examinations for DELE (Diploma for Spanish as a Foreign Language), which is an official qualification certifying a level of skill and fluency in Spanish language. The Consorci per a la Normalització Lingüística (www.cpnl.cat) provides similar services for Catalan. The first stage is free, and the rest heavily subsidised.

Government Resources

There are a number of local, regional, national and EU resources with details of workers' rights, legal information and job-hunting services. Within Barcelona, SAIER, Servei d'Atenció a Immigrants Estrangers i Refugiats (93 292 40 77, Avinguda del Paral·lel 202-204) is a good place to start. Catalonia's Generalitat (www.gencat.net) has a wealth of information, often linked to its Oficines de Treball de la Generalitat (Labour Offices or OTG), and the Servei d'Ocupació de Catalunya (Occupation Service or SOC, www.oficinatreball.net).

The Spanish Public Employment Service (Instituto de Empleo Servicio Público de Empleo Estatal or INEM), overseen by the Ministry of Work and Social Affairs (Ministerio de Trabajo y Asuntos Sociales), has advice, intermittently written in English, about working in Spain. It also has related legislation and downloadable guidebooks on its website (www.inem.es).

EURES (European Employment Services, http://europa.eu.int/eures) is brimming with information about working in EU countries. It also serves as a job portal, where you post CVs.

Working Hours

The hours you work will depend on the industry you're in and your contract. The standard working week is 40 hours, with a nine-hour day (eight-hours for those under 18 years old), but can run longer. Office workers start at about 08:00 or 09:00, break for

---

Baristas & Barristers

For many new residents, work in Barcelona is almost an after-thought. Often, it is the lifestyle that attracts people, rather than career development. They come first to soak up the sun and surf, enjoy the vibrant nightlife and take in the culture. And there are enough odd-jobs – bar work, call centres, teaching English – to keep a lively, youthful community honest. The expats you meet are as likely to be baristas as barristers.

The Complete **Residents'** Guide

an hour or two at 14:00 and then plug away until 18:00 or 19:00. Shops open around 10:00, generally close for two or three hours in the afternoon and re-open until 20:00. Shops in tourist areas are more likely to skip the siesta.

Government offices and banks tend to open from 08:00ish until 14:00, though some may have a late opening day, when they manage to stay awake until late afternoon. Not much is open on Sundays, except for small delis, bars and restaurants.

Some contracts and collective bargaining agreements only allow workers to punch in a maximum of 80 hours of overtime per year. This must be paid in time off or with extra money. There are 12 national public holidays and two local holidays annually, with a few tied to Christian festivals.

Come Back in the Autumn

During the summer, opening hours may fluctuate. Some small businesses close for the whole of August, while others take longer breaks in the middle of the day.

Business Councils & Groups

American Society of Barcelona	www.amersoc.com
Associació Independent de Joves Empesaris (AIJEC)	www.aijec.es
Barcelona Activa	www.barcelonactiva.cat
Barcelona Women's Network	www.bcnwomensnetwork.com
BarcelonaNETactiva	www.barcelonanetactiva.com
British Chamber of Commerce in Spain	www.britishchamberspain.com
British Society of Catalunya	www.bsce.ch
Business Angels Network Catalunya	www.bancat.com
Camerdata	www.camerdata.es
Centre d'Innovació i Desenvolupament Empresarial (CIDEM)	www.cidem.com
Consejo Superior de Cámaras de Comercio, Industria y Navegación	www.camaras.org
International Women's Club of Barcelona	www.iwcbarcelona.com
Micro, Petita i Mitjana Empresa de Catalunya	www.pimec.es

Health Card

If you're coming from another EU or EEA country, bring related 'E' forms or the European Health Card issued by your country's social security agency. Spanish employers or government officials may ask for this. Also, E-301 forms are required to credit work accrued in your country.

Finding Work

Finding work in Barcelona, particularly for non-EU citizens, offers a Catch22. Having a job will help speed the visa process. But, in order to get a job you love, or at least one you could live with for a while, you have to be here networking, building contacts and listening to the local grapevine. With Barcelona becoming a more desirable place to live, the labour market grows more competitive every year. To win the bid, work on your CV; highlight prior experience, advanced degrees and any languages you speak.

Unemployment Benefits

EU citizens are entitled to unemployment benefits in Spain should they find themselves out of work. They will need to complete an E-303 form before leaving their home country.

Finding Work Before You Arrive

While many people just pitch up with their fingers crossed, you'll save time, money and aggravation if you research beforehand. Check with the Spanish consulate in your home country to find out about work and residence visas, what types of documentation you'll need to provide and if special international seals or translations are required. Put your CV in good order, get it translated into Spanish and Catalan and research the local and international companies you'd like to work for, double-checking if they do indeed hire foreign workers. Sometimes, competition within Spain and the EU is so fierce, international candidates will immediately be discounted.

Scour the job boards and online classifieds for leads, too. Some of the main online search engines are: Empleo (www.empleo.com); Laboris (www.laboris.net); Loquo (www.loquo.com); Monster (www.monster.es) and Trabajo (www.trabajo.org).

The main newspapers for job ads are *Avui* (www.avui.com), *El Periódico* (www.elperiodico.es) and *La Vanguardia* (www.lavanguardia.es). See p.38 for more on local media.

Catalonia's Generalitat has a thorough list of job portals and useful hints on its website (www.cat365.net); click on the Your Life (Fet Vitals) link and then to the 'Getting a Job' (Trobar Feina) section. INEM, the Spanish public employment service, has a downloadable 'Working in Spain' guide (www.inem.es/inem/ciudadano/empleo/pdf/trabEsp_en.pdf) filled with information, industry-specific job boards and everything you need to know about living and working in the country. If you can, plan a short-term visit to Barcelona to attend interviews ahead of your move.

Finding Work in Barcelona

If you're already here, it is easier to line up interviews and dash around town to meet people. Take advantage of the government resources that have been created to help foreigners find work. Long queues may be a turn-off, but you're sure to walk away with piles of useful information. Just wait at SAIER (Servei d'Atenció a Immigrants Estrangers i Refugiats, 93 292 40 77, Avinguda del Paral·lel 202-204) and the Oficina de Extranjeros/Oficina d' Estrangers (www.map.es, 93 520 14 10, Avinguda Marquès de l'Argentera 4). If you already have a work and residence permit, head over to your neighbourhood Oficines de Treball de la Generalitat (Labour Offices or OTG, www.oficinatreball.net) and add your name to the roster of job candidates.

Recruitment Agencies

Local CVs
A concise, well-structured and targeted cover letter and CV, both written in Spanish, will make a stronger, and longer lasting impression on your prospective employer. For templates and advice about creating the perfect CV, browse the European Centre for the Development of Vocational Training's (CEDEFOP) europass site (http://europass.cedefop.europa.eu).

In a town like Barcelona, you'll want to make use of all the resources you can, including recruitment and temporary work agencies. These licensed firms connect prospective employers with employees. You'll be considered an agency employee and your services will be 'loaned out' to companies. Ask about fees; some do charge a small amount for their services. In Catalonia, temporary employment agencies are registered with the Department of Employment and Industry (Departament de Treball, www.gencat.cat/treball) and will be identified by the initials ETT. Agencies working more broadly in Spain are registered with the Spanish Ministry of Employment and Social Affairs.

Recruitment Agencies		
Adecco	93 488 22 23	www.adecco.es
Alta Gestion	93 245 40 80	www.altagestion.es
Attempora	93 490 05 04	www.attempora.es
Flexiplan	93 448 17 09	www.flexiplan.es
Manpower	90 212 10 93	www.manpower.es
Page Personnel	93 390 16 16	www.pageinterim.es
People	93 247 85 10	www.people-ett.com
Randstad	93 587 75 04	www.randstad.es
Select	90 249 04 90	www.select.es
Starjob	93 426 78 88	www.starjob.es

Voluntary & Charity Work

If you'd like to make a difference and give back to the community, there are plenty of volunteering opportunities in Barcelona. You could work with the Red Cross (Creu Roja), do environmental projects along the Llobregat River or work with sufferers of Parkinson's disease. Some groups are geared towards international visitors wanting to spend time abroad, while others rely on locals wanting to volunteer in their spare time.

Volunteer Organisations

Federació Catalana de Voluntariat Social is a private, non-political and non-religious organisation that connects 1,300 local associations with more than 300,000 volunteers (www.federacio.net/en or 93 314 19 00). Servei Català del Voluntariat (www.voluntariat.org) informs volunteers about projects, events and institutions that are seeking assistance. Volunteer Abroad runs a portal geared at international visitors who want to offer their services for a few weeks or a couple of months. It lists various groups working in Barcelona and Spain at www.volunteerabroad.com/Spain.cfm.

Working as a Freelancer/Contractor

Who doesn't like the idea of being a freelancer? You set your own hours and pick your projects. The downside, though, is the constant waiting for pay cheques (or bank transfers, as is more common here) and coughing up your own social security and tax contributions, which are not deducted from any client payments you receive. Freelancing, however, is becoming more appealing to employers, as it frees them from long-term contractual obligations while still getting work done. As in many matters, if you aren't an EU citizen, you must apply for a combined self-employment work and residence visa.

En Español
*For a list of official
translators, see
the table on p.53.*

All self-employed workers, regardless of nationality, must register for the Impuesto de Actividades Económicas (Economic Activity Tax) at the provincial Delegación de Hacienda (Tax Agency, www.minhac.es) where you must also submit a Declaración Censal de Inicio de Actividad (business start-up declaration). You also have to add your name to the local Social Security (www.seg-social.es) within 30 days of starting work. For more information about what you'll be expected to contribute, look at the Institut Municipal d'Hisenda site at www.bcn.cat/hisenda/guiacontribuent/ca. If the paperwork becomes too overwhelming, you can always hire a local accounting firm (*gestoria*) to handle Spanish tax law.

Employment Contracts

Once you've been offered employment and negotiated terms, you should receive a formal contract. Although Catalan law allows verbal contracts, the majority will come in written form, and will be registered with the Oficines de Treball de la Generalitat (Labour Offices of the Generalitat – OTG, see www.oficinatreball.net). Your contract should include information about:

• Salary (base pay, bonuses, profit sharing, supplemental pay, transport allowance and, very ocassionally, a private education allowance for children)
• Frequency of pay (monthly pay is common, though some workers opt for their salary to be split into 14 installments)
• Holidays and days off (turn to p.40 of the General Information chapter for more on Catalonia's many public holidays)
• Duration (temporary, indefinite, or for a fixed period)
• Hours of work
• Details about how the contract can be terminated by either the employer or employee, and what notice must be given

Also, clarify if you are being employed for a trial period. The maximum trial period for qualified technicians is six months, and two months for other workers. If the company has fewer than 25 workers, a three-month trial period is allowed, except for qualified technicians.

Ensure you understand the contract. If the employer doesn't provide a copy in your native language, it's worth getting it translated. Official translators are listed in the table on p.53. You don't want to sign something which you don't understand, but will be obliged to live up to.

Labour Law

Under the Spanish statute of workers' rights (Estatuto de los Trabajadores), all workers, regardless of origin, have the same rights and obligations and cannot earn less than the minimum wage, which is set annually by the central government. In 2007, the minimum wage for any activity was €19.02 per day or €570.60 per month. The annual minimum amount was €7,988.50.

Wages are typically paid monthly, but workers can opt for 14 annual payments, with the extra two made in July and December. It is the employer's responsibility to deduct appropriate income tax and social security from your wage. You'll receive a monthly salary sheet showing your contribution breakdown.

The working week is 40 hours long, with nine hour days, although this may vary at private companies. Overtime may be available in certain jobs. It often cannot exceed 80 hours a year and must always be compensated financially or with equivalent time off. Full time workers are entitled to 30 days annual leave. In addition, there are 12 national holidays and two local holidays each year.

Get Away
For a list of public holidays, turn to p.13. For potential destinations, see Weekend Breaks (p.190).

If you get married, you are entitled to 15 days of paid leave. Some companies require that you take these days right after the nuptials, while others are flexible, allowing you to schedule this time off at your convenience. Maternity leave is 16 or 18 weeks, depending on whether it is a multiple birth, and fathers may be able to take part of this if both parents work.

Contracts may be terminated if both parties agree, if the contract expires, the worker resigns, or is dismissed either in a series of redundancies or an individual disciplinary-related sacking. In contract expiry or dismissal situations, notification from the employer is always required, and should be made 15 to 30 days in advance. If the dismissal stems from the worker's failure to fulfil their duties, the employer must provide written notification detailing the reasons for dismissal and the effective date. To dispute the decision, the worker must file a request for conciliation, within 20 working days, at the regional Mediation, Arbitration and Conciliation unit (Unidades Territoriales de Mediacion, Conciliacion y Arbitraje) before complaints can be filed in Social Court.

Unions are legal in Spain, and may be able to provide more information on labour legislation. The bigger unions are the Confederación Sindical de Comisiones Obreras (CCOO, www.ccoo.es) and Unión General de Trabajadores (UGT, www.ugt.es).

Changing Jobs

While locals value some degree of longevity in the workplace, it's a market economy, and changing jobs for better pay, improved working conditions or other career advancement opportunities isn't uncommon. As in other places, it's customary to give at least two weeks notice before jumping ship.

There may be a catch for international workers, and you'll want to review your existing contract and visa data before hopscotching to another job. Your visa may restrict work outside a set geographic area, limit the kind of work you do, or only be valid for a specific amount of time. Your contract may have wording about how to properly terminate an agreement, or what your obligations are to the company.

Company Closure

If your company goes belly-up and declares insolvency, you may have some protection from the central government. The Ministry of Employment and Social Affairs has established a Wage Guarantee Fund (Fondo de Garantía Salarial, or FOGASA) which guarantees payment of pending salaries and wages affected by insolvency, bankruptcy or liquidation. There are restrictions on how paperwork is filed, and you may find it worth the effort to contact a lawyer regarding proper filing procedures.

Bank Accounts

There are plenty of banks in Barcelona, with regional, national or international branches in every neighbourhood. All banks are regulated by Banco de España and operate under the auspices of the European System of Central Banks. They provide the services you'd expect, like account maintenance, deposits and withdrawals, ATM cards and money transfers. They may also offer retirement accounts, insurance and financial planning, help with property transactions and provide new business loans.

Fees are lobbed onto almost everything – annual ATM and account maintenance, inbound and outbound transfers, cheque cashing and withdrawals from other banks. Fees vary widely, so you'll want to shop around to see which bank has the services you need at the best price. Try to negotiate the fees as well. Sometimes you may be able to knock down certain costs if you agree to keep a higher balance, for instance.

Typically, most banks will have a resident or non-resident account option. Residents can open an account with their foreign identification number (NIE), and non-residents – even non-visa holding visitors – can get an account with their original passport.

Non-resident accounts tend to have higher fees because you're considered a higher risk. Some banks want minimum balances, and some offer foreign currency accounts. Most have online and phone banking services.

Saving for the City

Caja/Caixa (in Spanish and Catalan respectively) are different kinds of financial institutions. They operate as savings banks, but with services very similar to traditional banks, and funnel part of their profits into social and cultural projects. For example, La Caixa's affiliated foundation supports the Caixa Forum exhibition centre, and Caixa Catalunya foots the bill for similar art and culture programmes at La Pedrera.

Banks

Name	Phone	Web	Online Banking	Tele-Banking
Banco Santander Central Hispano	93 401 11 00	www.gruposantander.es	✓	90 224 24 24
Banesto	93 270 20 89	www.banesto.es	✓	90 230 70 30
Bankinter	93 495 26 00	www.bankinter.com	✓	90 236 55 63
Barclays	93 481 20 23	www.barclays.es	✓	90 114 14 14
BBVA	93 301 43 86	www.bbva.es	✓	90 222 44 66
Caixa Catalunya	93 484 50 00	www.caixacatalunya.es	✓	90 242 55 42
Caixa Penedès	93 237 02 33	www.caixapenedes.com	✓	90 244 24 24
Citibank España	90 224 12 00	www.citibank.es	✓	90 218 05 16
Deutsche Bank España	93 042 21 02	www.deutsche-bank.es/pbc	✓	90 224 01 24
Grupo ING Direct	90 110 51 15	www.ingdirect.es	✓	90 102 09 01
La Caixa	90 240 04 10	www.lacaixa.es	✓	90 222 32 23
Sabadell Atlántico (STET)	93 482 39 00	www.sabadellatlantico.com	✓	90 232 37 77

Financial Planning

Living abroad can be expensive. You spend a lot setting up and taking advantage of your new home, and don't always know the money saving tricks of the locals. A stint in any exciting foreign city can leave you with empty pockets when it's time to go home, however good your job or intentions.

But, saving in Barcelona is possible. The euro is stable, and there are plenty of people willing to advise you on how to spend it. Local banks and advisors offer savings accounts, individual retirement funds, stocks, annuities and all the usual portfolio

Cost of Living

Apples (per kilo)	€1.30
Aspirin (pack of 20)	€3.36
Bananas (per kilo)	€1.69
Beef (per kilo)	€8.60
Beer (in a bar)	€3
Bottle of house wine (restaurant)	€10–€15
Bottle of wine (supermarket)	€3–€8
Bus (10km journey, zone one)	€1.25
Cafe con leche (coffee with milk)	€0.80–€1.40
Camera film (36 exp)	€3
Can of soft drink (supermarket)	€0.50–€0.75
Chicken (per kilo)	€1.85
Chocolate bar	€0.69–€1.09
Cigarettes	€2.55–€3.10
Cinema	€6.50
Eggs (pack of 18)	€1.15
Film developing (36 exposures)	€10
Fish	€4.90–€12.90
Loaf of bread	€0.80
Local postage stamp	€0.78
Milk (litre)	€0.95
New release DVD, CD album	€15–€20
Newspaper (international)	€2–€3
Newspaper (local)	€1
Orange juice (litre)	€0.80
Postcard	€0.50
Rice (per kilo)	€0.70
Salon haircut (male)	€9–€15
Salon haircut (women)	€9–€30
Six-pack of beer (supermarket)	€3–€4.50
Strawberries (per punnet)	€3
Sugar (1 kilo)	€0.90
Takeaway pizza	€7–€8
Taxi (10km journey)	€9.25–€11.55
Tube of toothpaste	€1.30–€1.95
Water (1.5 litre, restaurant)	€3
Water (1.5 litre, supermarket)	€0.65–€0.80

options. A common alternative for many international residents is to invest in a property in Barcelona or elsewhere in Spain. Plenty of agents are ready to help you seal a deal. For more details on buying property, see p.71.

One important consideration is your tax liability at home. There could also be capital gains payments and currency fluctuations to consider. In many cases, you will have to report your worldwide income to both the Spanish government and the tax agency in your home country, in order to avoid paying taxes twice.

While you may be able to manage on your own, particularly if there is less complexity involved, it may give you some peace of mind of talk to a financial adviser in your country of origin or once you arrive. See the table on p.66 for a list of local financial advisers with international experience.

Pensions

Pensions are a must for long-term financial security. While there is social security, in many western countries an ageing population means a diminishing public pot. Often, companies provide some sort of retirement account, with matching contributions, but they are not legally required to. The burden, then, comes back to you. Banks and other financial institutions will be able to help you set up your own individual retirement accounts.

Also, given the great climate, it's not surprising to find throngs of retirees living out their golden years along the Spanish and Catalan coastlines, relying on pensions drawn from other countries. Under Spanish law, if you are a taxpaying resident here, your pension could be subject to Spanish taxes. This liability may influence whether or not you want to keep your pension going in your home country or move it here.

Off-Shore Savings

With so many expats coming here, off-shore accounts are becoming more popular. A number of websites specifically address off-shore options for people living in Spain. Click around the following sites: The SFC Group (www.scfgroup.com); Bradford and Bingley International (www.bbi.co.im); Money Facts (www.moneyfacts.co.uk), and Shelter Offshore (www.shelteroffshore.com).

Taxation

Although Spanish taxes may be lower than those in other European countries, they have a way of sneaking into most facets of life. City, regional and national governments pull from several pots, including personal income, property, sales, corporation, wealth, capital gains, motor vehicle and inheritance taxes.

Regardless of whether you are a citizen or an immigrant, if you live in the country for 183 days or more during a calendar tax year, you'll have to declare, in many cases, all of your worldwide income.

Taxes are based on a percentage of your annual income, and, for property taxes, the amount levied will vary by city. Tax forms must be filed during May or June of the following year to the Hisenda/Hacienda (Tax Authority). If you dodge this responsibility, you risk being fined.

Financial Advisers		
Abec	93 218 48 12	www.abecsl.com
Cays	93 414 71 77	www.caysbarcelona.com
Gabinet Segura Illa	93 416 14 29	www.segurailla-sa.es
Lliteras	93 241 90 80	www.lliteras.com
Maturana & Asociados	93 487 85 24	www.maturanayasoc.es

Legal Issues

Spain's legal system is slightly different to the northern European and US model. It's based on the Napoleonic Code, which has also shaped systems in France, Italy, Portugal, and Belgium. In 1978, as Spain was moving from dictatorship to democracy, a new constitution was adopted and a number of changes were made to the legal system.

While central government sets laws and has broad legal responsibilities, many police and judicial powers are distributed to the autonomous regions. In Catalonia, for example, the Mossos d'Esquadra does much of the work that in other parts of Spain is handled by the Policia Nacional.

As in other countries, there is a hierarchical court system, with jurisdiction divided by the severity of the civil or criminal violation.

As a resident, you will eventually have some run-in with the Spanish legal system. The most common issues for expats involve property ownership, tax obligations, residency status and family law issues related to marriage, divorce and inheritance.

On the criminal side, while violent crime exists, visitors or international residents will be more likely to deal with petty thieves and pickpockets. If you are robbed, the Mossos d'Esquadra are the people to contact. You'll find assistance in English in the police station at Gran Via de les Corts Catalanes, 456, near the Rocafort metro station (phone: 93 424 27 27, or 088 for a patrol car).

El Forum

Financial & Legal Affairs

I'm an Expat, Get Me Out of Here
Your embassy or consulate will not be able to get you out of prison if you have broken the law. But they will be allowed to send a representative to visit you, and make sure all your rights are met.

Getting Arrested

If you find yourself in a legal tussle and get arrested, you should be informed immediately about the reasons for your detention, your legal rights and your right to an attorney. You may remain in police custody for no more than 72 hours, at which point police must either charge you with a crime or release you.

For a comprehensive overview of the Spanish legal system, in English, browse the Abogado Servicios Jurídicos site (www.spainlawyer.com).

Law Firms

Baker & McKenzie	93 280 59 00	www.bakernet.com
Faus & Moliner	93 292 21 00	www.faus-moliner.com
Garrigues	93 253 37 00	www.garrigues.com
Gomez-Acebo & Pombo	93 415 74 00	www.gomezacebo-pombo.com
Marti & Associats	93 201 62 66	www.martilawyers.com
Osborne Clarke Europe OWA	93 419 18 18	www.osborneclarke.com
Ramos & Arroyo	93 487 11 12	www.rya.es
Rodríguez Molnar & Asociados	93 416 09 39	www.rm-as.com

Adoption

Adoption is often a drawn out and costly court procedure. If the adoption involves overseas children, it can cross complicated international legal boundaries. However, adoption is not uncommon here, and is a good option for married, live-in or same-sex couples. There is, of course, a list of prerequisites, including being legally capable to adopt, being over 25 years old and being at least 14 years older than the adopted person. For information about international adoptions and other related legal matters, the Servicio de Protección de Menores from each Spanish Autonomous Community is a good starting point.

Making a Will

Spanish inheritance laws and procedures are quite different to other EU countries. For example, there are laws of succession that establish 'compulsory or obligatory' heirs, namely children. It's advisable to research the legal process to ensure that your property and wealth is distributed as you intended it to be.

Generally, however, making a will is a rather easy process. An open will is the most common type of document, and it's made before a notary, who keeps the original document in their files. If the person making the will is deaf, blind or has other physical (or mental) limitations, the notary may request two witnesses. The notary also notifies the Central Registry of Spanish Wills (Registro Central de Última Voluntad) in Madrid, which issues a certification number. This is helpful if family members or heirs do not know if a will has been made, or if it has been lost. Using the deceased's name, they can request the certificate and find out which notary has the will on file.

Divorce

Divorce has only been legal in Spain since 1981. Foreigners who married in other countries can file for a divorce here if one of the parties is a legal resident. It will be a faster and simpler process if the parties break ties amicably and jointly agree (forming a governing convention or *convenio regulador*) on property division, custody of children and other financial arrangements such as alimony.

However, if there is a dispute, a judicial authority will resolve all issues not spelled out in the governing convention. A judge's decision can be appealed. When finalised, divorces must be registered with the local Civil Registre.

Housing

Barcelona's accommodation is among Spain's most expensive. Whether you're aiming to buy or rent, prices are high. Whichever factors weigh on your mind when choosing where to live, remember that this is a compact city with good transport links, making each neighbourhood very accessible.

So, looking for the right area is not as difficult as it might be in a huge city like London or New York. Because of this urban compactness, accommodation tends to be in the shape of one, two or three bedroom apartments. Although renting will save you money in the short run, buying a property is, as everywhere, worthwhile if you plan to stay in the city long term.

Renting in Barcelona

Some international companies will provide accommodation for employees moving to the city. For those arriving without such a boon, real estate agent's windows can be a good way to gauge prices and general standards of accommodation in an area. Going to an agents is probably the most common way of finding an apartment, but increasingly, young flat-hunters are logging on to community noticeboards on websites such as www.loquo.com. Posts here are often by private landlords, cutting out the middleman. Doing it this way removes the safety net an agency provides if difficulties arise with a landlord, but it will eliminate the need to pay commission each month, making rent cheaper. English-language community boards can also be found in print form in the *Metropolitan* magazine and *Barcelona Connect* pamphlet. See p.38 for more on these. Both are free, and distributed in bars and cafes around the city. *La Vanguardia* newspaper provides extensive listings in Spanish and there are also numerous free publications outside shops all over the city, which advertise accommodation.

What's Included...

Flats normally come ready furnished (*amueblado*) with all mod cons (*electrodomoesticos*) such as washing machines, refrigerators and other white goods. If you want to look for your own furniture and appliances, rent is slightly cheaper. Rent sometimes, though not often, includes utilities such as electricity, gas and water, and on very rare occasions, a parking space. Usually though, you will have to pay for utilities separately. The IBI property tax, as well as service charges for the property, should be paid by the landlord.

Unless you make a special agreement, landlords are responsible for all property maintenance, though they can be notoriously reluctant and you might have to press them to repair anything. It is also expected that tenants keep the property in good order. Otherwise, the deposit may be withheld at the end of the tenancy. In some cases, you can save money on your rent by agreeing to do your own maintenance.

The normal length of a contract tends to be one year, although many landlords will be glad to make it as long as a five. Rent is paid in advance each month. You can either set up a direct debit agreement with your bank or pay

Housing Abbreviations	
a/a.	Aire acondicionado/air conditioning
asc.	Ascensor/elevator
bñ.	Baño/bathroom
calef.	Calefacción/central heating
ext.	Exterior/exterior
h	Habitación/room
int.	Interior/interior
pkg.	Parking/parking space
s.gres	Suelo de gres/tiled floor
s.parquet	Suelo de parquet/parquet floor
sal.	Salón/living room
trast.	Trastero/store room
v.alum	Ventana de aluminio/aluminium windows

Housing

Casa de les Punxes

Diagonal del Mar developments

Avinguda de Gaudi

Passeig de Gracià at night

it personally into the landlord's account. Sometimes the negotiation of rent is possible, particularly when there is no agency involved. There are no tribunals in place to protect tenants, but the Cambra de la Propietat Urbana de Barcelona (www.cambrapropbcn.com) oversees paperwork regarding accommodation in the city and monitors disputes between landlords and tenants.

After an eight year period of spiralling rents, things finally seem to be stabilising. Locals had found themselves priced out of their own city by an influx of foreign, highly paid professionals, pushing the rent up, but over the next few years the forecast suggests that rents will increase at a much slower rate.

Shared accommodation is easy to find. Look on www.loquo.com or keep your eyes open for message boards in internet cafes and bars.

Real Estate Agents

Free Views

Most agents have a free magazine outside their office, listing properties. The A4 sized 100% Inmobiliaria is a common one. For English-langauge magazines (which often have listings) see Media & Communications, p.38.

There are several reasons why renting through an agent can be better than going direct to a landlord. For a start, agents will have a broad range of places, normally available to show immediately.

Agencies will also (normally) have a higher standard of accommodation at a fair price. If you don't speak the language or don't have time to devote to searching, it can make things a lot easier.

But, if you choose to rent through an agent, you will be charged a fee of one month's rent plus 16% IVA (tax). Some agencies differ, by charging 10% of the year's rent plus 16% IVA. An agent should never charge for a property viewing.

To find one, either visit the area you fancy and wander the streets, or search online. No accreditation is needed to be a Spanish estate agent. A popular online agency is www.fincasadosmil.com

Real Estate Agents

Ad Infitinitum	93 209 34 14	www.adinfinitum.es
Aguirre Newman Barcelona	93 439 54 54	www.aguirrenewman.es
Altafinca Real Estate	93 467 63 24	www.altafinca.com
Barcelona Home Search	93 443 64 85	www.barcelonahomesearch.com
John Taylor	93 241 30 82	www.john-taylor.com
Loco Locations	93 540 25 98	www.locolocations.com
Lucas Fox	93 356 29 89	www.lucasfox.com
Monika Rusch	93 204 55 20	www.monika-rusch.com

The Lease

Before you move into a flat, it's normal to pay a refundable deposit of at least one month's rent, along with the first month's rent in advance. Both the tenant and the owner, or a representative, need to sign the lease and register with the Cambra de la Propietat Urbana de Barcelona. Upon signing the agreement, the tenant accepts the current state of the property. So, check whether the electricity, gas and water, *suministros* (utilities), are connected. If they're not, it could set you back as much as €200 for each installation. Also, it is a good idea to ask for a copy of the *escritura* (proof of ownership) and the owner's DNI (National ID card), just to make sure they really are the owner.

They will request your passport, DNI or NIE and a *nomina*, or proof of salary. Some landlords will demand an *aval bancario*, or bank guarantee, for as much as six month's rent. Negotiation over the price is a possibility, but not the norm. Contracts are in Spanish, but if you pay for a translation you can get an English copy. If you want to vacate the property before the contract has expired, the common notice period is one month. When a renewal of the lease is made the price will normally rise slightly, which makes long-term contracts better value.

Housing

Main Accommodation Options

Lodging ◀
Rooms are also available in private homes, where you share facilities with the owner. The cheaper cost of living this way if offset by the lack of privacy.

A Place of Your Own

For anyone who prefers their own space, or is arriving with family or friends, taking the lease on an apartment will be preferable. Apartments are available through individual landlords or the estate agents representing them. Normally, you will be offered a one-year contract, although shorter term lets are also available. Price ranges depend on location, quality and size.

For a fully-furnished studio apartment of 30-45sqm in the centre of town, ideal for a single young professional, you're looking at €700-800 per month. A one bedroom apartment consisting of a lounge with built-in kitchen and bathroom is in the region of €700-850. For a two bedroom place with lounge, kitchen and bathroom, prices begin at around €800. A three or more bedroom place is unlikely to be less than €900. Included in any rental will be essentials such as sheets and bedding, while modern conveniences and furniture will also usually be provided if the apartment is advertised as *amueblado* (furnished).

House or Flatshare

Young people and students on a tight budget often opt for a rented room in a *piso compartido*, or flatshare. This involves having your own bedroom, but sharing the bathroom, living room and kitchen with other inhabitants. Flatshares are a great way for new arrivals to make friends and learn the language. They often throw people from different cultures into the same living space (witness the film *Una Casa de Locos*, which covers this theme). For a single room in a flatshare, monthly prices begin at around €250. For a double, prices begin at around €350 per month.

Other Rental Costs

One thing to check is whether the electricity, gas, water and all *suministros* (utilities) are connected. If not, it could set you back as much as €200 for each installation. Phone lines can also be expensive to arrange, although Telefonica does sometimes offer deals involving free installation. Community tax and other municipal charges should be handled by the landlord. Service charges within the building should also be the landlord's responsibility. The real estate agency fee is included in the cost of your rent.

Buying Property

A buzzing economy, low interest rates and enormous foreign demand has helped the housing market grow phenomenally since the late 90s. Double-digit price rises have been registered every year in virtually every neigbourhood of the city since 1999, bringing prices in line with other European cities. Property availability is limited by the natural physical boundaries of the city. A boom in tourism has also created a huge demand for temporary accommodation in central areas. Hopefully, though, the period of spiralling prices is at an end. Since 2004, annual growth has slowed down considerably. In 2006, there was only a rise of 8.2%, compared to 2004's 18.3% increase. In the next few years a gradual stabilisation of prices is anticipated, although due to continuing investment by northern European, British, Irish and Russian buyers, it is unlikely prices will actually go down. Legally speaking, buying land to build a house on is possible, although building plans are tightly supervised by the council and there is very little space available.

The cheapest properties are the one or two bedroom flats and studios to be found in the old city, while in the Eixample and Les Corts, flats are on the whole larger and a bit more expensive. Gràcia lies somewhere in the middle. Sant Gervasi and the neigbourhoods of Barcelona's upper reaches, or *Zona Alta,* such as Pedralbes and Sarriá are the most expensive, with €4,000 per square metre a typical minimum.

House Hunters
For a list of some of the main estate agents in Barcelona, turn to p.70.

The Process

After finding the ideal property, financial arrangements must be made. In most cases, a mortgage must be agreed. You will also need the services of a lawyer (p.67) or *notario.* Then you can make an offer. If this is agreed, you must pay a reservation agreement. This is up to 2% of the price, and means the property will come off the market. If you then back out, the seller keeps your cash. If they back out, you should get your money back. If the offer is accepted you should then get a professional survey done, and begin the legal process of transferring the property over from the current *proprietario* (owner). Your lawyer can also check if there are any outstanding debts on the property. Make sure they do this. If they don't, and you find out later, you can get stung. The debts may become your responsibility, even though the property has changed hands.

If all is clear, a 10% deposit is paid. You should only pay this after seeing proof (signed by your lawyer and the seller) that no outstanding debts are on the property. Then you can complete the purchase and move into your new home.

Your tax obligations and other fees are likely to add on about 10% to the cost of the property. You will also need an NIE, see p.52 for details.

As anywhere, a common and frustrating impediment is the 'chain', when the buyer or seller (or both) are waiting for other sales to be completed so they can move house themselves.

Buying to Rent

Buying a property in order to rent it out is a good way to provide a reliable source of income. It is advisable to investigate the possibilities with a lawyer though, as regulations vary from area to area. In the strictest legal terms you must have a licence from the Ajuntament to be able to rent out accommodation on a short-term basis. Licences are no longer available for properties in Ciutat Vella, so a property there would need to already hold one. If you decide to rent out a property unofficially, as many landlords do, you risk being reported to the authorities. Short-term rentals are plentiful, and because of high competition it is increasingly difficult to fill apartments on a regular basis. Many landlords try to do it through rental agencies, which can lead to major problems. Some of the short-term rental agencies are good on marketing and poor on actual management services. Some have even been known to pocket undeclared rent. Long-term rental to students and young professionals is more manageable, with lower agency costs, but the gains are also considerably lower.

Selling Property

Selling property can be a stressful experience, so enlisting an agent is a wise move. See p.70 for a list of agents. You should expect brochures, advertising and promotion on the internet for your property, as well as regular showings and constant updates. Unlike in the UK, Spanish agents don't give keys to clients, but they dedicate a lot of time and energy to finding a buyer. Generally, they expect between 3% and 5% commission on the sale. In your initial contract there will be details of all extra costs, including advertising and agency tax charges.

Even if you choose to go it alone, it's a good idea to approach some agents, just to get a range of opinions on the value of your property. Although formal evaluations involve a fee, many agents will do a quick assessment for free. However you go about selling your property, be certain to know the ins and outs of your tax obligations so there are no unpleasant last minute surprises when you begin negotiations. Also, beware of agents who give unnecessarily high evaluations of your property just to get you on their books.

Mortgages

If you don't have sufficient funds to buy a property outright, you can arrange for a mortgage (*hipoteca*), a large-scale loan using your property as security. Capital is borrowed and repaid over a set term of up to 30 years, in monthly instalments with variable interest charges. Mortgages are available at most of the major banks in Barcelona.

Mortgages are attached to properties, not to the people who take them out. So, when buying, you may be able to take over the existing mortgage. If not, you will have to pay mortgage costs of between 1% and 1.5% of the total amount borrowed. A non-resident is generally able to borrow up to 60% of the property's value. Should you become a Spanish resident, this rises to 80%. Some banks are now offering 100% mortgages, while there are even agencies specialising in housing development that will offer deals including the costs of renovation in the mortgage.

If you borrow in a currency other than the euro, fluctuating exchange rates could make your mortgage more or less expensive. The rate of interest is normally about 6% for the first year. Be aware of the small print, as this rate will change from the second year onwards. Interest rates are normally tied to and slightly higher than the Euro Interbank Offered Rate, or Euribor (www.euribor.org). For example, the mortgage's interest rate might be the Euribor rate plus 1.25%. Fixed rate mortgages allow you to pay at a stable but slightly higher rate of interest. You may be charged an early redemption penalty of around 1% if you pay off your mortgage early. Lenders vary on what they require as documentation, but usually you will be asked to provide a work contract, three recent payslips and your last tax declaration. If you don't have one of these, you can use a guarantor (*avalista*).

Mortgage Providers		
BBVA	93 301 43 86	www.bbva.es
Caixa Catalunya	93 484 50 00	www.caixacatalunya.es
Casa Hipoteca SL	96 574 90 78	www.casahipoteca.co.uk
La Caixa	90 240 04 10	www.lacaixa.es
The Spanish Mortgage Lender	95 131 73 42	www.thespanishmortgagelender.com

Other Purchasing Costs

On top of the agreed price of the property, a 7% property tax fee, or IVA, must be paid, which goes to the Spanish Treasury. The notary (*notario*) must also be paid, normally around 1% of the purchase cost. The property registration fee is 40-50% of the notary fee. The agency fee will be approximately 5%, and is included in the sale price. Once you are installed in your new home, you'll have to pay for repairs to the building, anything from rewiring the interphone to painting the façade. A bi-monthly service charge for maintenance (*gastos de la comunidad*) will also be due. Service charges will vary according to the size and quality of the complex; whether there are lifts, a swimming pool, gardens, tennis courts and other facilities. Add to this the annual IBI (Impuesto sobre Buenos Inmuebles), another property tax dependent on the value of your property and payable annually to the Ajuntament. Installing a telephone line can be a lengthy and exasperating business. Telefónica is the only company that can do this, and is renowned for unsatisfactory customer service. For the installation of Cable and Satellite TV try EasiSat at www.easisat.net and see p.105 for more.

Real Estate Law

When there is an agreement between buyer and seller and a survey has been completed, the *traspaso*, or legal transfer, begins. A *precontrato*, or pre-contract, can be signed stipulating that if the owner accepts an offer from a third party, he is legally bound to pay you your deposit back twice over. If it is you who finds another property and fails to complete the deal, you will have to stump up compensation. Solicitors will arrange the exchange of contracts and set a date for the completion of the deal.

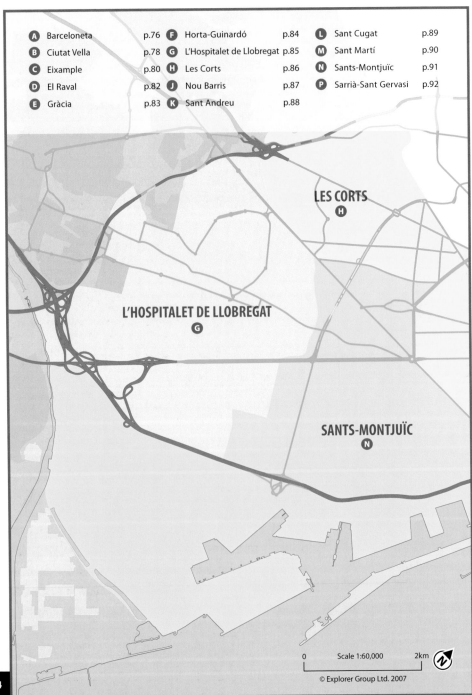

LES CORTS
H

L'HOSPITALET DE LLOBREGAT
G

SANTS-MONTJUÏC
N

0   Scale 1:60,000   2km

© Explorer Group Ltd. 2007

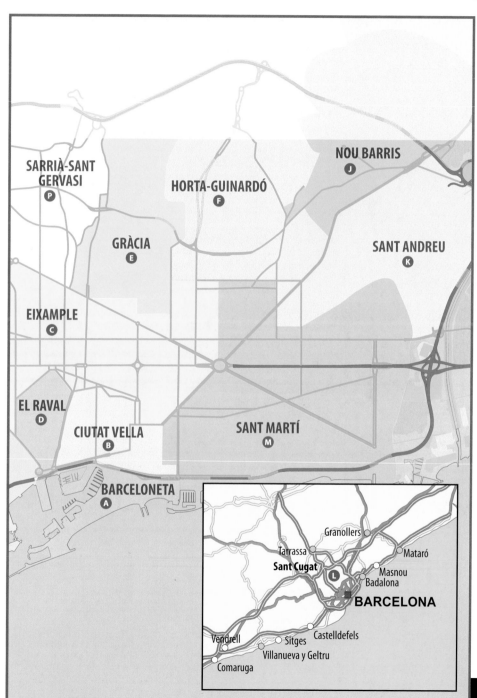

Map p.409
Area **A** p.75

Barceloneta

Seaside Barceloneta has an easygoing charm that's hard to resist. The most striking features are the broad promenades, lined by a yacht filled marina on one side, and stylish apartments on the other. Just one street away is a different Barceloneta; a tight grid of 18th and 19th century workers' cottages that was once the city's fishing district. Sheer density means that most social activity happens in the street and in bars, making this a lively barrio with a strong sense of community, best displayed during the local *festa major* (last week of September).

Best Points
A pretty, atmospheric quarter that has good facilities and an unbeatable location.

Worst Points
With hordes of tourists and tiny living conditions, it can get cramped.

Accommodation

Space is limited in Barceloneta. The older houses have some of the city's smallest flats, with two-bedrooms squeezed into 35sqm. But, this makes them affordable. Prices start at around €280,000 (€800 a month rental) for a 45sqm, two-bedroom flat. For larger flats and flashy seafront properties, expect to pay more than twice as much.

Entertainment & Leisure

Unsurprisingly, Barceloneta specialises in seafood. It dominates the menus in the restaurants lining the marina and Passeig Joan de Borbó, and inevitably features in an evening in the lively tapas bars scattered throughout the backstreets. The biggest daytime draw is the beach. There is a park with a children's playground on Passeig Maritim, and a large open-air pool at the end of the spit. The barrio's civic centre on Carrer Conreria hosts exhibitions, concerts and events for children and the elderly.

Shopping & Amenities

The recently renovated market is Barceloneta's best shopping experience, and includes 30 stalls of fresh produce. There are small supermarkets and a sprinkling of corner stores, and several banks on the busy Passeig Joan de Borbó. The central post office, at the base of Via Laietana, is also nearby. The major fashion lines reign at Maremagnum (p.312), a large shopping centre, while the hip boutiques and designer stores of the Born district are even closer.

Transport

Barceloneta is served by the metro station of the same name (Line 4), and is within easy walking distance of the Barri Gòtic and Born. Estació França, one of Barcelona's main railway terminals, is on Barceloneta's northern edge, and the area has good bus links that cross the city. However, the neighbourhood is not car friendly. The narrow streets make parking impossible, and the elderly apartment blocks have no underground spaces.

Healthcare

There are two public health centres, and the Hospital del Mar has an accident and emergency department (93 248 30 00, Passeig Maritim Barceloneta 25).

Education

There are no international schools in the district; however, there are a number of private schools in and near to Barceloneta. There are several state primary and secondary schools within easy reach.

Safety & Annoyances

Violent crime is rare in Barceloneta's bustling streets, but petty theft is rife. Bicycle theft is a particular favourite, but pickpockets who target tourists at the beach, metro stations and promenade can also be a problem.

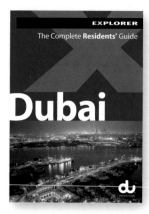
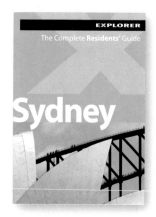
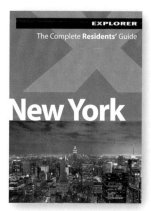
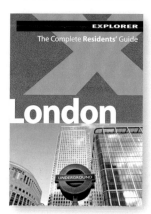

Map p.403
Area ⓑ p.75

Ciutat Vella

Perhaps Barcelona's most famous area. On the left, it is bordered by La Rambla, at its heart is the Gothic cathedral and five minutes from there is the Picasso Museum (p.165). The Ciutat Vella (old city) is where Barcelona began, as a walled Roman settlement called Barcino, and many historic institutions are located here. The streets are narrow and winding, and buildings were clearly thrown up according to residents' needs, with not an inch of urban planning. And this is what gives it its appeal.

Best Points

This central area is rich in history and culture, and has good places to eat, drink and have fun.

Worst Points

A lot of people crowd into this neighbourhood until the small hours. Many are not residents and they will not necessarily be respectful of those who are.

Accommodation

Buildings are fittingly old, so although they will have character, with tiled floors, wooden beams and high ceilings, they are unlikely to have a lift and the gas supply should be checked. House prices have spiraled here, as in most areas. In the Barri Gòtic, a two-bedroom flat has an average cost of €444,000; even a studio flat could be as much as €300,000. The highly desirable large flats of Born cost more. The closeness of buildings can cause a lack of natural light. Renting here starts at about €750 a month, and rises to more than €1,000.

Entertainment & Leisure

There are an excellent array of restaurants and bars, with regular new openings and an eclectic selection in this maze of streets. The whole area is bursting with culture, including the Palau de la Música (p.170), the history museums for both Barcelona and Catalonia and the attractive architecture of the Frederic Marès museum.

Shopping & Amenities

Santa Caterina market is striking, as much for its curvy roof as the array of foods on sale. Born is the focal point for those seeking independent designers and one-off gifts. Just off La Rambla and Plaça Catalunya are Portal de l'Angel and Carrer Portaferrissa, where famous Spanish and international high street brands can be found.

Transport

The narrowness of the streets and many pedestrianised areas mean that there is really no point having a car here. Instead, walking, moped and cycling are the best independent options. There are bus stops and metro stations on the main thoroughfares (line 4 on Via Laietana and Line 3 down La Rambla).

Healthcare

This area has two CAP surgeries, one each in the lower and upper part of the neighbourhood and the nearest hospital is in Barceloneta.

Education

There are four public primary schools and just two secondary schools. There are three private primary schools and five secondary schools. All teach in the local languages.

Safety & Annoyances

On Passeig del Born, Carrer del Comerç and nearby streets, there are lots of bars and restaurants that can be quite noisy. Touristy areas such as this are prime targets for pickpockets and scam artists, who will target residents if they can. Although the council has tried to 'clean up' here, there are still drug dealers and prostitutes earning their livings in spots like Plaça Reial. It is also a neighbourhood popular with stag and hen parties, who can be disruptive and noisy until the early hours of the morning. Full rubbish bags are often left outside by residents between 20:00 and 22:00, but if you're caught leaving your rubbish early, you will be fined.

Residential Areas

Carrer de la Riera Alta

The Barri Gòtic

Carrer de Fontaneda

La Rambla apartments

Map p.392-p.394
Area **C** p.75

Eixample

This neighbourhood is full of character, granduer and some of the city's most distinctive and photogenic icons.

It contains five segments that make up the central swathe of the city. Eixample itself is the 19th century project of architect Ildefons Cerdà. See the General Information chapter, p.4, for more on his grand plan and the boom that encouraged it. Eixample is divided between right (*dret*) and left (*esquerra*). Sagrada Familia includes the famed cathedral-in-progress, Sant Antoni has its popular market, and the fifth (and least well-known) area is Fort Pienc.

Across these, there are wide, bustling avenues like Passeig de Gràcia, quiet, tree lined side streets and Barcelona's principal square, Plaça de Catalunya. It is also home to one of Barcelona's main gay communities, the 'Gaixample'.

Best Points
There is something for everyone, from buzzing Sant Antoni and stylish broadways to the living history of the Sagrada Familia.

Accommodation

If you get a flat in the left or right Eixample, and parts of the Sagrada Familia, it may have original features like tiled floors, glass doors and cornices. In the left Eixample is the Model Prison, whose presence can result in cheaper housing prices, the pay-off being a view of the barbed wired wall.

Prices vary, but are usually higher in the right Eixample, which is considered a little grander (the average price for a two-bedroom flat is €700,000). Anywhere near one of the big streets such as Gran Via or Passeig de Gràcia will have raised its price accordingly. Sant Antoni tends to be the cheapest part, with the average price of a two-bedroom flat being €330,000.

Another issue is the current construction of the high speed train line under the centre of the Eixample, making residents nervous about the stability of their apartment buildings.

Worst Points
This is a very built-up area and as beautiful as many of its buildings are, there are few good parks. The neighbourhood has a lot of noise from traffic, building work and revellers.

Entertainment & Leisure

You will never be bored in this area. Not with the mass of restaurants, bars, theatres, cinemas and buildings by master architects such as Gaudí. Plaça de Catalunya often hosts concerts and other events, while Passeig de Gràcia and Rambla Catalunya attract many people on Sant Jordi, Catalonia's national day. In January, Sant Antoni has a big day-long fiesta called Els Tres Tombs (the three turns). In general, Eixample's bars, clubs and restaurants are a little fancier than their equivalents down in Ciutat Vella and up in Gràcia.

Shopping & Amenities

Spending is not a problem in this neighbourhood. It is home to most of the 5km long 'shopping line' that runs from La Rambla and up Diagonal. It is estimated that there are 35,000 shops along this mighty strip.

There are designer labels on Passeig de Gràcia, other well-known names on Rambla de Catalunya, a 24 hour flower market on Valencia, and the modernista Sant Antoni market, which sells food and clothes during the week, and books, music and collectables on Sunday mornings. For a flea market bargain, you can visit Els Encants near Glories.

Transport

Eixample is very well served for metro, buses and trains. The Estació del Nord is a large coach station and Passeig de Gràcia is on the main train line for many routes out of the city. Parking is not easy though, as there are restricted on-street places, and limited parking garages. And if you get a taxi, the area you are heading to is pronounced 'eye-sham-play'.

Healthcare

In the centre of the Eixample Esquerra is Hospital Clínic (see p.108), a large public teaching hospital. Emergency facilities are available at the Hospital Clínic, Sagrat Cor (private) and Dos de Maig (private). There are another eight private facilities in the neighbourhood, including the Barcelona Children's Hospital. Eixample has six CAP primary care centres. For more general information on private and public healthcare, go to the Health section, p.106.

Education

There are two private foreign schools, Collège Ferdinand de Lesseps (French) and Liceo Italiano. Of the local primary schools, there are 30 private and only 11 public. Secondary schools divide between 29 private and just six public. The University of Barcelona (p.127) has its main buildings here and there are a number of private universities in the area as well.

Safety & Annoyances

With many tourists, Plaça de Catalunya and Passeig de Gràcia attract groups of young pickpockets and petty thieves. Near Sant Antoni market, prostitutes can be seen day and night; disagreements sometimes break out between them, and locals regularly complain about their presence.

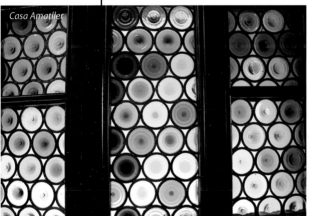

Casa Amatller

Passeig de Gracià

Carrer Rosello

Map p.402
Area **D** p.75

El Raval

El Raval was once Barcelona's seediest area, but this is changing fast. A former red-light zone with deprived immigrant communities, it has become increasingly upmarket over the years. The area's *festa major* has become a trendy, fusion-heavy music event and parts of the area have become quite chic. This doesn't mean Raval has fully cleaned up its act though. Prostitution is still quite open and there are dubious types behind the Boqueria and towards Drassanes to scare off tourists.

Best Points
An eclectic and exciting neighbourhood deep in the historic heart of the city.

Worst Points
Elements of Raval's criminal past remain, and it's still an area where you need to be vigilant.

Accommodation

The student-scruffy flats that fill Raval's old buildings remain plentiful, but smarter, renovated apartments are coming onto the market as well. Expect to pay around €380,000 (€1,000 a month rental) for a stylishly renovated two-bedroom flat in the trendy streets near the MACBA, or around €280,000 (€850 a month rental) for the same towards noisy Ronda Sant Antoni and in the dilapidated streets towards Drassanes.

Entertainment & Leisure

The district is crammed with little restaurants offering local and international foods, usually in scruffily hip surroundings. The local bar scene is found around the MACBA museum and Carrer Joaquim Costa. For late-night dancing, there is La Paloma (Carrer Tigre, p.365), an old establishment that offers ballroom at tea-time and then DJs until dawn. There are dozens of art galleries, from the gleaming CCCB (p.163) and MACBA (p.164) modern art museums, to tiny white spaces in the backstreets. The area lacks open spaces aside from skateboard-heavy Plaça dels Angels.

Shopping & Amenities

Raval boasts one of Barcelona's best shopping experiences – the enormous Boqueria market, housing scores of stalls, selling every food imaginable. It is always crowded with tourists and locals, but the stalls at the back have fewer crowds and better prices. There is a large supermarket on La Rambla, but it is very busy and has none of the Boqueria's charm. The area is rife with boutiques, second hand shops and local designers near the MACBA museum. Record stores can be found on Carrer Bonsucès, and there are pricey designer shops on Carrer Doctor Dou. Services are within easy reach, including post offices, banks, hairdressers and a couple of gyms.

Transport

There is no metro and a limited bus service in Raval itself, but the barrio is so compact that this doesn't really matter. Within a few minutes' walk are the metro stations of Paral·lel (Line 2), Liceu and Drassanes (Line 3), and Catalunya, (Lines 1 and 3). Suburban trains leave from Catalunya station. Car ownership is tricky as narrow, rowdy streets make street parking risky, and private car parks are overcrowded.

Healthcare

The district has two medical centres and an accident and emergency facility at Urgències Perecamps (93 441 06 00, Av Drassanes 13).

Education

There are private schools in and near to Raval (many of which are church schools), as well as a number of state schools, but no international schools.

Safety & Annoyances

Raval's hectic, gritty appeal has a downside: pickpocketing, theft and prostitution are serious issues, and the bar scene means that late-night noise is also a problem for residents.

Map p.385
Area **E** p.75

Gràcia

Gràcia is a hip, vibrant district with a traditional core. A separate town for centuries, it has kept its sense of identity through its local art scene and community groups. It's a pretty part of town, made up of narrow streets and wide plaças lined with bars and cafes, which are massively popular during the festes de Gràcia (last week of August).

Best Points
Thriving social activities, cultural scene and nightlife make for one of Barcelona's most distinctive and vibrant areas.

Accommodation

Housing in Gràcia consists mostly of elderly, period apartments, many of which lack lifts. There are also larger, less attractive blocks from the 60's and 70's with balconies and lifts. Prices have rocketed recently. Expect to pay around €330,000 – €400,000 (€900 a month rental) for a two-bedroom flat (€450,000 or €1,100 rental if recently renovated). Much larger flats are also available on the main thoroughfares.

Entertainment & Leisure

Worst Points
Noisy bars and thin walls cause constant sleepless nights, especially in summer.

Gràcia has a good range of small Catalan restaurants and international eateries, and a number of quirky, intimate bars with eclectic soundtracks. Much socialising goes on in the cafes around the main plaças, making them an enjoyable place to spend the evening. There are plenty of small art galleries and theatres. However, the live music scene has suffered from a local government crackdown, and the 'cultural associations' that functioned as unofficial bars are also under pressure. Cine Verdi (93 238 79 90) shows films in their original language and for those wanting greenery, there is easy access to the Parc de la Crueta del Coll. Park Guell (p.179) is also nearby.

Shopping & Amenities

In many ways, Gràcia remains an independent town, with supermarkets, post offices, banks, salons and other services in its village centre. Its three large markets, Mercat de l'Abaceria (Central Travessera de Gràcia 186), Mercat de la Llibertat (Plaça Gal·la Placidia) and Mercat de Lesseps, (Carrer Verdi 200) sell fresh food. There are also offbeat, individual boutiques, bookshops, and gift shops.

Transport

Metro stations at Fontana and Lesseps (Line 3) and Joanic (Line 4) provide quick access to the city centre and further out, while the train from Gràcia FGC station takes commuters to Plaça Catalunya in minutes. Gran de Gràcia, Avinguda Princep d'Asturies and Pi i Margall each have good bus services, including night buses. Streets are almost too narrow to park scooters, let alone cars.

Healthcare

There are two doctors' surgeries in Gràcia and two in Vallcarca. Hospital de l'Esperança (93 367 41 00, Avinguda Santuari S Josep Muntany 12) has an A&E department.

A Gràcia plaça

Education

There are plenty of state and private schools for all ages throughout the district. There are also a number of international schools within easy reach, in neighbouring Sarrià.

Safety & Annoyances

The annual festes de Gràcia seems to bring most of Barcelona to the neighbourhood for a week of noisy festivities. While it is undoubtedly the high point of the Gràcia community calendar, the mess, disruption and constant noise can make it a trying week for residents.

83

Map p.387
Area **F** p.75

Best Points
A tranquil, green
neighbourhood that's
family orientated.

Worst Points
A lack of transport links
and entertainment
options can make
things too tranquil
for some.

Horta-Guinardó

This large residential district spreads up the hillside to the west of Eixample, consisting of several neighbourhoods linked by parks. Guinardó is a tranquil city suburb that has much in common with Eixample, while working-class Horta, further up the hill, was once a farming village (horta means 'vegetable patch' in Catalan). Small vegetable patches still occupy the rare patches of flat land between apartment blocks. Guinardó's festa major takes place in early June.

Accommodation

Most of the district's housing has been built in the last 50 years, and spacious apartments suitable for large families are quite easy to find. Because of the distance from the city centre, prices are still affordable. A two bedroom flat costs €250,000 – €300,000 (€800 a month to rent).

Entertainment & Leisure

For exhibitions and cultural activity, there are civic centres in Guinardó, El Carmel and Horta. There are also a handful of museums on the Ronda del Dalt, including a tennis museum (93 428 53 53, Passeig Vall d'Hebron, 196). Horta-Guinardó has some of Barcelona's loveliest and least visited parks, such as the recently renovated Parc del Guinardó and Horta's neo-classical Parc del Laberint, which has a maze.

Shopping & Amenities

The district lacks major commerce, but there is a small selection of supermarkets, banks and other services at the heart of each area. There are markets in El Carmel (Carrer Llobregos 149), Guinardó (Passeig Llivia 34), Horta (Carrer Tajo 75), and Vall d'Hebron (Carrer Trueba 1). For more extensive shopping, there is the large Corte Inglés department store nearby at Can Dragó (Passeig. Andreu Nin 51).
Slightly further is Encants Nous at Glòries (Carrer Dos de Maig 225), which has a range of high street fashion branches and a computer superstore. To the north, the Vall d'Hebron public sports complex (Passeig Vall d'Hebron 166) was one of the main Olympic sites and has extensive sports and fitness facilities. There are several other sports clubs nearby.

Transport

A number of bus routes and night buses run through, but there is relatively little access to the metro. Horta and Guinardó each have metro stations (Lines 5 and 4 respectively), while Line 3 serves Vall d'Hebron and Mundet. Parking is available in many apartment blocks.

Healthcare

Carmel, Horta and Guinardó have healthcare centres. There are accident and emergency departments at the Hospital Universitari de la Vall d'Hebron (93 274 61 00, Passeig Vall d'Hebron 119) and Hospital de la Santa Creu i Sant Pau (93 291 91 91, Carrer Sant Antoni Maria Claret 167).

Education

The district is well-served by private and state schools, but its appeal for foreign families is its closeness to Sarrià's cluster of international schools.

Safety & Annoyances

While crime is higher in deprived El Carmel and on the fringes of Horta, street crime is rare. On the busier roads, traffic noise can be a serious problem.

Map p.390
Area **G** p.74

Best Points
*Residents have a
strong sense of
community and are
keen to maintain some
independence from
Barcelona.*

Worst Points
*The disruption caused
by redevelopment
projects, some of which
are due to last
until 2015.*

L'Hospitalet de Llobregat

L'Hospitalet is a self-governing municipality and the second biggest Catalan city, with around 250,000 inhabitants. However, the journey from Barcelona is seamless, apart from signs proudly announcing where you are. It is a largely working-class area that grew considerably during the 60s. The town is currently in a period of serious urban redevelopment and, hopefully, improvement.

Accommodation

Despite being outside Barcelona's city boundary, L'Hospitalet has not totally escaped the recent hike in house prices. A two-bedroomed flat in the centre has an average price of €280,000, although it's possible to pay up to €200,000 more than that. Collblanc, which borders directly with Barcelona, is cheaper, with an average cost of €240,000. Renting has an average rate of €850 per month, similar to many other neighbourhoods.

Entertainment & Leisure

L'Hospitalet has a busy cultural life, founded by Andalucian migrants who began arriving in the 60's. For the same reason, it's a good place to find flamenco and tapas. The town has its own theatre, and La Farga exhibition centre hosts regular shows, including one of erotica and another of manga. For fine dining, the Hesperia Tower hotel on Gran Via has a UFO-shaped restaurant that overlooks the sea. The hotel also houses a branch of the upmarket Metropolitan gym.

Shopping & Amenities

L'Hospitalet is well-served by indoor markets, with eight dotted around, including two in Bellvitge. Rambla Just Oliveras is one of the town's principal thoroughfares and the tree-lined street has cinemas, shops, banks, restaurants and bars. Not far away is a small shopping centre, La Farga, with cinemas and familiar high street shops. However, it is tiny compared to the mega-mall at Gran Via 2. (NB. Don't look for Gran Via 1, it doesn't exist). Almost next-door to Gran Via 2 is Catalunya's second, and slightly quieter, IKEA.

Transport

Metro (lines 4 and 5), FGC and Renfe trains, taxis and buses (day and night) run between L'Hospitalet and Barcelona. It is easy to reach the airport and Catalonia's southern coast, by car.

Healthcare

The Bellvitge (its official name is Hospital dels Principes d'Espanya) is one of the major hospitals in the metropolitan area, and there is also an important oncology centre, the Hospital Duran i Reynals. There are 12 CAP general surgeries.

Education

There are no English-language schools in L'Hospitalet, but the private school Xaloc offers the International Baccalaureate. It should be noted that the religious and spiritual teaching of Xaloc is associated with the Catholic organisation Opus Dei. There are 25 private schools (20 covering all ages, with five for primary age children only) and 48 public schools (34 primary and 14 secondary).

Safety & Annoyances

L'Hospitalet has a problem with overcrowding in some areas (such as Collblanc-La Torrassa and Florida-Pubilla Casas) due to a recent rapid influx of migrants. This has had an effect on public services. There has been some tension between new arrivals and those already living in L'Hospitalet, partly due to the lack of a common language.

Map p.383
Area **H** *p.74*

Les Corts

In the recent past, Les Corts was an isolated farming village, some distance from Barcelona. Although now firmly in the grasp of the city, it remains largely self sufficient and the abundance of amenities mean you may never need to go into town. The most famous local landmark is the Camp Nou. There are really two areas here; Les Corts itself and the upper part, Pedralbes.

Best Points ◄
Everything you need is to hand, but just in case, 15 minutes by metro and you're in the centre of Barcelona.

Worst Points ◄
It can lack atmosphere in the evenings and is dominated by modern buildings, with few traces of its history left.

Accommodation

Housing prices vary according to which side of Avinguda Diagonal you base yourself. North of this road is Pedralbes, the most expensive single area in Barcelona for housing. A Spanish infanta (princess) lives here; a good example of the tone of the area. It is full of large houses and plush apartments, many with a pool and communal gardens. Three and four bedroom flats start at €1,200,000. However, below the Diagonal, life is more down-to-earth. The average cost of a two-bedroom flat is €400,000 and if renting, you'll be lucky to get change from €1,000 a month.

Entertainment & Leisure

While not really known for its nightlife, there are clubs like Bikini (www.bikinibcn.com, 93 322 08 00) and Elephant (www.elephantbcn.com, 93 322 08 00), and some quality restaurants. There is an original version cinema, the Renoir Les Corts (www.cinesrenoir.com) and the Palau Reial Pedralbes and Cervantes parks both have landscaped gardens.

Shopping & Amenities

Apart from the seven floors of El Corte Inglés, there is also L'illa (p.312) shopping centre and the posher Pedralbes Centre, all on Diagonal. Small, independent shops are dotted about. Gym chains DIR and Europolis have branches here, the Metropolitan gym has a rooftop running track and there's the Royal Polo Club.

Transport

Les Corts is connected to most parts of the city. Metro Line 3 has five stations here. Many buses stop on Diagonal, and tram lines 1, 2 and 3 connect with nearby towns Esplugues de Llobregat and Sant Joan Despi. By car or taxi, it is 15-20 minutes to the airport.

Healthcare

The private Hospital de Barcelona and public maternity hospital are here. A couple of English speaking doctors are based at the private Googol Medical Centre. There are only two public CAPs, and there is no public 24-hour A&E facility.

Education

Many of Barcelona University's faculties are here, along with IESE and ESADE business schools. Pedralbes has English language private schools (e.g. Saint Peter's and

El 'Camp Nou' (p.250)

Kensington, p.125). Zurich School, in the same area, teaches in German. The American School of Barcelona (p.125) and German school Sant Albert Magne are nearby. Les Corts has three public secondary schools and seven primary schools.

Safety & Annoyance

When Barça play at home, there are traffic problems and the metro gets very busy. Diagonal is prone to congestion. Pedralbes is largely residential with few amenities; even finding a cafe can be difficult.

Map p.389
Area **J** p.75

Best Points
The area's strong community spirit and its emphasis on multiculturalism make foreigners feel welcome.

Worst Points
The distance from the city centre and lack of local entertainment makes it tricky to enjoy Barcelona to the fullest.

Nou Barris

Nou Barris is an area of former hamlets that grew rapidly and messily into a full-blown suburb. Long a poverty-stricken area of slapdash apartment blocks, in recent years a regeneration has begun. Retail facilities have been built, dilapidated housing has been knocked down and parks created. The tight-knit community, which has a rebellious history, remains a potent force, seen at its most active during the June and July festival season.

Accommodation

Despite the redevelopment work, many of the buildings in Nou Barris are still large blocks of hurriedly built apartments. These are on the small side and can be dark, but it's an affordable district, with prices ranging from €220,000 – €260,000 (€800 a month rent) for a 65sqm flat with two bedrooms.

Entertainment & Leisure

Nou Barris has a lively, integrated multicultural community and much happens around its civic centres. The Ateneu Popular (Carrer Portlligat 11) often stages productions in collaboration with the nearby circus school. The area's immigrant population means that restaurants are a mixed bag, with many international options. The Heron City complex, next to Avinguda Meridiana, is a cluster of bars and chain restaurants, with a bowling alley and a handful of *discotecas*. Even Nou Barris's urban parts are well-served by parks, several of which have recently been redeveloped. One popular spot is the Mirador de Torre Baró with its spectacular views across Barcelona and beyond.

Shopping & Amenities

The large Mercat de la Mercé (Passeig Fabra i Puig 270) is unattractive but useful. Roquetes, Canyelles and Ciutat Meridiana each have their own local markets, as well as small commercial centres with banks, post offices, hardware stores and bakeries. Fitness opportunities are limited beyond the numerous local football clubs, but include the large Virgin Active gym at Can Dragó, and Barcelona's biggest swimming pool, also at Can Dragó.

Transport

At the far end of metro Lines 1, 3 and 4, Nou Barris is relatively isolated. Although it has many bus services, most of them only go to outlying areas. A separate metro line (Line 11) serves the district's hilltop suburbs. There are suburban trains from Torre Baró FGC and Sant Andreu Arenal that reach Plaça Catalunya within 15 minutes, and there are night buses to Placa de Catalunya (N1 and N3). Most homes lack parking spaces but privately-owned facilities are easy to find.

Healthcare

Each of the district's barrios has a healthcare centre. The nearest accident and emergency department is at the Hospital de la Santa Creu i Sant Pau (93 291 91 91, Carrer Sant Antoni Maria Claret 167).

Education

Nou Barris has several private and state schools. It is far from the international schools, which tend to be based in Sarrià, but they can be reached easily, via the Ronda del Dalt.

Safety & Annoyances

Nou Barris is smartening up, largely due to the civic spirit of its citizens. But, it remains one of Barcelona's poorest areas and suffers from low-level crime, such as vehicle theft and damage.

Map p.397
Area **K** p.75

Sant Andreu

Covering a large area on Barcelona's north side, Sant Andreu is unapologetically residential. Its large apartment blocks and industrial estates have little to tempt the tourist, but enough commercial developments, amenities and services to keep locals content. The area is set to achieve new importance with the opening of the AVE station, which will make Sagrera one of Barcelona's twin hubs for the high-speed train network. Sagrera is under massive redevelopment in preparation.

Best Points
Central Sant Andreu has a quaint, small-town feel, minutes from the city centre.

Worst Points
Heavy traffic and a lack of nightlife can make the rest of the area feel like a commuter town.

Accommodation
Mostly apartment buildings from the past 30 or 40 years. In central Sant Andreu there are also a handful of small, sought-after houses. Prices are high considering the distance from the city centre; a 70sqm flat with two bedrooms costs €290,000 – €340,000 (€950 a month rental). Larger, more expensive flats are quite common.

Entertainment & Leisure
Entertainment revolves around small, local restaurants and bars, and trips to the smattering of late-night venues around Passeig Andreu Nin. For outstanding drinking and dining, you need to venture towards the city centre. The Parc de la Pegaso is the biggest green space in the area. Can Fabra cultural centre houses a library and hosts concerts, exhibitions, courses and children's activities.

Shopping & Amenities
The Mercat de Sant Andreu (Plaça Mercadal 41) is a pretty, local market. Fresh produce is also available from the Mercat Bon Pastor (Carrer Sant Adri'a 154) and Mercat de Felip II (Carrer Felip II 148). For more prosaic grocery shopping, there is the large Corte Inglés owned Hipercor (Avinguda Meridiana 350) and a Carrefour in La Maquinista shopping centre. This huge, open-air mall also has fashion and homeware stores. The recently opened Corte Inglés department store is in nearby Can Dragó (Passeig Andreu Nin 51). Local services, such as banks, salons and bakeries, are found in central Sant Andreu, Sagrera, Bon Pastor and Ciutat Vella. There are private gyms in La Maquinista and central Sant Andreu.

Transport
Sant Andreu lies on several of the main railway routes out of town, and so has frequent, rapid trains to the city centre from Sant Andreu Arenal and Sant Andreu Comtal stations. Aside from this, transport is tricky, with only the far end of metro Line 1 reaching the district. The area has good bus links, day and night, to the city centre and outlying areas. Car parking is fairly plentiful in local apartment blocks, and although the main thoroughfares can get busy, driving and car ownership are fairly easy.

Healthcare
Sant Andreu's public healthcare provision is scant, with just four health centres and no major hospitals. The nearest accident and emergency department is at the Hospital de la Santa Creu i Sant Pau (93 291 91 91, Carrer Sant Antoni Maria Claret 167).

Education
Sant Andreu has many private schools. There is also a decent choice of state schools, but the neighbourhood is a fair distance from any of Barcelona's international schools.

Safety & Annoyances
Constant construction work around Sagrera causes noise and traffic diversions, while congestion on Avinguda Meridiana further adds to the decibel level.

Residential Areas

Area **L** p.75

Sant Cugat

Set beyond Collserola, 15km north west of Barcelona, this town has been greatly influenced by the big smoke's increased accessibility. In the late 19th century, improved road connections made the town popular as a summer escape. When the train arrived in 1917, Sant Cugat took a huge leap economically and more than 70 years later, the opening of a new road tunnel gave further impetus. Thanks to an influx of international firms, the traffic between Sant Cugat and Barcelona is largely made up of commuters, and has become a popular area for affluent young families.

Best Points

The high quality of life in an independent town near enough to Barcelona to be able to take advantage of everything the city has.

Worst Points

There is little atmosphere, as the population is dominated by young families, which are less likely to be interested in nightlife.

Accommodation

The town is divided into different areas. Eixample, Parc Central, Coll Favà, Valldoreix, Mirasol, and Golf-Can Trabal all provide different housing. Historic Valldoreix has early 20th century houses, built as second homes for wealthy citizens. Parc Central has modern apartment blocks that are more likely to have communal gardens, a pool and parking. Prices here are not low. A three bedroom flat in Parc Central averages €600,000, while in Valldoreix the same size flat or a house would cost more than €800,000.

Entertainment & Leisure

There are two cinemas, three civic centres and a theatre. There is an international women's group that meets weekly, various art galleries and a museum of the town's history. Thanks to the high number of families, there are excellent facilities for children, including playgrounds and play centres. A large municipal sports centre has just opened.

Shopping & Amenities

The 12th century monastery is the town's principal landmark, and a sign of Sant Cugat's long past. As well as the monastery's grounds, there are many parks and the greenery of Collserola. Shopping in Sant Cugat is an upmarket experience, with small, independent shops the norm, particularly in the pedestrianised historic centre. There are two markets and a shopping centre on the road to the nearby town, Rubi.

Transport

FGC trains to Plaça de Catalunya in Barcelona leave every five minutes, and take just 25 minutes. There is also a Renfe station, for a line that runs into the centre, but takes a bit longer. It's also useful for going to towns on the outskirts of the Catalan capital. The Tunels de Vallvidrera road to Barcelona has a toll with variable prices. It is most expensive during rush hour.

Healthcare

There is one CAP in the centre of Sant Cugat and another in Valldoreix, which can provide emergency care. Private medical services include the Capio Hospital General and Policlinic Sant Cugat.

Education

The Col·legi Internacional Europa is a private school that teaches two thirds in the local languages and the rest in English, with French and German also important. It accepts pupils from 12 months to 18 years. The Japanese School of Barcelona is in Sant Cugat, while the Autonomous University of Barcelona is nearby.

Safety & Annoyances

The tiger mosquito has been an unwelcome visitor in Sant Cugat since 2004. Its repeated bites can be more painful than the ordinary mozzie, although in Europe it is not dangerous. Local buses are infrequent, with a typical wait of 30-45 minutes.

Map p.412
Area **M** *p.75*

Sant Martí

Sant Martí has come a long way in recent years. The renovation of this once-dilapidated industrial district was started for the 1992 Olympics, and continues apace. It has several distinct barrios, including Vila Olímpica, Poblenou, Besòs, and Clot. These days it has much to offer: beaches, futuristic architecture, regeneration projects and some startlingly pretty old streets around Poblenou and Clot.

Best Points

A relaxed and friendly district with good transport links and decent beaches.

Worst Points

There's a baffling lack of restaurants and decent bars.

Accommodation

The most affordable housing is in the huge 70s and 80s blocks of Clot and Besòs, where conditions are often cramped. A 65sqm, two-bedroom flat costs €300,000–€350,000 (€800 a month rental). Poblenou has post-industrial lofts and smart, spacious seafront flats with suitably high price tags; expect to pay upwards of €800,000 (€1,700 a month). The 90's-built Vila Olímpica is also pricey.

Entertainment & Leisure

For a district of its size, Sant Martí lacks nightlife. Port Olímpic's marina has seafood restaurants and identikit bars, while in Poblenou the huge Razzmatazz nightclub (Carrer Almógavares 122, p.366) hosts gigs and late-night dance sessions. Rock-themed bars have surfaced in the streets surrounding it. The Ramblas del Poblenou and Prim are good in the summer months, with cafes offering al fresco drinking and dining. On the beach, chiringuito bars have light meals and strong drinks. English language films are shown at Yelmo Cineplex in Centre de la Vila mall (Carrer Salvador Espriu 61). The Parc del Diagonal Mar features enormous plant pots suspended on metal spider-legs, whilst Jean Nouvel's nearby park is walled-in, like a giant room. The Parc de la Ciutadella and its zoo are close, and there's an open-air pool at the asphalt-covered Parc del Fòrum.

Shopping & Amenities

Each of Sant Martí's neighbourhoods has its own nucleus, with supermarkets, banks, salons, and delis. There are local markets and the Mercat de Provençals (Carrer Menorca 19), and the Mercat de Sant Marti (Carrer Puigcerdà, 206). Encants Nous at Glòries (Carrer Dos de Maig 225) and Diagonal Mar, both offer high street brands and hypermarkets. The huge flea market of Encants Vells, under Glòries roundabout, has cheap vintage items for those willing to rummage. There are affordable municipal gyms in Poblenou, Besòs and Clot. For more upmarket facilities, try Fitness First at Glòries (Avinguda Diagonal 208).

Transport

Metro Lines 1, 2, 4 and 5 connect Sant Martí to the centre in under 15 minutes. The FGC Renfe line links Clot and Passeig de Gràcia in less than five minutes, and the new tramline connects the Fòrum to Badalona and Vila Olímpica. The district is relatively car-friendly.

Healthcare

There are healthcare centres in Vila Olímpica, Poblenou, Clot, Diagonal Mar and Sagrera. The nearest accident and emergency department is at the Hospital del Mar (93 248 30 00, Passeig Marítim Barceloneta, 25).

Education

There is no international school, but there are 12 private schools, several offering the international baccalaureate, including institutions in central Poblenou, Clot, and Besòs.

Safety & Annoyances

The *botellon* (drinking in the street) can be accompanied by noise, vandalism and broken glass. Construction along Diagonal and elsewhere is set to last for some time.

Map p.391 & 399
Area *p.74*

Best Points
It's a busy place with lots to do. Despite the tourists, you can escape and enjoy an authentic neighbourhood.

Worst Points
Traffic is a problem, while trade shows at the Fira can put a strain on public transport.

Sants-Montjuïc

Despite being Barcelona's largest neighbourhood in terms of space, only a quarter of Sants-Montjuïc is actually residential, with the rest divided between the port, the neighbouring industrial area, and the 'mountain' of Montjuïc. The latter is a great bonus for local residents. There are museums, sports facilities and expansive grounds with spectacular views of the city. Plaça Espanya, between Sants and Montjuïc, is an important junction and a nightmare to drive around. The inhabited areas can be a little bit cramped, a reflection of its working-class past when factories and their workers were based in Sants and neighbouring Poble Sec.

Accommodation
Residential areas are divided up into Sants-Hostafrancs, Poble Sec, La Bordeta and Font de la Guatlla. The first two of these tend to have the best availability. A two-bedroom flat in Sants costs on average €350,000, whereas in Poble Sec you could spend up to €100,000 less. A two or three bedroom flat costs around €940 per month to rent. Some buildings are modern, but there are also a lot of older apartments, possibly without lifts and in varying states of disrepair.

Entertainment & Leisure
Montjuïc has lots of cultural and sporting action. There is the emblematic pool used for the 1992 Olympics, the Fundació Joan Miro, the Palau Sant Jordi (for concerts and live shows) and the Teatre Grec (an open-air amphitheatre). Poble Sec has a mix of fast food chains and excellent tapas bars; to find the latter, go off Avinguda Paral·lel. Poble Sec is also where a lot of Barcelona's theatres are found. The festa major of Sants (last week in August) is popular among locals.

Shopping & Amenities
The Carrer de Sants is the principal shopping venue. As well as a market, there are high street shops and independent vendors. In the former bull-ring in Plaça Espanya, an entertainment and shopping centre is being developed that could soon outshine the more traditional atmosphere of Carrer de Sants.

Telefèric de Montjuïc

Transport
Barcelona's biggest mainline station, Estació de Sants, has local and long-distance services. The high-speed AVE train will soon pass through on a route connecting Barcelona to Madrid and France. Three metro lines serve the neighbourhood (1, 3 and 5) and there are lots of city buses, including the one to the airport.

Healthcare
There are eight public CAP health centres, but no casualty department. However, the Numancia CAP is open throughout the night and the Doctor Carles Ribas CAP is open until midnight.

Education
The area is well-served for schools, with more public than private. Of the former, there are 21 primary and 10 secondary, while there are 16 private primary schools and eight secondary. Sants also has a good number of nurseries, with 21 public and 16 private.

Safety & Annoyances
When a big trade show is on at the Fira de Barcelona, the area can grind to a halt, as taxis fight for clients or vice versa. Some areas of Montjuïc are popular for cruising at night. Back streets are best avoided after dark.

Map p.384-p.385
Area **P** p.75

Best Points
History, a big park and
great shopping.

Worst Points
Limited public
transport means the
area is somewhat
isolated, and private
vehicles cause
congestion.

Sarrià-Sant Gervasi

Sarrià and Sant Gervasi were outlying villages that Barcelona absorbed during the 19th and early 20th centuries, when they swapped their farmhouses for tall, modern apartment blocks. This area is part of the Zona Alta (along with Pedralbes). The term means 'high area', an apt name for this barrio, both geographically and in terms of cost and reputation.

There are some remnants from the past that give it charm, particularly Major de Sarrià, a pleasant, partially pedestrianised road that runs through the area, parrallel to Via Augusta. The neighbourhood is divided into three main sections; Sarrià on the west, Sant Gervasi on the east, and to the north within Collserola park, Vallvidrera-Les Planes.

Accommodation

Sarrià-Sant Gervasi is the most expensive neighbourhood in Barcelona, although you often get a big apartment for your money, or even a house with a garden. The average price for a two-bedroom apartment in Sarrià is currently about €550,000, and for a house is €2,500,000. Sant Gervasi is cheaper, with an average of €470,000 for a two-bedroom flat. The further out of town you get, the more likely you are to find a house. In Vallvidrera-Les Planes, a three-bedroom house costs approximately €500,000, but this area is much further from the centre of town, and has very few amenities of its own.

Entertainment & Leisure

Sarrià-Sant Gervasi has small parks, like the pretty Parc Turó, and the extensive Collserola. This forested area overlooking Barcelona has running, walking and cycling tracks, as well as the old-fashioned amusement park in Tibidabo. In and around the street of Marià Cubí are lots of bars and clubs. These only get going after midnight and are very popular with the young and wealthy. If you enjoy reading, the British Council has its library in Carrer Amigó, from which, for an annual fee, you can borrow books and DVDs.

Shopping & Amenities

Sarrià is free of shopping centres. Instead, specialist shops and designer boutiques are the norm. Streets like Avinguda Pau Casals, Muntaner and Via Augusta have a good selection of stores (although your budget may allow window shopping only). Delicatessen-style food shops abound, and for those with the time, a stroll down Major de Sarrià is a pleasant way to do the weekly shop.

Transport

This is not Sarrià-Sant Gervasi's strong point. The Generalitat train service (FGC) has 12 stations in the neighbourhood, but these are best for heading down into Plaça de Catalunya or up out of town. Bus services run along the main roads of the neighbourhood, but the metro doesn't currently touch it. A new line is being constructed that will cross through Sarrià to the airport, but is not expected to be finished until 2013. However, if you have a car, there is good access to the ring road and main motorways that run past Barcelona.

Healthcare

This is a very good area for private healthcare, with a number of clinics, such as the Teknon (p.109) and the Corachàn (p.109). Various English-speaking dentists are based here as well as some doctors of differing specialties. There are four public CAP centres, with one each for Vallvidrera and Les Planes.

Education

Anyone seeking private schooling for their children will find a good variety here, including some foreign options. These are Oak House British School (primary), Benjamin Franklin International School (p.125), Lyceé Français de Barcelone, Scuola Elementale Statale Italiana and the Swiss School. There are over 40 different institutions teaching in the local languages, most are private and many offer schooling from four to 18 years. A number of international universities are here, such as La Salle and the European University.

Safety & Annoyances

With so many schools, traffic can be a big issue in the morning when the school run is in full flow.

The streets of Sarrià

Setting up Home

You are now in the land of siestas, late night parties and a very lovely, but often frustrating, *mañana* attitude. Patience is an essential virtue in Spain; whether it's sorting out home insurance or organising an electrician, nothing is done with a sense urgency. Take advantage of English-speaking companies where possible. The work won't necessarily be better than the locals, (it's certainly unlikely to be cheaper) but the more efficient attitude should be less frustrating. The number of English services available in Barcelona is ever-increasing, which makes setting up home in the Catalan capital a slightly less daunting experience.

Moving Services

Relocation companies tend to offer a little more than removals firms, which just tend to shift boxes. Relocation firms can find schools for your children, arrange your pet travel and certification, and they even shred documents if necessary. If moving from within Europe to Spain, there are no special censorship laws on items such as DVDs and CDs.

If you chose to ship goods yourself, think hard about sending over any large, heavy items like furniture. They are expensive to send, and can normally be replaced quite cheaply once you get here. Also, bear in mind that getting a crate across from far flung spots like Australasia could take up to three months. You should always make sure everything is suitably insured.

Smooth Moves

Do not rush your packing. Take as long as necessary to securely wrap and pack each item individually, especially those that are fragile. Insurance covers only so much and even 'secure shipping' can result in damaged items at the other end. Always stick around when the removals firm is collecting your boxes, so you'll be there to witness any damage caused by them. If a claim is necessary, lodge it in writing within seven days. Take out as much insurance as you can. Be really ruthless about what you need in Barcelona. It's tempting to bring everything that reminds you of home, but if you aren't planning on staying for long, put the unnecessary, sentimental bits in storage.

Removal Companies

Allied International Removals	93 244 44 27	www.allied.com
David Dale Removals	96 678 47 13	www.davidedale.co.uk
La Vascongada	93 673 00 40	www.lavascongada.com
Purias Impact	96 865 46 67	www.puriasimpact.com
Ramsey Douglas	95 211 53 22	www.ramseydouglas.com

Removal services will generally shift anything, from small fragile items to large pieces of furniture. If you're moving within the city, there's normally a 'man with a van' in most barrios, who will typically be cheaper, though less secure in terms of insurance. Check local papers for ads.

Relocation Companies

Citrus Iberia	96 649 72 34	www.citrus-iberia.com/relocation
Crown Relocation	91 878 24 10	www.crownworldwide.com
ET Brokers Relocation Consultant	+44 (0)175 221 2375	www.etbrokers-removals.com
Relocate to Spain	95 126 07 81	www.relocatetospain.com
Relocation España	90 219 03 17	www.relocationspain.com
Stacks Recloation Spain	667 432 122	www.stacksrelocationspain.com
The-Eurogroup.com	0800 435 246	www.the-eurogroup.com

Furnishing Your Home

If you buy a home in Barcelona, it is likely to come with basic white goods such as a fridge and freezer, but washing machines and dryers may need to be negotiated into the contract. Rentals come both furnished and unfurnished. The website www.loquo.com has homes to rent, and you can advertise yourself there as a potential tenant.

Stores such as Habitat (p.293) tend to be expensive as all items are imported, but Barcelona's independent shops can offer delightful, reasonably priced items for the home. As everywhere, there is an IKEA (see p.294).

Employers often pay some sort of furniture allowance for those moving to Barcelona from abroad. Not all Spanish companies do this, but international companies based in Spain usually will.

Furniture manufacturers can be found to make unique, individual pieces, but these are expensive. They often promote themselves as artists, so you'll get one of their creations rather than a bespoke piece.

Second-Hand Items

English language magazines in Barcelona (see p.38) will often advertise sales around the city, where fantastic bargains can be found on home furnishings. Again, www.loquo.com is a great source for buying and selling everything from a wardrobe to a bicycle. Garage sales are rare, but people often leave items on the street outside their apartments. These are available to whoever wants them, and some amazing pieces can be picked up.

There are second-hand stores dotted about the city and antique shops are definitely worth looking in. Everything from furniture to clothes, stamps and old electrical goods can be found, often in excellent condition and at a very reasonable price.

Tailors

There are a plethora of cloth shops in Barcelona. The city's former success as a textiles centre has left plenty of materials shops, offering anything from treated leather to itchy synthetics. You'll have a good choice for soft furnishings, curtains, sofa covers and the like.

Word of mouth, as always, is the best way to find a decent seamstress who can pull together the big items that may be slightly out your scope. Some fabric shops will also offer to make items for you and, if they don't do it on the premises, they'll have excellent contacts, so will be perfect for recommendations. The specialists mentioned in Tailoring and Textiles (p.302) in the Shopping chapter will make anything from beanbags to monogrammed linen.

Household Insurance

The most common crime in Barcelona is pickpocketing on the streets, but home thefts can occur.

Household insurance generally includes the building, its contents and third party liability, all of which are contained in a multi-risk insurance policy. Foreign coverage is generally more comprehensive than Spanish versions and covers valuables such as jewellery, which aren't always covered by local policies.

Buildings insurance isn't a requirement but it is advisable. Options include coverage against fire, smoke, lightning, water, explosion, storms, freezing temperatures, snow, theft, vandalism, acts of terrorism and natural catastrophes such as fallen trees. This will cover all glass, the external building, aerials, satellites, the garden and its contents. Premiums are determined by the cost of rebuilding. The cost of your insurance is likely to increase each year with inflation. Make sure the amount you are covered for also increases.

Household Insurance		
Abbeygate	95 289 33 80	www.abbeygateinsure.com
Brumwell Brokers	93 238 44 99	www.brumwell.com
Costainsurer.com	64 634 65 81	www.hsnr.co.uk
Dagmar Schittenhelm Barcelona	93 630 21 90	na
HIFX Insurance	95 276 31 39	www.hifxinsure.com
Neil Rowley Insurance	69 688 88 98	www.rowley-insuracne.com

For more expensive items, it is always advisable to keep photographs, receipts and even video when possible, in order to prevent dispute over the value of an item if a claim has to be made. One other important point is that theft is only covered if a visible sign of forced entry can be proven. All ground floor windows must have bars on them.

Laundry Services

Laundry services and launderettes (*tintoreria*) are available across the city and are commonly used by residents. Most apartments come with a washing machines and dryers though and, in the heat of the summer, you'll be grateful not to be lugging hot, heavy laundry through the streets. However, if you don't have facilities or you're looking for an excellent dry cleaner then you won't have to go far. Prices are very reasonable – clothes can be washed and dried for only €2 or €3, and dry cleaning is cheap too.

Laundry Services		
Jordi Joan Tintorers	Eixample	93 435 72 37
Quick Sec la Concepcio	La Ribera	93 458 41 32
Tintoreria en Casa	Eixample	90 245 55 55
Tintoreria Solanes	Eixample	93 440 10 44

Cashmere sweaters, cleaned and professionally folded, can be brought back to life for as little as €3 each. Larger items such as duvets run at around €10, but can be done for less. If the laundry service loses items, you'll be lucky to get compensation, as they have disclaimer signs posted on every wall.

Domestic Help

Other options **Entry Visa** p.49

Part-time, full-time or live-in domestic help are all available in Barcelona, with cleaners and childcare the most commonly used services. Because these are comparatively cheap compared to other western countries, they're not uncommon among expats. Cleaners, child carers and live-in helpers advertise locally in shops and small, free papers. Rates vary, but around €5 an hour for childcare and cleaning is about average. Rates for live-in help will vary according to the standard of accommodation offered, working hours and whether weekend work is expected.

In Barcelona, superheroes clean the beach

Clean Visa ◀

If you hire someone illegally, you can face a serious fine. If your prospective cleaner or child carer has come into Spain from outside the EU, be sure to check whether they have a work visa.

Live-In Domestic Help

Few families have live-in help, but it is still available. Although it may seem fractionally less expensive than in other western countries, it does mean restrictions on your privacy. But, childcare, cleaning and general household help are usually offered, and if your 'live-in' happens to be local, chatting in Spanish (or Catalan) will help with your language skills.

Referrals, again, are the best way of finding help. Alternatively, check out local notice boards in supermarkets and shops or the table here.

Domestic Help Agencies	
Agencia Nueva Dimension	93 450 04 48
Infinity Cleaning services	93 552 87 24
Jacky	93 589 14 33
Marta Gallardo	93 200 51 67
Myriam Campo	625 142 866
Tecno Cleaners	93 478 50 72

Pay must be negotiated from the outset and you may want to suggest a four to eight week trial period before committing to a longer contract.

If you want to bring someone to Spain from abroad, you can act as their sponsoring company, which will help with securing a work visa. See p.51 for more on these. But, if they're coming from outside the EU, this is likely to be very tricky. Contracts aren't essential, but are advisable.

Babysitting & Childcare

Tender Loving Caguros is excellent for both childcare and babysitting services. Aside from them, there are few agencies that are not nurseries. Teenagers who want to earn some extra money will always be willing to help (as long as you know and trust them, obviously). Cleaners and live-in help often look for extra work and may take care of your children; ads are often placed in local shops.

Women's groups are another good resource, and will also offer the opportunity to meet new people. The Barcelona Women's Network (www.bcnwomensnetwork.com) has mother and baby mornings every Wednesday. *Barcelona Metropolitan*

Babysitting & Childcare	
Apolo 10 Escola Infantil	93 329 06 68
Betlem Escoles	93 424 41 74
Collegi Tecla Sala	93 337 35 66
E. I. Verdaguer	97 732 62 73
Escola Infantil Trencapins	93 218 87 34
Formacion Infantil S.A.	93 457 80 47
Guarderia Babet	93 323 14 92
Sol Ixent	93 741 54 14
Tender Loving Canguros	64 760 59 89
Tutor Kids	93 253 10 66

magazine (www.barcelona-metropolitan.com) usually has ads for women's groups and mother and baby groups. Another useful resource is www.expatica.com where 'mother and tot' discussion forums take place online. Nurseries are a good source for finding help too. See p.123 for more on these.

Domestic Services

Apartment buildings usually have caretakers who are available to give advice and help with repairs. These are often tenants who have volunteered for the position. If something such as pest control isn't covered, it'll be up to you to sort out.

Websites like www.angloinfo.com (see p.39 for more online directories) are helpful resources for finding English or French speaking plumbers, electricians and so forth. ATA Servicios Urgentes are particularly useful, as they are on call 24 hours a day and they speak English, French and Arabic.

Rossell S.L. are a company focused on all types of building construction, design and carpentry, so are good for big jobs beyond your own DIY skills.

Unless you're living on the outskirts of Barcelona you're unlikely to have a pool but, should you, the list of maintenance companies is lengthy; Europiscines La Noguera,

97

listed in the table below, is one firm that comes highly recommended.

Pests are a part of life and unless there is a particularly nasty swarm, Catalans tend to just get used to it. You will need to handle this on an individual level, unless your entire apartment building has been infested, in which case the building manager will make arrangements, and split costs evenly among tenants.

There are no restrictions on which companies you use, although those called in from further afield may charge more. Look locally for the best rates on plumbing, electrical care, gas repairs and pest control. Always try to negotiate a fee in advance.

Domestic Services			
Air Confort	Eixample	93 405 04 05	Air conditioning and heating maintenance
Apinsa	Barceloneta	92 264 55 55	Pest control
ATA Servicios Urgentes	Vall d'Hebron	93 447 18 19	24 hour plumbing, electrical and gas emergencies
Bauhaus	Sants-Montjuïc	93 223 19 23	Garden design, maintenance and care
Ciape DD S.L.	Eixample	93 433 02 52	Pest control
Climsa	Eixample	93 231 05 52	Air conditioning and heating maintenance
Daniel Iuhas	Eixample	93 384 30 69	Painting and carpentry
Europiscines La Noguera	Eixample	97 344 64 45	Swimming pool maintenance
Ficlima	Eixample	97 267 21 90	Air conditioning and heating maintenance
Green Class	Sarrià-Sant Gervasi	93 583 06 10	Garden maintenance and care
Iberia Sericios Globales	Eixample	90 233 06 66	Plumbing and heating repairs, and general repairs
Kenryc	Eixample	93 218 38 66	Garden design, maintenance and care
Laminotech	Sarrià-Sant Gervasi	67 759 44 99	Window lamination for heating and air conditioning efficiency
Piscinas Waterair	Sarrià-Sant Gervasi	90 222 26 22	Swimming pool construction and maintenance
Rains Control de Plagas	Eixample	93 432 24 64	Pest control
Reformas en General	Sant Antoni	93 405 18 13	Electrical and plumbing repairs, painting and decorating
Rossell	La Sagrera	93 455 93 32	Carpentry, interior design, building work, and architectural projects

DVD & Video Rental

Rental options for DVDs and videos are not inspiring. Most DVDs can be played in English (or at least with English subtitles), but the selection is a little limited, and new titles take longer to hit the shelves here than elsewhere.

International films do normally make it here, but when is anybody's guess. The majority of video shops are independent, and they buy titles when they can afford them, so there's no guarantee of finding what you are looking for.

Recent releases are sometimes easier to buy rather than rent, from stores such as FNAC or El Corte Ingles (see p.305 for more on these). If you do join a local DVD rental shop, you may have to pay up to €15 deposit, but this is returned when your account and any remaining debts are cleared.

DVD & Video Rental		
Films Video	Eixample	93 424 53 06
Mediabank Cinestore	L'Hospitalet de Llobregat	90 222 23 03
Videoclub	Sant Andreu	93 385 73 58

Pets

Pets are extremely welcome in Barcelona and it isn't rare to see people taking dogs into restaurants with them. The most common pets are cats and dogs although in certain areas, such as Barceloneta, birds are kept in cages on balconies overlooking the street.

The conditions in which animals are kept in pet stores are often pretty shabby, and many people choose not to support such stores with their custom. All domestic pets are identified by microchip or (until 2011) a clearly readable tattoo. These should come with your new pet when you buy it, along with an ID card, called a *formulario de identificación canina* and a certificate of sale (*contrato de compra-venta*). That even moggies require ID should clarify for new arrivals the seriousness with which Spain views its paperwork. For a list of reputable firms offering pet services, see the tables on this page.

Vaccination against rabies is compulsory for dogs, and it may also be worth getting them jabs for hard pad and distemper. Cats should be immunised against typhus and feline gastroenteritis. Generally, dogs are allowed to travel on trains. They normally travel at half the fare of a second class ticket, payable directly to the conductor.

If you rent your home, check with the owner whether or not you can keep pets; it's ultimately their call. Montjuïc and the beach are perfect places for walking a dog and, while there is no law against dogs fouling public places, there are rules within urban parks. Birds and fish can all be bought from local pet shops or on one of the endless pet stalls on the Ramblas, though again, the standard of care here is questionable. Pets in Spain are known as *animales domésticos, animal de compania* or *mascota*.

Veterinary Clinics	
Adan Milanes	93 284 63 15
Agrupacio Veterinaria	93 426 87 46
Centre Veterinari Animals	93 349 41 15
Centre Veterinari Ciutat Vella	93 319 45 97
Centre Veterinari Galvany	93 200 33 40
Centre Veterinari Les Corts	93 430 56 96
Centre Veterinari San Jose	93 349 61 02
Clinica Maragall Exotics	93 436 58 88
Consultari Veterinari	93 217 08 94

Pet Boarding/Sitting		
A Font Freda	93 779 03 11	Boarding, daily walking service and vet clinic
Can Mir Residencia de Animales	97 256 10 74	Boarding, breeding and daily walks
Hostal Mascotas	93 645 00 38	Boarding, training, grooming, home delivery and pick up of animals
Rolke	93 633 11 84	Kennels and cattery, training and German Shepherd breeding
Tropics	649 787 812	Long and short term boarding
Vila Descans	97 251 62 80	Boarding, training, breeding of Jack Russel terriers

Pet Passport

If you're moving to Spain from within Europe, the European Pet Passport allows qualifying domestic animals (dogs, cats and ferrets included) to freely cross EU borders. It is a booklet with the animal's ID number, proof of vaccination against rabies and is valid for the life of the pet. It may only be issued by a licensed vet. You may bring up to five pets into Spain, but a valid EU passport must be carried for each one at all times when travelling. An animal will not be allowed to enter if its rabies jab has been done in the previous 21 days. On leaving, you'll need to get your pet an anti-rabies booster.

Pet Grooming/Training		
Animal's Park	93 408 04 13	Grooming
Artgos	93 441 06 12	Grooming and training
Ca La Tara	93 416 11 44	Grooming and kennels
El Super des Animals	93 419 91 53	Grooming
Euroanimals	93 284 69 39	Grooming and kennels
Lovedogs	93 532 26 89	Grooming
Saki	93 211 57 45	Grooming and vet services
Uau	93 455 75 63	Grooming
Veterinary Clinic Bonavet	93 211 02 04	Grooming and vet services

Utilities

The distributor of Barcelona's electricity is Fecsa Endesa. The main gas distributor is Gas Natural. For years, both these companies had the monopoly here, charging tariffs fixed by the central government every January.

Then, in 2003, came utilities deregulation. Fecsa and Gas Natural remained the distributors, but in competition both with each other and new rivals, principally Iberdrola.

Power Suppliers

Fecsa Endesa	90 250 77 50	www.endesa.es
Gas Natural	90 225 03 65	www.gasnatural.com
Iberdrola	90 120 20 20	www.iberdrola.es

Consumers could either stick with the annual fixed tariffs, or opt for the new, 'free-market' packages with variable rates. Complicating the picture further, these companies can also offer combined gas and electricity deals. In the run-up to deregulation Fecsa was frequently threatened with fines by local authorities for power cuts affecting private homes and public transport.

Water here is supplied exclusively by Aigues de Barcelona (Grupo Agbar). Shortages are rare in the city, though water bills are among the highest in Spain.

It's common practice in Barcelona for landlords of small apartments to pay water bills. Some landlords 'incorporate' electricity and/or gas into the rent too. Most contracts allow landlords to increase the rent a little every year, but only in line with inflation. If rises exceed this, and the reason is increased utilities bills, you should demand to see those bills over a preceding period.

Electricity

If you are the owner of a new house, and the electricity has not been installed or connected, you will need to phone Fecsa customer services (*atención al cliente*) on 90 250 77 50 (English spoken on request). You will need the following documents from the seller or constructor: Certificado de Instalación de Baja Tensión (this may also be called the Boletín de Instalaciones Eléctricas) and the Documento de Primera Ocupación. You may also be asked for the Cédula de Habitabilidad, a document that confirms a space is fit for habitation. If you do not have this, you can fill a form out at www.cedulahabitabilidad.com, and an inspector will be sent. Fees vary from €130 to €200, depending on the size of the apartment.

If the apartment you have bought or rent is already supplied with electricity, you only need to change the name of the account, *la titularidad*, to your own. If the electricity supply came from one of Fecsa's competitors, then these are the people you must get in touch with (see table above).

It's often quicker to fill out forms on company web sites (see table above). To do this, you'll have to register for their clients' area, the *oficina virtual* or *area de cliente*, which provides you with a username and password.

Bills

Bills are usually sent every two months. Amounts vary, and will depend on your choice of company, consumption levels, and whether you opt for fixed tarif, known as *tarifa regulada*, or free-market tarif, usually called *tarifa libre*. It will also depend on whether you have mains gas, and if you want to combine gas and electricity with the same company. There is a useful energy calculator (*calculadora*) on Fecsa's website which will help you work out your electrical energy needs in megawatts, and your likely consumption (megawatt hours). Armed with this information, you can then shop around for the right deal.

Using the *tarifa regulada* as a benchmark, the average Spanish household falls into the three to five megawatt band, generating two-monthly bills of around €60, including VAT and charges. Heftier bills can round out to €80 for two months.

Water

Aigues de Barcelona, the water concession here, estimate a one-child family in an average flat consumes 12 cubic metres of water a month, for which they are billed just more than €18. Compared nationally, Barcelona has high water bills. Connection can be arranged by phoning *atención al cliente* on 900 710 710. You'll need your NIE (Numero de Identificación de Extranjeros), your sale or rental contract (*contrato de compra o alquiler*), the Cédula de Habitabilidad (see explanation for this in Electricity, above) and your bank details.

On signing the contract, you should get water within four days. A connection fee of €50 will be charged to your first bill. Bills are sent out every three months. While it's perfectly safe to drink, tap-water in Barcelona has a famously unpleasant taste. The general wisdom is that the cafe solos in bars here are made as strong as possible to mask the chemical tang. Bottled water is not seen as a luxury item, and many people buy eight-litre kegs from supermarkets, costing anywhere between €1 and €2.

Gas

Bottled Gas
Some households opt for butane bottles for cooking, especially in the city centre. The main supplier in Barcelona is Repsol Butano (90 110 01 00), which offers a package of delivery and maintenance.

If you do not have mains gas already, you will have to install the unit by calling out a registered installation engineer (*instalador autorizado*). Once a certificate has been issued, it will automatically be registered with Gas Natural, regardless of which company you then opt for. Phone the local Catalan body (Ferca; 93 453 69 06) for details of the nearest certified engineers to your neighbourhood.

Costs vary, but typically include a €30 callout fee and €65 an hour for the inspection itself, after which the technician will quote you the actual installation cost. There is an additional charge of around €120, which covers both the production of the *certificado* (sometimes called a *boletín*), and registering the new unit with Gas Natural. You may also need to present your Cedula de Habitabilidad (see explanation for this in Electricity, left).

Again, gas bills vary, and will depend on your gas/electricity combination, whether you opt for the fixed tarif, known as *tarifa regulada*, or the free-market tarif, *tarifa libre*. Gas Natural provide the table here as a guide, based on the governmnet-fixed *tarifa regulada* (prices per month, excluding VAT).

Tariffs
Low usage
Gas Básica (cooking and hot water) €2.44 per month
Medium usage
Gas Óptima (cooking, heating and hot water) €5.46 per month
High usage
Gas Plus (cooking, central heating and hot water) €42.31 per month

Sewerage

Barcelona is on mains drainage, linked to an intricate sewage system 1,596 kilometers in length. This is under the control of the Barcelona municipality (Ajuntament de Barcelona).

Rubbish Disposal & Recycling

Rubbish collection in metropolitan Barcelona is the job of the Ajuntament. Every street or block is assigned one or several large grey dumper bins (*contenedores*). These are placed on the street, and rubbish is collected every night from around 10pm. The Ajuntament is encouraging domestic recycling, distributing terylene bags to each household, all labelled in Catalan. Green is for glass (*vidre*); yellow for plastic packaging and cans (*envasos i llaunes*); and blue for paper. These colour codes relate to the recycling bins scattered throughout every neighbourhood.

Large unwanted items, such as old furniture, will be taken away for free by the Ajuntament. There are set days for this service in every district. Call the city helpline on 010 to find out when this is.

Refrigerators, air conditioning units, ashes or organic waste can be left at Punts Verds, found in various fixed points across the city. The Ajuntament is committed to disposing ecologically of items left here. Phone 010 to find out where the nearest Punt Verd is. The Ajuntament is not bound by law to encourage recycling, but the advantages are obvious. They get the returns on recycled material, but also reduce the density of waste: one tonne of rubbish destined for landfill costs from €30 to €36 to process.

Telephone

Nationalised by Franco in 1945, Telefonica de España was the classic Mediterranean monopoly. The winds of change came as late as the 90s, when EU-led plans to

Mobile Service Providers		
Movistar (Telefonica)	1485	www.movistar.es
Orange	90 201 22 40	www.orange.es
Vodafone	60 712 30 00	www.vodafone.es
Yoigo	80 062 28 00	www.yoigo.com

liberalise Spain's telecoms spurred the newly privatised giant into action, sinking huge sums into infrastructure in the run-up to the 1998 deregulation.

A decade on, competitors fill the field, but Telefonica still covers over three-quarters of the Spanish fixed-line market. The less-than-thriving competition is in part due to the 90s assumption that faster internet would need new fibre-optic networks to challenge the old monopoly. Instead, ADSL came along, and Telefonica realised it could just use its own existing network, dissuading any investment in alternatives. Telefonica's complacency in the marketplace is reflected in its hefty set-up charges and fees. The mobile market has been challeneged by the arrival of big UK firms Orange and Vodafone.

Landlines

Phone & Internet Packages
Telefonica's rivals (see table) all offer internet deals along with their fixed line services.

Installing a phone line can only be done through Telefonica. Call 1004 for Telefonica customer services (English-speakers available). The fee for call-out, installation of a socket, and provision of number, cabling and telephone itself is around €112. This includes the set-up fee. Look out for occasional promotions waiving or reducing this fee. If you wish to set up an account (*darse de alta*) with Telefonica themselves, you will have to pay €112, regardless of whether or not

Telephone Companies		
Jazztel	1565	www.jazztel.com
Orange	90 201 22 40	www.orange.es
Tele2	80 076 07 70	www.tele2.es
Telefonica	1004	www.telefonicaonline.com
Ya.com	90 290 36 33	www.acceso.ya.com

you have a line already installed. Incredibly, you will still have to pay this even if you wish to switch to Telefonica from a competitor (though there is a reduced rate if you were a Telefonica client less than a year before).

You then have to choose a package. Most opt for the Línea Basica, which covers line rental (maintainance and repairs), the phone itself, voicemail and call waiting. Línea Basica costs around €17 a month, excluding of course, the actual calls you make. Tariffs for these calls can be seen on Telefonica's web site. Economy rates start from 22:00. Peak times are from early to mid-afternoon.

Inertia probably plays a role in Telefonica's Linea Basica's continuing hegemony. If you take the time to shop around the competition (see table), there are much better standalone telephone deals.

Hello Mum ◀
Another increasingly popular option, particularly among UK expats, is the internet phone service offered by British supermarket chain Tesco. With a broadband connection, calls between Tesco internet phone account holders anywhere in the world are free. See www.tesco.com/intern etphone for more.

Cheap Overseas Calls

One of the cheapest ways to make an international call is by using a calling card. These can be purchased in local newsagents, tobacconists and internet cafes, normally in dominations of €5. They will include a local number which you dial (and are normally charged for) and instructions to follow. Have a look around when shopping for calling cards however, as some brands will offer cheaper rates to particular countries. Most internet cafes and small local shops carry these cards, with posters on display that list the number of minutes a €5 call will get you to your chosen country.

Another good alternative is using Skype (www.skype.com), a software program which allows you to make cheap calls from computer to computer. If the recipient of the call is also a Skype subscriber, your conversation is free. Calling landlines is also possible, and there will be some charge, but this is still considerably reduced.

Internet

Other options **Internet Cafes** p.344, **Websites** p.39

The same people that compete with Telefonica for fixed line services (see table of telephone companies) also offer internet. The best deals are increasingly coming in the form of *ofertas combinadas*. These offer a monthly set fee for an all-in package of ADSL internet, calls to Spanish landlines, and (a regular tactic by Telefonica's competition) no set-up fee or monthly line-rental, with modem and router delivered free.

Internet Cafes

Fast public internet access is widespread in Barcelona, ranging hugely from the touristy haunts in the centre to the scruffier but better value *locutorios*. Generally €1.50 an hour is a good deal. Tickets with re-usable time codes are becoming the norm, though some places are still only providing one-off sessions. It's increasingly common to see Skype installed on public internet terminals.

Internet Censorship

Internet censorship in Spain is very limited. However, it is known that web sites 'glorifying' terrorism are monitored and can be banned, including those related to ETA and Batasuna (considered by many to be ETA's political wing).

Bill Payment

Monthly bills for phone and internet are the norm. You can pay by standing order (*domiciliación*), by individual card payments through a company's web site, by phoning the billing department (usually accessible through customer services), or direct transfers from your bank (which can involve fees of around €2 or €3).

If bills go unpaid, you are likely to be cut off, with service only restored after a fax of the bank transfer receipt is sent to the company in question. This can often take several days. Fees for restoring the service are usually added to the next bill. Many companies offer a registration scheme on their web site, often called the *oficina virtual* or *area de clientes*, where you can keep track of your bills.

Post & Courier Services

The heavy-package end of the Spanish postal market was opened up to competition in 1998, but the state postal service, Correos, still has the monopoly over most postal activity. Correos, a conventional 'to the door' postal service, once had a reputation for delays, though things have improved. With a state-of-the-art radio control system, registered deliveries can be tracked all the way.

Barcelona's General Oficina de Correos, on Placa d'Antonio López at the port end of Via Laietana, is open 24 hours. Dozens of post offices throughout the city can be located on the Correos web site (see table) or by phoning *atención al cliente* on 90 219 71 97. Stamps can also be bought in some tobacconists (*estancos/estancs*). Postboxes (*buzones*) are yellow and found throughout town.

Letters can take up to three working days to reach destinations within Spain, four working days for Europe, and eight working days for the US and Australia.

Parcels to the US and Australia will take either a month (*economico*), 12 days (*prioritario*) or seven days (*postal expres*). Parcels to European destinations, even using *postal expres*, take from four to five working days.

Post & Courier Services		
Correos	90 219 71 97	www.correos.es
DHL	93 481 41 48	www.dhl.es
FedEx	90 210 08 71	www.fedex.com
Moldexpress	93 504 14 00	www.moldtrans.com
Skynet Worldwide Express	93 289 46 20	www.skynet.es

The registered (*certificado*) scheme tracks every stage of delivery for packages (up to two kilos) sent abroad. An insurance service (only for use with the registered scheme), called *valor declarado*, costs €2.15 for every €50 of value.

There is no gift service option. Correo Digital allows you to send Word or PDF documents from your desktop, which will then be posted on. Register for this at the *area de clientes* at www.correos.es. A PO box (*apartado postal*) costs €25 for a three month subscription, or €60 annually.

Radio

Barcelona now has no English radio station. The excellent talk-based venture Radio Free Barcelona, set up in 2007, was unable to attract investment. Even the cheap and cheerful English stations of the Costa del Sol can't be found here, which may reflect the different expat demographic.

Spanish radio, like TV, is nevertheless a good way to listen in to the national conversation. State broadcaster Radio Nacional de Espana offers Radio 1 (88.3FM, talk, news and music), Radio Clasica (93FM, classical music), Radio 3 (98.6FM, eclectic rock and pop with home-grown emphasis, including Flamneco, rap, folk and world music), Radio 4 (100.8FM, local affairs in Catalan) and Radio 5 (99.0FM, 24-hour news and sport).

Independent stations include the pro-Socialist Cadena Ser (96.9FM), with its landmark morning show, *Hoy por Hoy*, presented by Carles Francino. On the other extreme is COPE (102FM) run by the Spanish bishops, whose in-house shock-jock Federico Jimenez Losanto thrives on lefty-baiting.

Television

Spain uses western European PAL format, and there is no licence fee. All terrestrial channels picked up in Barcelona are in Spanish or Catalan, and there are no plans at present for ventures in English. Films and comedy originally in English can be viewed undubbed by hitting the 'original version' mode on your remote control.

State broadcaster Television Espanola (TVE) offers TVE 1, mainly entertainment and news and TVE2, a shade more highbrow with some drama and children's programming. Independent channels Antena 3, Cuatro and Telecino, offer similar, light entertainment, histrionic soaps, and the odd documentary.

Operated by the Catalan autonomous government, Televisió de Catalunya (TVC) broadcasts in Catalan. Its mainstream terrestrial channel, TV3, has notably higher production values than the nationals. Unlike the other channels, its late-night films are not interrupted by commercials.

Spain is committed to switching off its analogue signal in 2010. Digital terrestrial TV can now be accessed in 80% of Spain, including Barcelona. Reception is free, with access to around 20 channels, including all the national stations and CNN+. A range of decoders (*decodificadores*) can be bought in audiovisual outlets, starting at around €50 for the basic set.

News Bias

Spanish broadcasting has come far since the censorship of the Franco years, but unhealthy political and business interests still play a role. The aftermath of the 2004 Madrid bombings was not TVE's finest hour, with evidence of (then conservative) government manipulation of the news agenda. Cuatro news programmes have a notably socialist bent, reflecting the political loyalties of its owners, Grupo Prisa.

Satellite TV & Radio

Barcelona falls just within the reach of Sky's Astra II satellite, so there is no need to opt for the mesh systems needed by expats in Spain's south. British satellite TV installers in the city (see table) say reception here is good with 80cm dishes.

Satellite & Cable Providers		
Digital+	90 211 00 10	www.plus.es
Easisat	93 845 98 74	www.easisat.net
ONO	90 085 51 23	www.ono.es
Smartsat	93 810 24 58	www.smartsat.tv

Most of the English language TV available in Spain comes from the UK. For a cheap fix of programmes, there is a free-to-air service of around 200 TV channels, including BBC 1-4 and ITV 1-4. Installation of an 80cm dish, cable and receiver is around €400 (excluding VAT).

The non-subscription Sky freesat will give you all of the above plus select Sky channels, and national and regional BBC radio. Sky freesat boxes come with upgradable card slots. Full installation (80cm dish, box and cabling) will work out at €600 (excluding VAT).

The advantage of going for Sky freesat first is the possibility of upgrading to the full range of Sky subscription products. The suppliers listed below are certified agents of Sky subscription cards and billing and delivery can be done through them.

Conservation laws in central Barcelona prohibit fixing dishes to facades, whether or not you own the property. There is scope for using roof terraces and sills where they are out of sight.

Sports fans that don't want to shell out for full subscriptions will find English and Irish pubs in the city centre with Sky Sports, especially around Carrer Ferran, La Rambla and Carrer Boqueria. One of the friendliest and longest standing is The Fastet in Barceloneta's Passeig de Joan Borbo.

Spanish language satellite TV is offered by the country's single satellite platform, Digital+, offering the full Canal+ range of channels, plus the usual satellite package (in Spanish) of Nickelodeon, Disney, Boomerang, National Geographic, Discovery Channel, Viajar y Canal Historia. Themed packages (documentaries, sport, new releases) are around €30 a month. A general package, Digital+ Familiar, is around €47 a month. Depending on offers, registration is less than €10 and installation is free. Spanish-language cable comes from ONO, with three main packages on offer: TV Familia, TV Estrella (Cinema), and TV Premium. Installation is free.

As everywhere, there is a trade in pirate DVDs in Barcelona. Though it's not as prevalent as in other cities, sellers occasionally enter bars, or tout their wares on street corners. As everywhere, quality is generally poor, there is no comeback if a virus damages your player or laptop and your money might end up funding other, more serious crimes.

105

General Medical Care

Spain's public health service (Sistema Nacional de Salud) is free at the point of use. While it often works well, sometimes better than private alternatives, the system is feeling the pressure of an ageing population and funding cuts, especially at GP level.

This, and Spain's growing prosperity, is increasing the popularity of private health care.

Going private may provide more comprehensive cover, especially as public healthcare offers only a rudimentary dental service and, of course, no added extras like cosmetic surgery. The culture of obstetrics and

Hospital de Barcelona, near Maria Cristina metro

pediatrics in the public system can prompt people to choose a private option, because while the service is attentive, the attitude can be one of 'doctor-knows-best' (though this is changing).

One key difference between private and public healthcare is language. Few doctors speak English, so you may prefer the English speaking services offered by Bupa, Sanitas or AXA PPP (see private health insurance, opposite).

Serious emergencies default to the public health services, taking patients by ambulance to the nearest hospital with A&E (*urgencias*). Public hospitals deal with emergency cases, regardless of the patient's social security status. Ambulance arrival times in Barcelona were poor a few years ago, and since 2004, the regional Catalan government (Generalitat de Catalunya) has committed extra funding to improve response times to within 10 minutes for the most urgent cases.

Health cover is not mandatory in Spain, but it's well-advised to opt for some kind of policy if you don't qualify for social security. If you can choose between public and private, though, it needn't be all or nothing: many here 'top up' public health with basic medical plans that can offer good value.

Get Well Soon
Hospital and clinic listings begin on p.110.

Public Healthcare

This covers visits to your GP, treatment in hospital, subsidised prescription drugs and dental check-ups (but not dental work). To access public healthcare, expats must be contributors to social security (Seguridad Social, www.seg-social.es), either as employees or as freelancers, or EU retirees whose pensions are paid to Spain.

EU citizens can use their European Health Insurance Card (EHIC, formally known as E111) for basic 'tourist' cover while they find their feet. If you qualify for public healthcare, you will be issued with a personal health card (Tarjeta Sanitaria Individual, www.scsalud.es) at the Social Security office (INSS, Oficina del Instituto Nacional de Seguridad Social). With this, you can register with a GP at the local health centre, known as the CAP (Centro de Atención Primaria).

On the whole, public facilities are clean. Barcelona has some of the best public hospitals in Spain, the Hospital Universitario Vall d'Hebron, for instance, hosting a level of specialist investigation and research with which most private hospitals can't compete. In certain areas, such as dermatology, public institutions are considered leaders in their field.

Private Healthcare

Barcelona is liberally supplied with private health institutions, and most are on the 'direct settlement' lists of major health insurers. These range from general clinics such as the Centro Medico Teknon (p.109) to maternity clinics such as the Clinica Instituto Dexeus, and speciality ophthalmology clinics such as the Clinica Barraquer, named after its revered founder, José Barraquer, the father of modern refractive surgery. Note that the public health system also sub-contracts some referrals to approved private hospitals.

Pharmacies

Barcelona abounds with pharmacies. Emergency after-hours service is provided by a neighbourhood duty pharmacy (*farmacia de guardia*), which changes every night according to a rotating weekly shift. Check out the notice board outside any pharmacy for the nearest one to you, or go to www.farmaciesdeguardia.com and run a postcode search.

Spanish pharmacies have long had a reputation for doling out antibiotics (or even anabolic steroids) without prescription. This is no longer the case, though the attitude to painkillers is relaxed, with large packets of 650mg paracetamol easily available over the counter.

Health Check-Ups

Check-ups and regular health screening (*chequeos* or *revisiones*) are covered on comprehensive private health plans, but not on some basic packages. Except for over-65s, well-man and well-woman clinics are less common in the health centres (CAPs) of the public health system. See Government Health Centres & Clinics, p.110, for how to find your nearest CAP.

Health Insurance

It's common for many employers in Barcelona to offer health insurance as standard and there are various packages tailored for the English-speaking expat, either in monthly or annual payments.

UK-based AXA PPP's 'International Health Plan' offers packages called Standard, Comprehensive and Prestige. In-patient treatment is well covered in the cheapest (Standard) package, but it does not include consultations, psychiatric treatment, vaccinations, prescribed drugs, pregnancy or childcare. Detailed quotes are available on request.

'Health Plan' from Sanitas, a Spanish company in the Bupa group, is also aimed at expats and offers three packages on monthly subscriptions: Basic (€11); Classic (€27); and Complete (€50). The Basic package covers GP consultations, tests and diagnoses, with hospitalisation only covered on the Classic and Complete plan.

For those moving regularly between their home in Spain and another country, Sanitas has joined with its UK parent company Bupa to provide Bupa-Sanitas Health Plan Complete. This offers total cover in Spain with partial cover in another country of your choice.

The Spanish insurance giant Mapfre is also worth considering, as it offers good full dental plans, and has the size and scope to offer plans that should cover most needs. Its insurance plan against long-term sickness or injury is a popular option for freelancers (*autónomos*).

Health Insurance Companies

AXA PP	+44 1892 508 800	www.axappphealthcare.co.uk
Bupa	+44 1273 208 181	www.bupa-intl.com
Mapfre	90 220 40 60	www.mapfre.com
Sanitas	90 223 02 20	www.sanitas.es

Donor Cards

Those wishing to donate will not need a card. With more than 30 donated organs per million inhabitants, Spain has one of the most successful organ donation records in the world. This is partly down to the so-called 'Spanish model', the central monitoring of near-death cases in intensive care, but also because of its 'opt out' system of donation, whereby those who do NOT wish to donate register with a national database.

Giving Blood

With a population that has grown very rapidly in recent years, Barcelona has a continual need for all blood types. Blood can be donated to the publicly run Bancs de Sang i Teixits (blood and tissue banks), which can be found at the following Barcelona hospitals: Hospital Vall d'Hebron (93 274 90 25), Hospital Sant Pau i Creu (93 291 92 18) and Hospital Clinic (93 227 54 00 ext. 2090). You can donate any time from 10:00 to 20:00 on weekdays.

Giving Up Smoking

If your Spanish is good, a free helpline has been launched by local authorities (90 211 14 44), offering free advice and evaluations.

Advice and therapy programmes are still relatively new in the public health system, but huge progress has been made since the nationwide 2006 ban on smoking in restaurants. Two-thirds of all Catalonia's public health centres (CAPs) now offer help to those wanting to quit. This comes in the form of eight sessions over three months. Continuing appointments are dependent on meeting targets, and in some cases, referrals will be made for group therapy. For those who do not have the public health option, the best alternative might be to sign up for paid sessions on the advice of your private GP. See also Alternative Therapies and Support Groups.

Main Government Hospitals

Not all hospitals that treat patients on social security are under direct local government control. Some, like Hospital de San Joan de Deu, are private institutions subsidised by the state through a grant known as a *concertada* (*concertat* in Catalan). *Concertada* hospitals are part of the network of public hospitals in Catalonia, known as the XHUP.

C/ Villarroel
Eixample
🚇 *Hospital Clinic*
Map p.392 C2 **1**

Hospital Clínic i Provincial

93 227 54 00 | www.hospitalclinic.org

This is the principal high technology hospital for central Barcelona. It has an A&E facility. It is organised into the following *institutos*: medical and surgical specialities, thorax, gynaecology and obstetrics, nephrology and urology, digestive and metabolic disorders, dermatology, radiology, haematology and oncology, ophthalmology and neuroscience. Casa de Maternitat, on a separate site on Diagonal (see Maternity, p.111), comes under the direct control of gynaecology and obstetrics.

C/ Sant Josep de la
Muntanya
Gràcia
🚇 *Lesseps*
Map p.386 A4 **2**

Hospital de l'Esperança

93 367 41 00 | www.imasbcn.org

Esperença, which comes under the same trust as Hospital del Mar, is focused on the needs of an ageing population, specialising in ophthalmogy and osteo-articular surgery, diseases of the locomotive apparatus and radiology.

Pg Marítim 25-29
Ciutat Vella
🚇 *Ciutadella/Vila*
Olímpica
Map p.410 B3 **3**

Hospital General de la Mare de Deu del Mar 'Hospital del Mar'

93 248 30 00 | www.imasbcn.com

This is a modern general hospital with A&E. Clean architectural lines and large windows exploit direct views on to the Mediterranean. It offers a general range of medical and surgical specialities, and is especially noted for its leading dermatologists.

Hospital San Joan de Deu (or San Juan de Dios)

**Pg de Sant
Joan de Déu**
Esplugues
Ⓜ **Zona Universitària**
Map p.382 C2 **4**

93 253 21 00 | *www.hsjdbcn.org*

A private institution with A&E (accident and emergency facilities), linked to the network of Catalan public hospitals. It focuses on paediatrics, adolescent health, obstetrics and gynaecology.

Hospital Santa Creu i Sant Pau

**C/ Sant Antoni
Maria Claret**
Eixample
Ⓜ **Guinardó**
Map p.395 D1 **5**

93 291 90 00 | *www.santpau.es*

A general research hospital with A&E and a full range of medical and surgical specialities, diagnostic services, obstetrics and neonatology. An ancient foundation, it has moved twice in the last six centuries, from its medieval origin in Carrer Hospital in Raval (now home to the Catalan National Library), to the modernista masterpiece built by Domènech i Montaner near Sagrada Familia. Some departments are still housed here, but the bulk of the hospital is now in a new complex just a little further up the hill.

Hospital Vall d´Hebrón

**Pg Vall
de Hebrón**
Vall d'Hebron

93 274 60 00 | *www.vhebron.es*

A modern research hospital with A&E and 1,400 beds, this is one of the best in Spain and the biggest in Catalonia, offering a comprehensive range of medical and surgical services. It is divided into four areas: general, maternity/paediatric, traumotology and rehabilitation, and a non-invasive surgery centre.

Other Government Hospitals		
Hospital de Bellvitge (Hospitalet)	L'Hospitalet de Llobregat	93 260 75 00
Hospital Universitari Germans Trías y Pujol	Badalona	93 465 12 00

Main Private Hospitals

The following institutions feature on the lists of approved hospitals used by most private insurance companies. They are large, general hospitals, many with emergency facilities and intensive care. These institutions also offer specialist treatment such as ophthalmology, covered later in this chapter (see Opticians & Ophthalmologists, p.116).

Centro Médico Teknon

C/ Vilana
Sarrià-Sant Gervasi
Ⓜ **Sarrià FGC**
Map p.384 C2 **7**

93 290 62 00 | *www.teknon.es*

This is a high technology clinic (hence the name) with 190 rooms and more than 300 specialists. It offers a pretty comprehensive service, with all the principal medical and surgical departments for adults and children, including gynaecology, obstetrics and neonatology. Full range of diagnostic services.

Clínica Corachán

C/ Buigas
Sarrià-Sant Gervasi
Ⓜ **Maria Cristina**
Map p.384 B4 **8**

93 254 58 00 | *www.corachan.com*

This is a 90-year old institution with an intensive care unit and 122 rooms. It has a strong patient-centred philosophy, describing its professionals as 'elite, not elitist'. It is equipped with the highest technology, and covers all the main medical and surgical specialisms, including gynaecology, obstetrics and neonatology.

Clínica Nuestra Señora del Pilar

C/ Balmes, 271
Gràcia
Ⓜ **Gracià FGC**
Map p.393 E1 **9**

93 237 00 44 | *www.clinicadelpilar.org*

This is a non-profit institution that belongs to a religious order with other branches dotted throughout Spain. It has an intensive care unit and 162 rooms. It offers the full

109

range of medical and surgical specialisms, including gynaecology, obstetrics and neonatology, and the full range of diagnostic services.

Pl Alfonso Comin, 5
Gràcia
🚇 *Penitents*
Map p.385 F2 🔟

Clínica Quiron

93 285 00 00 | *www.quiron.es*

This is the flagship clinic of the Quiron group, a private healthcare provider with outlets throughout Spain. The Barcelona Quiron moved into expansive new premises in June 2007. It has 252 rooms, of which 33 are suites, and 20 operating theatres. It provides all the main medical and surgical specialisms, including gynaecology, obstetrics and neonatology, and a full range of diagnostic services.

Other Private Hospitals

Clinica Fundacio FIATC	Les Corts	93 205 32 13	www2.clinicafiatc.com
Clinica Plato	Sarrià-Sant Gervasi	93 306 99 00	www.clinicaplato.com
Clinica Sagrada Familia	Sarrià-Sant Gervasi	93 212 23 00	www.doctoralia.com
Clinica Tres Torres	Sarrià-Sant Gervasi	93 204 13 00	www.gruptrestorres.com
CRC Corporacio Sanitaria	Les Corts	93 221 21 80	www.crccorp.es
Fundacio Puigvert	Horta-Guinardò	93 416 97 00	www.fundacio-puigvert.es
Instituto Clinica Dexeus	Sarrià-Sant Gervasi	93 227 47 47	www.idexeus.es

Government Health Centres & Clinics

There are 55 public health centres (*centres d'atenció primària* or CAPs) in Barcelona, distributed across every neighbourhood. You can find your nearest CAP by the street and postcode search on the official CatSalut web site, www10.gencat.net/catsalut. Select *Els serveis sanitaris*, then *atencio primaria*.

You can make appointments in advance at public CAPs, with the first slot being at 08:30. Most CAPS provide a daily walk-in service in the morning and/or late afternoon, though these can often mean long waits, especially on Mondays or after public holidays. Children usually see a paediatrician, though in very busy periods, staff might suggest the child sees the family GP instead.

CAPs are also staffed by nurses, and some have extra services such as family planning (see Gynaecology and Obstetrics). Additional services such as hearing specialists are also available in some public centres.

Hospital Santa Creu i Sant Pau, (p.109)

Private Health Centres & Clinics

Your choice of private medical centre may depend on the approved list of your health insurer. The following private centres are accredited to the main health insurance firms. All offer GP services (*medicina general*) and paediatrics, often as part of a much wider series of specialist services such as neurology, ophthalmology and even alternative treatments such as acupuncture.

Private Health Centres & Clinics		
Algori Salut	Barceloneta	93 221 45 88
Assistencial Montaner	Sarrià-Sant Gervasi	93 218 82 12
Cemedic	Eixample	93 226 78 13
Centre Mèdic Assistencial Catalònia	Eixample	93 215 39 00
Centre Mèdic Bunyola	Nou Barris	93 354 37 81
Centre Mèdic Busquier	Gracià	93 237 83 01
Centre Mèdic Robresa	Eixample	93 415 43 43
Centre Mèdic Lisboa	Sarrià-Sant Gervasi	93 427 91 21
Centre Mèdic Vila Olimpica	Vila Olímpica	93 225 19 48

Maternity

Other options **Maternity Items** p.296

Tiny Tots
For mother and toddler groups, go to p.227 of the Activities chapter.

The primary criticism of Spanish maternity care, both private and public, is that it is overly reliant on medical intervention. Yet for every horror story of women pressured to accept inducing or epidurals, there are happier accounts of good care in clean and calm wards. Giving birth in Spain can be a shock to some foreign residents, but the culture is beginning to change in some institutions. Comprehensive care including pre-natal, labour, delivery, post-natal and paediatric check-ups is automatically provided free under the public system. This includes scans, which are sometimes contracted out to private clinics. Private plans cover maternity but usually only in the more comprehensive packages, and there are important exceptions and conditions (see Private Maternity Care, p.112). Once you find out you are pregnant, your GP will set you up with your antenatal timetable, which involves a gynaecologist, midwife, scans, and tests (see Antenatal Care). Women over 38 will be offered amniocentesis. There is a high rate of elective caesarians here; in private clinics, the c-section rate is twice that of public hospitals. Both public hospitals and private clinics might ask the father (or birthing partner) to leave in the case of sudden complications. If you wish your partner to be present under all circumstances, make it crystal clear to staff in your birthing plan.

What happens in hospital depends on whether you want a natural or water birth, or whether your pregnancy is shaping up to be normal (*emabarazo normal*) or potentially complicated (*embarazo de alto riesgo*). Casa de Maternitat, a specialist maternity hospital that is part of Hospital Clinic, is the most likely option for difficult pregnancies in the public system. Under private cover, clinics like the Quiron, Dexeus or Corachàn are equipped with sophisticated technology in case of complications.

Home births are still regarded by many medical professionals as either dangerously hippy or some kind of masochistic throwback to Spain's austerity years. But it is not impossible to find private gynaecologists who encourage home births.

Generally speaking, mothers who have given birth vaginally and without complications can leave hospital between 24 hours to three days later. For those who have had complicated pregnancies or caesareans, a three-day minimum stay is the norm. The procedure once the baby has been born is to register in the Registro Civil within eight days. This is located in the Barri Gòtic in Placa Duc de Medinaceli. See p.54 for more on registering a birth.

Public Maternity Care

Delivery is usually made by a doctor, and in the case of 'non-natural' birth, stirrups are the norm. Pain relief is all or nothing: gas and air (*óxido nítrico*), the most basic form of relief, is not given in public hospitals, though pethidine is. Epidurals are extremely common. Hired TENS machines that offer electrical pain relief are not available in Spain, but can easily be ordered from the UK or US. Check beforehand whether hospital staff will consent to its use.

Although recovery rooms are usually shared with one other person, they tend to be spacious, clean and cool, with a fair degree of privacy. A change in the attitude to 'natural birth' is underway in some institutions. The Spanish Federation of Midwives called in 2007 for all women to be able to have a natural birth if they choose. Barcelona's Hospital Clinic i Provincial and Casa de Maternitat are pioneering *parto natural* for those deemed at low risk of complications. This method doesn't use inducement, episiotomy or epidural. Women are attended to only by midwives (*comadronas*), doctors only intervening if problems arise. Women can walk around, and take up any position they like, with birthing baths (*bañeras*) also made available. Despite interest in the pilot scheme, other hospitals lag behind. Hospital del Mar, for instance, is still known for what some consider excessive intervention.

Stay at Home Mamas
Reactionary attitudes towards working mothers linger. As recently as 2000, a conservative Spanish business association suggested women employees should pay into an insurance fund to cover the costs of any future maternity leave. To the great credit of Spanish society, uproar ensued and the suggestion was savaged by all the political parties. As many pointed out: why should potential mothers pay into such funds, and not potential fathers?

Private Maternity Care

More comfort, more privacy and the most modern technology. Birthing partners can use facilities and mothers-to-be can lower the lighting and bring in their own music. The drawback is that private clinics working on tight rotas lack the large staff of a public institution, giving rise to complaints of a 'speeded-up' labour. However, some private clinics, (the Clinica Instituto Dexeus for example) do offer natural birth. Gas and air is not offered in all private clinics, with epidurals remaining the norm. Prenatal and postnatal fees depend on the type of pregnancy and the needs of the mother. Labour, delivery and recovery alone is estimated at around €4,000 (pain relief included), so it's not surprising most people rely on private health insurance. Maternity care (from pre to postnatal, and through labour) is usually only offered on comprehensive plans. Some firms only give maternity coverage if the policy is more than ten months old. It's vital to check the small print on caesareans: they are not covered on some comprehensive plans, which given the high c-section rate in Barcelona clinics, is a significant exclusion.

Antenatal Care

Antenatal testing and monitoring is attentive here, both in the private and public system. Tests carried out as a matter of course (such as for streptococcus) would have to be specially requested on, say, the British NHS.

As soon as you know you are pregnant you should have a general check-up with your GP. He or she will assign you a gynaecologist, usually based at the hospital where you will give birth, though you can opt to see your usual gynaecologist if you already have one. You will also be assigned a midwife (*comadrona*), and be set dates for tests and scans (*ecograficos*).

There are usually three scans, corresponding with each trimester. In the case of a routine pregnancy, check-ups (*controles*) with gynaecologists are usually monthly until week 36, then fortnightly to week 41, and then weekly or more until delivery. More regular check-ups would be likely for older women, or those deemed to be at risk from complications. Blood tests for Downs Syndrome are always recommended. Women over 38 are offered amniocentesis, though these can also be requested by younger women with other risk factors.

This timetable is roughly the same whether you attend a private clinic or use the public system. In the public system there will be ten or so ante-natal classes for first-time mothers, usually coordinated by the midwife assigned to you. Women in private care are likely to have access to additional services, such as swimming therapy and relaxation classes.

Postnatal Care

There is no system in Spain for home visits by midwives or healthcare workers. Paediatricians will examine your baby in hospital with the first appointment usually two weeks after birth. You will then normally see your gynaecologist 40 days after birth. Breastfeeding mothers are still a minority in Spain, though huge efforts are being made by health authorities to promote natural feeding, and your GP should offer advice. Alba (www.albalactanciamaterna.org, 93 311 82 80) is a free, independent Barcelona-based support service for breastfeeding mothers. Barcelonins are not prudish about breastfeeding in public.

Maternity Leave

Spain has long languished at the tail-end of the European benefits league. Things are improving though, and paternity leave was brought into line with the rest of Europe in 2007. Mothers formerly working full-time are guaranteed sixteen weeks statutory maternity leave (*baja por maternidad*). An extra two weeks are granted in the case of twins. As is common in other European countries, the sixteen weeks need not be taken in one block. In consultation with employers, it can be used before or after the birth, in part-time blocks, or shared with the father. The six weeks following birth are, however, an obligatory rest period.

From March 2007, the paltry two days that fathers were allowed was extended to 15 days statutory leave, although this looks set to increase.

Gynaecology & Obstetrics

Talk to your GP about choosing a gynaecologist, especially if you'd prefer yours to be female and/or English-speaking, though in the public system the latter is not that likely. Most public CAPs have a family planning unit (*planificacion familiar*), known officially in Catalan as *programa d'atenció a la salut sexual i reproductiva*.

Contraception is not free on the public health system, and you will need a check-up with a gynaecologist in order to obtain prescriptions for certain types.

Maternity Hospitals & Clinics

Centro Médico Teknon	Sarrià-Sant Gervasi	93 290 62 00	Private
Clínica Corachán	Sarrià-Sant Gervasi	93 254 58 00	Private
Clínica Nuestra Señora del Pilar	Gràcia	93 237 00 44	Private
Clínica Quirón	Gràcia	93 285 00 00	Private
Hospital Clínic i Provincial	Eixample	93 227 54 00	Public
Hospital de l'Esperanca	Gràcia	93 367 41 00	Public
Hospital General de la Mare de Deu del Mar 'Hospital del Mar'	Ciutat Vella	93 248 30 00	Public
Hospital San Joan de Deu (or San Juan de Dios)	Esplugues	93 253 21 00	Public
Hospital Santa Creu i Sant Pau	Eixample	93 291 90 00	Public
Hospital Vall d´Hebrón	Vall d'Hebron	93 274 60 00	Public
Instituto Clinica Dexeus	Sarrià-Sant Gervasi	93 227 47 47	Private

113

Abortion

Abortion on demand is officially illegal, with four exceptions: a woman has conceived after being raped, is psychologically unfit to bear the child, is physically unfit to bear the child, or carries a severely impaired foetus.

However, as is often the case in countries that have 'strict' abortion laws, the reality is very different. The potential for doctors to exploit loopholes on the second of those conditions means that abortion is very common in Spain. And because elective abortions are officially banned, there are only vague parameters governing when a termination should or shouldn't take place. As a result, there has been much coverage of the city as a focus of 'abortion tourism' from countries with supposedly more liberal laws. One unscrupulous clinic hit the UK press in 2004, for offering abortions to British women at very advanced stages in pregnancy.

If you need an abortion, you must approach a private clinic, as none are carried out in public centres. Fees can range from €300 to €500. If you have public health cover, you can get free advice from your GP or from the family planning centre.

Mammograms

In the mid 70s, breast cancer was the primary cause of death for women aged between 35 and 65 in Catalonia. Universal, free screening saw a drop in mortality from the beginning of the 90s. Under this scheme, any woman, whether or not she is a social security contributor, can have a free mammogram (*mammografia*). Ask at your nearest public hospital for details.

Contraception

The pill (*la pildora*) and inter-uterine device (*dispositivo intrauterino*, or *diu*) are only available on prescription after seeing a gynaecologist. The same goes for emergency contraception. If there is an urgent need for the morning-after pill (*pildora del dia despues*) outside hours or at weekends, you may have to go to A&E (*urgencias*). Condoms are not generally dished out on the public system either, and will have to be bought in pharmacies, supermarkets, or from vending machines in bars and clubs.

Fertility Treatment

Reproduccion asisitida or *tratamiento de fertilidad* is one area of health that shows perhaps the biggest gulf between the private and public systems. Barcelona has some of the most sophisticated, and expensive, fertility clinics in Europe. Yet for couples with fertility problems that rely on public health cover, Catalonia is one of the worst places to be in Spain, with waiting times as long as four years.

Gynaecologists

Diatros	Eixample	93 457 02 00	www.diatros.com
Instituto Guilera	Les Corts	93 211 11 45	www.doctoralia.com
Medical Service Ishtar	Sarrià	93 205 09 11	na
Twobagesa	Sarrià	93 393 31 68	www.doctoralia.com

Additional Gynaecologists

Many of the health centres and main private clinics offer gynaecological services. The table here is an additional list of centres accredited with the main health insurance companies, and which have not been covered elsewhere in this guide.

Paediatrics

Those using the public health system can choose one of the paediatricians at their local CAP (see Government Health Centres, p.110). The recent baby boom is putting pressure on public paediatricians, and in busy periods they will prioritise children with more serious cases. In this event, more routine consultations will fall to the family GP.

Vaccinations

Polio 2, 4, 6, 18 months
Diptheria, Tetanus 2, 4, 6, 18 months, 14 yrs old
HIB 2, 4, 6, 18 months
Measles, Mumps, Rubella 15 months
Hepatitis B 2, 4, 6 months, 12 years
Meningitis 2, 6, 15 months
Chickenpox 12 years

For those with private health insurance, there is now a large English-speaking parents' network online (see Support Groups, p.120), which can offer advice on selecting a paediatrician. Much will depend on your parenting ethos. Some people like their paediatrician to dish out the antibiotics; others don't, so look around for like-minds. While you will have a freer choice of paediatricians on private health plans, this can only be within centres that have a contract with your insurer. Most of the comprehensive packages offer cover for your children, but this may exclude vaccinations that are not considered essential. Restrictions may apply for adopted children, or children born as the result of assisted conception.

Some parents in the public system may have reservations about the heavy vaccination load, especially in the first few months. Jabs are also given rather early here; the MMR jab comes in one shot at 15 months, considerably earlier than in Britain and other countries. Chickenpox vaccinations are given at 12. The vaccination programme varies slightly throughout Spain, and something similar to the list here will be followed in private clinics.

As a parent you have the right, of course, to decline a vaccination for your child, though Spanish public doctors can take a rather forceful, paternalistic view. Refusing vaccinations could also pose difficulties for enrolling your child in the state education system.

Additional Paediatricians

Many of the health centres and main private clinics offer paediatric services. Paediatricians named by expat groups as speaking English include: Dr. Thorsten Faust (Centro Medico Teknon, Sarrià, 93 393 31 29), Dra. Maria Dolores Terradas (651 747 664), and Dra. María de la Iglesia (93 200 65 85). The table here shows specialist paediatric centres accredited with the main health insurers, and not covered in other sections.

Paediatricians

Clinica Infantil Stauros	Horta-Guinardó	93 427 10 00
Equip Pediatric	Eixample	93 436 84 88
Hospital de Nens de Barcelona	Eixample	93 231 05 12
Kindatares	Eixample	93 405 17 88

Dentists & Orthodontists

There is limited dental cover in the public system. It consists of education and preventative care for children, and limited preventative care for adults, thorough dental examinations for pregnant women and extraction of teeth for patients in acute pain. Health insurance policies tend to pay partial dental fees for treatment, though with a hefty list of conditions. Routine check-ups, hygienist, straightening and cosmetic treatments are sometimes excluded even in comprehensive plans.

Mapfre's 'Salud Dental' standalone dental plan costs around €70 per insured family member, with optional supplements in case of hospitalisation, so annual family cover is likely to come out at nearly €300. Orthodontist fees for children are subsidised. Sanitas offers a similar plan, 'Sanitas Dental', which works out more expensive per adult. A yearly premium comes to €260 for a couple, but children under six are free. Existing general policyholders with Sanitas get reduced rates. See Private Health insurance, p.107 for contact details for both. Most dentists recommend the age of 1 for the first appointment, and parents in the public system should take advantage of the cover. The dental practices listed here are suggested by various diplomatic missions in Barcelona, and many of them speak English.

Dentists & Orthodontists

ADE, Asociación Dental Española Clínicas Dentales	Eixample	93 457 31 62
Clínica Dental Barcelona	Eixample	93 487 83 29
Clinica Dental Bonanova	Sarrià-Sant Gervasi	93 212 75 36
Clínica Dental Dr. Stefan Leonard Tingsvall	Sarrià-Sant Gervasi	93 205 19 03

Opticians & Ophthalmologists

There are over 400 opticians (*opticas*) across the city, including major chains such as General Opticas and Opticas 2000. Contact lenses (*lentillas*), solution, and prescription sunglasses are available in most centres. Eye tests are generally free, and frames and lenses work out considerably cheaper than in other European countries. Optica Universitaria is considered to be excellent value.

Specialist ophthalmology treatment is best sought in the many excellent ophthalmology departments of the main private and public hospitals (see hospitals, p.108). Of specialist eye clinics and ophthalmologists, the most famous is the Centro Barraquer, named after the great Catalan ophthalmologist José Barraquer who invented Keratomileusis, the basis of modern-day laser eye surgery (*cirugía ocular láser*). Prices vary, though typical fees for laser surgery are around €1,150, usually with an additional €65 fee for the first visit. Patients can usually return to work after two to three days.

All non-EU licence holders who are required to apply for a Spanish driving licence (see Driving, p.53) will need to have an eye test (*examen ocular*) as part of a general medical (*examen medico*). These can only be carried out by one of a list of doctors approved by the Direccion General de Trafico (DGT). To find the nearest, phone the Barcelona office of the DGT (93 298 65 00) and ask for the *centros de reconocimiento de conductores* in your neighbourhood. This can also be found on their web site (www.dgt.es) under the section *Tramites*.

Opticians & Ophthalmologists	
Centro Barraquer	93 209 53 11
Clínica Baviera Instituto Oftalmológico Europeo	93 362 49 90
Cottet Òptics	93 301 22 32
General Optica	90 062 66 26
Instituto Oftalmológico de Barcelona	93 241 91 00
Instituto Oftalmológico Tres Torres	93 200 98 79
Multiópticas Florit	93 302 02 96
Optica 2000	93 487 19 11
Optica Oftalmica – Centro Auditivo Corachan	93 205 68 59
Optica Universitaria	93 224 70 15

Dying to Look Good

There has been a great deal of publicity about cosmetic surgery related deaths in Spain, especially following liposuction operations. Two women died in a Barcelona clinic within four days of each other in 2007, and although there was no evidence of negligence, this generated much press interest. The Spanish national statistics bureau estimates that there were 76 deaths in Spain following complications in 'personal improvement surgery' in 2006.

Cosmetic Treatment & Surgery

Spaniards have more cosmetic surgery than any other Europeans, with 400,000 operations last year, at an average price of €2,000. According to the Spanish news agency EFE, some 20% are men, who mainly seek abdominal surgery and liposuction. The number one operation for women is breast enlargement followed by liposuction, then rhinoplasty (nose jobs).

This national enthusiasm is clearly reflected in the 120 or so cosmetic surgery (*cirugía estética*) centres and clinics across Barcelona, offering general plastic and cosmetic surgery. Non-surgical treatments include cosmetic dermatology (rehydration), cosmetic medicine (i.e. botox) and laser treatment for wrinkles, tattoos and birthmarks.

The following clinics host surgeons recognised by the Sociedad Española de Cirugía Plástica, Reparadora y Estética. See its web site for more information on the surgeons and their specialist areas (www.secpre.org).

Cosmetic Treatment & Surgery		
Centro Médico Teknon	Sarrià-Sant Gervasi	93 290 62 00
Clínica Beltrán y Obradors	Gracià	93 284 83 03
Clínica Corachán	Sarrià-Sant Gervasi	93 254 58 00
Clínica Nuestra Señora del Pilar	Gracià	93 237 00 44
Clínica Planas	Sarrià-Sant Gervasi	93 203 28 12
Clínica Quirón	Gracià	93 285 00 00
Clinica Sagrada Familia	Sarrià-Sant Gervasi	93 212 23 00
Clinica Tres Torres	Sarrià-Sant Gervasi	93 204 13 00
Hospital San Joan de Deu (or San Juan de Dios)	Esplugues	93 253 21 00
Instituto Clinica Dexeus	Sarrià-Sant Gervasi	93 227 47 47

Alternative Therapies

Terapias naturales/alternativas are hugely popular not just among Barcelona's expat community, but also among local residents, especially middle class Catalans. Some 5,000 people are employed in the industry in Catalonia and 20% to 30% of the population use these therapies alongside mainstream medicine. In a pioneering move in January 2007, the Catalan regional government (Generalitat de Catalunya) passed legislation to register the 3,500 or so centres and 60 schools that train practitioners, with a view to monitoring the qualifications and training of staff. There are few aspects of alterative medicine not offered by somebody, somewhere in the city. From Rolfing to Bach flower remedies, and moxibustion to applied kinesiology, it's probably here.

An excellent resource is www.terapeutas.es, in which a wide range of alternative therapies can be searched for using Barcelona postcodes.

Aromatherapy		
Blau Naturset	Les Corts	93 409 86 05
Body Max	Eixample	93 207 44 55
Centro Medico Matterhorn	Horta-Guinardó	93 347 65 29
ESSEP	Eixample	93 412 15 74
Teràpies Naturals Bryonia	Sant Andreu	93 354 88 13

Acupressure/Acupuncture		
Apac Asociacion Profesionales Acupuntura	Eixample	93 323 04 19
Cento Médico Diagonal	Les Corts	93 207 05 47
Centro de Acupuntura y Manopuntura	Eixample	93 323 32 28
Instituto Superior de Medicinas Tradicionales	Eixample	93 426 50 50
Integral Centre Medic i de Salut	Eixample	93 318 30 50
Societat d'Acupuntors de Catalunya	Eixample	93 268 13 62

Homeopathy		
Centre TerapèuticBlau Naturset	Les Corts	93 409 86 05
Body Max	Eixample	93 207 44 55
Centro Medico Matterhorn	Horta-Guinardó	93 347 65 29
ESSEP	Eixample	93 412 15 74
Centro Teràpies Naturals Bryonia	Sant Andreu	93 354 88 13

Reflexology & Massage Therapy		
Centre Namaste	Eixample	68 795 24 61
Equilibri	Gracià	93 218 34 68
Fisiovital	Gracià	93 415 99 09
Happy Massage	Port Olímpic	699 704 247
Instituto de Reflexologia Podal Lone Sorensen	Eixample	93 265 57 00
Saifis	Eixample	93 459 46 50
Sattva	Gracià	93 368 37 31

Addiction Counselling & Rehabilitation

Professionals who provide alcohol and drug addiction counselling in English can be accessed through Barcelona NEST (see Counselling & Therapy, p.119).

Hospital de la Santa Creu i Sant Pau is noted for its research and treatment of addiction. This is carried out at the Addictive Behaviours Unit in the department of Psychiatry, headed by Dr. J. Carlos Pérez de los Cobos.

Barcelona Alcoholics Anonymous is an English-speaking support group with no dues or fees. There are no rules for joining, except the 'desire to stop drinking'. It meets three times a week in the churches of San Miquel (Barceloneta), Santa María Del Pi (Gòtic)

Sant Josep (Plaça de Lesseps), and also in Plaça d' Espanya, but is not linked to any religious movement.

Narcóticos Anónimos is a nationwide group comprising 'recovering addicts who meet to offer support to stay off drugs'. An English-speaking group (*grupo habla Ingles*) has twice-weekly meetings in the Church of Santa María del Pi (Gòtico) and in the Sant Pere district of La Ribera. The regional Catalan government runs an anonymous telephone helpline (93 412 04 12) known as *linea verd*, 'the green line'. It's a useful first port of call for those who wish to talk anonymously about drug addiction, although counsellors who speak English might not always be available.

There is, as yet, no English-speaking service or support group for those worried about compulsive gambling. The Barcelona based FACAJOC provides support groups and services for compulsive gamblers or their relatives, but good Spanish would be essential. Making direct contact with the UK organisation GamCare is another option (www.gamcare.org.uk). GamCare is often recommended to Spanish gamblers anyway.

Addiction Counselling & Rehabilitation

Addictions Unit (Hospital de la Santa Creu i Sant Pau)	93 291 91 31	www.santpau.es
Alcoholics Anonymous	616 684 338	www.aabarcelona.org
Barcelona NEST (founder Jill Jenkins)	93 586 35 30	www.barcelonanest.com
FACAJOC	93 318 04 07	www.ludopatia.org
Narcóticos Anónimos	90 211 41 47	www.na-esp.org

Rehabilitation & Physiotherapy

Physiotherapy in the public system can be accessed through the major specialist hospitals, such as Hospital Vall d'Hebrón (p.109). But it is lacking in the CAPs, where fewer than 100 of Catalonia's 6,000 physiotherapists practice. There are numerous private clinics dedicated to sports rehabilitation and physiotherapy, many offering electrotherapy and ultrasound as well as manual physio. An English-speaking service is offered by Zoe Queally, a specialist in muscular and skeletal problems and rehabilitation of spinal and sport injuries (www.thebigproject.co.uk/pilates/index.htm).

Rehabilitation & Physiotherapy

Centre de Gimnàstica Terapèutica	Eixample	93 215 62 71
Centre Medic Terapeutic	Sants	93 490 66 66
Centre Medicina Esportiva	Eixample	93 487 43 74
Centre Recuperación Funcional y Fisioterapia	Eixample	93 207 45 13
Centre Rehabilitació Vila Olímpica	Vila Olímpica	93 221 37 22
Centro Medico de Recuperación Funcional	Sarrià-Sant Gervasi	93 218 42 83
Complex Esportiu Municipal Marítim	Barceloneta	93 224 04 40
Eurosport	Sarrià-Sant Gervasi	93 200 73 55
Servimèdic Rehabilitació i Traumatologia	Les Corts	93 490 62 33
Unidad Terapeutica Biofisica	Sarrià-Sant Gervasi	93 237 71 22

Back Treatment

Barcelona is well supplied with chiropractors (*quiropractos*) and osteopaths (*osteopatos*). Some centres, like the Centro Kineos, offer an integrated osteopath and chiropractic service. Other osteopathic surgeries include cranial therapy (*terapia craneosacral*) and visceral therapy (*terapia visceral*). Prices for both are around €70 to €80 for the first consultation and around €50 for subsequent sessions. Shiatsu is also widely available in alternative medicine clinics.

Back Treatment

Acumedic	Les Corts	93 321 44 16
Blau Centre de Teràpies Manuals	Eixample	93 325 75 74
Centre Chiropractic de la Columna Vertebral	Eixample	93 487 50 35
Centro Osteopathia y Terapias Integradas	Les Corts	93 241 12 02
Fisioterapia i Terapies Alternatives Fernando Molina	Sarrià-Sant Gervasi	93 368 18 06
Gabinet de Fisioterapia i Osteopatia FIOST	Sarrià-Sant Gervasi	619 070 599
Osteopatia BCN	Gracià	606 041 211

Nutritionists & Slimming

Weightwatchers (www.weightwatchers.es) runs meetings in Barcelona for those wanting to lose weight. Availability of sessions in English changes with demand. Phone 90 230 02 10 for English-speaking groups.

For those with digestive disorders, the Centro Medico Teknon (93 290 62 00, www.teknon.es, p.109) and the hospital Vall d´Hebron´s Servicio de Aparato Digestivo (93 274 61 00, www.vhebron.es, p.109) have a good reputation for treating IBS, as well as serious disorders such as Crohn´s Disease.

Nutritionists & Slimming

Centro de Estudios Vipassana	93 459 27 66
Dr. Eduardo Malo Romero	93 215 90 68
Dra. Susana Möller Roca	93 200 85 72
Kore	93 425 44 40
Medicina Estética Balmes	93 323 25 20
Sthetic Integral	93 302 41 48

Individual nutritionists can be consulted at their practices; home visits are not the norm.

Companies such as Sthetic Integral offer treatments such as facial nutrition, while Kore and the Centro de Estudios Vipassana offer alternative slimming therapies.

Counselling & Therapy

To request a consultation with a psychologist (*psicologo*), you will have to get a referral (*volante*) from your family GP. There are several public mental health centres (*centres de salut mental*) in Barcelona, as well as psychology units in main public hospitals. Some specialise in child and adolescent mental health. There is also a public network of *centres d'atenció psiquiàtrica* for adults and children with more acute psychiatric needs. The main private hospitals also have psychology and psychiatric units.

A common complaint of the Spanish mental health establishment (private and public) is its use of drugs over psychotherapy. Anti-depressants are all too often doled out for depression, and there is reported unwillingness on behalf of some public GPs to make referrals to psychologists. This, together with the need to communicate complex feelings (no matter how good your Spanish or Catalan) may prompt you to find an English-speaking therapist or counsellor.

Barcelona NEST (Network of English Speaking Therapists, www.barcelonanest.com) is a group of qualified English-speaking psychologists, psychotherapists and educational specialists who live and practice in the city. They offer a range of advice to adults and children, including dance movement psychotherapy and couple and marriage therapy. They also address child behavioural and adolescence-related problems such as anorexia.

Sometimes foreign residents do experience depression related to culture shock in Barcelona, which comes in different forms and levels of severity. There are those who

Counselling & Therapy

Connie Capdevila (clinical psychologist, family therapy)	93 217 98 41
Jill Jenkins (child psychologist, founder of NEST)	93 586 35 30
Peter Zelaskowski (psychotherapist, family therapy)	628 915 040

feel initial euphoria followed by sudden disillusionment, or those who have roundly rejected their own culture, but fail to find anything to replace it. Children may feel especially alienated or lost at school. Many of these are generic expat experiences, but Barcelona can also trigger idiosyncratic responses. There is the struggle with not one but two languages; feelings of rejection by the host culture, exacerbated in a city dominated by Catalan national identity; an obsessive tendency to criticise the host culture or, at the other end of the extreme, over identification.

Sign Up
For more groups,
classes and other
options for joiners,
hobbyists and
general keen beans,
go to the Activities
chapter, p.197.

Support Groups

Culture shock and related depression can happen here, as anywhere (see 'Counselling & Therapy', above), but Barcelona is not challenging enough to need a specific support group. However, groups relating to family life and relationships do exist among English speaking expats.

The Family Matters Forum on the established AngloInfo Barcelona website (barcelona.angloinfo.com) is a useful place for parents 'to exchange views, share useful information on parenting, schooling and kid's fun'.

The US web site meetup.com has a major presence among expats in Barcelona, especially Americans and Canadians. Go to www.meetup.com/cities/es/barcelona for an index of subjects that will put you in touch with likeminded expats. These include childcare, mothers' support groups, language exchanges, general parenting, education and alternative health.

Parents of children with learning difficulties and special educational needs often use India Knight's ongoing blog on the web site of the British newspaper The Times. Go to www.timesonline.typepad.com/india_knight to find the discussions between expats based in Catalonia. You can enter into email contact with individuals through the site itself.

Social Groups

English-speaking social groups can often be a good way to settle in, make contacts, and pick up advice. Anglos form a stable and long-established community in Barcelona, so there is an abundance of such groups here, many linked to shared nationality. Groups such as The British Society of Catalunya (93 688 08 66) and the American Society of Barcelona (www.amersoc.com) organise events, mixing traditions from back home with Catalan customs. The Australia Spain Business Association (asbabarcelona@australiaspain.com) is a networking group for business people. There is even a lunch club for old foes here, the Oxford-Cambridge Society of Barcelona (roygwaters@hotmail.com).

*'Place of prayer,
silence please'*

Dry Cleaners p.74
Divorce Lawyers p.108

Written by residents, these unique guidebooks are packed with insider info, from arriving in a new destination to making it your home and everything in between.

Explorer Residents' Guides
We Know Where You Live

Education

Any fair assessment of Spanish public education has to take into account its dismal situation under Franco. In this sense, Spain's provision of universal, free education is a marked achievement, and is steadily improving.

Spain still has worryingly poor science and maths scores on the OECD league tables, though, and there is ongoing criticism of unimaginative teaching methods across the curriculum.

On the positive side of the balance sheet, Spain pays teachers well, and has sustained an even standard across state schools, avoiding disparity that can divide neighbourhoods in other parts of Europe.

Concertat Schools

An important concept to grasp is the *concertat* school. These are private (often religious) institutions, where fees are paid by the state through a per-pupil grant known as a *concertat* (*concertada* in Spanish) and which follow the state curriculum. This odd arrangement arose from a lack of public institutions after the death of Franco. It is estimated that 30% of Spanish state schoolchildren attend *concertat* schools. Academic results are not necessarily higher than in state-run schools, though they might offer more in the way of excursions and after-school clubs. Such extras come at a price, though, and parents can usually expect to receive bills upwards of €100 a month.

Private Schools

School Ages

Compulsory schooling in Spain starts at the age of 6 and ends at 16. More academic pupils study for the Batxillerat (Bachillerato in Spanish) until 18, while others can stay in the education system for more vocational training.

The second category is independent schools proper. These often teach in Spanish (rather than Catalan) and tend to be expensive. Many are found in the well-set areas of Pedralbes and Sarrià, and can have a religious ethos. Some of these schools are closely connected to Opus Dei.

International Schools

The third category is the British, US and other international schools, where the majority, or a large minority, of pupils are native-English speakers (these are listed from Nurseries and Pre-School, p.123, onwards).

Choosing a School

Choice of school will depend greatly on linguistic factors. If you decide to enroll your child in the state school system, (and this is a popular choice among English-speaking parents in Barcelona) bear in mind that teaching is nearly exclusively in Catalan. Enrolment in state or private education can be undertaken on arrival, though this would depend on availability of places in individual schools. Waiting lists are common in the over-subscribed state-run nurseries.

In the state system, the process of choosing a school and enrollment is called *preinscripció*, and takes place in May, in time for the start of the academic year in September. Choice of school is limited to catchment area. *Barcelona és una Bona Escola* is an excellent annual guide listing all state-run and *concertat* schools, with photos and information on each. It is distributed free in the information office of the Ajuntament de Barcelona in Plaça San Miquel in the Barri Gòtic. The Ajuntament website, www.bcn.es/english, is another useful resource, and has a facility that allows you to search for schools by area.

Forms for enrolment can be picked up in any state school. When these are complete, return them with the originals and photocopies of the following documents: your residency card (see TIE, p.52), your health card and the child's birth certificate (or Libro de Familia if your child was born in Spain).

Nurseries & Pre-Schools

State nursery education is in two stages: from 0 to 3 years and 3 to 6. Children in the first phase go to *escolas de bressol*. Places are not guaranteed and are awarded by lottery, although factors such as siblings who previously attended, distance from the school, and parents' earnings are also taken into account.

Barcelona's *escolas de bressol* are often purpose-built and considered excellent, so expect long waiting lists. Staff have state qualifications and are often very experienced, overseeing a variety of structured and unstructured play, outdoor activities and occasional excursions. It is not entirely free: the Catalan regional government (Generalitat) and Barcelona Municipality (Ajuntament) subsidise about two thirds. The remainder, which includes lunch and tea, works out at around €230 a month per child.

Every child resident in Spain has the right to a place in the second phase of state nursery, known as *parvulari* (from age 3 to 6), though you may not get a place in the school of your choice.

Parvulari centres are usually housed within a state primary school (known in Spain as CEIP), and while it could be understood as 'pre-school', it is much like school itself. Children sit at desks, do drawing and art-based work, and later are introduced to reading, writing and basic numeracy in preparation for primary school proper. Some parents feel uncomfortable at this early introduction of structure, but many also recognise that it is an excellent way of integrating. This second phase of nursery education is free, though children who eat in the school dining room (*menjador*, or in Spanish, *comedor*) are billed by the AMPA (a parents' association), which runs the catering arrangements.

The notion of the drop-in nursery, or even a flexible timetable, is an alien one here. Timetables are long and, especially in the second phase, rigid, though parents can opt to bring their children home for lunch. Both *escolas de bressol* and *parvulari* open from 09:30 until 16:30. The length of the day is often quite a shock to people from the English-speaking world, but is regarded as perfectly normal by Catalans.

The Ajuntamet-distributed guide *Barcelona és una Bona Escola* (see Choosing a School, left) is an excellent resource for choosing a state nursery.

There are plenty of private nurseries and pre-school groups in the city, though parents who want a more unstructured environment shouldn't assume that private institutions are necessarily more progressive.

Below are the details of nurseries popular with foreign residents, either because they are English-speaking, or because they take a less rigid approach to play and timetables. There is only one Montessori nursery in Barcelona itself, the Scuola Primaria Montessori in Sarrià (www.simontessori.com, 93 203 00 06), where only Italian is spoken.

Fees are usually charged monthly, and vary from €380 to €490 per month for all-day attendance, excluding food, which adds from €70 to €140 on top. Most private nurseries are much more flexible in their timetables, allowing parents to opt for morning or afternoon sessions, or a few days a week. Waiting lists are likely, especially for nurseries nearer the city centre (such as The Playhouse or BCN Kinder).

Note too, that the international and English-speaking schools detailed in the Primary & Secondary Schools section (p.124) also offer nursery facilities.

C/ Bellafila, 4
Ciutat Vella
🚇 *Jaume I*
Map p.403 D4 **11**

BCN Kinder

93 268 25 78 | *www.bcn-kinder.org*

Nursery from 1 to 6 years, founded by German parents. Based in central Barcelona, it runs groups in German or Catalan, the latter popular with English parents for its progressive ethos of unstructured play. Organic food is available. Parents can opt for the morning or afternoon sessions, or combine both for all-day care.

Av de la Miranda, 18
l'Hospitalet de
Llobregat

Blossom

90 299 55 37 | www.blossom-kindergarten.com

Nursery and pre-school from 4 months to 6 years, based on the progressive Reggio Emilia method. Mainly English-speaking children, supervised by a multilingual staff of English, Spanish and Catalan speakers. Blossom offers spacious facilities and a huge garden. Organic food. Flexible timetable or 09:00 to 17:00 all-day care.

C/ Doctor Ferran, 74
Esplugues

Noah's Ark

93 473 53 71 | www.noahsark.es

Offering daycare up to 3 years old, Noah's Ark has a multilingual environment of English, Spanish and Catalan. It has a large outdoor space with open play areas, and operates on the 'active methodology' model, where teachers respect the natural rhythms of each child, while also encouraging the children to develop positive habits. Organic food. Timetable is all day, or there is a short-term drop in service.

C/ Mozart 10, bajos
Gracià
🚇 Diagonal
Map p.393 F2 92

The Playhouse

661 469 419 | www.theplayhousebcn.net

Child-centric daycare for 1 to 3 year olds, with a maximum teacher-child ratio of 1:7. There are three English-speaking teachers and one Catalan, with the aim that native English-speaking children will become 'balanced and happy bilinguals'. Ethos is based on Montessori, with unstructured, creative and free play. Organic food. Flexible timetable.

Primary & Secondary Schools

State primary education follows a core curriculum of Catalan and Spanish language and mathematics. Note, though, that nearly three times as many hours are devoted to Catalan, as part of the regional government's policy of 'linguistic immersion'. The rest of the curriculum is given over to music, art, nature, physical education and optional religious studies. There is no entrance exam for state primary or secondary schools. The state secondary curriculum places the same heavy emphasis on Catalan language, and students are expected to learn at least one foreign language. Compulsory secondary education from 12 to 16 (known in Catalonia as Educació Secundària Obligatòria, or ESO) works on a credits system, the final score contributing to the leaving certificate (Graduat en Educació Secundària). Academically able pupils go on to study the Batxillerat until the age of 18. Following new legislation in 2007, the Batxillerat divides into three areas: arts; science and technology; humanities and social sciences. Core subjects that are covered in all three areas include: Spanish and Catalan language and literature; philosophy and citizenship; history of philosophy; history of Spain; a foreign language; and 'sciences for the contemporary world'. Less academic pupils who wish to remain in the education system can opt for Formació Profesional, a vocational scheme divided between school and hands-on experience in the workplace.

Private and international schools in Barcelona integrate nursery, primary, secondary and sixth form or upper school. Facilities are generally of a high standard, and good sports facilities are the norm. Class sizes range between 16 and 22. Many parents feel the level of English teaching in the state sector is poor, and may feel uncomfortable with Catalan language 'immersion' in state schools. Because of the high number of local students, many international schools offer the Batxillerat. So, while the state system is unbeatable for those parents who would prefer their children to integrate totally, the international schools are by no means Anglo ghettos.

Most curricula are structured around either the US or British systems, though many also offer sixth-formers the option of taking the Spanish Batxillerat or the International Baccalaureate (see individual schools for more).

Fees range from €5,000 in the pre and primary schools, to €9,000 for upper school. Note that these are basic annual tuition fees, excluding food, medical insurance, after-school activities or travel to and from school. The latter is an important consideration, as many international schools are far from the centre or, in the case of ESCAAN and The British School, not in Barcelona at all, but in the southern seaside towns of Sitges and Castelldefells.

C/ Jaume Balmes, 7
Esplugues

The American School of Barcelona

93 371 40 16 | www.a-s-b.com

Set in two hectares of grounds in suburban Esplugues, ASB is accredited by the US Middle States Association of Schools. With places for 500 pupils from nursery level to High School, ASB follows a basic US curriculum with the option of studying for the International Baccalaureate. Sports facilities include two basketball courts, a 'soccer' field and gym. There is also a bus service to and from the school.

C/ Martorell i Pena, 9
Sarrià-Sant Gervasi
Reina Elisenda I
Map p.384 B1 **16**

The Benjamin Franklin International School

93 434 23 80 | www.bfischool.org

Founded in 1986 by US parents, BFIS is a school of 400 students accredited by the Middle States Association of Schools. The school, which runs from nursery to grade 12, has a mainly US-trained teaching body and follows the American curriculum, though it also prepares students for the Spanish high school diploma and the Batxillerat.

C/ Ginesta, 26
Castelldefels

British School of Barcelona

93 665 15 84 | www.britishschoolbarcelona.com

Founded in 1958, BSB moved into its current premises in 1999. It follows the British curriculum, but also places a strong emphasis on Spanish studies. Students in the upper school are prepared for Batxillerat, and the Selectivitat process. The complex includes extensive libraries, three laboratories, an IT suite, music rooms, gymnasium and outdoor sports facilities. Special bus services run to and from Barcelona.

Pg Isaac Albeniz
Sitges

ESCAAN

93 894 20 40 | www.escaan.com

Founded in 1994, ESCAAN takes pupils from 1 to 18 years. Secondary level follows the British curriculum (GCSE and A-Level) with the option of International Baccalaureate in the upper school. It has an extensive, well-stocked library, sports facilities, full medical service and after-school clubs, with transport to and from Barcelona. Extra academic support classes are also offered.

C/ Cavallers,31-33
Pedralbes
Zona Universitària
Map p.383 E2 **19**

The Kensington School

93 203 54 57 | www.kensingtonschoolbcn.com

Founded in 1966, The Kensington School moved into its current, purpose-built premises in 1988. It is a non-selective school that follows the British curriculum, and has a strong tradition of sport and drama. A relatively small school of around 230 places, most of its pupils are sons and daughters of business people, consular or diplomatic officials.

University & Higher Education

Although home to some of the oldest institutions in Europe, Spain´s universities are where the Franco legacy is said to have lingered longest. Complaints include a semi-official system of patronage between established and young academics, dismal pay for junior teachers and researchers, poor publication records and limited investment in scientific research.

125

This is a generalised, national picture, though, and there are individual centres of excellence. In the most recent survey of the world's top 200 universities, the single Spanish university on the list scraped in at 190. Bad news for Spain, but good news for Catalonia, as this one high-flyer was its very own Universitat de Barcelona, see opposite page.

Expats deciding whether to study here or go 'home' will have to take language into consideration, as most (though not all) courses in Barcelona's universities are taught in Catalan. Unlike US and British universities, students here tend to live with their parents, creating an atmosphere that some may find narrow and lacking the extra-curricular intensity of campuses in Anglo states. Some institutions, such as Universitat Pompeu Fabra, see right, are considered too nationalistic and Catalo-centric for some tastes.

For admission to university (from either state or private schools), students must sit two sets of exams. Firstly, the Batxillerat (see Primary and Secondary Schools, p.124) and secondly, an exam set by the university itself, known as Selectivitat.

Admission of students whose educational qualifications were acquired outside Spain is notoriously bureaucratic. To study a first or second degree here, high school diplomas and/or first degree certificates must be formally approved by the Delegación del Gobierno, which is located in Carrer Bergara 12 (93 520 96 03), near the Estació de França in El Born. For helpful details (in English) on this process, phone the Barcelona Centre Universitari, the information service for the city's universities, on 93 23 89 049. EU nationals do not need a visa to be resident or study in Spain. Non-EU citizens will need to apply for a Visado de Estudios for a Spanish embassy or consulate in their home country. See Visas, p.51 for more.

Student Digs

There are a few useful websites for students hoping to find a home. The CIAJ (www.bcn.es/ciaJ) is an Ajuntament-run organisation that helps arrange student accommodation. The site www.bcn-housing-students.com is useful and www.brighter place.com is focussed on Erasmus exchange students.

Student Life

Barcelona's student population is huge, with around 200,000 of the scruffy tikes spread across its several universities. The cultural, cosmopolitan and arty draw of the city attracts students from all over the world and for a variety of reasons. Whether you're on an Erasmus exchange, a TEFL programme, studying for a Masters or embarking on a full undergraduate course, there will be plenty of opportunity to get involved in this enriching city. Students doing an undergraduate degree at larger universities can expect to be housed in halls of residence based on campus. The Universitat Autònoma de Barcelona, for example, houses students in the University Village (Vila Universitària), which is designed to feel like a self-contained city with parks, leisure centres and so on. It is worth contacting your university's accommodation office well before you arrive. The universities also have an affiliation with Barcelona Housing Services (www.bcn-housing-students.com), which specialises in accommodation for students. Options vary from shared flats and rented apartments, to university halls.

Your social life will, at first, be determined by where you live, who you meet and what societies you decide to join. The Universitat de Barcelona, for example, has a good range. It has one of the largest sporting venues in the city and caters for those that want to join a sports team, drama club, music society or get involved in one-off events. Beyond campus life, a lively student social scene can be found in Gràcia. It is one of Barcelona's hippest areas, with narrow streets, busy bars, bustling street cafes and lots of life.

Further Education

The Barcelona Business School (www.bbs-edu.org, 93 452 22 30) offers corporate training and executive education to business people, in English. For those with good Spanish, Barcelona´s ESADE business school offers open programmes for continuing career development (www.esade.edu, 93 280 40 08), as well as partnership programmes in which business people can customise their own course, either as individuals or through their companies.

Universities

Various locations

Universitat Autònoma de Barcelona

93 581 11 11 | www.uab.es

Founded in the heady and optimistic last years of the Franco dictatorship, the Universitat Autònoma consists of 11 faculties and three university schools. It offers 77 degrees and diplomas, plus 90 doctoral programs. The main campus is outside the city, in Bellaterra, with affiliated centres in Barcelona, Manresa, Sant Cugat, Terrassa and Mollet del Vallès. It has over 50,000 students enrolled.

Gran Via de les Corts
Catalanes, 585
Eixample
🚇 *Universitat*
Map p.393 D4 **21**

Universitat de Barcelona

93 403 54 17 | www.ub.edu

Venerable and highly respected, the Universitat de Barcelona was founded in 1450. Its 20 faculties and university schools are distributed over four campuses, the principle one centred in stately premises on the Plaça de la Universitat. A large university, it offers 75 undergraduate degrees, over 90 doctorate programmes, 390 postgraduate courses and has nearly 70,000 students.

C/ Jordi Girona, 31
Les Corts
🚇 *Palau Reial*
Map p.383 E3 **22**

Universitat Politècnica de Catalunya

93 401 73 96 | www.upc.edu

Created in 1971, The Universitat Politècnica de Catalunya has campuses in Barcelona, Manresa, Sant Cugat del Vallès, Castelldefels, Terrassa and Vilanova i la Geltru. UPC specialises in technology and science for degree, doctorate and continuing education courses, and has a strong research record. Over 50,000 students enrolled.

Pl de la Mercè
Port Olímpic
🚇 *Barceloneta*
Map p.409 D1 **23**

Universitat Pompeu Fabra

93 542 28 81 | www.upf.edu

Named after the Catalan linguist who died in exile during the civil war, Pompeu Fabra´s main campus is near Parc de la Ciutadella. Since its founding in 1990, this young institution consistently yields high academic results, with a comprehensive range of degrees and postgraduate courses attracting diligent students with an eye to the top-end job market. Over 11,000 students enrolled. Quite Catalo-centric.

Universitat de Barcelona

C/ Claravall, 1-3
Port Vell
🚇 *Av Tibidabo FGC*
Map p.385 D1 **24**

Universitat Ramon Llull

93 602 22 00 | *www.url.es*

A private university with Catholic leanings, Universitat Ramon Llull is named after the great medieval Catalan philosopher, and places a strong emphasis on architecture and engineering degrees. Founded in 1990, URL is housed in several established educational centres, such as the business and law school, ESADE. Over 16,000 students enrolled.

Special Needs Education

Barcelona has several schools dedicated entirely to children with special educational needs (*necessitats educatives especials*, or in Spanish, *necesidades educativas especiales*). The general policy is to integrate children with such needs in mainstream schools, ensuring that extra assistance and resources are supplied as needed.

All children in Spain thought to have special needs (regardless of what type of school they attend) have the right to be assessed by a team of qualified professionals. Parents and teachers opinions are taken into consideration, and at the end of the evaluation the team will decide if the child will fare better in a special or mainstream school. If the latter is decided, the team will also advise on what extra resources will be needed.

A special school is only advised in rare cases, usually when the school curriculum and routine would have to be modified so drastically that being in a mainstream school would be of negligible advantage. At present, less than 1% of Spanish children attend special schools.

Access to assessment is normally arranged through the playgroup or school the child attends; individuals we consulted reported that teachers who know the child well form a vital bridge between parents and the relevant professionals.

Learning Catalan

Other options **Language Schools** p.223

The Catalan conundrum strikes most new residents within a few weeks of arriving. To become fully immersed in any city, it is always a good idea to try and learn the language. And most new arrivals are desperately keen to try out the Spanish they've been practicing at home. The trouble is, the locals aren't always quite so keen to reciprocate. The inhabitants of Barcelona are very proud of their heritage and you'll find that Catalan is widely used, with over 90% of the population having a good understanding of it. The difficulty for visitors is the prevalence of Spanish (and limited use of Catalan) abroad, or even in the rest of Spain. Most visitors go for Castilian first, for these reasons. But, learning some Catalan, even a few phrases and pleasantries, will be a great help. Though be aware that Catalans don't tend to like hearing the two mixed, and to really feel at home here, and properly mix with the locals, you'll need a bit more than the odd *si us plau*.

The Ajuntament offers free starter lessons and there are a range of language schools around the city for the more dedicated student.

Language Schools		
Barcelona Ajuntament	93 402 70 00	www.bcn.cat
BCN Spanish Language	93 238 45 16	www.bcnspanishlanguage.com
c2 barcelona	93 272 16 34	https://sslsites.de/c2-barcelona.com
Camino Barcelona	93 467 85 85	www.caminobarcelona.com
International House Barcelona	93 268 45 11	www.ihspain.com
Speakeasy Language School	93 342 71 97	www.speakeasybcn.com

Transportation

Other options **Car** p.33, **Getting Around** p.30

Cars are a wonderful luxury, but not that necessary for daily life in Barcelona. The metro is air conditioned, often filled with the gentle sounds of classical music, and both efficient and cheap. Buses are a good alternative too, running convenient routes across the city at reasonable prices. Parking can be a nightmare in Barcelona as there are very few car parks (those that exist often sell spaces to locals so there is never any availability) and because a lot of the streets are narrow, parking on them is often illegal. The further from the city you get, the better the parking conditions, but in the centre it's very limited. Cars are great for getting out of the city for a weekend, but car rental is cheap (see Vehicle Leasing, p.131). If choose to keep a car, however, the road system is good and the cost of driving is inexpensive compared to many places.

Taxis

Taxis are a great option for travel, especially at night. They are relatively inexpensive and found on almost every street corner. If you take a taxi from the airport there is a €5 surcharge added to your metered total and from bus stations, a €2.50 surcharge is added on.

His 'n' her's thrones, €6

A red Tibidabo tram

Barcelona's bumble-bee-coloured taxis

Driving Habits ◀

Local drivers are pretty relaxed, but they like to use their horn so be prepared for a good beeping. They aren't necessarily getting angry, just impatient.

Driving in Barcelona

Petrol in Spain is relatively cheap, making driving a less expensive option than in many countries. The challenge, especially in the very centre of the city, is with parking. One increasingly popular way around this is to share the journey to work with colleagues, and hire out a long term space in one of the few parking garages in the city.

Drivers in Barcelona are fairly considerate, so the driving experience shouldn't be too overwhelming. Even Plaça de Catalunya is less daunting than it looks and, once you are accustomed to the road signs, you shouldn't have any problem at all. Maneuvering through the tiny cobbled streets will be your biggest challenge. Those that opt for a scooter ahead of a car will find this much easier. Just beware of ambling tourists that think they're in a pedestrian zone. Journey times will increase around rush hour, so early mornings or from 18:00 to 20:00 should be avoided where possible. The DGT (Direccion General de Tráfico) is roughly equivalent to what other countries call a roads and transport authority. Its website, www.dgt.es, has lots of useful information for drivers, but this is only available in Spanish and, occasionally, Catalan.

Importing Vehicles

If you drive into Spain with an EU registered vehicle, you will need your driving licence, valid insurance and registration documents. Spanish regulations mean you have to carry some basic repair kit in your car, including two red warning triangles (as approved by the Ministerio del Interior; www.mir.es), a spare tyre, light bulbs, and the tools to change them. If you keep the car in Spain for more than six months, you will need to get Spanish plates fitted and register with the DGT to pay car tax (*impuesto municipal sobre circulación de vehículos*). You'll need a standardisation certificate if yours is a right-hand drive car. You can get this from any Spanish ITV (Inspección Técnica de Vehículos) centre. Even if you're bringing in a left-hand drive car, you'll need to do an ITV test. This checks that your vehicle is roadworthy. ITV garages are dotted about the city. Just put "ITV" in the *actividad* field on www.paginasamarillas.es. Otherwise, try www.rvsa-itv.com for sites outside Barcelona.

Traffic Rules & Regulations

Cars drive on the right-hand side of the road. Speed limits in town vary from 15 – 60kph. If you find yourself involved in an accident, call the police immediately and get a full report done for insurance purposes. Speeding fines tend to be issued on the spot, and if you are not yet resident in Spain, police may take you to an ATM to get the necessary cash. Overtaking is allowed on very few roads (these are all clearly marked) due to space restrictions.

Car Hire

Those with a licence from an EU country can hire cars without any other documents. Those from outside the EU will need to show an international licence, along with the licence from their home country. To apply for this, go to www.international-license.com; the whole process can be done online.

Parking

As mentioned before, parking can be problematic. Spaces are limited and parking garages are far and few between. Some spaces are free, others (such as those near the beach) are metered, but the cost is only a few euros for an afternoon. Those who live on the outskirts of the city tend to drive, but those within the center do not always rush to get wheels. The metro and bus can be less costly and far less hassle.

Traffic Updates
If your Spanish is up to scratch, you'll get good traffic reports on the radio. Radio 5, at 99FM, is a good place to start.

Petrol Stations

The big name petrol stations in Barcelona, as in much of Spain, are Repsol, BP and Regasoil. Some are self-service and others have pump attendants. There aren't many in the city center, but they are easy to find once you move away from the hubbub of Eixample and Cuitat Vella. Oil refills, car washes, refreshments, car supplies and accessories are almost always available, and the food isn't bad either. Unleaded, diesel and leaded petrol are available.

Vehicle Leasing

Different firms have slightly different procedures, but in general, before you lease a car, your driving record and credit history will be checked. If you've come from within the EU, your credit history in your home country may do. If you've arrived from further afield, you may have to establish a local credit history first. See p.64 for details of how to open a bank account.

Leases are by the month or annually, with the cost affected accordingly, but these should cover everything from maintenance, insurance, and the actual use of the car. Car leasing can be done through any of the manufacturers listed in the Buying a Vehicle section below. If a second-hand or independent dealer offers you a leasing option, do a little research on them before entering in to any sort of contract. You are likely to get the best deal (and save time) knowing what sort of size, power and type of vehicle you want, before entering a showroom.

Company Cars

Company cars are common in Barcelona, but whether or not you get one will obviously depend on who you work for and your seniority. These cars are either leased, or owned by the employer, leading to tax implications and wage issues. Your employer's HR team should be able to help with this.

Vehicle Leasing Agents		
Avis	93 298 36 00	www.avis.es
Ballestero Alquiler	93 757 99 18	www.ballesteroalquiler.com
Central Rent A Car	90 215 10 83	www.alquiler-de-coches-barcelona.com
Easycar.com	+44 (0)871 050 044	www.easycar.com
Europcar	90 210 55 55	www.europcar.es
Hertz Car Rental	93 298 36 37	www.hertz.es
National Atesa	93 298 34 33	www.atesa.es
Pepe Car	80 741 42 43	www.pepecar.com
Sol-Mar	97 777 84 80	www.solmar.es

Buying a Vehicle

A foreigner may buy a locally registered vehicle in Spain if they have one of the following: a residence visa, title deeds to a Spanish home, proof that they are resident in one particular town (a Certificado de Empadronamiento, available from the local town hall) or a property rental contract for a minimum of one year.

If you buy from a dealership, the sales staff should handle the registration and ownership transfers. The dealer may also offer insurance, but foreign firms tend to offer greater coverage and, unless your Spanish is good enough to understand a contract, are probably a safer bet.

Cars, motorbikes and scooters are generally more affordable in Spain than in many other European countries, especially high end, luxury brands. Most big brands are represented and easily available in Barcelona. See the table of New Car Dealerships on p.132. There are some excellent used cars advertised in magazines such as *Auto Seminal, Coche*

Used Car Dealers

Central Poblenou	Poblenou	93 300 00 16
Peugeot Barcelonesa	Sant Martí	93 307 74 43
Red de Concesionarios	Eixample	93 200 29 22

Actual, Mi Coche, or *Motor en Mano* and on websites such as Ebay. It is always worth taking the vehicle you're considering to a trusted mechanic, who can check the car over and verify mileage, before you purchase. See the list of garages offering repairs on p.134.

If you are arranging the transfer yourself, the current owner must give you proof of road worthiness (an ITV certificate), proof the chassis number matches the registration document (Permiso de Circulación), a transfer of ownership form (Transferencia), and a receipt to show proof of paid-up car tax. If you buy from a dealer you should get a warranty and service history. You must then apply for the renewal of the vehicle's registration document (Jefatura de Tráfico) within 30 days. One copy of the Transferencia stays with the seller, and you must send your copy to the traffic office that issued it (the address will be on the form).

New Car Dealers

Audi	Mogauto Audi	93 278 13 33	www.mautomocion.com
Citroen	Barnacit	93 457 88 87	www.barnacit.citroen.es
Fiat and Alfa Romeo	Italsol Motors	93 668 93 92	www.italsol.es
Ford	A-Car	93 247 05 02	www.acarsa.com
Hyundai	Tecno Dinamic	93 320 83 22	www.tecnodinamic.com
Jaguar	V. de la Oliva	93 209 59 09	www.boicar.com
Jeep and Chrysler	Dream Motors	93 243 17 00	www.jeep.es
Mazda	Vilacar 2000	93 244 42 18	www.viacar2000.com
Mercedes Benz	Automoviles Fernandez	93 363 29 70	www.afsa.mercedes-benz.es
Mini and BMW	Cano Catalunya	93 587 71 00	www.bmw.com
Nissan	Cobo	93 296 72 84	www.nissan-global.com
Renault	Tallers Arnalot	93 237 67 11	www.arnalot.com
Rover and MG	British Motors	93 452 74 50	www.rover.co.uk
Seat, Chevrolet and Subaru	Lesseps Motos	93 285 75 75	www.gruplessep.com
Toyota	Mastertrac	93 436 55 55	www.mastertrac.toyota.es
Volkswagen	Mogauto Barcelona	93 498 78 78	www.mautomocion.com
Volvo	Autocat	90 222 72 27	www.volvo.com

Vehicle Finance

New and used car dealers usually offer financing, but interest rates depend on your driving record, your credit history and your employment status. Banks tend to offer a slightly lower rate on financing, but have stricter criteria for eligibility. Again, this depends on personal history. Interest rates can run from anywhere between 10% and 20% APR, depending on the driver and the amount borrowed. The main Barcelona banks such as Caja Madrid, Caja Santander and Barclays are the best people to speak to, see p.64 for details. Shop around before committing to anything.

Vehicle Insurance

You cannot get local insurance on a vehicle if it is not registered in Spain. You will have to get insured through a firm in your home country, which may mean they bump up your premiums. See the following section for details of registering a car.

Insurance is compulsory in Spain and, at a minimum, drivers must purchase third party, fire and theft insurance, known as *seguro de terceros o de*

Vehicle Insurance

Andrew Copeland Group	+44(0)208 656 8435
Balumba	90 250 42 44
Buena Vista Insure	96 648 14 42
Dragon Insurance S.L.	96 649 27 62
Hyperian	95 289 52 16
Knight Insurance Brokers S.A.	95 266 05 35

responsabilidad civil obligatoria. If a vehicle is leased, drivers are often required by the leasing agency to get full coverage.

Registering a Vehicle

Registration of new cars should be handled by your dealer. When registering a second-hand vehicle, you will need to organise a change of registration. This is called *cambio de titularidad*, and must be done within 10 days of the purchase. You will need to go to your local traffic department (www.dgt.es). Look for the counter marked *vehículos*, and be prepared to wait with a stack of papers under your arm.

You will need your NIE (see p.52). If you don't have one, a copy of the lease on your home will do, but an NIE really is worth getting anyway. Take the registration document (*permiso de circulación*) with you. This should have been signed by the seller when you bought your car. You will also need proof of an ITV (Inspección Técnica de Vehículos). This certifies that your vehicle is roadworthy, and should come with the car. If you need to arrange one yourself, ITV garages are dotted about the city. Just put "ITV" in the *actividad* field on www.paginasamarillas.es. Otherwise, try www.rvsa-itv.com for sites outside Barcelona.

You will also need a road tax receipt (*impuesto sobre circulación de vehículos*). Again, this should come with the car. If it has expired, arrange payment at your local town hall. You will also need to show a receipt for payment of transfer tax (this should be paid by the seller, and it's in their interest to provide it, otherwise you can rack up fines in their name).

Finally, complete an application form (you can get this on the day), known as a *notification de transferencia de vehiculos* and handover a stamped, self-addressed envelope which can be used to return your new registration documents.

EU Cars
You can drive an EU-registered car in Spain for up to six months before registering it locally. Go to www.dgt.es and register online or head to your local English-speaking information centre and they will be able to advise you. The DGT (Direcion General de Trafico) in Barcelona is at Gran Via de les Corts Catalanes, 184, or you can call on 93 298 65 39.

Traffic Bodies

Dirrecion General de Trafico (for Catalonia)	93 298 65 39	www.dgt.es
Ministerio de Interior (nationwide)	90 012 35 05	www.mir.es

Traffic Fines & Offences

Double Parking
If you find yourself blocked in by somebody double parking, call the police on 112. Trying to remove the car yourself may be illegal, and with a towing firm it will be expensive.

Traffic fines vary according to the driving offence committed. You can face prison time for the most serious offences, such as causing death by dangerous driving. All motorists should know their Codigo de la Circulacion, the Spanish Highway Code.

If you get pulled over for speeding and receive an 'on the spot' fine (*muitas*), this must be paid within 30 days, in order to receive a 30% discount. If you are not a resident in Spain, then fines really must be paid 'on the spot', otherwise the police can immobilise the vehicle. They may accompany the driver to a cash machine to get the money.

Drink Driving

Drinking and driving is a serious offence in Spain, where a 'zero tolerance' attitude is enforced by law officials. A driver with a blood alcohol level of 0.5 grams per litre (or, a blood alcohol level of 0.3 grams per litre where the driving licence is under two years old), will be considered under the influence.

Police have the power to carry out random alcohol tests on drivers at any time, and will immediately confiscate the licence of a person caught over the legal limit. A sizable fine will also be imposed, and multiple offenders face prison. All of this is decided in court. Insurance is automatically void if an accident is caused by someone under the influence of drugs or alcohol. All the same rules apply to cyclists.

Speed cameras are rare in the centre of the city but can be found out towards the motorways. They are small black cameras, similar to those found in other countries. Tinted windows are allowed in Barcelona, but driving without a seatbelt is illegal. Infants should always be placed in child safety seats, fitted according to their instructions, in the back of the car.

Breakdowns

If you break down, either push the car out of the flow of traffic, or call RACE immediately (www.race.es, 90 240 45 45). This is the only big, national recovery service. In more remote spots and along motorways, you can find SOS phones. They are free and will put you straight through to a recovery service. Mobile phones are obviously far more convenient, so always take one on long trips.

Traffic Accidents

Other options **Car** p.33

Traffic accidents tend to be scratches and scrapes that occur in heavy traffic and narrow streets. More serious crashes do occur, especially on the motorways outside the city. The very centre of the city, around Plaça de Catalunya and down towards the port, is a hot spot for prangs. If you are involved in a traffic accident, it is worth calling the police immediately (112), even if no one is hurt. You'll need police reports for insurance, and if you are relying on the other party to pay then you need proof of the accident to ensure coverage. If someone is injured, 112 can be dialed for an ambulance as well. Always travel with your driving licence, a copy of your insurance papers and your registration. Road rage is not prevalent, but it does occur. If someone gets aggressive, the best thing to do is remove yourself from the situation as soon as you can, and leave them steaming.

Accident reports include the date and place of the accident, vehicle information (make, model and registration numbers), drivers' information (full names, addresses and driving licence details including number, category, date and place of issue), details of insurance companies and policies, witness names and addresses, injuries, vehicle damage, and an explanation of the accident. If you plan to bring charges against other parties, you have to file these charges within two months.

Repairs (Vehicle)

A legitimate mechanic will ask you for a copy of your car's registration to ensure legal ownership of the vehicle. If you have had an accident, no matter how minor, you will need a police report to claim insurance coverage. If you are paying for the repairs yourself, then a police report won't be necessary. Insurance companies will usually offer a list of

Repairs (Vehicle)		
Euromaster	Port Olímpic	93 300 26 50
Garaje Espana	Eixample	93 426 13 56

recommended establishments that they prefer, but they rarely insist that these are used. Manufacturer's dealers are a good choice for repairs but, they are often much more expensive than a local mechanic. The only advantage is speed. If you need a part replaced urgently, for example, the dealer will often have greater supply and access to parts. Air conditioning checks, tyre repair and cleaning (due to all the dust) tend to be common areas that need attention. Euromaster has multiple branches. See http://es.euromaster.com for others.

Not big, but very clever…

Perfectly proportioned to fit in your pocket,
this marvellous mini guidebook makes sure
you don't just get the holiday you paid for
but rather the one that you dreamed of.

Paris Mini Visitors' Guide
Maximising your holiday, minimising your hand luggage

Exploring

Exploring

Barcelona has three defining features: the sea, the city and the hills. The Collserola range echoes the coastline with the metropolis tucked between. This urban playground has nine Unesco World Heritage Sites, more than any other city on earth. Barcelona's buildings come from a trio of defining eras. The Gothic old town was built by bullish merchants as Barcelona flourished as a trading port, the Eixample grid coincided with the emergence of the *modernisme* movement, and the 1992 Olympics brought new facilities and enough reinvigorated confidence to ensure future projects stayed true to Barcelona's adventurous spirit.

City of Counts

Barcelona is known as the Ciudad Condal (Ciutat Comtal) or City of Counts. This is a legacy of the days when an independent Catalonia was ruled by the powerful Counts of Barcelona.

The Olympics came at a time when the city needed reinvigorating. Prior to 1992, the seafront, in particular, was a dilapidated industrial wasteland. Olympic investment brought better beaches, a ring road, new airport terminal, revamped public spaces and world class sporting venues. The games were a huge success, and Barcelona rode the momentum, continuing to renovate the port and open up Raval. In 2004, as the World Forum came to town, the Avinguda Diagonal was extended down to a neglected zone around the mouth of the Besòs River. Next on the agenda is the clumsy Plaça de les Glòries Catalanes, where a new design museum should provide a boost.

Since 1992, tourism has more than tripled and Barcelona is now the third most popular European city to visit, after London and Paris. The visitor mix of conference attendees, stag and hen parties, couples, clubbers, music lovers, foodies and cultural visitors is synonymous with the makeup of the city itself. The repressive Franco years still weigh heavy, and so Catalans are a very tolerant bunch, embracing all forms of freedom of expression. This makes for a cosmopolitan city, where the elderly brush shoulders with the young, Catalans with immigrants, and businessmen with artists.

Barcelona comprises 10 districts, each subdivided into separate barrios (note that compass points describing their location in this section refer to how Barcelona appears on a city map, with the coastline to the south, as opposed to how it geographically lies, with the coast to the east). The barrio concept is very important here. Local people shop at the local market, convene in the local square and residents are proud of the barrio they live in. This spirit is strongest in the suburbs that were former villages: Sants, Sarrià, Horta, Les Corts, Gràcia, Sant Martí, Sant Andreu and Sant Gervasi. Each one is its own little universe. A visitor to Barcelona is more likely to start with the central districts: the Barri Gòtic for its historical sites, Montjuïc for its sports and culture facilities, Eixample for its architecture, Barceloneta for its beaches and the Raval for its nightlife. All find a magic formula of being boldly innovative while nurturing tradition.

*The roof of
La Pedrera (p.166)*

Go Gòtic p.146

Barcelona was first settled by the Romans and the walled boundaries they created stood for many years, hemming the city's very oldest buildings into a tight area. Here you will find not only Catedral and the Santa Maria del Mar church, but also narrow streets and squares, ancient fountains and passageways. Put your map away and see what you discover.

Tram it to Tibidabo p.160

The views from Tibidabo mountain, the highest point within metropolitan Barcelona, are simply breathtaking. Looking to the sea, the city sprawls out in front of you in all its glory. In the opposite direction lie the rolling hills of Catalonia and on a clear day you can see as far as the Pyrenees. Riding the Tramvia Blau up to the top is an experience in itself, as this historic tram has been winding up the hill for over 100 years.

Walk La Rambla p.146

From the ancient Canaletes fountain at the top, passing the human statues, flower stalls and news stands, taking in the Virreina Palace, the Boqueria food market and the Plaça Reial to finally arrive at the Columbus Column and the sea, La Rambla is Barcelona's emblematic pedestrian artery. Note that La Rambla extends beyond Plaça de Catalunya as La Rambla Catalunya, an equally engaging and less-touristy stretch.

Eat Catalan Cuisine p.322

It doesn't quite enjoy the reputation it merits, but Catalan cooking deserves to be explored. Grilled meats, roasted vegetables, pork sausages and salted cod fish are staples, as is the signature pa amb tomàquet, bread soaked in tomato juice. If you happen to be around in spring, go for the calçots, giant spring onions cooked over a wooded fire. The region's Penedès wines, particularly the sparkling white cava, are a treat for any palette.

Watch Barça p.253

The Barça fans may not be the most raucous, but attending a match at the Camp Nou is an unforgettable experience. The football club is a huge part of the city's fabric, a social, political and cultural phenomenon and symbol of Catalan pride. At the very least, non sports fans can visit the club's museum and tour the stadium.

Revel at Festes Majors p.173

Join in the fun of the many outdoor festivals held throughout the summer. The city-wide Nit de Sant Joan in late June is a firework extravaganza. La Mercè in September offers three nights of more pyrotechnics and live music on stages across the centre. Each district throws its own party, with open-air food, drink and parades of papier maché giants. Those of Gràcia and Sants, both in August, are the most renowned.

Hit the Beach p.176

Barcelona's beaches may have been artificially engineered, but at least this means they have good facilities. There are different vibes to each stretch of sand, from sporty, to relaxed, to nudist, so everyone should find something to suit them. For those wanting to escape the crowds, there are more isolated spots just a short train journey out of town.

Go to Market p.309
Barcelona is a city where people still shop at a local market. Every barrio has its own, each with unique character and colour. La Boqueria on La Rambla is as good a place to start as any, while the recently renovated Mercat Santa Caterina is worth a visit, if only for its impressive new roof.

Discover Gaudí p.166
Barcelona is blessed with stunning architecture, much of it either by Antoni Gaudí or inspired by his bold sense of creativity. The Sagrada Familia remains the maestro's signature piece, albeit still a work in progress. His Park Güell is not far behind on the must-see list, as are his two masterpiece houses on Passeig de Gràcia: La Pedrera and Casa Batlló.

Catch the Castellers p.252
Taking in a human castle-building contest is an incredible sight, though slightly alarming as you watch a tiny child climb up to the seventh or eighth layer. Competitions are taken seriously and it is intriguing to compare the different tactics of each team, along with the reactions of the crowds that support them. The world record is an amazing ten layers.

Swing Over the Port p.180
The Port Vell has undergone major changes in the last decade and there is no better way to get a view than via its cable car. The Transbordador Aeri, as it is known, has been making the trip from Barceloneta beach up to Montjuïc, via a stop-off half way, since 1929.

Shop p.305
More relaxed than London and less self-conscious than Paris or Milan, Barcelona is fast gaining a reputation as a shopper's paradise. A 5km stretch known as the 'shopping line' has chic boutiques on Avinguda Diagonal and quirky independent stores off Plaça de Catalunya and into the Born.

Get Funicular p.159
Montjuïc is a mix of parkland and cultural and sporting institutes. The Olympic stadium, the castle, Miró Foundation and the National Museum are here, along with several gardens. Tibidabo has its own, gently climbing hill train too. Either one offers breathtaking views across the city and down the coast.

Have a Menú del Día p.322
The menu of the day is one of the few positive legacies of Franco. He believed that every worker had the right to a substantial lunch with a glass of wine and insisted that all standard bars and restaurants provide one. The custom lives on and most places still offer a three-course set menu, often for under €10. So join local workers for a leisurely midday meal.

Explore a Former Village p.144

The districts of Gràcia, Sarrià, Poble Nou, Sant Andreu and Horta were once towns in their own right, before being swallowed up by Barcelona, around the turn of the twentieth century. They've all kept a villagey feel, offering a real contrast and different pace to the Barcelona of the Eixample and centre.

Catch a Classical Concert p.370

In the Liceu (p.370), the Palau de la Música (p.371) and the Auditori (p.370), Barcelona has some of the best classical music venues in the world, both from an aesthetic and acoustic perspective. The city also boasts a long and celebrated singing tradition, particularly in the fields of choral and opera. Local heroes Montserrat Caballé and José Carreras regularly come to town.

Find Hidden Modernism p.151

While Gaudí's signature pieces merit their fame, there are hundreds of other modernist gems across the city. His Casa Vicens, down a side street in Gràcia, is a real marvel, while Domènech i Muntaner's Hospital de Sant Pau is just up the road from the Sagrada Familia and almost as impressive. Searching out these hidden treasures is a good way to explore different suburbs.

See the Magic Fountains p.159

Witness the spectacular light, water and sound shows of the dancing fountains by Plaça Espanya. They have been performing their routine since the Universal Exhibition of 1929, and continue to enchant today. The Palace of Montjuïc makes for an inspiring backdrop to the show.

Nibble Tapas p.335

A plate of patatas bravas, a dish of olives or a seafood snack with a cold glass of beer is a delightfully civilised way to end a hard day's work. Pintxos, the Basque variety of tapas, are even more ornate and a healthy source of competitiveness among the city's Basque bars.

View an Art Gallery p.165

Very few cities in the world can compete with Barcelona's artistic output. Pablo Picasso and Joan Miró are two of the city's favourite sons and both have galleries dedicated to them. For more of a mix, the MNAC in Montjuïc Palace has a superb collection spanning most major movements, while the likes of the Caixa Forum, MACBA and CCCB are the places to head for contemporary work.

Drink Until Dawn p.364

If you are planning a proper night out, be prepared to go to bed in daylight. Barcelona is a city that gets going late: restaurants tend to be empty before 10pm, bars don't truly fill up until midnight, nightclubs by 2am; even the metro runs all night on Saturdays. The best areas for an all-nighter are the Born, Raval, Gràcia and Poble Nou or for something a bit more hip, the Zona Alta.

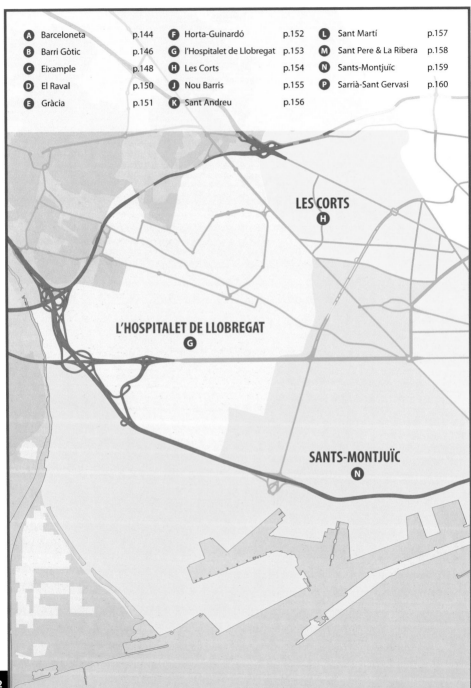

LES CORTS
H

L'HOSPITALET DE LLOBREGAT
G

SANTS-MONTJUÏC
N

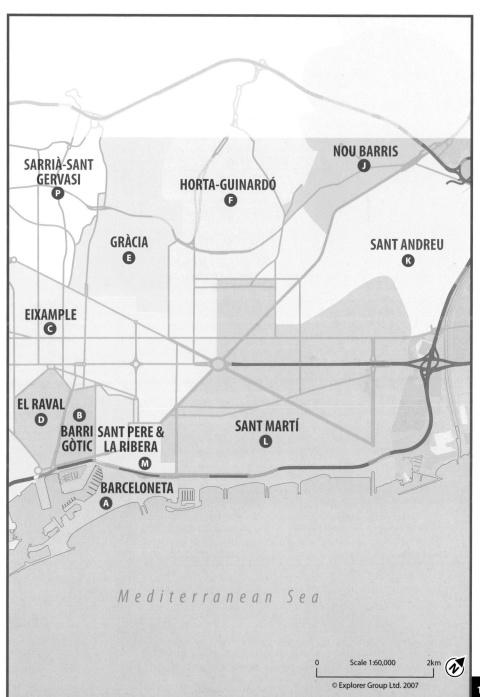

SARRIÀ-SANT GERVASI ⓟ

NOU BARRIS Ⓙ

HORTA-GUINARDÓ Ⓕ

GRÀCIA Ⓔ

SANT ANDREU Ⓚ

EIXAMPLE Ⓒ

EL RAVAL Ⓓ

BARRI GÒTIC Ⓑ

SANT PERE & LA RIBERA Ⓜ

SANT MARTÍ Ⓛ

BARCELONETA Ⓐ

Mediterranean Sea

0   Scale 1:60,000   2km

© Explorer Group Ltd. 2007

Barceloneta

Map p.409
Area **A** p.143

Barceloneta and Port Vell are two of the city's most popular and vibrant areas, but it hasn't always been so. This seafront has undergone dramatic changes over the past fifteen years and it is almost impossible to imagine what the area once looked like. Before the 1992 Olympic Games, this was a filthy, neglected wasteland. Now, it's a model, modern beachfront, with a revamped and fully functioning seaport. Barceloneta marks the beginning of a run of city beaches, and Port Vell is a purpose built commercial zone.

When the Ribera neighbourhood was raised in 1714, to make space for the new citadel, many of those made homeless ended up here, slumming in shacks by the beach. It was a logical place for a new housing project, and a series of cheap blocks, based on military barracks, were thrown up. They quickly filled with fisherman and sailors until massive overcrowding lead to each living space being halved, then quartered, then extended higher. It remains a predominantly working class area with a strong community spirit, and its Festa Major celebrations are among the city's best.

Places of Interest

Port Vell meets the city at the bottom of La Rambla, where the Monument a Colom points out to sea. Built to commemorate Christopher Columbus' discovery of the Americas, you can get a lift to the top to admire the view.

Boat trips out to sea depart from here too, just beside the Rambla de Mar footbridge which leads to the Moll d'Espanya, home to the Imax cinema (p.369), the Aquarium (p.181) and the Maremagnum (p.312). Across the water sits the World Trade Centre, a new conference and office block supposed to resemble a ferry. From the Port Vell or Born, the first building you come across is the Palau de Mar, a converted warehouse made of red brick which now houses the Museu d'Historia de Catalunya (p.172) and marks the beginning of Barceloneta proper.

Barceloneta's main attraction is its neighbourhood. As well as many colourful bars and restaurants there is the Sant Miquel del Port church, the oldest building (1753) in the barrio, and the recently refurbished market.

Gas production has had a long tradition in Barceloneta and provides a great opportunity to compare the old and the new. First up is the Torre Catalana de Gas, a cooling tower dating from 1900, that stands in Barceloneta Park. Almost right beside it, though away from the sea on the Ronda del Litoral, is the new Gas Natural headquarters, a mirrored jumble of blocks and shapes that play tricks of perspective on your eyes.

Back along the waterfront is the more impressive, if less striking, Genome Research Centre, a circular structure, hollowed to the core. This sits next to the Hospital del Mar (p.108), itself awarded several architectural prizes on opening in 1992. Where better to recover than inside a designer building in a room with a sea view.

Continuing along the beachfront, Frank Gehry's popular fish sculpture twinkles in the sunlight and marks the start of Vila Olimpica.

Must Do
Join members of the Club Natació Atlètic Barceloneta (p.258) for their traditional Primer Bany de l'Any, *a New Year's Day swim in the sea at Sant Sebastià beach. Usually 300 or so enthusiasts brave the chill to enjoy the first dip of the year.*

The Good
The restaurants on Passeig Joan de Borbó, and especially some of those tucked away on the backstreets, offer superb seafood and some of the finest dining in the city, all at good prices.

The Bad
The beaches suffer from the usual problems associated with city beachfronts, namely litter, pollution and petty-theft. The beaches along the front at Mar Bella offer a more rewarding all round experience.

The Lowdown
Now the very model of a modern seaside resort, before the Olympic Games came to town this was but a grimy wasteland.

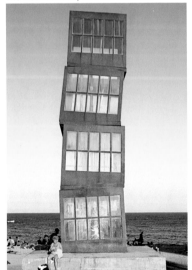

The Wounded Star, Barceloneta Beach

Is getting lost your usual excuse?

Whether you're a map person or not, this pocket-sized marvel will help you get to know the city like the back of your hand – so you won't feel the back of someone else's.

Barcelona Mini Map
Fit the city in your pocket

Map p.403
Area B p.143

Barri Gòtic

El Barri Gòtic is the oldest and most central area of Barcelona. Enclosed between La Rambla on one side and Via Laietana on the other, and stretching from Plaça de Catalunya down to the sea, it incorporates Barcelona's earliest structures and most important administrative sites. It is also the commercial centre and the main tourist focus. In fact, some locals grumble that the neighbourhood caters too much to outsiders and not enough for natives. New proposals to ban shops from selling irrelevant souvenirs (like Andalucian castanets or Mexican sombreros) seem to have placated them. La Rambla has a very touristy feel, but may be the best way to begin exploring. The iconic, kilometre long boulevard links Plaça de Catalunya to the Columbus monument and the sea. Just remember to amble off down side streets as you go, to enjoy the atmospheric alleyways.

Must Do

Barri Gòtic is a treasure trove of historic buildings, pretty courtyards, narrow winding alleyways and traditional shops and bars. The best way to experience it is to wander aimlessly and let yourself get lost.

La Rambla

Starting at the top, near Plaça de Catalunya, is the Rambla de Canaletes, named after the famous old fountain. Drink from it, and you will forever remain part of Barcelona, or so the legend goes.

The Good

La Rambla may be a little too much at times, but it is still great fun and one of Barcelona's most emblematic attractions.

To the right stands the Teatre Poliorama (p.371). It was on the roof of this building that George Orwell spent three months during the Civil War, staking out a Civil Guard position, as described in *Homage to Catalonia*. This section of La Rambla perfectly illustrates one of the modern paradoxes of Barcelona: the stalls selling rare birds have been around for more than a century, but the cramped cage conditions are putting off tourists; yet part of the reason La Rambla attracts visitors is its rougher edges. The next stretch is more pleasant. Rambla dels Estudis was once home to several colleges, and the 17th century Betlem church of an old Jesuit school remains, at the corner of Carrer Carme. Next door is La Boqueria (p.310), Barcelona's much loved food market. It is always worth a wander, to see what produce is in season or stop for a tapa at one of the cafes. On the other side of the road is the modernist shop, Casa Bruno Cuadros, once an umbrella shop but now a bank. Underfoot is a colourful Miró mosaic marking the halfway point of La Rambla.

The Bad

Locals are concerned that the area has become so tourist-focussed that residents will soon begin to avoid it. The balance between catering to visitors and protecting citizens' lifestyles is delicate, but something the city is managing – for now.

The Liceu metro station is found here, although it is currently being refurbished and this is causing some disruption. The Liceu Theatre (p.370) is on the right. Across the street is the Café de l'Ópera, an established and popular meeting place. On the same side begins Carrer Ferrán, which leads up to Plaça Sant Jaume, the heart of the Barri Gòtic. Off Ferrán is Plaça Reial, a beautiful 19th century courtyard with terrace cafes. The next stretch of La Rambla is where painters and caricaturists work and home to Plaça del Teatre, a small square with a modernist monument honouring local playwrite Frederic Soler. With the end of the road now in sight, there are a number of sex shops to the right, before smartening up again with the Centre d'Art Santa Mónica (93 316 28 10, www.centredartsantamonica.net), a contemporary art space that hosts temporary exhibitions and performances. On the left is the Wax Museum (Museu de Cera, 93 317 26 49, www.museocerabcn.com), with its slightly surreal Café Bosc de les Fadas (Fairy Forest Café). There is a craft market at the weekends, while most weekdays see an assortment of street performers (capoeira acrobats, Michael Jackson impersonators, break-dancers), performing in the shadow of the Columbus monument.

The Lowdown

The commercial, administrative and historic heart of the city, the Barri Gòtic perfectly demonstrates Barcelona's sometimes effortless, sometimes bold ability to combine the old with the new.

Gothic Quarter

To investigate the old town, begin at Plaça Sant Jaume, Barcelona's geographical and spiritual heart. On the square itself, the Palau de la Generalitat (p.170) sits facing the Ajuntament (p.169); the Catalan Government and Barcelona Town Hall respectively. The latter of these two dates from 1373. The Town Hall balcony is the best vantage point for the *castellers* contest held in the square during the La Mercè festival, although you need to move in the right circles to get an invite. Next to the Ajuntament sits Sant Just, said to be the oldest church in the city. Carrer Bisbe leads to Catedral (p.168). Enter from this side via the charming cloisters. A cathedral has stood on this site since the fourth century, though the current Gothic version dates from the late 1100s. In December, a Christmas market fills the surrounding streets. On the other side of the cathedral is the delightful Plaça Sant Felip Neri square and church, with Civil War bomb damage visible in its walls.

Barri Gòtic is also one of the city's main commercial zones. The area framed by La Rambla and Carrer Ferran, from Plaça de Catalunya down Avinguda Porta de l'Àngel, is a shopper's paradise. Most of the streets are pedestrianised and all the top high street fashion stores can be found, including Spanish institutions, Zara, Mango and El Corte Inglés. For something a bit more original, head to Carrer d'Avinyó, a parade of alternative, independent designers. It was once synonymous with brothels, and Picasso's seminal *Les Demoiselles d'Avignon* was really a French translation of the Catalan *Les Senyoretes d'Avinyó* and based on a bordello here. The bottom part of the Barri Gòtic is rough and the bars are all colourful hole-in-the-wall affairs with Sin Copa a favoured haunt of Manu Chao, among others. Picasso himself preferred to drink in Els Quatre Gats (p.323) on Carrer Montsió, back in the top part of Barri Gòtic, off Avinguda Porta de l'Àngel. This bar staged his first ever exhibition.

Picasso Museum (p.165)

A Gothic doorway

Plaça Reial

147

Map p.392–p.394
Area **C** p.143

Must Do

Sandwiched between Carrer de Balmes and Passeig de Gràcia is the Rambla de Catalunya, a beautiful tree-lined boulevard with terrace bars, cafes and a central pedestrian area.

The Good

While almost every block in Eixample has its own modernist gem, it is hard to argue with La Sagrada Família's claim as the most iconic building in all the city.

The Bad

Ildefons Cerdà's plan was only half completed, with most of the areas designated as open spaces eventually built upon. The area can become claustrophobic and the traffic in some parts is overbearing.

The Lowdown

The expansion of the city via Ildefons Cerdà's grid system coincided with the emergence of modernisme, making the Eixample a theme park of architectural delights.

Eixample

As Barcelona grew, the cramped conditions within the city walls became unsustainable. So, the Ajuntament held an urban-planning contest to design the Eixample (the expansion), which was won by Antoni Rovira i Trias. However, the central government over-ruled the decision and commissioned a design from military engineer Ildefons Cerdà. The locals hated being dictated to by Madrid and there was bitter opposition to the new scheme.

Nevertheless, Cerdà's plan was practical, in keeping with rational ideas of the time. It was also something of a utopian dream and aimed, through a uniform grid system, to create neighbourhoods entirely equal to each other in terms of amenities and services. To a degree his vision was a success, and the block network functions perfectly well to this day.

Eixample was created in prosperous times however, and the nouveau riche were keen to indulge. If the street plan was to be uniform, then flamboyant decorative touches would be added to ensure buildings stood out. A wave of one-upmanship rushed through the new area, and Eixample developed as a playground of modernist architecture.

La Dreta de L'Eixample

The 'right' of Eixample was the first part of the project to be built. The houses at the Carrers Consell de Cent and Roger de Llúria crossroads lead the way. Today it encompasses almost all the Quadrat d'Or, the so-called golden square mile, which contains 150-plus protected buildings, most of them modernist. It is full of *modernisme* delights like cast iron lampposts and hexagonal paving stones, but its highlight is undoubtedly the Mançana de la Discòrdia. This block offers typically flamboyant works by the era's three main protagonists. There is Antoni Gaudí's Casa Batlló (p.166), Lluís Doménech i Montaner's Casa Lleó Morera, and Josep Puig i Cadafalch's Casa Amatller. Around the corner from the Discòrdia block, is the Fundació Antoni Tàpies (p.163), housed in Doménech i Montaner's building, which is believed to be the first modernist offering in the Eixample.

Continue along Aragó and you get to the Rambla de Catalunya, a pedestrianised boulevard which leads to Plaça de Catalunya. This square became the city's main point of reference, but this was never part of Cerdà's plan. He envisaged Plaça de les Glòries Catalanes as the city's heart, but Plaça de Catalunya, as the spot where the old town met the new, naturally evolved into the city's central hub.

L'Esquerre de L'Eixample

The 'left' of Eixample developed many years after the 'right' had taken off. L'Esquerre became home to many of the practical, less glamorous buildings the Eixample required, such as Hospital Clínic and Modelo prison. Many such buildings have been redeveloped: the slaughterhouse is now Miró Park (93 413 24 00, www.bcn.es/parcsijardins), and the Can Batllo textile factory (93 402 27 15, www.diba.cat/educacio) became an adult education centre. One of the most intriguing redevelopments is that of the Arenas bullring on Plaça Espanya, which is set to become a new commercial and leisure centre.

The Universitat de Barcelona continues to function as the city's main university. Built in 1882, in the neo-romantic style, its courtyard cloisters offer a perfect retreat from the bustle of nearby Plaça de Catalunya. Higher up in the Esquerre, the so-called Gaixample (p.146) is home to most of the city's gay bars and night clubs. Further on still, Diagonal leads to Plaça Fransesc Macià, the city's main business district and gateway to Zona Alta, party central for the trendier crowd.

La Sagrada Familia & Beyond

It is worth reiterating how stunning Gaudí's ongoing masterpiece is and how it shapes life in the area. Tourists boost local commerce while the towers of the temple itself draw attention from all over the district. There are other attractions too: the Hospital de la Santa Creu i Sant Pau (p.170) by Domènech i Montaner is a work of modernist genius and also a Unesco World Heritage Site. Heading back down the hill along Carrer Marina is the Monumental bullring. Although not as popular or traditional as in other parts of Spain, *corridas* are still held here most summer Sundays (p.252). Cross Gran Via de les Corts Catalanes and you enter the neighbourhood of El Fort Pienc, one of Eixample's most evolving areas. It is home to the Estació Nord central bus station as well as the Auditori and Teatre Nacional de Catalunya (p.371). Another interesting development is the emergence of a major Chinese presence in the area. Around Estació Nord there is a dense gathering of Chinese textile shops, restaurants and hairdressers.

Modernist facade

Inside Casa Batlló (p.166)

Gaudí's La Pedrera (p.166)

Casa Batlló (p.166) at night

Map p.402

Area **D** p.143

El Raval

Raval is the area to the right of La Rambla when walking towards the sea. Many of La Rambla's main attractions are here, including the Betlem church, the Palau de la Virreina, the Boqueria, the Liceu theatre and the Centre d'Art Santa Mónica (see p.146). There are visitor attractions located within Raval too, but its main appeal lies in the vibe of the barrio. Raval is one of the most colourful areas in the city, and a melting pot of cultures. North Africans, Filipinos and Pakistanis have stamped their mark on the neighbourhood, with curry houses, Asian food shops and children playing cricket in the streets. More recently, a wave of Andean immigrants has added to the mix. There is still an edge to the area, and the darker, more isolated alleyways, with open prostitution and some seedy characters, are best avoided at night, especially if alone. But, some alternative, anything-goes bars and a buzzing music scene have also emerged. It's too buzzing for some though; Raval is at the heart of a new city-wide struggle by authorities to clamp down on noise pollution.

Places of Interest

The best place to start a tour of the Raval is the Sant Pau del Camp monastery, on Carrer de Sant Pau, the oldest building in the neighbourhood, dating from around 912. The shipyards date from 1378 and make an impressive structure, now housing the Museu Marítim (p.173). The streets retain their narrow and cramped character, the Can Ricart, an old textile factory on Carrer Sant Oleguer, has kept its façade although it is now a fitness centre.

The section where Carrers Nou de la Rambla and Arc del Teatre meet Paral·lel was the area which filled up with cabarets and bordellos. The legacy today is heavy prostitution around La Marsella bar (said to be the oldest bar in Barcelona – see p.348) on Plaça de Salvador Seguí. Nevertheless, the Nou de la Rambla does throw up a diamond in the rough: Antoni Gaudí's Palau Güell (p.166), built in 1890, a six-storey mansion declared a Unesco World Heritage Site in 1984. Further up on Carrer Sant Pau is another modernist classic: the Hotel España by Domènech i Montaner. Carrer Sant Pau leads to the bottom of Rambla del Raval. Markets gather here and many an open-air concert takes place in the summer while bars operate all year round. Fernando Botero's statue of a giant cat adds a touch of artistry. Although the lower Raval has always been the poorer relation, the top part has shared many of it problems. These days it is thriving, or at least the streets surrounding the showpiece MACBA (p.164) and CCCB (p.163) are. These two modern art spaces opened up in the mid 1990s in and around a former convent and orphanage and it's hard to imagine the area without both. Several historical establishments have likewise been reinvented, such as the 15th century Antic Hospital de la Santa Creu, now a library and Catalan studies centre.

The Iglesia de Betlem

Must Do

The bars between Rambla del Raval and Plaça de Salvador Seguí are some of the best in town, but for a truly authentic Raval experience, eat in one of the Ecuadorian-Pakistani or Cuban-Moroccan crossover restaurants by the junction of Carrers Joaquín Costa and Carme.

The Good

The MACBA and CCCB play host to all manner of artistic activity. An exhibition or show can be highly rewarding, but so can simply sitting outside in one of the cafes, watching the world go by.

The Bad

Raval hasn't completely shaken its 'rough' tag but is generally safe these days. The clampdown on noise has seen institutions such as La Paloma and London Bar shutdown or lose their music licence.

The Lowdown

Raval has reinvented itself as a hot-spot for nightlife and creativity, after years of squalor and underworld activity.

Map p.385
Area **E** p.143

Gràcia

Gràcia used to be a town in its own right, separate and distinct to Barcelona until the Eixample expansion of 1897. Removed from the laws and norms of Barcelona, Gràcia had developed a spirit it was determined to protect. Today, Vila de Gràcia lies straight down the middle of Barcelona, beginning just above the Eixample, and stretching through Vallcarca i els Penitents. New Gràcia, known as Camp d'en Grassot i Gràcia Nova, sits alongside the original one and incorporates nineteen blocks of the Eixample grid-work. The mid-part of Gràcia, above the old town, is characterised by steep slopes and comprises two areas dominated by parks. El Coll is home to the Parc de la Creueta del Coll, while La Salut houses the jewel in the district's crown, Gaudí's Park Güell. Vila de Gràcia retains a village feel, with narrow streets and squares and an independent spirit, with a staggering 800 or so bars in the old town. But, Gràcia's reputation for being both dissident and cool has caused conflict. As one of the city's most popular neighbourhoods, property is overpriced while its status as a party hub attracts late-night noise. Despite such problems, Gràcia's liberal tradition means that balance and compromise usually prevail, making the area one of the most attractive and vibrant in the city. This is perhaps best displayed during the Festa Major in August when all of Barcelona descends upon Gràcia to join in the neighbourhood's annual celebrations.

Casa Vicens, Carrer de les Carolines

Must Do
Every August, the whole of Barcelona pours onto Gràcia's streets to join in the Festa Major celebrations. There are castellers contests, competitions for the best decorated streets, and drinking and dancing until dawn.

The Good
Gaudí's Park Güell is not just an amazing fairytale garden, conjured from the maestro's wild imagination, it also offers some of the best views in the city.

The Bad
A victim of its own success, property prices are high, causing grief among locals who fear the area is losing its essence and selling out.

The Lowdown
Effortlessly cool bars and independent shops characterise this former village, which has kept its old narrow streets and pretty squares as well as its independent spirit.

Places of Interest

Tucked away on Carrer de les Carolines is the Casa Vicens, one of Gaudí's very first works and one that is often overlooked. Although private, the building is intriguing enough from the outside to demand a visit. Further down the hill sits the Casa Fuster (93 255 30 00, www.hotelcasafuster.com) by Domènech i Montaner. The Llibertat market is close by, designed by Gaudí's apprentice, Francesc Berenguer. It is now Barcelona's oldest covered market and is worth a visit. At the top of Gran de Gràcia is Plaça Lesseps and its newest addition, the Jaume Fuster library (93 368 45 64, www.bcn.es/biblioteques). Opened in 2005, its innovative design won it Spain's top architecture prize. Up the hill from Plaça Lesseps is Kasa de la Muntanya (www.nodo50.org/kasadelamuntanya), one of the most established of around 200 Okupa sites and certainly one of the most beautiful buildings held by the movement. Okupa is a large, loose collection of squatters with anarchist and leftist political leanings. Just around the corner is Park Güell (p.179), Gaudí's masterpiece of landscape gardening. Besides such attractions, the real reason to visit Gràcia is to wallow in its old village charm: there are few areas of Barcelona quite so pleasant to while away the hours in. You can stroll along streets such as Carrer de Verdi, which is home to Cinema Verdi, one of best places in the city to catch a film in its original language. Alternatively, head to Carrer Torrijos and browse the windows of the quirky, independent designer shops, or stop for refreshment and watch the world go by in one of several leafy squares, each of which has a character all of its own. Perhaps the prettiest is Plaça de la Virreina, with its terrace cafes in front of the Sant Joan church. Plaça Rius i Taulet is almost as enchanting, and features a 33m bell tower, as well as the district town hall. Plaça del Sol is more alternative, and the place to head for a night-time beer.

Map p.387
Area ① p.143

Horta-Guinardó

The Horta-Guinardó district is to the north-east and stretches from Eixample to the Collserola. Characterised by green spaces and hills, as well as close knit communities, it marches to a slightly different beat than the rest of the city. It didn't become part of Barcelona until 1904, and locals remain content to maintain a sense of separation. Neighbouring Carmel is a fairly tough working class barrio populated by many immigrant Andalusians. It leads to La Teixonera and La Clota, neighbourhoods that grew from makeshift housing on the slopes of La Creueta del Coll in the early parts of the 20th century. The whole area lacked infrastructure and had long been deprived and neglected. Although Olympics-induced regeneration was sometimes clumsy and superficial, the area has been lifted. Carmel will soon get its own metro station as Line 5 extends and links with Line 3 at Vall D'Hebron. However residents might be forgiven for asking if it is all worth the trouble: a tunnel collapsed during construction work in January 2005, toppling homes and forcing the evacuation of everyone living on or around Passieg de Calafell.

Must Do

Finding the remains of old Horta is essential when it comes to grasping an understanding of this once extremely separatist area.

The Good

As one of the three main Olympic areas, the district boasts some first class sporting facilities, not least the Vall d'Hebron Tennis Centre and city Velodrome.

The Bad

Many areas behind Carmel hill feel slightly left behind: out of sight, out of mind as far as the central authorities are concerned. Improvements to infrastructure are finally being made, but slowly and carelessly.

The Lowdown

The area spreads out from the edge of the Eixample, through the working class, hillside barrio of Carmel and on to Horta, the former village from which the whole district takes its lead.

Places of Interest

Horta grew around the church of Sant Joan, which was originally near the Can Cortada farmhouse at the top of Carrer Campoamor. Today's version was rebuilt in the 80s and can be found close by on Carrer de la Rectoria.

Horta was a farming community for many years and has developed as a popular spot for Barcelona's wealthier citizens to build summer retreats. Set in a valley between several hills, water was abundant in the 19th century, and Horta carved itself a niche as the city's primary washing outlet. By the early 20th century almost all of Barcelona's laundry was done there. Take a trip to Carrer Aiguafreda (the word itself means cold water) and witness the remains of all the open-air wells, where washerwomen scrubbed and bleached the city's linen.

Today the commercial hub of Horta is where Passeig de Maragall meets Carrer del Tajo, and the metro emerges at Plaça d'Eivissa, a leafy square with bars and cafes spilling onto the patio.

The Guinardó area is where the district meets the rest of the city and is dominated by two parks, Guinardó itself and les Aigues (93 413 24 00, www.bcn.es/parcsijardins). The first offers magnificent views from the top of a hill; the second features the neo-Arabic Casa de les Altures, dating from 1890, and acts as the district headquarters.

Above Guinardó Park, at the top of the Turó de la Rovira hill, are the ruins of a Civil War lookout from where three cannons would try to ward off German and Italian bombers. The views are magnificent and the remains intact enough to give a sense of what it must have been like when under attack. Further up, towards Collserola (perhaps the district's most natural and popular leisure space), the Vall d'Hebron Tennis Centre (p.245) periodically attracts international tournaments and the Pavello (93 428 39 52) hosts volleyball events and concerts. In fact, sports facilities flourish in this area. Further along the Ronda de Dalt is the Velodrome (p.253), which sits behind the delightful Labyrinth park (p.179). Near the back of the park, the Palau de les Heures (93 567 74 00, www.heures.fbg.ub.es), a palace dating from 1895, now forms part of the university. The city's main hospital buildings are also found here. Back the other way, as far as architecture is concerned, there is the Patronat Ribras building on Ronda de Dalt, built as an orphanage in the 1920's and now the L'IES Vall d'Hebron training college. The Pavelló de la Republica on Avingunda Cardenal Vidal i Barraquer in Montbau stands opposite the giant 'matches' sculpture, a reconstruction of Spain's pavilion at the 1937 Paris World Exhibition (where Picasso's Guernice painting was first shown) and hold a library.

152

Map p.390
Area **G** p.142

L'Hospitalet de Llobregat

Strictly speaking, L'Hospitalet de Llobregat is not a district of Barcelona, but a city in its own right. However, it is joined to Barcelona's west flank and there are several L'Hospitalet stops on the metro network. It is divided into six districts of which Centre, the administrative and commercial heart, is the oldest and most important. It incorporates the barrios of Sant Josep and Sanfeliu along with one known as Centre itself.

Most neighbourhoods are tucked in between the site of the original Hospitalet in Centre and metropolitan Barcelona. They include Les Planes, La Florida, Collblanc and Torrasa. Further west are the areas of Can Serra and Pubilla Cases, while to the south of Centre lies Bellvitge and Gornal. The city's south used to stretch to the sea but L'Hospitalet traded in its coastal areas to Barcelona, which has used the space to create the docks and free port. Several railway lines leave Barcelona and cut through L'Hospitalet, dividing its districts from one another. There are plans to resolve this by covering the tracks with parks. Developments like the tower blocks of Bellvitge were typical of rushed housing thrown up in the middle of the last century with little regard to infrastructure. The citizens of L'Hospitalet campaigned long and hard until service improvements began in the 80s. Today it is a modern and attractive city with impressive parks and cultural centres, sports facilities, schools and hospitals. Its people, meanwhile, keep a reputation for communal campaigning.

Must Do
Take a trip to the Santa Eulàlia de Mérida church and observe the sculpture bestowing honour on the young soldiers who fought in the civil war.

The Good
Few cities can boast such otherworldly charm near a commercial centre as L'Hospitalet, courtesy of Carrer Xipreret and its surrounding buildings.

The Bad
While the idea of placing a flash new hotel complex in Bellvitge may have been well intended, there is something slightly distasteful about the way the opulence of the Hotel Hesperia tower rubs against its surroundings.

The Lowdown
Not just a tag on to Barcelona, but a city in its own right. After many years fighting its cause, L'Hospitalet is now a modern, fully-functional urban space with a bright future.

Places of Interest

The Plaça Ajuntament is the heart of L'Hospitalet, a square which holds the town hall, dating from 1895, and the Santa Eulàlia de Mérida church and clock tower, from 1492. Beside the town hall is the Porto Rico cafe, a building dating from 1912, with walls lined with photos of L'Hospitalet through the ages. Next to the church is a sculpture honouring the Lleva del Biberó, a squadron of boys aged just seventeen who fought for the Republican cause in the Civil War.

Behind the church, off Carrer Barcelona, is L'Hospitalet's best visitor sight, a group of historical buildings clustered around Carrer Xipreret. The street itself is narrow and cobbled, lined by houses dating from the 16th century. Their elderly occupants sit outside their front doors on summer afternoons, giving the impression of having been transferred to a country pueblo. At the bottom of the Xipreret is L'Harmonia, a stately home from 1595, part of the original Torre Blanca estate. Here also stands La Talaia, a lookout tower built in 1587 on the outskirts of the city but moved to its current location in 1972. Other significant buildings include the Casa Espanya, another stately home, now the Museu de L'Hospitalet (93 338 13 96), and the Can Sumarro (93 337 20 82, www.l-h.es/biblioteque), an old farmhouse which has been converted into a library.

Continuing on from the top of Xipreret, on the other side of the train tracks, is the Can Buxeres park, which features the Casa Alta, an old farmhouse that was later converted into a modernist palace. Back through Centre, the Rambla de Just Oliveras is a pretty, tree-lined boulevard which runs down as far as Bellvitge. Half-way along, at the junction with Carrer Major, is the old casino (1873) and two old farmhouses awaiting renovation. Outside of Centre is the stately home of Pubilla Cases, on Carretera Collblanc. Within Collblanc itself is the Gratacels 'skyscraper'. This narrow, high-rise column of flats was built in 1927, as the first attempt to solve the housing shortage, and was the only premises in L'Hospitalet to feature a lift. Somewhat away from the architectural appeal of the area is the draw of fine restaurants. Waves of Galician and Andalucian immigrants have brought with them some of the best tapas restaurants in the Barcelona area. Make a bee-line for Plaça Eivissa in Pubilla Cases and indulge.

153

Map p.383
Area ❶ p.142

Les Corts

The Les Corts district is synonymous with FCBarcelona. The football club has been based in the district for over 80 years and the locals are fanatical Barça fans, for most this is more than just a club, it's a symbol of strength and pride. Other major institutions include the University of Barcelona campus and the Catalonia Polytechnic. One of Barcelona's most appealing qualities is the way it effortlessly mixes old with new and Les Corts is a case in point. Avinguda Diagonal, which reaches the end of the line here, is home to some of the city's most modern shopping malls and the headquarters of La Caixa bank, while just a few blocks away are historical monuments such as the Pedralbes monastery and the Palau Reial.

Must Do
A trip to Les Corts cannot pass without seeing the Nou Camp. After this however, wind down with some live jazz at the Can Deu

Places of Interest

Les Corts was one of the towns previously separate to Barcelona. The last remains of the old town are to be found in and around the Plaças Can Rosés, Comas and de la Concordia. The latter features a 40m bell tower and the Can Deu (93 410 10 07), which has seen life as a farmhouse and town hall. These days it is a civic centre that hosts exhibitions and workshops and has a popular bar with live jazz. Around the corner on Carrer Remei is a church, one of the very oldest buildings in Les Corts, dating from 1849, it boasts a distinguishing clock tower. On the other side of Travassera Les Corts, is the Colonia Castells, a workers village dating to the 20s. Back on Diagonal, lies El Corte Inglés, Spain's largest chain of department stores, and the huge L'Illa mall (p.312). These mark the start of what is known as the Barcelona shopping line, which runs all the way to the sea.

The Good
A refreshing mix of old town values, modern commerce, historic homes and, in the shape of Barça, a splash of international glamour.

The Bad
While transport links to the area are great, on match days the metro becomes packed and all roads grind to a standstill.

FC Barcelona (p.250) dominates the neighbourhood. The facilities include an indoor arena, ice skating rink and a mini version of the main stadium. The club has big plans to become more focused on the local community. Besides hosting football matches, the Nou Camp stadium houses one of the most visited museums in Catalonia, the Barça club museum (p.172). A trip to 'Camp Nou', as it's known locally, is essential for understanding what Barça means to the city, and how the club has almost become a representative side for Catalonia. A match is ideal, the museum a good second best, but also look out for training sessions held on the pitch outside the ground.

The Lowdown
A mixed district that spreads from the urban barrio of Les Corts to the expansive Pedralbes and its swanky upmarket mansions. The area is also home to Barça and indelibly linked with the football club and cultural phenomenon.

Across the road is the Les Corts Cemetery and behind that the Bederrida park, parts of which are said to date from 945. Today, it is the centre piece of the south campus of the university, which stretches as far as the Royal Polo Club. From here, Carrer del Pintor Ribalta winds down to the Sant Ramon Nonat church, designed by Enric Sagnier i Villavecchia, in 1935.

The neighbourhood of Pedralbes is one of the swankiest in the city and there are some huge properties on Avingudas Pearson, Pedralbes and d'Esplugues. All three roads lead to the Pedralbes monastery (p.168). Built in 1327, at the behest of Queen Elisenda de Montcada to house an order of Poor Clare Nuns, the building is the jewel in Barcelona's Gothic crown. Carrer de Joan d'Alòs leads from the monastery to La Mercè, a curious gathering of modest houses which was one of Barcelona's first ever housing estates. Back then, it was situated in the middle of nowhere but with the city's expansion, the fantastic views and the neighbourhood's status these houses became much sought after, and even protected. On the other side of Ronda de Dalt lies the Parc de Cervantes (93 413 24 00, www.bcn.es/parcijardins) home to an extensive rose garden, and one of several impressive parks in the Pedralbes barrio. Another is to be found at the Finca Güell, a former estate of Gaudí's patron. The cast iron dragon at the gate and the fountains inside are both the works of the maestro himself. The Palau Reial on Diagonal was also designed for Eusebi Güell but was later used as a royal palace, which now houses the ceramic and decorative arts museums (p.171).

Map p.389
Area **J** p.143

Nou Barris

Nou means nine in Catalan, although there are actually 13 barrios that comprise Nou Barris. In the recent reorganisation, several communities demanded recognition and former neighbourhoods were split up. But *nou* still works, as its other meaning is 'new' and this part of town, in Barcelona's extreme north-east, is the youngest. Most estates were built between the 50s and 70s and the apartment blocks were a marginal improvement on the homemade hillside shacks they replaced. On one infamous occasion, a cemetery was to be built on the hillside, but it was decided that the location was too humid – so they built the Ciutat Meridiana housing estate instead. Those who ended up there could only marvel that they lived in an area deemed not worthy of the dead.

Local residents have had to fight for improvements, often taking the initiative themselves. Public transport wasn't simply inadequate, it was non-existent. The municipal authorities claimed the streets were too steep to get a bus up, and so local residents took to hijacking buses and driving home to prove them wrong.

These days, the Ajuntament is more responsive and the whole area is improved, with redeveloped urban spaces, better transport and infrastructure. There are also plenty of parks and squares, not to mention the Collserola hillside itself. It is a district where life is lived to the full.

Must Do
Given its immigrant background, the annual World Food Fair on the last Sunday of February is an ideal way to sample the district's variety. Everyone prepares a dish from the motherland and assembles at the Ángel Pestaña square.

The Good
The views from the park on top of the Turó de la Peira hill are great. Those from the Torre Baró 'castle' are particularly good. It is said you can see to Mallorca on a clear day.

The Bad
Although blessed with urban parks and green hillside behind, some areas of Nou Barris are just a swathe of characterless tower blocks, all thrown up in the last 50 years.

The Lowdown
A gathering of 13 different barrios, mostly linked to slapdash housing projects built from the 50s onwards to provide homes for the growing immigrant population. Community spirit is strong following decades of shared struggle.

Places of Interest

The oldest section of the district is Vilapicina, and a sense of the past can be gained by heading to Passeig de Fabra i Puig. Between the market and La Esquinica tapas bar (one of the best in the entire city) is a patio where the Can Basté (93 420 66 51, www.noubarris.net/cccanbaste) presides over a gathering of historic buildings. Once a farmhouse, it is now a civic centre, hosting regular photography exhibitions.

The Turó de la Peira hill, at the top of Passeig de Fabra i Puig, has a peaceful park and provides fantastic views. The path to the side ends up at the Can Peguera housing estate. Back in 1929, immigrant workers were forced to abandon their huts and were moved to four hastily built housing projects which came to be known as the Cases Barates neighbourhoods. It means cheap houses in Catalan. The other three (Eduardo Aunós in San Martí, Baró de Viver in Sant Andreu and Bon Pastor in Nou Barris) have been replaced by modern facilities, making those at Can Peguera the last of their kind. Row upon row of uniform, white-washed bungalows gives the impression of a seaside holiday complex, but they do exude a certain charm. They run as far as the Parc Central de Nou Barris, an urban plot that shows Barcelona town planning at its best. With ponds and fountains, grass areas and children's playgrounds, it is a hive of activity once school is out.

The park also combines the old with the new. The Fòrum Nord technology centre jets out over a water feature, and the huge former psychiatric facility beside it dates from 1889. It is a marvellous stone building of several wings, transformed into the district headquarters and library (93 291 48 50, www.diba.es).

La Trinitat Nova is the main commercial thoroughfare. It has become a transport hub since the metro arrived in 2000, but is most intriguing for a community project on Carrer de Portlligat. In another example of locals taking matters into their own hands, in 1977, hundreds of residents dismantled an abandoned asphalt factory, an eye-sore which was quite probably toxic too. In its place they built a cultural centre which thrives today as the Ateneu Popular (93 353 95 16, www.noubarris.net). It runs theatre, dance and circus workshops (there is a big-top tent out back) and regularly puts on shows and performances for the public. The emphasis is very much on community participation and the centre has made huge strides in reducing delinquency in the area.

155

Map p.397
Area **K** p.143

Sant Andreu

The district of Sant Andreu is located to the north-east of the city and is another with independent roots, where the locals feel themselves to be separate from the Barcelonins. The neighbourhoods of La Sagrera and Sant Andreu were villages incorporated into Barcelona in 1897, via the Eixample expansion. By then, both communities had become heavily industrialised after years dedicated to agriculture. La Sagrera and Sant Andreu are connected by the shop-lined Carrer Gran de Sant Andreu, an old Roman road, although the Avinguda Meridian thoroughfare now dominates this part of the city. The barrios of El Bon Pastor and Baró de Viver are cut off from the others because of the tracks but this is all about to change: La Sagrera will be one of two Barcelona stop-offs for the high-speed AVE train to Madrid; the new track will be covered over and a park built on top. The whole area around the station is going to be redeveloped, bringing new housing and service centres. Frank Gehry is in charge of the plan and blueprints show five striking tower blocks of different heights, each one covered in metal and glass. The AVE Route will also pass through the neighbourhoods of Bon Pastor, Baró de Viver and El Congres i los Indians (named after the Catalans who returned to Spain after the Spanish colonies were lost).

Places of Interest

The best places to visit are the former villages. In La Sagrera, this means the market square of Plaça de Masadas, a delightful arched courtyard with cafes in its alcoves. The nearby Plaça de la Assemblea Catalana is a fairly standard residential square most interesting for its name, which honours the aborted attempt at holding the first ever meeting of the Catalan assembly, in 1971. Nearby is Parc Pegaso (93 413 24 00, www.bcn.es/parcsijardins), a pretty spot with a bridge over a small lake, built where a truck factory once stood. Many more of the district's old factories have made way for new developments: The old La Maquinista in El Bon Pastor abandoned its machinery making days to become an open-air shopping centre (www.lamaquinista.com). The Can Fabra (93 360 05 65, www.bcn.cat/canfabra) building still stands in Sant Andreu, but the former thread manufacturing plant has been converted into a cultural centre with exhibition spaces, a library and a popular bar. Its sister complex, the fast Fabra i Coats next door, awaits a similar reinvention after a popular campaign prevented its destruction. Incidentally, the Coats part of the name relates back to a partnership with Scottish firm J&P Coats Ltd, begun in 1903, then marking the first ever foreign investment in Catalan industry.

Sant Andreu's old centre is based around the Plaça de Orfila, home to the Ajuntament, the metro station and Sant Andreu de Palomar church which, with its huge domed roof, is quite imposing. The streets behind the Ajuntament are all of a different era, narrow, winding and home to traditional shops. Plaça de Comerç (known as Plaça del Rellotge to locals due to the giant clock outside the watchmakers shop) is home to the Can Vidal modernist building which houses the Bar Versalles (93 345 10 21, www.versalles.info). Recently renovated, it has been a Sant Andreu institution since 1928. Its basement served as a bomb shelter during the Civil War and a gambling den both before and after. Around the back is the Mercat Sant Andreu, similar to that of La Sagrera but with a covered market in the middle, and this is where to go to see the neighbourhood in full swing. A few blocks up, Carrer Basconia has managed to preserve a row of traditional two-storey houses, while the Casa Bloc, a model workers villiage back in 1932 when Catalan President Francesc Macià laid the first stone, offers a spin on the theme of the modern apartment block. A more typical redevelopment is the residential block built on the site of the Can Galta Cremat, all that remains of the former factory is a token chimney on the patio.

Must Do
In an area so rich in political history, where better than the Bar Versalles to discuss politics over a beer. In doing so you would be following a long established tradition; the bar was a meeting point for anti-Franco rebels throughout the dictatorship.

The Good
The market squares of La Sagrera and Sant Andreu are as fine as any found in the city. The bars beneath the arches of La Sagrera's make an ideal spot to retire to for an after-lunch coffee.

The Bad
The AVE will bring a high-speed rail link from Barcelona to Madrid, but there are many who argue the route should be heading around the city's outskirts and not through it, disrupting everything in its path.

The Lowdown
Both La Sagrera and Sant Andreu are former villages and are proud to keep their distance from central Barcelona. Sant Andreu in particular is a vibrant town all on its own.

156

Map p.412
Area **L** p.143

Sant Martí

The district of Sant Martí lies to the city's south-east. On the seafront closest to the city centre is Vila Olímpica, boasting state of the art tourist facilities. Further down the coast at the city limits is El Besòs i el Maresme, one of Barcelona's most deprived barrios. In between is Poblenou, the once booming industrial heartland now looking to reinvent itself.

Factories monopolised Poblenou from the 18th century, dedicated to all sectors of industry. By the end of the 19th century the zone had acquired the nickname of the 'Catalan Manchester,' in honour of northern England's then industrial powerhouse. By the 60s, times had changed. Industrial decline brought closures and buildings became derelict. This attracted artists and several abandoned premises were converted into basic studio spaces: by the late 80s, a creative community had formed. This helped inspire a new urban regeneration project, the 22@ plan. The aim is to create new business and office spaces and establish centres of technological innovation.

Must Do
Poblenou old town is an unexpected treasure. The Rambla del Poblenou is a real haven of tree-lined tranquillity while the Plaça de Prim belongs to another era.

The Good
Torre Agbar is striking in appearance and bold in design, just what Barcelona is all about. At night it brightens the city skyline as it lights up in blues and reds.

The Bad
There is something slightly vulgar about the riches on display at the Diagonal Mar development, less than a five-minute walk from the marginalised La Mina housing project.

The Lowdown
The future and the past of Barcelona: Poblenou was the city's industrial engine and is the site of a new technology-based regeneration project. Vila Olímpica shows just how an area can reinvent itself.

Places of Interest

Plaça de Prim, though now surrounded by construction chaos, has an almost surreal sense of belonging to another time and place. Single-story white houses huddle around a small patio. It is also home to a first-class fish restaurant, Els Pescadors (p.335).

The Can Ricart is a factory saved from destruction by popular protest. Covering several blocks between Carrer del Perú and Carrer del Marroc, it is now protected as a heritage site although it is unclear exactly how it will be redeveloped. Many other industrial hangars have been turned into bars and clubs, and one of the main reasons to visit Poblenou is for a night out. Live music venue and nightclub Razzmatazz (p.366), restaurant, bar and disco Oven and the enormous L'Oveja Negra all pull in the punters.

For a more modern flavour, there is Torre Agbar (93 342 21 29, www.torreagbar.com). French architect, Jean Nouvel's phallic tower standing 142m high. Similar in appearance to London's gherkin, the design of the Torre Agbar was actually conceived first. There are plans to open it up to visitors but nothing has yet been finalised. Also reaching for the skies is the Piramidón (93 278 07 68, www.piramidon.com), a contemporary art space for the La Verneda i La Pau area. You can watch the artists at work then visit their showroom. This is a rare break from the norm in the eastern blocks, which offer little to entice the visitor, though the Rambla de Prim is a pleasant boulevard and gives a sense of the redevelopment taking place. The tram has recently extended through Besòs, improving the roads and parking.

Cross the Ronda de Sant Ramon de Penyafort and you enter La Mina. The area is distinctly different and has a rough, and partially undeserved, reputation. If you are lucky enough to bag an invite, the best flamenco in the city can be heard here, courtesy of La Mina's strong gypsy (gitano) community. There is also a mosaic of a gitano guitar player on the bottom of the last block of old La Mina. Granted, it is no Gaudí, but it does provide a much-needed splash of colour to the drab blocks – though there is no shortage of colourful characters.

Five minutes walk from La Mina is the new Diagonal Mar development of luxury hotels, air-conditioned shopping malls, offices and apartment blocks. A little down the coast is Vila Olímpica, marked out by its twin towers. One is the swish Hotel Arts (p.27), the other the Mapfre Tower, with shops on the ground floor, offices up above. At 153.5m each, they are the highest buildings in Spain and they formed the basis of the Athlete's Village during the Games.

Sant Pere & La Ribera

Map p.403
Area **M** p.143

Must Do

Away from the more fashionable Born, some of the squares and patios further up, such as Plaça Sant Pere and the Carrer d'Allada-Vermell, are perfect spots for relaxing.

The Good

The best in Barcelona's creative energy finds its way to El Born, be it in the bars or the boutiques. Given that the Picasso museum is also here, such originality and artistry seems highly appropriate.

The Bad

El Born is another barrio in which there is a good deal of friction between local residents and those who come to party or do business. Complaints about noise levels are a nightly occurrence, while house prices have gone through the roof.

The Lowdown

Separated from the Barri Gòtic by the Via Laietana, it is similar to its neighbour, combining some of the city's oldest buildings with some of the freshest shops and bars. This is particularly true in El Born, currently the trendiest part of town.

Snappily known as Sant Pere, Santa Caterina i la Ribera, this area brings together several different barrios, the most well known being Born. Barcelona has always been adept at reinventing itself, and El Born epitomises why. It is home to some of the city's most ancient buildings, housing institutions such as the Picasso Museum, but its shops and bars set the very latest trends. Recent initiatives have focused on spreading some of El Born's magic to its poorer cousins, Sant Pere and Santa Caterina, although some locals question if that's what they want: house prices in El Born have rocketed over the last decade.

Places of Interest

This neighbourhood takes its name from the church located on Plaça Sant Pere, a pretty little shaded square with a beautiful art deco fountain. The Carrer Sant Pere Més Alt leads from the church to Domènech i Montaner's stunning Palau de la Música Catalana (p.170). It is considered by some to be *modernisme's piece de resistance*. It is a wonder to behold from outside and inside.

The Santa Caterina market (p.310) recently re-opened after a huge renovation project, begun back in 1998. Once work began, significant Roman and medieval remains were discovered in the foundations (some of the artefacts are now on display below a glass floor in one corner of the market). But they got there in the end and the finished product is a real breath of fresh air for the neighbourhood.

Thanks to the maritime trade of the 13th century, when locally made products were distributed all over the Mediterranean, El Born was once the wealthy centre of high society. The palaces that line Carrer Montcada, built by rich merchants at the peak of their powers, bare testimony to the brio of the era. Several of these magnificent buildings now house some of the city's best museums: Museu Picasso (p.165), The Textiles Museum (p.173) and the Museu Barbier-Mueller (p.172). Almost every street name refers to the trade once practised there: Carrer Sombreres (hat-makers), Carrers Argenteria (silverware), Corders (rope makers), Assaonadors (tanners), Vidrieria (glass). For a taste of something traditional, try Casa Gispert (93 319 75 35, www.casagispert.com), a tea and spices store with an ancient roasting oven, located next to the Santa Maria del Mar church on Sombreres.

A beautiful masterpiece of Catalan Gothic, the Santa Maria del Mar (p.168) is the focal point of El Born, and has been for centuries. It is also the centrepiece of the historic novel, *La Catedral del Mar* by Ildefonso Falcones. At the church front a pretty square, known as the Fossar de les Moreres, pays homage to the spot where the last defenders of the city were executed at the end of the War of the Spanish Succession, in 1714.

At the end of Passeig del Born is the Antic Mercat del Born. It closed in the 70s after one hundred years as Barcelona's main food market, but when work began to convert the cast iron shell into a library, all manner of medieval remains where unearthed. The plan is to keep the market's framework but convert the site into an archaeological attraction, a project set for completion by then end of 2007.

Estació de França (p.35)

Map p.391–p.399
Area N p.142

Sants-Montjuïc

This district is the city's biggest in terms of land mass, though much is taken up by Montjuïc mountain and the container port. The main residential barrios can be split into two areas, with the Gran Via de les Corts Catalanes dividing them. Sants was one of the independent towns which became annexed to Barcelona with the Eixample project. These days, it is best known for its transport links: almost all trains pass through Sants Estació and its bus terminal is one of the most important in the city. Montjuïc was not part of the original Cerdà plan for Eixample (see p.148). So, those who owned the land pleased themselves, and built simple workers houses as they saw fit. Thus, Poble Sec became the first of Barcelona's new suburbs. Above the new residences, makeshift shacks began to appear, hanging off the inclines until the 70s. These days, Poble Sec is a colourful and vibrant area, testimony to the influence of its newest immigrants: a wave of Latin Americans have populated it, opening bars and restaurants to provide a taste of home.

Must Do
The Civil War bunker in Poble Sec can be followed by a trip to the Castle at Montjuïc to reflect on who the people were hiding from. Tucked away behind the castle is the Caseta del Migdia bar, with a stunning sea view.

Montjuïc

There are several ways to reach the top, including the cable car (p.180) and funicular, but most people approach via the Plaça Espanya gateway. One building to look out for is the striking Pavelló de Barcelona (93 423 40 16, www.miesbcn.com) by Mies van der Rohe. Demolished after the trade show in 1929, it was lovingly rebuilt in the 80s. At night, the parade's fountains – also relics of 1929 – come to life with the Font Màgica show, a spectacular light, water and music extravaganza (http://fonts.bcn.es). Nearby is Poble Espanyol (p.180), a model village from 1929, designed to showcase Spanish handicrafts and building styles. The Olympic ring (p.250) is also a must see, housing the Olimpic Stadium, the Palau Sant Jordi arena and Picornell Swimming Pools, along with the Catalan Sports Institute and the curious communications tower, Torre Calatrava.

The Good
Montjuïc offers all manner of attractions, from the sporting (Olympic stadium and arena) to the cultural (Miró foundation, the MNAC and Caixa Forum), not to mention great views and parkland, including the botanical gardens.

Poble Sec

Poble Sec was once a poor, working class barrio, its name means dry village and running water didn't arrive until 1894. The first fountain still exists on the corner of Carrers de Margarit and d'Elkano.
Perhaps the most fascinating testimony to the past can be found below the Nou de la Rambla. The Civil War anti-air raid shelter (p.171) here was built by the people of Poble Sec themselves and can be visited at selected times.
In the years preceding the war, Avinguda Paral·lel was the heart of Barcelona nightlife and so Poble Sec developed a similar bohemian ambiance to Raval. Theatres, nightclubs and music halls abounded, of which two of the most emblematic, Teatre Arnau and El Molino, closed at the end of the 80s. Theatre life has not completely deserted the area though, on Carrer Lleida towards La Fira, is the Ciutat del Teatre, a complex of theatres and drama schools.

The Bad
Some of the hillside of Montjuïc and slopes down to Poble Sec are dark and isolated and provide opportunities for thieves. Crime is not rife, but caution is advised when off the main drags late in the day.

Sants

There are few attractions to pull visitors to Sants, but the appeal lies in the stories of its past. The Vapor Vell, or old steam factory, off Plaça de Sants, was a major textiles house built in 1842. In 1897, it was the scene of *Baralla en un Café* (brawl in a cafe), believed to be the first ever film shot in Spain. These days it is a library (93 409 72 31, www.bcn.cat) and primary school. The Casa del Mig, once home to the factory owners, and the Casa Cuna, a nursery for the workers' children, still stand.
The Sant Medir Church is next door to the Can Battló textile factory. As well as fulfilling its religious obligations, it is an all-round community centre and was a major hub of clandestine politics in the city from the Civil War through to the last years of Franco.

The Lowdown
A huge district that covers the heights of Montjuïc, the vibrant barrio of Poble Sec and the no nonsense, working class Sants.

159

Map p.384-p.385
Area ℗ p.143

Sarrià-Sant Gervasi

This is one of Barcelona's wealthiest areas, characterised by green spaces, prestigious schools and Sarrià old town. Sarrià and Horta were the only two towns beyond the city limits which managed to avoid annexation to Barcelona as part of the Cerdà plan. They retain a village charm, and locals will still say they are 'going to Barcelona' rather than 'popping into town'. The old town of Sarrià is wedged between Via Augusta and Avinguda de JV Foix, both of which follow the course of a former river (Sarrià is believed to mean 'two rivers'). Sant Gervasi shares much of its history with Sarrià, having grown steadily as an area of summer residences for the moneyed classes. The irony is that these days, local residents spend the working week in their Sant Gervasi city pads and then head out of town to their second homes at the weekend; on Saturdays and Sundays, the streets are quite deserted. The neighbourhoods of Putget i Farró, Vallvidrera and el Tibidabo i les Planes, meanwhile, are mountainous and sparsely inhabited.

Sarrià

The Sant Vicenç church on Plaça de Sarrià is the neighbourhood's oldest building, dating from the 10th century. Inside are some fairly uninspiring murals by Josep Obiols; more interesting is the painting and statue dedicated to Pere Tarrés. Behind the church, and just off Carrer Major de Sarrià, is the Plaça del Consell de la Vila, home to the Sarrià Town Hall and plentiful barrio life. Around the corner, Carrer de Canet has a row of traditional two-storey houses. On the corner with Carrer Major is a larger building, once the home of a textile factory owner. The smaller houses were part of a village constructed by the owner for his workers to live in. The Foix de Sarrià bakery (93 203 07 14, www.foixdesarria.com) on Carrer Major offers a slice or two of history itself. First and foremost, the cakes and pastries are delicious, but the shop is also renowned as the home of JV Foix, one of finest ever poets in the Catalan language. His father opened the bakery in 1886, but the wordsmith eventually took over the family business and it became something of a gathering point for intellectuals. On the other side of Via Augusta is the neighbourhood of Les Tres Torres, so-called because three large houses with turrets were the first buildings built in the region. Only one survives, on Carrer del Doctor Roux.

Sant Gervasi

From Via Augusta to Diagonal you are never far from designer stores and chic boutiques. Something a bit more traditional can be found at the Galvany market, a magnificent modernist structure of brick and cast-iron, dating from 1868. But to truly escape the materialism, head for the hills. The higher section of the neighbourhood includes Tibidabo, with the theme park (p.180), Fabra Observatory (93 847 95 12, www.observatorifabra.com) and Torre Collserolla (93 406 93 54, www.torredecollserola.com). There is also the Parc de la Collserola (p.181) and a walk along the Carretera de les Aigües mountain path is especially rewarding. Avinguda Tibidabo crosses the Ronda de Dalt near the CosmoCaixa (p.171) science museum.

The whole area spread between Ronda de Dalt and Passeig de la Bonanova is a treasure trove of architectural delights. Most buildings here are private properties, though you can usually peak through the gates. For Gaudí, try the Santa Teresa College on Carrer de Ganduxer. The modernist master built the convent and, although not usually open to the public, admission to the gardens and grounds is often possible outside term time, but call ahead (93 212 33 54).

Must Do

Order a coffee and croissant in the Cafe San Marco on Carrer Major de Sarrià: the croissants are from the Foix bakery opposite and made from a secret butter-based recipe. Further down the street is Café Tomas which produces some of the best patatas bravas in Barcelona.

The Good

Be it the spectacular views from Tibidabo, the breath of fresh air that is the Collserola park or Sarrià's sleepy squares and back streets, no district offers a better escape from the stresses of city life.

The Bad

With their plush housing, private schools and hospitals, some parts of the district are fairly snooty and tend to have limited interaction with residents of other parts of the city.

The Lowdown

Once an independent village, Sarrià has preserved its sense of otherness, while Sant Gervasi is one of the city's most wealthy areas. Both stretch up the Collserola foothills to Tibidabo.

Tibidabo

Museums, Heritage & Culture

How Barcelona spent so much time in the doldrums before 1992 really is a wonder. Quite apart from its natural beauty and pleasant climate, its culture and heritage are wonderfully rich. Here is a city built by the Romans, which developed into a prosperous Mediterranean trading port, saw battles for independence won and lost, witnessed one of the most exciting architectural periods (thanks to the *modernistes)* and provided inspiration for some of the 20th century's greatest artists, including Picasso and Miró.

But the Olympics concentrated minds on presenting the city's many attractions in as attractive a manner as possible; something that now benefits tourists as much as residents. Barcelona's museums, galleries and other heritage sites are slick affairs. They are accessible but well maintained, and informative but rarely overbearing. Prices are also generally reasonable.

The star attractions, such as the Picasso Museum and the Sagrada Familia, do get busy at peak times, but their hours are extended in summer (most stay open until 20:00) and the queues have usually dispersed by 18:00. Visitors also tend to flock to the showstoppers, meaning you will tend to have the run of the lesser known spaces. As well as the Articket (see p.163), another promotion worth considering is the Barcelona Card, which can be bought for two to five days (price ranging from €24 to €36). It gives free or discounted admission to almost all museums and galleries listed here, as well as on public transport, some shops, restaurants and leisure facilities. Consult the city's tourist office for details: www.barcelonaturisme.com.

Archaeological Sites

Barcelona was initially settled by the Romans, and the old town is littered with remnants. The Museu d'Història de la Ciutat houses a vast underground excavation site, while adjacent Carrer Tapineria has the best preserved section of the original Roman walls. The four remaining columns of the Temple Roma d'Augusti, in a side courtyard off Carrer Paradís, can be visited free of charge (every day but Monday) as can the remains of the Roman round tower at Centre Cívic Pati Llimona, on Carrer Regomir. A scheme to develop the Antic Mercat del Born site and show off its artifacts is ongoing. Archaeology enthusiasts will also be interested in the Museu d'Arqueologia (93 424 65 77, Passeig de Santa Madrona 39, www.mac.es), dedicated to Catalonia, and the Museu Egipci (Carrer València 284, 93 488 01 88, www.fundclos.com), which focuses on Egypt.

Pl del Rei ◀
Barri Gòtic
🚇 *Jaume I*
Map p.403 E3 **1**

Inside the museum

The Museu d'Història de la Ciutat
93 315 11 11 | www.museuhistoria.bcn.es

The lift to the excavation site below the museum counts down the years as you descend, finishing at -12, the BC era when what would become Barcino was first settled by the Romans. The city remains are impressive and there is something quite magical and unexpected in their being underground. Audio commentary is available for those keen to learn about the origin of every ruined wall and column, while labels do the job for those after a more general idea. There are also interactive screens to show how the city once looked, and further relics on display upstairs. The highlight of the above ground section is the Saló del Tinell great hall. Entrance to the museum is €5.

Art Galleries

Other options **Art** p.277, **Art & Craft Supplies** p.277

Given that artists such as Pablo Picasso, Salvador Dalí, Joan Miró and Antoni Tàpies have all called Barcelona home at some point in their lives, few cities can boast a modern artistic heritage to rival the Catalan capital. Modern art emerged out of the Renaixença, a revival of Catalan culture in the 19th century. *Modernisme*, which lasted from the 1880's through to the 1910's, was both an artistic and architectural movement. The French-influenced artists Ramon Cases and Santiago Rusiñol lead the way, with Pablo Picasso later picking up the baton. The next movement to emerge reacted against the decorative excesses of modernism and was known as *noucentisme* (nineteen-hundreds style). It sought to revive classical techniques of the past. Both Picasso and Dalí were caught up in this wave of nostalgia, with cubism and surrealism becoming their favoured fields. Then came Joan Miró, who went on to become a leading light of the avant-garde scene.

Many galleries open for free on the first Sunday of each month, while the Articket is also a good option: costing €20, it is valid for six months and allows admission to the MNAC, Picasso Museum, MACBA, CCCB, Tàpies Foundation and the Caixa Catalunya Foundation in La Pedrera. All participating galleries sell the ticket, as do tourist offices and braches of Caixa Catalunya bank. Alternatively, call 902 101 212 or visit www.telentrada.com.

Av Marquès de Comillas, 6-8
Montjuïc
🚇 **Espanya**
Map p.400 A1 **2**

CaixaForum

93 476 86 00 | www.fundacio.lacaixa.es

This gallery offers four art spaces located inside the magnificent brick building of the former Casaramona textile factory and houses temporary exhibitions of various shapes and forms, most of them refreshing and worth a gander. Sponsored by La Caixa bank, the emphasis is on modern art in all its facets with photography particularly well represented. Recent shows have also looked at sculpture, conceptual art, video installation, even fashion design and there is the occasional step back in time too: summer 2007 brought a retrospective of the work of English painter and cartoonist William Hogarth. Admission is free.

C/ Montalegre, 5
Raval
🚇 **Sant Antoni**
Map p.402 B1 **3**

CCCB

93 306 41 00 | www.cccb.org

Directly next door to the MACBA, the CCCB (Centre of Contemporary Culture for Barcelona) is in a former almshouse, from which the impressive Pati de les Dones courtyard remains. The CCCB is a multi-discipline centre that holds temporary exhibitions, debates, courses, music shows, cinema festivals and many other cultural activities. Exhibitions vary from the established, such as The World Press Photo Awards, to the experimental, of which many are mixed media. Film festivals include the Docúpolis International Documentary Festival in October and the Barcelona Independent Film Festival every November. Exhibition entry costs €4.40 although there is no charge for those under 16, the unemployed or on the first Wednesday of the month. Out back is a cafe with loungers, while in the basement there is a bar which opens up for events in the main hall.

C/ Aragó, 255
Eixample
🚇 **Passeig de Gràcia**
Map p.393 E3 **4**

Fundació Antoni Tàpies

93 487 03 15 | www.fundaciotapies.org

The building in which the Fundació Antoni Tàpies resides is fascinating in itself. Designed by Lluís Domènech i Muntaner, it is said to be the first modernist building constructed in Barcelona. Today, the red brick, art nouveau framework is topped by a silver tangle of Tàpies wire sculpture. He is considered one of the finest modern artists of his generation, and this is home to the most complete collection of his work. There is also an extensive, and quite beautiful, modern art library. As well as the permanent collection there are regular touring exhibitions, although it is worth noting that when one is on, the number of Tàpies works on display diminishes. The touring exhibitions are usually rewarding, varying in range and format, and usually quite contemporary. Access to all areas costs €6.

C/ de València, 284
Eixample
🚇 *Passeig de Gràcia*
Map p.392 F3 **5**

Fundació Francisco Godia

93 272 31 80 | www.fundacionfgodia.org

Francisco Godia was a Formula One racing driver with a keen interest in art collecting. From such unlikely roots comes a somewhat unlikely museum, housing work collected by Godia (and others acquired by his foundation since his death in 1990) in a small apartment off Passeig de Gràcia. While only modest in size, it is worth a look primarily for its collection of modernist paintings, with the likes of Santiago Rusiñol, Ramón Casas, Joaquín Mir, Isidre Nonell and Joaquín Sorolla – Picasso's drinking buddies from Els Quatre Gats. In 2008, the museum will move to larger premises in the Casa Garriga i Nogués on Carrer Diputació. The entrance fee for now is €5.50.

Av de Miramar, s/n
Montjuïc
🚇 *Sant Antoni*
Map p.399 F3 **6**

Fundació Joan Miró

93 443 94 70 | www.bcn.fjmiro.es

Up at the top of Montjuïc, the Miró Foundation offers probably the best collection of work by Joan Miró found anywhere in the world. A selection of paintings, sculptures, tapestries, prints and sketches show the maestro's development as an artist, his favourite themes and preoccupations. There are also regular temporary exhibitions of work by his contemporaries. As well as pleasing modern art aficionados, architecture enthusiasts will love Josep Lluís Sert's 70s building design, and even the most philistine visitor will enjoy the view from the surrounding gardens and refreshments in the courtyard cafe. Admission to the museum is €7.50.

Pl dels Angels, 1
Raval
🚇 *Catalunya*
Map p.402 B1 **7**

MACBA

93 412 08 10 | www.macba.es

Since opening in 1995, the MACBA has been criticised as a victory of style over substance, the argument being that the slick, striking white building, designed by US architect Richard Meier, is far more impressive than the exhibits held within. This is slightly unfair, but its dedication to experimentation and eagerness to be as broad as possible, does sometimes neglect duties of quality control. The MACBA has its own permanent collection of modern work, beginning from 1950, from which chosen items are shown on the ground floor. Upstairs is reserved for a rolling programme of temporary exhibitions, while there are also workshops, conferences, audiovisual experiments and talks, as well as an attractive first-floor terrace bar. Admittance to the MACBA collection costs €4, while access to the whole building, including any temporary exhibitions is €7.50.

Museu d'Art Contemporani de Barcelona (MACBA)

MNAC

Palau Nacional
Montjuïc
Espanya
Map p.399 F2 **8**

93 622 03 60 | *www.mnac.es*

The MNAC (Museu Nacional d'Art de Catalunya – National Catalan Art Museum) is one of those museums that you could spend days inside and still not take everything in. The extensive collection spans the 10th to 20th centuries, all neatly divided into different period sections. The majority of artists are Catalan, while the non-natives all have some connection to the region, having lived or worked here. The range of medieval art is vast and the Romanesque frescoes are a particular curiosity: paintings have been removed from church apses and then refitted in the style of the original inside the gallery, complete with reconstructed columns and arches. Nevertheless, Barcelona is a modern and dynamic city and the modern art collection is perhaps the most pleasing element. All the modernist masters are here with Santiago Rusiñol and Ramón Casas particularly well represented. Elsewhere, there is a room dedicated to photography, another to a vast coin collection, while the basement is reserved for temporary exhibitions. The building itself is also worthy of a mention: the Palau Nacional of Montjuïc provides magnificent high ceilings and domed hallways as a backdrop to the exhibits while the view from the front entrance is stunning. All in all, art lovers will find a visit well worth the €8.50 admission fee.

Museu Picasso

C/ de Montcada,
15-23
Born
Jaume I
Map p.403 F4 **9**

93 319 63 10 | *www.museupicasso.bcn.es*

The most popular gallery in the city offers one of the most complete Picasso collections found anywhere and, with its chronological arrangement, is a unique perspective of the development of the artist's influence and technique. Picasso moved to Barcelona in 1895, and there are many observation pieces painted in the city. Most works in the permanent collection come from his Blue Period (1901-1904), a spell when the artist divided his time between Barcelona and Paris. From the Rose Period, his portrait of Senyora Canals is a highlight. There are also frequent temporary exhibitions, which look at particular themes in his work. The museum is in a series of medieval mansions and some rooms are left bare, to be admired as the once opulent homes of rich merchants. Entrance to the permanent collection costs €6 while for temporary shows the charge is €5; a combined ticket is €8.50. At peak summer times, queues can get long but tend to have died down by 18:00.

Palau de la Virreina

La Rambla, 99
Raval
Catalunya
Map p.402 C2 **10**

93 316 10 00 | *www.barcelona.es*

Located on La Rambla next to the Boqueria market, the Palau de la Virreina is a 19th century town house built around a pretty courtyard. It was occupied by the viceroy of Peru's widow for several years (Virreina means viceroy's wife). It has two art spaces: the Espai 2 usually shows contemporary art while the Espai Xavier Miserachsis is generally dedicated to photography. A third gallery called La Capella is housed in the Antic Hospital de la Santa Creu around the back and focuses on new work by contemporary artists. Exhibitions tend to be compact, interesting and original and worth the €3 entrance fee.

Forts

The castle at Montjuïc has had a long and troubled history. It was originally developed from a maritime watchtower in the 17th century, in anticipation of the Thirty Years War (a Europe-wide conflict based on France-Habsburg rivalry). It was re-enforced in 1714, when Catalonia lost its independence, and rebuilt in 1751. Since then, it has towered over the city, acting as Madrid's eyes and enforcer. Bombs were fired on the city from here in 1842, to repress an uprising while, under Franco, it became a political prison.

165

The journey up the hill was often the last one the General's opponents ever made. Only in 2004 did the Spanish government actually cede the castle to the city of Barcelona. Today, you can reach the fort by the funicular cable car or via a steep walk. The castle is an impressive structure and affords magnificent views of both the city and the port. Outside its walls are moats, gardens and several cannons, while inside is the Military Museum (93 329 8613, www.ejercito.mde.es) with a collection of weaponry and uniforms old and new, admittance to which costs €3 and permits entrance to the castle grounds.

Historic Houses

Many of the city's best museums are in what were once distinguished houses: the Picasso Museum covers five former merchants' homes on Carrer de Montacada, the MNAC is housed inside Montjuïc Palace, and the Ceramics and Decorative Arts museums are in King Alfonso XIII's former royal palace. However, most of Barcelona's historical houses date from the *modernisme* period. As the city expanded, wealthy industrialists contracted local architects to design new homes and a wave of flamboyant buildings were erected. One of the best is Gaudí's Palau Güell on Nou de la Rambla (93 317 39 74) although it will remain closed for refurbishment until January 2009.

Gaudí's other two signature houses, Casa Batlló and La Pedrera, are listed below, but for a full list of modernist houses in Barcelona, visit www.rutadelmodernisme.com or call 90 207 66 21.

Pg de Gràcia, 43
Eixample
🚇 ***Passeig de Gràcia***
Map p.393 E4 **11**

Casa Batlló
93 488 06 66 | www.casabatllo.es

Part of the Mançana de la Discòrdia (p.148), Gaudí's Casa Batlló is one of the most emblematic modernist buildings in the city. Created for industrialist Josep Batlló, Gaudí was hired to spark some life into what was formerly a mundane apartment block, and his facelift certainly did that. One theory is that its mysterious design represents St George and the dragon, in honour of Barcelona's patron saint (Jordi in Catalan), and the surface does resemble a reptile's skin, with an elaborate shimmy of mauve and turquoise tiles. Down below come bone-like archways, while the rooftop is similar to the same architect's so-called gingerbread houses in Park Güell. The interior is equally impressive: the stairway basks in the reflected blues of the tiled walls, all harmonious curves, the attic is a labyrinth of cool white arches and the roof is peppered with Gaudí's trademark mosaic chimneys. Mind you, at €16.50 a time, entrance does demand something exceptional.

C/ de Provença,
261-265
Eixample
🚇 ***Diagonal***
Map p.393 E3 **12**

La Pedrera
93 484 59 00 | www.fundaciocaixacatalunya.org

Gaudí's Casa Milà is more popularly known as La Pedrera, which means stone quarry. The locals were less than impressed when it was unveiled in 1912, and dismissed it as resembling a pile of old rocks. Gaudí was clearly ahead of his time as the block, which sprawls over a corner of Passeig de Gràcia and seems to be inspired by the mountain range of Montserrat, is now one of the city's most iconic buildings, and has been a Unesco World Heritage site since 1984. Inside, the first floor is home to the Fundació Caixa Catalunya, host of regular, free exhibitions. Admission to the main building costs €8 and includes access to an exhibition in the arched attic, honouring the architect and his creations. There is also a show-flat furnished in the modernist style and up onto the roof, a typically playful array of swirls and curves and ornate chimneys, one of them topped with broken cava bottles – all with a stunning cityscape view.

Gaudi's creations

Religious Sites

It is hard to escape monumental churches in Barcelona. The image most associated with the city is the Sagrada Familia and the cathedral can be seen from any hilltop or high-rise building. From down below, El Sagrat Cor on Tibidabo mountain is equally ever-present. As well as the landmark religious buildings listed below, other churches worth looking out for include Sant Just i Pastor, off Plaça Sant Jaume, and Sant Pau del Camp, in Raval. Elsewhere, the Pedralbes Monastery is a marvel but the whole of the Sarrià-Sant Gervasi district is full of splendid religious schools and orders; many are private and so can only be viewed from their gates but some do cater to visitors. Consult the Architecture & Monuments search facility in the districts section of www.bcn.es for more.

Pl Santa Maria
Born
🚇 *Jaume I*
Map p.403 F4 **13**

Basílica de Santa Maria del Mar

93 310 23 90 | www.bcn.es/turisme

This Gothic church in El Born is one of Barcelona's finest. Built in the 14th century, its beauty is understated, unlike most religious buildings in the city, and is all the more charming for it. The interior is surprisingly cavernous with a highlight being the stained glass rose window. A fine way to contemplate the space is by attending one of the classical music concerts held here. Beyond its architectural appeal, the church is historically significant too; sailors would come to prey here before the trading voyages, establishing the city as a merchant power. The arches were damaged in the siege of 1714, which finally cost Catalonia its independence and a monument to the fallen defenders stands next to the church.

Pl de la Seu
Barri Gòtic
🚇 *Jaume I*
Map p.403 D3 **14**

La Seu Catedral

93 315 15 54 | www.website.es/catedralbcn

Barcelona Cathedral, or La Seu Catedral to give it its proper title, is one of the great Gothic buildings of Iberia. Work began in 1298 and was completed in 1448, although a final flourish was added to the front in the 1880s. Unfortunately, much of its beauty has been hidden behind a giant tarpaulin for the last few years, as extensive restoration work has been delayed by funding trouble. The inside can still be visited though, and it is an impressive and imposing space to behold. Around its edges stand 29 chapels, while the tomb in the crypt of the high alter holds the remains of the martyr Santa Eulàlia, one time patron saint of Barcelona. Perhaps the best feature of all is the cloister courtyard at the back complete with palm trees and a gaggle of geese. Admission to the cathedral is free, but in summer months they have begun to ask for a €5 contribution towards renovation work.

Pedralbes Monastery

Baixada del Monestir, 9
Les Corts
🚇 *Reina Elisenda (FGC)*
Map p.383 F2 **15**

Pedralbes Monastery

93 203 92 82 | www.museuhistoria.bcn.es

This monastery of the Poor Clare Nuns, the female version of the Franciscan Order, is an extremely beautiful monument which, though open to visitors, remains a peaceful and dignified space of contemplation. Pedralbes (from the latin *Petras Albas*, meaning white stones) was founded in 1327 by Queen Elisenda de Montcada. Recently widowed, she ploughed her inheritance into the monastery's formation before joining the order herself. It is a true treasure of Gothic architecture, with its medieval walls and gateways, dormitory, refectory, abbey and chapterhouse. The basic day cells, which acted as the nuns' own private retreats, open out onto a pretty

cloistered courtyard with three levels of arched terracing. There is also a simple church in which Elisenda de Montcada was laid to rest in a superb marble tomb. Entrance costs €5.

C/ de Mallorca, 401
Eixample
🚇 *Sagrada Familia*
Map p.394 B3 **16**

Sagrada Familia

93 207 30 31 | www.sagradafamilia.org

In a city blessed with stunning architecture, the Sagrada Familia is the most emblematic building of all. This towering monument, something of a giant fairytale sandcastle, is Gaudí's masterpiece. But, it remains a work in progress. The maestro dedicated all his energies to the project for 14 years until he was killed by a tram in 1926. Work eventually recommenced in the 50s although some argued it shouldn't. All Gaudí's models and plans were destroyed by the anarchists in the Civil War (the church being the very symbol of the conservative enemy) and the

La Sagrada Familia

Sagrada Familia was supposedly only spared for aesthetic purposes. Nevertheless, Gaudí's vision lives on. One day, the current eight spires, each more than 100m high, will be joined by four more of the same stature (representing the 12 Apostles), another four on a larger scale (honouring the Evangelists), and a further one in homage to the Virgin Mary plus a huge 180m domed tower in the centre, a symbol of Jesus himself. A visit today allows the guest to travel up the completed towers (from where the views between the cranes are stunning), watch the next generation of architects at work and learn about the building's progress in the basement museum, all for €8.

Heritage Sites

Other options **Museums – City** p.171, **Art** p.277

Pl de Sant Jaume
Barri Gòtic
🚇 *Jaume I*
Map p.403 D3 **17**

Ajuntament

93 402 73 64 | www.bcn.es

The Ajuntament is Barcelona's city hall, and sits bang opposite the Palau de la Generalitat on Plaça Sant Jaume. Dating from 1373, it is the older of the two administrative centres, but both have been altered over the years. The building was initially the seat of the Consell de Cent (Council of the One Hundred) which governed Barcelona between the 13th and 18th centuries. The Sala dels Cents Jurats council chamber is one of the original features. Another highlight is the Saló de Cròniques (Hall of the Chronicles), its walls covered in murals of epic adventure. Until recent years, when crowds became too much (and the football club fell out with them), Barça would commemorate their titles from the Ajuntament balcony. The balcony is also the best vantage point for the Castelling contest held in the square during the La Mercè festival, although getting an invite may prove difficult. Generally speaking, the Ajuntament can be visited on Saturday and Sunday mornings via guided tours, and pre-booking is essential.

169

Hospital de la Santa Creu i Sant Pau

Sant Antoni Maria Claret, 167-171
Eixample
🚇 *Hospital de Sant Pau*
Map p.395 D2 **18**

93 256 25 04 | *www.santpau.es*

Just up the road from the Sagrada Familia, the Hospital de la Santa Creu i Sant Pau is another Unesco World Heritage site. Designed by Lluís Domènech i Montaner, it combines red brick with intricate mosaic and tile work and bares a great resemblance to the Palau de la Música by the same architect. In its day (built between 1902 and 1930), it was one of the most advanced hospitals in Europe. It still functions as a hospital, but conditions have become cramped and it has run into funding problems as it tries to expand. There is no need to fake injury to visit, as the public are free to wander about the gardens and admire the various pavilions. There are also guided tours every morning. Phone ahead to book a place or consult the www.rutadelmodernisme.com website.

Palau de la Generalitat

Pl de Sant Jaume
Barri Gòtic
🚇 *Jaume I*
Map p.403 D4 **19**

93 402 46 00 | *www.gencat.net*

The Palau de la Generalitat is the seat of autonomous government in Catalonia. Work on the building first began in the 14th century but it was tinkered with right through to the 17th, meaning it is a mixture of styles, including gothic, renaissance and baroque. The Pati dels Tarongers courtyard, complete with orange grove, is its highlight, while other impressive stately rooms include the Golden Room (Sala Daurada) and St George's Hall (Saló de Sant Jordi). The Palau de la Generalitat can be visited at weekends but by appointment only, so telephone ahead.

Palau de la Música Catalana

C/ de St Pere Més Alt, 1
La Ribera
🚇 *Urquinaona*
Map p.403 E2 **20**

90 244 28 82 | *www.palaumusica.org*

Many argue that the Palau de la Música is the most complete modernist building in the world, and it is hard to argue. Designed by Lluís Domènech i Montaner, it is protected as a Unesco World Heritage site, which made recent renovation and expansion work very sensitive. But, the extension is faithful to the original (stylish and in red brick) and imitates the modernist style. The delightful decorative touches in colourful tile can be appreciated from street level but elements such as the terrace of mosaic columns deserve to be viewed up close, as does the stunning stained glass skylight in the main concert hall. Of course, the best way to see them is to attend a concert (check the website for the programme) but failing that, there are daily guided tours costing €9 and lasting just under one hour.

Palau de la Generalitat

Palau de la Música Catalana

C/ Nou de la
Rambla, 169
Poble Sec
🚇 *Paral·lel*
Map p.406 D1 🔢

Refugio 307

93 256 21 00 | www.museuhistoria.bcn.cat

During the Spanish Civil War, bombs from German and Italian planes rained down on Barcelona. At that time such attacks were the new tactics of warfare and the city's citizens had to improvise how best to cope. Makeshift air-raid shelters were built by residents all over the city. At the end of the war, Franco ordered them to be destroyed or filled in. But some survived, and the shelter in Poble Sec is among the best preserved and has been recently opened to visitors. An informative guided tour of the tunnels lasts about one hour and costs €3. It is best to call ahead and book, as spaces are limited.

Museums

Other options **Art** p.277, **Heritage Sites** p.169

This city, so rich in history and culture, has an abundance of top class museums. Variety is certainly the watchword, with museums dedicated to chocolate, perfume, shoes, music, erotica, the '92 Olympics, and even undertaker transport. For details on these spaces, see the city tourism website (www.barcelonaturisme.com). Most city museums are very accessible in terms of price (very rarely does admission reach €10), and most open their doors for free on the first Sunday of each month, when they can get quite crowded.

Park Güell
Gràcia
🚇 *Penitents*
Map p.386 A3 🔢

Casa Museu Gaudí

93 219 38 11 | www.casamuseugaudi.org

One of only three buildings completed in the Park Güell (p.179), which was originally conceived as a luxurious housing estate, the museum is in a house designed by Francesc Berenguer, one of Gaudí's chief collaborators. Built in 1905, Gaudí moved in the following year and kept it as his home until just before his death in 1926, by which time he had installed himself on site at the Sagrada Familia. The museum contains personal belongings and memorabilia associated with Gaudí, as well as many items of furniture designed by him. The house is in a pretty little garden inside the park, which features artefacts from other Gaudí projects and can be explored free of charge. Entrance to the building itself costs €4.

Palau Reial, Av
Diagonal, 686
Les Corts
🚇 *Palau Reial*
Map p.383 E3 🔢

Ceramics Museum

93 280 16 21 | www.museuceramica.bcn.es

This extensive collection of ceramics ranges from 12th century Arabic items through to late 19th century local pieces. There are examples of tiles from all the Spanish regions and a good collection of pots, including a room dedicated to the work of Joan Miró and Pablo Picasso. The casual observer may wish to hurry through to the Decorative Arts Museum across the hall (entrance to both is included in the €3.50 ticket), but ceramics enthusiasts will enjoy tracing the craft's development in Spain. Both the Ceramics Museum and the Decorative Arts Museum will move, along with the Textiles Museum, to a new Design Museum in Glòries, in 2011.

C/ de Teodor Roviralta,
47-51
Sarrià-Sant Gervasi
🚇 *Vall d'Hebron*
Map p.385 E1 🔢

CosmoCaixa

93 212 60 50 | www.cosmocaixa.com

Barcelona's science museum is perfectly designed for young, inquisitive minds. Countless interactive features guide the visitor towards discovering scientific principles for themselves. Its highlights are the Geological Wall (a cross-section that looks at the history of the world through its rock formations) and the Flooded Forest (a reproduction of an Amazon rainforest inside a greenhouse), complete with wildlife,

171

some of which can be picked up in the Toca Toca section. Other segments deal with the Big Bang, the birth of humankind and scientific progress through the ages. The emphasis is on having fun and inspiring learning. it is undoubtedly one of the best museums in the city for children. Entrance costs €3 with an additional supplement for some activities.

Decorative Arts Museum

Palau Reial, Av Diagonal, 686
Les Corts
🚇 *Palau Reial*
Map p.383 E3 **25**

93 280 50 24 | *www.museuartsdecoratives.bcn.es*
The Decorative Arts Museum shows developments through the ages in furnishings and trinkets. Beginning in the 13th century, it starts out with furniture, glasswork, jewellery and other ornaments before moving on to an 'industrial design' section which features office equipment and household appliances. The building itself is as intriguing as the museum. It was constructed in 1924, as a palace for Alfonso XIII to stay in when visiting the city. By 1931, the Spanish Republic had been declared and the property passed into the hands of the city authorities. But much of the royal splendour remains, particularly in the gardens. Entrance to the Decorative Arts Museum costs €3.50 and allows entry to the Ceramics Museum on the same site. You can explore the gardens for free.

Museu Barbier-Mueller

C/ de Montcada, 12-14
Born
🚇 *Urquinaona*
Map p.403 F4 **26**

93 310 45 16 | *www.amicsmuseuprecolombi.org*
The Barbier-Mueller Pre-Columbian Museum offers a superb collection of Latin American artefacts, the legacy of Iberian adventurers in the New World. Exhibits are well chosen, with only the very best making the cut, all carefully displayed with appropriately moody lighting. The museum is fairly compact but its display offers a fine introduction to ancient American civilisations for anyone not overly familiar with Inca, Aztec and Mayan cultures. Entrance costs €3.

Museu Barça

Av Arístides Maillol
Les Corts
🚇 *Collblanc*
Map p.391 D1 **27**

93 496 36 08 | *www.fcbarcelona.cat*
The Barcelona Football Club museum will impresses its visitors, as it gives access to the magnificent Nou Camp. Officially known as the President Núñez Museum, it has all manner of memorabilia spanning the club's 100-plus years. There are trophies galore, shirts, photos, artefacts, even the boot worn by Ronald Koeman when he scored the winning goal in the 1992 European Cup final. Three audiovisual displays trace the club's origins and show footage of some of the best players to have put on the *blaugrana* shirt. Entrance to the museum costs €7 for adults while a tour of the stadium (including the museum) is €11.

Museu d'Història de Catalunya

Pl de Pau Vila, 3
Barceloneta
🚇 *Barceloneta*
Map p.409 F2 **28**

93 225 47 00 | *www.mhcat.net*
Housed in the former warehouse of the old port now known as the Palau del Mar, the Catalonia History Museum opened in 1996. Two floors are dedicated to the permanent exhibition, which charts the region's history from pre-historic settlers, through the War of Succession and Catalonia's loss of independence in 1714, to the Franco years, the dictator's death and the 1979 Statute of Self-Government. The display is varied, from historic artifacts to everyday items, and there are interactive options that children will appreciate. The other two floors are dedicated to temporary exhibitions which tend to focus on twentieth century history. All in all, the €3 entrance fee is money well spent.

Museu Frederic Marès

Pl Sant Iu, 5-6
Barri Gòtic
🚇 *Urquinaona*
Map p.403 E3 **29**

93 310 58 00 | *www.museumares.bcn.cat*
This curious museum throws up all sorts of surprises. Frederic Marès was a sculptor, historian and teacher, but most of all he was an obsessive collector. While children

172

might dismiss the medieval sculptures and crucifixes on the ground floors, they will certainly find something of interest on the top floor. Displays of old toys and games, playing cards, miniature theatres, bikes, fans, clocks, keys, smoking pipes and much more; its a true treasure trove. The museum, which costs €3 to enter, stands next to the cathedral and is housed in the former Royal Palace of the Counts, which boasts a sumptuous courtyard garden, with a cafe in summer.

Museu Marítim

Av de les Drassanes
Raval
🚇 *Drassanes*
Map p.408 B1 **30**

Museu Marítim

93 342 99 20 | *www.museumaritimbarcelona.org*
Barcelona has a rich seafaring culture, and the Museu Marítim pays tribute to this heritage. The museum is housed inside the city's Reials Drassanes (the Royal Shipyards), a complex which served as a dockyard until the first half of the 18th century, and an arsenal and artillery park thereafter. There are regular temporary exhibitions, while the permanent collection has a huge array of model ships, nautical instruments, a fine selection of maps, a replica of the royal galley of Juan de Austria, and the Santa Eulàlia schooner, a vessel from 1918. Entrance costs €6.50.

C/de Montcada 12-14
Born
🚇 *Jaume I*
Map p.403 F4 **31**

Museu Tèxtil i d'Indumentària

93 319 76 03 | *www.museutextil.bcn.es*
Located in El Born, an area renowned for both its museums and fashion boutiques, the Museu Tèxtil i d'Indumentària (Museum of Textiles and Clothing) carries a heavy resonance, as Barcelona's industrialisation was founded on textiles. The oldest item in the permanent collection is a 7th century Egyptian tunic, but most pieces date from the 16th century through to the present day. Temporary shows tend to look at current trends. Exhibits are well displayed, English guides can be picked up at reception and the progress of embroidery techniques is well explained. The non-enthusiast might still prefer to head for the delightful patio cafe, although admission to the museum is just €3.50.

Festivals

Catalans appreciate the right to party and to celebrate their identity. The city's main festivals are enthusiastically participated in and attended. The most important celebrations are linked to the city's patron saints, both the current incumbents Jordi and Mercè and the previous protector Eulàlia, while each district also has its own *feste major*. Such events might typically involve *correfocs* (firework weilding 'devils' running down the street with revellers dancing in the sparks), *castellers* (see p.252), *gegants* (parades of papier-mache giants), *sardanes* (a folk dance peformed in a circle) and *havaneres* (a popular local song).

New Year festivities get the calendar under way but foreigners be warned: the local's eat their 12 grapes at midnight at home with friends and family, then head out to party from around 02:00 or 03:00. The Diada Nacional (National Day of Catalonia), on 11 September, is also worth noting. It marks the loss of independence in 1714, and is a day of remembrance for those who died defending the nation and a celebration of all things Catalan. There may be more political posturing than actual revelry, however.

173

Various locations ◀ Diada de Sant Jordi

www.bcn.es/festes

The Diada de Sant Jordi (St. George's Day) is hard to miss. Every 23 April, the city's streets are filled with stalls selling books or red roses. Tradition dictates that men give their lover a rose, while females give a book. St George is said to have been a very chivalrous man, and both Miguel Cervantes and William Shakespeare died on 23 April. This all adds up to something of a Valentine's Day come World Book Day hybrid. The rules are hardly set in stone, and it is common for people to buy friends and family flowers or paperbacks too, while patisseries make George and the Dragon chocolates and bakeries produce pastries in the colours of the St George Cross.

Various locations ◀ El Grec

93 316 10 00 | *www.barcelonafestival.com*

El Grec is a huge summer festival that starts at the end of June and runs through to August. Begun in 1976, as a modest programme of theatrical performances based around the Greek amphitheatre at Montjuïc, it now incorporates a spectrum of cultural events across the city. There are dance performances, concerts, plays, circuses, films and talks. A dose of prestige is provided by inviting international acts to showcase new work. Tickets vary in availability and price according to the reputation of the acts. It's best to consult the website or pick up a programme, which you will find at any of the city's cultural institutions. To book a ticket, head to any of the participating venues, use Telentrada (902 101 212, www.telentrada.com) or visit a branch of the Caixa Catalunya bank.

Various locations
Gràcia ◀ Festa Major de Gràcia

www.festamajordegracia.cat

The second half of August brings the Festa Major de Gràcia. The streets of the former village compete for the honour of best dressed, with Carrers Verdi and Puigmartí covered in streamers and papier-mâché models. The local residents work on the decorations and theme all year round. Meanwhile, the Plaças Sol and Diamant erect stages for live music and bars to keep the crowds in the party spirit. All of Barcelona descends on Gràcia and the Graciencs, who still consider themselves separate to the rest of the city. Graciencs welcome all and do their best to show off their independent, liberal spirit. There is a *castellers* contest in Plaça Rius i Taulet and activities to suit all ages, from games for the smallest child to dances for the oldest grandparent.

Various locations
Sants ◀ Festa Major de Sants

www.bcn.es/festes

The district of Sants throws this festival at the end of August, and encourages everyone out on to the decorated streets. There is live music in the squares at night and plenty to keep the little ones entertained in the day, with children's picnics, clown shows and games. In this most Catalan of neighbourhoods, all the usual outbreaks of local revellery are found, including *castellers, sardanes, havaneres* and *gegants*.

Various locations ◀ La Mercè

www.bcn.es/festes

While all the city districts have their own *festes*, La Mercè is Barcelona's own street party, and appropriately bigger and more organised. Held on the days surrounding 24 September, there is a wide programme of events which include a huge *correfoc* down Via Laittana followed by a firework display. The city's main *castellers* contest is in Plaça Sant Jaume on the Sunday, and there's free live music events all around the city centre.

Stages are erected in almost every downtown open space, including Plaça Sant Jaume, the Cathedral patio and behind the CCCB. Acts range from the well established to the obscure. All concerts are free.

Parc del Forum
Sant Martí
 Maresme Fòrum
Map p.403 D3 **14**

Primavera Sound

www.primaverasound.com

Primavera Sound is an indie rock and electronica festival held at the start of June. Hosted on several stages in the Parc del Forum down by the sea, the line-up is a mix of established acts and the latest scene-setters in European alternative music. Both bands and DJs play. The festival runs for three days (although there is no camping – you come and go to the site each day). A pass for the whole extravaganza costs €125, for one full day €65 and for just a night €20. Tickets can be bought in advance via Tick Tack Ticket (90 215 00 25, www.ticktackticket.com) or Atrapalo (90 220 08 08, www.atrapalo.com).

Various locations

Sant Joan

www.bcn.es/festes

Sant Joan, held on 23 June, is a pyrotechnic extravaganza. The night of St John the Baptist commemorates summer solstice, the shortest night on the calendar, and marks the arrival of summer. Traditionally, bonfires were lit in all the barrios, cava was drunk, coca cake eaten and everyone danced the night away to live music. Things haven't changed too much, although fewer neighbourhoods put on events. Barceloneta is where there's an official firework display, although most people just head to the beaches and make their own fun. In fact, the whole city is filled with anarchic crackles and bangs. The aim is to party through until dawn. The number of people out and about can spell transport chaos and it's best not to be too ambitious with your schedule, or be prepared to walk.

Various locations

Santa Eulàlia

www.bcn.es/festes

Santa Eulàlia was one of the city's patron saints before being dethroned by Mercè in the 17th century, but she has not been forgotten. What the La Mercè *feste* does for the summer, Santa Eulàlia pulls off for the winter, although on a smaller and less raucous scale. Her feast day is on 12 February and the week around it is dedicated to the usual Catalan festival shenanigans – *correfocs, castellers, gegants*. There is a craft fare and other children's activities outside the cathedral, where Santa Eulàlia is buried. The annual City of Barcelona Prizes for Science and the Arts are awarded during this festival too.

Various locations

Sónar

www.sonar.es

Sónar is a long-weekend festival (three days, two nights) in June, celebrating the best in cutting edge music and electronic culture. Activities include music concerts, DJ sets, VJ shows and multimedia installations. The programme is split into Sónar by Day and Sónar by Night. The former is held in the Sónar Village, based around the CCCB and MACBA, and mixes lower-key performances with a market. The latter is at a site which tends to change annually (in 2007 it was held at the Fira Gran Via) and involves headline acts performing until the sun comes up. Tickets for the whole event cost €140. Specifically, for Sónar by Day it's €28 and Sónar by Night €45. Due to limited availability, advance purchase is recommended (go to www.ticktackticket.com or call 90 215 00 25). During the festival the Palau de la Virreina sells tickets if there are any still on offer.

175

Beaches

Other options **Parks** p.178, **Swimming** p.243, **Beach Clubs** p.258

Within the city limits, there are six beaches; Sant Sebastià, Barceloneta, Nova Icària, Bogatell, Mar Bella and Nova Mar Bella. Each has unique characteristics and its own feel, although they've all had some sort of artificial sculpting.

What they lack in authenticity, they make up for in modern facilities. All have places to buy refreshments or rent sun loungers, are well watched by lifeguards and have showers. Only the Nova Icària lacks toilets, but is right next to Port Olímpic in any case. Five of the six beaches have been awarded a Blue Flag (www.blueflag.org) over the last few years, the only one to miss out being Barceloneta, the most urban. This worldwide seal of quality control evaluates various factors, from accessibility for disabled visitors to the number of bins, and from watchtowers to general cleanliness. Each beach also has a safety system, whereby a green flag indicates calm waters, a yellow flag suggests caution and a red flag warns of dangerous currents.

Nevertheless, these are inner-city beaches and, at their worst, do become crowded, dirty and polluted. It is worth noting that cleaner, prettier ones are but a short trip away.

C/ de l'Almirall Cervera
Barceloneta
🚇 *Barceloneta*
Map p.409 F4 **41**

Barceloneta
93 481 00 53 | www.bcn.cat/platges
The nearest beach to Passeig de Joan de Borbó and the marina, this is a first port of call for most tourists and local residents. Old men playing dominoes in the shade are as much a part of the makeup as visiting sunbathers. The recent installation of a wall out at sea has meant better sand retention and has considerably increased the size of the beach itself, so overcrowding is not such a problem. Given its location, Barceloneta beach is also well served with information points and toilet facilities, although queues at the latter can get very long.

Xiringuito beach bars are dotted along this stretch and there is a row of restaurants at the Port Olímpic end, where there is also a children's climbing frame and outdoor exercise gym.

Espigós Bogatell to
Ferrocarril
Poblenou
🚇 *Poblenou*
Map p.412 B4 **42**

Bogatell
93 481 00 53 | www.bcn.cat/platges
This long and narrow stretch of sand is similar in feel to Nova Icària. The area around the beach's only *xiringuito*, at the part nearest to its neighbour, is something of a spill-over, popular with the beautiful people of Barcelona. Heading away from the city, the beach empties out, both in terms of people and facilities, and attracts more families. Sea currents here are choppy enough to draw body-boarders and even a handful of surfers.

Espigós Ferrocarril to
Bac de Roda
Sant Martí
🚇 *Poblenou*
Map p.412 B4 **43**

Mar Bella
93 481 00 53 | www.bcn.cat/platges
This is the official nudist beach, although nakedness is not compulsory. The nude area is tucked in on a narrow strip of sand, just after Bogatell, where the surrounding dunes and foliage provide a modicum of privacy. The beach is relaxed, its bathers – mainly male – lounge in liberation rather than exhibition. As the beach moves away from the city, it widens out with more space (and more clothes) the closer you get to La Oca restaurant.

There is also a decent *xiringuito* playing chilled-out beats. Back the other way, there is a wind-surf club next door to the nudist section, and the sea is rough enough to reward keen board surfers too.

Life in the fast lane?

Life can move pretty quickly so make sure you keep in the know with regular updates from **www.explorerpublishing.com**

Or better still, share your knowledge and advice with others, find answers to your questions, or just make new friends in our community area

www.explorerpublishing.com – for life in real time

Espigó del Bogatell
Port Olímpic
🚇 **Ciutadella / Vila Olímpica**
Map p.411 F3 **44**

Nova Icària

93 481 00 53 | *www.bcn.cat/platges*

Just after the Port Olímpic development, this beach attracts a young and local crowd; people of all nationalities who call Barcelona home. It gets busy at peak times down towards the water edge but it is a people-watching sort of place, so that kind of the appeal. The strip is also wide and curved and so, to its periphery, there is space for beach volleyball, to throw a Frisbee, or kick a ball around.

North of Espigó de Bac de Roda
Sant Martí
🚇 **Poblenou**
Map p.412 C4 **45**

Nova Mar Bella

93 481 00 53 | *www.bcn.cat/platges*

This is the furthest beach from the centre, and the most relaxed and clean of the six city beaches. It starts out as a fairly narrow, well-equipped strip, but fills out the further away from the city you go and facilities soon peter out. Overall, there is ample space and a mixed crowd of local families and individuals prepared to go that extra distance for a bit of peace. Peace, but not necessarily quiet, as a string of *xiringuitos* play chilled out tracks well into the evening with summer beach parties featuring Groove Armada beats as a staple.

Off Pg de la Escullera
Barceloneta
🚇 **Barceloneta**
Map p.409 F4 **46**

Sant Sebastià

93 481 00 53 | *www.bcn.cat/platges*

Tucked away in the corner, Sant Sebastià is close enough to be served by the nearest watchtower but far enough out of reach of the Guàrdia Urbana to make it an anything-goes area. It is not officially a nudist beach but many bathers do choose to be naked. Others come here to smoke weed or just enjoy the sense of freedom. There is a very mixed crowd, with a considerable gay contingent. The huge Bofill Hotel complex is taking shape next door and will probably completely change the mood once it is complete.

Parks

Other options **Beaches** p.176

Barcelona's Mediterranean climate makes it a very outdoorsy place. From late afternoon, spring through to autumn, every square, patio or park is usually full of children playing or elder generations simply sitting and watching the world go by. Each district has a local park, all are well looked after, free of charge and usually come equipped with toilet facilities and fountains. The flip-side to the warm climate is that a lack of rainfall means there are none of the vast, sweeping grassy parks to be found in cities such as London. Nevertheless, what they lack in greenery they more than make up for in architecture and design: Gaudí was the brains behind Parc Güell and also had a hand in the Finca Güell and the Parc de la Ciutadella. Another characteristic of Barcelona's parks is their stunning views: as well as the mountains of the Collserola and Montjuïc, there are six hills within the city – Carmel, Peira, Rovira, Putget, Monterols and Creueta del Col – each one with a park at its crest.

Tarragona, 173
La Ribera
🚇 **Espanya**
Map p.392 A3 **47**

Parc de la Ciutadella

93 413 24 00 | *www.bcn.es/parcsijardins*

As well as having Barcelona's best grass spaces, pretty, flower-lined pathways and a fountain, Parc de la Ciutadella is also home to the zoo and the zoology and geology museums. The most central of Barcelona's parks, it was built on the site where the citadel once stood and some of the old buildings remain. What was the arsenal is now the seat of the Catalan parliament. The World Exhibition of 1888, was held here. Look out for the The Umbracle (it means shaded house), a brick and wood greenhouse full of tropical plants, and The Hivernacle, an iron and glass pavilion. In the summer, evening concerts are performed at the Glorieta de la Música bandstand, and up the Passeig de Lluís Companys, stands the Arc de Triomf. There is no charge to enter the park, and facilities include ping-pong tables, boat and bike hire, drinking fountains, children's playgrounds, a cafe and toilets.

Parc de Montjuïc

Montjuïc
Espanya
Map p.399 F2 **48**

93 413 24 00 | *www.bcn.es/parcsijardins*
Parc de Montjuïc is 250 hectares of green leisure space covering the Montjuïc mountain, with cultural and sporting institutions held within. This mountainside has experienced many transformations over the years, not least in 1929, for the Universal Exhibition, and 1992, for the Olympics. There are several cultural and sporting attractions, but it has retained its forests and parkland and there are different gardens to explore. The botanical gardens, old and new (p.180), the Jardins del Teatre Grec (inspired by the Hanging Gardens of Babylon), the Jardins de Joan Maragall (designed in the French neoclassical style) and Montjuïc Park itself. Meanwhile, children will love the space which the Funicular passes over. There are climbing frames and adventure playgrounds as well as giant musical instruments to play with.

Parc del Labarinthe

C/ Germans Desvalls,
Pg dels Castanyers
Horta

93 413 24 00 | *www.bcn.es/parcsijardins*
At the foot of the Collserolla, the Labyrinth Park offers fun for all the family. The oldest park in Barcelona, it used to be part of an estate owned by a Catalan aristocrat and it still has the feel of an exuberant private garden. Open to the public only since 1971, it is a fine example of an eighteenth century neoclassical garden, albeit one with Arabic, Mediterranean and Romantic touches. Spread out over the hillside on three levels, the gardens feature ponds and fountains. There are Moorish arches, sculptures of Greek gods, terracotta potting and the maze that gave the park its name. The park's periphery is a less organised expanse of pine forest and sprawling foliage. There is a €1.85 admission charge, though this is waved on Sundays, and guided tours are available. In the summer, there are classical music concerts. Dogs, bikes and picnics are not permitted within the park itself but just outside the gate is a children's play area complete with cafe and picnic tables, as well as the city's velodrome, which hosted the Olympic cycling events.

Park Güell

C/ d'Olot and Av Coll
del Portell
Gràcia
Vallcarca
Map p.386 A3 **50**

93 413 24 00 | *www.bcn.es/parcsijardins*
Antoni Gaudí's fairytale playground is the city's most emblematic park, offering stunning views and breathtaking design. Named after Eusebi Güell, the industrialist and politician who sponsored much of Gaudí's work, the original idea was to create a private luxury housing estate. Only two houses were ever constructed – Gaudí himself lived in one, now a museum (p.171) – and the whole site ended up being donated to the city in 1922. In 1984, it was declared a Unesco World Heritage zone. Straight lines have been avoided wherever possible: everything is undulating, from the paths to the benches, which are fashioned from broken tiles. A jumble of slanted pillars support a viewing-platform while further below sits the iconic ceramic salamander and fountain. Admission is free yet caters for all needs including guided tours, drinking fountains, a children's play area, a basketball hoop, a cafe and toilets. There are several entrances to the Park Güell, but the easiest way of getting there is from Vallcarca metro station. Walk down the main road (Avinguda de Vallcarca) until you come to a steep street on the left (Baixada de Glòria), with escalators up to the top.

179

Other Attractions

Various locations
Port Vell
Map p.409 D4 **51**

Transbordador Aeri Cable Car

93 225 27 18 | www.bcn.cat

This cable car ride links the harbour with Montjuïc and offers stunning views of the city and the coast. Commissioned for the city's 1929 exhibition, delays in its construction meant that it was actually launched in 1931. It was fully renovated in 2000. There are three stops: the Sant Sebastià tower (at the beach of the same name in Barceloneta), the midpoint Jaume I Tower (outside the World Trade Centre), and the Miramar (on top of Montjuïc mountain). At its highest point, the car climbs 70m above street level. The total distance travelled is some 1,300m. At peak times, cars run every ten minutes and a round trip costs €12.50 per person.

Amusement Centres

Other options **Amusement Parks** see below

Marquès de Comillas
Montjuïc
🚇 *Hostafrancs*
Map p.399 F1 **52**

Poble Espanyol

93 508 63 00 | www.poble-espanyol.com

This model village was designed for the 1929 Expo, to celebrate and promote Spain's many different architectural styles and crafts. There is a town hall, a church, a monastery and several houses around a central plaza, with all the typical building styles of Spain's different regions represented. Most of them function as artisan workshops or as craft shops, other as cafes, bars and restaurants. There are art exhibitions, street performers, theatre shows and games for children. Admission is €7.50 for adults and €4 for children over 7.

Amusement Parks

Other options **Amusement Centres** see above, **Water Parks** see opposite

Pl de Tibidabo, 3-4
Sarrià-Sant Gervasi
🚇 *Hostafrancs*
Map p.399 F1 **53**

Tibidabo Amusement Park

93 211 79 42 | www.tibidabo.es

This is the oldest amusement park in Spain and second oldest in Europe. The Castle of Terror and the Russian Mountain Big Dipper have been going for 100 years. This does mean that the rides are not state-of-the-art, white-knuckle affairs, but what it loses in thrill-seeking it gains in quaint charm. While there are enough attractions to satisfy children of all ages, adults will revel in the antique collections of fairground memorabilia or simply enjoy the view. Prices for children begin at €9 while full price admission is €22. There are discounts for groups, families and schools. To get to the park from the Avinguda Tibidabo train station, take the Tramvia Blau (it's as old as the park itself) up the hill, and then connect to the equally ancient art-deco funicular. The experience of arriving is all part of the fun.

Botanical Gardens

Montjuïc has been home to the city's botanical gardens since 1930, but building and access work for the 1992 Olympics threatened their stability to such an extent that it was decided to create a new and improved version up the road; today's Jardí Botànic. What remains of the original gardens, the Antic Jardí Botànic, can still be visited at Avinguda dels Muntanyans (near the palace), where you'll find the tallest trees in Barcelona. Also located on Montjuïc is the Mossèn Costa i Llobera garden, on the side of the mountain facing the ferry port. This has Europe's most complete cactus collection, with over 800 species.

C/ Doctor Font i Quer, 2
Montjuïc
🚇 Hostafrancs
Map p.399 F3 **54**

Jardí Botànic
93 426 49 35 | *www.jardibotanic.bcn.es*
The new Botanical Gardens are located behind the Olympic Stadium. They are dedicated to the conservation and study of Mediterranean flora, however, Australian, African, Chilean, Californian and Canary Island plant-life all get a look in. The pathways run horizontally, following the hill's contours, and are modern in layout and design. Facilities include study areas, and there are guided tours. Admission is €3, though free at weekends, and a visit might typically last an hour.

Water Parks

Other options **Amusement Parks** see opposite

Pl Llevant
Rambla Prim
Sant Martí
🚇 Passeig de Gràcia
Map p.413 F3 **55**

Zona de Banys
93 356 10 50 | *www.bsmsa.es*
A collection of swimming pools created by walling in sections of the sea. As well as safe swimming, protected from the strong sea currents, and easy access to the water (including wheelchair ramps), there are various watersports options. Canoes, kayaks, rafts, and water polo goals are available for hire. Boat trips out to sea are another option.

Aquariums & Marine Centres

Moll d'Espanya del
Port Vell
Port Vell
🚇 Drassanes
Map p.40 D3 **56**

L'Aquarium de Barcelona
93 221 74 74 | *www.aquariumbcn.com*
The aquarium is on the commercial island in the city harbour and one of the largest in the world. The highlight is the Oceanari, an 80-metre long glass tunnel, which allows you to walk through a giant shark tank. Twenty tanks in all, ranging from sea horses to star fish to plant life. Plenty of interactive options, while different floors cater to younger and older children. Admission is €13 for adults and €9 for children under 12.

Nature Reserves

Above the Rda
de Dalt
Sarrià-Sant Gervasi

Collserola Nature Park
93 280 35 52 | *www.parccollserola.net*
Forms Barcelona's natural western barrier, covering almost 8,000 hectares, 1,800 of which are within municipal Barcelona; providing thick forest just fifteen minutes from the centre. You can wander among 10 million trees and 1,000 different plant species, 200 natural springs and masses of animal life including reptiles, mammals, fish, birds and wild boar. There are even archaeological remains, old farmhouses and chapels. A protected zone since 1976, several segments have been declared nature reserves. Facilities include information and educational centres, the latter also home to the Rural Life Museum.

Zoos & Wildlife Parks

Parc de la Ciutadella
🚇 Bogatell
Map p.404 B4 **58**

Barcelona Zoo
93 225 67 80 | *www.zoobarcelona.com*
There are over 7,000 animals of 500 different species at Barcelona Zoo, which makes for a fulfilling visit, but also means that some of the enclosures are a tight fit. The star turn used to be Snowflake, an albino gorilla, though he sadly passed away in 2003, and now the dolphins, monkeys, elephants, hippos and panthers take centre stage. For smaller children, there is a petting farm and there are plenty of areas to stop for refreshments. Adult price is €14.50, children €8.75. There are also group packages and guided tours.

Tours & Sightseeing

Other options **Activity Tours** p.182, **Weekend Break Hotels** p.195, **Out of Barcelona** p.191

Barcelona is not overwhelmingly huge, and is very accessible and safe to explore. Many places of interest fall within pedestrian zones, so it is easy to move around on foot, making it an ideal city to wander on your own. There are many ready-made routes, mapped out and easy to follow. The official city tourist website has some good suggestions (www.barcelonaturisme.com) as does the Institute of Urban Landscape. Marked throughout town by small red paving stones with a flower emblem, these trails lead around Barcelona's major Art Nouveau works, visit www.rutaldelmodernisme.com for more information.

Local knowledge will also go a long way and touring the city with a guide can be a hugely rewarding experience. Tourism is big business in Barcelona, so there are all manner of options for getting to know the city and its charms, from walking to cycling tours, seeing the sights aboard a boat or a horse-drawn cart. Versatility is the name of the game for tour operators. All offer a range of transport possibilities, have standard whistle-stop-tour packages, allow you to design your own private itinerary, operate inside and outside the city and offer themes such as shopping or gourmet too. A standard tour of the city centre will take in all the city's main heritage sites while typical trips out of town are to Montserrat and the Penedès vineyards.

Tour Operators

Name	Address	MRT Station
ALSA	Plaza Peiro	L3, L5 Sants Estació
Barcelona Guide Bureau (BGB)	Via Laietana, 54	L4 Jaume I
Julià Travel	Plaça Universitat, 12	L1,L2 Universitat
Pullmantur	Gran Via de les Cortes Catalanes, 645	L2,L3,L4 Passeig de Gràcia

Activity Tours

Other options **Tours & Sightseeing** p.182

Barcelona is a great city for exploring on foot or by bike (see Bike Tours and Walking Tours) while its immediate surroundings offer plenty of hiking and watersport action (see the Out of the City section). For diving, Nautitracción (93 309 75 74, www.gymsub.com) run training courses in Barcelona itself, with dives on the Costa Brava, or even in the shark tank at the Barcelona Aquarium. Meanwhile, Spanish Trails Adventure (93 317 41 60, www.staexcursions.com) have an office by Plaça Reial, at Carrer Vidre 7, where you can arrange trekking trips around Catalonia.

C/ Balboa, 3
Barceloneta
🚇 *Barceloneta*
Map p.410 A2 59

Scenic

93 225 22 30 | www.scenicbcn.com

Scenic provides guided tours of the city streets by bike, scooter (kick-scooters as opposed to the motorised variety) or roller-blade, as well as mountain bike trips into the hills and paint-balling excursions out in the sticks. They are based out of Barceloneta, from where they also run kayak tours and schooner trips around the harbour and out to sea.

Bicycle Tours

With over 100km of cycle lanes and large parts of the town centre and sea front pedestrianised, Barcelona is very bike-friendly. Away from the more obvious tourist

Plaças of Barcelona

draws, it is full of history and architecture. Many modernist buildings are tucked away off the beaten track and hiring a bike allows you to discover areas you might not otherwise see. Given that it is also a food-lovers paradise, burning off a few calories as you explore excuses your indulgence once you are ready to rest. Barcelona's downtown zones are generally flat, while hills crop up if you to choose to visit the suburbs.

Biciclot

Pg Maritim de la Barceloneta, 33
La Ribera
🚇 *Barceloneta*
Map p.410 C3 60

93 221 97 78 | *www.biciclot.net*
Biciclot is dedicated to promoting cycling as a healthy, and environmentally friendly urban transport. They offer education, tourism or leisure programmes. Guided tours depart from their bike shop in Barceloneta on one of five thematic circuits (Ciutat Vella, Modernist, Collserola to the Sea, Montjuïc to the Fòrum and Barcelona Contrasts). Groups can map their own routes too. Trips last around three to four hours.

Classic Bikes

C/ Tallers, 45
Raval
🚇 *Catalunya*
Map p.402 C1 61

93 317 19 70 | *www.barcelonarentbikes.com*
Classic Bikes brings a splash of originality with their types of bikes and the tours they offer. In terms of the cycle itself, you can choose from the traditional model (known here as the Dutch design) or a fold-up bike; handy if you plan to take the metro and start your ride in the suburbs. Two hours outright rental will set you back €6 while their guided CycloTours cost between €21 and €30 for a morning or afternoon. There are four themes: the Classic takes in all the favourite sights while Beaches covers the waterfront. Markets & Tapas caters to foodies while the Divine route explores Barcelona's gay and lesbian scene.

Fat Tire Bike Tours

C/ Escudellers, 48
Barri Gòtic
🚇 *Drassanes*
Map p.402 C4 62

93 301 36 12 | *www.fattirebiketoursbarcelona.com*
Perhaps the most popular of the bike tour companies with English-speaking visitors, and part of a network spanning most of Europe's major cities. Their shop is on Plaça George Orwell and rents bikes and equipment, sells t-shirts and offers basic advice for getting around town. The emphasis here is on socialising and having fun, and the bikes are designed to be as user-friendly as possible. A tour lasts around 4 hours and covers the old town and seafront, where there is a stop-off for a drink and a snack – even a dip in the sea if you need to cool off – and costs €22.

Un Cotxe Menys

C/ Esparteria, 3
La Ribera
🚇 *Drassanes*
Map p.403 D4 63

93 268 21 05 | *www.bicicletabarcelona.com*
This is the most established bike tour operator in the city, boasting ten years experience and membership of the Barcelona Tourism Convention Bureau. Rent your own bike or join one of their morning, afternoon or night tours, which focus on the old town and the waterfront and include a guide, mechanic and an aperitif, for €22 per person. Special tours with lunch or dinner stop-offs can be arranged for larger groups, as can trips out of town, catering to all levels of cycling proficiency.

Boat Tours

Barcelona has a beautiful marina and busy functional port. A trip out to sea provides good views of harbour life, the city's beaches and an entirely different perspective of the landscape. From the Mediterranean, you can look back at the sprawling metropolis to see landmarks such as the Columbus monument, Montjuïc with it's spectacular palace and the castle, the Cathedral, Torre Agbar, the Sagrada Familia and Tibidabo mountain.

Pl Portal de la Pau
Port Vell
🚇 *Drassanes*
Map p.408 B2 64

Barcelona Orsom

93 221 82 83 | www.barcelona-orsom.com
Orsom run cruises on their catamaran boats. The standard trip heads out to sea and back again, lasting around 80 minutes, but you can also charter vessels for private use and a run down to Sitges or up to the Costa Brava. Either offers impressive scenery. In the evening, they organise themed cruises: choose from jazz, singles, sunset or wine tasting.

Pl Portal de la Pau
Port Vell
🚇 *Drassanes*
Map p.408 B2 65

Las Golondrinas

93 442 31 06 | www.lasgolondrinas.com
In operation for over 100 years, Las Golondrinas (meaning swallow in Spanish) boats depart the marina where La Rambla meets the sea. The Trimar and Omnibus services are catamaran trips which head out of the bay and out to sea, dropping you at Bogatell beach further down the waterfront or bringing you back again for a one and a half hour round trip. Adult tickets cost €10.50.
They also run excursions as far as the breakwater and back. These last just over half an hour and cost €5 for adults. All services are hourly (and on the hour) during the week but more frequent at weekends.

Bus Tours

Other options **Walking Tours** p.188

It may feel a little tacky, but there is often no better way to see the sights than from an open-top, double-decker bus. In Barcelona this is especially so, given the undulating cityscape, with lots of low, flat buildings interspersed with tall, landmark buildings and hilltop suburbs. Several companies provide a hop-on hop-off service and some also offer private coach tours.

Various locations

Barcelona Bus Turístic

93 285 38 32 | www.barcelonaturisme.com
With 44 stops dotted around the city, Barcelona Bus Turistic is the leading tour operator. There are three routes – North, South, Forum – which connect at six points, and you can jump on and off as many times as you like. A straight run of the North or South circuits would last two hours. A one-day adult ticket costs €19 while a two-day pass comes in at €23. Discount vouchers for some sights are included in the price.
Each bus has a multi-lingual guide on board to answer questions, and offer local history and directions. There is a detailed timetable at each stop, but generally busses hit the road from 09:00 and run until 19:00; 20:00 in summer. At peak times they pass by every five minutes, or 25 minutes during the leanest hours. Tickets can be bought on board, at tourist information points and most major transport stations, as well as online.

Rda de la
Universitat, 5
Sant Antoni
🚇 *Universitat*
Map p.393 D4 67

Barcelona Tours

93 317 64 54 | www.barcelonatours.es
This is the other major open-top bus tour service, boasting 50 years experience. It provides the same service as the Bus Turístic, but with fewer stops (around 20) and no discount vouchers. This means that they are often less crowded. These bright orange and blue busses operate one huge loop around the city, beginning at Universitat and ending at Plaça de Catalunya, which lasts three hours on a continuous ride. The bus has an eight language audio guide. Price for the day is €20.

Pg Olímpic, 5
Montjuïc
🚇 *Universitat*
Map p.399 F2 **68**

Bus Montjuïc Turístic
93 441 49 82 | *www.bsmsa.es*

There is a special tourist bus service for those who wish to visit the many delights on Montjuïc mountain. Two lines intertwine and, for the €3 euro ticket, passengers can hop on and off as much as they like. The Blue Line sets off from and terminates at Plaça Espanya, the Red Line to and from Portal de la Pau, and their paths cross at five junctions. This service operates daily in the summer months and at weekends all year.

Culinary Tours

Determined to cater to all tastes, most of the general tour operators offer trips with a culinary theme. Otherwise, a gourmet tour is one of the four official walks organised by the Barcelona Tourist Board. You wander the old town and learn the history of Barcelona's cuisine while stopping off for samples at various restaurants, grocers and markets (see Walking Tours, p.188 for details).

The Institute of Urban Landscape, meanwhile, has a design route you can follow yourself, with food and drink as part of the deal (see Novelty Tours, below). As well as shopping trips, Blai has a gourmet route too, so if you wish to be driven around in one of their luxury cars, give them a go (see Shopping Tours, p.188). If cycling is more your thing, have a look at the Markets & Tapas tour run by Classic Bikes (see Bicycle Tours, p.182).

Helicopter & Plane Charters

Moll Adossat
Port Vell

CAT Helicòpters
93 224 07 10 | *www.cathelicopters.com*

For a unique perspective of the city, treat yourself to an aerial view of Barcelona with a helicopter ride. The CAT choppers take off from the port (the helipad is tucked away at the back of the cargo terminal) and fly along the coast before soaring over the Sagrada Familia and the Parc Güell, up to Tibidabo, passing the Camp Nou and Olympic stadium, before returning to the port. Trips last around 10 minutes and cost €80 per person with cabin capacity for up to five.

Novelty Tours

There are all sorts of weird and wonderful ways of getting to know Barcelona. The Association of Licensed Tour Guides of Catalonia (see Walking Tours, p.188) has experts happy to wax lyrical on many specialist subjects.

To go it alone, the Institute of Urban Landscape (www.bcn.es/paisatgeurba, 93 256 25 25) has plotted three courses to go with its modernism route: the women's route, exploring the city's historical females; the liberty route, a tour of the city's flashpoints, including sites of Civil War scrapes; and the design route, highlighting the fields of architecture, shopping, food and drink. The last one has its own link (www.rutadisseny.com) while tourist offices and the town hall bookshop on La Rambla stock their guide books.

C/ Muntaner
185, 1º, 2a
Eixample
🚇 *Diagonal*
Map p.393 D2 **70**

Icono
93 221 25 01 | *www.iconoserveis.com*

Icono covers the classic tourist trails but also offers a popular ghost walk. The group is lead around the gothic quarter by a theatrical guide in costume, who is ever keen to spook the audience with ghost stories and legends. For lovers of Carlos Ruiz Zafón's novel, *The Shadow of the Wind*, they also do a tour which visits many of the locations mentioned in the bestselling book.

Various locations ◀

My Favourite Things

637 265 406 | www.myft.net

For something even more off the wall, My Favourite Things offers original takes on the city. A Love Birds tour steers couples on a romantic trail and for bohemians, there is a bar crawl around some of the old town's more choice establishments. A furniture design special takes in antique shops and flea markets, while families will enjoy the children's special, which keeps the nippers entertained with games and stories while giving the parents a bit of local history.

Other Tours

Barcelona's winning formula is its ability to blend the old and the new. To step back in time, horse-drawn carts can be hailed from the bottom of La Rambla, while the Segway HT offers a glimpse of the future, though, there's still no denying that this electronic, wheeled pedestal makes you look extremely daft.

Try and follow the lead of the locals and get a moped. Barcelona recently overtook Rome to become Europe's most scooter-riding city, so why not join them and tour town on a *moto*?

Baixada del Caçador, 2 ◀
Barri Gòtic
🚇 *Jaume I*
Map p.403 E4 71

Barcelona Glides

93 268 95 36 | www.spainglides.com

An increasingly common sight in Barcelona, albeit still a head-turning one, is that of groups exploring via the Segway HT, a futuristic apparatus which suggests a cross between a hoverboard and a lawnmower. Guided tours of the old town and seafront begin in Plaça Sant Jaume with a 30-minute training session and then last around two hours. There are morning or afternoon outings and each cost €60 per person.

Pl de la Sagrada ◀
Família
Eixample
🚇 *Sagrada Família*
Map p.394 B3 72

Barcelona Scooter

93 285 38 32 | www.barcelonaturisme.com

One of the most unique ways to see the city can be arranged through the Barcelona Tourist Board; a guided tour from the hot seat of an automatic 125cc scooter. Outings depart every Saturday morning and cost €45 euros per driver, €30 euros as a passenger. Drivers must be aged 21 years or over and present their driving licence (valid for at least three years), passport or other ID, and a credit card as guarantee. The trip lasts around four hours and takes in all the city's leading attractions.

Pl Traginers, 4 ◀
Barri Gòtic
🚇 *Jaume I*
Map p.403 E4 73

Trixi

93 455 58 87 | www.trixi.com

A popular and alternative way to see the sights is to hop into a Trixi rickshaw. Your driver will whisk you and a companion around the top attractions, or just follow your directions, with prices fixed at €18 for one hour. The same company can arrange group tours by kickbike, something of a kick-scooter and penny-farthing hybrid. An eight hour day trip on one of these original contraptions also works out around €18.

Private Tours

Cta Real, 103,1º, 2ª ◀
Sant Just Desvern
🚇 *Trinitat Nova*
Map p.389 E1 74

Guias de Barcelona

93 468 24 22 | www.guiasdebarcelona.com

Although based on the city periphery in Sant Just Desvern, Guias de Barcelona come to you and offer a choice of transport, ranging from chauffer-driven luxury cars to mini-buses and coaches. They provide a selection of set routes, both in Barcelona and beyond, or you can set the agenda yourself.

187

Various locations

Taxi Van Class

687 537 751 | www.taxivanclass.com

Offer personalised tours around the city, either to destinations of your choice or following the recommendations of the drivers themselves. Prices start at €40 per hour with executive cars and seven-seaters available. They also offer out-of-town trips to the likes of Sitges, Figueres and Montserrat.

Pub Crawl Tours

A few companies run pub crawl tours, although their aims do vary somewhat. Smashed! (93 342 52 52, www.smashedtravel.com) operate out of their Travel Bar on Carrer Boqueria and run a crawl which takes in four bars and ends in a nightclub, with a drink in each place included in the €15 price. The emphasis here is more on providing a good night out for visiting backpackers than any local insight. Likewise, Barcelona Tours (93 368 05 62, www.barcelonatours.net) cater to stag and hen parties, mostly from northern Europe.

For something a little more cerebral, My Favourite Things (see Novelty Tours, p.186) do a lap of the Bohemian bars of the Barrio Chino.

Shopping Tours

The official Barcelona tourism website (www.barcelonaturisme.com) has special maps and suggested routes, depending on what's on your shopping list. Shopaholics will also be interested in the Tombus, a hop-on and hop-off service which runs from Plaça de Catalunya up Avinguda Diagonal, guiding you along the Shopping Line. The website above has further details, or call 93 415 60 20.

C/ Maresme, 111-113
Poblenou
🚇 Besòs
Map p.413 E1 76

Blai Limousines

93 303 43 34 | www.blailimousines.com

Barcelona has plenty of chic boutiques and designer stores, and with this firm, you can arrive at them in chauffeur-driven style. With the choice of their executive fleet or limousine range, there will be no shortage of space for shopping bags. Blai provides expert advice on the most exclusive shops in town or will simply listen to your instructions and hit the road. They also have Cultural and Gourmet agendas.

Walking Tours

Part of the beauty of Barcelona is its everyday street life. The best way to get a feel for the city's spirit is to lose yourself to it, literally, and wander the back streets. Although there are thieves who prey on tourists, they tend to stick to La Rambla and its surrounds, so an aimless wander is highly unlikely to lead you anywhere uncomfortable, and you may find your dream bar, cafe or shop.

However, if you do prefer a little guidance, several companies provide all manner of themed walking tours.

Pl Ramon
Berenguer el Gran, 1
Eixample
🚇 Jaume I
Map p.403 E3 77

APIT

93 319 84 16 | www.apit-barcelona.org

The Association of Licensed Tour Guides of Catalonia offer a whole range of themed full or half-day tours – from the general sights, to panoramic views and sports – with most languages covered. Their website also has a list of the names and contact details of over 100 registered guides. All are based in the city and have their own specialist subject. The best plan is to send an email with an idea of what you are looking for and let them assign you a guide and programme. At weekends, the number to call is 93 310 40 11.

Park Güell (p.179)

Tourist Office
Pl de Catalunya
Eixample
🚇 *Catalunya*
Map p.403 D1 79

Barcelona Walks

93 285 38 32 | *www.barcelonaturisme.com*

Run by The Barcelona Tourist Board, Barcelona Walks offer four different guided tours: Gothic, around the old town, Modernism, in the Quadrat d'Or of L'Eixample, Gourmet, as mentioned in Culinary Tours, and Picasso, taking in the museum but also the places he lived, worked and hung out. All depart from the Tourist Information office at Plaça de Catalunya, and cost between €9.50 and €14, generally lasting two hours.

Wine Tours

Other options **Alcohol** p.277

Estrella Damm is the biggest brewer in Catalonia and it is possible to tour their main factory in El Prat de Llobregat with a minimum booking of 15 people (90 230 01 25, www.damm.es). Several of the tour operators arrange excursions to the nearby Penedès vineyards, as does Catalunya Bus Turístic (93 285 38 32, www.barcelonaturisme.com).

Pl de L'Oli, 14
Vilafranca del Penedès

Vinomadas

60 931 46 22 | *www.vinomadas.com*

Vinomadas is an enotourism company run by wine industry professionals. This means that their tours provide expert advice on everything from wine production to tasting. Based in the heart of the Penedès valley, in Vilafranca, they can also arrange trips to other grape-growing regions. Tours can be customised to suit any occasion. As well as trips to visit wineries, they also provide beginners wine-tasting courses.

Tours Outside Barcelona

Catalunya Bus Turístic (93 285 38 32, www.barcelonaturisme.com) organises tours to Figueres, Girona, Montserrat, Sitges and the vineyards. All the tour operators listed in the Tours & Sightseeing introduction on p.182 (Alsa, BGB, Julià, Pullmantur) do day-trips out of Barcelona, typically covering the same destinations, along with the Costa Brava and Tarragona. For more information on Barcelona's out-of-town visitor options see the Out of the City section (p.191).

Tour Operators

As can be seen throughout the chapter, there are as many operators as different ways to tour the city, and given that tourism is big business in Barcelona, competition ensures that standards of service are generally consistent and high, with prices reasonable. Nevertheless, Barcelona is an easy city to manage and with a minimum of planning and studying of either street or metro map it is fairly straightforward to organise your own day's independent exploring. Where tour operators come into their own is when groups are large or time is of the essence and, of course, most provide guides offering local knowledge and expert commentary. While there is no standard citywide seal of approval, all operators listed in the table below are recommended by the Barcelona Tourist Board. All can be booked direct – there is no real need to go through agents – both over the phone or online.

Tour Operators

APIT	93 319 84 16	www.apit-barcelona.org
Barcelona Bus Turístic	93 285 38 32	www.barcelonaturisme.com
Barcelona Guide Bureau (BGB)	93 268 24 22	www.bgb.es
Barcelona Walks	93 285 38 32	www.barcelonaturisme.com
City Guides BCN	93 412 06 74	www.city-guides.net
Guies de Barcelona	93 473 92 24	www.guiasdebarcelona.com
Icono	93 221 25 01	www.iconoserveis.com
Julià Travel	na	www.julia-tours.com
Pullmantur	93 318 02 41	www.pullmantur.es
Un Cotxe Menys	93 268 21 05	www.bicicletabarcelona.com

Out of Barcelona
Other options **Weekend Break Hotels** p.195

Although Barcelona is packed full with delights, sometimes there's nothing better than escaping the big city, particularly in the heat of summer. The favoured local options are the coast and the hills. More natural and less crowded beaches can be found at Sitges, Garraf and Castelldefels, a half hour train ride from Barcelona and easily reached by car. Girona and Lleida are beautiful historic cities, as is the university town of Vic, while Tarragona boasts impressive Roman remains. For art enthusiasts, the main Salvador Dalí museum is located up in Figueres while his former residence in Port Lligat, Cadaqués, is also open to visitors. Wine lovers can tour the vineyards of the Penedès region, or the modernist Anís de Mono factory in Badalona.

All Aboard
Before planning your trip, visit the Renfe website (www.renfe.es) for up to date information on train timetables and fare prices.

For getting out of the city, the Catalonia-wide Cercanías train system is excellent. Regular services cover a wide network at very reasonable prices. A return trip anywhere in the region will rarely be more than €10. Timetable and ticket information can be found at Sants station, or by contacting rail provider Renfe (90 224 02 02, www.renfe.es). For the places the trains don't reach, coach operators usually fill the gap, especially along the coastline and into the Pyrenees. Most coaches leave from Estació Nord (90 226 06 06, www.barcelonanord.com). Otherwise, renting a car is the best way to get off the beaten track. The main roads are tolled but this does mean they are generally in good nick and easy to navigate.

Sitges, Castelldefels & Garraf
Heading south along the coastal road from Barcelona you hit Castelldefels, then Garraf, then Sitges. Castelldefels has a huge stretch of sand and seafood restaurants. Many Barça footballers live here, Ronaldinho included, although Castelldefels itself is nothing special. Garraf is much prettier, its beach is lined with art deco huts and there is more modernist fun at Gaudí's Celler de Garraf. Sitges is the main port of call along this stretch of coast, offering golden sands and picturesque cobbled streets in the old town and banging bars and discos elsewhere. It is also Spain's principal gay resort and there are numerous cultural events, including the Sitges Film Festival in October and a huge fancy dress parade. Sitges is just 41km from Barcelona. The direct train takes 33 minutes; the stop-off service is a little slower at 41 minutes but calls at Garraf (35 minutes from Sants) and Castelldefels (22 minutes).

Girona, Figueres & Cadaqués
Head north from Barcelona and you'll find Girona, an ancient walled city, sitting proudly on top of a hill above the River Onyar. Getting here is easy, with regular train and bus services. The airport is also served by budget carrier Ryanair.
For those wanting to spend a weekend away from Barcelona's bustle, the Girona Cathedral should be first on the agenda. An absolutely stunning building with the widest gothic nave in the world, it's at the end of Rambla de la Liberat. You can take a pleasant walk along the riverside afterwards. Travel further north and you'll hit Figueres, and Dalí territory. It's here that he was born and died. The Teatre Museu Dalí (97 267 75 00) is definitely worth a visit and displays the famous face of Mae West created using furniture.
Further along the Costa Brava (*brava* means rugged, an apt description of the coast's magnificent cliff faces and coves) lies Cadaqués, the holiday retreat of Dalí. A former fishing village which now has a ban on high-rise buildings, it feels a million miles away from Barcelona, and is a base for the higher classes. Visit Dalí's former house, which has been converted into a museum (97 225 10 15), and see an array of outlandish furniture and fittings, giving an incite into his mind.

191

Weekend Breaks

Catalonians are keen to highlight their differences with the rest of Spain, but each Spanish region has its own characteristics and unique reasons to visit. The Basque Country, as fiercely separatist as Catalonia, has many selling points: its foods and wines are amongst the very best, its countryside amongst the prettiest, its sports and customs as quirky as they come.

Andalusia offers the perfect antidote, embracing all that is considered quintessentially Spanish by the outsider: bull fights, *abanico* fans, flamenco dancing and castanets. Madrid is home to some of the finest art galleries in the world, and has bars that open longer than anywhere else. For those looking for somewhere less obvious, Galicia is a sparsely populated region of fishing communities, Asturias has rugged mountains and seaside coves, Castilla y León has great castles and historical cities, Valencia has its orange groves, and Aragón the Mudéjar monuments.

Each region has its own particular visitor appeal, but also its own distinctive culture, traditions, food and drink. Besides the changing of the seasons, the festival agenda is the other factor to consider when deciding where and when to go. Many people head to Valencia for Las Fallas in mid-March, to Buñol on the last Wednesday of August for La Tomatina, and to Pamplona for the San Fermines in early July. All are fantastic fun but if you intend to stay overnight, book somewhere well in advance. The Spanish Tourist Board lists the various festivals on its website, along with other helpful information: www.spain.info.

Viva la Diferencia

Spain is an extremely varied mix of cultures and traditions. Make sure that you sample the regional specialities of each area that you visit, as you may not be able to find certain quirks and attitudes back in Barcelona.

The Pyrenees

The Pyrenees is a haven for outdoor sports enthusiasts. As well as skiing in the winter, there are excellent camping, hiking, mountaineering and rock climbing opportunities in the summer. Parc Nacional d'Aigüestortes i Estany de Sant Maurici (97 362 40 36 or www.mediambient.gencat.net/eng for info) is the only one of Spain's 12 national parks located in Catalonia. With jagged peaks (including the twin peaks of Els Encants), beautiful valleys, rolling rivers, waterfalls and lakes, a trip can be as active or relaxing as you wish. The website www.spain.info has details on this and other national parks, as does www.reddeparquesnacionales.mma.es/parques/aiguestortes.

In terms of skiing, the biggest resort is Baqueira Beret (www.baqueira.es) which caters to most abilities, including some tough black runs and good off-piste action. The second largest is La Masella (www.masella.com), which is near La Molina. La Molina is easy to get to on public transport: trains leave from Sants (Line 3 on the Cercanías network) and drop you at the La Molina train station, from where busses connect to the slopes. Travel time is around three and a half hours. You can get from Barcelona to the lifts by road in less than three hours with light traffic but, at their worst, the roads can really clog up. The ski season runs from December through to April (weather permitting – although snow machines can provide a boost in desperation). The Tour de France cycle race usually crosses into Spain at some point during its Pyrenees jaunt, drawing the Catalans – and particularly the Basques – to the mountains in their thousands. For all sorts of information on outdoor sports, places to stay and the region generally, the Palau Robert is full of advice (93 238 80 91, www10.gencat.net/probert). For more specialist knowledge try the Spanish Mountain Sports Federation, (93 426 42 67, www.fedme.es), based in Barcelona at Carrer Floridablanca, 75.

Andorra

The small principality, tucked between France and Spain in the Pyrenees, is home to outdoor sports and tax-free shopping. From December to late April, skiing is king. There are five resorts in Andorra: Arinsal, Pas de la Casa, La Rabassa, Ordino Arcalis and Soldeu i el Tarter. The latter is the busiest for skiing, the first on the list has the liveliest après ski. Given the altitude, temperatures are mild in the summer making it a great place for hiking, with views as good as anyone might hope for. The Juberri to Sispony route has been divided into seven trails, each around 14km and based around a network of mountain refuges. Andorra's valleys are sprinkled with small villages while Andorra la Vella is its major town, and a bizarre one; it resembles an out of control border market full of duty-free electronics and luxury goods stores. As with duty-free airport shopping, the savings are not what they once were, but there are still bargains to be had. There are no rail or air links to Andorra, the only way of entering being by road. It is a 200km journey from Barcelona and coaches leave from Sants or the airport (37 680 37 89, www.andorrabybus.com) or you can take the train as far as Puigcerdà and connect to a bus there. To plan a trip, drop by the Andorra Tourist Office on the ground floor of the World Trade Center (93 508 84 49, www.turisme.ad) down by the port.

Stocking Up
Prepare for your trip by having a read over our shopping chapter (p.273). Here you will find information on all your travelling essentials and maybe even find that perfect backpack.

The Balearic Islands

The islands of Mallorca, Menorca, Ibiza and Formentera are part of Catalonia and extremely popular holiday destinations for the mainlanders. They are also highly favoured by northern Europeans, the Brits and Germans in particular, and it is largely for this crowd that monstrous developments of tower-block apartments and happy-hour bars have been built.

On Mallorca, the biggest of the four islands, is the Bay of Palma; best avoided unless you are looking for a sun, sea and sangria sort of trip, possibly with the odd brawl and STI thrown in. The north-west coast, on the other hand, is much more scenic, with small villages and unspoilt beaches. Mallorca's main city is Palma, which has a pretty old town. The island has been slowly developing a luxury reputation. Michael Douglas and Catherine Zeta Jones have a pad here, and the Stein Group have two hotels. The word boutique gets a bit overused, but Son Net and Son Julia (www.steinhotels.com for both) are genuinely lovely, with some very grand, unique touches.

On Ibiza, the package-tour excess can be found at San Antonio, while Ibiza Town has its old quarter and shops, bars and restaurants with a bit of character. Most of Ibiza's super nightclubs are found nearby. It can get busy and chaotic during peak season but the island has loads of tiny little beaches to choose from, so those who want to can spread out. Formentera is the smaller of the islands and more an excursion from Ibiza than somewhere to stay itself, but it does have some good trekking and cycle paths. Menorca is something of a scaled down Mallorca and has some ancient monuments along with its beaches. Besides flying, ferries leave Barcelona from down by the World Trade Centre. To Palma it is four hours, Ibiza seven, Mahon on Menorca five – although there are also overnight services which take a little longer. Prices start at €72 return to Mallorca: (902 454 645, www.trasmediterranea.es).

Travel Agencies

Atrapalo.com	90 220 08 08	www.atrapalo.com
Barceló Viajes	93 317 02 20	www.barceloviajes.com
eDreams	90 288 71 07	www.edreams.es
Halcón Viajes	80 722 72 22	www.halconviajes.com
Iberia	90 240 05 00	www.iberia.es
lastminute.com	90 252 52 52	www.es.lastminute.com
Rumbo	90 212 39 99	www.rumbo.es
Viajar.com	90 290 25 22	www.viajar.com
Viajes El Corte Inglés	90 230 40 20	www.elcorteingles.es

193

South of France

Two of the easiest cities to get to from Barcelona are Toulouse and Perpignan. Both are pretty towns set on rivers, offering fine wining and dining. Toulouse is most notable for its magnificent Capitole square and town hall, while Perpignan – part of French Catalonia – boasts an interesting castle. A far more impressive castle can be found at the fortified city of Carcassonne. The fort has been restored and a visitor's village created, with craft shops, bars and restaurants. All three places are very tourist friendly and particularly popular with families in the summer. For a more genuine French experience, Marseille is another three and a half hours by train from Perpignan. Based around its port, Marseille is rough about the edges but full of vitality. A good time to visit France is Bastille Day, July 14, its national day of celebration with fireworks and music in the streets. Otherwise, the Tour de France always passes through the Pyrenees in July, ideal for cycling aficionados and a great opportunity to explore mountain villages. Train links to Perpignan are straightforward, although you often have to change at the Portbou – Cerbère border crossing, and the journey takes around three hours. By road it is less than 200km. The train to Toulouse goes via the Puigcerdà – Tour de Carol border and usually takes a little over five hours. For times and ticket information on the French side consult SNCF (www.sncf.com). The French tourist board has two sites; www.franceguide.com, and www.francetourism.com.

Sail Away

While in Valencia, try your hand at sailing. The weather conditions and sea breeze are perfect for taking a trip out to sea.

Valencia

For a long time, the only real reason to visit Valencia was to witness the pyrotechnic mayhem of its Las Fallas festival. However, in the last few years it has done a great job of reinventing itself as an attractive stop-off for a weekend break. The whole initiative was based around the impressive City of Arts & Sciences (www.cac.es), a huge complex with a planetarium, Imax cinema, aquarium, science museum and opera house, all designed by local hot-shot architect Santiago Calatrava. All these new projects have helped Valencia attract major sporting events too. It hosted the Americas Cup sailing event in 2007, and will feature a Grand Prix on the city's streets annually from 2008. More traditionally, the Museo de Bellas Artes (www.cult.gva.es/mbav) has work by all Spain's greats (El Greco, Goya and Velázquez) while the Palacio del Marqués de Dos Aguas is well worth a peak too. Amidst all the exploring, settle down for a Paella – the *valenciens* invented it – and maybe even an Agua de Valencia cocktail: Cava, Grand Marnier and orange juice. The website www.turisvalencia.es contains useful information.

The Basque Country

El País Vasco (www.basquecountry-tourism.com) is one of the best places to visit in Spain, due to the strong regional identity of the Basque people. There is much affinity between the Catalans and the Basques, a product of mutual respect and empathy from the struggle against Madrid. The Basques speak their own language too, although it is not as widely spoken in Bilbao as Catalan is in Barcelona. Bilbao is the state capital and most obvious city to head to, with a charming old town (Casco Viejo) and the Guggenheim Museum. Bilbao possesses an alternative streak, best witnessed during its Aste Nagusia (www.astenagusia.com) festival in August. The Basque country is a gourmet's paradise; the south of the region is Rioja country, full of vineyards and wineries, many offering tours and tasting. The region's second city, San Sebastián is a rather upmarket, picturesque seaside resort. There are good city beaches, although for surfing, Mundaka along the coast to the west is best. Traditionally one of the most popular family holiday resorts, San Sebastián gets very busy in summer as well as late September, when it hosts one of the world's leading film festivals. Even busier though is Pamplona in early July, when the bull running

194

takes place, as part of the San Fermines festival. Renfe (www.renfe.es) trains run direct from Barcelona to Bilbao, but flying, particularly with a budget carrier is much quicker, and usually only a little more expensive.

Madrid

Madrid is a good destination for a weekend break, with plenty to do both day and night. The top draws are the art galleries: the Prado (www.museoprado.mcu.es) is simply one of the best in the world, and the Reina Sofía (www.museoreinasofia.es), is home to many a masterpiece. The other main attractions are the Plaza Mayor and the Palacio Real (www.patrimonionacional.es) while the Bon Retiro park is also worth exploring. Madrid is not a classically beautiful city in the manner of Barcelona, or steeped in history like other European capitals; rather its appeal lies in the way the city goes about its business. As befits a capital city, most major banks and corporations have offices in Madrid but the city is also synonymous with long lunches and even longer nights out; few cities in the world go to bed as late as Madrid. As well as business visitors, Madrid is a fixture on the budget airline circuit and so attracts a real range of guests, some for the galleries, some for the bars and restaurants, many for a bit of both. The city does get very hot in summer but generally speaking, anytime is a good time to visit. The third week of May is particularly popular as the city celebrates its Fiestas de San Isidrio. Again, until the high speed train link is established, flying may be more appealing than going by train, which typically takes five hours, for around €70 each way.

Southern Spain

Seville (www.andalucia.org) is a wonderful city, with winding streets, charming patios, the Cathedral and the Alcázar. But the main appeal lies in Seville's spirit and its exaggerated lust for life. This is best demonstrated at the huge Semana Santa (Easter Week) and Feria d'Abril (last week of April), festivals which really fill the city up. Granada is another great place to head, with its stunning Alhambra (www.alhambra.org) and its Albayzín Moorish quarter, as is Córdoba, with its Mezquita.

For beaches, the Costa de la Luz offers some of the least developed coastline, while the opposite can be said about the Costa del Sol, an area almost as British as nearby Gibraltar. For something entirely different, the Alpujarra hills provide great hiking, while the Sierra Nevada has ski-runs in winter. In the summer, the south of Spain gets intensely hot, meaning that the cities empty as locals retreat to their cooler *pueblos*, or country homes. The heat also contributes to the overall pace of life, which is slower and more laid back than in Barcelona.

Weekend Breaks

Casa Imperial	Seville	95 450 03 00	www.casaimperial.com
Gran Hotel Domine Bilbao	Bilbao	94 425 33 00	www.hoteles-silken.com
Hotel Atzaro	Ibiza	97 133 88 38	www.atzaro.com
Hôtel de la Cité	Carcassonne	+3346 871 98 71	www.hoteldelacite.com
Hotel Maria Cristina	San Sebastiàn	94 343 76 00	www.mariacristina.es
Hotel Montarto	Baqueira Beret	97 363 90 01	www.montarto.com
Hotel Princesa Parc	Andorra	90 293 20 01	www.hotelprincesaparc.com
HPAM	Madrid	91 744 54 00	www.hotelpuertamerica.com
Ibis Perpignan Centre	Sóller	+3346 835 62 62	www.ibishotel.com
Ibis Toulouse Centre	Neptuno	+3561 636 163	www.ibishotel.com
L'Avenida	Sóller	97 163 40 75	www.avenida-hotel.com
Neptuno	Valencia	96 356 77 77	www.hotelneptunovalencia.com
Palacio de Santa Inés	Granada	95 822 23 62	www.palaciosantaines.com

Jump over the daily grind.

Fly over nagging thoughts.

Glide into your own space.

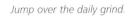 Cut through monotony.

Ski Dubai. Leave it all behind.

ESCAPE EVERY DAY

SKI DU

an unforgettable snow exp

Activities

Sports & Activities

Barcelona's warm Mediterranean climate leaves the avid sportsman or amateur enthusiast utterly spoilt for choice. With hot summers and mild sunny winters, bad weather is rarely a viable reason for avoiding sport. Gyms are of a high standard but membership is usually required; this is certainly the case for health clubs and country clubs. Municipal sports centres (known as *polideportivos/poliesportius* or *centros deportivos/centres esportius*) often offer a 'pay and play' system as well as formal memberships. When summer arrives, gyms become significantly less busy, as members flock to the beach or nearby mountain areas such as Montserrat. The city's reputation as an artistic and cultural centre is justified by the huge number of courses and exhibitions. The website www.aprendemas.com is good for general information on academic courses in subjects like photography. If you're looking for a sports team or a social group made up of fellow foreigners, try magazines such as *Barcelona Metropolitan* (www.barcelonametropolitan.com, p.38) and other English-language publications (see p.280). Lifestyle Barcelona (93 270 20 48, www.lifestylebarcelona.com) also organises one-off sports activities and cultural events. Finally, for sports club listings around the city, the Ajuntament categorise all clubs by sport on their website, www.bcn.es.

Activity Finder

Aerobics & Fitness Classes

Aerobics is excellent for improving circulation, burning fat, reducing cellulite and feeling healthy. Most gyms offer a wide range of classes, from spinning to legs, bums and tums (*glutis, abdominals i cames*). Generally, you need to join a gym or health club, as few take drop-ins. Spinning classes are hugely popular, so make sure you book in advance. The clubs in this table all offer aerobic and aqua aerobic classes, including aquafit, aquapower, aquarelax, aqua-tó (aqua toning) and aquaerobics. The same goes for the reasonably-priced municipal gyms, such as Can Ricart in the Raval (p.261). The city's main swimming pools and clubs (see Swimming, p.243) also tend to have offer aqua aerobics. For more classes, look in the city council directory (www.bcn.es).

Aerobics & Fitness Classes		
BonaSport	93 254 15 00	www.bonasport.com
Club Feminí Iradier	93 254 17 17	www.iradier.com
DiR	90 210 19 79	www.dirfitness.es
Holmes Place	93 272 20 00	www.holmesplace.es

Art Classes

Other options **Art Galleries** p.163, **Art & Craft Supplies** p.277

Art in Barcelona is omnipresent. From street art to high-brow galleries, caricaturists on La Rambla to independent shows in the Barri Gòtic, it is everywhere. Art classes are no different, with a veritable buffet available. Most community centres have art courses in some form or another, costing between €50 and €100 for the trimester. Bear in mind that these do not provide you with a qualification, and are often only for two hours per week. If you want to learn more rapidly or gain a professional qualification then it is best to study at an official teaching institution. Arte-en-Barcelona (www.arteenbarcelona.com) lists courses.

C/ Ferlandina, 26
Raval
🚇 **Sant Antoni**
Map p.402 A1 **1**

Artists Love Barcelona

93 302 27 79 | *www.artistslovebarcelona.com*

Artists Love Barcelona is a working studio and private contemporary art gallery, just off La Rambla. The attraction is that all courses are given in English and Spanish. Courses for all levels are offered in sketching, painting and life drawing. There are also art-orientated weekend breaks. Weekly life drawing classes, held on Saturday and Wednesday, are run on a five or 10 week basis (five weeks €100, 10 weeks €180). The main areas covered during the course are proportion, chiaroscuro and anatomy.

La Carboneria
C/ Groc, 1
Barri Gòtic
🚇 **Barceloneta**
Map p.409 D1 **2**

DrapArt

93 268 48 89 | *www.drapart.org*

DrapArt want to turn your 'rubbish' into something altogether more beautiful, while encouraging us to recycle and think green. They are bursting with ideas and always looking for artists or those keen to participate in their festivals, exhibitions and workshops. Membership costs €30 for the year. The organisers run recycling workshops in jewellery-making, accessories, fashion, toys and instruments. So, before you throw out that empty cereal box, just think; it is potentially a work of art.

Inspirational Audrey

199

EINA Escola de Disseny i Art

Pg Santa Eulália, 25
Gràcia
🚇 **Verdaguer**
Map p.394 A2 **3**

93 203 09 23 | www.eina.edu

A prestigious art and design school founded in 1967, EINA focuses more on the design side of things than art, but it is an excellent centre for those wanting a further studies or postgraduate course. EINA has gained a reputation as one of the city's most avant-garde art schools, always at the forefront of international trends and artistic innovations. The school of advanced studies, principally offering postgraduate courses and masters as well as specialist workshops, is linked to the Universitat Autónoma de Barcelona. The most commonly followed courses here are Interior, Graphic and Product Design, although various courses are also available in Illustration. ELISAVA Escola Superior de Disseny (www.elisava.net), part of the Universitat Pompeu Fabra, is also excellent in terms of teaching and reputation.

Nuria Duran

C/ Abaixadors, 10, local 1
Born
🚇 **Sant Antoni**
Map p.403 E4 **4**

619 875 072 | www.nuriaduran.com

This intimate gallery in the Born gives small-sized classes (maximum of six pupils) to an international mix of students. The courses are taught in a relaxed, experimental way that aims to let pupils express themselves through their work, by concentrating less on theory and more on practical trial and error. Classes focus on the four basic elements of fine art – composition, shading, colour and technique – and at the end of the course the students' artwork is exhibited in the gallery. You can sign up for classes anytime between September and June, for €45. The monthly course fee of €95 includes one two-and-a-quarter-hour class per week and all painting materials for the month.

Taller d'Art Maño

Rda Sant Pere 22, 1°, 2ª
Eixample
🚇 **Urquinaona**
Map p.403 E1 **5**

93 310 63 53 | www.tallerartmanyo.com

Taller d'Art Maño is a small, friendly school in the centre of Barcelona. More notably, it offers some of the most reasonably priced art classes in the city. Workshops are given in drawing, sculpture, painting and how to prepare material for applications to study fine art at university. The annual registration fee is €48, but there are various different schemes depending on how many hours per week you want to study. One two-hour class per week costs €68 monthly, whereas five two-hour classes per week (40 hours per month) costs €98 monthly. Courses become more interesting price-wise when you opt for three weekly classes and above.

Ballet Classes

Other options **Dance Classes** p.211

Many are put off ballet by the tight, flesh-coloured leggings and tutu, but it is an excellent activity for toning the lower body and improving poise and elegance. In Barcelona, there are a number of dance schools that offer ballet lessons (often referred to as *clásica* or *danza ballet*). For information on where to find classes, head to Danza Ballet (www.danzaballet.com), a forum for ballet dancers where information is shared on upcoming performances, auditions and productions. The World Dance Web (www.ladanse.com/auto/wlduk.mv) is also a good reference for schools, associations and ballet or contemporary dance festivals in Spain and around the world.

Ballet Barcelona

Various locations

626 091 064 | www.balletbarcelona.org

This is not a school, but a ballet company and non-profit association. Classes are open to all, with no distinction between abilities – and are included in the monthly membership fee. It works towards five performances per year and encourages ballet dancers of all ages and levels to participate. You can become a member of the company either as a dancer (€12 per month) or as a contributor (€10 per month), which involves helping with backstage aspects of the performance such as front of house, couture and clothes design, set design and lighting. All students and over 60s receive a discount of €4. You can participate in a free trial class (Wednesday 20:00 to 22:00, Friday 19:30 to 21:30) before committing to monthly membership.

C/ Torres i Amat, 5
Eixample
🚇 **Catalunya**
Map p.402 B1

Carolina de Pedro

685 877 797 | www.carolinadepedro.com

Carolina is a professional ballet dancer from Argentina who, having travelled the world performing with the Bolshoi Ballet and others, now shares her experience as a teacher. She gives classes in Points and Classical Ballet to adults and children of all levels. Classes take place at the Happy Yoga centre, near Plaça Universitat, on Tuesday and Thursday, from 19:00 to 20:30 as well as at the Escola de Dansa Rosita Mauri. Contact Carolina directly to find out which course suits you best in terms of level, location and price.

C/ de la Nació, 50
Clot
🚇 **Clot**
Map p.395 E3 8

Escola de Ballet Classic David Campos

93 347 73 40 | www.escuelaballet.com

This ballet school was founded in 1988 and has been producing some of the country's finest ballet dancers ever since. They specialise in classical ballet for all levels and ages, starting from 4 years of age. Classes start at 17:45 in the afternoon for 4 year olds and run until 23:45 at night for the advanced level (16 to 22 year olds). The David Campos dance company has been running for just four years. See their website to find out how you can get involved in performances and touring productions (www.balletdc.com).

C/ d'Ali Bei, 113
Eixample
🚇 **Marina**
Map p.405 D1 9

Escola de Ballet Eulàlia Blasi

93 246 59 62 | www.escoladeballet.com

This is one of the oldest ballet schools in Barcelona, with over 40 years of experience in teaching ballet, contemporary and jazz dance. The school regularly invites world-class foreign ballet dancers to teach for a semester or two, so the standard is very high. Two one-hour weekly classes cost €63 per month and classes run from mid-September to the end of June, with a signing-up fee of €65 in October. From July to September, the school runs intensive summer courses for both adults and children.

La Granada del
Penedés, 27
Sarrià-Sant Gervasi
🚇 **Diagonal**
Map p.393 D2 10

Escola de Dansa Rosita Mauri

93 217 26 48 | www.cmagnet.com

Ballet classes are taught from Monday to Friday, with separate classes for children, teenagers and adults and their varying levels of experience. Flamenco, jazz, corporal re-education and creative dance for children are interesting alternatives. Beginners' ballet classes are slightly shorter in length than at intermediate level, but all courses cost €60 per month for two weekly lessons, with a €65 signing-up fee.

Basketball

Spain are currently ranked number one in the world after the national team won the 2006 FIBA World Championship (www.fiba.com). This win has given basketball a much-needed boost in Spain, and caused basketball fever. Many sports centres in the city (*polideportivos/polesportius*) have at least one basketball court or multi-purpose pitch. Rental of the court for one hour will cost around €20, although lighting may have an additional cost. The Federación Española de Baloncesto (www.feb.es) and the Federació Catalana de Basquetbol (www.basquetcatala.com) are both worth consulting for information on national and regional updates and club rankings.

201

AE Bàsquet Pratenc Femini

*C/ Riu Guadal
quivir, 1-13
Sants
🚇 Plaça de Sants
Map p.399 D1 11*

93 478 76 60 | www.basquetpratenc.cat

This club specialises in basketball coaching for all ages from 6 years and up, with a particular interest in encouraging women's contribution to the sport. As a result, the club is female friendly with most teams in all age categories being female. However, there are boys' teams as well. Coaching for children and teenagers is payable in semester chunks: €50 September to February or March to June (two practice sessions per week). Adults should contact the school to find out which training session is most suited to their level.

JAC Sants

*C/ de Begur, 8
Sants
🚇 Plaça de Sants
Map p.391 E2 12*

652 089 701 | www.jacsants.com

One of the oldest basketball clubs in Barcelona, JAC Sants has a very well established reputation and a high standard of coaching. Dedicated wholly to basketball since 1935, it maintains excellence through a rigorous selection of team players. If you think you have what it takes, contact the club to see if you can join in trials. Adult training sessions are only open to team players and teams are male-only. Children's classes and training sessions (boys and girls) run throughout the year.

Birdwatching

Other options **Environmental Groups** p.214

Studies made by the Institut Català d'Ornitologia (ICO – www.ornitologia.org) show that in total, nearly 400 bird species are found in Catalonia. The region's broad variety of biotypes, including high mountains, rocky coastal areas, headlands, wetlands and sierras, are rich in year-round birdlife. As a result, Catalonia is a favourite spot for keen twitchers from all over the world. Despite city fumes, there is an abundance of birdlife in the city too. Most species are concentrated in the parks; Parc del Labarinthe (p.179), in the Horta-Guinardó area is a prime spot for catching sight of the Great Tit. The Vall d'Aran and Aigüestortes National Park (p.192) are famed for their stunning scenery and birdwatching possibilities. The ICO is the official source of information on birdwatching in Catalonia, but a useful English language website is www.fatbirder.com. For all manner of birdwatching equipment, Oryx store (www.weboryx.com) sells binoculars, guides, outdoor wear and books on naturalist pursuits.

Audouin Birding

Various locations

640 286 086 | www.audouinbirding.com

Audouin Birding organises weeklong birdwatching and wildlife tours of Spain and Catalunya (€950 full board). Tours focus primarily on Catalonia and the areas surrounding Delta del Ebre, the best being 'The Pyrenees, Steppes and Ebro Delta' and 'The Ebro Lands and Islas Columbretes.' These are professional and entertaining excursions with English and Danish guides, and come highly recommended.

Catalan Bird Tours

Various locations

93 818 82 72 | www.catalanbirdtours.com

Catalan Bird Tours are a good option for family holidays, as kid-friendly packages are tailored to allow enough time for non-birding activities. Self-catered accommodation comes with a swimming pool and games room, and is located just 30 minutes from Barcelona, next to Garraf National Park. Excursions take birders as far as Cap de Creus, Aigüamolls, the Pyrenees, Lleida Steppes and Ebro Delta, with the option of exploring these regions over the space of four or five days.

Sports & Activities

Delta del Ebre ◀

Delta del Ebre
www.ebre.com

Delta del Ebre, situated 200km south of Barcelona, boasts a population of between 50,000 and 100,000 individual birds from more than 300 species. Usually the first stop on the map for foreign birdwatchers, the delta covers an area of 320sqkm, making it one of the largest wetlands in the western Mediterranean. The delta's landscape encompasses many natural habitats and biotypes uncommon to the rest of Catalunya; as a result, you will find bird species here that are unique to the Delta del Ebro, such as the rare red-crested pochard. If organising your own trip, www.ebre.com provides essential information on rural tourism, hotels, restaurants, beaches, national parks and leisure pursuits.

Delta del Ebre ◀

Ebro Tours
97 726 73 82 | www.ebrotours.co.uk

Ebro Tours is an English company that organises birdwatching and hiking excursions in the Ebro Delta and the deep canyons of nearby El Ports national park. One-day birding tours cost €115 per person and self-catered country cottages have magnificent views and a terrace for catching a glimpse of raptors and griffon vultures. Ebro Tours are highly recommended, and guides, Margaret and Rob, are experienced and friendly.

Bowling

While bowling is popular in Spain, it has not taken on the same proportions as in the USA. In Barcelona, though, it is an increasingly popular pastime. Bowling Pedralbes (93 333 03 52, www.bowlingpedralbes.com) is the biggest indoor bowling centre in the city, open from 10:00 to 02:00. Many of the city's shopping centres have bowling alleys as well; the most modern of these is located in La Maquinista shopping mall (93 504 21 00, www.lamaquinista.com) where UV bowling balls are a quirky novelty. If you bowl professionally, contact the Club Bowling Barcelona (93 204 58 01) for information on membership and club nights.

Camping

Other options **Outdoor Goods** p.298

Catalonia's mild climate makes for a pleasant camping experience, but avoid winter months(November to February) if you're sleeping in a tent. Temperatures can drop below zero at night. The best time to go is from April to September, avoiding the sweltering summer months of July and August when temperatures can reach 37°C. Camping is prohibited in the region's national parks, such as Aigüestortes Parque Nacional. Instead, look for one of the many designated camping sites in the surrounding villages (www.campingscatalunya.com). The most popular campsites in summer however, are those that run along the Costa Brava and the Costa Daurada. A light to middleweight tent should be fine for both coastal and mountain camping. Good places to buy tents include El Corte Inglés (p.305) and the sports megastore Decathlon (p.302), which both have sales at the beginning of July. Essential items to take with you include a torch, Swiss army knife (with all-important bottle opener), lighter, basic first aid kit and sleeping bag.

Campsites in Catalonia are generally equipped with a range of leisure facilities. Many have swimming pools, a small supermarket and a bar or entertainment in the form of tennis, volleyball, beach football and games in the pool. For those who don't fancy roughing it, you will find many campsites have fully-equipped bungalows available. For more information consult the Federació Catalana de Campings i Ciutats de Vacances website: www.campingscatalunya.com.

203

Cta N-230, km174,4
Bossost

Camping Bedura-Park
97 364 82 93 | www.bedurapark.com

Set in the stunning surroundings of Vall d'Aran, the views of the valley from this campsite are reason enough to go. It is open all year round, including the winter months, when bungalows equipped with heating become very popular among skiers, snowshoers and hikers who enjoy extreme conditions. The site has a swimming pool, and activities include mountain biking, rafting, mountaineering and horse riding. Tents cost €13-18 in summer months. There are also wooden and concrete bungalows available from €35 for two people.

Av Montgó, s/n
l'Escala

Camping Cala Montgó
97 277 08 66

This campsite is just five minutes from the beach at the quaint and cosy enclave of Cala Montgó. The hill overlooking the cove is dotted with white, typically Mediterranean houses and the waters are clear. It is particularly popular with families, owing to its relaxed atmosphere and child-friendly beach. There are ample facilities, including a swimming pool, tennis court, mini-golf course and bar. It costs €5 per day for adults and four-person bungalows cost from €37.50.

Pja de Sa Riera
Begur

Camping El Maset
97 262 30 23 | www.campingelmaset.com

El Maset is right next to the beach. Not just any beach though; a nudist beach. However, it's not obligatory to be a naturist to stay. The site is popular with families, couples and travellers alike for one simple reason; the beach is stunning and slightly hidden from view, lending the place a sense of privacy. The campsite offers a number of water sports, diving and fishing activities, as well as onsite games and sport. There is also a restaurant, bar and pool room for après-sun fun. Tents costs €5 per day; adults pay €6.70 daily in high season (July and August), and children €4.70.

Ctra Arboç, km 2,5
Vilanova i la Geltrú

Vilanova Park
93 893 34 02 | www.vilanovapark.es

Vilanova Park is one of the best-equipped campsites in the region. Just 15 minutes by train or 40 minutes by car from Barcelona, it is a practical option for those wanting to visit the centre of Barcelona and relax on the beach at the same time. There is pretty much everything you could want here, including a sauna, gym and Jacuzzi onsite, while kids can amuse themselves playing tennis, ping-pong, football or splashing about in the large swimming pool. Camping in style comes at a price, but there are many options and tariffs available; contact the site directly for prices.

Canoeing
Other options **Outdoor Goods** p.298, **Kayaking** p. 221

You will find that most rafting companies and water sports clubs offer kayaking (*piragüismo/piragüisme*). River kayaking is particularly popular along the Noguera Pallaresa rapids near Lleida. On average, a half-day excursion should cost between €35 and €45, depending on the distance covered and the level of difficulty. ROCROI and Rafting Llavorsí both offer kayaking trips (see Rafting, p.232).

Sea kayaking is an excellent way to discover otherwise inaccessible coves along the Costa Brava. Excursions are typically half-day or full day affairs, giving you time to explore. Kayaking Costa Brava (97 277 38 06, www.kayakingcb.com) runs half-day excursions that leave from Cala Montgó near L'Escala; they last four hours and cost €45 per person. Full day excursions (€51) leave from Cap de Creus.

Cercle d'Aventura (902 170 593, www.cercleaventura.com) organise wakeboarding, sailing and half-day coastal kayaking trips (€40) as well as snow sports in the winter. If you would rather kayak in the Pyrenees mountains, contact Berguedà Nautic (617 698 984).

Near Barcelona, Canal Olímpic de Catalunya (93 664 57 73, www.canalolimpic.com) is an Olympic-standard water sports centre in Castelldefels offering kayaking classes (€38 for one-hour), beginners' courses and competitive team and club training. However, if you are already experienced and are simply looking to join a club, contact Kayak Club Premià de Mar (625 538 714, www.kayakbarcelona.com) as they organise regular excursions, including kayak surfing.

Canyoning

Other options **Hiking** p.218

Canyoning is an extreme sport that is often practised in remote and rugged settings. The sport is particularly popular in the French and Spanish Pyrenees because of the numerous caves, potholes, gorges and unusual rock formations. The Spanish website www.barranquismo.net lists all of the caves in the region with weblinks provided for each. Canyoning is often more about fun than tough physical endurance, and is enjoyed worldwide by people of all ages and skills. If you are curious about canyoning, but aren't ready to sign up to a club, Spanish Trails Adventure (www.spanish-trails.com) organise day trips.

Various locations

Canyoning Club Punto Límite

www.canyoningclub.com

Canyoning and descending gorges are the principal activities taken on by club members in both Catalunya and the French Pyrenees. The club's adventurous members are always on the lookout for new challenges and as a result, they organise sideline activities in mountaineering, rock climbing and alpine hiking expeditions. Once you sign up as a member on their website, you receive regular information on upcoming excursions and social events. Canyoning Club is a group of athletic, full-of-life characters who enjoy pushing themselves to the limit as sugested by the *punto límite* part of their name.

La Rambla 41, pral
Ciutat Vella
🚇 *Liceu*
Map p.402 B4 22

Federació d'Entitats Excursionista de Catalunya (FEEC)

93 412 07 77 | www.feec.org

The Canyoning Committee forms part of the Federation of Catalan Expedition Entities (FEEC), organising canyoning (*barranquismo/descens de barrancs*) expeditions on a regular basis. Members of the FEEC itself and partner associations, such as the Catalan Caving Federation (www.espeleologia.cat), can sign up. Usually there is a fee of around €20 for participation. Participants must bring their own helmets, appropriate clothing and canyoning material. Depending on the difficulty of the descent, it may be necessary to use abseils, ropes and wetsuits. Contact the FEEC directly for information.

Castelling

Castells (building human towers) originated in the 18th century. The ancient tradition embodies the essence of what it means to be Catalan – solidarity, fraternity, and strength – stirring feelings of pride among locals and disbelief among foreigners. Essentially the castell is divided into three parts. The *pinya* (pineapple), at the base of the castle, provides support if anyone should fall, and can be made up of as many as 100 people (the higher the castle, the bigger the *pinya*). The *tronc* (trunk) is the vertical structure made up of between one and nine people on each level. The *pom de dalt* at the top usually provokes a few gasps, as the youngest castellers form a bridge and another climbs up and over to raise a shaky hand. Without doubt, it is a gruelling physical challenge for all involved (especially those at the core of the *pinya*) and demands discipline and concentration and rigorous practise.

If you would like to join a castellers group, bear in mind that communicating in Spanish is not an option, and English even less so. Being a staunchly Catalan tradition, it could come across as insensitive, especially as castellers represent the preservation of a strong Catalan national identity and language.

Most groups will be happy to let foreigners watch but be reluctant to allow them to participate. To have a go yourself, you'll need an invite, because this is not an activity that has been altered to accommodate tourists in the way others in Barcelona have. But, once you show your enthusiasm, communicate in Catalan and show an interest in the cultural aspects of castelling, you will find people very welcoming.

C/ Bilbao, 212
Sant Martí
🚇 *Bac de Ronda*
Map p.395 E4 23

Els Castellers de Barcelona

93 232 55 56 | www.castellersdebarcelona.cat

Castells have a significant following in the comarcas of Tarragona and Vilafranca del Penedès: the castelling strongholds where the tradition originated. Castellers de Barcelona was formed as recently as 1969, to try to uphold the city's tradition, where previous castellers groups had failed. Today, the group has quite a following, with training sessions three times a week, from February to November (except August); Tuesday and Thursday 19:30, Saturday 19:00. The group is happy to let visitors come along and see how they train for the key castell events of the year (see their website for dates). During La Mercé is your best bet for seeing them in action.

Caving

Other options **Out of Barcelona** p.190

For extreme sports junkies who have tired of throwing themselves off tall structures, caving may be the adrenaline-filled answer. Known in Spanish as *espeleología* (*l'espeleologia* in Catalan), caving combines physical endurance, mental strength and exploration of underground geographical wonders. It is important to take necessary health precautions and first-timers should seek out a guide.

The Catalan Caving Federation (www.espeleo-cat.org) can inform you of upcoming group expeditions. Tailored trips are usually led by experienced and qualified instructors, but for those who are experienced enough, self-guided solo excursions are also an option.

Centre Excursionista de Catalunya (www.cec-centre.org) is an excellent organisation that regularly organises trips incorporating caving, hiking, camping, skiing or climbing. The CEC attracts members of all nationalities; try their multi-lingual website for upcoming events and trips.

C/ d'Asturies 83, 1º,1ª
Gràcia
🚇 *Fontana*
Map p.393 F1 24

Espeleo Club de Gràcia

93 415 04 60 | www.ecgracia.com

This 25 year-old caving club runs a number of courses; caving for beginners, caving for intermediate level, alpine caving, underground photography and canyoning at both beginner and intermediate level. Courses are run in prime caving season, between March and October. The three main caving spots that have been explored in past excursions are El Salí de Cardona (187m depth), La Falconera (80.9m depth) located near Garraf and the nearby La Fou de Bor (61m depth) in Badalona. Cave diving into the region's crystal clear underground pools is gaining popularity in Catalunya but the sport remains rather unconventional as a choice of hobby.

206

Chess

Chess has been played in Barcelona since the fleeting ascendancy of the Moors in the early 700s. It is not surprising then, to find that it is an avidly followed game, played by all ages. You often see chess played in squares and outdoor terraces, but if you prefer a livelier atmosphere, there are bars that keep a games selection in-house. Denver bar (Plaça Tetuan 16), has chess and Monopoly games available. For listings of chess clubs in Barcelona, visit www.chessclub.com. Alternatively, consult the Federacio Catalana d'Escacs (www.escacs.cat) or the World Chess Federation (www.fide.com). The English Speaking Club also holds chess nights from time to time (www.englishspeakingclub.com) if you're intimidated by all-Catalan clubs. When browsing the net, bear in mind that Spanish (ajedrez) and Catalan (escacs) translations of chess differ quite dramatically.

C/ de Francisco Giner, 42
Gràcia
🚇 *Diagonal*
Map p.393 F2 25

Escuela de Ajedrez Miguel Illescas (EDAMI)
93 238 53 52 | www.edami.com

This school specialises in encouraging chess-playing in younger ages. In the central office, near to the Plaça Rius i Taulat, EDAMI offers children's classes on a daily basis and adult classes on a weekly basis. Lessons are given by a team of over 20 teachers, most of which are, or have been, professional chess players.

C/ de Francisco Giner, 44
Gràcia
🚇 *Diagonal*
Map p.393 F2 26

Unió Gracienca d'Escacs (UGA)
93 237 13 48 | www.gracianet.org

Founded in 1924, the UGA is a long-standing, prestigious institution that has developed many regional and national champions. The staff and players are friendly, and the atmosphere warm. If you're interested in joining, pop along to club nights. All abilities are welcome, and there are a number of FIDE-rated (World Chess Federation) players to test stronger opponents. The club is open from 18:00 to 22:00 on weekdays and classes are available for both adults and children.

Climbing

Rock climbing is a hugely popular sport in Catalonia, because of the fantastic formations and climbing conditions. With over 3,500 climbing routes, covering all levels of difficulty, Montserrat is the prime spot for aficionados. All climbing *vias* (pathways) are graded in terms of difficulty, much like ski pistes. Within the city itself, climbing walls, known as *rocòdroms* are used for practise sessions throughout the week, while climbers wait until the weekend to visit out-of-town places. *Vias ferratas* (roughly translated as 'iron paths') were introduced here in 1990. These *vias*, made up of a series of ropes, harnesses and footholds, involve following a marked route combining hiking and climbing skills.

Climbing is a year-round sport here, although the ideal climbing period is from autumn to spring. The national governing body of the sport, Federación Española de Deportes de Montaña y Escalada (www.fedme.es) can give you pointers on which routes to follow and clubs to join.

Another invaluable contact is the FEEC (Federació d'Entitats Excursionistes de Catalunya, www.feec.cat). This group regularly organises climbing excursions all around Catalonia.

A useful English-language website is www.escuelasdeescalada.com. It catalogues all climbing spots in Spain, providing information on levels of difficulty, refuges in the area, routes available and how to get there. In terms of equipment, Decathlon (www.decathlon.com) has a wide range of climbing footwear, harnesses and other necessary equipment at reasonable prices.

207

Climbat Barcelona

C/ del Moianés, 19-21
Montjuïc
🚇 *Espanya*
Map p.391 F4 **27**

93 432 99 08 | www.climbat.com

Climbat is an indoor climbing centre with an artificial climbing wall (*búlder*), equipment hire, specialised library and a shop. The centre offers courses and excursions to nearby climbs, normally at Montserrat. One climbing session costs €9 in the morning and €12 in the afternoon, but for beginners, there are short courses (€35) that include two climbing sessions, footwear hire and one hour of teaching per session with a qualified instructor. For more experienced climbers, rock climbing courses and excursions to Monserrat are available, in association with the Federacio d'Entitats Excursionistes de Catalunya. In the summer, they also offer guided climbing tours around the region in English and Spanish.

Esportec

Various locations

635 199 126 | www.esportec.net

Esportec organises various extreme sports activities, but their specialities are canyoning and *vias ferratas*. With *via ferrata* routes formed by a set of footholds, bridges and ropes, you climb up a vertical face. Set up in Montserrat, Andorra, the Pyrenees and St. Feliu de Guíxols, you can enjoy the region's beautiful scenery without needing prior climbing experience or training. Climbs range from two-hour excursions for first-timers to two-day trips for those more experienced in the sport. There are a number of different routes and locations, so contact Esportec directly for more information.

Foment Excursionista de Barcelona

C/ de Creu dels
Molers, 6
Montjuïc
🚇 *Paral·lel*
Map p.401 D3 **29**

93 441 50 21 | www.foment.cat

This outdoor sports association organises excursions in skiing, rock climbing, hiking and caving. There is a small 'boulder' wall with a number of plastic footholds, used for climbing practice within the centre. Climbing excursions usually take place once a month in various locations around Barcelona, such as Garraf and Montserrat. Don't forget to take along your 'cat feet' (*pies de gato*); the Spanish for climbing shoes.

La Fuixarda Montjuïc

Av de l'Estadi, 30-38
Montjuïc
🚇 *Universitat*
Map p.399 F2 **144**

93 423 40 41 | www.picornell.com

This is the largest urban climbing area in Europe and the most popular area among climbers in Barcelona. So popular, in fact, that in summer there can be as many as 300 people on the outdoor rock faces at once. With 150 routes for all levels, you shouldn't ever find yourself fighting over footholds. Natural outdoor rock walls are the preferable climbing surface, although there is also a climbing tunnel, which is used when it is raining. The main climbing wall, with an average height of 15m and a maximum of 40m, is lit until 23:00 every night. It is an excellent place to meet people, as the atmosphere is very friendly and if you're alone you won't ever have trouble finding a climbing partner. And even better; it's free.

Cookery Classes

To Catalans, gastronomy is synonymous with the region's culture. Barcelona prides itself on the quality of fresh goods and the upholding of market shopping. Lunch and dinner are appreciated as sociable activities. There is no finer example of this than *calçotadas* – a semi-primal culinary experience in which families, friends and whole villages feast on calçots (similar to large onions) dipped in a traditional sauce. Whether you want to study cookery as a hobby or gain a professional qualification, there will be a course to suit you. For information on where to find your nearest school, look at www.escuelasdegastronomia.com. Alternatively, community centres are excellent for studying recreational courses at reasonable prices. Barceloneta Centre Cívic (www.civicbarceloneta.com) offers cooking courses in Moroccan cuisine (*cuina Marroquí*), local cuisine (*del mercat a la cuina*) and cooking therapy (*el valor therapeutic dels aliments*) for €48.50 per trimester.

La Rambla, 58, 3ª
Ciutat Vella
🚇 *Liceu*
Map p.403 C4 **31**

Cook and Taste
93 302 13 20 | www.cookandtaste.net
This school offers classes in traditional Catalan cuisine taught in English, French and Spanish. It uses local produce and recipes, providing information on where to find the best seasonal fresh goods. Half-day courses last three and a half hours and are run twice a day (at 12:00 and 18:00) from Monday to Sunday. Each session costs €50 and includes the class, a meal with Spanish wine and a booklet of translated recipes. Contact Cook and Taste directly for information on their private party and corporate packages.

C/ de Ferrer de Blanes, 7
Gràcia
🚇 *Diagonal*
Map p.393 F2 **32**

Jamón my son

Coquus
93 368 02 29 | www.coquus.es
Coquus offers classes in English, Spanish and German that explore typically Spanish and Catalan cuisine. Using fresh market ingredients (bought during a tour of the market) the group makes its own tapas, which are then enjoyed with a good Rioja. It is a particularly nice way to have a get-together with friends or as a team-building business event. It is a good choice for those who want to learn cooking in Barcelona, but don't have the time to dedicate to a weekly class.

C/ d'Aribau, 83
Eixample
🚇 *Passeig de Gràcia*
Map p.393 D3 **33**

Escola Bell-Art
93 451 79 65 | www.escuelabellart.com
The teaching standards are high at this well-known cooking school, which has been producing gastronomic geniuses for over 30 years. Luckily for mere 'dabblers', there are a number of alternatives to the professional chef training. Two-week summer courses cover all of the basics: salads and hors d'oeuvres, pasta and rice, fish and meat, soups and sauces and, finally, desserts. Each course consists of six evening classes and costs €230 (€410 for four weeks). Alternatively, year-long courses specialising in a particular area are run throughout the year.

Pg del Taulat, 243
Poblenou
🚇 *Selva de Mar*
Map p.413 D3 **34**

Escola Superior d'Hosteleria de Barcelona
93 453 29 04 | www.ferhb.com
Founded in 1985, this cooking school has made a name for itself as one of the most prestigious culinary institutions in Barcelona. If you are looking for formal training, this place is fully-equipped to help you master the arts of gastronomy and oenology. Month-long summer courses, and six to 12 month courses are available, as well as three-year degree and postgraduate qualifications. Contact the school for information on fees for specific subjects.

Pl Sant Pere, 5
La Ribera
🚇 *Arc de Triomf*
Map p.404 A2 **35**

Mescladis
93 295 50 12 | www.mescladis.org
Mescladis is a restaurant and cooking school all rolled into one. Classes are aimed at children aged 5 to 14, although there are also classes for adults. Classes encourage cultural integration and draw on different culinary traditions from around the world,

209

letting each child explore different cultures through cooking. Weekly classes run on Wednesday, Thursday and Friday afternoons from September and cost €25 for the semester. Summer classes are particularly popular and cost €50. Prices are extremely reasonable as one of the association's policies is to make it possible for everyone to take part. The restaurant also hosts birthday parties.

Cricket

Barcelona is poorly equipped with pitches and large spaces to play and it is extremely difficult to find clubs. The Pakistani and Indian communities keep cricket alive in the Raval, and you often seen groups of men and boys playing in the street or on municipal tennis courts. Not much help however, if you want to join a club.
The Barcelona International Cricket Club (605 562 047, cricketinbarca@yahoo.com) is the best bet for keen cricketers. They play friendly matches throughout the season (March to July). Players hail mainly from cricket-playing nations such as England, Australia, India and South Africa. It is best to contact the club directly for practice information because they have no cricket ground and, as a result, venues tend to vary. For general information on clubs and upcoming events, Cricket España (www.cricketeurope.net/spain) is an affiliate of the European Cricket Council (ECC).

Cycling

Other options **Sports Goods** p.302, **Mountain Biking** p.229

Some 50,000 people use the healthy, two-wheeled form of transport for getting around the city. By cycling, you avoid traffic jams, get fit and save money. This is precisely why the Ajuntament has recently launched a new form of public transport called Bicing (see Getting Around, p.30). The cycling system aims to promote the use of bicycles as a greener alternative to cars. Bicycle theft can be a problem though, and some people prefer to buy second-hand bikes over new ones, as they don't draw as much as attention. On a professional level, Spain is one of the leading cycling nations. Six of the top 10 2007 Tour de France finalists were Spanish, as was the winner, Alberto Contador. La Volta Ciclista a Catalunya (The Cycling Tour of Catalunya, www.voltacatalunya.cat), first started in 1911, and is the third oldest in the world after the Tour de France and El Giro de Italia. La Volta takes place every year around the end of May, followed by the national tour, Vuelta a Espana, in September. For information on cycling clubs, competitions and upcoming tours, the Federació Catalana de Ciclisme (www.ciclisme.cat) is a useful organisation, and it also runs a number of one-day courses and competitions. The Centre Excursionista de Catalunya (93 315 23 11, www.cec.cat) also organises regular cycling excursions.

C/ Demóstenes, 19
Sants
🚇 **Plaça de Sants**
Map p.391 E2 **36**

Bicing (p.34)

Amics de la Bici

93 339 40 60 | *www.amicsdelabici.org*
Amics de la Bici is an association that works to encourage people to use bicycles and adopt eco-friendly ways of living. They hold regular pro-bicycle campaigns in the city, as well as group outings to nearby coastal and mountain areas. Annual membership costs €25 but excursions may cost extra. The club explores nearly 20 different routes around the region during the year, and there is usually an out-of-town excursion at least once a week. Alternatively, if you prefer to explore by yourself, you can use the routes and mountain refuge listings on their website.

C/ Esparteria, 3
La Ribera
🚇 **Drassanes**
Map p.403 F4 63

Un Cotxe Menys

93 268 21 05 | www.bicicletabarcelona.com

This cycling company organises tours in and around Barcelona. Individual city tours (€22 per person) for small groups tend to cover about 15km, visiting all of the main sights and passing through areas such as Ciutat Vella and Port Olímpic. The tour is mostly flat (suitable for kids and adults) and all guides speak English and Spanish. Rural bike tours ranging from 12 to 52km long can be organised for groups of 20 to 50 people, and can include a traditional meal or cultural excursion on request. None of the routes are too challenging, making Un Cotxe Menys (One Less Car) a good option for families and inexperienced cyclists.

C/ de Riego, 2
Sants
🚇 **Plaça de Sants**
Map p.391 F3 38

Unió Esportiva Sants – Secció Ciclisme

93 431 82 98 | www.uesants.cat

Cycling and football are the main activities at this well known sports centre in Sants. The club is key to the cycling world in Catalonia, because it organises the all-important Volta a Catalunya every year, and has done so for over 80 years. There are activities organised for all levels, but club training and excursions are aimed principally at experienced cyclists. Sessions run from early September to late July; contact the club directly for timetable information. If you want to participate in the 'Volta' (30km) contact Unió Esportiva Sants for information on when time-trial qualifiers will be held.

Dance Classes

Other options **Music Lessons** p.230

There are many booty shaking options in Barcelona. Community centres are the most reasonable (€50 per trimester), often offering an extensive selection of classes. Funk, contemporary dance, belly dancing, flamenco, salsa, tango and African dance are all available at Drassanes and Barceloneta community centres (*centros cívicos/centres cívics*). Consult the Ajuntament's website (www.bcn.es) for listings of your nearest community centre. Dance schools are generally of a high standard and occasionally have special discounts, particularly in summer. Courses are usually held in trimester periods (September-December, January-March, April-June) during the academic year. In July, intensive summer courses run for periods of one to four weeks.

C/ Salvador Espriu, 27
Vila Olímpica
🚇 **Ciutadella/Vila Olímpica**
Map p.411 D2 38

Asi Se Baila

627 566 930 | www.asisebaila.com

This school regularly tours Spain and other European countries exhibiting its star performers. Specialising in Latin rhythms, you are sure to get hot under the collar here. Meringue, Cuban rumba, cha-cha-cha and bachata are particularly spicy; non-dancers can opt for percussion lessons. The Latin fever of it all can get a bit stifling, so if you're interested in movement and toning rather than Latin music, pilates classes are also available.

C/ Sants, 82-96
Sants
🚇 **Plaça de Sants**
Map p.391 F3 39

Ball Centre

93 296 90 17 | www.ballcentre.com

This five storey school near Plaça de Sants has 172sqm of practise rooms and a 1,300sqm ballroom that is used for shows and official competitions. Trimester courses will set you back €80 (10 weeks, one hour each week) and July's courses cost the same price, running for four weeks, with two hour-long classes each week. The diversity of courses does not disappoint, but for some it is necessary to sign up with a partner. If you don't have one, the school can link you up with a fellow class member.

211

Culturart

C/ Sant Salvador, 113
Gràcia
Alfons X
Map p.386 A4 **40**

93 213 75 86 | www.culturart.eu

Established in February 2007 under the direction of Brazilian actress and professional dancer Milena Trasmonte, this school focuses on artistic expression through dance and theatre. Culturart offers some of the most reasonable prices around, even compared to community centre courses. The cozy school has a distinctly bohemian vibe, with artists' work exhibited on a regular basis. Courses cater to both ends of the age spectrum (there are theatre for the over 60s sesions), and mime and clown courses are original additions to the programme. Theatre and dance programmes are held regularly and vary in length from week-long intensive blasts to full trimester affairs.

Open Dance

C/ Villarroel
204, 10a
Eixample
Hospital Clínic
Map p.392 C2 **41**

93 410 33 33 | www.opendance.es

As well as offering courses in salsa, tango, samba and hip hop, this school teaches some of the less common forms of dance, including lambada, breakdancing, country dance and house. Courses cost €110 for 10 classes. All levels are welcome; if you have done some dance before, you will need to pass a short exam to identify what level you are. The standard of teaching is high and the school is contracted at Holmes Place gyms, so if you can't make it to Hospital Clinic, Holmes Place Balmes (Carrer Balmes 44-46) is a more central solution.

Salsa Buenavista

C/ del Rosselló, 217
Eixample
Diagonal
Map p.392 E3 **42**

93 237 65 28 | www.salsabuenavista.com

In addition to lessons in almost every aspect of salsa, this school also provides salsa choreography courses, professional teacher training, private classes and the opportunity to undertake study exchanges abroad. It has a lively social scene, regularly organising dinners, parties and group events. Trimester and intensive (July only) courses will set you back €120 each, covering 10 hours of classes.

Diving

Exploring the mysteries of the Mediterranean, with fish swimming inches from your face is a mind-blowing experience. It can also be rather daunting and slightly claustrophobic at times, which is why training is required before plunging into the big blue. Open Water Diver is the standard course that first-time divers opt for: it involves theory classes over three to four days and training sessions in a swimming pool or at the beach. Once the training is out of the way, you will do three or four open water dives. 'Bautizos subacuáticos' are for those who want to get a feel for diving by literally just dipping their head in. During 'underwater baptisms', as they are translated in English, you are accompanied by a qualified instructor and will probably not dive lower than four or five metres. The official organisation behind the sport is the worldwide Professional Association of Diving Instructors, commonly known as PADI. For more information on professional courses, visit their website (www.padi.com). For general information on diving centres and companies in Spain, check www.bajoelagua.com.

Aquàtica

l'Estartit
Illes Medes

97 275 06 56 | www.aquatica-sub.com

Illes Medes is the daily destination of this first-rate diving school on the Costa Brava. As well as exploring this cluster of seven islands (a must for all diving aficionados), Aquàtica dive along the coast north of L'Estartit, exploring underwater caves, tunnels, walls and soft beds. Many of the dive spots are 20m down, which requires a PADI qualification. First-time divers on the PADI Scuba Diver course (€235 low season, €260 high season) will visit soft beds no deeper than 12m, accompanied by a qualified instructor, after lessons in the pool. PADI Open Water Diver courses (€395 low season, €410 high season) are slightly more expensive than other schools in Barcelona, but it is well worth paying the extra to learn at Illes Medes, one of the best diving destinations in the Mediterranean. Tariffs include equipment, transport to the dive spots from L'Estartit and insurance for one year.

C/ Joan de Sada, 42, 1a
Vilanova i la Geltrú

Aquatics Diving School
93 815 60 92 | www.aquaticsds.com

Aquatics Diving School differs from others in Barcelona in that it is both a school and a diving club. Learners and qualified divers have free membership to the club, which organises regular excursions to spots on the Costa Brava. Many of the students stay on to take part in club activities, and as a result the school has a sociable atmosphere. It runs PADI courses throughout the year, even in the winter chill. Open Water Diver involves five theory modules over the course of four days (although you can do it over a longer period) and four open sea dives. Members get discounts on equipment at some shops.

Cta Begur-Aiguablava Km 3.6
Girona

Gym Sub Aiguablava
97 262 26 59 | www.gymsub.com

This diving centre has a host of different diving courses, covering every possible aspect of the sport, from underwater photography to night diving. The standard courses – Scuba Diver (€230) and Open Water Diver (€380) – are also on offer, and there is even a 'bubblemaker' course aimed at giving kids a taste of diving. The website is in eight different languages and most of the instructors speak an impressive array of foreign languages themselves. The only downside to this school is that it is a two-hour drive from Barcelona (see the website for directions). But, it is a winner if you are looking to train professionally in a specific area of diving, or you fancy an underwater weekend away from the city.

C/ Almogávers 169, 6
Eixample
📍 **Llacuna**
Map p.412 A1 46

Rayas Diving School
93 309 94 61 | www.rayas-diving.com

Rayas Diving School in Eixample runs 12 official PADI courses. Training sessions take place in a local swimming pool and open water dives are practised in Palamós, north of Barcelona. Theory classes are given from Monday to Thursday and on Saturday students are driven to Palamós to put theory into practice. The 'underwater baptism' course, held on Tuesdays and Saturdays, costs €70 and Open Water PADI costs €330 including insurance, transport and equipment. 'Scuba Diver', taking you to 12m, is an intermediate option (€225) if your budget won't stretch to the Open Water PADI course. July and August get booked up fairly quickly, so try to book well in advance.

Drama Groups

Barcelona is thriving with drama groups. Finding English speaking ones though, is not so easy. Most of those that do exist are listed below. However, if you feel your Spanish or Catalan is up to the challenge, don't hesitate to sign yourself up to one of the many theatre courses offered in local community centres. While lessons in monologue performance may be a bit ambitious, Barceloneta (www.civicbarceloneta.com), Drassanes (www.ccdrassanes.tk) and Fort Pienc (www.fortpienc.org) community centres run theatrical improvisation classes. Courses cost between €50 and €70 per trimester, which covers one weekly class for a period of roughly three months. If you want to study official postgraduate or degree courses in theatre studies, consult www.aprendemas.com.

Actors Workshop

Sala Anaglifos
C/ Mònec, 17
La Ribera
🔲 *Urquinaona*
Map p.403 F2 **47**

63 715 53 99 | *www.actorsworkshop.info*

Actors Workshop was founded in 2004 to give novice and professional film and TV actors the opportunity to train and work on a weekly basis. One of the unusual aspects of this workshop is that all classes are given in English and Spanish. Classes on Wednesdays are predominantly English and some classes are even in French. Improvisation, song and dance, monologues and script analysis are just some of the themes for weekly classes. Running from 10:00 to 14:00 or 19:00 to 23:00, beginner, intermediate and advanced courses cost €135 per month (one four-hour class per week). During the summer, there are a number of intensive four-day courses.

The Drama Factory

C/ Ros de Olano, 9
Gràcia
🔲 *Fontana*
Map p.393 F1 **49**

93 301 43 01 | *www.thedramafactory.com*

The Drama Factory offers drama classes to native and non-native English speakers, aimed at both adults and children. The children's classes are geared at 6 to 14 year olds. For native English-speaking children, classes are on Thursdays from 18:00 to 19:00 and for non-native kids they are on Mondays at the same time. Dance, music, spontaneity, improvisation and educational games are key elements of the classes. Adult courses are open to those with or without theatre experience.

Estudis de Teatre

C/ Cid, 10
Raval
🔲 *Drassanes*
Map p.408 A1 **48**

93 324 82 28 | *www.teatrestudis.com*

This truly international theatre school has teachers and students from all parts of the globe. Teachers come from countries as far away as Canada, Tunisia and Cuba as well as the rest of Europe. The school has a reputation for being a multi-cultural mixing pot of young and promising talent looking to pursue professional theatre training. The school's official three-year course requires serious dedication. Alternatively, there are weekly clown, movement, voice lab and interpretation classes taught in Spanish. These run from September to June.

Environmental Groups

Other options **Voluntary & Charity Work** p.61

Spain suffers heavily from drought and desertification. The most recent campaign to reduce traffic pollution is Bicing, and it is expected to encourage people to adopt greener methods of transport while getting fit at the same time. For those who want to be actively involved in environmental campaigns, there are many organisations to join. Greenpeace (93 310 13 00, barcelona@greenpeace.es) is a good starting point. Club Universal Amics del Arbres (Friends of the Trees Club, 93 442 76 44, amicsdelarbres@yahoo.es) organises regular activities and excursions. Failing that, the Generalitat (www.gencat.net/mediamb) provides a list of environmental groups in each area. Online environmental communities are an increasingly popular way of keeping up to date with climate change concerns and new sustainable technology. Treehugger (www.treehugger.com) is an important reference, providing news on ecological breakthroughs in the domains of design (industrial and interior), architecture, transport, fashion and food.

Fishing

In Spain, to go fishing inland or in the sea you need a licence (*permiso de pesca*). These can be obtained through the Generalitat de Catalunya (www.gencat.cat). Available to anglers aged 16 and above, general licences for free waters (non-private areas) are valid for up to four years, include a sea fishing licence, and cost around €16. There are

Parc de la Ciutadella (p.178)

three main water categories where you can fish – *libros*, *cotos* and *intensivos*. *Cotos* and *intensivos* are private establishments. One of the most popular fishing spots is the River Ebro delta. Roughly two hours south of Barcelona, it is famous for its wild carp and large catfish. The season runs from February to October. The Federación Catalana de Pesca Deportiva provides information on the various clubs in the area (93 330 48 18, www.fcpeic.cat/societats) and the Reial Club Marítim (www.maritimbarcelona.org) organises group sea fishing excursions.

C/ Doctor Trueta,
195
Vila Olímpica
🚇 **Llacuna**
Map p.412 B3 50

Associació Pescadors Esportius de Barcelona
635 925 090 | www.apdbcn.com

Established in 1941, this fishing association has a host of regulars who have been with the club for over 20 years. It has a heavy Catalan and Spanish contingent, so you might want to brush up on your language skills before going. Excursions incorporate trout and salmon fishing and sea fishing, with competitions held on a regular basis. Annual membership costs €35 for men and €18 for women and children.

Various locations

Club Esportiu de Pesca La Lanzada
669 386 398 | www.ceplalanzada.com

This club specialises in sea fishing and attracts a number of young people every year, creating a lively atmosphere. Club leagues and competitions are held for all age categories: under 16s, under 21s, men, women and veterans. Annual membership costs €150 for 17 to 21 year olds and senior men and women. Under 16s and veterans pay €70. Club competitions take place along the coast both to the north and south of Barcelona, at seaside locations such as Gavà, Castelldefels and Ebro Delta.

Flamenco Classes

The origins of flamenco are steeped in myth and mystery, making it such a fascinating art form. An accepted truth is that flamenco originated in southern Spain in the late 1700s. 'Invented' by gypsies (*gitanos*) in Andalusia, its character reflects the history and cultural evolution of the region itself, which is hugely influenced by Muslim culture. It is created by four main elements: dancing, guitar playing, singing and hand clapping, conducted by the *compás*. A Catalan version of flamenco, named rumba Catalana, emerged in the 40s. In Barcelona, you will find that most dance schools and community centres offer flamenco courses. De Flamenco – www.deflamenco.com – is an invaluable reference for all things flamenco: guitar lessons, concerts, dance performances, private classes and even where to buy the best maracas.

C/ Marquès de
Barberà, 6
Raval
🚇 **Liceu**
Map p.402 B4 52

Flamenco Barcelona
670 437 577 | www.flamencobarcelona.com

Flamenco Barcelona covers all aspects of flamenco: classes are available in dance, guitar, song, *compás* (hand clapping) and *cajón* (rhythm). All dance classes are given by professional flamenco dancers, most notably by the famous Barcelona-born gypsy,

215

'El Chato.' Classes are given weekly to groups of 10 to 15 and cost €110 for eight monthly sessions. Weekly guitar lessons for groups of five or six cost €72 for four monthly sessions, with individual classes costing €30 each. Singing lessons cover more than 15 types of *palo* such as *buleria*, *soleá*, *cantiñas* and cost €64 for four monthly classes.

Gràcia Flamenca

C/ Burgos, 55
Sants
🚇 *Mercat Nou*
Map p.391 E3 53

651 090 177 | *graciaflamenca@gmail.com*
Gràcia Flamenca is a flamenco and sevillanas (a type of folk music) school in the popular area of Plaça de Sants, offering group and individual dance classes from September to June. The school has a lively atmosphere and prices are reasonable: €40 monthly for one weekly class, €60 monthly for two weekly classes and €80 monthly for three. And there is no joining fee. The first courses in the evening concentrate on the basics; arm, hand and foot technique. The second courses of the evening work on choreography. The school has a relaxed attitude and if you miss a class, you can make it up without paying any extra.

Flamenco icon Jose Camaron

Flower Arranging

Other options **Gardens** p.180, **Flowers** p.289

Flower arranging is not common here and non-professional courses are hard to find. It is always worth checking with your local church or community centre to see if they have one-off activities. Also, Barcelona International Women's Club (93 204 02 31, www.iwcbarcelona.com) may be worth a look. An interesting alternative is the Bonsaikebana school (93 265 31 54, www.bonsaikebana.com). Ikebana floral art is an ancient Japanese tradition steeped in myth and spirituality. Similar to the philosophy of feng shui, the correct arrangement of flowers is meant to make you feel at peace. For those looking to gain a professional qualification, the Escola d'Art Floral de Catalunya (93 332 95 00 or 93 232 28 99) offers degree and postgraduate training. Try www.emagister.com for general course information.

Football

Football is king in Barcelona: the beloved FCBarcelona ('Barça', p.251) winning or losing a match can determine the atmosphere in the city. The sheer size of Camp Nou stadium, the third largest in the world, with a capacity approaching 100,000 and set to be extended, speaks for itself. And for social players, the sport is played as passionately as it is watched. Most local sports centres (*polideportivos / poliesportius*) have multi-surface pitches that are used for football and hockey matches and many also have a futbol salon (indoor football, see p.254). Below are leagues and clubs that you can join. For general information on team and league progress, the Federació Catalana de Futbol (www.fcf.cat and www.futcat.org) is a good place to start. In terms of children, it is the main sport practised in schools for boys. Football for females is also on the rise; see www.futfem.com for the latest national and international news.

Various locations

Barcelona International Football League

93 218 67 31 | www.bifl.org

This amateur 11 a side tournament has grown in strength, reputation and numbers since being founded in 1992 by British expats living in Barcelona. Amateur players of various nationalities compete in what has become a highly competitive tournament. Despite being an informal, non-federated league, it is taken seriously by the participating teams. What began as a small get-together organised by a group of English teachers now has over 18 teams vying for the cup. If you're keen to join, post a message on their website under the new players section, and hope that you get invited to a training session to show off your skills.

Golf

With the mountain backdrop, beautiful coastal coves and mild climate, golfing in and around Barcelona is a pleasure. Whereas in southern Spain many of the plush golf courses are in holiday colonies, golf in Catalonia is appreciated by both Catalans and foreigners. Most clubs allow non-members to play and green fees average €70 on weekdays and €140 on weekends. If you want to plan a golf trip around the region, consult www.barcelonagolf.com, an English-language website with extensive information on courses and accommodation. The Catalunya Golf portal (www.catalunyagolf.com) is a good reference for club listings and regional competitions. Failing that, try the regional golf federation, Federació Catalana de Golf (www.catgolf.com).

Sant Feliu de Llobregat

Can Cuyàs Golf

93 685 55 66 | www.cancuyasgolf.com

This nine-hole course is ideal for beginners and not too far from Barcelona. Each hole is between 80m and 150m long, with wide greens to allow room for error. A particularly popular option for families keen to introduce their children to the sport, the school has a range of classes available for 6 to 16 year olds. Courses are run on a trimester basis and cost €195 for non-club members. The summer school for 7 to 13 year olds is also a popular option, as classes run intensively in June and July when parents are not yet on holiday.

Sant Esteve Sesrovires, Costa Dorada

Masia Bach Golf Club

93 772 88 00 | www.golfmasiabach.com

Designed in 1990, this is one of the more modern and challenging courses found near Barcelona. The 18 hole course, situated 25km from Barcelona, can prove difficult even for the club's best players. Luckily, the gentler nine hole course provides some respite for less experienced players. Green fees for the 18 hole course are €75 on weekdays and €170 on weekends, public holidays and Fridays from 13:00 onwards. If you are planning to play regularly, it may be worth joining for a trimester (€475).

Plans de Bonvilar Terrassa

Reial Club de Golf El Prat

93 728 10 00 | www.rcgep.com

Founded in 1954, this elite club has hosted prestigious championships such as the Spanish Open, and boasts two meticulously maintained 18 hole, par 72 courses. Located in Terrassa, roughly 30 minutes by car from Barcelona, Reial allows non-members to play under one condition: they must show current membership of a golf club in their home country, or they must have a handicap officially validated by the governing golf body at home. Members can enjoy the use of the swimming pool and two padel (similar to 'real tennis') courts. However, the club's nine hole course and driving ranges are open to the public. Green fees cost €114 on weekdays and €228 on weekends. If you go with a member it is half-price.

217

Sant Cugat

Sant Cugat Golf Club

93 674 29 08 | *www.golfsantcugat.com*

Founded in 1917 this club is the oldest in Catalonia, priding itself on its history and the quality of the 18 hole, par three course. Each hole has an English name as it was created by English construction workers employed to build the Spanish railway line to Sant Cugat. Green fees cost €65 from Monday to Thursday and €150 from Friday to Sunday and on public holidays. You have to show some form of identification that proves you play golf, like membership at a local or foreign club. Children's classes run on Saturdays and there is a crèche for families with tots.

Handball

Handball is a popular sport in Spain, and is played both indoors and on the beach. Catalonia has two teams in the top 10 of the national handball league; ASOBAL F.C. Barcelona (93 496 76 05, www.fcbarcelona.com) and Club Balonmano Granollers (93 879 28 62, www.bmgranollers.org). FC Barcelona only has three teams, for which the managers sign up players. Club Balonmano Granollers, one of the oldest handball clubs in the country, has several teams of all levels and ages and is more accessible for club-standard players.

The best way to get involved in the handball scene, is to place an ad on the *borsa jugadores* (players' draw) on the Catalan Handball Federation website (www.fchandbol.com). Also contact the teams and clubs directly to find out whether they are still looking for players, as sometimes they forget to remove their ad from the *borsa*. If you would like to contact your local club directly, the Catalan Handball Federation (Federació Catalana d'Handbol) provides contact details of all listed clubs in the region.

Hiking

Other options **Canyoning** p.205, **Out of Barcelona** p.190, **Outdoor Goods** p.298

Hiking, known as *senderismo* (*senderisme* in Catalan), is a popular activity in Catalonia. There are a number of hiking options available, including guided day trips, multi-day group excursions and self-guided, marked trails that you can navigate yourself. The most extensive and well-marked trail near to Barcelona is Montserrat. Consult the Federació d'Entitats Excursionista de Catalunya (FEEC) website (www.feec.org) for maps of these.

Guided excursions are a popular alternative to going it alone, because with a knowledgable guide you learn about the history, culture and biodiversity of the region in more depth. If you want to seek advice from fellow hikers or alpinists, www.senderisme.org is an online mountaineering community with hiking-related discussion forums.

Various locations

Catalonia Adventures

93 890 45 14 | *www.cataloniaadventures.com*

This English, Spanish and Catalan-speaking company organises guided trails in the Pyrenees, Aigüestortes, Montseny and Montserrat, finishing up with tasty traditional grub in a local restaurant. If you opt for a multi-day excursion, there is always the possibility of combining hiking with other activities such as canyoning, skydiving, climbing, bungee jumping, caving or mountain biking. Catalonia Adventures also has a mountaineering school which offers courses in climbing, orienteering and alpine adventure sports. The range of activities on offer make it a good option for families and those who enjoy the thrill of adventure sports.

La Rambla 41, pral
Ciutat Vella
🚇 *Liceu*
Map p.402 B4 🔢

Federació d'Entitats Excursionista de Catalunya (FEEC)
93 412 07 77 | www.feec.org

Organising hiking, camping, climbing, caving trips and more, the FEEC is an essential point of reference for information on trails and excursions. On their website, they list all of the hiking trails that you can follow. The trails are divided into three different colour-coded categories: *senders locals* (marked by green signs), *senders de petit recorregut* (short trails between five and 50km long, marked by yellow signs), and *senders de gran recorregut* (long trails between 50km and 500km long, marked by red signs). The most popular trails, and those for which the FEEC organise group excursions, are marked in bold. For each trail the inscription and trip prices vary, so it's best to contact them directly for trip specific information.

Various locations

Follow the Baldie
617 039 956 | www.followthebaldie.com

Follow the Baldie is a small local company that offers one-day hikes around off-the-beaten-track corners of Catalonia, avoiding tourist hot spots. The experienced 'baldie' is a fountain of knowledge on local culture, biodiversity and celebrations, and speaks English, Dutch and Spanish. Most excursions include a visit to a local bar or restaurant, an isolated castle, a hidden cave or traditional village fiesta. Exploring the beauty of the region seems to be as much a priority as eating a good lunch, and the local farmhouse or village cuisine is tasty and generously served. Given that the 'baldie' is often away on excursions (and without mobile network coverage), the easiest way to contact him is by posting a message on the website.

Online only

Viatge Addictes
www.viatgeaddictes.com

Viatge Addictes (travel addicts) works in conjunction with the Generalitat to provide detailed information on all of the various hiking routes in each part of Catalonia. Purely an information point and not a travel agent as such, you can not book your excursion through Viatge Addictes. Instead, for each route they provide you with contact details of local tourism offices and mountain refuges. For those who want to organise their own excursion, it is a useful source.

Hockey

Hockey is popular in Spain. Catalonia is a leader of the national hockey scene, and boasts a fair number of grass hockey clubs. Most of these also play hockey *sala* (indoor, seven-a-side hockey). Clubs are usually members-only, rather than 'turn up and play'. Hockey clubs tend to be affiliated to tennis, polo and football clubs, and, occasionally, local sports centres have hockey pitches, or all-weather pitches that can be used for hockey. For further information on clubs, beside those listed below, see www.fchockey.org (Federació Catalana de Hockey).

Cta Castellar
Terrassa

Atlètic Terrassa Hockey Club
93 787 03 51 | www.athc.cat

While this club also has racquet sport facilities, hockey is the main focus. There are numerous teams fro men and women all playing in different divisions. This club takes hockey extremely seriously, achieving outstanding results and upholding an unshakeable reputation. There are also youth teams for all ages, even for children aged 6 and 7. Training times are staggered for the different divisions, so if you are interested in joining a team, contact the club for information on whether you can attend a training session or team trials. Oh, and brush up on your Catalan – you'll need it.

219

Catalònia Hoquei Club

Parc Migdia
Passeig Olimpic, 4
Montjuïc
Poble Sec
Map p.399 F3 **64**

93 426 38 58 | www.cataloniahoqueiclub.com

This is a grass hockey club that plays at the municipal sports centre Pau Negre on Montjuïc. The club has men's and youth 15 a side teams that play on astroturf pitches as well as seven-a-side indoor hockey teams (*sala*). Training sessions for young players are on Mondays from 18:00 to 19:00 and Fridays from 18:00 to 19:30. For adults there are no casual training sessions; practice is for team players only. But if you would like to join the adult team and sign up for the new hockey season in September, send them an email with details of whether you have played previously and, if so, at what level.

Reial Club de Polo de Barcelona

Av Doctor Marañon
17-31
Les Corts
Zona Universitària
Map p.383 D4 **65**

93 448 04 00 | www.rcpolo.com

The Barcelona Polo Club has a reputation for producing some of the region's finest hockey players. Teaching standards are excellent, as are the facilities. The hockey school boasts over 300 pupils, and there are girls' and boys' teams for youngsters aged 7 to 18. It costs €610 to join for the season, which covers lessons, competition entries and the complete team kit (shirt, shorts and socks). Training sessions are held daily from Monday to Saturday, 18:00 to 20:00, organised by age category. To join the adult men's and women's teams, contact Ana Mari.

Horse Riding

Other options **Polo** p.232

Horse riding in Spain is immediately associated with Andalusia, conjuring up vivid images of Carmen, flamenco and beautiful white stallions. While Andalusia is home to some of the finest pure breed horses and riding schools, Catalonia mustn't be overlooked. Equestrian activities are hugely popular here, hence the exhaustive number of riding clubs and schools. Federació Catalana de Hípica (www.fchipica.org) can help you to locate all of them. Group riding classes usually cost between €15 and €25 per person, whereas private classes can set you back as much as €50 per hour. Exploring Catalonia on horseback is a great way to make the most of the region's natural beauty, and to get fit.

Escola Municipal d'Hipica La Foixarda

Av Montanyans, 14-16
Montjuïc
Espanya
Map p.399 F1 **66**

93 426 10 66

This is the only riding school in Barcelona itself. Despite being central, the Escola Municipal d'Hipica is set in surprisingly green grounds, high up on Montjuic, with stunning views of the city. The school's facilities include three equestrian jump circuits, one outdoor course, an indoor arena and a riding school open to all ages and abilities. Classes in show jumping, dressage and general schooling are available, starting from €15 per hour for group lessons. The school itself doesn't have a website, but you can find out more information by phone or through www.picornell.com.

Hipiclub Internacional

Cta Barcelona a
Santan Creu a Calafell
Gava

93 662 10 62 | www.hipiclub.com

Hipiclub Internacional has been providing training and holding competitions since it first opened in 1960. The 15 hectare grounds border Garraf National Park, a short drive from Barcelona. The centre has two outdoor arenas, one beginners' outdoor area and an 80m by 100m show jumping circuit. Pupils participate in regular excursions into the surrounding countryside and classes are open to all ages (adult classes from €20 per hour). The club is open to the public and there is no membership or joining fee. An outdoor pool and ping-pong table are also available and there is a play area for children.

Various locations

Natural Hípic

609 438 080 | www.naturalhipic.com

Natural Hípic's Three Breeze Ranch could be straight out of a wild west movie. The equestrian centre specialises in horse breaking and western-style mounting, incorporating complex horsemanship, reining techniques, trail, pole bending and barrel racing. Building trust and communicating with the horses is crucial. Some courses are taught in groups only, while others are two-day affairs. All courses vary in price depending on the duration and chosen training method. If you have experience in horse riding and want to try something wild and adventurous, get in touch.

Camí de Vallvidrera
Sarrià-Sant Gervasi

Poni Club Catalunya

93 371 63 64 | www.poniclubcatalunya.com

This riding school is particularly suitable for children, as pony and horse riding classes are available for 3 year olds upwards. It is a popular venue for birthday parties and school visits. The Petita Escola de Ponis (Little Pony School) incorporates pony paddocks, boxes and over 20 Shetland ponies that were introduced into the school for the 3 to 6 year olds. Classes are aimed at adults as well and cater to all levels: group classes cost €90 per month with one class a week, and private classes cost between €35 and €45 each depending on the pupil's level. If none of that appeals, *equinoterapia* (roughly translated as equinetherapy) is an interesting alternative.

Ice Skating

Ice skating rinks (*pista de hielo/pista de gel*) are not a common sight in Barcelona. Although around Christmas time, when decorations are up in full glory, many of the shopping malls install rinks. La Maquinista shopping centre (902 248 842, www.lamaquinista.com) houses the biggest outdoor ice rink in winter. The indoor ice rink at Pedralbes Centre (93 410 68 21, www.pedralbescentre.com) is smaller and more geared to children. The only permanent ice rink of note is Skating Club (93 245 28 00, Roger de Flor 168, www.skatingclub.cat) in Eixample. It is open all year round and is a good venue for children's birthday parties (minimum 10 children). But the best feature is the school: children's courses are given in ice skating and ice hockey, following the ISIA (Ice Skating Institute of America) training method. It is hard to find centres that provide training in the Olympic sport of curling, but Skating Club does so, with a seal of approval from the World Curling Federation.

Kayaking

Other options **Canoeing** p.204

Inland kayaking (*piragüismo/piragüisme*) on rivers and lakes and coastal kayaking are both possible in Catalonia. Most rafting companies and water sports clubs offer one or the other. River kayaking is particularly popular along the Noguera Pallaresa rapids near Lleida. On average, a half-day excursion should cost between €35 and €45, depending on the distance covered and the level of difficulty. Kayaking Costa Brava (97 277 38 06, www.kayakingcb.com) run half-day excursions that leave from Cala Montgó, near L'Escala. They last four hours and cost €45 per person. Full day excursions (€51) leave from Cap de Creus.

Cercle d'Aventura (90 217 05 93, www.cercleaventura.com) based in Puigcerdà, Cardedeu and Blanes, organise wakeboarding, sailing and half-day coastal kayaking trips (€40) as well as snow sports in the winter. If you would rather kayak in the Pyrenees mountains, contact Berguedà Nautic (617 698 984).

221

Near Barcelona, Canal Olímpic de Catalunya (93 664 57 73, www.canalolimpic.com) is an Olympic-standard water sports centre in Castelldefels offering kayaking classes (€38 for one-hour), beginners' courses and competitive team and club training. However, if you are already experienced and are simply looking to join a club, contact Kayak Club Premià de Mar (625 538 714, www.kayakbarcelona.com) as they organise regular excursions, including kayak surfing.

Kids Activities

Barcelona is one giant playground for children and teenagers, not only because of the sea and the mountains, but also because of the numerous clubs and teams in each area. Most sports centres have a range of clubs, with swimming and football being the most popular. In summer months, the most popular way for kids to burn some excess energy is at the beach or local outdoor swimming pool. Below are indications of some fun family activities for full-day outings. Check entertainment guides such as El Guía del Ocio (www.guiadelocio.com) and the Ajuntament's website (www.bcn.es) on a regular basis for upcoming children's activities. Barcelona Turisme (www.barcelonaturisme.com) is also a useful source of information.

Camí de la Riera, s/n
Santa Susanna

Activ Natura Adventure Park
93 769 53 24 | www.activ-natura.com

This outdoor adventure park is ideal for family outings, children's birthdays and school trips, because there are distractions for all ages. 'Adventure in the forest' involves exploring the woodland on nets, cables, zip wires and rope bridges, and starts from €10 per person. Other activities include the challenging high rope course (€35 per person) and the 'pamper pole', both sure to get the heart pumping. Mountain biking circuits, quad bikes and archery are also available and there is a picnic area too. Activ Natura is situated about 50 minutes from Barcelona by car, in the direction of Girona; contact the park for directions.

Finca les
Basses-Albinyana
Tarragona

Aqualeon
97 768 76 56 | www.aqualand.es

Aqualeon (water-lion) combines water park attractions with safari adventure. Free buses regularly tour the safari section of the theme park, but you can visit at your own pace by car. Lions, zebras and Siberian tigers can be spotted. The animals have, in many cases, been brought in from Africa. Throughout the day, there are shows such as 'reptile encounter' and 'exotic birds'. Entrance fees of €18.50 for adults, €16.50 for senior citizens and €13.50 for children include access to the water park, which has a selection of exciting and sometimes hair-raising water slides. 'Black hole', 'kamikaze' and 'rapids' are particularly popular. The park is open from June 16 to September 11. It is best to avoid the manically busy July and August weekends.

Climbing frame near Maremagnum

**Moll d'Espanya del
Port Vell**
Port Vell
🚇 *Drassanes*
Map p.409 D3 56

L'Aquarium de Barcelona

93 221 74 74 | www.aquariumbcn.com

The aquarium has been one of the city's key family highlights since it opened in 1995. With 35 tanks and some 450 marine species, there is plenty to keep kids entertained for an afternoon. In summer, children's activities such as 'sleeping with sharks' are held, where kids can sleep-over and watch the beasts all night. All activities are geared for 8 to 12 year olds and vary in cost depending on the nature and length of activity. Entrance fees cost €16 for adults, €11 for children and €12.50 for seniors, and the centre is open every day of the year from 09:30 to 21:30, 23:00 in July and August.

Tarragona

Port Aventura

www.portaventura.es

One of the most renowned theme parks in the country, Port Aventura is a must-see for many families. Well-serviced transport wise, Renfe trains run from Barcelona Sants-Estació or Passeig de Gràcia, taking about one hour and 20 minutes, and buses also run from Sants-Estació directly to the park. Attractions are divided into five themed areas; China, Far West, Mediterrània, México and Polynesia; each with hair-raising rides such as the much-feared Dragon Khan. For those with young children, there are various kids' rides and gentle water slides. A one-day pass to the theme park allows access to all of the attractions: adult pass €39, junior (4-10 years old) and senior pass €31. Children under the age of 3 qualify for free entry.

Language Schools

Other options **Learning Catalan** p.128

Arriving in a foreign city and not understanding the language can be a nerve-wracking experience. Luckily, Barcelona is full of language schools. Consult the Spanish language courses directory – www.europa-pages.com/spain – for details of those in Barcelona. If you are looking for private classes, conversation groups or a tandem exchange pal, community centres and the language faculty noticeboards in universities make good starting points. Private classes usually cost between €15 and €20 per hour. Teachers and students also post personal ads on the Loquo community site – www.loquo.com.

Pg de Gràcia, 51
Eixample
🚇 *Passeig de Gràcia*
Map p.393 E3 74

Barcelona Escuela de Estudios Internacionales (BEEI)

93 394 46 60 | www.beei.es

BEEI is a British Council certified school right in the heart of the city centre. The school gives classes in over 10 different languages, including Spanish and Catalan. For private and intensive courses, pupils propose a timetable and the school finds a teacher to fit your schedule as closely as possible. Intensive Spanish group courses (€125) comprise 20 hours of teaching per week from 09:30 to 13:30 every day. BEEI has a cosy feel and teachers are friendly, but it does lack a café or communal social area.

**Agustí Durán i
Sanpere, 2**
Raval
🚇 *Liceu*
Map p.402 B2 75

Barcelona Lingua

93 329 22 04 | www.barcelona-lingua.com

Barcelona Lingua is just off La Rambla and offers competitive prices for 20 hour intensive Spanish courses. Two weeks of classes cost €195 and the four week programme costs €360. The school lends out tennis rackets, footballs and volleyballs should you want to head down to the beach. The main advantages of Barcelona Lingua are the reasonable course fees and the school's central location.

223

Centre per a la Normalització de Lingüística

C/ Quintana, 11
Ciutat Vella
🚇 *Plaça Catalunya*
Map p.402 C4 76

93 412 72 24

Most foreigners who come to work, study or live in Barcelona choose to learn Spanish over Catalan. It is understandable given that Spanish is the third most spoken language in the world. However, as part of the Generalitat's initiative to preserve local Catalan language and traditions, this centre gives low-cost Catalan classes to foreigners and Spaniards. Just to make sure there is no excuse for not learning Catalan, level one is free.

International House Barcelona

C/ Trafalgar, 14
Born
🚇 *Urquinaona*
Map p.403 F1 77

93 268 45 11 | www.ihspain.com

In addition to Spanish language courses, this prominent school hosts a number of social events usually centering around the pub quiz held at the bar on Friday nights. The school is particularly popular with professionals who need to learn Spanish quickly and efficiently. Courses include business Spanish and Spanish immersion (a five day course consisting of 30 hours of private tuition and business lunches). Overall, teaching standards are high, but so are course prices. The intensive Spanish course costs €190 for 20 hours of classes per week and €760 for four weeks. If you're looking for a language course with a little more prestige, International House is for you.

Kingsbrook

Trav de Gràcia, 60
Gràcia
🚇 *Fontana*
Map p.393 D1 78

93 209 37 63 | www.kingsbrookbcn.com

Kingsbrook Spanish Academy is a well-established, Cervantes Institute-accredited school, which has been in business since 1985. As well as offering top-notch Spanish courses, the school runs work placements and study abroad programs. Over 13 different languages are taught including Russian, Catalan, Japanese, Swedish and German. Spanish courses run on a four-week basis and are good value for money given the superior standard of teaching; intensive courses (20 hours per week) cost €465 for four weeks.

L'Escola Oficial d'Idiomes Drassanes

C/ Arc del Teatre, 24
Raval
🚇 *Drassanes*
Map p.408 B1 79

93 329 24 58

This language school offers the cheapest classes in the city but expect long queues at the start of term. A lottery system is in place for sitting the exam; take a ticket to see if you win a place for that day. It is worth the wait though as standards are high, courses are reasonable and the school has a lively buzz to it. Spanish, Catalan, English, French, Japanese, Russian, Chinese, German, Italian and Portuguese classes are all up for grabs. Places go quickly.

Libraries

Other options **Books** p.280, **Second-Hand Items** p.300

There are hundreds of public libraries in Barcelona, but you need to be a member to borrow books. Non-members are free to use books on a reference-only basis. For general information on your nearest public library, you can find contact details on the Ajuntament's website (www.bcn.cat/biblioteques). Some of the municipal libraries are very small and specialise in certain subjects, such as the Fundació Tàpies library (www.fundaciotapies.org), where the emphasis is on modern and contemporary art. For statistical or administrative information on the city, the Biblioteca General de l'Ajuntament (93 402 74 68, www.bcn.cat/bibliotecageneral) is useful. A good alternative, however, is to use the university libraries. For non-university members, books are for reference only. See the Universitat de Barcelona (www.ub.es/biblioteques) website for information on their various libraries. On a general note, you will find that most libraries use an online catalogue, through which you can search for and reserve books.

C/ de Hospital, 56
Raval
🚇 *Liceu*
Map p.402 B3 80

Biblioteca de Catalunya

93 470 23 00 | www.bnc.es

Located in the heart of Ciutat Vella, just off La Rambla, Biblioteca de Catalunya stocks one of the largest collections of books in the city. Housed in a beautiful 15th century building that was previously the Hospital de Santa Creu de Barcelona, it was converted into a library in 1931. Ask one of the assistants to explain the sometimes daunting shelving system, and to help you find the appropriate section. It is open from Monday to Friday 09:00 to 20:00 and Saturday from 09:00 to 14:00. Loan times on books vary, but the standard borrowing period is 15 days, which can be prolonged for an extra 15 days on demand.

Raval Library

C/ de l'Arc del
Teatre, 24
Raval
🚇 *Drassanes*
Map p.408 B1 81

Biblioteca de l'Escola Oficial d'Idiomes Barcelona

93 329 24 58

This library is small but extremely useful for those struggling to get to grips with their Spanish or Catalan. Located in the city's official language school, you have access to books in over 15 different languages including Japanese, Russian and Arabic. There are also video and audio tapes available for use within the school. Staff are usually helpful and will explain how to use the individual video and audio stations. The biggest advantage of attending this library is the direct contact with Catalans and Spanish-speakers from different parts of the world, who are often looking for language exchange partners. Books are great, but practice makes perfect.

C/ del Portal
de Santa Madrona,
6-8
Sant Antoni
🚇 *Paral·lel*
Map p.408 B1 82

Biblioteca de la Filmoteca de Catalunya

93 316 27 80 | http://cultura.gencat.net/filmo/filmo3.htm

For film and documentary boffins, the Filmoteca is paradise. No matter how obscure, old, alternative or anti-Hollywood the film may be, Filmoteca will probably have it. It is a hugely popular hangout with film and documentary students, not to mention passionate cinema-goers. There are regular film screenings and festivals and the fact that Filmoteca has a reference library is a little-known secret. Books are available for reference only but films, audios, video tapes and DVDs can be taken out on loan. Contact the library directly to find out current Filmoteca loyalty and membership benefits.

Martial Arts

There are many martial arts disciplines available in Barcelona and it can be overwhelming deciding which one to follow. It's best to attend a trial class, something that is offered by most schools. Taekwondo, ju-jitsu, karate, kickboxing, judo, aikido, hapkido, jeet kune do (a variation of kung fu) and kung fu are the most common choices. Some centres specialise in one discipline, while others offer a whole range. Many local gyms, sports centres, health clubs and community centres offer classes too. Martial arts that focus more on self-defence than combat, such as

225

hapkido, are particularly popular with women. But these sports also relieve stress, increase flexibility and improve balance. Useful organisations include the Federació d'Arts Marcials de Catalunya (93 533 11 11), the Federació Catalana de Karate (www.fckarate.com) and the Federació Taekwondo de Catalunya (www.taekwondocatala.com).

The Barcelona Martial Arts Academy

Various locations

www.bma-academy.com

Inspired by the agility of Bruce Lee, jeet kune do is one of the main martial art disciplines taught here. Even though its bases are drawn from the art of kung fu, jeet kune do introduces other combat disciplines such as boxing. Jun fan gung fu (kung fu) is the other major martial art taught. The school does not have a physical space, instead the academy professors teach in various schools, gyms and sports centres around Barcelona. Kali, silat, ken kyu do and tai chi chuan are also taught. Have a look on their website to see where they give classes near you.

Club Bushido

C/ d'Emili Roca, 18-22
Nou Barris
🚇 *Fabra i Puig*
Map p.388 A4 83

93 351 00 01 | www.clubbushido.com

Club Bushido is a school that also holds local and regional competitions. It is one of the best in Barcelona, and has a reputation for high teaching standards. The school specialises in the karate discipline wado ryu; a form of karate that demands a more upright and natural body position. Club Bushido opens during the working week from 17:00 to 21:00.

Club-Gimnàs Judo Condal

C/ Consell
de Cent, 44
Sants-Montjuïc
🚇 *Tarragona*
Map p.392 A4 84

93 325 49 34 | www.judo-condal.org

Judo Condal has been running since 1967 and focuses purely on judo. Classes for adults, youths and children are held every Monday, Wednesday and Friday evening between 18:00 and 21:00. On Tuesdays and Thursdays the club holds general fitness and dance classes. From the outside, the school looks deceptively small but inside the two judo rooms – one for recreational use and one for competitions – and the weights room, are more than adequate.

Escola Budo Sensei

C/ Melcior
de Palau, 119
Sants
🚇 *Plaça del Centre*
Map p.391 F2 85

93 490 62 09 | www.budosensei.net

Budo Sensei is well-known on the Barcelona martial arts scene. Running since 1976, the school now has over 30 years of experience teaching judo, ju-jitsu, taekwondo and tai chi chuan. Separate classes in each of these disciplines (except tai chi chuan) are tailored for adults and children. For the more advanced students there are competitive training sessions. Classes run all year (except August) and are reasonably priced: €44 monthly for a minimum of three hours of classes per week (you can participate in as many as you like), including the joining fee.

Mugendo Kickboxing

C/ d'Alfons XII, 92
Sarrià-Sant Gervasi
🚇 *Sant Gervasi (FGC)*
Map p.384 E4 86

93 209 45 25 | www.mugenryu.com

This school only teaches mugendo, which is a mix of karate, boxing and self-defence. There are classes to suit all levels and paces and if you want to improve rapidly, sign up for individual classes. Mugendo has three schools in the centre of Barcelona – Sarrià, Bonanova and Molina – and several more in the outskirts, for example Gava and Viladecans. Classes are held every evening from 17:00 to 22:00; morning classes run on Tuesday, Thursday and Saturday. Prices start from €80 monthly for two classes per week, but before signing up call to get a free trial.

*C/ Carreras
i Candi, 40*
Sants
🔵 *Badal*
Map p.391 D2 88

Won's Barcelona

93 533 11 11 | www.telefonica.net/web2/wonsbarcelona/default.htm

Some of the ex-pupils here have gone on to become regional, national and international champions of taekwondo and kickboxing. It is an excellent place to learn, as the atmosphere is diligent, yet laid back. The school is open from 16:00 to 22:00 Monday to Friday, during which classes are taught in taekwondo, kickboxing, jeet kune do and hapkido. The latter is a Korean martial art form that is a cross between taekwondo and self-defence and is not commonly taught here. For classes starting in September, sign up before August and the inscription fee (€40) is free. Monthly membership starts from €40.

Mother & Toddler Activities

It isn't easy to find English-speaking mother and toddler groups in Barcelona, which is why there is a certain solidarity among foreign resident mums. Groups also provide an outlet for mums to vent frustrations on the Spanish birthing system, which has a tendency to favour caesarean methods over natural birth. Hospitals do not use TEN machines either during labour, as they do in other western countries. You can hire these pain-relieving machines from the Born-based shop Mujer (93 315 15 31, Carders 28). Other mothers find the additional support of a *doula* reassuring both during and after labour. Meaning 'mother who serves the mother' in Greek, a *doula* provides emotional and practical support to a woman (or couple) in all stages of childbirth. Contact Manuela Garcia (627 994 328) at Doulas BCN for more information. See also p.111 of this book for more on giving birth.

Aside from the groups listed below, many creches encourage parental participation in toddlers' activities, so it's worth finding the nearest one to you (see nurseries and Pre-School, p.123). El Cigaronet d'Or (93 246 94 63, www.cigronetdor.com) is a cheerful and relaxed place that keeps children entertained, charging just €5 per hour. Also, the Fira Allada Vermell artisan market (Saturdays from 10:00 to 21:00) hosts drama and games for children once a month. Pop down to find out when the next performances are taking place. Finally, if it's you that needs entertainment rather than your baby, Tender Loving Canguros (647 605 989, www.tlcanguros.com) is an invaluable contact for English, Spanish and Catalan speaking babysitters. See p.97 for more.

Various locations

Baby Rock English

653 924 542 | www.babyrockenglish.com

Run by international mums, this group organises music and movement workshops in English, for parents with toddlers aged 1 to 4 years old. Activities and games in the workshops include painting, action songs, cooking and drawing, emphasising the importance of parental involvement. At the Baby Rock centre, one trimester of classes (10 sessions each, one hour long) costs €180 or you can opt for the taster course of three sessions for €75. Baby Rock also organises groups sessions in private homes, community centres and schools.

C/ Carders, 28
Born
🔵 *Jaume I*
Map p.403 F3 90

Babyboogieloo

93 315 15 31 | loumelotte@hotmail.co.uk

From her funky babywear shop in the Born – Mujer – Lulu runs mother and baby groups. She has created a 'chill out' space upstairs, open all day, where mothers can relax, breastfeed and meet other mums while the toddlers play. Babyboogieloo 'mums and tots' classes will start from September and are split into two groups: sing and sign, happy clapping for naught to one year olds and action songs for the one to threes. Classes last around 40 minutes and cost €5 per mum. Organisations are invited to speak on a range of issues, such as natural birth, in monthly talks.

Baby massage classes will be starting soon. To find out more contact Lulu; she is a walking encyclopedia of information on childbirth and can help you with any queries you have.

Various locations

BCN Tots
bcntots@hotmail.com / BCNTots@groups.msn.com

BCN Tots is a large support network organising baby and toddler activities so parents can meet on a regular basis. The group often gathers in the city's parks and swimming pools or on out-of-town excursions. One of the most popular meeting points is Parc Ciutadella. The group is English-speaking, but is open to families of all nationalities. Parents regularly contact each other through the BCN Tots forum, an extremely useful portal through which parents share ideas and advice on issues such as where to find a good dentist or where to buy the best cots. Email the group to find out when and where its next meeting is.

C/ Mozart, 10
Gràcia
🚇 Diagonal
Map p.393 F2 92

The Playhouse
66 146 94 19 | www.theplayhousebcn.net

The Playhouse is a bilingual daycare centre (English-Catalan) for children aged 1 to 3 years old. The school's highly trained staff are of both English and Catalan origin, which exposes the children to bilingualism from a young age. Children can stay at the daycare centre from 09:00 until after their lunch (all meals are organic), and will participate in a number of games and activities. Every Saturday morning from 10:00 to 12:00, the Playhouse runs a 'jack in the box' playgroup for 4 to 11 year olds. All activities are in English and to take part it costs €60 per month, per child.

Motorsports

Catalans love motor sports, as evidenced by the number of professional racing drivers the region produces. The Centre d'Alt Rendiment (CAR) in Sant Cugat is where the most promising talents from across Spain receive specialised training, in the hope that one day they will reach the Circuit de Catalunya (www.circuitcat.com). The prestigious circuit in Montmeló hosts World Motorcycling and Automobile Championships and Formula One races.

On a non-professional level, motorcycling is incredibly popular – the city has the highest number of motorcycles per inhabitant in Europe – and it is common to see groups of bikers travelling up and down the coast. It is worth planning road trips between April and October, when the weather is milder and there is less rainfall. The Federació Catalana de Motociclisme (93 217 55 01, www.fcm.cat) has information on motorcycling regulations and listings of all of the clubs in the region. For general car and motocycle information though, the RACC Automóvil Club (www.racc.es) is the most useful source.

Circuit de Catalunya
Montmeló

Barcelona Driving
www.barcelonadriving.com

Ferrari, Porsche, Lamborghini, F1-V10: there are scores of sexy cars on offer. It is a dream come true for Formula One fans or James Bond wannabies, as they race around the championship Circuit de Catalunya. Professional instructors take you round the track on a trial round (*bautizo*) before you're set free on your own. Prices vary according to the number of laps you do. In a Formula One V10 prices range from €2,145 (three laps) to €4,229 (10 laps). For Ferrari F430 and Aston Martin DB9 prices start at €369 for five laps. The most efficient way to contact them is through their website.

228

GoldWing Club Catalunya (GWCC)

C/ d'Arenys, 55
Vall d'Hebron
🚇 *Vall d'Hebron*
Map p.386 A1 94

www.gwcc.net

This motorcycling club organises regular excursions, often including additional sporting activities or entertainment. Skydiving is a particularly popular choice, especially as the club wangles discounted group prices. To become a member there is one condition though: you have to drive a GoldWing motorbike or similar model. And when you first sign up, you have to pay two years' membership (€60 per year) up front. Pop along to one of their weekly meetings, held in Vila Olímpica (Salvador Esríu 23), to find out more. Don't forget to brush up on your Spanish or Catalan before you go.

Penya Motorista Barcelona (PMB)

C/ Trav de Les
Corts, 63
Les Corts
🚇 *Collblanc*
Map p.391 D1 97

93 330 78 22 | www.pmbarcelona.com

Penya Motorista is a Barcelona-based club that consists of, and is supported by, a stalwart community of motorcycle and automobile aficionados who regularly meet for one or two day excursions, competitions, rallies and social events such as *calçotadas*. It is at this club that the '24 hours around Montjuïc' was first initiated in 1955; the endurance race continues to be held every year. Annual membership costs €28, with a sign up fee of €28 in the first year.

RACC Automóvil Club

C/ Diagonal, 687
Les Corts
🚇 *Zona*
Universitària
Map p.382 C3 96

93 495 50 35 | www.racc.es

The RACC is the official Catalan automobile organisation that deals with everything from driving regulations and schools for learners to insurance policies and rally competitions. It is the organisation to contact for the latest on all things automobile, motorcycle and scooter related. Information on the World Rally Championships and the yearly calendar for rallies around the world are available through the RACC at www.rallycatalunya.com. Members receive benefits such as roadside assistance and reduced insurance costs for an annual fee of €132.30.

Mountain Biking

Other options **Cycling** p.34

Mountain biking or BTT (*bicicleta todo terreno*) as it is known in Spain, is a thriving activity, and fans have the Pyrenees mountain range, numerous national parks and beautiful coastal routes to explore. Popular cycling spots near Barcelona include El Montseny, Collserola and Ribera d'Ebre. Most adventure companies that organise rafting, climbing and other activities also offer mountain biking excursions, ranging from half-day taster tours to four-day breaks. Catalonia Adventures (www.cataloniaadventures.com) are a highly recommended adventure company that organise trips for groups of four people and above, for all abilities. If, however, you are a serious mountain biker looking to join a club, then www.solobtt.com is an extremely useful website, with information on national competitions, regular excursions (*marchas*), courses, clubs and mountain biking federations. Amigos del Ciclismo (www.amigosdelciclismo.com) provides route maps with explanations of levels of difficulty, and www.cicloide.com offers a general overview of 541 mountain trails in Catalonia.

A Golpe de Pedal

Various locations

www.agolpedepedal.com

This group of experienced mountain bikers goes on regular excursions. Details of their outings, giving map, distance and price information are clearly marked on their website, along with full contact details. Excursions take place in Aragón and

229

Catalonia, with the majority in Barcelona, Lleida, Girona, and occasionally Huesca. Excursions cost an average of €18, never exceeding €30, and cover distances up to 40km. If you're something of an adrenaline junkie and would like to get involved, drop them an email.

C/ Numància, 73
Les Corts
🚇 **Sants Estació**
Map p.392 A2 `98`

Open Natura

646 962 121 | www.opennatura.com

Open Natura is a centrally-based mountain biking club that organises regular weekend excursions around Catalonia for all ages and abilities. There are children's circuits (*circuit infantil*), intermediate circuits (*circuit intermig*, suitable for teenagers and adults who don't want to push themselves too hard), and long circuits (*circuit llarg*). Excursions cost between €14.50 and €21 depending on whether you are a member of the club and the Catalan Cycling Federation (Federació Catalana de Ciclisme, www.ciclisme.cat). If you plan to participate regularly, paying the annual membership fee of €14 could save you money. You're also entitled to discounted prices in bike shops, sports stores, ski resorts and hotels.

Andorra

Vall Nord-Andorra

+37 687 80 00 | www.vallnord.com

Vall Nord–Andorra is a mountain park in the Pyrenees offering biking, hiking, climbing, archery and off-road challenges. The park's most distinguishing features are the freestyle snow park and the internationally-recognised bike park (www.vallnordbikepark.com). Hosting the Mountain Bike World Cup in 2008, the park comes with cross country and downhill circuits and bike trail areas. In summer, one-day lift passes cost €25 for adults and €20 for children. They cost substantially less in the winter season (which runs until the end of April). One hour mountain biking classes cost €24 each in a group of one to five people and €36 in a group of up to 10 people. It's best to bring your own bikes if possible, as bike hire is pretty steep. Specialist 'four cross' mountain bikes cost €25 for a day and free ride bikes cost €50.

Music Lessons

Other options **Dance Classes** p.211, **Music, DVDs & Videos** p.297

Music is everywhere in Barcelona. With the highest number of public holidays in Europe, you can always find a free concert somewhere in the city. Percussion lessons are available in most community centres and many run musical interpretation classes, which are basically free-for-all jamming sessions where you bring along whichever instrument you play. If you're looking for one-on-one classes, personal ads offering private music lessons are posted on the Loquo community website (www.loquo.com). Other good sources of tutors for private lessons are noticeboards in the music faculties of the various universities and in community centres. For professional training, www.aprendemas.com and www.emagister.com provide general information on degree courses.

Edifici L'Auditori
C/ de Padilla, 155
Eixample
🚇 **Monumental**
Map p.405 E1 `100`

Escola Superior de Música de Catalunya

93 352 30 11 | www.esmuc.net

This prestigious music school in L'Auditori, is for those looking to gain a professional music qualification. The school is reputed to have excellent teaching standards. The academic year runs from mid-September to mid-June and courses are given in jazz, modern, classical, contemporary and traditional music. The rigorous application process includes a 30 minute recital. Teachers and students are of native and foreign origin, creating a melting pot of international talent.

Taller de Músics

Requesens, 5
Raval
⊞ Sant Antoni
Map p.401 F2 **101**

93 329 56 67 | www.tallerdemusics.com

Taller de Músics focuses purely on jazz, Latin and flamenco music. A member of the International Association of Schools of Jazz, this Raval-based institution has been teaching young musicians for years. Open to all levels, from beginners to postgraduates, the school offers individual and group classes in brass, string and wind instruments and piano. Classes run for three months at a time, with one 50 minute class per week. Individual classes cost €520; group classes cost €285. There are discounts available if you choose to study a second instrument or a theory class. And join the big band or marching band (marching band) if you want to put theory into practice.

Paintballing

Paintballing involves firing balls of paint at friends, siblings, work colleagues or complete strangers. It is an invigorating way of relieving stress, hilarious fun and appeals to all ages. Paintballing is good for any celebration that calls for childlike tomfoolery. Most centres are on the outskirts of the city or further afield, so make sure you check the location before booking with a company that claims to be 'in Barcelona'.

Anoia Paintball

C/ Igualada
Gràcia
⊞ Diagonal
Map p.393 F2 **102**

655 877 914 | www.anoiapaintball.com

This company near Igualada specialises in stag and hen celebrations (*despedidas de soltera / soltero*). Paintball groups participate in all day activities, followed by a celebratory dinner and entertainment of your choice in the form of clowns, cabaret singers, go-go dancers or, as stated matter-of-factly on their website, 'sexy boys and girls'. Contact the company directly for information on package prices.

Barcelona Paintballing

C/ Sant Cristofol, 8
La Palma de Cervelló
Baix Llobregat

607 860 458 | www.barcelonapaintball.es

Set in large grounds 15km from Barcelona in Baix Llobregat, this company has the necessary space to manage groups of up to 100 people. The basic package costs €27, comprising camouflage equipment, insurance and 100 paint balls. 100 balls run out quickly, so you'll probably have to fork out for extra (€7 per 100). When hunger pangs kick in, there is a picnic area and the company can arrange catering for an additional cost. Directions in English are on the website.

Duaka Adventures

C/ Moragas i Barret,
38 -40
Pineda de Mar

617 024 145 | www.duaka.com/paintball

Paintballing is not the only activity organised by Duaka. If you want to make a day of it, you can also try quad biking, horse riding or kayaking after splattering each other. Although it is a little out of the way, the lower prices make it worthwhile for large groups (€22 for equipment, €6 for an extra 100 balls) and Duaka arrange transport to and from the site.

Photography

Perhaps because it is such an incredibly photogenic city, where avant-garde fashion, architecture and artwork catch the eye, Barcelona has become one of the most important European centres for photographic studies. The city is bursting with talented young snappers trying to get their break. There are hundreds of different photography courses in the city, ranging from trimester-long weekly courses at local community centres to two year, internationally recognised Masters. For photography equipment, ARPI (93 317 95 73, La Rambla 38-40) and Casanova (Pelayo 18 and 9 and Tallers 68, www.casanovafoto.com) are the most professional photography

231

stores, selling everything you could possibly need, including second-hand manual and digital cameras. Fotografia Barcelona (www.fotografiabarcelona.com) is a virtual community of photographers based in the city, where professionals post job offers and course information.

Institut d'Estudis Fotografics

C/ Comte d'Urgell, 187
Eixample
🚇 *Hospital Clínic*
Map p.392 C2 **105**

93 494 11 27 | www.iefc.cat

This photography school is a non-profit organisation, established to make photography studies more accessible. There are range of specialist courses available that run for three months, some with a fine arts slant, such as portait photography (*retrato*), fashion (*moda*) and nude portrait (*figura y desnudo*), while photojournalism (*fotoperiodismo*), social commentary and reportage (*reportage social*) and travel photography (*fotografía de viajes*) focus more on the journalistic aspects of snapping. The general photography course covers a wide range of subjects, including reportage and portrait, and lasts for the whole of the academic year.

Polo

Other options **Horse Riding** p.220

The origins of polo are thought to trace back to China and Persia, some 2,000 years ago. It was only in the 1850s that British tea planters first discovered the game in Manipur on the Burmese border with India.

Today, polo is played in over 70 countries. While polo clubs are more frequent in Andalusia and Madrid, the Reial Club de Polo de Barcelona hosts internationally acclaimed tournaments such as the Torneo Ciudad de Barcelona. The Real Federación Española de Polo (www.rfepolo.org) provides information on all of the major polo clubs throughout the country.

Club de Polo Sant Antoni de Viladrau

Cta de Vic, Cami de
la Sala 'Finca
Masvidal'
Viladrau

93 743 02 07 | www.santantonipoloclub.com

Set in the Montseny National Park, roughly one hour from Barcelona by car, the club is in an idyllic location. Lessons are held on weekends throughout the year and a summer school runs in July and August. The polo season runs from March to November and players of a six to 10 handicap can sign up as a team. For non-polo players, the club organises horse riding excursions into the surrounding countryside. This club is less famed than the Reial Club de Polo, but no less distinguished.

Reial Club de Polo de Barcelona

Av Doctor Marañon,
17-31
Les Corts
🚇 *Zona Universitària*
Map p.383 D4 **55**

93 448 04 00 | www.rcpolo.com

This prestigious and highly reputed club is often the first point of reference for polo enthusiasts arriving in Barcelona. The club was founded in 1897 and has been a pillar of world-class coaching ever since. The 1992 Olympics equestrian competition was held here, for which some of the club's older facilities were revamped. As a result, the grounds now house some of the most luxurious sporting facilities the city has to offer. Coaching standards are extremely high, and there are schools for horse riding (private classes cost €40 with use of a school pony) polo, paddle tennis, hockey and tennis.

Rafting

Rafting involves teamwork and is considered one of the 'softer' adventure sports (in comparison with diving or canyoning, for example). The best place to go rafting is the Noguera Pallaresa river near Lleida, known as '*Aguas Bravas*' (brave waters), because of the strong rapids. Considered one of the best rafting spots in Europe, the region boasts rapids ranging from level II to VI (the highest). The only downside is that most spots on the Noguera Pallaresa involve a two to three hour drive from Barcelona. Realistically, you need a car to get there, although if you take the train to Lleida some rafting companies will pick you up.

There are so many firms in the region offering this adrenaline-pumping experience, that it can be hard to choose which one to invest your money in. Some suggestions are listed below. Bear in mind that the season begins in March and runs until November, but the best time to go is normally in May and June, because the rivers are then at their fullest.

Boi Taüll Resort

C/ d'Amigó, 14-16
Sarrià-Sant Gervasi
🚇 **Hospital Clínic**
Map p.392 C1 **108**

90 240 66 40 | www.boitaullresort.com

This converts into a ski resort in the winter months, but during the summer hosts sailing, rafting, kayaking and hydrospeed. Rafting excursions last three hours and go 12km downriver. There is only one main rafting route available. However, excursions are open to children from 5 years old and the level of difficulty is not high, making it a good option for families. Be sure to ask about the baby raft option if you are with young children.

Rafting Llavorsí

Camí de Riberies
Llavorsi
Llieda

97 362 21 58 | www.raftingllavorsi.com

Despite the competition with other companies along the Noguera Pallaresa, Rafting Llavorsí has kept prices slightly high, but accommodation standards are good. Multi-activity weekends, combining half-day rafting (€34 per person) with other activities, are the most popular with guests. Bungee jumping (€25 per person) and Busbob (€46 per person), a bizarre cross between a raft and a banana boat, are alternatives. There is a wide range of accommodation available, including a hotel with a swimming pool, a hostel, camping site and self-catered apartments that sleep two to six people.

ROCROI

Pl Nostra Senyora
de Biuse, 8
Llieda

97 362 20 35 | www.rocroi.com

Trips range from five kilometre runs suitable for children (€18 per person) to 52km full-day excursions with lunch (€77 per person). The most common are the 16km rafting trips that cost between €38 and €45. The multi-activity offers are particularly worthwhile, as they combine rafting, caving and an activity of your choice – kayaking, *hidrospeed* or *topo-duo* (two-man kayak). *Hidrospeed* involves shooting down the river with the aid of flippers, while holding onto a large swimming aid or float. Year-round activities include climbing, paintballing, quad biking, trekking and horse riding.

Turisnat Pirineus

Pg de les Vernedes
s/n, Sort
Pirineu de Lieda

97 362 10 08 | www.turisnatpirineus.com

Turisnat Pirineus is a rural tourism and adventure resort on the Noguera Pallaresa. Guests rent out cottages for a reasonable €25 per night (€15 for children under 12), with breakfast, and can choose to take part in all of the activities offered at the resort (at an additional cost). The country cottages are equipped for up to 50 guests with rooms for two, four and six people. Rafting is one of the favourite activities among guests; half-day descents cost €40 per person and full-day descents with a picnic lunch cost €75. Special family holiday and weekend break packages are good value for money.

233

Roller Hockey

Roller hockey (*hockey patines* in Spanish and *hoquei patins* in Catalan) is rapidly gaining on traditional field hockey in terms of popularity. It is much like ice hockey (and can be just as boisterous). Catalonia – the region where the sport is most rigorously played and followed – is home to most Spanish roller hockey clubs. And these top-level teams, most notably FC Barcelona and Reus Deportiu Hockey, set the standard for the rest of Spain. In fact, roller hockey is so popular here that it was included in the Olympic Games programme for the first time in Barcelona in 1992, as a demonstration sport. If you want to give it a try, check out the Spanish Association for Roller Hockey Trainers (www.aeehp.com) as they list the principal clubs in Spain. Buscahockey.com is also a useful website. In terms of playing, FC Barcelona (93 496 36 00, www.fcbarcelona.com) has a number of professional men's teams competing in national and international leagues. Alternatively try one of the following, more low-key clubs: Sants-Montjuïc Club Hoquei Patins (93 491 05 49, santsmontjuic-@esportbarrio.com), Patí Hoquei Club Sant Cugat (www.phcsantcugat.com) or Club Patí Congrés (93 408 13 34, Carrer Portugal 1, Sant Andreu).

Rollerblading & Rollerskating

Other options **Parks** p.178, **Beaches** p.176

Rollerblading is becoming popular as a fun alternative to cycling. Every Friday night, hordes of rollerbladers take to the streets with the group 'Rollerbladers of Barcelona', and every day more people can be seen using blades as a means of transport. Unfortunately, rollerbladers are in a bureaucratic no-man's land: they are considered pedestrians, which mean that roads (apart from quiet streets) are off-limits; yet they can't use cycle lanes either, although the Rollerblading Association (APB www.patinar-bcn.org) is campaigning to change this. The boulevards of Diagonal and Passeig de Gràcia are ideal spots for pros and beginners alike, because of their broad promenades and smooth paving. For freeskate fans, http://fskportal.blogspot.com explains tricks using video demonstrations. If you want to put theory into practice, the skate park at Platja Marbella is a freeskate hot spot.

C/ Nàpols, 42
Poblenou
🚇 *Arc de Triomf*
Map p.404 C2 112

Escola Oficial de Patinatge

93 300 50 70 | www.escolapatinatge.com

This rollerblading school, located in L'Estació del Nord sports centre, gives competitively priced adult and children's classes. Roller hockey and dance classes are entertaining alternatives. All classes cost the same price: €12 per hour session or €35 for the month and blades and pads are included in the course fee. Adult classes are free with Patinadores de Barcelona (see next entry), so it is only worth forking out for paid classes if you want to learn quickly or your children want to learn, as they may struggle to keep up with the pace on rollerblading tours.

Various locations

Patinadores de Barcelona

www.patinar-bcn.org

Scores of rollerbladers of all ages and nationalities meet every Friday night to tour the city. The Friday routes are free and open to all abilities, starting from Baja Beach Club in Vila Olímpica at 22:30. Experienced rollerblading monitors lead the group on one of their seven different routes. Free beginners' classes run every Tuesday from 22:00 to 23:30 in Parc Clot (Metro Clot). Intermediate and advanced levels are free for all members who have paid the €25 annual membership fee. For all activities you have to bring your own blades and pads; the website provides information on where to buy or rent equipment. This is by far the most sociable and fun rollerblading group in town and an excellent way to meet new people.

Rugby

Spain has never been thought of as a rugby-playing nation. But, rugby fans will be pleased to know that Catalonia is an exception. It is a region that avidly follows and plays rugby, together with the Basque Country. Perhaps it is to do with Catalonia's proximity to the rugby-mad French south west, where world-class teams like Toulouse, Bayonne and Montpellier fight for top spot in the league. Whatever the reason, there are several clubs in the city that you can join. A good place to start is the Catalan Rugby Federation (www.rugby.cat) where you will find all Catalan clubs listed. They also have a ballot system for clubs looking for players, and vice-versa. Gòtics Rugby Club (93 332 39 86) is one of the most centrally located in Barcelona, together with Club de Rugby Químic (93 455 79 72 or 618 627 370). These clubs require a high level of proficiency, demand that players attend regular training sessions and competition for places is fierce. Club de Rugby Bonanova (www.terra.es/personal/rugbybonanova) is open to new players.

Running

Barcelona is full of idyllic places to go for a jog. First and foremost, there are the main parks (p.178): Ciutadella, Montjuïc and Parc Güell. The latter is the most challenging to run, due to the steep uphill slog, but the view from the top makes for an exhilarating reward. The many jogging tracks in Montjuïc are pleasant, and you can enjoy clean air and magnificent views. The beachfront promenade is a hot spot for tanned, toned and lithe individuals running to the pace of their iPods. From Barceloneta to Bogatell, there is a long enough stretch to test your endurance. The Club Natació Montjuic (www.cnmontjuic.com) has a running circuit through the grounds of Montjuic, again with stunning views. The best place to find information on athletics training and running tracks is through the governing body of the sport: Catalan Athletics Federation (www.atletisme.com/fca).

Various locations

Barcelona Hash House Harriers
93 415 97 38 | www.geocities.com/barnahhh
Officially, hashing is a more energetic form of the traditional British paper chase during which participants run after a 'hare' (the person nominated to run ahead, leaving clues en route). Unofficially, hashing is an excuse to give each other crude names and drink large quantities of post-run beer. Barcelona Hash House Harriers does all of the above on the last weekend of each month; no-name adult harriers pay €5, named harriers €4.

Av Diagonal, 716
Les Corts
Pubilla Cases
Map p.382 C3 115

Circuit Footing Parc de Cervantes
Set in a park, this 1.5km running track is ideal for a quick jog in your lunch break. Those training for competitions or as part of a fitness regime prefer to do the course several times over. However hard you want to push yourself, running in a park beats the treadmill any day.

C/ del Roser, 15
Poble Sec
Paral·lel
Map p.401 E4 116

Club Atlètic Running
93 346 55 55 | www.carunning.blogspot.com
Founded in 1979, this Poble Sec running club works in conjunction with the Coordinadora d'Entitats de Poble Sec (Poble Sec community centre), an organisation that hosts multi-cultural initiatives. The Club Atlètic Running has a blogspot where regular feeds are entered on recent runs and competitions. It is a sociable club for serious runners, who enjoy pushing themselves to the limit on 10km mountain runs, coastal excursions and 42km marathons. Port Olímpic is a popular meeting point for training sessions all year round. Contact the club directly between the hours of 16:00 and 22:00 to find out about upcoming runs and training sessions.

235

C/ Polvorí, 5
Montjuïc
📍 **Hostafrancs**
Map p.399 E1 **117**

Estadi Municipal Joan Serrahima Pista Atletisme

93 423 80 35

Used for training and warm-up sessions during the 1992 Barcelona Olympics, many world-class athletes have left their mark on this 400m athletics track. The only other facilities are a small gym, shower and snack kiosk. Set in beautiful grounds, high up on Montjuic, the air is clear and pleasant. The one-off entrance fee is €4.54. Season tickets of 10 admissions cost €35 but if you plan to train on a regular basis it may be worth subscribing to yearly membership of €184.66. There are regular training sessions and personal trainers are on hand.

Sailing

Spain is famous for its boating scene and Barcelona is no exception. Sailors and travellers flock from all over the world to enjoy the calm Mediterranean water and many residents enjoy nautical activities like jet skiing, motor boating or sailing on a yacht. These are available for rent at many beaches along the coast, as are catamarans and other types of sailing boats that allow you to enjoy the sea at a slower pace. For those who want to learn to sail, there are plenty of schools where you can take courses. The Centre Municipal de Vela (93 225 79 40, www.velabarcelona.com) is an important organisation offering reasonably priced courses. If you are interested in participating in upcoming races and regattas, the Real Club Naútico de Barcelona (www.rcnb.com), the Reial Club Marítim de Barcelona (www.maritimbarcelona.org) and the Catalan Sailing Federation (www.fcv.cat) are useful organisations.

Nautical Base, Marina
Port Vell, Gate B
Port Vell
📍 **Barceloneta**
Map p.409 E2 **118**

Business-Yacht Club

610 766 511 | *www.business-yachtclub.com*

At this exclusive establishment, J/80 regatta sailboats are available for a few hours' charter from Port Vell Marina. You can sail the J/80 with or without a skipper (for those with a sailing licence). Inexperienced sailors can take a boat out with a skipper on Wednesdays and Fridays during specific time slots and Saturdays all day. For those with a license, you can sail J/80s from Monday to Sunday – prices vary between €50 and €75 for a three-hour sail, depending on the time and day of the charter. The maximum capacity allowed on board is six individuals. The basic monthly fee of €35 (and member signing up fee of €190) covers a three-hour sailing session with a professional skipper every month. Contact the club for information on other membership tariffs.

Pg de Gràcia, 18
Eixample
📍 **Passeig de Gràcia**
Map p.393 E3 **119**

Escuela Naútica de Catalunya

90 232 59 02 | *www.enc.es*

The Nautical School of Catalunya is an excellent option for studying sailing, as prices are reasonable and there are several courses. Whether you are looking to gain a professional nautical qualification as Yacht Captain (98 hours of study) or specialise in a particular aspect of sailing on a short 20-hour course (€250 to €295), this school should accommodate. Standard beginner, intermediate and advanced sailing courses run from September to July. The beginner course (*iniciación*) costs €300, which comprises 140 hours of teaching split

Yachts at Port Vell

between theoretical and practical modules. Classes are from 14:00 to 16:00 or 20:00 to 22:00 twice per week, or once a week on Friday from 14:00 to 17:00 or 18:00 to 21:00. The intermediate course costs €295 and the advanced course (€690) qualifies you to sail a boat independently.

Real Club Naútico de Barcelona

Moll d'Espanya, s/n
Port Vell
🚇 *Barceloneta*
Map p.409 D2 `120`

93 221 65 21 | www.rcnb.com

With over 130 years of experience, this club offers a range of professional sailing courses taught by experienced skippers. Courses aboard cruise ships and other vessels are available for all levels, ranging from beginners to private lessons and family excursions. *Bautizo del mar* (sea baptism – €16 per person) is an introductory trip for beginners, familiarising them with the basics of sailing. Trips last about two hours, are supervised by experienced skippers (English-speaking on request) and take place every Saturday and Sunday afternoon. If you want to gain a deeper understanding of the sport, there are monthly sailing courses that involve attending a weekly four-hour class at the weekend (€160 per person). Each session is evenly split between theory and practice. On a competition level, the club hosts and organises several regattas and boat races.

Reial Club Marítim de Barcelona

Moll d'Espanya, s/n
Port Vell
🚇 *Barceloneta*
Map p.409 D2 `121`

93 221 48 59 | www.maritimbarcelona.org

This club, the oldest in Barcelona and one of the oldest in the country, has an outstanding sporting record and an excellent nautical sports academy. Reial Club Marítim offers group and private sailing courses for adults and children, in conjunction with the Catalan and Spanish Sailing Federations. Once students have completed their courses, they can continue their training through the club's highly successful boat race teams. Also, this is one of the few centres in the city that teaches rowing, as well as holding regular training sessions in the sport.

Scouts & Guides

Sir Robert Baden-Powell, former Lieutenant General in the British Army, founded the scout movement in 1907 in England. Today, scout and guide organisations exist in 216 countries around the world. And in Spain, particularly in Catalonia, scouting and guiding are popular. The names for scouts and guides can vary quite dramatically: *exploradores*, *guías / guies* and *escoltes* are all possibilities. Being aware of the different terms for scout groups will make it easier when looking for one to join. In Catalonia, a scout group is often referred to as an *agrupació escolta* or association of *l'escoltisme* (scouting). Escoltes Catalans (Catalan Scouts, 93 268 91 10, www.escoltes.org) and Acció Escolta de Catalunya (Scout Action of Catalonia, www.accioescolta.org) are key scout associations in the region, providing useful contact details and links to the many groups in and around Barcelona. The website will direct you to your nearest scout or guide group.

Skateboarding

Barcelona is a skater's paradise. Smooth pavements, ramped walkways, beachfront promenades, granite benches and graded banks have earned the city a reputation as one of the hottest skateboarding destinations in Europe. Skateboarding over street furniture is technically illegal, and being caught can land you a fine of up to €750. Rarely does it come to this though. Occasionally, sessions end with police telling skaters to move on, and in the worst-case scenario, the odd board may be confiscated. Around the MACBA museum, you can see flips, 360s, grinds and ambitious jumps executed day and night, with varying degrees of finesse. Pros and eager amateurs, some armed with

237

video cameras, come to try their luck on the museum's skater-friendly paved surfaces. Other popular hangouts include Port Olímpic, Plaça Universitat, El Fòrum, Parallel and Sants-Estació. There is a skate park in Poble Nou (Pamplona 88, Mon-Sat 10:00-14:00, 16:00-20:00) where you can grind all day long without any hassle. If you need a board or accessories, visit La General Surfera Surf Shop (93 209 05 39, Balmes 308) which sells longboards, skateboards and snakeboards, or the newly-opened Cub Skateboards (93 459 13 99, Torrent de L'Olla 46, www.cubskateshop.com).

Skiing & Snowboarding

Comparisons made between the Alps and the Pyrenees often sell the latter short. The Pyrenees might not have the nightlife or variety of slopes, but they are accessible and good value for money. Their proximity to Barcelona makes weekend breaks easy. Most of the ski and snow resorts (*estaciones de esquí / estacions d'esqui*) are a two hour drive away and if you don't have a car, trains run regularly from Sants-Estació. Remember to take snow chains if you do travel by car. There are many resorts in the Catalan Pyrenees, but for more challenging slopes it is worth popping over to Andorra (www.andorra.es). For information on all of the Catalan ski resorts and their winter and summer activities, consult www.catneu.net. If you prefer participating in a group excursion, Spanish Trails Adventure (www.spanish-trails.com) organises multi-day ski, snowboard and snowshoe tours.

Av Diagonal, 652-656
Eixample
Maria Cristina
Map p.384 A4 **122**

Baqueira Beret
97 363 90 10 | www.baqueira.es

A favourite with the Spanish Royal family, Baquiera Beret is the most exclusive Pyrenean resort. It is frequented by well-to-do Catalan families and some non-skiers who come solely for the elite ambiance and vibrant après-ski. Day passes cost more than in other Catalan resorts (€40.50 for adults and €27 for children) but they do cover all 72 pistes and 33 ski lifts. Snow cover is usually quite thick, as the maximum altitude is 2,500m and snow canons guarantee action in mild winters. The town has family-orientated facilities such as ice rinks and a snow park for toddlers. Vielha Ice Palace, a large spa and commercial centre, is a favourite for its relaxation rooms, massages and indoor heated pools. There are quite a few bars in town but most après-ski nightlife revolves around the pijo and studenty Pachá club.

Andorra

Grandvalira, Andorra
37 680 10 74 | www.grandvalira.com

This is the biggest resort in Andorra, boasting 200km of green, blue, red and black runs. The range of slopes, animated après-ski, excellent ski schools and family activities make the extra distance (186km from Barcelona) worthwhile, especially for a long weekend. Grandvalira incorporates three different valleys: Pas de la Casa, Gran Roig and Soldeu El Tarter. Ski passes for the whole area are available (€35 per day in high season), so even the most experienced skiers will be challenged. Transport is efficient; trains run from Barcelona to Puicerdà, where buses take you up to Grandvalira resorts. Andorra is an excellent place to buy tax-free ski and snowboard gear, particularly at the end of the season (end of March to mid-April) when prices are reduced in a bid to shift the stock.

Vall d'Aran
Sant Andreu
Sagrera
Map p.397 B1 **124**

Heliski Aran
64 613 36 21 | www.heliskiaran.com

This firm will fly experienced, adventurous skiers to some of the best off-piste action. The mountains in the Val d'Aran reach over 3,000m, making the snow conditions better than in resorts down in the valley. A typical trip includes flying by helicopter to the top of the mountain. From there you will descend with a guide (all guides have expert

238

qualifications in skiing, canyoning and mountaineering) through the woodland and pine forests. Trips also tend to end with a sociable lunch. This is not a suitable activity for the inexperienced, as the level is comparable to red runs. Three heliski descents cost €180 per person and six descents (approximately 3,500km in total) will set you back €350 per person. Four-day helicamps, snowshoeing and cross country skiing are alternative options. For other mountain jaunts, Pyroutdoor (www.pyroutdoor.com) can organise canyoning, rock climbing and heliskiing tours.

La Molina

La Molina
97 289 20 31 | *www.lamolina.cat*

This resort is the closest to Barcelona, and easy to reach (trains run from Sants to La Molina). It is also a safe bet for good snow compared to other Catalan resorts, because the mountains peak over 2,500m. With 42 slopes and 16 lifts (almost four times that of Vall de Nuria) there is enough variety to test all abilities. Snowboarders will be happy in the snow park, mastering tricks on the numerous jumps or showcasing their talents on the half-pipe. Après-ski is lively, so after hitting the slopes sink a glass or two of mulled wine. Make sure you book well in advance as this resort can become extremely crowded in high season, particularly around New Year.

Vall de Núria
Pyrenees

Vall de Núria
97 273 20 20 | *www.valldenuria.cat*

One of the smaller ski resorts of the region, with 11 slopes and four lifts, Vall de Núria is ideal for beginners and inexperienced skiers who want to gain confidence. The slopes are not too challenging, with just enough to be able to explore the resort in a day trip or over a weekend. Adult day passes are reasonably priced at €25.75. If you want to polish up your snow plough and parallel turns, group classes (minimum six students) cost €19.50 for two hours, while the going rate for a one-hour private class is €30. Non-skiers need not despair: the gentle slopes easily lend themselves to sledging, snowshoeing and cross country skiing. RENFE trains run from Sants to Ribes de Freser, from where you get the tramway (*cremallera*) up to Vall de Núria.

Skydiving

Skydiving was only recognised as a sport in 1950, even though the first jump was successfully carried out in 1897 by American, Tom Baldwin. Today, skydiving is not just for adrenaline junkies and thrill-seekers. Many people enjoy it as a stress busting hobby, however counter intuitive this may sound. But, once you are in the air your mind is focused on the jump alone, and terrestrial worries evaporate. There are about 20 different skydiving clubs around Barcelona. Most of these are located in Empuriabrava, the biggest drop zone in Europe. First-time jumpers will do a tandem jump strapped to the chest of a qualified instructor, during which the freefall period typically lasts for about 55 seconds. Check out www.skydiveworldwide.com for videos of past jumps from the Empuriabrava drop zone.

Empuriabrava

Jump Europe
690 606 747 | *www.jumpeurope.com*

Operating from the same drop zone as Skydive Empuriabrava, Jump Europe is a family-run business with Australian skydiving champion Richie Pym at the helm. The school offers a range of services: tandem jumps, IFF (intro freefall) courses, AFF (complete freefall) and advanced training. Prices for tandem jumps and introductory skydiving courses cost the same as Skydive Empuriabrava and during the week there is a €25 discount per person (except in July and August). Accommodation of all varieties is available, from the bunkhouse onsite (€15 per person) to nearby three star hotels.

239

Sector Aeroclub s/n
Empuriabrava

Skydive Empuriabrava

97 245 01 11 | www.skydiveempuriabrava.com

Skydive Empuriabrava is the largest skydiving centre in Europe. A whopping 130,000 jumps take place every year. The basic tandem jump costs €182 in the summer months and additional costs for photos or video footage range from €60-100. A €25 reduction is available on weekdays. If you fall in love with the sport after one jump, you can train to skydive solo. The Mini PAC course costs €492 and includes one tandem jump, one level one solo jump and 50% discount on accommodation during the course. The school also imparts professional training in freefly, freestyle and group formations. Consult the website for directions on how to get there.

Social Groups

Other options **Support Groups** p.120

An inability to speak Spanish or Catalan makes it harder to socialise, network and meet new people, but there are a number of expat societies to help counter these lost feelings. Language is the key to integrating, although the Catalan versus Spanish play-off can sometimes make this harder. Finding a tandem language partner or group is a great way to combine language learning with socialising. But if you need a break from all the multiculturalism, there are a number of English-language social groups that you can join.

Various locations

7para7

617 287 793 | www.7para7.com

7para7 organises speed dating evenings where you will speak to seven different partners for seven minutes each time. The rounds take place in bars across the city, from Baja Beach Club to Jazz Bar Bel-Luna, and are aimed at a different age category each week. It attracts a broad range of participants, averaging 30 to 40 years old, with the occasional appearance of an early twentysomething. Granted, most speeddaters are Catalan, but French, English and American participants have been known to make an appearance. In any case, how complex can a conversation get in just seven minutes?

Various locations

American Society of Barcelona

69 675 16 45 | www.amersoc.com

This non-political society, founded in 1974, organises social events, the most popular of which is a Sunday brunch. Traditional American midday grub is laid on by Si Senor restaurant on the last Sunday of each month, with entertainment for young children. Parties, Independence Day celebrations and Thanksgiving are also favourites among members. Membership for one year – €29 per person and €49 for a couple or family – covers the costs of the society's activities, although for some events you may need to pay a supplementary fee.

Various locations

Barcelona Business Lunch

www.thebizlunch.com

If you are looking for a business lunch conducted in true British fashion (and preceded by a whisky or gin and tonic) then Barcelona Business Lunch will appeal. Lunches, held once a month, are open to all English-speaking professionals looking to network and meet new people in Barcelona. Usually organised in a central restaurant, the average cost is €18 per person. In summer, the group makes the most of the weather by occasionally organising lunch on board a catamaran.

The English Speaking Club Catalunya

607 113 737 | www.englishspeakingclub.com

This club has been running since 1994, organising dinners, leisure pursuits, parties, sports events, family outings and excursions around Catalonia. It is free to join and is open to English-speakers and English-learners who want to practice. The club has a Madrid branch, with more than 4,500 members split between Barcelona and the Spanish capital. Parties are held throughout the year for key Catalan and international celebrations such as *calçotadas*, San Juan and Halloween.

International Women's Club of Barcelona

93 204 02 31 | www.iwcbarcelona.com

Established in Barcelona in 1945 as a multicultural voluntary organisation, Barcelona International Women's Club is the equivalent of the WI (Women's Institute) in the United Kingdom and other English-speaking countries. The club is open to all English-speaking women of all nationalities. Coffee mornings are held every Wednesday from 11:00 to 13:00 and wine and cheese soirees on the first and third Monday of every month. Other activities include art courses, bridge, golf and tennis; some of these are organised rather sporadically, so it is best to contact the club directly for information on current events.

Prestigious Speakers

680 423 790 | www.prestigiousspeakers.com

Prestigious Speakers is a registered Toastmasters International Club for native and foreign English-speakers. The objective of the discussions – held on the first and third Tuesday of every month – is to improve public speaking skills and network with fellow professionals resident in the city. Held in Marcblau restaurant, group members often stay for a meal afterwards. Annual membership costs €86 and includes all printed material for the year and a contribution to the global non-profit organisation, but guests and potential new members can go along free of charge for a taster session. As most members are native English-speakers, a high level of English is necessary. Alternatively, Barcelona Toastmasters (www.bcn-toastmasters.com) is both a Spanish and English public speaking club that meets every Wednesday evening.

Special Needs Activities

Barcelona is not an easy city for people with disabilities to navigate. There are narrow streets, small doorways, endless flights of stairs and few ramps. But, newer hotels and the more expensive restaurants are usually equipped for wheelchair-users. Equally, most museums, buses and some metro stations are wheelchair friendly. Transports Metropolitans de Barcelona (www.tmb.net) has information on all bus and metro lines and their accessibility. For housing information, www.gencat.es/probert (Generalitat) and www.bcn.es (Ajuntament) have lists of establishments that have been adapted to suit the needs of people with disabilities. Federació ECOM (www.ecom.es) is one of the most informative associations in Barcelona, with links to transport, accommodation, sport and travel websites. If you want to get away for a few days, Valinet (95 491 54 44, www.valinet.org) organises personalised trips, depending on each person's disability, to Andalusia and Extremadura, providing detailed information on hotels in the region.

Accessible Barcelona

93 476 63 43 | www.accessiblebarcelona.com

Accessible Barcelona, started by wheelchair-user Craig Grimes, is a key source of information for foreign residents and tourists with disabilities. While the hotel section is clearly aimed at tourists, the entertainment and going out section is also a useful resource for residents. The site gives pointers on restaurants, bars and clubs that have

241

disabled access, covering most central areas of the city. Accessible Barcelona can also arrange hire of electric scooters, manual or electric wheelchairs and electric hoists. You can book the tailored, disabled-friendly tours around the Barri Gòtic and the main Gaudi sites as well.

Online only

Esplaya.com
www.esplaya.com

This website provides useful information, in English and German, on which beaches are accessible nationwide. By clicking on a region and then a *comarca* you will find lists of wheelchair-friendly beaches and resorts. On some beaches the Red Cross has a wheelchair-bathing service. The chair is specially designed to allow users to bathe with the aid of lifeguards. For precise information on which beaches offer this service, email discapacitados@esplaya.com.

C/ Francesc
Tàrrega, 48
Sant Andreu
🚇 **Congrés**
Map p.395 F1 137

Federació Catalana d'Esports de Minusvàlids Físics
93 340 92 00 | www.fcemf.org

For sportsmen and women, the Catalan Federation of Sports for Those with Physical Disabilities has a wealth of information on clubs that you can join. It covers everything from cycling and athletics to hockey, skiing, swimming and basketball. The federation has a particularly good teaching scheme set up with the Escola Oficial de Tennis en Cadira de Rodes (93 428 53 53). The tennis centre, to the north of Barcelona, runs a number of classes throughout the week, for adults and children.

Av Diagonal, 233
Eixample
🚇 **Monumental**
Map p.394 C4 138

Institut Municipal de Persones amb Disminució
93 413 27 75 | www.bcn.es/imd

This is the city's official organisation for people with disabilities. It has information on access to venues and can provide a map with wheelchair-friendly itineraries. Cultural and social events are organised intermittently, so call to find out about upcoming events.

Squash
Other options **Leisure Facilities** p.258

Squash received yet another blow in its campaign to be recognised as an Olympic sport when it was denied inclusion in the 2012 Olympic Games in London, its city of origin. While squash loses out in terms of recognition to other racket sports, like tennis, it remains hugely popular. Most centres and health clubs have squash courts, although membership is sometimes required to play. You may struggle to get a court at the most popular times (18:00 to 22:00), so do book in advance if possible. The best option, if you only want to play occasionally, is to head to one of the tennis centres (such as Centre Municipal de Tennis Vall d'Hebron, p.245) as many have a 'pay-and-play' system. The average price for a one-hour session is €15 to €20.

C/ Almogavers,169
Sant Martí
🚇 **Llacuna**
Map p.412 A1 139

Alfa 5
93 320 94 92 | alfa5@alfa5.com

Alfa 5 is a cheap and cheerful sports club offering the best prices in town. The club entrance fee is €7 and enables you to use all of the facilities available: seven squash courts, a small gym, swimming pool and sauna. Although not obligatory, you can book a court by calling the club two hours before playing. On Tuesday and Thursday evenings (18:00–22:00), it is impossible to get a court, as league games are played. The only way to get round this is to sign up for the social league yourself.

Club Natació Catalunya

C/ Ramiro de Maeztu, 25
Gràcia
🚇 *Mercat Nou*
Map p.386 B3 **140**

93 213 43 44 | www.cncat.org

One of the best deals in the city, you can use the squash courts, indoor and outdoor swimming pools and solarium for €7.35 on a 'turn up and play' system. The facilities are good and if you want to be able to use the gym or attend one of the numerous classes available, monthly adult membership is reasonably priced at €29.50. The signing-up fee is nearly €100.

Club Natació Sant Andreu

Rla de Fabra I Puig, 47
Sant Andreu
🚇 *Sant Andreu*
Map p.388 B4 **141**

93 345 67 89 | www.cnsandreu.com

Tournaments are held here every year on the four courts, check out www.openbcnsquash.com for more information. You have to be a member to play at this club but prices are reasonable: monthly fees are €23.01 for adults, €21.20 for 15 to 17 years old and €19.45 for children aged 14 and under. There are reduced tariffs for families. Squash courts cost an additional €4.20 per hour on top of monthly membership, although many people find half an hour is tiring enough. Aside from squash, the centre has eight tennis courts, six petanque surfaces and two badminton courts.

Esportiu Rocafort

C/ Floridablanca, 41
Poble Sec
🚇 *Espanya*
Map p.401 D1 **142**

93 426 47 17 | www.esportiurocafort.com

This health club offers many different services, but its most prominent feature is squash. Coaching is of an excellent standard and group or private classes are available for all levels. There is a children's squash school where separate classes for boys and girls are held on alternate nights from 17:30-19:30, Monday to Friday. Open from 07:00 to midnight during the week and from 08:00 to 22:00 on weekends, few centres have such long opening hours. The club regularly hosts international and national squash competitions on its seven courts. For club standard players, there is a social league.

Squash Marconi

C/ Marconi, 240
Terrassa

93 780 26 00 | www.squashmarconi.com

If squash is your passion, then this squash-only club could be for you. Don't expect to be able to go for a swim, relax in a Jacuzzi or use a gym though: four well-maintained squash courts and one activities room (used for toning classes) are the only facilities available. The club organises private classes, leagues, and a ranking system that partners you up with someone of the same level. Courts for non-members cost €22 per hour (€18 morning rate) and the club is open from 11:00 to 23:00. Membership varies depending on when you play, but the most common is the €38 monthly tariff, which comprises four hours weekly play during the most popular times (18:00-22:00).

Swimming

Swimming is a popular pastime in Barcelona and the city has many indoor and outdoor pools. The city's gyms (p.261) and sports centres (p.258) tend to have swimming pools attached to them, and some of the quieter beaches (p.176) are good, as lifeguards are present even when crowds are not. The Club Natació Catalunya (p.259) in Gràcia is a popular spot, with indoor and outdoor pools. The beach clubs listed in this book (p.258) also have pools. There are many others, just try www.bcn.es for the nearest to you. Almost all have an outdoor sun patio, so you needn't worry about losing out on tanning time. Centres with indoor pools empty out dramatically in July and August, but when September comes around the lanes start to fill up again. The busiest times are after work hours (19:00 to 21:00) or in the lunch period, between 13:00 and 15:00. Sundays are extremely quiet but be aware that many pools are closed in the afternoon between 14:00 and 16:00.

243

Team Building

Bridging cultural differences is fundamental in Barcelona. Muddling Catalan and Spanish words in the same phrase is a grave insult to defiant Catalan nationalists, and knowing whether to kiss or shake hands with business acquaintances can be daunting. Team building activities are an increasingly popular way to break the ice between work colleagues. Barcelona is well established on the conferences circuit, attracting a number of foreign multinationals and corporations who come for company incentives. In 2006, the city received nearly 500,000 conference visitors.

C/ Legalitat, 8
Gràcia
🚇 *Joanic*
Map p.394 A1 **145**

Amfivia

902 998 314 | www.amfivia.com

Amfivia, an outdoor events firm offers extreme sports and adventure challenges. Options include four wheel drive (4WD) off-road expeditions, pot holing, white water rafting, dog-sledding, art workshops (including painting with your feet), beach volleyball and human castle team challenges. Sailing (yachts, catamarans, schooners and motor boats are all available) excursions range from day trips to week-long adventures. English, Spanish and Catalan are all spoken.

Various locations

Barcelona Adventure Company

93 215 32 85 | www.bcn-adventure.com

This locally-based British company handles corporate event management, hospitality, adventure sports and accommodation, in addition to team building activities. A treasure hunt around the city is perhaps one of their more original activities, and is designed to encourage group work and communication. Human castles, high rope challenges, dragon boat racing and who-can-make-the-best-paella competitions are other options.

C/ Vidre, 7, 3
Barri Gòtic
🚇 *Liceu*
Map p.402 C4 **147**

Spanish Trails Adventure

93 317 41 60 | www.spanish-trails.com

Spanish Trails Adventure focuses on out-of-the-city activities. Adventure trails and excursions in the Catalan countryside are their specialty. One day wine tasting tours are as popular as multi-day Costa Brava excursions, where sea kayaks and bikes are used for getting from cove to cove. The firm will look after companies or private groups.

Tennis

Other options **Leisure Facilities** p.258

Spain has a long tradition of tennis stars; Rafael Nadal being the most recent example. In Catalonia, the Federació Catalana de Tennis (FCT – www.fctennis.cat) has worked hard to change perceptions of tennis as an elite sport. They have tried to encourage universal access, with initiatives like tennis sessions in local schools. With 275 courts in the city, you won't have trouble finding a place to play. Many sports complexes have courts, for example, Europolis Health Club (Travessera de les Corts, 252-254).
The best time to play is on Sunday afternoons, when Catalan families are at the beach or tucking into a big family lunch. Some clubs, like Centre Municipal de Tennis Vall d'Hebron, even offer reduced rates after 15:00 on Sundays. At normal times, non-members should expect to pay €13-20 for one hour on court. Bear in mind though, that prices vary between clubs and some are members only.
Most clubs offer private and group lessons with qualified coaches. For budding young professionals in-the-making, the prestigious tennis academy Elitennis (www.elitennis.com), in nearby Castelldefels, runs summer camps and regular training programs.

Barcelona Tennis

Various locations

650 499 997 | www.barcelona-tennis.com

Quintus Snapper is the brains behind this social and competitive tennis ladder. Players of all nationalities and levels who share a love of the sport are matched up against each other. It is a great way of keeping in shape and meeting people with similar interests. The site is multi-lingual and extremely open: each match is written up on the website with a short commentary on how it went, ranging from tips for future players to gentle banter. The signup fee for competitive matches is €9 while the Open Social Ladder is free to join.

Centre Municipal Tennis Vall d'Hebron

Av Vall d'Hebron, 178-196
Vall d'Hebron

93 427 65 00 | www.fctennis.org

Some of the country's best players have sent passing shots and smashes flying down the lines of these courts. The club has 24 in total; 17 are clay and seven are hard. Set high up on the road to Tibidabo, you can enjoy magnificent views as you play. More reasonable in price than Vall Parc Tennis Club (see below), clay courts cost €18 per hour and hard ones are €13, with special reduced rates on Sunday afternoons. The FCT is the club's governing body, organising regular competitions for adults and children.

Club de Tennis Vall Parc

Cta Rabassada, 97
Tibidabo

93 212 67 89 | www.vallparc.com

This elite tennis club in Tibidabo has fantastic views over the city. Of course, this comes at a price (€20 per hour) but the facilities are in exceptionally good condition. The changing rooms, with jacuzzis, are a mark of the club's high standards. There are 13 clay courts available, together with five paddle courts (€26 per hour), two for fronton and three for squash (€20 per hour). There is also a gym, swimming pool, multi-surface indoor pitch and ping pong tables. Try to book courts in advance, as it can get busy.

David Lloyd Club Turó

Av Diagonal, 673-685
Les Corts
🚇 *Zona Universitària*
Map p.383 D3 151

93 334 20 12 | www.davidlloyd.es

The British firm David Lloyd Leisure is considered one of the leaders in the sports industry for its facilities and standards of coaching. This centre in Diagonal is no exception. It has 14 tennis courts, five paddle tennis courts, three swimming pools (one outdoor) and a spa centre. Classes are given for swimming, tennis, paddle tennis and there are also personal fitness trainers available.

Reial Club de Tennis Barcelona (RCTB)

C/ Bosch i Gimpera, 5-13
Les Corts
🚇 *Palau Reial*
Map p.382 F3 152

93 206 35 83 | www.rctb1899.es

As one of the longest-standing and most prestigious clubs in the country, this is the place to come if you want to catch a glimpse of the next Nadal. RCTB has seen some of Spain's greats. Arantxa Sánchez, Conchita Martínez, Carlos Moyà and Albert Costa have all played in the club's high-brow Trofeo Conde de Godó. The ATP-listed club holds regular tournaments that attract highly ranked players from all over the world. A strictly members-only club and very exclusive, this is not the place to come for a casual knock-around, and there is a strict dress code.

Reial Societet de Tennis Pompeia

C/ de la Foixarda, 2-4
Montjuïc
🚇 *Hostafrancs*
Map p.398 F1 153

93 325 13 48 | a13158@hotmail.com

This 100 year old club operates a 'turn up and play', no booking system, which can often mean waiting for a court if you arrive between 18:00 and 21:00 during the week. Members (*socios*) are given priority over non-members, but still abide by the same no pre-booking system. The atmosphere is rather adult-dominated, but the seven clay courts are in good condition and a bar and restaurant are available. Quarterly membership fees of €150 include use of the swimming pool. For non-members, courts costs €13 per hour and €17 for courts with night lighting.

Triathlon

The first triathlon race (swimming, cycling and running) was called an 'ironman' and took place in Hawaii in the 70s. It remains, for many, the most challenging of all international triathlon competitions. The sport made its first Olympic appearance during 2000 at the Sydney games. For the Olympics, the ironman distances (a 3.8km swim, 180km cycle and 42km run) were reduced to a 1.5km swim, 40km cycle and 10km run. If you're a beginner and this all sounds far too ambitious, don't be put off; the 'sprint' is popular with newcomers and consists of a 750m swim, 20km cycle and 5km run. In Barcelona, the sport is growing rapidly; every year there is a 30% increase in the number of participants in the Barcelona City Triathlon (Triatlo Ciutat de Barcelona). To get involved, consult www.tri-trials.com.

Complex Esportiu
Sagnier
Federica
Montseny, s/n
El Prat de Liobregat

Club Prat-Triatló
93 478 31 76 | *www.prat-triatlo.com*

Club Prat-Triatló has produced some of the finest triathletes in Catalonia, gaining a reputation as one of the top training clubs in the region. Over recent years, the club has attracted international triathletes from France, Australia, Argentina and Haiti. The annual inscription fee is €55 and membership payments are payable each trimester. It's €75 for team-members, which covers sessions with a professional trainer three times a week and use of Complex Esportiu Sagnier facilities (sauna, swimming pool, gym and athletics tracks) and €55 for non-team members. This allows you the same involvement in national and regional competitions but not an unlimited use of complex facilities.

Various locations

Ironcat
www.ironcat.org

This is the only ironman triathlon in Catalonia that covers the awe-inspiring traditional distances: 3.8km swim, 180km cycle and 42km run. Starting in the small and picturesque fishing village of l'Ampolla, the race explores the Mediterranean coastline and the Delta de l'Ebre national park. Held once every year in springtime, the competition runs over two days, with a one-night stay in l'Ampolla before the big day. The website is in several languages, including English, French and German, and clearly explains the event with maps of each leg of the race. Contact the Federació Catalana de Triatló (93 307 93 32, www.triatlo.org) for more detailed information on accommodation, costs and transport.

Volleyball

There are two forms of volleyball played here: indoor volleyball (*volei de pista*) and beach volleyball (*volei de platge*). While it is a popular hobby in Barcelona, it tends to be played informally, among friends or colleagues. Vila Olímpica beach volleyball club (www.geocities.com/voleyplayabcn) is a friendly international group of enthusiasts. The group don't take themselves too seriously, which is a refreshing change from the sometimes cliquey, Catalan dominated, official volleyball clubs. In summer, you will see members playing at Vila Olímpica from 17:00 every day. In Spring, the group play on weekends from 15:00 and in winter play is shifted to 13:00. If you want to brush up your technique, there are beginner, intermediate and advanced master classes, taught by experienced beach volleyball professionals. Also, there is a large Brazilian contingent in the multi-national group, making the samba social nights just as lively as the volleyball games. If you'd like to get involved, send an email to icariavoleyplaya@yahoo.es or go down to Vila Olímpica beach and chat to the players directly.

Watersports

Windsurfing (*surf a vela*), body boarding, wakeboarding, waterskiing and kitesurfing are all popular. There are water sports centres within the city where you can hire equipment or take lessons, but the better centres, offering a wider range of activities, can be found along the Costa Brava (particularly around Empuriabrava, Sant Pere Pescador and L'Escala). If you're serious about surfing, the Atlantic coast in northern Spain has much bigger waves. Barceloneta and Port Olímpic are the best spots in the city for renting out windsurfing equipment. It can cost as little as €60 per day for equipment and the help of an instructor. Aside from the clubs entered below, useful organisations to contact are the Real Club Naútico Barcelona (93 231 65 21, www.rcnb.com, p.237) and the Reial Club Marítim Barcelona (www.maritimbarcelona.org, p.237). Bear in mind that most sailing clubs (see Sailing, p.236) offer other watersports. Official organisations include the Catalan Windsurf Association (www.windsurfcat.com) and the Catalan Kitesurfing Association (www.ack.cat).

Rio Ebre
Amposta

Barcelona Wakeboard School
97 131 85 75 | www.nomadsurfers.com

Set 100km to the south of Barcelona, this camp is the only one in Spain that focuses entirely on wakeboarding and wakeskating. Both sports are relatively new and, as a result, wakeboard centres and equipment are something of a novelty. Wakeboarding is similar to kiteboarding, except that you are pulled by a motor boat; this avoids having to rely on wind conditions. A 30 minute ride costs €50 and one hour costs €100. If you would like to spend the weekend in Amposta, one night's stay costs €25 (or €40 full-board) and the school also runs week-long wakeboard camps that involve five days of wakeboarding and two days of excursions.

Paseo Maritimo, 163
Castelldefels

Bunker Wind, Surf and Kite Club
650 808 211 | www.bunkerwind.com

At first glance, the annual membership of €450 seems quite expensive, but it does include use of the club's exclusive beachfront facilities (swimming pool, sunbathing area, garden, changing rooms, showers, individual lockers and storage space) and partners and children are also welcome to use the facilities. The downside is that the club is extremely popular: there is always a waiting list to join, which you could be on for up to six months before becoming a member. Storage space is provided for each member's kitesurfing and windsurfing equipment.

Av Canal Olímpic, s/n
Castelldefels

Canal Olímpic de Catalunya
93 636 28 96 | www.canalolimpic.com

Canal Olímpic water sports centre was created for the 1992 Olympics, when it hosted the kayaking. Eight to 10 hour courses are available in kayaking, windsurfing and water skiing, with 50% reductions for club members. Membership costs €62 per person (14 years and above) per trimester and family membership (includes partner and children below 12) costs €71 per trimester. Standard membership includes the water sports facilities, gym, sauna and hydromassage pool, but use of the swimming pool is payable separately each time you visit (or with separate pool membership). Non-members can hire canoes, kayaks, rowing boats, windsurfing boards and Optimists (little sailing boats) at a cost of €10 for one hour.

247

Centre Municipal de Vela

Moll de Gregal, s/n
Port Olímpic
Llacuna
Map p.411 F4 **159**

93 225 79 40 | www.velabarcelona.com

This centre is run by the Catalan Sailing Federation, and offers windsurfing classes as well as sailing courses. These are good value and well taught. Windsurfing courses (€159 plus €25 signing-up fee) consist of eight intensive hours of teaching, either from Monday to Thursday or over two weekends. Lessons are taught between the following times: 10:00 to 12:00, 12:30 to 14:30 or 18:00 to 20:00. If these hours don't suit you, private lessons are also an option. Annual membership costs €186 and entitles you to full use of the club facilities as well as discounted courses. There are regular socials, regattas, sporting activities and family events organised for club members.

Flyworks

Sant Pere Pescador
Girona

629 224 559 | www.flyworks.net

This club and school is focused purely on kitesurfing. Trained instructors give classes for different levels and at different paces. One hour private classes cost €65, but if the pupil is a first-timer, an initial theory lesson on the beach is obligatory (€45). The school also offers intensive courses that comprise 10 hours of classes over two days. The course, which costs €266 including insurance, teaches all the theory and practical understanding needed to enable you to kitesurf independently. The school is open from April to September and is just over 100km from Barcelona.

Wind 220

Paseo Marítimo con
Pontevedra
Barceloneta
Barceloneta
Map p.409 F4 **161**

93 221 47 02 | www.wind220.com

Wind 220 is the most centrally located windsurfing and surf club in Barcelona. Set on Barceloneta beach, the club is popular with residents more because of its easy access than because of the quality of surf. It's not everyone's first choice though, because of the overwhelming number of tourists on the beach during the summer. Yearly membership costs €400, which can be divided into monthly payments. Members are entitled to use all club facilities: changing rooms, personal locker space, sauna, showers and board rack. There is also a chill-out area upstairs equipped with hammocks. Unfortunately, the membership waiting list can be very long, so get in there quick.

Wine Tasting

Catalan wines are sometimes unjustly overlooked. Over the last 10 years the region has increased wine exportation and Catalan wines are now present in many countries, including Germany, Holland, Britain, Scandinavia and Japan (the French are yet to be convinced). A tip when buying: check that all wines have the Empordà - Costa Brava DO (*denominación de origen*). Penedès, Empordà and Priorat wines are reliable reference points. Competition is rife between the city's tour companies, so you can get a good deal on excursions that combine fine wine with other activities such as cycling, walking and hiking through the countryside. Tours cost a lot more than if you go independently, so you may want to try www.do-catalunya.com for direct contact details of wine cellars in the region. Also worth a visit is the Catalan Wine and Cava Show, held each September at Maremagnum (93 225 81 00) where some 400 wineries, *bodegas* and merchants from all over Catalonia parade their goods.

Albet i Noya, Can Vendrell

Can Vendrell de la
Codina
Sant Pau d'Ordal

93 899 48 12 | www.albetinoya.com

Albet i Noya winery has been producing wine and cava on its 210-hectare estate for 100 years. It specialises in organic wines with great success since 1979. Just over 30 minutes from Barcelona, it makes for a pleasant day trip into the Penedes wine region. Visits can be in Catalan, Spanish or English and take place during the week from 09:00

to 13:30 and 15:00 to 18:00, and on weekends from 10:00 to 14:30. There are two tours available: the 'tourist' (€5.50 per person, 90 minutes) includes a tour of the cellars and the opportunity to taste three of the wines produced on-site. While the 'technical' (€11 per person) includes a tour of the cellars and vineyards, takes two to three hours and requires a minimum of 20 people. The estate now uses 100% organic farming methods.

Cavas Rovellats

Vilafranca del Penedès

93 488 05 75 | *www.cavasrovellats.com*

It would be unfair to discuss Catalan wine without mentioning one of the region's most famous drops; Cava. Cavas Rovellats is a 15th century farmhouse just outside Vilafranca del Penedès specialising in Cava production. The farmhouse, set in beautiful surroundings, houses the winery, underground cellars (12m deep), a picturesque chapel and wine museum. Basic tours last just under an hour and are given by local experts. They finish with a tasting session of the Cava Gran Reserva on the farmhouse terrace. In production for over 500 years, this pioneering Cava cellar set the standard for many that followed. The winery closes in August and December.

Mas Comtal

Mas Comtal, 1 Avinyonet de Penedès Penedès

93 897 00 52 | *www.mascomtal.com*

This rustic wine farm in Alt Penedès is constructed around a 12th century Roman tower. Production is limited in favour of quality over quantity, which seems to work very well; Mas Comtal has been gathering a good reputation for the quality of its wines, particularly Petrea, a 100% merlot. Their Xarel·lo, a grape variety originally introduced by the Greeks, is also exceptional. You can visit the vineyard independently during the week, but make sure you call ahead. Alternatively, Food Wine Tours (www.foodwinetours.com) organises guided tours. One of them starts with a tour of Mas Comtal, followed by a traditional Catalan lunch and another vineyard tour with tasting and tapas. Prices include transport to and from Barcelona.

Park Güell (p.179)

Spectator Sports

To its people, Catalonia is a stateless nation, with FCBarcelona the most recognised symbol of Cataln nationhood abroad. Under the repressive dictatorship years, the Catalans attended FCBarcelona matches and found an environment in which they could express themselves freely. This quickly developed into a powerful representation of regional identity.

Catalans have strong sporting traditions, and castle-building contests are major components of any summer festival. Similarly, the Barcelona Marathon, held the first weekend in March, takes place on the city streets, as does the final stage of the Tour of Catalunya bike race.

To find out what's on, there are two Barcelona-based sports dailies: *El Mundo Deportivo* and *Sport*. When purchasing tickets, the easiest option is often to go through ServiCaixa, a sales system operated by La Caixa bank. This can be done online at www.servicaixa.com (you collect your tickets at the venue) or via the bank's cash points (which print a ticket). The main venues are listed below.

Av Arístides Maillol
Les Corts
🚇 *Les Corts*
Map p.391 E1 **169**

Nou Camp
90 218 99 00 | www.fcbarcelona.com

FCBarcelona stands for Football Club Barcelona, and while the football team is the most popular and visible element, it also incorporates the city's top basketball, handball and roller-hockey teams. There are also athletics, cycling, rugby, baseball, volleyball, field hockey, ice hockey and ice dance divisions, though these are not professional. Football is the top draw and witnessing a Barça match at the Nou Camp (or El Camp Nou, as the locals say) is an unforgettable experience. Few grounds are quite so football orientated with its sweeping bowl design and steep tribunes ensuring an enclosed feel and superb view from every seat. And it is set to become even more spectacular. UK architect Lord Foster recently won the commission to redesign the existing stadium, taking its capacity to 106,000, and adding Gaudi-inspired shells of colour to the outside. The redesign begins in 2009, and should finish in time for the 2011/12 season. Within the ground is a museum (p.172) and sometimes (usually weekdays, mid-morning) you can even watch the players run through their routines.

Pg Olímpic
Montjuïc
🚇 *Hostafrancs*
Map p.399 F3 **166**

Estadi Olímpic Lluís Companys
93 426 20 89 | www.bsmsa.es

There has been a stadium at Montjuïc since 1929, when a new facility was unveiled at the International Exhibition. In fact, the stadium was originally conceived as part of Barcelona's bid to host the 1936 Olympic Games, eventually losing out to Berlin. Some 50 years later, work began on an upgrade for the 1992 Olympics, rebuilding the stadium itself but retaining the old façade. All athletics events were held here, along with the opening and closing ceremonies. These days it still plays host to international athletics meetings as well as football matches and concerts. As a football stadium, UEFA classifies it a five star venue, the top grade: Espanyol use it as

The Olympic stadium

250

their home ground and internationals are occasionally played here. Capacity stands at 56,000 for sporting events, rising to 70,000 for concerts. The website www.agendabcn.com has details of what's on, both sporting and musical.

Palau Blaugrana

Av Arístides Maillol
Les Corts
Les Corts
Map p.383 D4 167

90 218 99 00 | www.fcbarcelona.com

Located on the same site as the Nou Camp, FCBarcelona's sports hall has the capacity for just over 7,000 spectators and hosts regular matches from the club's basketball, handball, roller-hockey and football salon divisions. The Palau Blaugrana was originally opened in 1971 and, with its domed roof, was then one of the most impressive, state-of-the-art arenas in Spain. These days it looks a little dated, but it is due to be rebuilt and expanded as part of the campus redevelopment project. The roller hockey, judo and taekwondo events at the Barcelona 1992 Olympic Games were held here. You can buy a Palaua Blaugrana season ticket for €76 which gives you access to any of the home games played by the four indoor professional Barça teams.

Palau Sant Jordi

Pg Olímpic
Montjuïc
Hostafrancs
Map p.399 E2 168

93 426 20 89 | www.bsmsa.es

Next to the Olympic Stadium, this indoor arena was built to host gymnastics, handball and volleyball at the 1992 games, but these days it also caters for basketball, indoor athletics, ice skating and music concerts. It even converted to hold a swimming pool in order to host the 2003 World Swimming Championships. Its design is particularly striking, especially the meshed metallic roof. Capacity is 17,000. To see what's on, visit www.agendabcn.com.

Basketball

Spain is the reigning World Cup holder, triumphing in Japan in 2006, and basketball is easily the country's second most popular sport. In this respect, Catalonia is no different. There are two major basketball teams in Greater Barcelona: the ubiquitous FCBarcelona and Joventut de Badalona.

FCBarcelona

Av Arístides Maillol
Les Corts
Les Corts
Map p.391 E1 169

90 218 99 00 | www.fcbarcelona.com

For Barça fans, the basketball team comes second in importance to football. There is also much rivalry with Real Madrid who also have a basketball team. Barça and Real Madrid dominate the domestic basketball scene in the same way as their football counterparts. Founded in 1926, Barça experienced more downs than ups until the 80s when a golden generation of players established the club as a real force both in Spain and Europe. In the 2002-2003 season, Barça achieved a historic treble: the domestic league and cup and a first-ever European Cup. Regular matches are played at the Palau Blaugrana, although big games are switched to Palau Sant Jordi. Ticket prices vary depending upon the importance of the fixture and go on sale to the general public a fortnight ahead of games. As well as the all-encompassing Palau Blaugrana season ticket, you can also buy individual sports season tickets; the basketball one costs €65.

Joventut de Badalona

C/ Ponent, 143-161
Badalona

93 460 20 40 | www.penya.com

Based just outside the city limits in Badalona (but on the L2 Metro line), Joventut compete in Spanish basketball's top tier, the Liga ACB. Founded in 1930, they began to establish themselves in the 40s and 50s, evolving fast enough to win the national league title in 1968. The 90s were then Joventut's golden era, as the team chalked up two league titles and a European Cup. Nicknamed La Penya, they play in green and

251

black at their home arena, the Palau Olímpic, so named for hosting the basketball events of the 1992 games, when the legendary US team of Michael Jordan, Magic Johnson and Larry Bird swept all before them. Tickets are available via the club website.

Bullfighting

Although not really a Catalan tradition, and despite symbolic declarations that Barcelona is anti-bullfighting, there remain enough tourists and enthusiasts (many of them displaced from elsewhere in Spain) to ensure that *corridas* do still take place most summer Sundays – at least for now.

The Plaza de Toros

Gran Via de les Corts
Catalanes, 749
Eixample
🚇 *Glòries*
Map p.394 B4 171

Plaza de Toros Monumental

93 245 58 02 | www.torosbarcelona.com

The Monumental is the last standing active bullring in Barcelona: the city's first *plaza de toros* was located in Barceloneta but is long gone, while the Las Arenas ring at Plaça Espanya is currently being converted into a leisure complex. Designed by the modernist Joaquím Raspall i Mayol in 1914, the Monumental is striking with its red brickwork, decorative tiles and giant eggs. The bullfighting season runs from April to September and prices start at €21 for a bench seat in the *sol*, with shaded ones in the *sombra* slightly more expensive. Tickets can be bought direct from the ticket booth at the ring itself, through ServiCaixa or from an outlet on Carrer Muntaner.

Castelling

Building *castells* (human towers) is a longstanding Catalan tradition, with contests held at all major festivals. A tower is formed by team members standing on one another's shoulders, and can reach up to 10 levels high. There are three parts: the base, which provides support, the trunk, and the *pom de dalt*, the crown, consisting of the lightest members of the team, usually small children. The smallest of these is called the *enxaneta*, and must reach the top and raise their arm to signify the castle being complete. There are four classic designs: the 1/5 pillar (five levels of a single person); the 2/7 (seven storeys of pairs); 3/8 (eight levels with three people to each) and 4/6 (six levels of four). There is a healthy competitive side to these spectacles. Points are awarded for how high the castle gets, how difficult the structure is and for how smoothly the castle is constructed and deconstructed. Consult the website www.lawebdelscastellers.com to see the latest contest schedule.

C/ Bilbao, 212
Sant Martí
🚇 *Bac de Ronda*
Map p.395 E4 23

Els Castellers de Barcelona

93 232 55 56 | www.castellersdebarcelona.cat

Founded in 1969 by a group of enthusiasts from Vilafranca, a true *castells* hotbed, Els Castellers de Barcelona pioneered the nine-storey tower, now something of a team speciality. They have a distinctive uniform – white trousers and red shirts with a black sash – and perform at most of the city's district festivals, including those of Sants, Gràcia and La Mercè. To see when they are next in action have a look at their website. Otherwise, you can go see them train at their base in El Clot most Tuesday, Thursday and Saturday evenings.

Cycling

Road racing has traditionally been one of the most popular sports in Spain and, although recent doping scandals have dampened enthusiasm, it remains a firm favourite in Catalonia. While the Pyrenees stages of the Tour de France trigger an annual pilgrimage to the mountains, there are prestigious races in Barcelona too. The Tour of Catalonia (Volta de Catalunya) is a seven day event held at the end of May that draws a pool of the world's top riders to the region. The Escalada a Montjuïc, meanwhile, is an October event, and one of the last of the European racing season. Held since 1965, the great Eddie Merckx won six of the first 10 races. It takes place over one day but is split into two stages: a 5km circuit followed by a 10km time trial up the slopes of Montjuïc. Meanwhile, the Horta Velodrome (93 427 91 42, www.agendabcn.com) holds regular track-racing events throughout the year, including the Championships of Catalonia in May.

Football

FCBarcelona dominates football in the city and attending a Barça match is an incredible experience. Fans from other football-mad countries may find the atmosphere a little tame, as being a Barça season ticket holder is something of a Catalan society affair. Everyone is welcome in the stadium though, and a capacity of 98,000 means that for some games you can just turn up on the day and get a ticket. The city has another top-flight side, RCD Espanyol (see next entry), who were Uefa Cup finalists in 2007. Throughout the football season (September to June), Barça and Espanyol play at home on alternate weekends, usually on Sunday evenings but sometimes on Saturdays (check newspapers for days and kick-off times, which can often change up to a week before a game). One or the other will ordinarily have a mid-week cup fixture too. Elsewhere, Europa of Gràcia and Júpiter of Poble Nou are semi-pro outfits with respectable stadiums and followings. A Catalan 'national' side plays occasional friendlies at either the Camp Nou or Montjuïc, as do Ecuador, Argentina, Morocco and other countries with large immigrant communities in the city. Spain do not.

Av Arístides Maillol
Les Corts
🚇 **Les Corts**
Map p.391 E1 169

FCBarcelona

90 218 99 00 | www.fcbarcelona.com

Futbol Club Barcelona was founded in 1899. Throughout the Franco years, Barça suffered many injustices (and crooked officiating decisions) at the hands of the regime's team, Real Madrid. Times have changed, but the rivalry has not. Another legacy of the dictatorship years is Barça's association with democracy and fighting the good cause. The club is answerable to its more than 150,000 members and sports the Unicef logo on its shirt in place of a sponsor. Barça's golden era came in the 90s, with the club's first ever European Cup triumph. Barça repeated the trick in 2006 with a squad inspired by its star player, Brazilian maestro Ronaldinho.

El 'Camp Nou' (p.250)

Season tickets are near impossible to come by (with a waiting list of several years) but you can still become a member and get priority on tickets and other preferential conditions, including discounts. Tickets for any given match go on sale to the general public one month before the fixture over the internet, 15 days before hand via other channels, namely ServiCaixa ATMs and over the phone. Even for the big games, when ticket availability seems limited, it is worth monitoring the website: season ticket holders who can't make the game are encouraged to release their seats (they get money off their ticket the following season) and these then go on general sale, meaning that a few thousand tickets might be made available the morning before the match.

Pg Olímpic
Montjuïc
🚇 *Espanya*
Map p.399 F3 **173**

RCD Espanyol

93 292 77 00 | www.rcdespanyol.com

Founded in 1900 by university students, the club was originally called Sociedad Española de Football (Spanish Society of Football) to differentiate it from other clubs in the city, which were then dominated by foreign players. Although the club changed its name to the Catalan spelling of 'Espanyol' in 1995, there remains a sense of loyalty to the Spanish flag amongst their followers, even an ugly fascist element to their ultras. For years, Espanyol played at their own ground in Sarrià but this was sold off in 1997 and, with a new home in Cornella-El Prat still under construction (March 2009 is the predicted completion date), home games currently take place at the Olympic Stadium. Though an impressive arena, the running track does somewhat dampen the atmosphere. Despite being homeless, Espanyol have enjoyed a run of unprecedented success in recent times, winning the Spanish Cup in 2006 and reaching the UEFA Cup final in 2007. Match tickets are relatively easy to get hold of, even for games against Barça or Real Madrid. The best bet is through the Espanyol website or the club's official agency site (www.rcdespanyol.eatb.es).

Football Salon

Football salon, *fútbol sala* or *futsal*, is an indoor, five-a-side version of the beautiful game. Played on a basketball-sized court and with field hockey-sized goals, it is very popular in Spain. Barça are the only major team within the city limits, but both Martorell and Marfil Santa Coloma are based close by.

Av Arístides Maillol
Les Corts
🚇 *Les Corts*
Map p.391 E1 **169**

FCBarcelona

90 218 99 00 | www.fcbarcelona.com

The football salon team at FCBarcelona were founded in 1978 by a group of former professional footballers. By then there was already a *futsal* league firmly established and so they had to join the Catalan Third Division. By 1980 they had already reached the top flight; by 1982 they had won the league, and by the late 80s, they were involved in pan-European competitions. Throughout its history, the *futsal* department has been considered something of a poorer relation in the FCBarcelona structure, regularly having its funding cut. But when the new board of directors took the club over in 2003, one of their manifesto pledges was to professionalise the football salon section and Barça now field some of the best players in the country.

Handball

Handball is one of the most popular sports in all of Spain and the national team were the world champions in 2005. In Barcelona, the only top level team is Barça, but there are other Catalan representatives in BM Granollers (www.bmgranollers.org), just a short journey from Barcelona itself.

Small but indispensable…

Perfectly proportioned to fit in your pocket, this marvellous mini guidebook makes sure you don't just get the holiday you paid for but rather the one that you dreamed of.

Barcelona Mini Visitors' Guide
Maximising your holiday, minimising your hand luggage

Av Arístides Maillol
Les Corts
🚇 Les Corts
Map p.391 E1 169

FCBarcelona

90 218 99 00 | www.fcbarcelona.com

The handball section of FCBarcelona was founded in 1942, back when the sport was an 11-a-side game played on full-size football pitches. In the 50s, numbers were reduced to seven and they moved indoors. In the 80s, under the leadership of legendary coach Valero Rivera, Barça came to dominate Spanish handball and by the 90s they were firmly established as Europe's best, winning an unprecedented five European Cups in a row between 1996 and 2000. Although the team gradually disbanded, Barça very much remained a competitive force, winning the Champions League and the Asobal national league title in 2006. They play at the Palau Blaugrana where, as well as the all-encompassing arena season ticket, you can also buy individual sports season tickets, for which the handball one costs €29.

Motorsports

Formula One racing has a colourful history in Barcelona. In the early 50s, two Grand Prix events were held on the city streets on what was known as the Pedralbes track: the longest stretch ran down Avinguda Diagonal. New rules governing spectator safety soon brought an end to the fun but F1 racing returned to the city in 1969 at a circuit around Montjuïc. Tragedy struck in 1975 when an accident killed four spectators, spelling the end for racing on the mountain. Sixteen years later, a new purpose built track at Montmeló played host to the Spanish Grand Prix and Barcelona is now a firm fixture on the F1 calendar. Popularity has soared in recent years, largely due to the success of Spanish driver Fernando Alonso.

Montmeló

Circuit de Catalunya

93 571 97 00 | www.circuitcat.com

The Circuit de Catalunya at Montmeló opened in September 1991, hosting the Formula One Spanish Grand Prix, and has done every year since. The first MotoGP at Montmeló followed in 1992 and the Catalan Moto Grand Prix is also now an annual event. The F1 Grand Prix takes place every May while its MotoGP counterpart follows in June. The 2007 F1 race set a new record for attendance at a Spanish motorsport event of 140,700. Facilities are superb, with 17 grandstands, three of them under cover, and 25 giant screens to keep spectators up to pace with events. The track is half an hour outside the city: to get there on public transport take the L2 Cercanías train to Montmeló station from Sants. F1 tickets go on sale a year ahead of the event and start at just over €100 for basic admission on race day to almost €500 for three days in the covered grand stand. MotoGP tickets range from €30 euros basic to just over €100 euros for the full package. To buy tickets, call the Circuit de Catalunya Ticket Hotline (93 571 97 71), go through ServiCaixa or consult the Montmeló website.

Roller Hockey

Roller hockey is a fast-paced game similar to ice hockey but performed on roller skates. The sport is very popular in Catalonia and was one of the three exhibition sports of the 1992 Olympic Games. In 2007, Spain won the World Cup with a team made up entirely of Catalans. Barça is the only major team in the city.

Av Arístides Maillol
Les Corts
🚇 Les Corts
Map p.391 E1 169

FCBarcelona

90 218 99 00 | www.fcbarcelona.com

The roller hockey section of FCBarcelona can lay claim to the most decorated honours list of any of the club's sporting divisions. Initially formed in 1942, they had a troubled first few decades, struggling to find a permanent home. However, in the '70s everything fell into place and the club began to win state titles, then national titles, then European ones – and lots of them: between 1978 and 1985, they won eight European Cups. These days, Barça always start as favourite for any title and in 2007 they won the national league for a record tenth time in a row. They play at the Palau Blaugrana with season tickets costing €29. Individual match tickets are priced at €11.

Tennis

Barcelona has become an important training base for professional tennis players, especially clay court specialists. The Sanchez-Casal Academy is particularly renowned; the likes of Andy Murray, Svetlana Kuznetsova, Rafael Nadal and Daniela Hantuchova have perfected their games there in recent years. Most of the top Spanish national players are products of the city's training programmes, and the affinity many of them have with the city means that Barcelona tournaments attract big names. Spain's Davis and Federations Cup home matches are usually held in the city too, at one of the venues listed below.

Av Vall d'Hebron
Vall d'Hebron

Centre Municipal Tennis Vall d'Hebron
93 427 65 00 | www.fctennis.org
In 2007, elite women's tennis returned to Barcelona in the shape of the WTA Tour Barcelona KIA Tournament in June, and the intention is for it to become an annual summer event. Former champion and Barcelona legend, Arantxa Sánchez-Vicario, is in charge of the initiative and Vall d'Hebron certainly has the pedigree, having hosted the tennis events during the 1992 Olympics.

Bosch i Gimpera, 5
Les Corts
Map p.383 F2 **175**

The Real Club de Tenis Barcelona 1899
93 203 78 52 | www.rctb1899.es
The city's oldest tennis club plays host annually to the country's most prestigious tennis tournament, the Trofeo Conde de Godó, played every April. This clay court competition was first played in 1953 and is now an ATP Gold tournament known as the Seat Open. Local hero, the Majorcan Rafael Nadal, has won the last three tournaments, becoming the first player ever to do so. In the week preceding the main event, there is a seniors exhibition tournament featuring stars of the past. Tournament passes and tickets for the big games go on sale from late February but day passes in the early rounds can usually be bought during the tournament itself. Tickets are acquired through the office at the club directly, by phone (902 332 211) or through ServiCaixa.

Port Olímpic

Leisure Facilities

There is something of a grey area when it comes to differentiating between sport and leisure facilities in Barcelona. Gyms sometimes have spas; health clubs and county clubs may have gyms, and sport centres tend to have a bit of everything. Municipal sports centres often run a 'pay and play' system alongside membership options. Swimming pools are also a reasonable option, particularly for families, and some of them have limited gym facilities. The most successful sports chain in the city is DiR (www.dir.es) considering itself neither gym nor health club, preferring the title of 'fitness club'. In general, use of health, fitness and country club facilities requires membership. To find out where your nearest sports facilities are, the Ajuntament provides complete listings at www.bcn.es.

Beach Clubs

Other options **Beaches** p.176, **Country Clubs** see opposite page

One of the luxuries of being in Barcelona is that you can combine your health and fitness regime with views of the big blue. Beach clubs tend to be around Barceloneta or Port Olimpic, which in summer can be so crowded that the view of the water is lost to sunburnt bodies. Nevertheless, clubs remain popular and tend to have an outdoor swimming pool, gym, and solarium. Typically you have to be a member, although some offer expensive one-day passes. Expect full adult membership to set you back between €30 and €40 per month.

Pl del Mar, s/n
Barceloneta
🚇 *Barceloneta*
Map p.409 E4 **176**

Club Natació Atlètic-Barceloneta

93 221 00 10 | www.cnab.org

Set right on the beach, this club's strengths are its swimming and waterpolo teams, which compete regularly with the prestigious Club Natació Barcelona. All the usual gym and fitness facilities are here, along with ping pong. There are three large pools, Jacuzzis and masseurs. The club is clean and well-run, staff are helpful and members seem excruciatingly bronzed. One-off entry (*entrada puntual*) costs €9.80 for adults and €5.70 for children, monthly membership is €33 and well worth it. The only downside is that in winter (from the beginning of October to mid-May) the club closes at 15:00 on weekdays and 14:30 on Sundays.

Pg Joan de Borbó, 93
Vila Olímpica
🚇 *Barceloneta*
Map p.409 D2 **177**

Club Natació Barcelona

93 221 46 00 | www.cnb.es

Club Natació Barcelona (CNB) is one of the biggest and longest running swimming clubs in Barcelona, having been around for over 100 years. Club facilities are located right on the beach and include squash courts, paddle tennis courts, beach bat and ball ('ta-ka-ta') and beach football pitches. The most exhilarating aspect of this club is the active and friendly atmosphere generated by the views; the main sea water swimming pool looks out over the beach and even the gym has a sea view. Sailing and PADI diving courses are also available. The club is members only.

Sports Centres

Sports centres, known as *polideportivos/poliesportius* or a *complex esportiu*, are a good option for those who are keen to do sport but are put off by the selective membership prices of some gyms. Sports centres are invariably more reasonable in terms of price, as they tend to offer both a 'pay-as-you-go' service and monthly membership. Facilities are usually generous, often comprising football and hockey pitches, basketball courts and squash or tennis courts, as well as the usual gym, fitness classes and pool combination. To locate your local sports centre, visit the city council website, www.bcn.es.

C/ dels Esports, 2-8
Sarrià-Sant Gervasi
 Palau Reial
Map p.384 A1 **184**

Can Caralleu

93 203 78 74 | www.claror.cat

This superbly equipped sports centre is well worth the monthly membership fee of €37.50. It boasts three different swimming pools, several fitness rooms (one separate room solely for spinning), four tennis courts, two paddle tennis courts, an astroturf football pitch and two small rock climbing walls. Entry costs €6.75 for use of the pools, water jets and solarium, and €10 for use of the pool and one other sporting activity. The one-off entrance fees are rather steep, so a better option is to opt for half-time membership of €25.20, which covers full use of the facilities either in the morning, afternoon or evening.

Av Alcalde Barnils, 3-5
Sant Cugat del Vallès

Centre d'Alt Rendiment Esportiu

93 589 15 72 | www.car.edu

The CAR has a reputation as one of the top training centres in the country for athletes and sportsmen. And with good cause; many regional and national teams come to train here in preparation for international tournaments. The centre has world class facilities in over 23 sports, including athletics, gymnastics, synchronised swimming, speed skating, pentathlon and table tennis. There are Olympic training facilities, numerous field sports and pitches and an indoor tennis pavilion. This comes with a hefty membership fee though and only likely to be worth it if you are a serious competitor.

C/ Ramiro de Maeztu, 25
Gràcia
Mercat Nou
Map p.386 B3 **140**

Club Natació Catalunya

93 213 43 44 | www.cncat.org

This municipal swimming centre in Gràcia is a favourite among locals. It is child-friendly and hosts a number of activities for families. The main focus is on the indoor and outdoor pools, where courses for adults and children are run throughout the year. Facilities include a gym, exercise rooms for fitness classes, solarium, sauna, climbing wall and squash courts. The latter is particularly popular with 'pay-as-you-play' enthusiasts as there is a pool and squash combined entrance fee of €7.35. Membership paid month by month costs €29.05 for adults and €20 for children.

Diagonal, 695-701
Les Corts
Pubilla Cases
Map p.382 C3 **186**

Servei d'Esports UB

93 403 93 70 | www.ub.es/esports

Part of the University of Barcelona, this sports centre is popular with professionals, students, families and sporting all-rounders who come to enjoy the many facilities and low prices. One-off entry costs just €6 for adults and €5 for children between the ages of 6 and 12. This enables you to use the swimming pool, tennis courts, gym and fitness classes. Paddle tennis courts cost €8 for four one-hour sessions. Perhaps the most surprising, however, are the prices for the rugby, football and hockey pitches. Football is from €39 and rugby from €49.80 – making this one of the best-priced places in town. Make sure you book in advance, as it can get crowded.

Country Clubs

Country clubs tend to be members only establishments. You usually find they are amalgamated with golf, tennis or polo clubs, or in some cases they can be exclusive health clubs.

The clubs are genuinely set in the country, offering a calm respite from the city buzz in lush, green surroundings. Facilities typically include tennis, paddle tennis or squash courts, a swimming pool (often indoor and outdoor) and a social area or clubhouse. Membership fees vary radically and the signing-up fee can be very hefty, so make sure you talk to the club directly regarding full membership costs.

259

Av 11 de
Septiembre, s/n
Sant Just Desvern

Can Melich El Club

93 372 82 11 | www.canmelich.com

Can Melich is an exclusive out-of-town, members only health club, with varied membership. Top Soci (€420 monthly) includes use of all club facilities, Mix Soci includes all facilities apart from the spa, Ball Soci (€160 monthly) includes all racquet sport facilities and Pool Soci (€125 monthly) includes only the swimming pools. There are seven clay tennis courts, four artificial-grass paddle tennis courts and 12 squash and soft racquet courts. The pool area includes Jacuzzis, thermal jets, a sauna, steam baths and a solarium. The fitness facilities, comprising one gym and two fitness rooms where over 70 classes take place weekly, are adequate, but it is clear that racquet sports are the main activity here.

C/ de les Escoles
Pies, 105
Sarrià-Sant Gervasi
🚇 *Sarrià*
Map p.384 C2 179

Deportivo Iradier Femíní

93 254 17 17 | www.iradier.com

Iradier Femíní is a large, women-only health club set in a stunning 19th century mansion. A haven of relaxation, with five large gym rooms, a fitness room used for classes, a cardiovascular training room, a weights room and a resistance machines area. This is a country club however, not a spa, so if the sports facilities are what interest you, try the two paddle tennis courts, three squash courts, driving range and putting green or one of the centre's two swimming pools. Membership tariffs vary according to age and how regularly you want to visit, but the standard monthly fee is €163.75, allowing full use of the facilities at anytime. There are price reductions for women aged between 15 and 28, or 65 and over. If you are not planning to go more than once a week you could opt for the Cuota Mini (five days per month) or the Cuota Fin de Semana (weekends only), which both cost €89.51 monthly.

Plans de Bonvillar, 17
Terrassa

Reial Club de Golf El Prat

93 728 10 00 | www.rcgep.com

This prestigious golf and country club draws its inspiration from traditional English equivalents, all done with Spanish flair. The clubhouse (Casa Club) has a cards and games room, and the main bar, Bar Inglés as it is ironically called, has an outdoor terrace with pleasant views overlooking the 18 hole golf course. Facilities include an outdoor swimming pool, two paddle tennis courts, gym, sauna, hydromassage pools and a track for running or cycling through the club grounds. The snack bar is a popular post-round meeting point. However, if you want something more formal, the club restaurant offers a la carte service. Regular bridge, domino and chess tournaments and social ladders are held weekly.

Av Doctor Marañon,
17-31
Les Corts
🚇 *Palau Reial*
Map p.383 D4 65

Reial Club de Polo de Barcelona

93 448 04 00 | www.rcpolo.com

Founded in 1897, Real Club de Polo is an elite institution that has been turning out champion jockeys and first-class hockey and tennis players for more than 100 years. Highly exclusive, the entrance fee to become a member is an eye-watering €25,500, followed by a monthly membership fee of €91.80. The usual fitness facilities are all present and correct: gym (open from 07:45 to 23:00 every day), squash courts, aerobic classes, indoor and outdoor pools, sauna and beauty salon. The games room is stocked with chess, backgammon, cards and dominos, and the club also caters for families with young children. There is a nursery open from 10:00 to 17:00 on weekends and public holidays (€3.65 per hour) and a lifeguard supervises the children's outdoor pool. Members are entitled to 12 free guest passes for non-members each year. After that, each supplementary invite costs €6.

Gyms

Gyms in Barcelona tend to have swimming pools and saunas, and in some cases spa facilities, which means that there is a crossover with sports centres and health clubs. 'Pure gyms,' that concentrate wholly on cardiovascular training, free weights and fitness classes are not as common as gyms with swimming pools, due to the hot weather. Outdoor pools and solarium areas are often packed during the summer, particularly in the pre-holiday months of June and July. At almost all gyms you will need to become a member, although day rates and pay-as-you-go options are available.

Can Ricart

Sant Oleguer, 10
Raval
🚇 *Paral·lel*
Map p.402 A4 180

93 441 75 26 | www.canricart.com

Can Ricart is an open-plan gym with a range of fitness classes. There's a large free weight and resistance area downstairs, with cardiovascular machines and exercise mats upstairs. There is a 25m indoor swimming pool, which can get very crowded in the evenings, and a small outdoor solarium with about 10 sunbeds. A spa pool with water jets and Jacuzzi is open to all, but for the spa area and sauna you have to pay supplementary membership. Unless you are willing to pay over the odds for use of the sauna, the higher monthly membership isn't worth it. Standard membership costs €33 per month for use of the facilities at anytime. There is also a half-day tariff of €24 per month, which allows use of the facilities until 14:00 everyday. One-off entry to the pool costs €10 per person.

DiR

Various locations

90 210 19 79 | www.dirfitness.es

This Catalan-owned fitness chain has gyms dotted all over the city. The most impressive of DiR's 13 branches is DiR Diagonal. The 12,600sqm spot has one large fitness room with cardiovascular equipment, three other rooms used for the many daily classes and one spinning room. The best feature has to be the 50m swimming pool. It is half-indoor and half-outdoor during the summer, and surrounded by a grassy area where gym-goers relax on sun beds. Membership costs vary between centres, depending on the facilities, but average between €42 and €48 per month. Day membership is available and from time to time there are special promotions for members to invite one guest free of charge.

Esportiu Claror

C/ de Sardenya, 333
Gràcia
🚇 *Sagrada Família*
Map p.394 B2 182

93 476 13 90 | www.claror.cat/esportiuclaror

This gym and sports centre in Gràcia has a number of activities for children and families; basketball, judo, aerobics and dance classes are aimed at children from primary school age to 16 years old. Swimming classes are also available for children aged three and above. Facilities include fitness rooms, a spinning room, space for judo and taekwondo classes, a weights room and a cardiovascular area with running, rowing and bike machines. Monthly membership costs €29.80 for adults and €16.40 for under 16s. Morning, midday or evening membership costs between €21.30 and €23.20.

Holmes Place

Various locations

93 272 20 00 | www.holmesplace.es

This reputable British chain has two centres in Barcelona: Balmes, 44-46 and Ausiàs Marc, 9-11. There are three different exercise rooms in each, one used for aerobic classes, one for spinning and one for relaxation (yoga and tai chi). Around 150 classes are given each week, so any time of day you will find something on and there is no need to pre-book. The 20m swimming pool is restricting if you want to train or are a serious swimmer. On the whole, the atmosphere is adult focused, and there are few family activities. Membership costs between €70 and €80, depending on whether you choose to use the facilities anytime, or the plan which allows use at restricted times.

Well-Being

The Catalan 'work hard, play hard' philosophy can be daunting when you first arrive, and it can be hard to find time for the recommended eight hours of sleep. For those who need a break, Barcelona offers more than enough respite in the form of massages, gyms and beauty treatments.

Yoga, Pilates and tai chi classes are very popular and reasonably priced. Beauty treatments, in particular facials and massages, are pricier, but this is starting to change as they become more mainstream. In Spain, facials, hair removal and massages are still perceived as treatments for women or slightly effeminate and overly vain men.

Generally, relaxation therapies are common in Barcelona, and no longer seen as a bourgeois extravagance. As a result, the range of treatments is more extensive, and prices much more competitive.

Beauty Salons

Other options **Health Spas** p.264, **Perfumes & Cosmetics** p.299

Regular beauty treatments, particularly waxing, are common and regarded as a necessity rather than an indulgence. Prices have become more competitive, with leg waxing treatments costing as little as €15 and facials €20. With the arrival of summer, beauty salons become busier, so if possible, avoid Saturdays. High-street salons in less well off areas such as Raval and the Barri Gotic may not seem too appealing, but they often offer special deals on leg wax, bikini wax and facial combos that will set you back around €30 for the works. Laser hair removal and medical beauty treatments are on the rise as weight, vein and cellulite removal treatments become more mainstream. Botox is also big business in Barcelona and is now found in most beauty salons; Doctor Inma Costa's centre is a good reference: www.inmacosta.com.

Centre d'Estetica Groc

C/ Topazi, 9
Gràcia
🚇 Fontana
Map p.393 F1 **187**

93 218 40 65 | www.grocestetica.com

This beauty salon in the centre of Gràcia has been in business since 1983, specialising in laser hair removal, facials, peeling and botox treatments. Be prepared to pay a small fortune for treatments though, as this is not the place to come for a quick 10 minute wax. Spa, massage and nail treatments are also available.

Centro de Terapias Naturales y Estética Hera

C/ Maresme, 243
Sant Martí
🚇 La Pau
Map p.396 B4 **188**

93 313 29 75

Located in Sant Martí, this centre focuses on natural, holistic treatments that draw on Asian influences, such as ayurvedic massages, as well as standard waxing and nail treatments. Acupuncture, reiki and homeopathic therapies are also available. This place has a more organic and natural philosophy towards beauty treatments. Contact the salon directly as prices vary depending on the length of time you need.

Consultorio Dermoestético Barcelona

Rda Universitat, 6
Eixample
🚇 Universitat
Map p.393 E4 **189**

93 302 57 51

The exterior of this beauty salon is deceptively unassuming. But the centre has all the usual beauty treatments – waxing (full leg €20), rejuvenating facials (€42), uplifting anti-age masks, massages (from €35) – in addition to waist-trimming body wraps and anti-cellulite scrubs. The range of waxes used for treatments is particularly impressive. Watch out for the salon's regular special offers on beauty packs that include waxing, massage, eye relaxation and facial treatments (€30–€45).

C/ Balmes, 44-46
Eixample
🚇 *Universitat*
Map p.393 E4 **190**

Zensations

93 272 20 23 | *www.holmesplace.es*

Zensations lives up to its name; the place is calming and smells lovely. Their specialities are wine and chocolate therapy treatments which include massages, facials and full body moisturising treatments. These start from €45, whereas their standard facial and massage treatments start from €30. The site (part of Holmes Place, p.261) is reminiscent of a wood cabin in the mountains, allowing you to leave feeling warm and glowing. Bridal packages, multi-treatments, manicures, pedicures and tanning are also offered.

Hairdressers

Hair is a big deal in Barcelona; it is a demonstration of identity, a fashion statement and even representative of a particular political stance. The Catalan mullet is surely the finest – and most contradictory – example of this. Hair styling in Barcelona is avant garde with a tendency to challenge the norm, and yet it has been home to the mullet since the 80s. Once a haircut that represented a defiance of mainstream trends, the mullet (and its numerous variations) quickly became über-fashionable. In terms of salons, Raffel Pages is probably the most well-known Catalan hair salon (*peluqueria*) in Barcelona. While there are an exhaustive number of salons, a strong culture of independent hairdressing exists. Alternative art and fashion magazines distributed in independent boutiques can enlighten you further. Average prices for ladies' haircuts in a salon are between €20 for a cut and blow-dry with an independent hairdresser or in a small salon, and as much as €50 for a full 'cut and blow' in a designer salon. Most salons are unisex (men's cuts rarely pass the €20 mark) and child-friendly.

C/ Balmes, 5°, 1ª
Eixample
🚇 *Universitat*
Map p.402 C1 **191**

5° 1ª

93 412 51 62

This is a highly imaginative combined beauty salon and hairdresser. Unexpected massages, aromatherapy treatments and even the sound of the waves while you wait are all pleasant surprises. Hair is washed with deliciously scented shampoo and a head massage to finish. A basic cut for women costs from €22 and the mini-beauty treatments are €1 per minute.

C/ d'en Bot, 3
Barri Gòtic
🚇 *Liceu*
Map p.402 C2 **192**

BOT

93 342 63 39

Bot hair salon has the latest in modern, non-punk Spanish cuts and highlights. Well groomed stylists advise you on what look complements your facial features and style. This salon's strongest point however, is the wide range of highlights, lowlights and all-over colour shades that are available. Cuts are on the pricier side at €38 for a cut and blow, €27 cut only (women) and €20 cut only (men). If you want to pamper yourself silly, the salon has a small beauty salon attached that offers hair removal, manicures and make-up services.

Various locations

Raffel Pages

93 215 14 69 | *www.raffelpages.com*

This salon is a household name in Barcelona. There are over 20 branches in the centre and a number of others in the outskirts popular with men and women alike. Edgy cuts, razor straight fringes and dramatic changes in image are specialities. Prices vary between salons, depending on location. In the Rambla de Catalunya, 99 branch, a cut and blow-dry starts from €28.90 (men´s cut from €15.50). Prices don't include conditioners, hair masks or any styling products that you wish to use on your hair, so watch out for the extra charges.

C/ d'Avinyo, 12
Barri Gòtic
Jaume I
Map p.403 D4 194

Salva G

93 302 69 86 | www.salvag.com

Standing out from the crowd is important at Salva G. Sharp layering, punk-esque mullets, off-centre fringes and anything that goes against the conventional is what this unisex salon aims for. Design is clearly thought out, down to the last detail; multi-coloured lighting sets off the Redken products the salon use, and the coloured montages and leather sofas seem more lounge bar than hair salon. A cut and blow-dry costs €36, cuts for men cost €25 and a good selection of highlights and lowlights are available.

Health Spas

Other options **Leisure Facilities** p.260, **Massage** p.265

Catalonia's love affair with health spas goes back a long way. Hot springs and natural spas (*aguas thermals*) can be found throughout the Pyrenees Mountains, most notably in Andorra. Try Caldea (902 932 025, www.caldea.ad), one of the largest mountain-based natural spas in Europe. The sodium-rich minerals found in the centre's thermal waters are excellent for relaxation and rejuvenation. In Barcelona itself, the swankiest hotels house some of the city's most luxurious (and most expensive) health spas. Exceptions do exist though, such as Aqua Urban Spa, a centrally located independent spa. The Aqua Diagonal O2 Wellness Centre (93 330 63 66) and Poliesportiu Marítim Talassoteràpia (93 224 04 40) offer no-frills facilities including hydro-jets, plunge pools and spa circuits at accessible prices. If you want to treat someone to a thoroughly different experience, Metropolitan Spa in Richard Rogers' state-of-the-art Hesperia Tower (93 413 50 00, www.hesperiatower.es) is the largest spa in town, offering numerous treatments and facilities.

C/ Gran de Gràcia, 7
Gràcia
Diagonal
Map p.393 E2 195

Aqua Urban Spa

93 238 41 60 | www.aqua-urbanspa.com

Treatments at this independent spa mix holistic trends, aromatherapy products and ancient Greek and Roman traditions. The main spa area has several different baths, hydro-jets and Jacuzzi pools, each catering to different needs, like tired legs, muscle toning, anti-cellulite treatment and psoriasis. The Vichy shower, a column with 16 jets at variable pressures and temperatures, is just one of the hydrotherapy showers that combines massage with a colour sequence. The combination of colours is designed to stimulate different parts of the body and inner emotions. There is also a steam room, Roman sauna and Turkish bath. One spa session, usually lasting up to 90 minutes, costs €51. For €74.90 you get a 30-minute massage with the spa session. Chocolate and wine massages and facial treatments (*'chocolaterapia'* and *'vinoterapia'*) start from €125 and always include a spa session.

Pg Marítim de la Barceloneta, 33-35
Barceloneta
Barceloneta

Poliesportiu Marítim Talassoteràpia

93 224 04 40 | www.claror.org

This fresh seawater spa, part of Marítim municipal sports centre, provides the opportunity to relax body and mind without having to empty out your wallet. The swimming and spa centre overlooks Barceloneta beach and for this reason it is particularly popular with families. During the week, the centre is calm, allowing you to enjoy the hydro-jets and massage pools. On weekends, however, be aware that the centre fills with excitable children. Weekday entry costs €14, and on weekends it's €16.50. The most basic monthly membership starts at €25.80; full use of the centre at all times will set you back €41.10 per month.

C/ Marina, 19-21
Port Olímpic
Ⓜ Llacuna
Map p.411 D2 **196**

Six Senses Spa, Hotel Arts

93 221 10 00 | www.sixsenses.com

This superb spa on the 42nd and 43rd floors of Hotel Arts offers invigorating and breathtaking views of the Mediterranean from its slick marble spa rooms. The separate ladies and gentlemen's areas include hot Finnish sauna and steam rooms, Jacuzzis, plunge pools and chilling 'ice fountains' to get the circulation pumping. Signature treatments include hot stone therapy (€190 for 80 minutes) and the Six Senses Sensory Journey four-handed massage (€120 for 50 minutes). Express facial, manicure and eye treatments (between €49 and €60) are tailored for

SpaciOmm

those with limited time, but if you really want to treat yourself the colour therapy treatments last over two hours, and can set you back as much as €325.

C/ Rosselló, 265
Eixample
Ⓜ Diagonal
Map p.393 E2 **197**

SpaciOmm, Hotel Omm

93 445 40 00 | www.hotelomm.es

SpaciOmm is the newest addition to this ultra-modern hotel. Treatments are mainly eastern: Tibetan head massages, shiatsu, ayurvedic full-body massages and a host of other treatments use natural plant-based oils and lotions. Aside from treatments, the spa has a water circuit with a series of spa pools, Jacuzzis, plunge pools, Turkish bath and tatami cabin. SpaciOmm combines ancient traditions with modern beauty trends – why not try the Inca ritual (€115), a holistic facial treatment (€70) or the four-handed massage (€140).

Massage

Other options **Leisure Facilities** p.260, **Health Spas** p.264

Massages and facials are generally more expensive than waxing treatments. Expect to pay between €50 and €70 for a one-hour massage. The latest massage treatments to emerge are *vinoterapia* (wine therapy) and *chocoterapia* (chocolate therapy). As a wine-producing region, the former is becoming increasingly popular throughout Catalonia. As for chocotherapy (they smear it on, then feed you a fresh batch afterwards) well, the combination of chocolate, massage and total relaxation is a fool-proof recipe for success. If you want to offer a treatment to someone special, you can book chocolate massages or wine therapy treatments through Lifestyle Barcelona (www.lifestylebarcelona.com).

Various locations
Ciutat Vella

Centro Kathmandu

680 210 596 | www.tantriconepali.galeon.com

This centre specialises in Oriental massages: ayurvedic, tantric, shiatsu, taoist and champi (upper body massage). Indian oils are used and Oriental music plays in the backround. The ayurvedic massage (€75) covers the whole body and lasts almost one hour; it is more suitable for general relaxation and posture correction than for serious back problems. Shiatsu (€60 for 45 minutes) focuses on key pressure points and can be tailored to target specific back pains. Reservations are made by appointment only, so call beforehand and the centre will reserve a treatment for you in either Universitat or Ciutat Vella.

C/ Floridablanca, 133
Eixample
🚇 Sant Antoni
Map p.401 F1 199

LifeStyle Healing Centre

93 423 76 77 | www.lifestyle-world.net

LifeStyle Healing Centre combines natural healing therapies and healthy eating. There is a restaurant that serves a vegetarian, low-fat set lunch menu as you walk through the door. Further back are the treatment rooms where masseurs practice shiatsu, Thai (€49) and ayurvedic (€41.40) one-hour massages. The centre also runs meditation classes and alternative medical treatments such as naturopatia – a combination of healthy diet, sunlight, water and massage treatments.

Various locations

Masajes a 1000

93 215 85 85 | www.masajesa1000.net

Functioning on a no-booking system, Masajes a 1000 is a walk-in and wait service for professionals of both sexes with little time to dedicate to beauty treatments. It is also one of the most reasonably priced options in town for massages, hair removal treatments and facials. Don't expect centres to be luxurious or queue-free though, especially on Saturday mornings. Masajes a 1000 works on a ticket system: one ticket costs €4.80. Massages range from five minutes in a relaxation chair (one ticket) to 90 minutes on a massage bed (12 tickets) and foot massages cost just two tickets. There are branches at Sardenya, 529, Mallorca, 233 and Travessera Les Corts, 178.

Meditation

Meditation is becoming increasingly popular here. It hasn't yet gained the same popularity as activities such as yoga, tai chi or Pilates, but it is no longer perceived as a kooky 60s throw-back. Many tai chi, yoga and martial art centres run meditation sessions. The Fundació Casa del Tibet (93 207 59 66, www.casadeltibetbcn.org) is also an important reference. The centre gives free talks and classes in meditation, yoga and the Tibetan language as well as celebrating Tibetan and Buddhist festivals.

Pl Sant Agustí Vell, 6
La Ribera
🚇 Arc de Triomf
Map p.404 A3 201

Centre Dojo Zen de Barcelona

93 268 39 55 | www.zenbarcelona.org

Founded in 1979, this meditation centre or '*dojo*' is a practicing Tibetan monastery. The doors are open to members every day except Sunday so they can take part in meditation and prayer sessions either individually or in a group. Each session is guided by a monk and intensive sessions can be organised on weekends. The €20 joining fee allows you to attend as often as you like. Opening times are Monday to Friday from 07:30 to 08:45 and 19:30 to 20:45 and Saturdays from 08:30 to 10:00.

Pl Gal la Placidia
8-10, pral. 2ª
Gràcia
🚇 Fontana
Map p.393 E1 202

Centro Budista Tara

93 217 04 74 | www.centrobudistatara.com

This non-profit organisation instructs people on the teachings of Tibetan Buddhism. There are free activities at 20:00 from Monday to Friday, ranging from group meditation sessions and topical discussion groups to philosophical teachings. The centre frequently runs weekend courses, but if this is not enough to relieve you of your daily stresses, Budista Tara has its own retreat in Asturias. Set in the Asturian Mountains, it is a lovely spot to reflect and meditate.

C/ Vallcanera, 28
Sils

Dojo Asai de Sils

97 285 63 48 | www.dojoasai.com

Dojo Asai is a Japanese meditation centre just outside Barcelona that teaches Nembutsu and Naikan. Nembutsu Meditation is taught through intensive weekend courses that begin on Saturday at 10:00 and end on Sunday at 12:00. The course is split into three main components; Nembutsu, Shinsei and Naikan. Shinsei is a form of meditation that incorporates movement of the arms and hands. Nembutsu and Naikan, however, focus more on techniques of internal reflection and meditation. The course costs €65 and includes board and breakfast. Five to 10 day retreats and personalised meditation programmes are alternative options.

Mahakaruna Buddhist Centre

C/ Girona 83, 3-2
Eixample
🚇 *Girona*
Map p.394 A4 204

93 487 69 17 | www.meditarabcn.org

This Buddhist centre, a member of the International Kadampa Buddhist Union, also has sister-sites dotted around Catalonia. Classes focus on teaching the Buddhist way of life. Prayer and meditation sessions are held every week in English and Spanish and tend to attract a multinational mix of people. For those new to the discipline, meditation courses and individual classes are available (€6 per individual class or €25 for five classes). Group meditation sessions are held every Tuesday at 20:00. The group also organise retreats ('*retiros*') to remote and thought-provoking places. There is usually one retreat per month and these can last anything from two to 14 days.

Nail Bars

Nails bars, as opposed to nail salons, are still new territory in Barcelona. The first nail bar (*barra de uñas*) to open in Spain was in Madrid not long ago, and then Bilbao. Barcelona is likely to be next in line. In the meantime, there are enough nail salons and institutes to keep cuticles primped. The most basic and quick manicure treatments typically cost around €15 to €20, whereas pedicures are usually slightly more expensive (around €25). Silicon and gel nail treatments are more expensive but increasingly popular. It is worth booking an appointment in advance as first class nail salons are scarce and highly sought after.

Master Nails Institut

C/ Castanyer, 21
Sarrià-Sant Gervasi
🚇 *Lesseps*
Map p.385 E2 205

93 254 13 53 | www.masternails.com

Master Nails Institut is a specialist in nails of every shape, colour and form. There are a range of beauty services, such as waxing and facials, but nail treatments are the main draw and cater to every taste. Gel nails, silicone nails, painted nails and recovery treatments for damaged nails range from €15 to €30 per treatment. Master Nails Institut also offers professional training courses. The nearest train stops are El Puxot or Av del Tibidabo (Ferrocarril Line 7). Being in the Zona Alta, it is not accessible by metro.

The Nail Concept

Various locations

90 236 67 70 | www.thenailconcept.com

Nail treatments are clearly the focus in this very fashionable, design-oriented salon with its trendy clientele. There are five nail salons in the city centre and a further three in the outskirts of the city; The Nail Concept just above Plaça Catalunya (93 481 63 33, Rambla Catalunya 20) is the most central. Manicure and pedicure treatments (€15-€20) last 30 minutes each. If you have the manicure and pedicure twin treat (€43) make sure you set an hour aside.

Pilates

Other options **Yoga** p.270

Pilates was first developed in 1945. Based on eastern traditions, European training methods and Greek and Roman exercises, it is an invigorating workout designed to strengthen body and mind. It is essentially a more rigorous form of yoga, centring on similar principles of flexibility, posture and strength, but the movements in Pilates are

267

quite different. It is beneficial for helping patients to prepare for and recover from surgery or pregnancy and is particularly popular with athletes because it helps to prevent injury. Many health clubs and gyms now offer Pilates classes. Failing that, all you need is a mat to practice Pilates at home.

C/ Laforja, 101
Sarrià-Sant Gervasi
Hospital Clínic
Map p.392 C1 207

Area Pilates
93 209 10 63 | www.areapilates.com
This centre uses Pilates equipment for individual and group classes (maximum four people). You can do allegro, fitball, bosu, elastic resistance or work with multi-sized balls. Each room is dedicated to a different Pilates method. One group class costs between €30 and €36 (depending on the chosen method) and the monthly fee is €105 to €130 for one 55 minute class per week. Located in the *Zona Alta* area, classes are used by professionals and well-to-do residents of the district.

C/ Girona, 15
Eixample
Urquinaona
Map p.403 F1 208

Centre Pilates Barcelona
93 301 08 46 | www.barcelona-pilates.com
Centre Pilates was first opened in 2003 by French former professional ballet dancer Fabien Menegon. The peculiarity of this centre is that all classes are privately tutored. Qualified Pilates instructors (many former professional dancers) design class structure, level of difficulty and use of equipment for each individual pupil. With classes being one-on-one, the level is more intense and the prices higher. One class costs €46 and a ticket valid for five classes costs €220. The centre is open from Monday to Friday, 08:00 to 20:00 (Saturdays 10:00-14:00).

Pg Francesc
Macià, 89
Sant Cugat

Pilates Powerhouse
93 544 16 94 | www.pilatespowerhouse.es
The name 'Pilates powerhouse' may evoke images of sweaty gyms and bulging muscles, but this is at odds with the centre itself. It is definitely focused on the physically challenging aspect of Pilates, but there are no excessively bulging muscles in sight. A wide range of equipment is used during the classes, including resistance ropes, large inflatable balls, bars and a number of contraptions designed to increase flexibility, strength and toning. If there's a chance of breaking into a sweat anywhere, it's here.

Reiki
Reiki is a Japanese healing technique used for stress reduction and relaxation. Meaning 'universal life force energy', it is administered by laying hands over parts of the body to release negative energy. The theory goes that by releasing this energy you are more capable of feeling happy and relaxed. Because of its mental, physical and emotional healing properties, it is often used with medical treatments to promote recovery. Compared to other relaxation practices such as yoga, Pilates and meditation, reiki is fairly new to Barcelona and there aren't yet many places that offer treatments. You are most likely to find reiki in beauty salons that specialise in eastern and oriental relaxation treatments.

C/ Sant Agustí, 5
Gràcia
Diagonal
Map p.412 A1 210

Associació de Terapeutes Reiki a Catalunya
93 217 31 78 | www.reikicatalunya.cat
This reiki-only association specialises in treatments and training. It offers what may be the best prices in the city; €25 for a 45 minute session, which usually lasts an hour in total. If you are new to Reiki and unsure whether it is for you, 15 minutes taster sessions are available for €5. And for those who want to specialise in the practice, the centre regularly holds training courses. It is best to call before booking as the association shares space with other treatment centres and opening times can be fluid. It is worth becoming a member if you plan to take regular courses or treatments.

Centre Namaste

C/ Calabria, 202
Eixample
🚇 *Entença*
Map p.392 B3 **211**

687 952 461 | *www.centrenamaste.com*

Centre Namaste (officially the Catalan Reiki Federation) focuses almost entirely on reiki treatments. But, it also has unusual courses that are difficult to find elsewhere. Interpretation of Dreams is the most abstract and original. Meditation sessions, yoga and tai chi are sideline activities. Reiki sessions officially last one hour, although they often overrun by 15 to 30 minutes. Considering the extra time, sessions are reasonably priced at €40. Reiki courses are popular as they teach you how to practice on yourself and others. Level one costs €135 and runs over a whole weekend.

Oxigen

C/ Borí i
Fontestá, 16
Sarrià-Sant Gervasi
🚇 *Hospital Clínic*
Map p.392 C1 **212**

93 200 73 33

A specialised group of masseurs, dieticians, physiotherapists and beauty therapists are on-hand at this luxurious and calming beauty salon. Body sculpting, firming treatments and facials are popular, as are reiki sessions. One-hour reiki treatments start at €50 but can cost more depending on the treatment given and the products used. Practitioners compose personalised programmes that you can follow at home.

Stress Management

Other options **Support Groups** p.120

Working long hours and balancing your professional and personal life can seem difficult at times. Stress management is a way of learning how to cope with these daily stresses so your health and general well-being are not affected. In Barcelona, stress manangement is a fairly new venture and as a result, there are few centres offering courses. The business school ESADE (http://exed.esade.edu) is ahead of the times; they offer two-day stress management courses at the not altogether stress-free sum of €1,850. Alternatively, most psychiatrists offer treatment and some hold group sessions during which you try to verbalise what is causing your stress. CAPP Centro de Atencion Psicologica y Psicoterapeutica (93 229 22 94, www.psicologoscapp.com) is a well-recognised and experienced centre.

Tai Chi

Tai chi is a self-paced form of gentle physical exercise combined with meditation techniques that originated in China more than 2,000 years ago. It involves performing a series of postures or movements in a slow, graceful manner. Appealing to all ages, although particularly popular with older adults, the level of intensity, pace and difficulty of movements can be adjusted to suit you. Health benefits include stress reduction, better balance and increased flexibility. Tai chi does not require large spaces or special equipment, and you'll often find it practised in gyms or community centres. As with yoga, you will usually be required to wear white clothing. For information on tai chi classes in the city and centres where classes are given, see the Catalan Tai Chi Chuan Association website: www.kungfuweb.org.

Centro Ceitai

C/ Jonqueres, 8
La Ribera
🚇 *Urquinaona*
Map p.403 E1 **213**

93 268 03 85 | *www.ceitai.com*

Centro Ceitai focuses almost entirely on tai chi (taiji quan) and its various teachings. The school is an excellent source of first-rate classes and high teaching standards. Founded in 2000 by Catalan Maestro Jose Luis Serra and his wife, Maestra Kazuko Onkai (both trained in the art) the centre today is a member of the International Taiji Quan Research Institute. Lessons are run all year round from Monday to Friday, in addition to regular two or three-day seminars and intensive courses. One weekly class costs €37 per month. For two it increases to €52. There is an inscription fee, as with most tai chi centres, but this centre also charges annual insurance of €50.

Instituto Wu Shu San Chai

C/ Joaquím Blume, 2
Poble Sec
🚇 **Universitat**
Map p.400 B2 **214**

646 019 606 | www.wushusanchai.org

In summer, this martial arts and tai chi school gives classes in the fresh air up on Montjuic (Monday, Wednesday and Friday). Tai chi chuan and kung fu are the principal courses taught from Monday to Thursday, between 08:15 and 21:30. Tai chi classes are very reasonably priced; €45 per month for two weekly classes and €65 for four weekly classes. Five types of acupuncture are also available. Alternatively, if you need to release frustrations in a more physical way, lessons in the use of Chinese weapons are also given.

UBK Ki Dojo Catalunya

C/ Acàcies, 17
Horta-Guinardó
🚇 **Maragall**
Map p.387 F4 **215**

93 351 22 55 | www.ubk-centre.com

At this centre, emphasis is placed on the spiritual aspects of tai chi, with aikido and free mediation classes three times a week. Perhaps UBK's most original aspect is the UBKids non-violent martial arts class held on Thursday afternoons from 17:45 to 19:00, for 7 to 12 year olds. One weekly class costs €37 per month and a monthly payment of €75 covers unlimited classes at the centre. There is a signing up fee but discounts are regularly on offer. With over 20 years experience, the school has support from various organisations and regularly hosts weekend breaks and intensive classes in nearby parks.

Yoga

Other options **Pilates** p.267

An Indian tradition dating back more than 5,000 years. Six different branches exist, but hatha yoga, also known as 'yoga of postures', is the path you are most likely to come across. It is excellent for toning muscles, strengthening the spine and improving circulation and flexibility. Barcelona is a great place to learn as a beginner because it is still relatively new here. Many of the studios offer one free taster class. Most centres require you to wear white clothing. If you are content with simply one weekly session of yoga, try your local community centre (www.bcn.es/centrescivics) for trimester-long courses, as they remain the most reasonably priced group classes in town.

Carlos Claramunt

C/ Muntaner, 22
Eixample
🚇 **Universitat**
Map p.393 D4 **217**

93 451 28 00 | www.carlosclaramunt.com

Carlos Claramunt is an extremely professional yoga institute, with over 25 years of teaching experience in Barcelona (Instituto Sundari) and Sant Cugat (Instituto Ganesha). Hatha yoga is the main discipline covered, with occasional meditation and belly dancing (*danza oriental*) sessions, each running for 75 minutes. Prices become more reasonable (and worthwhile) once you opt for the higher monthly tariffs; €70 for three classes per week, €85 for four. As a final tip; ayurvedic, Thai and holistic massages are highly recommended.

Escola Yoga Vida

C/ Sant Guillem 27, entlo 1ª
Sarrià-Sant Gervasi
🚇 **Fontana**
Map p.385 E4 **218**

93 209 33 98 | www.escolayogavida.com

This school has been providing an introduction to yoga since 2000, under the direction of Habib Ba. Group classes cost a monthly fee of €56 (two 75-minute classes per week, at any time). The limited classes are timetabled to suit working hours, starting at 07:15, 14:30 and 18:00. This is ideal for professionals but if you would rather practise yoga during the day to avoid the post-work rush, this may not be the place for you.

Well-Being

Various locations

Happy Yoga

93 318 11 07 | www.happyyoga.com

Happy Yoga may have the most extensive number of classes in the city and yes, overall, they do have a happy vibe. The yoga-only centre has five branches in the city specialising in kundalini, hatha and Tibetan yoga; the most central of these is in Plaça Universitat. All levels are welcome, from beginners to advanced. The first trial class is free, but do try to wear white cotton clothing if possible. Monthly membership costs about €50, depending on the number of monthly classes that you take. Classes in meditation, tai chi, Pilates and specially compiled children's classes are also available.

C/ de Sicilia, 236
Eixample
🚇 **Monumental**
Map p.394 B4 `220`

Nectar Kundalini Yoga

93 265 89 26 | www.nectarkundaliniyoga.com

Nectar Kundalini is for those who are looking to practice a more spiritual form of yoga, incorporating mantras, music and active and passive meditation techniques. This intimate setting, complete with floor cushions and incense, may not be to everyone's taste but it certainly awakens the senses. If you want to maintain good habits at home, courses in healthy eating and vegetarian cooking run throughout the year.

Pl Universitat, 4,
1º 2ª
Eixample
🚇 **Glòries**
Map p.393 D4 `221`

Yoga Studio

93 451 29 28 | www.estudiodeyoga.com

Hatha yoga and ashtanga vinyasa are the two variants that Yoga Studio work with. Beginner, intermediate and teacher-training classes are given. One of the advantages of this school is the flexibility over prices and when you can attend. Monthly payments of €80 cover an unlimited number of lessons, at any time except Sunday. If you would rather take part in yoga classes sporadically, there are cards available in blocks of four, eight or 12 two-hour lessons (€52, €96, €120 respectively). A one-off two hour class costs €14.

Palau Reial gardens

271

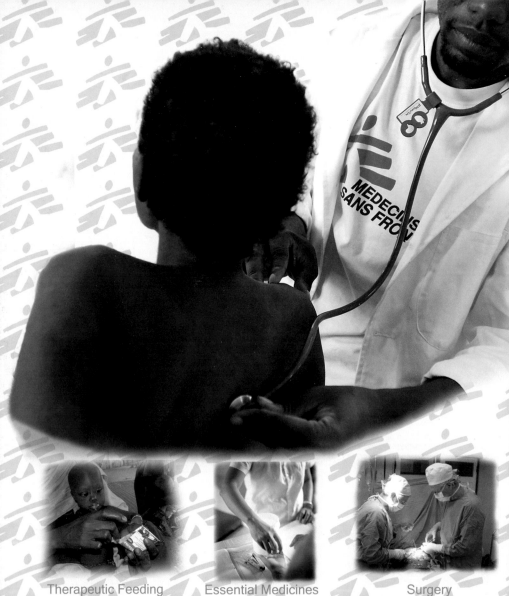

Therapeutic Feeding   Essential Medicines   Surgery

MEDECINS SANS FRONTIERES
أطبـاء بـلا حـدود

Providing emergency medical
relief in over 70 countries.

help us help the helpless

Shopping

Shopping

Barcelona is a top European shopping destination. Passeig de Gràcia offers the finest in couture and designer brands, Born, Gràcia and Barri Gòtic are havens for one-off pieces from new Catalan designers, while Eixample is a hot spot for those seeking the lowest prices on big name Spanish labels such as Massimo Dutti, Zara and Mango. International brands bought here will almost certainly be cheaper than cities like London, Paris and Milan. Certain companies that import goods from abroad, however, can be more expensive than in their home countries. Habitat, p.293, is one example. Tax is included in all items, so the amount on the ticket is the price you pay. If you buy from a market stall, prices can be haggled over, so do feel free to offer an alternative price, and be aware of not being overcharged. If sales assistants or vendors get over zealous, feel free to get defensive and walk away. They're highly unlikely to take offence and are less likely to take advantage of you on price. Sales are impressive, especially for clothes, when items can be reduced by up to 80%. Barri Gòtic, though better known for its architecture, has some wonderful independent boutiques, while the centre of the city is where the brand name shops are found. Simply wander the cobbled lanes and you'll stumble across all sorts of shopping treasures.

Clothing Sizes

Women's Clothing

Women's Clothing						
Aust/NZ	8	10	12	14	16	18
Europe	36	38	40	42	44	46
Japan	5	7	9	11	13	15
UK	8	10	12	14	16	18
USA	6	8	10	12	14	16

Women's Shoes						
Aust/NZ	5	6	7	8	9	10
Europe	35	36	37	38	39	40
France only	35	36	38	39	40	42
Japan	22	23	24	25	26	27
UK	3.5	4.5	5.5	6.5	7.5	8.5
USA	5	6	7	8	9	10

Men's Clothing						
Aust/NZ	87	90	93	96	99	102
Europe	46	48	49.5	51	52.5	54
Japan	S	-	M	M	-	L
UK	35	36	37	38	39	40
USA	35	36	37	38	39	40

Men's Shoes						
Aust/NZ	7	8	9	10	11	12
Europe	41	42	43	44.5	46	47
Japan	26	27	27.5	28	29	30
UK	7	8	9	10	11	12
USA	7.5	8.5	9.5	10.5	11.5	12.5

Measurements are approximate only; try before you buy

What & Where to Buy – Quick Reference

Online Shopping

As more people get an internet connection at home, online shopping is increasing in popularity. But, postal rates in Spain are relatively high, so while hours may be saved by not traipsing around shops, you won't necessarily save money. Some local sites do offer free delivery when spending over a certain amount, however. For example, electrical goods stores and supermarkets tend to charge only a nominal fee to deliver goods to your door. Buying things like books from domestic sites can be expensive, as the delivery charge is determined by weight. Payment options vary from site to site; some accept credit or debit cards, while others only use PayPal. Many expats frequent online shopping sites in their home country for items they can't get here. Goods arriving from overseas may be inspected by customs on arrival.

Online Shopping	
Website	Type of Goods
www.amazon.co.uk	Discounted books, CDs, DVDs, toys, videogames, vinyl
www.capraboacasa.com	Groceries
www.carrefour.es	Groceries, cameras, electrical goods, home furnishings, mobile phones, wines, food
www.casadellibro.com	Books
www.condisline.com	Groceries
www.eBay.es	New and used books, cameras, CDs and DVDs, clothes, games
www.elcorteingles.es	Groceries, flowers, gifts, wines
www.freshcurry.com	Fresh curry sauces
www.ukshoppinginspain.com	Products from British shops, including Argos, Boots, Mothercare, Next

Refunds & Exchanges

Retailers are required by law to exchange faulty goods. But they don't have to accept the return of non-faulty items. Returns policies vary greatly, as each independent store or chain sets their own rules. But, once they've made them, they have to honour them. If they do accept returns, you'll receive a credit note or an exchange. Time limits will be specified, which again vary from company to company (usually between seven days and a month) and you will need to present the receipt as proof of the date of purchase. Most stores stipulate the item must not have been used or worn. Some shops display their policy in-store, but others do not, so it's always a good idea to check with the sales assistant whether or not you'll be able to return an item. During sales periods, shops can change their returns policies, except in the case of faulty goods.

Consumer Rights

If a shop refuses to exchange faulty goods, you need to ask for a complaints form (*hoja de reclamación*, or *full de reclamació* in Catalan). All shops have to supply these and carry a sign clearly stating that they have them. The form is in triplicate; a copy for you, one for the shop and the third goes with an original receipt and any other relevant paperwork to the Oficina Municipal d'Informació al Consumidor (OMIC). Their office is at Ronda Sant Pau 43 (93 402 78 27, www.omic.bcn.es). Similarly, if a shop with a returns policy for non-faulty goods refuses to refund your money, exchange the item or give a credit voucher, and you are within the time limits and terms set by them, you can also make a complaint, following the same procedure. The Agència Catalana del Consum (ACC) can also help (www.consum.cat).

Mini Marvels

Explorer *Mini Visitors' Guides* are the perfect holiday companion. They're small enough to fit in your pocket but beautiful enough to inspire you to explore. With detailed maps, visitors' information, restaurant and bar reviews, the lowdown on shopping and all the sights and sounds of the city, these mini marvels are a holiday must.

275

Shipping

Any of the relocation companies mentioned on p.96 will be able to offer quotes for large items that need to be sent abroad. El Corte Inglés can organise shipping, but no other large name shops or department stores offer a 'shop and ship' service. If you do opt for a private shipping service, be aware that quicker tends to be costlier. Air freight can be much more expensive than shipping. Even with the latter, the money saved on buying in Spain will often be lost in the cost of transport. Redhead International is a British company that offers competitive rates on delivery from Spain by truck (www.redhead-int.com) while DHL and UPS are, usually, highly efficient. See Post, p.103 of the General Information chapter, for contacts. Avoid posting things from the local Correos (post office), as rates are extremely high for even low weight packages.

How to Pay

All shops and markets in Barcelona accept cash payments in euros. However, it's a good idea not to carry around large wads of folding money, as pick-pockets are quite common. Large shops and some smaller ones accept payment by Visa and Mastercard as well as Visa Electron and Maestro debit cards. Other cards like American Express, Diners Club and JCB are also accepted in many shops. As a precaution to minimise fraud, most shops insist customers provide photographic ID such as a passport or driving licence when paying by credit or debit card. Some shops are set up to take payments by the 'Chip and PIN' system but may also require a signature. Many small shops will only accept card payments for purchases over a certain value and most markets only accept cash.

Bargaining

Bargaining is out of the question in brand name shops, where the price on the tag is the price you pay. However, in a city filled with wonderful independent shops and markets, bargaining does happen. Furniture shops are also open to offers, and a respectable alternative price will always be considered. Paying in cash, especially if you're buying in bulk or dealing with high prices, may help. If you don't ask, you won't get. Simply be up front and ask vendors if they would be willing to negotiate on the price. If they are, just tell them what you're willing to pay and ensure you're alternative is not insulting. If they're open to negotiation, they are likely to give you a counter offer. If you're buying food in the big markets you can't bargain with stallholders, but do keep an eye on the price. Those believed to be tourists have occasionally been overcharged for their fruit and veg.

Santa Caterina (p.310)

Alcohol

Other options **Drinks** p.317,
On the Town p.346

Traditional wine pouches

Alcohol is easy to come by in Barcelona. Supermarkets stock a selection of cheap and medium-priced wine, beer and a range of spirits, while many corner shops also sell cans of beer and a less dependable selection of wines and cava. Many independent delicatessens and upmarket *colmados* (grocers) stock a handful of pricier wines and are happy to offer advice as to which bottle matches your cheese. The specialist *botigas* (wine shops) that scatter the city are the place to find that truly special bottle. Try Mas Bacus for a huge range of Spanish and Catalan wines, or Los Vinos del Mundo for imported wines. Prices are cheap; a six-pack of beer costs less than €2, fair-quality wine starts at €5 and a bottle of spirits costs €8 to €15.

Alcohol			
Los Vinos del Mundo	C/ Gran De Gràcia, 202	Gràcia	93 368 65 98
Mas Bacus	C/ Enric Granados, 68	Eixample	93 453 43 58
Torres	C/ Nou de la Rambla, 25	Raval	93 317 32 34
Vila Viniteca	C/ Agullers, 7	Born	93 327 77 77

Art

Other options **Art Galleries** p.163, **Art Classes** p.199

Barcelona's art scene is buzzing, with the dominance of veterans like abstract expressionist Antoni Tàpies (whose foundation stands imposingly on Carrer Aragó) increasingly being challenged by the bold, graffiti-influenced works of Boris Hoppek and his contemporaries. At times it seems like every trendy café and bar in Barcelona secretly wants to be a gallery, so common are small solo shows by emerging artists. Iguapop sells work by some outstanding urban artists, including Hoppek (93 310 07 35, www.iguapop.net, Comerc 15). Prices start at around €500 but go far higher for collectible and particularly promising artists. For more established names, there is a run of galleries on and around Carrer Consell de Cent, including the Galeria Toni Tàpies, which boasts a prestigious little collection of local and international talents, including Sol LeWitt (93 487 64 02, www.tonitapies.com, Consell de Cent 282). Prices start in the thousands. Galeria Kowasa (93 215 8058, www.kowasa.com, Carrer Mallorca 235) specialises in photography, with prices for original images starting at around €600.

Art & Craft Supplies

Other options **Art Classes** p.199, **Art Galleries** p.163

C/ Ferran, 39
Barri Gòtic
🚇 *Liceu*
Map p.403 D4 **1**

Belles Arts Ferran
93 302 38 98
This shop sells practically everything related to arts and crafts. Apart from leading brand names in oils, water colours and acrylics, they also stock textile and glass paints, staring from around €2. Easels, canvasses and mannequins in a range of sizes

277

are available, as are craft papers and drawing pads. Brushes and other specialist tools are plentiful. There are also painting by numbers sets and books on technique. The art boxes and sets are particularly good value; Staedler drawing pencils are around €7, 12 Derwent water colour pencils cost €13 and a wooden case of 24 Titan oils is €115. The interior looks pretty chaotic but the staff seem to know exactly where everything is.

Spanish ceramics

C/ de Sepúlveda, 81
Eixample
🚇 *Rocafort*
Map p.392 B4 **2**

Pepar
93 424 54 01

Paper is the speciality in this store. It comes in a huge variety of shades and textures, from A1 sheets of card in dozens of colours, to decorative handmade pieces and wrapping paper, as well as art pads. There's a section of ready-cut and folded card in various sizes (with matching envelopes) for those who want to make their own greetings cards. Staff are keen to help or happy to let you browse.

Baby Items

Carrefour hypermarkets (p.306) are a good option for everything baby related, from baths and bottles to pushchairs and car seats. Their own brand products, including the Tex Bebé range of clothes, are very affordable. Babys R Us (93 356 23 04, www.toysrus.es) in Diagonal Mar's shopping centre also stocks a wide selection of baby goods, and although slightly more pricey, in-store entertainment for kids and regular baby care demonstrations make it a popular choice for many parents. Italian company Chicco, (93 356 03 74, www.chicco.es) another all-rounder, has a number of stores around the city (Ronda de San Pedro 5, Diagonal 35, and Ciudad de la Asunción s/n) and their products are also available in other shops such as El Corte Inglés (p.305).

When it comes to baby food, most supermarkets have a limited choice. Pharmacies tend to have a larger variety and Veritas (90 266 77 89, www.veritas.es) stocks a good selection of organic foods. There are nine stores in Barcelona, including Via Laietana 28, Gran Via 539 and Travessera de les Corts 271.

High factor sun creams for babies are widely available, as are Johnson's Baby products. Most baby shops have list services to register for gifts for new arrivals. Some companies, like Prénatal (www.prenatal.com), also offer special discounts on future purchases once the list has ended.

Beachwear

Other options **Sports Goods** p.302, **Clothes** p.282

As April arrives, summer diets begin and beachwear appears in fashion boutiques and high street stores. It tends to stay on the shop floor until the end of September, although the selection becomes more limited.

But you shouldn't have a problem getting hold of beachwear out-of-season, as sports shops, surf shops and lingerie vendors stock beachwear all year. At Decathlon (p.302) you can purchase a bikini for as little as €8 and kids' swimsuits for €4. It has nine stores in Barcelona, including Carrer de La Canuda 20 (93 342 61 61) in the old town and

Avinguda Gran Vía, 75 (93 259 15 92) in L´Hospitalet. They also sell all manner of beach accessories, snorkelling gear, rash vests and fins at competitive prices.

Quiksilver (www.quiksilver.com, 93 552 56 06) surf shop is always a safe bet in terms of style and quality. Bikinis and board shorts here can cost as much as €80, which may seem expensive, but you're paying for quality material designed to withstand surfing wear and tear. There are six stores, including those at Avinguda Diagonal 617 and down the road at 545. Another can be found at Portal del Angel 19 or Plaça de Catalunya 14.

Lower prices (and quality) are to be had in high-street shops such as Zara, Bershka, Mango, and H&M (see Clothes, p.282), where you can usually pick up a bikini for less than €10.

For a wider range of styles, the lingerie stores Calzedonia (www.calzedonia.it) and Women's Secret (www.womensecret.com) have a generous selection of colourful and sexy bikinis at reasonable prices. Women's Secret stores are dotted about the city, including sites at Avinguda Diagonal 399 and 463, at Fontanella 16 and Portal del Angel 38. Call 93 318 70 55 for the last store.

Bicycles

Cycling is increasingly popular in Barcelona, both as a sport and as a means of transport. Affordable bicycles are available in many of the sports chains, such as Decathlon (p.302), and in the sports department of El Corte Inglés (p.305). There are also plenty of specialist shops and repair places throughout the city, where prices and quality tend to be higher.

Helmets (which cost around €30) are not compulsory, although front and back lights and bells are, and sturdy locks are essential (expect to pay upwards of €35). It's illegal to chain bikes to lamp-posts or other street furniture, although many people still do so. Bike parking facilities are widely available, and the city hall is working to install more. One recent but highly visible addition to the city's cycling landscape has been the launch of the municipal bike hire scheme, Bicing (p.34), in which card-holders can pick up retro-styled, bright red and white bikes from one of the special stations around the city and leave them at any other. Membership costs €24 a year and cards can be obtained from www.bicing.com. The bikes are free for the first half hour and 30 cents for each half hour after that.

Second-hand bicycles are usually sold privately, through websites such as www.loquo.com and www.bikezona.com.

C/ Santa Tecla, 5
Gràcia
 Diagonal
Map p.392 F2 **3**

Bicitecla
93 368 69 78 | *www.bicitecla.com*
A small, friendly outfit in Gràcia that specialises in urban bikes and accessories, Bicitecla sells foldable and upright bikes, with prices starting from €475 and €325 respectively. There is also a repairs workshop that fixes simple problems on the spot. Bicitecla also offers bike hire (from €16 for five hours or €24 for 24 hours), including delivery to your hotel or home.

C/ Diputació, 369
Eixample
Tetuan
Map p.394 A4 **4**

Bikeland
93 246 03 62 | *www.bikelandsl.com*
If you're looking for disc brakes, aluminium frames or specialised tyres, Bikeland is the place to head. The cavernous store caters to serious mountain biking enthusiasts, with a huge selection of bikes, accessories, clothing and tyres, and a knowledgeable staff. Prices for basic models start at around €300 but can go much higher. There is also a range of BMX (from €500), foldable (from €250), urban (from €200) and electric bikes (from €500), as well as children's models (from €100).

279

C/ Sepúlveda, 109
Eixample
🚇 **Urgell**
Map p.392 C4 **5**

Tomas Domingo, The Bike House

93 452 16 16 | www.tomasdomingo.com
This long-established specialist stocks comprehensive ranges of mountain bikes (from €350), BMX (from €300) and road bikes (from €300), as well as accessories and a handful of urban, foldable and children's bikes. Tomas Domingo offers financing schemes and will give a discount in exchange for your old bike; there is also a repairs workshop. A second, equally large branch is at Passeig Sant Gervasi 12, which can be called on 93 416 47 87.

Books

Other options **Second-Hand Items** p.300, **Libraries** p.224

Being such a cosmopolitan city, many local bookshops not only stock Catalan and Castilian language texts, but also cater for the needs of the many foreign residents living here. Fnac (p.306) has a decent English language section. Books on the whole are not that cheap and original language texts imported from overseas can be quite pricey. Most bookshops will do individual orders for titles they don't stock, but if you are ordering from overseas it may take a while for your book to arrive. Some stationers and newsagents also sell books and you can usually pick up bargains like pocket cookery books and classics for a few euros. Sant Antoni Market (p.310) on Sunday mornings has some good deals on new and second-hand books and comics (see Markets, p.309).

C/ Gran Via de
les Corts Catalanes, 616
Eixample
🚇 **Universitat**
Map p.393 E4 **6**

Altaïr

93 342 71 71 | www.altair.es
This claims to be the biggest travel bookshop in Europe, and has guides and maps on hundreds of destinations. Handily divided by continent, it has everything from small guides for a few euros, travelogues (literary and photographic) and volumes on obscure cultures, street maps and atlases. The ambience is chilled, with soft lighting and world music playing in the background (CDs are available) with comfy chairs to read on or to plan your next trip. They also stock a good selection of books on food, wildlife and wine as well as travel-related accessories like rucksacks and bum-bags. English, Spanish and Catalan books are the most common, and there's a comprehensive section on Catalonia in various languages. The message board outside is filled with hundreds of ads by travellers offering lifts or those hoping to catch one. The shop also hosts photographic exhibitions.

Bookish Barcelona

C/ Roger de
Liúria, 118
Eixample
🚇 **Verdaguer**
Map p.393 F3 **7**

BCN Books

93 457 76 92 | www.bcnbooks.com
This long established bookshop carries all the usual teaching (and studying) products for those involved with TEFL and ESOL courses. It also has a very good range of fiction and travel books. There is a 'cash and carry' at Rosselló 24, for those that want to purchase in bulk.

280

C/ Montseny, 17
Gràcia
🚇 *Fontana*
Map p.393 F1 **8**

Hibernian Books
93 217 47 96 | *www.hibernian-books.com*
This second-hand, English bookshop is a relatively new addition to the city and offers some real bargains on genre fiction for under €2. The antique section exudes that old book smell (as does the rest of the shop), although they do sell a few new books too. There's a good selection of non-fiction on all subjects as well as English teaching books.

C/ Mallorca, 237
Eixample
🚇 *Procença (FGC)*
Map p.393 E3 **9**

La Central
93 487 50 18 | *www.lacentral.com*
A huge variety of books are on offer in this two storey shop. All the latest international fiction titles are available, some in their original language, others as translations. Extensive non-fiction sections include art, social history, cinema, biography and literary theory, with many titles in English and French. The staff are often busy behind their desks in one of the shop's many nooks, but are happy to help when prompted. La Central has two other branches in the city, one in MACBA, and it also sells CDs.

C/ Pau Claris, 85
Eixample
🚇 *Catalunya (FGC)*
Map p.393 F4 **10**

Laie Pau Claris Llibreria Cafè
93 318 17 39 | *www.laie.es*
Books on practically every subject can be found here, with large sections of poetry, plays, art, architecture, music, cinema and history, mainly in Catalan and Spanish, but also some in English and French. There's a good selection of English and French fiction from around €10, as well as English translations of Spanish texts. Barcode scanners fixed to the walls let customers check the prices themselves. Personalised gift vouchers are available that the recipient can spend in one of Laie's five bookshops or on a meal in this branch's café. They also stock children's books and accessories on sale include reading glasses and Penguin Classics mugs. Staff are knowledgeable and helpful.

C/ Balmes, 129
Eixample
🚇 *Provença (FGC)*
Map p.393 E3 **11**

Libreria Inglesa Come In
93 453 12 04 | *www.libreriainglesa.com*
The Libreria Inglesa is a decent resource for students and teachers of English as a foreign language. There are some audiovisual materials for teaching kiddies, and more formal texts for those involved in teaching (and learning) business English. You should find all your TEFL and ESOL kit here too.

Car Parts & Accessories
Barcelonins like a well-pimped ride. 'Car tuning' is a noisy and very visible passion among some of Barcelona's younger motorists, with chrome hubcaps, elaborately shaped spoilers, vinyl stickers and turbo-charged sound systems all popular. A huge car tuning expo is held each November, and speciality shops such as Totcar sell high-tech accessories and parts (Totcar also has a separate branch, Totmoto, devoted to scooters). The city is also well-served with shops selling less exotic, more mundane car parts. Self-service and drive-through carwash establishments are common throughout the city, away from the Ciutat Vella.

Car Parts & Accessories

Autorecambios Rocla	C/ Corcega, 240	93 218 10 50	www.recambiosrocla.com
Beyco Union (Grupo Belloc)	C/ Ciutat Asunció, 4	93 360 06 01	www.grupobelloc.com
Marco Racing	C/ Comte de Borell, 142	93 451 27 27	www.marcoracing.com
Totcar	C/ Girona, 183	93 207 35 14	www.totcar.com
Totmoto	C/ Còrsega, 380	93 207 40 61	www.totmoto.com

281

Cars

Other options **Buying a Vehicle** p.131

Barcelona has a number of car dealerships, selling both new and used cars in specific brands (see table below). Second-hand cars (*coches de ocasión* in Spanish, or *cotxes de segona mà* in Catalan) are also widely bought and sold privately, often through websites such as www.coches.net and www.segundamano.es. Whether new or second-hand, cars are reasonably priced in comparison to other European countries. See the Driving section on p.130 of the Residence chapter for details on the formalities of ownership.

New Car Dealers			
BMW Muntañá	C/ Numancia, 22	Sants	93 600 12 00
Cataluña Motor	Zona Franca, 51	Sants-Montjuïc	93 298 25 00
Peugeot Barcelonesa	Pg Sant Gervasi, 72	Sarrià	93 212 33 42
Citroen	Av Paral·lel, 164	Eixample	93 325 69 28
Catalana d'Automoció (Ford concession)	C/ Santander, 50	Sant Andreu	93 498 70 00
V de Oliva (Jaguar concession)	C/ Dr Fleming, 9	Sarrià	93 209 59 09
Mercedes Peribañez Rufas	Ronda Universitat, 19	Raval	93 301 66 13

Scooters

Scooters (known locally as *motos*) are incredibly popular as a means of getting around. They are manoeuvrable, easy to park, and easier to drive through the narrow Ciutat Vella streets than a car. Any scooter of less than 125cc can be driven with a standard driving licence. See Driving, on p.130 of the Residence chapter, for more on ownership rules. Like cars, scooters are often bought and sold privately, with vendors advertising their vehicles online, for example via www.motos.net. There are also a couple of dedicated scooter establishments.

New Motorbike & Scooter Dealers				
Vespa Balart	C/ Còrsega, 201	93 419 26 11	Eixample	www.vespabarcelona.com
GR Bikes	C/ Neptuno, 36	93 217 25 99	Gràcia	www.grbikes.com

Clothes

Other options **Sports Goods** p.302, **Shoes** p.301, **Lingerie** p.296, **Beachwear** p.278, **Tailoring** p.302

As you'd expect for such a stylish city, Barcelona has a huge range of clothes on sale, from international designer labels to kooky independent stores. Head to Born for little boutiques selling one-offs by local designers, the top end of Raval for alternative and street fashions, Passeig de Gràcia and the middle of Diagonal for serious designer gear, and Portal de l'Angel or Rambla de Catalunya for high street chains. Areas to Shop, p.304 has more details. It's possible to spend lots of money on clothes, but even many of Barcelona's mid-range stores are very fairly priced in comparison to other countries. For the chance to buy quirky, one-off garments straight from local designers, look out for ModaFAD fairs, organised by a local, non-profit fashion body (www.modafad.org).

Pg de Gràcia, 32
Eixample
🚇 *Passeig de Gràcia*
Map p.393 E4 🔢

Adolfo Dominguez

93 487 41 70 | www.adolfo-dominguez.com

The classic cuts and subdued colours of Adolfo Dominguez's clothes are given a slight streetwise twist through little logos and details, but generally this clobber is conservative. There are no wacky asymmetrical hemlines or exaggerated shoulder pads here. Instead, there's a reliable, smart-casual feel, and fairly affordable pricing. There is an impressive range of Adolfo Dominguez product lines, including menswear, womenswear, accessories, shoes, plus-sizes, and children's clothing.

C/ Consell de Cent, 349
Eixample
🚇 **Passeig de Gràcia**
Map p.393 E4 **13**

Antonio Miro

93 487 06 70 | *www.antoniomiro.es*

The undisputed king of Catalan fashion design, Antonio Miro's menswear and womenswear lines are slick, classic and luxurious, with well-cut shirts and suits for men, in great fabrics and, at times, in vivid colours. Prices reflect the designer's local prestige: men's shirts start from around €75. There is also a clean, modern accessories range and a casual range, Miro Jeans. There are also small Antonio Miro sections in some of the larger department stores and menswear shops.

Pg de Gràcia, 49
Eixample
🚇 **Passeig de Gràcia**
Map p.393 E3 **14**

Armand Basi

93 215 14 21 | *www.armandbasi.com*

This is a sleek, upmarket fashion brand offering contemporary cuts and elegant, if rather monochrome, styling for men and women. Armand Basi is particularly strong on men's suits and women's eveningwear, although there are also some lovely pieces for more casual dressing. The firm makes accessories, shoes, watches and glasses as well. Stores are elegant and staff are courteous.

Av Portal de l'Angel, 15
Ciutat Vella
🚇 **Catalunya**
Map p.403 D2 **15**

Bershka

93 302 01 04 | *www.bershka.es*

With its gaze firmly fixed on the youth market, this lively chainstore offers funky, fashionable clothing and wardrobe basics at knockdown prices, with basic vest tops costing under €5. Clothes aren't especially durable and service could be more attentive, but Bershka is adored by teens nonetheless. It's owned by Inditex, which also has other Spanish high street brands, including Zara and Oysho.

C/ Rec, 42
Born
🚇 **Jaume I**
Map p.403 F4 **16**

BoBa

93 310 67 43 | *www.boba.es*

Primary colours and bold outlines characterise this plucky little local label, which specialises in chic but funky womenswear. Run by design duo Gimenez & Zuazo, the firm's cheerily modern boutiques (another is in the Raval, 93 412 33 81, Carrer Elisabets 20) make browsing fun.

Traditional Spanish shawls

C/ Notariat, 8
Raval
🚇 **Liceu**
Map p.402 B2 **17**

Comité Shop

93 317 68 83 | *www.comitebarcelona.com*

This is a funky, friendly little boutique run by a collective of local designers who use it to sell their own products. The group includes Swedish designer Cecilia Sorensen, who has been steadily building herself a cult following on the local scene. Comité stocks small and eclectic men's and women's ranges, with plenty of one-off pieces. The premises are something of a destination in themselves, hosting art exhibitions and selling a small, fashion-savvy selection of books and magazines.

Cortefiel

Av Portal de l'Angel, 38
Barri Gòtic
🚇 *Catalunya*
Map p.403 D1 **18**

93 301 07 00 | *www.cortefiel.es*

Although Cortefiel's menswear can be rather on the conservative side, it's a reliable and affordable choice for wardrobe staples such as plain T-shirts or sweaters, and suits, which start from around €150. Tailoring services are available. Larger branches also have a small selection of other brands, such as Polo by Ralph Lauren. Their womenswear offers the same classic styling and reasonable prices. Further branches are throughout the city.

Custo Barcelona

C/ Ferran, 36
Barri Gòtic
🚇 *Jaume I*
Map p.403 D4 **19**

93 342 66 98 | *www.custo-barcelona.com*

The bright colours, distinctive outlines and cartoonish patterns that are Custo's hallmarks have won this Catalan brand an international fanbase. Look closely and the designs are considerably more wearable than they may initially seem: in between all those out-there garments lie a number of well-cut, edgy pieces. Their stores (which stock both men's and women's lines) continue the wonderland theme with huge, imaginative window displays, and staff are just as snooty as you'd expect when the prices are this high (a women's T-shirt costs around €100).

Desigual

C/ Argenteria, 65
Born
🚇 *Jaume I*
Map p.403 E4 **20**

93 310 30 15 | *www.desigual.com*

For bright colours, loud patterns and funky, asymmetric cuts, look no further than this chain, whose highly distinctive designs have something distinctly Barcelonin about them. The look is certainly youthful, but both the menswear and womenswear collections are well-made and the post-industrial shop fittings and imaginative window displays set the tone well. The prices are mid-range (a skirt will cost around €50), and the brand's popular, 'distressed' clothes have seen it open stores across the world. There are 17 branches throughout the city, inlcuding three outlet stores.

Dou 16

C/ Doctor Dou, 16
Raval
🚇 *Catalunya*
Map p.402 B2 **21**

93 318 99 47

A small, newly-opened boutique, used by owner Joan Bernaus as a showcase for young, emerging local designers, Dou 16 specialises in breathtakingly pretty frocks. The style tends to be feminine in the extreme, but garments are often beautifully cut, and it's a great place for picking up one-offs and supporting local talent.

Friday's Project

Pg de Gràcia, 91
Eixample
🚇 *Diagonal*
Map p.393 E3 **22**

93 215 62 60 | *www.fridaysproject.com*

This large, chic shop, sells trendy clothes and shoes from a variety of hip designers, with a large womenswear section and a smaller choice of menswear. The selection is definitely geared towards the casual, with a fairly large choice of jeans and casual tops. Prices aren't the cheapest (expect to pay upwards of €15 for a vest top) but the clothes are funky.

Jean-Pierre Bua

Av Diagonal, 469
Eixample
🚇 *Hospital Clinic*
Map p.392 C1 **23**

93 439 71 00 | *www.jeanpierrebua.com*

For those who take their fashion very seriously indeed, a trip to Jean-Pierre Bua is something akin to a pilgrimage. Its impossibly sleek, modern interior houses two floors of forward-thinking fashion by some of the more daring designers on the international circuit, stocking labels including Miu Miu, Temperley, Dior Homme, Matthew Williamson and Alexander McQueen.

La Roca del Vallès

La Roca Village

93 842 39 00 | www.larocavillage.com

This kitsch collection of faux-village buildings houses a surprisingly upmarket selection of labels, just a half hour drive from the city centre. The trek is worthwhile considering the bargain prices on Burberry, Diesel, Tommy Hilfiger, Calvin Klein, and many others. There's also an ample selection of shoe sellers, beauty and accessories shops and several homeware stores. Four buses a day connect La Roca to Barcelona's Fabra i Puig bus station in around 30 minutes. On the Renfe train, go from Barcelona Sants Station to Granollers, where you can catch a special La Roca bus. If driving, it's exit 12 (marked 'Cardedeu') of the AP7 motorway.

Av Portal de l'Angel, 7
Ciutat Vella
Urquinaona
Map p.403 D2 25

Mango

93 317 69 85 | www.mango.es

This is one of Spain's biggest high-street chains, focusing on womenswear. Fabrics can tend towards the synthetic and the staff aren't always too helpful, but the clothes are on-trend and fun. The tone is possibly more funky and youthful than that of its great rival, Zara, but the two have much in common. It is easy to buy in bulk and on impulse, at prices that range from the merely affordable to the ridiculously cheap.

Av Portal de
l'Angel, 15-17
Ciutat Vella
Catalunya
Map p.403 D2 26

Massimo Dutti

93 301 89 11 | www.massimodutti.com

A chain (there are further outlets across Barcelona) offering classic – almost preppy – well-tailored clothes in great fabrics and muted colours. The emphasis is on elegance rather than the very latest trends, while prices are very fair considering the quality (a cashmere sweater will set you back around €40). There are both men's and women's lines, and staff are courteous and attentive.

C/ Portaferrisa, 11
Born
Liceu
Map p.402 C2 27

McQuinn

93 317 53 83

An urban clothing chain stocking jeans, hoodies, T-shirts and hats by skate and streetwear brands including Dickies, Quiksilver, Billabong, and Loreak. There is also a wide range of bags and skating paraphernalia, and a smaller range of womenswear, with brands including Roxy and Miss Sixty. Surfing and snowboarding clothes are also available, depending on the season.

Rla de Catalunya, 77
Eixample
Passeig de Gràcia
Map p.393 E3 28

Oysho

93 488 36 09 | www.oysho.es

Part of the Inditex empire that also owns the Zara and Massimo Dutti chains, Oysho sells good quality underwear and nightwear at reasonable prices (an underwear set can be purchased for as little as €20). The designs are varied, ranging from a reliable selection of staples to funky, more youthful pieces with quirky little details.

Pg de Gràcia, 93
Eixample
Diagonal
Map p.393 E3 29

Santa Eulalia

93 215 06 74 | www.santaeulalia.com

A venerable institution that has been dressing Barcelona's moneyed classes since 1843, Santa Eulalia sells high fashion brands such as Balenciaga, Stella McCartney and Marc Jacobs in an atmosphere of hushed reverence. Belts, bags, scarves and wallets are sourced from a label junky's wish-list of accessory designers, including Jimmy Choo. There is also a bespoke tailoring service for men.

C/ Fontanella, 16
Ciutat Vella
🚇 *Urquinaona*
Map p.403 E1 🔟

Women's Secret

93 412 70 19 | *www.womensecret.com*

The brightly-coloured underwear, bikinis and nightwear that fill the branches of this affordable chain are great for a cheap pick-me-up, with large coordinated collections providing plenty of choice. The styles tend to be flirty and fun, while prices are reasonable, with a nightdress costing around €25. There is also an extensive collection of basics, and a small kids' line.

Av Diagonal, 606
Sarrià-Sant Gervasi
🚇 *Maria Cristina*
Map p.392 C1 🟥

Zadig & Voltaire

93 209 22 45 | *www.zadig-et-voltaire.com*

This French boutique combines trendy, casual styles in luxury fabrics: expect to find gorgeous, funky cashmere sweaters, lace trims and carefully distressed cotton. Womenswear is especially beautiful with floaty, bohemian styles and classic but fashionable silhouettes. There is also a highly desirable menswear and children's range, as well as shoes and accessories. The store is slick and the service is laid-back but attentive. However, prices are high; women's T-shirts start at €80.

Av Portal de
l'Angel, 32-34
Ciutat Vella
🚇 *Catalunya*
Map p.403 D2 🟥

Zara

93 301 08 98 | *www.zara.es*

The grand dame of the Spanish high street, Zara has conquered the world with its convincing, wearable and highly affordable imitations of catwalk designs. Although it now has men's and children's lines, womenswear is still dominant, with everything from casual outfits to evening dresses. There is a particularly strong line in smart, everyday clothing with the current season's twist. The fabrics can sometimes feel a little nasty, and garments aren't always the most durable, but the up-to-date tailoring and prices make it easy to see how Zara has achieved such popularity, in Spain and across the world. There are more than 40 branches dotted across the city, just visit the website, and click on *tiendas* to find the branch nearest to you.

Clothes		
Adidas	C/ Avinyó, 6	93 317 55 79
Armani Collezione	Pg de Gràcia, 68-72	93 487 95 44
Benetton	Av Portal de l'Angel, 4	93 318 61 35
Billabong	C/ Canuda, 31	93 481 38 25
Burberry	Pg de Gràcia, 56	93 215 81 04
Carhartt	C/ Rec, 71	93 268 85 01
Carolina Herrera	Pg de Gràcia, 87	93 272 15 84
Chanel	Pg de Gràcia, 70	93 488 29 23
Diesel	Pg de Gràcia, 19	93 445 83 60
Dolce & Gabbana	Pg de Gràcia, 95	93 467 22 56
Donna Karan	Av Diagonal, 618	93 414 12 00
G Star	C/ Provença, 257	93 272 38 54
Gucci	Av Diagonal, 415	93 416 06 20
H&M	Pl Catalunya, 9	90 112 00 84
Lacoste	Pg de Gràcia, 51	93 487 44 64
Levi's	Pg de Gràcia, 18	93 412 55 66
Muji	Rla de Catalunya, 81	93 467 65 60
Naf Naf	C/ Portaferrissa, 28	93 412 22 78
Net-a-Porter	www.net-a-porter.com	Online only
Puma	Pg de Gràcia, 11	93 342 85 04
Quiksilver	C/ Portaferrissa, 25	93 304 06 43
Top Shop	C/ Bergara, 1	93 301 53 43
Yves Saint Laurent	Pg de Gràcia, 102	93 200 39 55

Computers

Other options **Electronics & Home Appliances** p.288

The latest technology is readily available in Barcelona, and desktop computer prices are generally comparable to those in the US. Laptops tend to be more expensive. The best deals are to be found on Ronda Sant Antoni (see map p.401), and the streets leading off it. The area is packed with specialist shops, all offering regular discounted deals, both on ready-to-go PCs and parts to construct your own desktop. Most brands are available, including Packard Bell, Toshiba, Sony, Acer, Compaq and LG. Although prices continually fluctuate, they are very competitive, so it's worth shopping around. In MegaStore DataSystem, prices for laptops start at €600. You can pick up desktops from around €400 in Green Megastore and Computer Videal. Macs are available in a few shops, including department stores Fnac (p.306) and El Corte Inglés (p.305); prices start at around €1,000. Others outlets, like Sony Gallery, only sell their own brand. Computers should be covered by a two year warranty, although in some stores laptops are only under guarantee for one year. Extended warranties are usually available, but can be pricey. Many shops have in-house repair services; the length of time repairs take depends on the individual shop and severity of the problem. The Apple website lists shops authorised to carry out repairs on Macs.

Computers

Apple Spain	Online	na	www.apple.com/es
Computer Videal	C/ Sepúlveda, 177	93 454 03 88	na
Green Megastore	C/ Sepúlveda, 178	93 451 43 42	www.pcgreen.com
MegaStore DataSystem	Rda Sant Antoni, 51	93 424 18 75	www.ds-datasystem.com
PC City	Various locations	na	www.pccity.es
Pricoinsa	Various locations	93 423 80 44	www.pricoinsa.es
Sony Gallery	C/ Gran De Sant Andreu, 248	93 274 47 88	www.sonygallery.es

Costumes

The fiestas and celebrations here provide ample excuses for dressing up. Sitges Carnival is the main fancy dress event of the year, when many people go to great lengths to put together an original outfit. There are several fancy dress shops (*tienda de disfraces*) where you can buy or hire complete costumes. Menkes (93 301 40 24, www.menkes.es, Gran Vía de les Corts Catalanes 646) specialises in flamenco attire. The company has branched out, however, and now offers a fancy dress rental service for adults and children. The outfits are imaginative, well-made and good quality; animals, period costumes and medieval knights are just some of the many options available. However, choice and quality come at a price, and Menkes can be expensive. A more reasonable option is the lively party shop in Gràcia, El Relámpago (93 237 26 74, www.elrelampago.es, Torrent de l'Olla 115 and 138). It has some imaginative offerings for kids' parties, including outfits and accessories. La Bolsera (www.labolsera.com) is a party and fancy dress chain that specialises in costume accessories. Bows and arrows, hula-hula skirts, ladybird wings and fire-fighters' helmets are just a few of the goodies on sale. There are a few stores, including one at Avinguda Paral·lel 115 (93 441 66 75).

In February, it gets extremely busy around the time of Sitges Carnival. Prohibited under the Franco regime, this public holiday is an important part of life here. If you find yourself fighting over feather boas, head to the expensive, but well-equipped shop Party Fiesta (www.party-fiesta.com), which has four Barcelona stores, including one at Avinguda Diagonal 288 (93 486 04 19).

287

Electronics & Home Appliances

Other options **Computers** p.287

Department stores (see p.305), and in particular El Corte Inglés are a good source for electrical equipment, from coffee makers to white goods and fancy home entertainment systems. The firms below are the best known electrical goods stores and tend to carry slightly more obscure, specialised kit, alongside the staples on offer at department stores.

Expert

Various locations

90 230 30 35 | *www.expert.es*

With over 70 branches in Barcelona province, around a dozen in the city itself, and more than 100 stores across Catalonia, Expert can afford to have regular promotions. An abundance of kitchen appliances are on offer including dishwashers, fridges, freezers, washing machines and small items like blenders and kettles. Microwaves and mini-ovens start at around €100 and portable heaters at €20. Other items sold include digital cameras, micro stereo systems from between €100 and €200 (Samsung and Sharp) LCD TVs (Panasonic 42" for €1,200, Sony Bravia 32" for €900) and mobile phones. Products come with a two year warranty and extended warranties are available. There are interest free payment schemes for some bigger items. Friendly staff are always happy to help. Free delivery within a 50km radius of the store.

Miró

Various locations

www.miro.es

A huge selection of household appliances, as well as electrical goods like computers, mobile phones, GPS navigation systems, car stereos, and mp3 players are available in this chain of stores. They also sell digital cameras, both compact and SLR, and camcorders. Regular in-store promotions on local and household brands make them very competitive. The type of goods you can expect to pick up for around €100 include portable TVs, DVD players (from €35 euros), mobile phones, mp3 players and portable air-conditioning units. Extras include after-sales service, installation on some products, interest free payment plans, extended warranties and free home delivery. Products are covered by a two year warranty as standard. Staff are extremely friendly and helpful. They also have a store online.

Eyewear

Other options **Opticians & Ophthalmologists** p.116

Most residential areas are home to a few independent opticians and larger chains are common in central areas and shopping centres. Most don't charge for standard eye tests and those that do (usually around €15) often waive the fee if you make a purchase. Treated lenses and custom-made glasses for special prescriptions are available in most, as are designer frames like Tous and Lacoste. They will all carry contact lenses, with many stocking a variety of types; daily, weekly, monthly, yearly, multi-focal and coloured.

Not surprisingly, sunglasses are big business, and in the run up to summer the promotions really start to hot up. Pre-summer 2007 saw opticians like Vista Optica offering free prescriptions sunglasses with the purchase of regular specs. Prices for prescription sunnies tend to start at around €50 and in some opticians you can have prescription lenses fitted into designer frames. Sun Planet has a massive choice of non-prescription sunglasses from designer names including Ray Ban, Dior and Hugo Boss; prices start at about €80. Online optician Visual Click offers some great discounts on designer sunglasses and prescription glasses. They also sell contact lenses at reduced prices and home delivery is free. But if your budget won't stretch to designer prices, there are plenty of shops, such as Bijou Brigitte (www.bijou-brigitte.com), selling shades from €10. At high-street fashion stores like H&M they can go as low as €6. If you're looking for designer fakes, street vendors all over the city will be more than happy to help.

Eyewear			
General Optica	Various locations	90 062 66 26	www.generaloptica.com
Grand Optical	Various locations	93 304 16 40	na
Optica 2000	Various locations	93 487 19 11	www.optica2000.com
Optica Boixadera	Eixample	93 257 67 16	na
Sun Planet	Various locations	na	www.sunplanet.com
Vista Optica	Various locations	na	www.vistaoptica.es
Visual Click	Online only	na	www.visual-click.com

Flowers

Other options **Gardens** p.292

Barcelona's most prominent flower market is along the middle of La Rambla; here, as in most other florists, cut flowers and potted plants are sold side-by-side. However, away from La Rambla, flowers can be tricky to find, especially if you're after something a little different from carnations and cellophane wrap. Carrer València is a good place to look, with a few large florists in quick succession, see table. Otherwise, flower vendors are dotted rather sparsely across the city's residential districts. Most florists sell accessories such as pots and vases alongside their blooms. Interflora can arrange deliveries within 24 hours through their website. There are a number of plant and flower stalls in Mercat de la Concepció, and nearby Floristeria Navarro is open 24 hours a day. Meanwhile, the soothing little boutique Au Nom de la Rose sells only roses.

Flowers			
Au Nom de la Rose	C/ València, 203	93 451 16 50	na
Floristeria Navarro	C/ València, 320	93 457 40 99	www.floristeriasnavarro.com
Interflora	C/ Julián Camarillo, 29	90 225 45 65	www.interflora.es
Just Flowers	C/ Enric Granados, 106	93 431 58 01	www.justflowers-bcn.com
Mercat de la Concepció	C/ Aragó, 313-317	93 457 53 29	www.laconcepcio.com

Food

Hypermarkets (p.306) such as Condis, Mercadona and Dia are gradually growing in popularity in Barcelona. But, for many Catalans these are just a supplement to the markets and the small fishmongers, greengrocers, butchers and bakers that pepper each area, where the real food shopping is done. It's easy to see why: many supermarkets have limited, lacklustre selections of fruit and vegetables, while meat and fish are slightly more expensive than in the markets. Still, even the smaller supermarkets will have a decent fish counter, where your purchase is gutted, filleted and scaled to order. There will also be smaller meat, ham and cheese counters, where products can be bought by weight. Many supermarkets also offer online shopping and home deliveries.

Catalan cookery revolves around the use of high-quality, fresh ingredients, which helps explain the lasting popularity of the markets. While shopping this way is

289

certainly time-consuming, it's fun, and offers a much wider range of goods. Stallholders are often fantastically helpful, offering tips on how to cook a certain fish, letting you sample olives or cheeses, or recommending which *jamon* to buy.

It's possible to eat very cheaply in Spain, but spending just a few more euros will often take the quality from great to sublime. Especially worth the extra money are *jamons* – look for dark, marbled Iberico ham, cut by hand straight from the black-hoofed *paleta* (leg) – manchego cheeses, and seafood. The rich red prawns from Palamos may be the most expensive crustaceans you'll ever consume, but will also be among the tastiest.

Despite all the gastronomic treats on offer, organic and international foods can still be tricky to find, although most residential areas have at least a couple of health-food shops.

Barcelona-Reykjavik

C/ Doctor Dou, 12
Raval
 Catalunya
Map p.402 B2 **35**

93 302 09 21 | *www.barcelonareykjavik.com*
The opening of Barcelona-Reykjavik was quite a cause for celebration in Barcelona's north European community. It's one of the only bakeries in Barcelona to make its bread from scratch in-store (the vast majority of bakery baguettes are made in factories then frozen to be re-baked). Using traditional methods and no artificial additives, Barcelona-Reykjavik produces a huge (if rather costly) choice of breads, including herb, nut and seed breads, as well as excellent wholemeal and wholegrain loaves.

Casa Alfonso

C/ Roger de Llúria, 6
Eixample
Urquinaona
Map p.403 E1 **36**

93 301 97 83
This charcuterie has provided locals with a massive choice of hams, dried meats, cheeses and other delicacies since the 30s. Staff are gruffly attentive and will point you in the right direction if you find the sheer mass of options bewildering. The quality of the produce is excellent, although the prices are rather steep.

Colmado Quilez

Rla de Catalunya, 63
Eixample
Passeig de Gràcia
Map p.393 E3 **37**

93 215 87 85 | *www.lafuente.es*
A splendid old-fashioned grocery store, stocked to the ceiling with Spanish and Catalan delicacies, and a small but gourmet charcuterie and cheese counter. There's a large selection of wines and olive oils, and charming, highly knowledgeable staff, who are happy to offer advice and carefully wrap each purchase in paper. Prices are surprisingly affordable.

Corte Inglés Food Hall

Pl Catalunya, 14
Ciutat Vella
Catalunya
Map p.403 D1 **38**

93 306 38 00 | *www.corteingles.es*
This large, upmarket food hall, in the basement of the department store, is a reliable choice for European imported delicacies and big brands, as well as luxury Catalan foods and wines. There's a large selection of charcuterie, cheeses, pates, and an adjoining cigar shop. You can also buy online.

Delaterra

Online only

97 216 01 90 | *www.delaterra.net*
This online retailer provides a pricey but guilt-free range of organic and fair trade products, delivered to your door. The selection is small but it does include a good choice of seasonal fresh fruit and vegetables, as well as things that can be hard to find elsewhere, like wholegrain pasta, free-range eggs, organic meat and poultry, and organic baby food. They also stock locally-produced wines, olive oils, meat substitutes, cheeses and dried meats.

EMBOTIT

Nice legs

C/ Mallorca, 241
Eixample
🚇 **Provença (FGC)**
Map p.393 E3 40

DeliShop
93 215 15 46 | www.delishop.es
A slick, modern little shop specialising in imported foods, with a small but useful selection of British, American, Thai, Japanese, Indian, Greek and French treats, and a range of gourmet Catalan products. DeliShop stocks comfort foods such as baked beans or cookie dough mix alongside hard-to-find ingredients such as seaweed sheets for sushi, imported soy sauce and curry pastes. Prices are not cheap, but the range is so well-chosen that it's impossible to leave empty-handed.

C/ Balmes, 6
Eixample
🚇 **Universitat**
Map p.393 E4 41

Dong Fang
93 301 25 87
For all manner of oriental produce, Dong Fang is a reliable bet. This long-established Chinese superstore has branched out in recent years and now stocks comprehensive ranges of Thai, Japanese, Filipino, Vietnamese and Korean foods, in the form of imported brands from the Far East, rather than western copies. Prices are extremely reasonable, especially as many of their products are very hard to find elsewhere.

Pl de la Llibertat, 12
Gràcia
🚇 **Gracià (FGC)**
Map p.393 E1 42

La Nostra Pasta
93 237 87 93
This is a small Italian delicatessen specialising in fresh pasta, including homemade tortellini and ravioli. La Nostra Pasta also sells homemade sauces, imported Italian cheeses, including mozzarella di buffala, Italian dried meats such as prosciutto, and traditional Italian cakes, biscuits and other delicacies.

Rla de Catalunya,
102-103
Eixample
🚇 **Provença (FGC)**
Map p.393 E3 43

Pastisseries Mauri
93 215 81 46 | www.pasteleriasmauri.com
This stately, long-established bakery and tea salon is a favourite for its luxurious hand-made chocolates and its expensive, extravagantly-decorated cakes, which have achieved something of a cachet locally as dinner party offerings. The ornate shop, the stern ladies behind the counter, and the fairytale confections make shopping here something of an experience, even if the prices ensure that it's not a very frequent one. There is also a small section devoted to upmarket prepared dishes and charcuterie.

C/ Tallers, 77
Raval
🚇 **Catalunya**
Map p.402 B1 44

Superstore Asia Food
93 317 61 70
This ethnic food store provides a wide selection of international goods. There are loads of Chinese, Indian and Thai sauces on offer, including Patak's and Sharwoods. There are also lots of different types of noodles and rice, fresh and tinned goods from around the world, as well as a few frozen convenience foods, including vegetarian products. Prices are reasonable, considering most products are imported.

291

Pg del Born, 13
Born
🚇 *Jaume I*
Map p.403 F4 **45**

Tot Formatge

93 319 53 75

The name translates as 'all cheese', which tells you all you need to know. Highly experienced, cheese-loving staff preside over long counters stuffed with a mouthwatering array of *queso* from all over Spain, as well as a small section of other European choices. There is a selection of other cheese-related produce, such as wine and *membrillo*, the quince jelly that often accompanies soft, mild *mató* cheese.

Various location

Veritas

90 266 77 89 | *www.veritas.es*

This chain of organic stores has a number of branches around the city. They stock their own range of products, and some imported brands. A good selection of vegetarian convenience foods, meats, snacks, fruits, vegetables, dairy products, organic foods and dry goods are on offer. Drinks include wine, tea, coffee and lots of interesting fruit juices. There is an in-store bakery, cafeteria and free-parking available in some stores. A home delivery service is available for purchases over €60 (with a small charge), and there are regular price promotions.

Gardens

Other options **Flowers** p.289, **Hardware & DIY** p.293

Private gardens are a rare sight in Barcelona, except occasionally in the Zona Alta (the wealthier northern suburbs of the city) where large town houses have private plots of grass. Balconies, terraces and patios decorated with plants and flowers are more normal. Arborètum (93 285 71 80, www.arboretum.es, Rabassa 63), Jardins Pedralbes (93 203 88 38, www.jardinspedralbes.es, Eduardo Conde 11) and Garden Center Babilonia (93 414 12 26, Santaló 110) are useful references. Each stocks a broad range of plants, garden tools, soil, accessories and furniture. Jardins Pedralbes offers a private gardening and landscaping service. Jardiland (www.jardiland.es), a garden and DIY chain, has two enormous warehouses selling all possible garden-related items at reasonable prices. These are at Ronda dels Països Catalans 11, along Autopista C-32 at the 100km exit (Mataró Oest) and the exit at 210km (Gavà-Platja) on the same road. For more upmarket and stylish furniture, Magic Garden (93 805 25 29, www.magicgarden.es) has a generous selection of wooden, mosaic, canvas and Java teak outdoor tables and chairs, as well as wooden sheds, summerhouses, cushions, parasols and barbecues. Failing that, large hypermarkets like Carrefour (p.307) and Alcampo (www.alcampo.es) stock garden basics, tools and some furniture, as does DIY and hardware giant Leroy Merlin (www.leroymerlin.es).

Gifts

There are plenty of other options in the city for finding gifts, apart from the often kitsch and tacky souvenir shops that crowd La Rambla. A good place to start is Carrer Avinyó (see map p.402 D4) in the Barri Gòtic, where you will find a number of small boutiques and quirky shops selling trinkets and boho-chic jewellery. Tomate (93 301 37 88, Carrer Banys Nous 22) an alternative fashion boutique, sells interesting accessories such as wallets and bags. For sweet-smelling bathtime treats, Delirium's (Boulevard Rosa, Passeig de Gràcia)

Marionetas

effervescent bath balls and soaps smell delicious enough to eat. They also sell natural massage oils and beauty products. Cereria Mas (93 317 04 38, www.cereriamas.com) on Carrer Carme in the Raval is a candle shop that moulds wax into all kinds of wonderful shapes and colours. Candles filled with roses (€20 for the smallest) make great presents.

Hardware & DIY

Other options **Outdoor Goods** p.298

When it comes to DIY, people prefer to support local business by visiting the *ferretería*, rather than going to the larger stores in out-of-town retail parks. Translated literally, *ferretería* means ironmonger in English, but today the term refers to general hardware stores. An excellent spot to find them is around Mercat Sant Antoni (p.310), either on Ronda Sant Antoni or before the market on Ronda Sant Pau. Ferreteria Mallol (93 442 00 98, Ronda Sant Antoni 24), in business since 1922, is one of the oldest in the city. Also in the Raval, Tot Pintura (93 441 14 90, Nou de la Rambla 68-70) is a family business specialising in paints (they claim to sell 150,000 colours). Suministros Carles (93 454 90 60, www.suministroscarles.com) is a local hardware business with five stores in Barcelona. DIY tools, power tools and locks are the main products sold here; the main branch is on Carrer Aragó 132-134 in Eixample. One of the most efficient and comprehensive DIY centres is Habitacle (www.habitacle.es). They offer a range of services including personalised carpentry orders and customised paints. Power tools, home furniture kits, garden accessories, doors and flooring are also available, and won't break the bank. There are two branches on the outskirts of Barcelona. Larger still, Leroy Merlin (www.leroymerlin.es), the French DIY superstore, has branches all over Spain, usually located in out-of-town retail parks.

Home Furnishings & Accessories

Other options **Hardware & DIY** see above

Considering that Barcelona is such a design-conscious city, there is a surprising paucity of places to buy affordable, stylish furniture, which helps to explain the enduring prevalence of IKEA in Catalan homes. However, if you're prepared to pay a little more there are some beautiful things on offer: try the run of interior design places where Carrer Mallorca meets Rambla de Catalunya for plush, pricey furniture (expect to pay upwards of €2,000 for a sofa). There is a series of charming little shops selling antiques in the Barri Gòtic, around Carrer Banys Nous. Second-hand furniture is largely bought and sold privately: see www.loquo.com or www.catalunya-classified.com. With a little patience, lamps and other decorative bits and pieces can also be unearthed at the flea market of Els Encants (see map p.394 D4).

Pl de Catalunya, 4
Eixample
🚇 *Catalunya*
Map p.402 C1 **47**

Habitat

93 301 74 84 | *www.habitat.net*

Terence Conran's home furnishings giant has been a recent but very influential addition to the Barcelona furniture scene. Habitat offers modern and well-designed furniture in a wide variety of styles. There is also a selection of crockery, kitchenware, lighting and rugs available. With sections devoted to bath towels and bathroom accessories, and bedrooms and bed linen, you're sure to find all you need. The downside is that furniture can tend to be rather expensive, but smaller household items are quite reasonably priced. A second branch is at Avinguda Diagonal 514. Call 93 415 44 55 for more details.

293

Gran Via, 115-133
L'Hospitalet de
Llobregat
🔲 *Magoria FGC*
Map p.391 D4 48

IKEA

90 240 09 22 | *www.ikea.com*

Love it or loathe it, the Swedish furniture behemoth is alive and well in Barcelona, with two massive branches on the city limits. The other is in Badalona, at Carrer Luxemburgo s/n (90 240 09 22). Stocking almost everything you could need for setting up a home, IKEA has a colossal range of understated, modern furniture and household wares, all at rock-bottom prices. They also provide a home delivery service. However, there are drawbacks: stores become nightmarishly crowded at weekends, service is nonchalant at best, and not all products are built to last.

C/ Enric Granados, 44
Eixample
🔲 *Provença*
Map p.393 D3 49

L'Appartement

93 452 29 04 | *www.lappartement.es*

This is a boutique design shop, stocking nifty little pieces and household objects by up-and-coming European talents, as well as bigger names such as Mathmos lamps. The tone is certainly geared towards beauty rather than function, but it's great for picking up stylish little objects like a digital cuckoo clock, handmade Danish glasses, funky lampshades or hand-painted coffee tables. Sylvain, the owner, is a willing source of design advice and can often order hard-to-find pieces.

Av Diagonal,
405
Eixample
🔲 *Provença*
Map p.393 E2 50

Maisons du Monde

93 368 32 07 | *www.maisonsdumonde.com*

A mid-priced shop specialising in international furniture, featuring Moroccan, Indian, and Indonesian ranges, as well as more modern pieces and traditional English and French furnishings. Maisons du Monde also stocks bed-linen, mirrors, children's furniture, and garden pieces. There is also an online shopping service, as well as home delivery.

Pg de Gràcia, 96
Eixample
🔲 *Passeig de Gràcia*
Map p.393 E3 51

Vinçon

93 215 60 50 | *www.vincon.com*

This large lifestyle store specialises in homewares and accessories, stocking unusual designer items alongside beautifully made furniture and a comprehensive range of high quality and kitchenware, including Le Creuset pans. There are small lighting, bathroom, bedroom and children's sections, and many desirable little trinkets. A graphics section upstairs has posters and prints.

Exotic interiors

Av Portal de
l'Angel, 24
Barri Gòtic
🔲 *Urquinaona*
Map p.403 D2 52

Zara Home

93 318 71 91 | *www.zarahome.com*

The home furnishings offshoot of the clothing giant has a distinctly Zara outlook: rather than aiming to set trends, it provides affordable copies of existing fashions. The overall style tends to be somewhat on the feminine side (think Arabesque prints, pastels and lots of white) and quality isn't always the best, but the prices are fairly low. Ranges include basic furniture, bed linen, cushions, crockery and glassware, and trinkets like candles and picture frames. There are further branches throughout the city.

Work Visas p.54

Weekend Breaks p.155

Written by residents, the Sydney Explorer is packed with insider info, from arriving in the city to making it your home and everything in between.

Sydney Explorer Residents' Guide
We Know Where You Live

Kids' Clothes

As with adult clothes, the most affordable kidswear is available from large branches of high street chains, such as Zara (p.286), Benetton (p.286) and H&M (p.286). They all stock clothing for ages 2 to 12. Bóboli is another reliable option for affordable everyday clothing and shoes. For special occasions, Jacadi Paris makes classic, pretty outfits and shoes for the under 6s, while French company Le Petit Bateau makes particularly good casualwear as well as party outfits for 6 to 12 year olds; both of these are rather pricey. Gocco makes slightly more trendy, high-quality clothing and shoes.

Kids' Clothes		
Babu	Eixample	93 185 14 88
Bóboli	Eixample	93 215 82 85
Carandra	Eixample	93 215 62 03
Caribu	Gràcia	93 237 94 67
Charanga	Sant Andreu	93 360 83 18
Chicco	Raval	93 301 49 76
Gocco	Sarrià-Sant Gervasi	93 240 14 82
Jacadi Paris	Eixample	93 487 58 40
Le Petit Bateau	Eixample	93 272 03 62
Oilily	Sarrià-Sant Gervasi	93 201 84 79

Lingerie

Other options **Clothes** p.282

There are several lingerie stores in Barcelona that offer brightly patterned underwear with teasing messages and quirky designs. Oysho (www.oysho.com) and Women's Secret (p.286), in particular, fall into this category. Many of their brightly printed combos are aimed at teenagers and young twentysomethings. However, both shops sell classic and comfortable no-frills bras in a range of colours, starting from €10, that are suitable for all ages and sizes. They also have simple designs to suit every kind of strapless, backless, see-through, or plain awkward top. Intimíssimi (www.intimissimi.it) is an Italian chain that is classic in style, with a number of sexy bra and French knicker combos. The collections cater for women of all ages, and men's underwear is also available. At the higher end of the scale, Le Boudoir (93 302 52 81, www.leboudoir.net, Canuda 21 and Diagonal 609) offers highly seductive silk and lace lingerie with collections and prices that are sure to get the heart racing. Alternatively, El Corte Inglés (p.305) is a sure-fire hit if you are looking to save yourself time and energy. Everyday comfort underwear and special occasion combos designed to provoke a jaw-dropping reaction are all available, in addition to collections that cater for larger or more unusual sizes. French designers Aubade (bras from €50), Triumph (bras from €25) and Calvin Klein, as well as other international names, feature in the department.

Maternity Items

Barcelona has a slightly scant choice for expectant mums. But, that doesn't mean you can't find some good, flattering and reasonably priced maternity wear. The scope and selection is not large but the shops mentioned here are lovely choices.

Maternity Items		
El Corte Inglés	Av Diagonal, 471-473	93 493 48 00
H&M	Pl Catalunya, 9	90 112 00 84
Lepreg	C/ Mallorca, 273	93 467 32 88
Prenatal	C/ Casanova, 153	93 419 56 56

Plus, with the internet and so many local tailors (p.302) in the city, you have some great options. Department stores have sizable maternity ranges too and offer all the additional necessities such as breast pumps, creams and swim wear. LePreg and Prenatal offer these with baby clothes too, so are effectively maternity and newborn departments rolled into one. Fashion chain Zara is rumoured to be planning a maternity range too.

Medicine

Other options **General Medical Care** p.106

Getting Well
For more information on health related issues turn to the Residents chapter, where you'll find information on doctors and hospitals (p.108).

You're never far from a pharmacy in Barcelona, and in some areas there's one on practically every block. You'll find them in shopping centres and department stores too. If you need to visit outside of normal business hours (which tend to be the same as shops) check the daily lists posted outside the pharmacy doors. Late opening is done on rotation, and these lists tell you which stores across the city will be open until 22:00 that day and those open from 22:00 until 09:00 the next morning. Alternatively, you can ring the 24 hour Sanitat Respon helpline (90 211 14 44). This can tell you where your nearest open pharmacy is. Pharmacists are well-qualified to give medical advice for minor ailments and will refer you to a doctor when necessary. As well as over-the-counter medicines, such as mild painkillers and cold remedies, antibiotics can also be bought in pharmacies without a prescription. There is no fixed price for medicines prescribed by a doctor, but in many circumstances people are entitled to a reduction on the normal price, such as those registered with the public health system CatSalut and EU visitors carrying an EHIC card. Pensioners in both the above cases are entitled to free prescriptions (see Health, p.106).

Mobile Telephones

Other options **Telephone** p.102

Mobile Phones	
Amena	656 001 470
Movistar	93 323 31 29
The Phone House	93 488 21 51
Retevision	656 155 000
Sinertec	93 241 65 81
Telefonica	1004
Vodafone	607 123 000

Stores such as Telefonica, Movistar or Orange generally offer quality phones, competitive contracts and some follow-up support. They can often also organise your home phone and internet service. El Corte Inglés (p.305) has a large mobile phone department, where new phones can be bought, despite the fact that they don't sell contracts. The area around Plaça de Catalunya is especially good for mobile phone providers.

Shops that sell electronic goods are all over Barcelona and they're an excellent option for items like replacement chargers, but be wary of second hand telephones. With new ones costing so little, you're better off going for something that guarantees quality and authenticity. 'Pay as you go' deals are a great option for new arrivals, but calls and texts are charged at premium rates, so you'll find yourself permanently topping up your credit. Pay as you go phones can be bought for as little as €30, which often includes €10 of free credit. Contract mobiles normally provide ample text and talk time for around €35 a month. Mobiles don't always come with a guarantee, but the provider of your phone and network will have its logo and name clearly printed on the handset. If you have any technical problems, sales staff in the shop should be happy to help.

Music, DVDs & Videos

In a city where music reigns, DJs inhabit almost every block, and residents love to party, it's unsurprising that there are so many music shops. Fnac (p.306) has an excellent music department, selling all the newest releases at very competitive prices. For vinyl, rare CDs and vintage records, independent, old school music shops, such as Planet Music and Revolver Records, are excellent choices. Often, if something isn't in stock, it can be ordered in, even if it's a rare album. Anything bought over the internet from Ebay or Amazon, for example, can be delivered without any trouble and you are able to bring your own DVDs and videos from abroad without any censorship issues. If

Music, DVDs & Videos

Blanco y Negro Music	C/ Llacuna, 11	93 230 09 00
CD Drome	Valldon Zella, 3	93 317 46 46
El Corte Inglés	Av Diagonal, 471-473	93 493 48 00
Fnac	Various locations	90 210 06 32
La Casa Discs	Pl Vicenz Martorell, 4	93 412 33 05
Planet Music	C/ Mallorca, 214	93 451 42 88
PTT Records	Floridablanca, 47, baixos 2	93 325 20 31
Revolver Records	C/ de Tallers, 11	93 302 16 85

you have an internet purchase shipped, you may pay a little more than normal to have it delivered to Spain, but it'll be just a few cents. The department stores mentioned are excellent for DVDs as well, and have a wide selection of foreign and English-language films. Most films are available in multiple languages when bought or rented on DVD, so don't fear if the title of your favorite old movie appears in Spanish on the DVD case. You may not yet be fluent in the local lingo but you can still get a taste of home with a favourite film in your native language.

Musical Instruments
Other options **Music, DVDs & Videos** p.297, **Music Lessons** p.230

Gràcia is the best area for buying musical instruments in Barcelona, with a mass of shops dedicated to little else. Everything from pianos to saxophones, flutes to clarinets should be available, as well as instruments, music paper, books, sound systems and accessories. Retrofonic is an excellent choice, as there is a shop in Barcelona and an online store where home deliveries can be

Musical Instruments

Josep Puig	C/ Progres, 42	93 285 04 09
La Clau del Sol	Pl Josep Maria Folch i Torres, 16	93 441 79 29
Retrofonic	C/ Llibrertat, 2	93 207 56 63

arranged. Spanish guitars are, of course, very popular and easy to buy. They are wonderful both for music lovers looking for a new challenge or bought as a gift or souvenir. And if you never master your G chord, they make pretty wall decorations. Department stores (p.305) also sell some pieces.

Outdoor Goods
Other options **Sports Goods** p.302, **Hardware & DIY** p.293, **Camping** p.203

Department stores (p.305) tend to be a good bet for outdoor equipment. The French sports store Decathlon has an excellent range of sporty kit at reasonable prices. Their successful own-brand names are excellent value for money; Tribord is watersports gear and Quechua is for those heading to the mountains. The Ciutat Vella's branch is the most crowded, so try heading to one of the less central stores if you are short of time or patience. Camping equipment, shooting gear, fishing tackle, rods and accessories can also be found

Outdoor Goods

Benitsports	Rla de Catalunya, 81	93 215 24 72
Decathlon	Av Diagonal, 545	93 444 01 65
Game Fisher	C/ Doctor Aiguader, 2	93 295 55 11

in smaller sporting goods shops, such as Benitosports. Equipment for a day in the sand dunes can usually be picked up at beach-front shops. El Corte Inglés (p.305) has an excellent floor dedicated to everything needed to enjoy the summer, from sun loungers to barbecues and swimwear to picnic sets. Game Fisher is a shop focused solely on fishing equipment and accessories. Hiking in any of the stunning surrounding hills and mountains is an activity enjoyed by many, so hiking equipment is readily available in most sports stores.

Party Accessories

Other options **Parties at Home** p.367, **Party Organisers** p.367

Party supplies and decorations can be picked up in department stores, small convenience stores and large supermarkets such as Carrefour (p.307), but Barcelona isn't a city with much in the way of dedicated party supply shops. Any of the companies listed in the Parties at Home section can offer help with sourcing decorations, marquees, children's entertainers, DJ's and cake makers.

Smelly soaps

Cakes can be bought from local sweet makers and bakers, where you'll get the finest quality for the best price. Simply wander in, tell them what you want, and they'll have it made in no time. They're unlikely to deliver though, so you'll need to pick up your purchase personally.

Perfumes & Cosmetics

Perfume and cosmetics can be bought in up-market pharmacies, but department stores and perfumeries tend to offer a better range. As with so much else, El Corte Inglés is an excellent choice, and has an entire floor dedicated to Lancome, Clarins, Chanel et al. Sephora offers both designer brands and younger, popular makes like Stila and Bourjois, which won't be found elsewhere. The Body Shop has branches across the city, although they're more expensive than in the company's native England. Duty Free is always an excellent option but even if you buy in Barcelona, designer names are cheaper than in a lot of other countries around Europe. Department stores (p.305) often offer makeovers and product advice. Specialist cosmetics are not very common, but treatments for sensitive or problem skin can be found in pharmacies and larger department stores. Older pharmacies will often stock Spanish perfumes that are no longer available elsewhere.

Perfume & Cosmetics		
Anti-Aging Store	C/ Guillem Tell, 51	93 238 49 68
The Body Shop	Diagonal, 280	93 486 02 19
Dr. Huuschka Skin Care	C/ Señeca, 31	93 238 60 80
Perfumeria Ella y El	C/ Pelai, 40	93 318 27 46
Perfumeria Julia	Rla de Catalunya, 97	93 487 95 91
Perfumeria Vall	Rda Sant Pere, 7	93 317 31 39
Regia	Pg de Gràcia, 39	93 216 01 21
Sephora	C/ Pelai, 3	93 301 14 63

Pets

Other options **Pets** p.99

There are plenty of pet stores around Barcelona with puppies looking longingly at passers-by. It's important to do some research before buying however. You can usually tell if an animal is pedigree or not but some pet shops are known for mistreating animals or keeping them in less than adequate conditions. While it may be tempting to 'rescue' animals by buying from such stores, the general attitude is that such establishments should not be supported. The pet shops listed are well known for their treatment of animals, after care and advice for new owners. All the domestic animals you'd expect, like cats, dogs, birds and fish, can be found. However, once you've found a pet and taken it home, there are certain steps that

299

Pets		
BCN Animals	La Ribera	93 349 67 27
Cuatro Patas	Sarrià-Sant Gervasi	93 212 84 55
La Fauna	Nou Barris	93 353 85 21
Superfauna	Sant Andreu	93 345 24 94
Yorky's	Eixample	93 415 89 88

need to be taken. All domestic pets must be identifiable by either microchip or a clearly readable tattoo. Any vet or local pet shop can offer advice. New pets must be registered at your local Ajuntament and if you own a dog classed as dangerous then you must have third party public liability insurance. See Pets in the Residence chapter (p.99) for more. There are no public dog fouling rules but people are becoming more sensitive to this as a health and safety issue, so if Fido does leave a deposit on La Rambla, you may find your ear bent by a passing citizen.

Portrait Photographers & Artists

Independent photographers will gladly do personal shoots for families and those needing pictures for commercial or business-related projects. Whether you want an intimate shot of your new baby or pictures of a big wedding, any of the photographers below offer competitive rates. The website www.exposr.com is an excellent source of photographers, allowing you to compare portfolios, prices and availability online. El Corte Inglés can organise family portraits, but if you want something unique and of fine quality, you're probably better off going with an independent. Street artists all along La Ramblas will do portraits while you sit and wait and some will do bigger portraits over a series of sittings, if asked.

Portrait Photographers & Artists		
Agrupacio Fotografica de Catalunya	93 301 65 81	www.afc.cat
Alula le Portrait	93 553 16 13	www.alulaportrait.blogspot.com
Diaz Wichmenn Photography	93 512 89 09	www.diazwichmann.com
Exposr.com	68 751 02 43	www.exposr.com

Second-Hand Items

Other options **Books** p.280, **Cars** p.282

Barcelona has a vast array of second-hand shops. Charity shops are abundant, and don't look as tatty as contemporaries in other countries. Clothes are beautifully displayed, china sets line window panes and everything from furniture to toys, garden seating to handbags can be bought in excellent condition and for little money.

On Riera Baixa in La Raval are a plethora of second hand and vintage clothes shops, where items can be bought and sold. The Saturday street market there is definitely worth visiting. Holala and Manados are well worth a look for hats, clothes, shoes and accessories from every era since the 30s. The online market is huge too. Local websites and magazines have excellent classifieds sections where anything can be offloaded or sought out. *Barcelona Metropolitan* is excellent (www.barcelona-metropolitan.com) as is www.angloinfo.com, which allows you to buy and sell around the country. See Websites, p.39 for more.

Second-Hand Items		
Bulevard dels Antiquaris	Pg de Gràcia, 55	93 215 44 99
Cash Converters	C/ Floridablanca, 145	93 453 99 00
Holala	C/ Carme, 72	93 441 99 44
Humana	Trav de Gràcia	93 415 78 88
La Trocante	C/ Comte Borrell, 22	93 443 60 37
Manados	C/ Carme, 39	na
Matador	C/ Hospital, 145	na

300

Shoes

Other options **Beachwear** p.278, **Sports Goods** p.302, **Clothes** p.282

Saving Your Soles
Shoe repair shops, often part of a launderette, dry cleaners or key cutters, are all over the city and for just a few euros can repair heel or sole problems and clean shoes.

Whether you want espadrilles or Manolo Blahniks, Barcelona is heaven for foot fetishists. *Zapaterias* normally offer men's, women's and children's shoes in a variety of styles, colours and prices. Foreign brand names can often be bought for less than elsewhere in Europe and there are a lot of Spanish shoe chains, such as Vogue, Tascon and Royalty. Many also sell their own designs blended with favorites like Jimmy Choos. Whether you're looking for a pair of decent leather shoes for €50, a €2 pair of flip flops or designer stilettos at €400, you should be satisfied. Aside from boutiques and *zapaterias*, supermarkets like Carrefour (p.307), and local markets (see p.309) often sell shoes. Pharmacies (p.107) will stock you up with Dr.

Zapatos rojos

Scholl's shoes. El Corte Inglés (p.305) occasionally has deals on summer shoes in winter and vice versa; it is also the best place to buy children's shoes and get children's feet measured properly. Custom made shoes are not easy to find, but one-off pairs from local designers can be seen in the funky boutiques of Born and Barri Gòtic.

Shoes		
Alvarez	C/ Ferran Agullo, 3	93 200 63 84
Camper	C/ Elisebets, 11	93 270 13 63
Casas Sabaters	Portal de l'Angel	93 302 11 12
Jorge Juan	C/ Valencia, 241	93 215 99 85
La Manual Alpargatera	C/ Avinyo, 7	93 301 01 72
Noel Barcelona	C/ Pelai, 46	93 317 86 38
Padevi Shoe Shop	Av Diagonal, 600	93 200 13 78
Royalty Shoe Shop	C/ Calvet, 23	93 209 51 32
Tascon	Pg de Gràcia, 64	93 487 90 84
Vogue	Pg de Gràcia, 30	93 301 90 35

Souvenirs

While souvenirs are unlikely to be top of a resident's wish list, Barcelona has a lovely range of Spanish ceramics, postcards, textiles and, unsurprisingly, Gaudi memorabilia. Eixample and Ciutat Vella have souvenir shops on every corner, some tacky, some pretty. For postcards, local tobacco shops (*tabacs*) often have the nicest selection. Local and national ceramics are found all over the city and, while some are covered in mock Gaudi or Picasso images, basic handmade olive dishes, bread bowls and water jugs can be purchased for little money and are often quite gorgeous. The galleries and museum shops often have a good selection of souvenirs. Carrer de Mallorca (see map p.394), just a few seconds from the Segrada Familia, is a souvenir hot spot with ceramics, place mats, candle holders, mini Sagrada Familias and posters of the great Spanish artists.

Souvenirs		
Escudellers Art	C/ Escudellers, 12	93 412 68 01
Souvenirs	C/ del Bisbe, 2	93 315 09 54

301

Sports Goods
Other options **Outdoor Goods** p.298

The tourist shops around La Rambla sell bundles of cheap sports kit, replica (and fake) football shirts. El Corte Inglés (p.305), Esports A.S. and Esports Nuria have excellent selections of equipment and clothing. Decathlon has several departments: watersports; mountain sports; cycling; fitness; team sports; nature (horseriding and fishing); racket sports and golf; health and adventure (diet) and running. There is no excuse for leaving ill equipped.

There are also some specialist sports centres. Match focuses on all things tennis, Ski Center says it all in the name and Attack Board looks after fans of surfing, skateboarding and skiing. Second hand items can be found in the classified listings of local newspapers notice boards in gyms, tennis centers and swimming pools. Home gym equipment is hard to find. For larger items such as treadmills, you're better off getting online and ordering direct from manufacturers; NordicTrack (www.nordictrack.com), and Horizon (www.horizonfitness.com) are among the better known brands.

Sports Goods		
Attack Board Shop	C/ Tecla Sala, 9	93 337 18 43
Decathlon	Pl Vila de Madrid, 1-3	93 342 61 61
El Corte Inglés	Av Diagonal, 471-473	93 493 48 00
Esports A.S.	C/ Esglesia, 25-27	93 337 13 45
Esports Nuria	Rda Sant Pau, 21-25	93 442 80 69
Ikara Sports	C/ Floridablanca, 122	93 423 09 87
Match	Via Augusta, 187	93 209 31 85
Ski Center	C/ Diputacio, 374-378	93 232 91 13

Stationery
Smaller, independent *papelerias* are old fashioned stationery stores. They can be found all over the city and can supply everything from writing paper to expensive Mont Blanc pens.

Stationery			
La Carpeta	C/ Comtal, 24	93 301 57 30	na
Libreria Baibars	C/ Muntaner, 337	93 201 00 62	www.baubars.com
Papereria Rovira	Rla de Catalunya, 62	93 215 20 92	na
Pepa Paper	C/Valencia, 266	93 215 92 23	www.epapaper.com

Tailoring
Other options **Tailors** p.95, **Souvenirs** p.301, **Clothes** p.282, **Textiles** p.303

Having clothes made to measure is common in Barcelona, despite the impressive selection of shops offering ready-made items. Finding a good tailor is easy; such is the abundance of talent. The list of tailors is lengthy (some excellent choices are below) but some specialise. Matex Iberica, for example, is known for curtains, while Camiseria Xanco tends to do just shirts. Some will provide material, while others will need you to bring your fabric of choice. Many will copy your existing items, and some will work from magazine pictures. Either way, you should be measured twice or more to ensure a piece that fits perfectly.

Tailoring		
Aramis (Tailoring and alterations)	C/ Ferran Agullo, 10	93 209 54 09
Camiseria Xanco (Shirt makers)	La Rambla, 78-80	93 318 09 89
Maria del Carmen Gorreto Sanchez (Seamstress)	Pg Mare de Deu del Coll, 102	93 210 04 13
Matex Iberica (Curtain making and installation)	Vallbona d'Anoia	93 771 90 75
Novamida (Tailoring and alterations)	C/ Provenca, 225	93 488 00 81
Oliveras Sastreria (Tailoring and alterations)	C/ Riera, 83	93 790 27 18
Sastreria de la Empresa (Tailoring and alterations)	Doctor Marti i Julia, 32	93 439 77 50

Textiles

Other options **Souvenirs** p.301, **Tailoring** p.302

The city was established as a major exporter of fine fabrics and textiles in the 18th century, and today there are plenty of tablecloths, towels, linens, curtains and fabrics available. There is even a Textile and Costume Museum at Carrer Montcada 12 in Ribera (www.museutextil.bcn.es). Independent, unadvertised textile shops are common, especially in Chinatown, which lies between Urqiunaona and Estacio de Nord, where the weekly markets are a great source for bright, light, reasonably priced fabrics. Feel free to haggle, especially if you're buying in bulk. Service in shops is traditional and impeccable, so you can count on talking to people with expertise. The price per metre will vary, but the cost of fabric is likely to be less than in other European cities, and the variety will be better. IKEA and other brands are here too, but with such independent, old fashioned stores, it seems a shame to buy modern copies.

Textiles		
CD Carpas & Tarimas	C/ Espronceda, 21	93 231 63 77
El Indio	C/ Carme, 24	93 317 54 42
Huntsman Textile Effects	C/ Balmes, 117	93 404 03 45
IKEA	Gran Via, 115-133	90 240 09 22
Rodin Tres	C/ Ausias Marc, 19	93 481 77 20

Toys, Games & Gifts

Barcelona has lots of little toy shops and boutiques that specialise in model army figures and other toys. For painting sets, Jordi Rubio Miniaturison Militar is very well established. Malda shopping mall near Plaça del Pi spreads across an entire block and has lots of independent toy boutiques. L'illa Diagonal (Diagonal 557) is another double level shopping centre, with lots of independent toy shops. Imaginarium is a wonderful chain with branches across Spain. The stores are designed with inquisitive kids in mind, and some have mini doorways that only children can use, next to adult-sized entrances. El Corte Inglés is excellent and Fnac (p.306), has a great computer game department.

Toys, Games & Gifts		
English & Me	Major de Sarrià, 20	93 206 00 94
Imaginarium	Rla Prat, 2	93 368 47 96
Jordi Rubio Miniaturismo Militar	Av Gaudi, 56	93 433 45 53
L'Illa Diagonal	Av Diagonal, 545-557	93 444 00 00
Xalar	Baixada Libretaria, 4	93 315 04 58

Wedding Items

The best known Spanish company is Pronovias. It offers custom made wedding dresses and the selection, quality and price is excellent. El Corte Inglés, though a department store, has a highly recommended wedding department. Wedding lists can be accessed from abroad, and it has a large selection of shoes and bridesmaid dresses. Massimo Dutti is also extremely popular for those looking for wedding outfits.

On local invitations, lace, frills and gilt lettering are hugely fashionable, so if that's not what you're after, get on the internet. For cakes, local bakers are often best. Companies specialising in wedding cakes aren't common, but the talent of Barcelona's many local bakers means that brides and grooms have an array of choice on their doorstep.

If the whole process is getting complicated, you can hire a planner to help book the church, find caterers and do all the other bits you may want to avoid. Fiesta Sol and D'Elite weddings (listed left) are both excellent options, run by professionals who can offer help anywhere in the country.

Wedding Items		
Aderzo de la Molina	Av Mques Comillas, 13	93 289 03 08
D'Elite Weddings	Various locations	93 212 18 99
Farah Novias	C/ Muntaner, 261	93 414 35 99
Fiesta Sol	Marbella	95 286 73 16
Jordi Auguera	C/ Muntaner, 269	93 201 52 68
Massimo Dutti	Pl de Catalunya, 4	93 412 59 16
Provonias	Pg de Gràcia, 74	90 010 00 75
Rosa Clara	Rla de Catalunya, 72	93 215 90 93
Tot Nuvis	Rla Modelell, 9	93 659 00 14

303

Places to Shop

Barcelona is a city that shops locally. Each barrio is likely to have its own baker, butcher and tailor, and this enduring sense of community often appeals to those from countries where local stores have been crushed beneath the economies of scale offered by dreary, strip-lit mega malls and hypermarkets. This shopping experience and the enthusiasm for supporting local trade is an important aspect of Catalan culture. It helps explain why Catalonia considers itself different to the rest of Spain. The local focus is endearing, but can also explain why other Spaniards sometimes consider Catalans insular and unfriendly. And while local markets and shopping areas are an important part of life, so is El Corte Inglés, and hypermarkets and department stores do exist, and often offer goods (such as uniquely British, Aussie or American items) that can't be bought elsewhere.

Streets & Areas to Shop

Av Portal de l'Angel
Barri Gòtic
Map p.403 D2

Avinguda Portal de l'Angel

This is a wide, busy, pedestrian strip, with the mammoth El Corte Inglés at the top, on Plaça de Catalunya. It's a great area for variety, however. As you head down, you are presented with a choice of posh nibbles, plush fashions and a good range of high street staples. Once you cross over Plaça Carles Pi i Sunyer, it all gets a little funkier, flamboyant and a bit more 'street'.

C/ Banys Nous
Barri Gòtic
Map p.403 D3

Carrer Banys Nous

In this part of the Barri Gòtic, modernity and tradition are thrown together in the labyrinth of narrow streets. Antique dealing was traditionally the trade here, but in recent years this has been replaced by alternative fashion boutiques. Tomate (p.292) and Glint are examples of the alternative fashion trends that are so characteristic of Barcelona. Some of the cuts and designs are a bit wacky and some of the materials are vintage-esque. Carrer Banys Nous sells stamps and stamp collector's items, second-hand books and other antique bits and bobs. For those with tired feet, Caelum is a relaxing shop-café that specialises in mouth-watering treats – cakes, biscuits, honey, marzipan bonbons and chocolates - from all over Spain.

C/ d'Avinyó
Barri Gòtic
Map p.403 D4

Carrer d'Avinyó

This street, which runs down from Carrer de Ferran, is one for young, fashion conscious shoppers who are interested in independent stores, new designers, and something a little more cutting edge. There are lots of boutiques hidden in the Gothic streets and choices are a little more eclectic than around Plaça de Catalunya. This makes for a great place to get lost and discover some unknown hidden outlets.

C/ Xucla
Raval
Map p.402 C2

Carrer Xucla

The junction of Carrer Xucla and Carrer Elisabets holds some of Barcelona's oldest, most well-hidden gastronomic secrets. First stop is La Portorriquena: a coffee specialist founded in 1902, it is the oldest shop on the street. The original coffee grinder is still used every morning to grind coffee beans from South and Central America, Africa and Puerto Rico (the house special). Next door, Forn Boix bakery has been in business since 1920. Their speciality is wholegrain biscuits made with raisins, walnuts and pine nuts. Herbolari pharmacy sells over 200 different herbs. For each ailment, specific prescriptions are made up using as many as 20 different herbs. Further along the street, Mantegueries Puig is a favourite among loyal local residents. The shop has been selling cheese from all over Europe for more than 60 years.

Plaça de Catalunya

C/ Doctor Dou and MACBA area
Raval
Map p.402 B2

MACBA area, Raval

Ravalejar ('to Ravalise') was an idea first introduced by a Catalan artist with a vision of a regenerated Raval. The upper part of the area sees new restaurants popping up all the time, whilst the lower area, around Carrer Nou de la Rambla, remains a little *chungo* (seedy). This too is changing though, and nowhere can it be seen more clearly than on the fashionable street Doctor Dou. The Raval's mix of hippy shops and edgy fashion boutiques reflect the changes that the presence of the MACBA (Museu d'Art Contemporani de Barcelona, p.305) has brought to the area. The lower Raval's ethnic shops, artisan jewellery stores, hippy fashions and kebab vendors reflect the area's diversity of identities. Second-hand clothing shops can be found on the streets that run perpendicular to Carrer Joaquin Costa.

Pg de Gràcia, Rla de Catalunya and Diagonal
Eixample
Map p.393 E3

The Shopping Line

This 5km stretch is a well travelled route for shopaholics. Passeig de Gràcia is often thought of as the Champs-Élysées of Barcelona because of its wide boulevards, architectural grandeur, designer institutions like Adolfo Dominguez and flagship high-street stores such as Zara and H&M. It is also rapidly gaining international recognition as one of the great shopping boulevards of Europe. Gaudí's fine architectural works, Casa Batlló (p.166) and La Pedrera (p.166), also attracts large numbers, creating a melee of determined shoppers and meandering tourists. Rambla de Catalunya and Diagonal are less of a tourist draw: the former is home to smaller specialty shops, lingerie stores, shoe shops, cosmetics and fashion boutiques; the latter is more designer.

Department Stores

El Corte Inglés is Spain's only department store of note. The name, meaning 'The English Cut', subtly demonstrates that department stores are not part of Spanish culture. A force to be reckoned with, the hegemonic commercial institution has managed to quash all possible competition over the years. Shopping malls and retail parks spring up, but not department stores. Even the Spanish word *grandes almacenes*, used to describe El Corte Inglés, is an umbrella word under which any large stores, such as IKEA, or even Carrefour hypermarkets, are classified. Department stores are usually open from 10:00 to 22:00 Monday to Saturday, and are closed on Sundays and public holidays.

Various locations

El Corte Inglés
90 112 21 22 | *www.elcorteingles.es*

This is by far the country's most successful and frequently visited department store. Barcelona's flagship site is a seven floor giant that overlooks Plaça de Catalunya. Fashion, beauty, home décor, domestic appliances, home entertainment systems, baby wear and accessories on different floors provide enough choice for an afternoon's work. Women's and men's fashions are designer label-orientated: Carolina Herrera, Ralph Lauren, Adolfo Dominguez and Calvin Klein are all here. Diesel and Pepe Jeans dominate the younger fashion department. The basement supermarket is home to some local products from Catalan and Spanish producers, and delicatessen counters selling cheese, cured meat and caviar. The Gourmet Club is good for finding

305

gifts. For those who want to make a day of it there is an exclusive restaurant on the top floor overlooking Plaça de Catalunya. There are other stores also, including two on Avinguda Diagonal, at numbers 617 and 471.

Various locations

Fnac
90 210 06 32 | *www.fnac.es*

Fnac has mastered the art of multi-tasking: from DVDs, CDs, hi-fis, TVs, computers, mobile phones and IT equipment to cameras and mp3 players, the French multimedia megastore has it all (and that's just the first floor). On the second floor, the generous and moderately priced selection of English and French books is reason enough to go. The bottom floor is dedicated to film processing and concert tickets, making it busy after working hours and on weekends. While you wait, there is an international newsstand and cafe-bar. The gig room on the ground floor of the Plaça de Catalunya branch is used on Saturdays to give up and coming bands the opportunity to be heard live. The groups are hit and miss, but you may just get lucky. Fnac has three stores in Barcelona; Plaça de Catalunya 4, Avinguda Diagonal 3-35 and at L´Illa, Avinguda Diagonal 549.

Hypermarkets

The geography of each area in Barcelona affects the availability of supermarkets. The narrow streets of Ciutat Vella and Gràcia lend themselves to convenience stores and smaller supermarkets; Carrefour on La Rambla is the only large supermarket in the area. Eixample's grid structure on the other hand, is much more suitable for housing multi-storey supermarket chains, municipal parking garages and indoor markets. Less central areas, or peripheral retail parks, are the only places where you are likely to find hypermarkets and large shopping malls. Convenience stores have become more common in Barcelona over the last few years. These are a practical option as they are open until late every day of the week. The best and most inexpensive option for household cleaning products and banal nick-knacks such as plugs, adaptors and light bulbs are the convenience stores found mainly in Raval, Poble Sec, Barri Gòtic and Eixample.

Various locations

Alcampo
93 356 20 00 | *www.alcampo.es*

Alcampo is a successful French hypermarket chain that can be found at retail parks on the perimeter of the city. The stores are invariably vast in size and range of products, both local and international. Prices are competitive and they would argue that they are cheaper than their competitors. In some cases this is true, particularly when it comes to fruit and vegetables, frozen foods and special offers. Mostly though, it is just fighting talk. Quality is high and home delivery, travel bookings and financial services are additional benefits; however, internet shopping is not yet available.

Various locations

Caprabo
90 211 60 60 | *www.caprabo.es*

This is the most expensive supermarket chain, found in the wealthier suburbs such as Sarrià, Vall d'Hebron and the northern parts of Eixample. Avinguda Mistral is the nearest branch to Ciutat Vella. The fresh meat and fish are particularly plump and flavoursome, and there are no shortages of cheese and fine deli produce. Fruit and vegetables look perfect but the taste is no better to what you find in the markets. Caprabo gains serious brownie points for its online shopping catalogue though. It is way ahead of the competition in terms of presentation and user manageability. You have two options when you order online: home delivery or pick up. When you spend more than €100, the delivery fee is €4; if you spend less, it costs €6. Caprabo is well served for parking.

Places to Shop

Various locations
Carrefour
90 220 20 00 | *www.carrefour.es*

The French giant offers the most comprehensive selection of food of all the supermarket chains. Carrefour also sells home entertainment systems, IT products, photographic equipment, household and electrical appliances and home furnishings. It boasts the broadest range of international products, together with Alcampo and El Corte Inglés. Being a French supermarket chain, the wine and cheese sections are well stocked, and feature many French household names. Supermarkets are called Carrefour Express, whereas stores on the outskirts of the city are hypermarkets that sell all of the above products in greater bulk. Carrefour provides financial advice, insurance policies, travel bookings and property services as well. Internet shopping through their website is efficient and gives you access to all of the shop's departments. The delivery fee is €8.99 for orders above €110 and €10.99 for orders below.

Various locations
Condis
90 226 63 47 | *www.condis.es*

This Catalan supermarket chain is middling on the price scale, resting somewhere between Caprabo and Mercadona. Condis is a pleasant and clean chain with a good selection of cheeses, meats, fresh olives, fruit and vegetables. If you are a fan of olives, check if your nearest branch has a fresh olive stand. The shelves are mainly stacked with Catalan and national products, apart from the cheese, yoghurt and confectionary sections, which have some international (mostly French) names.

Various locations
Dia
602 453 453 | *www.dia.es*

Low price products abound here. Dia is the cheapest supermarket chain in the city and prides itself on being so. A good option for non-dairy products, preserved foods, base foods such as pasta, household products and buying in bulk, Dia is particularly popular among students and families. Usually located centrally, it is a one-stop convenience store. However, in some stores (in Raval particularly) the fruit and vegetable selection can look rather weary.

Various locations
Mercadona
93 226 53 47 | *www.mercadona.es*

This is probably the best value for money option in town. You can buy good quality meat, fish and fresh produce for around half the price of the international supermarket chains. Mercadona's own-brand range offers good choice at low prices. The only letdown is their website: constant referral back to the homepage makes online shopping rather difficult. There are only 30 stores around the city, but with such good deals on offer, it is worth finding your nearest branch. Paradoxically (given its bargain prices), most stores are situated in the wealthier areas of the city.

Various locations
Schlecker
90 288 85 41 | *www.schlecker.com*

Boasting more than 100 stores in and around Barcelona, Schlecker is a low-cost leader in the cosmetics and toiletries market. The pharmacy chain sells everything from men's facial creams to pedicure sets. Originating in Germany, Schlecker is now present in over 25 European countries. While their prices are not radically different from those in the supermarkets, the main draw is the stream of constant price reductions on brand names such as L'Oreal or Nivea, and the two-for-one offers. Schlecker's own-brand products are even cheaper.

Independent Shops

The maze of narrow streets in Ciutat Vella lends itself to speciality stores and boutiques; you are as likely to find a 19th century candlemaker, as you are an über-trendy designer store. Shops change hands in the Born at a rapid rate, and it's not uncommon to see them close after six months. Nevertheless, the boho-chic area continues to attract new business. Raval is the spot with most promise; rent and mortgage prices are lower than in the Born, encouraging alternative, edgy young designers to set up shop. With high-street chain stores popping up everywhere, it's refreshing to see that small-time specialists are surviving.

C/ Dagueria, 16
Barri Gòtic
🚇 *Jaume I*
Map p.403 E4 77

Formatgeria La Seu

93 412 65 48 | *www.formatgerialaseu.com*

Katherine McLaughlin opened this fine cheese shop over six years ago and has never looked back. Her gourmet collection of over 20 Spanish farmhouse cheeses has gained a reputation as the best of its kind. Through word of mouth and taster sessions held at the shop, she has acquired a strong local client base. Cheese from goat, cow and sheep's milk, together with cheese flavour ice cream, olive oil, red wine, and her newest addition, house sherry, are the products on offer. Taster sessions are held every Saturday afternoon from 12:00 to 15:30. By keeping the range of products focused, Katherine ensures that quality, and not quantity, is the priority.

C/ Canuda, 21
Barri Gòtic
🚇 *Catalunya*
Map p.403 D2 78

Le Boudoir

93 302 52 81 | *www.leboudoir.net*

Reminiscent of scenes from Moulin Rouge, this exclusive lingerie store is erotic and taboo. It sells La Perla and Agent Provocateur lingerie, luxurious Venetian masks, saucy literature, sex toys and cosmetics. Principally a lingerie store, the clientele are exclusively women, on some occasions accompanied by their enlightened, if slightly daunted, boyfriends. For those who want to work on their moves, Le Boudoir also organises courses in striptease.

C/ Nou de la Rambla, 40
Raval
🚇 *Drassanes*
Map p.402 B4 79

News Times

93 481 55 79

News Times, an intimate fashion boutique, seems rather incongruous with the kebab joints and the call centres that stand opposite. Business suffers from the surroundings, which is a shame because the clothes deserve more recognition. Designed by students from the renowned BAU Escola de Disseny and by independent French designers, the style and quality of clothes is a cut above some of the other newly-opened, but better located, fashion boutiques. Alternative and edgy, with usually only one item in each size, it is the ideal place for those who want to stand out from the crowd. Popular with well-heeled students and trendy twentysomethings, as prices are not much higher than high-street names.

C/ de la Palla, 8
Barri Gòtic
🚇 *Jaume I*
Map p.403 D3 80

Oro Liquido

93 302 29 80 | *www.oroliquido.es*

Ana Segovia, French-born of Andalusian parents, and business partner Patricia Elkhoury, are both of olive-growing lineage. Since opening in 2005, their objective has always been clear: to emphasise the true value of good quality extra virgin olive oil. The bottles are presented in the same way as wine: stylish and individually designed, with the appellation clearly marked on the bottle. Not just for cooking, anti-oxidants and vitamins found in olive oil contain anti-ageing properties. Oro Liquido takes advantage of this by offering a luscious range of beauty products and skin creams.

Av Diagonal, 520
Eixample
🚇 *Diagonal*
Map p.393 D2 **81**

Sans & Sans

93 414 56 23 | *www.sansisans-finetea.com*

This upmarket tea shop exudes a sense of calm and relaxation from the moment you walk through the door. Aromatic teas, fruit teas, blends, white tea, green tea and rooibos (red bush tea); you name it, they'll have it somewhere. The fruit teas and exotic blends, such as Pearl of the Orient (infused with rose petals), are well worth trying, or sniffing at the very least. They also offer an elegant range of teapots and other tea making accessories. Their other shop in the Born (Carrer Argenteria 59) offers an equally extensive selection.

Markets

Market shopping here is a way of life. It is a social outing and a chance to discuss everything, including the fruit and vegetable season's highs and lows. However, large supermarket chains have been threatening the survival of smaller market vendors. In a venture to rejuvenate the city's markets, the local government launched a huge municipal advertising campaign and multi-million euro project. Of the central markets, Santa Catarina and Poblenou are newly completed and Barceloneta recently re-opened its doors to an impatient public. It doesn't stop there though: plans are afoot to renovate Mercat Sant Antoni, one of the oldest markets in Barcelona. Encants Vells, the city's largest flea market, will also be relocated to the now disused bullring. Today, markets are seen as a national heritage and a cultural landmark, which is why the local government is working hard to preserve them. There are also specialised markets, such as the book fair Dominical Llibre at Mercat Sant Antoni or Flors de la Rambla, the permanent flower market. To locate your nearest local market, consult the City Council's website (www.bcn.es) under the section *Comerç*.

Markets

Mercat de Canyelles	C/ Antonio Machado, 10	Nou Barris	93 427 71 86
Mercat de La Sagrada Família	C/ Mallorca, 425	Eixample	93 436 34 52
Mercat de Les Corts	Trav Corts, 215	Les Corts	93 330 97 02
Mercat de Sant Andreu	Pl Mercadal, 41	Sant Andreu	93 345 11 48
Mercat de Sant Gervasi	Pl Joaquim Folguera, 6	Sarrià-Sant Gervasi	93 417 78 74
Mercat de Sant Martí	C/ Puigcerdà, 206	Sant Martí	93 313 34 49
Mercat de Sants	C/ Sant Jordi, 6	Sants-Montjuïc	93 339 55 53
Mercat de Vall d'Hebron	C/ Trueba, 1	Horta-Guinardó	93 428 31 84

Pl Glòries Catalanes, 8
Eixample
🚇 *Glòries*
Map p.395 D4 **82**

Fira de Bellcaire

93 246 30 30

Fira de Bellcaire, commonly known as Encants Vells (Old Charms), is the oldest flea market in Barcelona, and just about everything goes. You can find all manner of things here from washing machines, hairdryers, shoes, African furniture and Moroccan carpets to stolen mobile phones and emptied leather wallets. Mind your own wallet as you're walking around as the place is a prime target for pickpockets. Encants Vells is not organised; clothes are left in piles on the ground, furniture spills out from under the stalls and toiletries overflow from their containers. If you want to find a real bargain though, this is the place to come. You may have to trawl through a lot of useless dross, but if and when you do come across something desirable, you can be sure that it will be cheap. This market is particularly good for picking up discounted furniture, shoes and toiletries. It's open all day Monday, Wednesday, Friday and Saturday.

La Rambla, 89
Ciutat Vella
🚇 *Liceu*
Map p.402 C3 83

La Boqueria

93 318 25 84

Among tourists, La Boqueria is considered the most colourful market in Barcelona. Among locals it is known as a tourist trap offering the same as other markets but at higher prices. Located off La Rambla, there are so many tourists that the market entrance becomes a bottleneck of shoppers. If you go, head to the stalls at the back, as the prices are lower and the atmosphere is less hectic. The central area of the market is dedicated to fresh fish and seafood, where one kilo of mussels costs €3 and a kilo of prawns costs €6. Market sellers on the whole tend to be friendly, although you can stumble across one or two who are so fed up of tourists that extracting a smile is impossible. If you come across a chatty stallholder, haggling is always worth a try.

Pl Font, 1
Barceloneta
🚇 *Barceloneta*
Map p.409 F3 84

Mercat de la Barceloneta

93 221 64 71

This market, open from Monday to Saturday, has recently had a good scrub up. It's setting between port and sea is reassuring, as this is a fresh food market. You can get fish that arrived that morning, or a healthy dose of fruit, meat and vegetables. Definitely one for foodies.

Comte d'Urgell, 1
Sant Antoni
🚇 *Sant Antoni*
Map p.401 E2 85

Mercat Sant Antoni

93 423 42 87

If you're after a tourist-free, traditional market experience, Mercat Sant Antoni might be the answer. Throughout the week (closed on Mondays) clothing and second-hand book stands can be found. Particularly fascinating (although more in terms of appreciation than usefulness) are the slightly kitsch flamenco stands selling brightly coloured skirts and fans. You can find a bargain here from time to time, particularly on smaller items such as socks (only €2). However, the best feature of this market is its authenticity, unchanged and untainted by the enormous number of foreigners that flood into the city every year. There are stands selling CDs, electrical accessories, baby clothing, books and trinkets of no practical use. It comes alive on Saturdays, the busiest time to visit, when there is an amicable buzz to the place. Bookworms and comic-lovers should visit on Sunday mornings between 08:00 and 14:00, when the second-hand book and comic fair takes place.

Av Francesc Cambó, 16
La Ribera
🚇 *Jaume I*
Map p.403 F3 86

Mercat Santa Caterina

93 319 57 40 | *www.mercatsantacaterina.net*

This is the one with the funky roof. The wave of colour that shelters this fine foods market is quickly becoming another heavily photographed architectural icon of the city. Beneath the glamorous rain shelter, you'll find fancy olive oils, meats, cheeses and vegetables. The crafty lighting allows shafts of sunshine to illuminate your prospective purchases.

La Boqueria market

Shopping Malls

Mall culture is not something that has traditionally been a part of life in Barcelona. The city prides itself on the diversity of choice hidden in the narrow streets of Ciutat Vella, or proudly displayed on the Passeig de Gràcia and Rambla de Catalunya. Nevertheless, mall shopping is on the rise. Over the last decade, developments have included Diagonal Mar, Glories (built in 1995) and L'Illa Diagonal. The latest project is the conversion of Les Arenes bullring in Plaza Espanya. The emblematic bullfighting arena is to be converted into a shopping mall. The prestigious British architect Richard Rogers is undertaking the architectural design, together with the Catalan studio Alonso & Balaguer.

Pg de Gràcia, 51-57
Eixample
🚇 *Passeig de Gràcia*
Map p.393 E3 59

Bulevard Rosa

93 215 83 31 | *www.bulevardrosa.com*
Bulevard Rosa differs from other malls; being smaller and attracting more boutique-style shops, it manages to maintain a more sophisticated image. You will not find large high-street or department stores here, nor will you find the bargain prices offered by stores such as Zara. Most of the shops are speciality boutiques, local designers and quaint, high quality children's garments. Despite this, Bulevard Rosa is not a child-friendly zone, with no children's facilities available. It is centrally located - serviced by five parking garages and Passeig de Gràcia metro station - thus catching the eye of many a tourist or passer-by.

C/Salvador Espriu, 61
Port Olímpic
🚇 *Ciutadella/Vila Olímpica*
Map p.411 E2 60

Centro Comercial El Centre de la Vila

93 221 09 09 | *www.elcentredelavila.com*
Soul-less in its character and shapeless in form, El Centre de la Vila is of no particular architectural or cultural merit. The usual names Zara, Mango and H&M are present, but the mall lacks character. A smattering of cafes, restaurants and a Burger King are on the second floor. Baby changing facilities are available but there aren't many activities for children. The 15 screen Icaria cinema, showing films in their original versions, is the mall's only redeeming feature. Sound quality is good and the seats are comfortable, but weekend queues can be tremendously long, so try to arrive at least thirty minutes before the film starts.

Av Diagonal, 3
Vila Olímpica
🚇 *Maresme Fòrum*
Map p.413 E2 61

Diagonal Mar

90 253 03 00 | *www.diagonalmar.com*
This mall has a distinctly airy ambience, helped by its seaside setting. Its best feature is the terrace, filled with fast-food cafes, restaurants, tapas bars and ice cream parlours. The hypermarket giant Alcampo, Fnac and high-street favourites Mango and Zara are all present. There are plenty of family-oriented activities such as a bowling alley, concerts and children's entertainment every Sunday at 12:30. Exhibitions and concerts for adults are regularly held, with details on the website. In summer months, the mall hosts a series of free concerts as part of a summer festival.

Pl Catalunya, 1-4
Ciutat Vella
🚇 *Catalunya*
Map p.402 C1 62

El Triangle

93 318 01 08 | *www.eltriangle.es*
Fnac and Habitat dominate this mini-mall in Plaça de Catalunya, dwarfing the smaller jewellery and cosmetics stores. Calvin Klein Lingerie distracts the gaze of determined shoppers, as does the ice cream parlour opposite. El Triangle's best feature is its central location, a stone's throw from La Rambla. Parking is available and particularly useful for those wanting to spend the afternoon in the heart of the city. However, parking spaces are keenly vied for, and come at a price, so try to arrive early in the morning.

311

Av Gran Via ◄
l'Hospitalet de Llobregat
🚇 **Ildefons Cerda FGC**
Map p.390 C4 **63**

Gran Via 2

90 230 14 44 | *www.granvia2.com*

One of the biggest, busiest and best equipped shopping centres in the city. Decathlon, Carrefour and IKEA attract customers from the suburbs looking to buy in bulk. This does not detract from the three floors and 180 shops dedicated to clothing, music, jewellery, books, technology and shoes. The children's facilities are more expansive than in other malls, with play areas both inside and out. Parking is not usually a problem, as there are 3,400 spaces, each with three hours of free parking. The mall is well-serviced by several train and bus routes; the most direct and frequent buses leave from Plaça Espanya.

Av Diagonal, 545-557 ◄
Eixample
🚇 **Maria Cristina**
Map p.392 B1 **65**

L'Illa Diagonal

93 444 00 00 | *www.lilla.com*

'The Island' is the work of architects Rafael Moneo and Manuel de Solà-Morales, whose design of a skyscraper lying down was inspired by the Rockefeller Center in New York. The €240 million project would seem rather outlandish if it weren't for the neighbouring business towers. During the week, a food market on the ground floor and Caprabo supermarket are popular lunchtime options for professionals and local students. Home to Fnac, El Corte Inglés, Diesel, Zara and Decathlon, as well as Adolfo Dominguez and Hermes. Within the complex, there is a small park and an infant care room, equipped with microwave oven, table, chairs and a diaper changing facility.

Av Diagonal, 208 ◄
Poblenou
🚇 **Poblenou**
Map p.412 B1 **64**

Les Glories

93 486 04 04 | *www.lesglories.com*

Les Glories is one of the most pleasant malls to shop in, because of its open-spaces, alfresco cafes and relaxed atmosphere. The most important feature is the large central square. Surrounded by cafes, restaurants and fast-food chains, it acts as a key meeting point and social hub. There are over 220 shops in total and a seven screen cinema, unfortunately, foreign films are all dubbed into Spanish. Children's play areas and a free pram-lending service make for an enjoyable family experience. In the evening, you have a fantastic view of the brightly lit Torre Agbar, which stands just across the road from the mall. Parking is free for the first two hours, €1.75 per hour thereafter.

Moll d'Espanya ◄
Port Vell
🚇 **Drassanes**
Map p.408 C3 **66**

Maremagnum

93 225 81 00 | *www.maremagnum.es*

Maremagnum underwent a makeover, replacing bars and clubs with upmarket stores such as Calvin Klein and Adolfo Dominguez. Even so, terrace bars and clubs remain, as does the large Miramax cinema. Mainstream high-street stores are punctuated by boutiques and new designer outlets. The ground floor sweet shops and children's clothing stores are geared for families and there is a small children's play area on the second floor. For good eateries, there are a number of restaurants within the mall, but better located are those with terraces, overlooking the port.

Diagonal, 609-615 ◄
Les Corts
🚇 **Maria Cristina**
Map p.384 A4 **67**

Pedralbes Centre

93 410 68 21 | *www.pedralbescentre.com*

When this shopping mall opened in 1989, the objective was to make it exclusive. Space was offered to prestigious national and international establishments, curtailing the involvement of high street chains. There are 74 establishments in the mall, many of which are Catalan designers, such as Samblancat and Lluis Guirau. The ClientCard is handy for those planning to burn a hole in their haute couture pockets, as it gives you a 5% or 10% discount in selected shops. Sophisticated architecture and design make it a popular venue for catwalk presentations of new fashions. In the winter months, an ice rink is installed, providing entertainment for families with young children.

Catalan chic

Giggling Guiri
Comedy Club
madrid - barcelona

Stephen K Amos

Michael McIntyre

Brendon Burns

Paul Sinha

Andrew Maxwell

Spain's premier comedy club bringing the premier comedians every month

January	Stephen K Amos
February	Michael McIntyre / Russell Howard
March	Andrew Maxwell
April	Paul Sinha / Reginald D Hunter
May	Brendon Burns
June	Cat Laughs Collaboration

+info and tickets at www.comedyinspain.com

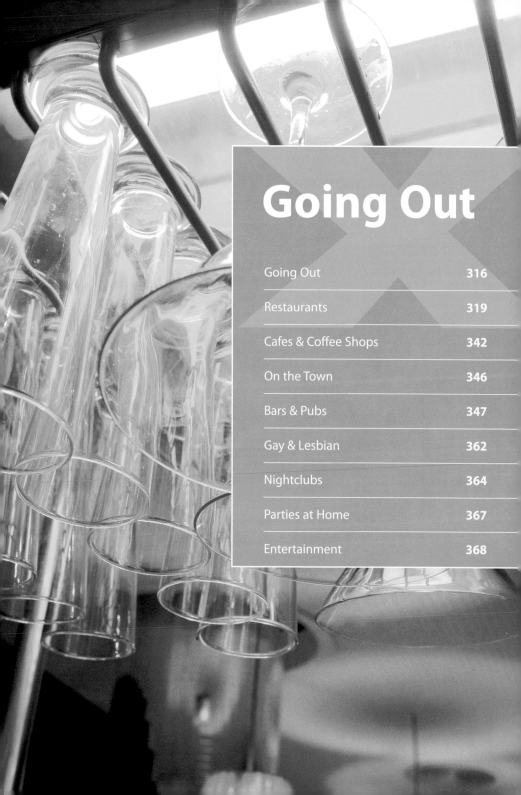

Going Out

Going Out

The social scene in Barcelona is eclectic, exciting, energetic and constant. Whatever you're looking for, whether it's a club at 07:00 on a Sunday, or a theme bar filled with old circus equipment, you'll find it here. Every taste is catered for, whether you're hoping to drink in a squat full of dreadlocked anarchists, or you want Europe's finest wines and foie gras. There is something for every demographic, but Barcelona is certainly a little more alternative and bohemian than other Spanish cities.

In Barceloneta you'll find bars perched on the waterfront, the Gothic district offers some wonderfully dark dens and underground jazz clubs, while Eixample and Port Olímpic are the clubbing districts. It's a relatively small city, so easy to get your bearings. Wander the streets and dip into watering holes, hit the clubs for some all-night action or wile away the hours drinking cocktails in any of the beautiful plaças. The Catalans are not considered the friendliest folk in Spain, but make an effort (especially with the language) and you'll be warmly welcomed. Alcohol is available all day, every day, often with complete disregard for licensing laws. Everything starts and finishes late, so you'll need to adapt to the siesta way of life (which is particularly easy in the hot summer months). Lunch is in the middle of the afternoon (although available earlier than that if you get hungry), restaurants are empty before 22:00 (many don't open before 21:00) and clubbing begins after the bars close at 03:00. To maintain an active social life in your new home, you may need to adjust your body clock. Just follow the natives.

Eating Out

With the world's number one restaurant (El Bulli in Cala Montjoi, Roses, according to *Restaurant Magazine*) just an hour away, Barcelona's culinary reputation is growing. Avoid the tourist traps and soggy paella, and you'll find a fantastic array of Catalan, Basque, traditional Spanish, French, Italian and, most often, fusion food. People eat late, and some kitchens don't open until 21:00. The earlier you eat, the less atmosphere you can expect. The only night of the week that restaurants are quiet is on Mondays, when many don't open at all. Every other night they'll be busy until the early hours.

Catalans are very family-orientated and restaurants tend to welcome children regardless of the time, although there are still many spots for business meetings or romantic suppers. Recent immigration surges have also seen lots of ethnic restaurants open, especially in Gràcia and Raval, but fusion foods (often Spanish and French, Catalan and French or Mediterranean and Japanese) are still predominant. In fact, the only potential complaint foodies may have is the limited range of non-European foods. The table below will show you where to find a specific cuisine, and info boxes like 'Al Fresco,' on the left of this page, will highlight a few gems.

Alfresco

Eating outside is a cornerstone of life in Barcelona and most places will have a few tables set on the pavement. Some are particularly worth noting for either the pleasantness of their setting or spectacular view. Agua, p.330 and Salamanca, p.335 both provide sea-view terraces without the corresponding dip in quality that many beachside restaurants suffer. For a drink surrounded by the greenery of the Parc de la Ciutadella, try Hivernacle, p.352.

Cuisine List – Quick Reference

Arabic/Lebanese	p.319	French	p.326	Pizzerias	p.333
Argentinian	p.319	Fusion	p.327	Portuguese	p.333
Basque	p.320	Indian	p.329	Seafood	p.334
Brazilian	p.321	Italian	p.329	Spanish	p.335
British & Irish	p.321	Mediterranean	p.330	Steakhouses	p.338
Catalan	p.322	Mexican	p.331	Thai	p.339
Chinese	p.324	Moroccan	p.332	Vegetarian	p.340

Delivery

While entertaining at home is extremely popular, home delivery is not. Choices beyond pizza are limited, but if you're willing to collect pre-ordered food, you'll have more luck. For excellent Sushi or Thai food, Matsuri (see p.339) is a great option and gladly serves takeaway. Dinner parties can easily be catered for and there are a plethora of private companies, especially if you want traditional Spanish or Catalan cooking (see Caterers, p.367).

Drinks

Other options **Alcohol** p.277

While licensing laws exist, they are barely noticeable. Alcohol is available at all times, although the minimum age is technically 16. Minors can drink at the discretion of their parents and buy alcohol if accompanied by one of them. It is widely available, from supermarkets and smaller outlets. Speciality wine shops are wonderful for learning about the incredible selection of regional grapes, but they don't sell spirits or beer. Alcohol is relatively cheap, but some bars and clubs demand higher prices. Cocktails such as mojitos and caipirinhas are popular but measures tend to be generous so drinks are very strong. Vichy Catalan is the local sparkling water. It has a salty taste that you'll either find delicious, grow to appreciate, or never want to touch again. Do not drink the tap water; lead pipes are yet to be replaced and besides the health worries, it tastes bad.

Hygiene

Most bars and restaurants are hygienic. The latter have to adhere to health and safety codes, even if they aren't as stringently enforced as in other countries. Bars often provide questionable bathroom facilities, but you don't generally need to worry about food poisoning. Just remember to avoid the tap water.

Special Deals & Theme Nights

With so many fiestas and public holidays, promotions on entry charges, drinks and food are steadily on offer. The Irish pubs will offer cheap drinks on St. Patrick's Day, the local bars will offer deals on any of their many saint's days, and clubs often have offers on for those arriving early. Ladies' nights aren't as common as in other cities and happy hours aren't a given either, mainly because men and women party till dawn without incentive and drinks are cheap anyway. Don't expect anything to be happening on either January 5th or New Year's Day - the former being the day when most Spaniards celebrate Christmas and the latter being when everyone spends the day in bed recovering from New Year's Eve.

Tax & Service Charges

There is no tax or discretionary service charge added to bills in restaurants, bars or clubs. Very high end hotel bars may make an exception and tag on a service charge.

Tipping

Tipping is not expected. In the brief days of republican unity at the beginning of the Civil War, tipping was considered an insulting assumption of class superiority. While no one likely to be insulted today, it still doesn't happen. Some say this is a throw back to the republic or a demonstration of the city's left-leaning, alternative outlook. Others say it's because Catalans are tight. Either way, taxi drivers, bar staff and waiters expect nothing. If you want to leave a little extra, 2-3% is reasonable and 10% or more is considered very generous.

Food Restrictions

There are few food restrictions in Barcelona, but some items are more common. Seafood, steak and hot padrones peppers are widespread, foreign foods (such as Indian) are not. Very little attention is paid to allergy foods such as nuts, except in expensive restaurants, so always check before you order.

317

However, charges do appear on restaurant bills for bread. Often it is served before a meal arrives, whether requested or not, and a charge for each person's portion will be added to the bill. If you want to avoid this, send the bread away before anyone gets their fingers on it. Once it's been nibbled, you'll be charged.

Independent Reviews

All of the outlets in this book have been independently reviewed by a team of food and nightlife experts who are based in Barcelona. Their aim is to give clear, realistic and unbiased views of each venue without any back-handers, special treatment or underhandedness on the part of any restaurant owner, nightclub promoter, crafty PR guru or persuasive barista. If there's one thing the Explorer team thrives on, it's feedback. So if any of the reviews in this section have led you astray, or if your favourite local eatery doesn't grace these pages, then drop us a line on info@explorerpublishing.com and tell us all about it.

Restaurant Listing Structure

The restaurants listed here run in alphabetical order by cuisine type. Some offer more than one cuisine, but we've tried to group them by what they are best at, and the cuisine that dominates the menu. While places for eating and places for drinking tend to merge in Barcelona, we've split bars, cafes and restaurants with the same criteria in mind. If somewhere does a mean mojito, but offers sit-down meals and exquisite food, it'll be listed in restaurants. If a venue does a decent bocadillo but is best known as somewhere to drink till dawn, it'll be under bars.

Vegetarian Food

In a country where meat and fish are so revered, there are few vegetarian restaurants. Barcelona has more than elsewhere because of the largely young, bohemian community that inhabits the city. The Maoz (www.maozveg.com) chain of falafel bars serves veggie fast-food at venues all over the city. Health-food shops and restaurants selling vegetarian snacks, such as those on p.340, are often committed to all things organic and healthy. If you are in a restaurant that isn't focused on vegetarian food, ask the waiting staff for a menu of non-meat or fish-based dishes. Their menu may not have many options, but they'll usually try to accommodate you. Catalan food is loaded with mixed vegetable varieties, so there should be something.

Discounts
Privilege cards are rare, but one recommendation is a local, monthly publication called *Guide Out*. As well as offering restaurant, club and bar reviews, it often provides one-off discounts and special offers.

The Yellow Star
The natty yellow star seen to the right is our way of highlighting places that we think merit extra praise. It might be the atmosphere, the food, the cocktails, the music or the crowd, but any review that you see with the star attached is somewhere that we think is a bit special.

'A full belly makes you happy'

Arabic/Lebanese

Other options **Moroccan** p.332

C/ València, 218
Eixample
🚇 *Passeig de Gràcia*
Map p.393 D3 1

Al Jaima

93 454 07 12

Apart from fantastic food, Al Jaima has a dancefloor that gets packed late into the night, with locals sashaying to Arabic-influenced music. Belly dancers emerge from dark corners, shisha waterpipes get passed around and cocktails are mixed by the dozen. Before this fun begins however, a delectable menu can be enjoyed. Al Jaima has been serving for over a quarter of a century, offering everything from classic lamb kebabs and veal to tabouli salad. There are many excellent vegetarian options and mint tea flows from ornate pots at the end of each course. With its thick red curtains and mass of gold, Al Jaima is aesthetically ornate (some would argue over-the-top) and a decadent place to eat, drink and dance the night away.

C/ Vila i Vila, 82
Sants-Montjuïc
🚇 *Paral·lel*
Map p.401 F4 2

Kasbah

93 329 83 84

If you manage to spend more than €20 on dinner in Kasbah, you've a greater appetite than most. With three separate dining areas and a mezzanine, it is a good choice for large groups and at such reasonable prices, you can split the bill equally and no one will feel aggrieved. The decor is quintessentially Arabic, with its tapestries and rugs across the floor, copper-topped tables and cushioned seating. The food has classic Arabic dishes such as fried lamb meatballs, tagine and even raw lamb. There is a touch of French food on the menu though, with entrecote steak in Roquefort cheese for those who want to avoid the spicier dishes. Fun, kitsch and easy on the wallet, Kasbah will require reservations at weekends, as it's hugely popular and people tend to end up staying all night.

Argentinian

Other options **Brazilian** p.321

C/ Consell de
Cent, 338
Eixample
🚇 *Passeig de Gràcia*
Map p.393 F4 3

El Boliche del Gordo Cabrera

93 215 68 81

The excellent steak and kebabs at El Boliche de Gordo Cabrera attract a mixed and very voluminous clientele, so reservations are recommended. If you decide on a whim to drop by, the service is efficient enough that you probably won't be waiting too long. The house speciality is red meat, grilled Argentinian style. There are thousands of bottles of wine lining the walls and the decor is comfortable and homely. A reasonable set menu is available on weekdays, but if you prefer to select your own cut from the menu, you can guarantee it'll be cooked perfectly. All the meat is cooked on an open fire grill, and served with classic chimmichuri sauce (a blend of parsley, garlic, oregano and olive oil).

Pl Doctor
Letamendi, 25
Eixample
🚇 *Passeig de Gràcia*
Map p.393 D3 4

Pampero

93 532 17 51 | www.pamperobarcelona.com

Tuesday is the night to head to Pampero because, apart from incredible beef, you can enjoy tango sounds played by Argentinian musicians. This is free, and offers both a lively atmosphere, and a peek into Argentinian culture. Serving specifically Andean cuisine, you can expect lots of empanadas, but if you're after proper beef, the Argentinian roast is a winner; chunks of charcoal-grilled cow served piping hot on a platter. It's a meat lover's heaven. The provoleta is an interesting speciality – it's a delicious cheese casserole with spices, and is now a permanent fixture on the menu.

Gran Via Corts
Catalanes, 660
Eixample
🚇 Universitat
Map p.393 F4 **5**

Patagonia

93 304 37 35

Argentina is known for producing some of the finest quality beef in the world and for lovers of meat, Patagonia is a treat. Very un-Argentinian in atmosphere, Patagonia is tranquil, peaceful and a gentle supper destination. The decor is sleek and sophisticated, and the meat is imported straight from Argentina. The dwelling originally housed a jewellery shop, and hints of this still exist in the form of glass cases along the dining room walls, alongside memorabilia and photographs from Patagonia itself.

C/ Vila i Vila, 53
Ciutat Vella
🚇 Paral·lel
Map p.401 E4 **6**

San Telmo

93 441 30 78

A very popular fixture on San Telmo's menu is the Asado de Tira; fine Argentinian meat roasted and served in strips. All ingredients and dishes are imported straight from Argentina, so there is nothing gimmicky about this restaurant. Very rustic and cosy in character, with a lovely interior garden, it's a fantastic place to enjoy real Argentinian food while listening to the gentle tango sounds that drift through the restaurant. The waiters, proud of the dishes they serve, usually promote the Bife de Chorizo (beef sausages) which they describe as 'the king of meats'. It's a classic Argentinian dish and an excellent choice for those unfamiliar with the country's food. This family-run spot is a treat, and not overly advertised to tourists.

Basque

C/ Sicilia, 135
Eixample
🚇 Monumental
Map p.394 B4 **7**

Asador Izarra

93 245 21 03

An *Asador* is a place that sells meat and fish, while the Izarra region is known for its liquors. The use of both words in the name here explains much of what you need to know about this centrally located restaurant. Basque classics such as sardines, jamon Iberica and giant gambas (prawns) are just some of the delights to be found on the menu. After which, you can enjoy the treats behind the bar.

C/ Montcada, 1-3
Barri Gòtic
🚇 Jaume I
Map p.403 F4 **8**

Euskal Etxea

93 268 40 80

This is a popular choice among those in the Born and Gòtic areas. The menu consists of pinchos, small meat, fish and dairy tapas placed on pieces of bread and held together with a toothpick. It's very elegant to look at, but the food is informal – you just select what takes your fancy, and the price is calculated by a toothpick count at the end. Wash each dish down with either a delicious txacoli (classic Basque white wine) or one of the other 25 bottles on the wine list. There is no outside seating, which is a shame when you're in such a stunning part of the city, but the atmosphere is always vibrant and the tapas are excellent. It's great for vegetarians too, as there are lots of options that don't include meat or fish. Save room for dessert, as their homemade delicacies are famous.

C/ Diputacio, 421
Eixample
🚇 Monumental
Map p.394 B4 **9**

Gorria

93 245 11 64

All the ingredients used by the chefs at Gorria hail from Navarra and the Basque country. Established by Fermin Gorria and now managed by his son, Xavier, this is a family-run institution. The traditional Basque way of cooking meat is respected, as the chefs use only wood fired ovens and, as with all Basque restaurants worthy of mention, the desserts are exceptional. The waiting list for a table is frustrating, and means you must plan ahead before visiting, but this just reinforces the quality of the place. A huge wine cellar lurks below the restaurant, stocking a very wide variety of both Basque other regional Spanish favourites.

La Granada del
Penedes, 14-16
Eixample
🚇 *Fontana*
Map p.393 E2 **10**

Laurak
93 218 71 65

Translated from Basque, Laurak means 'four', a simple reference to the number of people who came together and created this wonderful culinary rarity. If you don't speak Basque, however, the name sounds sophisticated and intriguing, which is a fair description of the restaurant itself. Laurak isn't stuffy in atmosphere, but regulars tend to get quite dressed up for a visit. If you don't know much about Basque food, an excellent and very reasonable tasting menu is on offer, which gives you samples of the most popular dishes. You'll get two starters, meat and fish main courses and dessert. You'll need a roaring appetite to finish all this, but it's a perfect way to learn about a new cuisine, as Basque food is not for the unadventurous.

C/ Valencia, 169
Eixample
🚇 *Urgell*
Map p.393 D3 **11**

Taktika Berri
93 453 47 59

Taxtiki Berri is closed for 21 days in August when the owners get a well-deserved break, after working their aprons off for the rest of the year. Considered by many to be the finest Basque restaurant in Barcelona, the place is packed through the remaining 11 months. Reservations are required, and if you can get a table, be sure not to miss your booking. Specialties such as battered cheek adorn the very traditional Basque menu, as does a fine cod omelette and hake. This is not up everyone's alley, but a must for those wanting to explore this northern Spanish cuisine. You can either enjoy pinchos in the bar area or the full culinary experience in the main dining room.

Brazilian

C/ Consell de
Cent, 403
Eixample
🚇 *Girona*
Map p.394 A4 **12**

El Rodizio
93 265 51 12

El Rodizio is a buffet-style restaurant, but don't let the inner snob deter you from visiting. It's fantastic for those watching their wallets, as the price is fixed, no matter what or how much you eat. For fans of Brazilian food, this is considered the finest choice in Barcelona. Excellent (and very strong) caipirinhas and caipiroskas are offered by waiters the second you step in the door. A sizable buffet spreads around the sides of the restaurant, but meat dishes are served directly to the table by the same friendly waiters that push alcohol your way regardless of the time. Do save room for the meat though – it's excellent quality and perfectly cooked by the Brazilian chefs.

British & Irish

Traditional British and Irish food can be found in the many pubs scattered around the city. Many of the same places that sate British and Irish appetites for Premiership football, Gaelic games, cricket and rugby, will also serve up beer-soaking comfort food. While these dishes are unlikely to be quite as Mum, Ma or Mam used to make for British and Irish residents, you'll get a half-decent stew or fish and chips to a standard similar to pub food in the British Isles. Carrer Ferran, just off La Rambla heading in to the Barri Gòtic, is a good place to start. There are no gastropub equivalents, or restaurants offering New British cuisine.

321

Catalan

C/ Gignàs, 16
Ciutat Vella
🚇 *Barceloneta*
Map p.409 D1 🔢

Agut
93 315 17 09
For more than 75 years, Agut has been serving Barcelona traditional Catalan dishes, such as eggplant terrine and pork feet stuffed with foie gras. In a city where Catalan food is often fused with French sauces and cooking methods, Agut remains popular for offering authentic, untouched and untainted Catalan dishes. With Maria Agut Garcia currently at the helm, this has been a family-run restaurant for more than 75 years. Its historical building and fairly unchanged decor gives it quite a 50s aura, with Catalan art on every wall and a tiny little bar tucked neatly into one corner. Dishes for two are available for those who are on a date or seriously hungry, and include Catalan classics such as ox.

Local Cuisine
Catalan cuisine is closer to French than Spanish and traditional Catalan dishes are often given a Gallic twist. One dish to try is bacala (salted cod). This is available in most restaurants, or from the fresh food markets around the city. The Catalans also lay claim to alliolo, a beaten garlic and oil dish that makes a wonderful alternative to olive oil. Rabbit, cuttlefish, and swordfish are also very popular. One way of sampling a variety of Catalan dishes is by ordering any one of the numerous *menus del dia* (menus of the day). One area to generally avoid is the throng of restaurants overlooking the port along the edge of Barceloneta. Overpriced paella dishes will leave a bad taste in your mouth, and a dent in your wallet.

C/ Doctor Trueta, 211
Poblenou
🚇 *Poblenou*
Map p.412 B3 🔢

Cala Blanca
93 221 07 79
Cala Blanca is a good lunchtime pitstop for those working nearby or wandering around the local area. Hordes of hungry locals can be found here at noon, all hoping to secure a seat on the terrace and sample the range of Catalan favourites on offer. Even the most sceptical of diners should be satisfied with something on the menu. The prices are extremely reasonable, and for the quality of food - all local market produce - you may find yourself checking the bill for mistakes. Surprisingly for Barcelona, this restaurant becomes quiet at night, drawing in the majority of its hungry customers when the sun is shining.

C/ d'Arago, 214
Eixample
🚇 *Universitat*
Map p.393 D4 🔢

Can Gaig
93 429 10 17
Originally in an ancient, rustic hostelry in the Horta Guinardò area, Can Gaig recently moved to a more central location. First opened in 1869 as a resting place for hungry travellers and their carts, it still offers homely, traditional Catalan dishes, as well as an impressive cigar and wine menu. A favourite among families, its house speciality is roast partridge with Iberian bacon. Carles Gaig, the latest owner in a long line of family members, has managed to maintain everything that was originally loved about the restaurant, despite moving it out of its authentic, rustic dwelling.

C/ Maria Cubi, 189
Sarrià-Sant Gervasi
🚇 *Lesseps*
Map p.392 C1 🔢

Can Punyetes
93 200 91 59 | *www.canpunyetes.com*
Can Punyetes' Catalan dishes are found across Spain and there is another outlet in Barcelona, on Carrer Francesc Giner. But, there is nothing about these places that feels franchised. Each one is family-run, and with the rustic, unpretentious charm and warmth shown here, you'd never suspect that there were other branches. The decor is quite shambolic and loaded with quirky antiques. Affordable, high quality dishes are served all day and night. The very best pâtés, cheeses, meats and anchovies pile out the kitchen by the platter-load and Catalan, Basque and Spanish wines are available.

El Glop de la Rambla

Rla de Catalunya, 65
Eixample
🚇 **Passeig de Gràcia**
Map p.393 E3 17

93 487 00 97

It's hard to believe when you're on the busy Rambla de Catalunya that a place like El Glop could be nearby. Reminiscent of a roadside country tavern, it has been serving locals for decades. With hundreds of pork legs dangling from the ceiling and an epic selection of both black and white Catalan ham, it offers fine quality pork and unfussy Catalan classics. It's perfect for festive dinners with large groups of people, as the atmosphere is relaxed and casual. You can make as much noise as you want - you'll only be adding to the bustling atmosphere of this family eatery anyway.

El Raco d'en Freixa

C/ Sant Elies, 22
Sarrià-Sant Gervasi
🚇 **Lesseps**
Map p.385 D4 18

93 209 75 59 | www.elracodenfreixa.com

El Raco d'en Freixa has proudly been run by the Freixa family for years, but when son Ramon took over it garnered a whole new level of buzz and excitement. Now a Spanish celebrity chef, published author and television star, Ramon has really put this Catalan delight on the culinary map. Maintaining respect for classic dishes, he has also added some innovative new choices, such as fennel ice cream. This is all very representative of the exciting, creative direction in which Catalan cuisine is headed. The restaurant has traditional, simple decor and, with its low lighting, is perfect for a romantic dinner for two. It is also somewhere you will need to book in advance.

Els Quatre Gats

C/ Montsió, 3bis
Barri Gòtic
🚇 **Catalunya**
Map p.403 D2 209

93 302 41 40 | www.4gats.com

If you fancy a bit of culture with your cappuccino, this place is for you. Els Quatre Gats was a regular haunt for many artists during the modernist heyday, including Picasso, who was reputedly commissioned to design the menu cover (everyone has to start somewhere). The interior reflects that heritage, a tribute to the turn of the 20th century, with paintings covering the walls, high pillared ceilings and dark wood furnishing. Come for a coffee, a drink and a snack from the toast selection, or a full Mediterranean lunch or dinner. Monkfish and prawn skewer, and pork fillet with apple, raisins and raspberry sauce, are two highlights. A selection of wines from the Castell del Mirall cellar are available. Sipping a glass or two while listening to the live piano and violin music and discussing the merits of the modernists makes for a fine, high-brow evening.

L'Encis

C/ Provença, 379
Eixample
🚇 **Sagrada Família**
Map p.394 B3 19

93 457 68 74

The red-walled setting of L'Encis is elegant, traditional and refined. Located near the Sagrada Familia, it is a good spot for lunch. It is open in the evenings of course, when tapas of poultry, pork or fish can be ordered, as well as larger, heartier dishes. The wine list is extensive and the staff are extremely friendly (remember: this can be rare with Catalans if you're not Catalan yourself). It's great for small tapas snacks, sandwiches and cold beer.

L'Imprevist

C/ Fernandina, 34
Raval
🚇 **Sant Antoni**
Map p.402 A1 20

93 342 58 59

L'Imprevist serves up the region's favourite traditional dishes in a modern, eclectic environment. This restaurant-cum-art gallery offers grilled meat dishes and lots of hams, and you can buy one of the many art works on display while dining. Owner and artist, Josep Bofill, has used his restaurant as an opportunity to also showcase his sculpture, painting, and photography. L'Imprevist is spread over two rooms. It's big but does have two seating times, one at 21:00 and another at 23:00, so it's not somewhere you can settle for the night.

Chinese

Av Parallel, 152
Sant Antoni
🚇 *Poble Sec*
Map p.400 C2 21

Dong Lin

Popular among the young fans of Chinese food in Barcelona, Dong Lin is good for a cheap and easy Oriental fix. If you're after delicious, fast food, without authentic decor or service, this is your place. Peking duck, special fried rice, noodles and spring rolls are all available. Prices are extremely reasonable, the service is friendly, and the food is simple but good.

C/ Lincoln, 17
Gràcia
🚇 *Fontana*
Map p.393 E1 22

Memorias de China

93 415 76 02

When owner (and former martial arts actor and director) Lam Cheun decided to open Memorias of China in Barcelona, his aim was opulence and first class food. With the decor of an ancient Chinese temple, superb favourites such as Peking duck, and endless dim sum, he's created some spectacular Chinese cuisine. The kitchen is open and Cheun himself is extremely friendly, so may approach you for a chat. He's very much a part of the experience and will happily guide you through food selections.

C/ Diagonal, 460
La Ribera
🚇 *Diagonal*
Map p.393 E2 23

Ming Dynasty

93 217 47 80

This is a popular venue for business lunches, as the service is impeccable. Aside from a Xi'an warrior that looms in the entrance of the restaurant, the interior is fairly simple and western. The food is the experience here, rather than the atmosphere, and the selection spans Pekinese, Cantonese, and Sichuan provincial cooking. The Pekinese ribs and sauteed vegetables are notable.

C/ Muntaner, 100
Eixample
🚇 *Passeig de Gràcia*
Map p.393 D3 24

Out of China

93 451 55 55

Barcelona is a long way from China, and this often shows in the local Chinese cuisine. This place is one exception. Owner Chenqui Wang wanted a restaurant far removed from the paper lanterns and silken chair coverings often found in aging Chinese restaurants. With bright red walls, and 20s perfume girl posters, that is what she has she has managed to achieve. The menu also offers a welcome break from chicken and cashew nuts. It will satisfy lovers of traditional Chinese food, but dishes are spiced up and sometimes given a slightly more western kick, like the spring rolls stuffed with salmon and prawns.

C/ Diputacio, 26
Port Olímpic
🚇 *Rocafort*
Map p.392 B4 25

Swan

93 488 09 77

Despite being probably the oldest Chinese restaurant in Barcelona, Swan is relatively unknown. If you're after some wontons in peace, without the hype and crowds of more central areas, Swan, located in Port Olimpic, is perfect. It offers what is referred to as a 'noodlefest' at weekends, with different noodles cooked any way you like and decorated with whichever meat, fish or vegetables take your fancy. The dim sum alone is worth the trip.

Restaurant Timings

There are many public holidays that affect restaurant and bar timings, but it's up to each place individually, and there is no fixed rule about opening. Everywhere tends to close for Christmas, New Year's Day and 5 January. Few Catalans go out to eat before 22:00, but most restaurant will open around 19:00 or 20:00 for dinner. While most places will stay open until the last customer leaves, those that offer live entertainment may usher you out of the way before their shows begin, or only serve in two sittings.

French

C/ Comte
D'urgell, 196
Eixample
⊕ Hospital Clínic
Map p.392 C3 **26**

Baravins

93 451 51 72 | www.baravins.iespana.es

Baravins offers French cuisine as it would be found in France. Snails, endless choices of cheeses and pates, roquefort fondue, duck carpaccio and sweet crepes for dessert. All can be enjoyed alongside an epic selection of French wines from regions such as the Loire Valley. Opened in 1999 by French expats Sophie and Gilbert, Baravins was intended to open Catalan eyes to true, sumptuous French delights. The lunch menu gives way to a sampling menu at dinnertime. The decor is delightfully Gallic without being gimmicky and it's clear that you're in the presence of people who love the food they serve.

C/ Aribau, 106
Eixample
⊕ Diagonal
Map p.393 D3 **27**

Bistro 106

93 453 23 23

With its marble tables, soft lighting and classic French offerings, Bistro 106 almost transports you to a Parisian sidewalk bistro. With lots of French stews and soups, as well as foie gras, oysters, vintage wines and baguettes, you'll quickly forget the Catalan surroundings. The prices are extremely reasonable, and the atmosphere really relaxed. You can spend many an hour there with a coffee and a newspaper or enjoy it for a formal meal.

C/ Provença, 88
Eixample
⊕ Entença
Map p.392 B3 **28**

Jaume de Provença

93 430 00 29 | www.jaumeprovenza.com

Rumoured to be a favourite of King Juan Carlos, Jaume de Provença has established itself as a high quality French restaurant. Close to Barcelona Sants train station, this little rustic spot has won three major European awards for excellence in gastronomy. With celebrity chef Jaume Bargues at the helm, the menu is sharp, modern and changes frequently. Favourites that do reappear are the sole stuffed with mushrooms and the rabbit loins. While the cuisine certainly has a hint of Catalan to it, Jaume de Provença is a tribute to great French cooking and remains extremely popular among French expats.

C/ Còdols, 29
Raval
⊕ Drassanes
Map p.408 C1 **29**

Mastroque

93 301 79 42

At the very hip and trendy end of Drassanes, Mastroque, which advertises itself as both a bar and restaurant, has become a top joint for food and a first class destination for drinks. Simple gastronomy graces the menu and reasonably priced French wines are available among the Catalan and Spanish selections. The cooking is a blend of Provençal, with a few Catalan dishes thrown in. Besides serving delightful, tasty food, its location and atmosphere make it a good place for a few drinks too.

C/ Paris, 196
Barceloneta
⊕ Diagonal
Map p.393 D2 **30**

Petit Paris

93 218 26 78 | www.granparis.com

With its multilingual waiters and French dishes blended with Catalan flavours, Petit Paris is cosmopolitan, chic and extremely popular. The owners have now opened Gran Paris on Carrer Muntaner to accommodate larger groups and business meetings, because the demand at Petit Paris was becoming unmanageable. Set menus are available, as are individually crafted dishes like the home made chocolate cake. The owners are friendly, and the seaside location adds to Petit Paris' charm.

C/ Carme, 7
Born
🚇 *Liceu*
Map p.402 C2 **31**

Quo Vadis

93 302 40 72 | *www.restaurantquovidas.com*

Located very near to the Liceu, Quo Vidas is a popular destination after the ballet, opera or a classical concert. During theatre season it organises a special menu. With deep red and blue walls, old-fashioned fanned linen napkins and charming waiters in tails and bow ties, this is a quintessentially French restaurant. Although it claims heavy influence from Catalan cuisine, the frog legs, cheese soufflé and liver that grace the menu show the bias towards Gallic flavours.

Food Stalls

The most noteworthy food stalls exist in the incredible food markets, such as La Boqueria (p.310) on La Rambla. Fresh fruit, piping hot raciones and delicious cold tapas dishes are just some of the delights that are served at the stalls (some with seating) that intersperse the market stands. The food, although not always served very glamorously, is always fresh and of the finest quality, representative of everything that can be bought from surrounding vendors.

Fusion

Other options **Mediterranean** p.330

Fusion has been the biggest food fad to hit Spain in decades. Popular current combinations include Spanish and French, Chinese and Spanish, Catalan and Basque and Japanese and Thai. There are now fewer restaurants that have a menu simply offering one food type. Some spots mix ingredients and flavours, others create hybrids of national dishes, and in general, restaurants are becoming harder to categorise. The following are well regarded and attempt to cater to many fused tastes.

C/ Rec, 79 - 89
Born
🚇 *Jaume I*
Map p.403 F4 **32**

Abac

93 319 66 00

The French-Spanish dishes of head chef Xavier Pellicer have even impressed members of Spain's royal family and, while it's not overly expensive to eat here, it does require some organisation. Book ahead, or you're unlikely to get a table. Located next to the beautiful 1948 Park Hotel in Born, Abac has an exquisite atmosphere. Fresh linen napkins are dropped onto your seat with tweezers each time you leave the table but the effect isn't stuffy pretentiousness; it just makes you feel appreciated. For fans of suckling pig, there are two types to choose from. These are so popular that they're permanently on the menu. Pellicer describes his menu as *cuisine d'auteur*, meaning every dish is designed to be unlike anything you've had before.

Mercat Santa Caterina (p.310), home to wonderful food stalls

Ca l'Isidre

C/ Flors, 12
Raval
🚇 Paral·lel
Map p.401 F4 **33**

93 441 11 39 | www.calisidre.com
Family-run Ca l'Isidre is part of
Raval's history and hugely popular
among art students and pop stars
alike. Very much part of the city's art
scene, it's a minute from the CCCB
(p.163) and MACBA (p.164). Julio
Iglesias is rumored to eat here when
passing through town. Favourites
such as the baby octopus and lamb
in truffle sauce remain ever-popular.
The wine list is huge and Isidre
himself will gladly give you advice
and some history on all the
varieties. His daughter, a master
pastry chef, is responsible for the

Ca l'Isidre

wonderfully wide range of desserts. If you have any space left, these really should be
tried. Everything here is home-made and comes fresh from the city's markets.

Jean Luc Figueras

C/ Sant Teresa, 10
Gràcia
🚇 Diagonal
Map p.393 F2 **34**

93 415 28 77
This Catalan-French restaurant strives continually to stay on top of what is becoming a
highly competitive market. In a city where food trends regularly change, Figueras
works hard to maintain his place as one of Barcelona's five top chefs. Dishes are quite
traditional, but always have Figueras' innovative touches. This is the place for special
occasions but also a great excuse to head into Gràcia for supper. The menu boasts
seafood but meat dishes are of excellent quality and the seven varieties of homemade
breads are a delight. The service is impeccable.

La Dama

Av Diagonal, 423
Eixample
🚇 Diagonal
Map p.393 D2 **35**

93 202 06 86
Set in a stunning 1918 building with an art nouveau lift that hauls visitors up to the
first floor dining area, La Dama is considered one of the most beautiful restaurants
in all of Spain. It's also one of the few in Barcelona to be awarded a Michelin star, so
you can order with confidence. The menu is sizable, with popular dishes including
the crayfish salad and salmon steak. Reservations are required and the dress code is
smarter than most eateries in the city, making this a tranquil and elegant restaurant.
It's far from stuffy though, and perfect for a romantic dinner date. The wine list is
excellent and focuses mainly on Catalan varieties, which the waiters know a great
deal about.

Santa Caterina Cuines

Av Francesc
Combó, 16
Barri Gòtic
🚇 Jaume I
Map p.403 F3 **36**

93 268 99 18 | www.mercatsantacaterina.net
Within the stunning Santa Caterina market lays Santa Caterina Cuines. After browsing
through the rows of seafood, meat, cheese and doughy bread, this is the best way to
enjoy the culinary delights of the market without having to cook for yourself.
Everything from tapas to sushi, cheeseburgers to fruit kebabs is available. The decor is
sleek and modern, with daily specials that flash across LED screens like stock market
reports. The atmosphere is buzzing, the wine list is extensive and the food, bought
fresh from the stall owners next door, warrants repeat visits.

328

Indian

Pg Colom, 22
Port Vell
🚇 *Drassanes*
Map p.408 C1 37

City Gate

93 317 12 79

Lamb rogan josh, korma, chicken tikka masala, pilau rice and naan bread. All the classics can be found here. The decor is basic, but the food is delicious and, if you're in fear of spices being toned down to cater to a Spanish audience, don't worry. Diners are asked if they want their food spicy, so be prepared; if you say yes, they load on the chilli. Authentic lime pickle with yogurt sauce is served with popadoms as soon as you take your seat. Those looking for Indian beer will be disappointed, as only local lagers are available, but with such a bevy of delicious dishes, it's easy to overlook this minor detail.

C/ Sant Pau, 39
Ciutat Vella
🚇 *Liceu*
Map p.402 B4 38

Kashmir Restaurant

93 441 37 98

While the decor of Kashmir Restaurant appears more like an unappealing, greasy English breakfast cafe, its food is exceptional. You'll be paying no attention to your surroundings once your meal arrives. If you want a spicy dish, you may need to specify when ordering, as the chefs are nervous about offending European palates, but if you ask, you'll get an authentic taste. The fact that it is often filled with Pakistanis is testimony to its authenticity. Basic in design but mind-blowing in terms of cuisine, Kashmir Retsaurant is a must for any die-hard curry lover.

Italian

Other options **Pizzerias** p.333, **Mediterranean** p.330

While most Italian restaurants in Barcelona are Spanish owned, there are a few authentic, family run places that serve up home made lasagne, pizza and antipasti. The good ones get busy and don't always take reservations, which, coupled with everything being home made, means you'll need to be patient. Traditional Italian dining is meant to be leisurely, so order a bottle of Chianti and relax.

C/ Comte D'Urgell, 247
Eixample
🚇 *Entença*
Map p.392 C2 39

Il Commendatore

93 322 55 53

The gimmicky decor of this lovely local Italian does not suggest great taste or sophistication. Designed to replicate a real street in Italy, the centre piece is a well with bucket and rope, and street lamps perch in each corner. Washing lines are painted daintily across the edge of each ceiling, but somehow it works. The homely, family-friendly atmosphere is one of the reasons why Il Commendatore is so popular. The Pizza Torpoedone is of epic proportions, so if ordered, you're unlikely to need a starter course as well. A porcini mushroom carpaccio is one of the permanent menu fixtures and the risotto is also extremely popular. Reservations are not taken, so you may want to get in early.

C/ Josep Anselm Clave, 11
Ciutat Vella
🚇 *Drassanes*
Map p.408 C1 40

Il Mercante Di Venezia

93 317 18 28

Il Mercante de Venezia has been a well-kept secret for some time, but news has finally leaked out. Popular among those in the know for years, it is now so highly rated that at weekends people queue around the building for a table. Nestled on the edge of a lovely tree-lined square, it is intimate, cosy, serves delectable Italian food and is a popular date venue. The house speciality is the gnocchi and although very heavy, it's justifiably popular. The interior is quite Baroque, with drapes, tassels, heavy wood and gold detail. This can make it feel like more of a winter venue, but that doesn't seem to put people off in the summer.

329

La Bella Napoli

C/ Margarit, 14
Poble Sec
🚇 *Paral·lel*
Map p.401 D3 **41**

93 442 50 56
The Neapolitan family who run La Bella Napoli create the buzzing atmosphere of this fantastically authentic Italian. Lots of yelling, Godfather-style hand gestures and excitement fill the four walls of this recently renovated eatery. Rather than modernising the place, red and white gingham tablecloths adorn wooden tables and raffia wrapped wine bottles line the walls. A house favourite is the arancini (rice balls stuffed with sauce, bread crumbed and fried). Pizzas, which can be ordered as eat in or takeaway, are also immensely popular, and are cooked in a proper wood-fired oven. Desserts are fresh, the tiramasu must be tried, and there are more than thirty Italian wines on the menu. There are two sittings per evening to accommodate the hordes of fans, the first at 21:00 and the second at 23:00.

Parking
Parking garages exist but spaces are often owned by local residents. Street parking is possible, but tricky. In Eixample and the Barri Gòtic there is almost none. Public transport is an excellent alternative. See Getting Around, on p.30 for details.

La Locanda

C/ Dr. Joaquim Pou, 4
Barri Gòtic
🚇 *Jaume I*
Map p.403 E2 **42**

93 317 46 09 | www.restaurantelocanda.com
For a slightly more chic Italian experience, La Locanda is ideal. The decor is a warm orange and yellow that is both intimate and sophisticated. Only the freshest ingredients are used in the home-made dishes (even the bread is baked fresh on the premises) and you can expect quality food without forking out your monthly budget. La Locanda is unpretentious and different to other places trying to replicate a restaurant in Naples. It has its own unique character, with food taken very seriously and of a consistently high quality.

Made in Italy

C/ Ample, 50
Barri Gòtic
🚇 *Barceloneta*
Map p.409 D1 **43**

93 319 85 54
Owned by Italo Sanguineti, Made in Italy has a sister restaurant of the same name in London's Chelsea. The cuisine all hails from northern Italy and Sicily. Antipasti, such as salmon rolls and mascarpone, are beautifully made by the chefs, who create everything by hand. The principle of Sanguineti is that authentic and fresh ingredients must be used at all times. The salads are excellent and a very wide range of pizzas and pastas are available. The cheeses are delivered twice a week, so freshness is guaranteed.

Mediterranean

Other options **Italian** p.329, **Spanish** p.335

Agua

Pg Maritim de la Barceloneta, 30
Port Olímpic
🚇 *Ciutadella/Vila Olímpica*
Map p.410 C3 **44**

93 225 12 72
What better name for a restaurant offering such spectacular water views? Agua, located near the Hotel Arts, has a wide terrace that slopes right onto the ocean. If there is a chill in the air, or you simply can't get seats outside, a large-windowed dining room guarantees you won't miss out on the natural surroundings. Agua is very popular, so reservations are recommended. But it isn't just the sea view that brings back loyal fans; the fresh seafood is spectacular. Huge display cases show off the catches of the day, which are all grilled over an open fire.

Brilliant Lounge

C/ Balmes, 314
Gràcia
🚇 *Lesseps*
Map p.385 E4 **45**

93 414 58 04
For dinner and dancing rolled into one, Brilliant Lounge is a prime destination. This is where you can fill up on fresh Mediterranean food and enjoy fantastic cocktails with

330

live DJs. This is a hip, bustling joint. Everything about it is new and vibrant - the decor, the contemporary sounds and the menu, which boasts ostrich fillet steak, among other adventurous culinary delights. The cocktail bar is separate to the restaurant, so those wanting a peaceful dinner aren't greatly disturbed and there is an area that can be booked out for private meetings or parties.

C/ Roger de Lluria, 35-37
Eixample
Ⓜ Passeig de Gràcia
Map p.393 F4 **46**

Noti

93 342 66 73 | www.noti-universal.com

Noti, with its black tables and gold panelling, is uber-glamorous. It looks more like the nightclub scene in the Al Pacino film *Scarface* than a Mediterranean restaurant. This design has earned Noti its name, rather than the food (although that's not bad at all). It isn't traditionally Mediterranean, despite labelling itself as such, because universal favourites such as tuna sashimi grace the menu. It's a hothouse for power lunches during the day and a haven for the beautiful at night. Jazz music plays endlessly, so it's more of a sophisticated hangout than other restaurants and bars. The Sala Noti is a side room available for private functions and the bar, called Goodbar, is a lovely area for an after-dinner caipirinha.

Ptge de la Concepció, 5
Eixample
Ⓜ Diagonal
Map p.393 E3 **47**

Tragaluz

93 487 01 96 | www.grupotragaluz.com

With a sliding roof that opens to the stars, and a reputation as one of Barcelona's finest culinary destinations, Tragaluz has become very successful. Owned by the Barcelona restaurateurs Grupo Tragaluz, this flagship establishment serves fantastic Mediterranean classics. The menu changes seasonally (as should be expected of any decent restaurant) and there are three floors to choose from, the Mezzanine lounge usually being the most popular. Tragarapid is downstairs, a more casual version of Tragaluz, and across the street you'll find the Japanese version. These are sleek, chic and very trendy, but reasonably priced.

Mexican

C/ Amigo, 57
Sarrià-Sant Gervasi
Ⓜ Fontana
Map p.392 C1 **48**

Bar Panchito

93 202 21 31 | www.panchito.com

More Tex-Mex than authentic Mexican, Bar Ponchito produces winning burritos, nachos, fajitas and enchiladas. Portions are enormous so whether it's beef, chicken or seafood you fancy, you'll get your hit here, wrapped in a floury tortilla and smothered in salsa and guacamole. The crowd is young and gets quite hectic, no doubt drawn to the various beer sizes that can be ordered. There is an XXL option that is so enormous it'll either last you the evening or leave you legless. Kitsch and bright, this is a wonderful place to mix with the local crowd.

C/ Torrijos, 47
Gràcia
Ⓜ Fontana
Map p.393 F1 **49**

Cantina Machito

93 217 34 14

Cantina Machito serves good, authentic Mexican food. Menus detail the history and cultural significance of every dish, and the decor includes a fountain, carved wooden pillars and gold walls. Authenticity is key and you won't find the menu watered down with Tex-Mex specials. Top shelf liquor is used to create the restaurant's infamous Margaritas. There is also a good range of tequila and Mexican beer. The atmosphere (no doubt enhanced by the strength and frequency of the cocktails) makes this a popular place and at weekends, when reservations are not taken, you will need to arrive a little earlier.

331

C/ Aribau, 207
Eixample
🚇 *Fontana*
Map p.393 D1 50

El Ultimo Agave

93 209 24 07 | www.elultimoagave.com

El Ultimo Agave is geared towards Mexicans. The bevy of them that gathers here and at the other branch (Carrer Aragon, 193) guarantees cracking food. The restaurant, with its deep red walls and elongated bar, serves up beautiful tacos, home made guacamole and more than 25 different brands of tequila. It's both a restaurant and a popular social hang out, partly due to the live mariachi performances on Wednesday, Friday and Saturday nights. The cocktails are incredible, the atmosphere is totally unpretentious, and the food has a perfect kick.

C/ Josep Anselm
Clave, 6
Sarrià-Sant Gervasi
🚇 *Drassanes*
Map p.408 C1 51

Margarita Blue

93 412 54 89 | www.margaritablue.com

Margarita Blue offers up an interesting blend of Mexican food with a Mediterranean twirl. Fried green tomatoes are just one of the popular features on the menu and the fajitas can be quaffed by the dozen. The Margarita Blue cocktail is lethal but very tasty and, with its relaxed, informal and vibrant atmosphere, the restaurant has become a favourite among young revellers. Aesthetically colourful, and daring in its culinary combinations, this is another south of the border establishment with reservations highly recommended.

Moroccan

Other options **Arabic/Lebanese** p.319

C/ Banys Vells, 21
Born
🚇 *Jaume I*
Map p.403 F4 52

El Pebre Blau

93 319 13 08

El Pebre Blau is a wonderful mix of Moroccan and Catalan cuisine and one of the few restaurants that blends the two cooking styles successfully. Space is tight, but you shouldn't feel as though you're sitting on the couple next to you. Dividing arches separate tables and create a wonderfully intimate arena for enjoying the food of head chef, Teresa Ferri. There are lots of sweet and savoury combinations and an entire section of the menu is dedicated to salads. Dishes of Indian food are also available, such as Rajasthan curry.

Pl Narcis Oller, 7
Gràcia
🚇 *Diagonal*
Map p.393 E2 53

Las Rosa del Desierto

93 237 45 90

No guide to Moroccan food in Barcelona would be complete without reference to Las Rosa del Desierto, the first restaurant of its kind to open here, more than 30 years ago. With a vast range of different tagines, 10 types of couscous, kemia (north African tapas) and home made Arabic pastries for dessert, this restaurant really pioneered the beginning of a wave in Moroccan eateries in the Catalan capital. Takeaway is available, and belly dancing shows can be booked in advance for parties. The interior is designed to resemble an authentic Moroccan tent, to help you feel transported to north Africa.

C/ Tamarit, 151
Eixample
🚇 *Sant Antoni*
Map p.401 E1 54

Volubilis

93 424 72 02 | www.volubilisrestaurant.com

All the Moroccan favourites adorn the Volubilis menu, like shawarma (mini kebabs), chicken or red meat tagines (stews) and pasteleta. The latter is a chicken pie with almond and onion and is delicious. Intimate, cosy and warm in feel, Volubilis is renowned for its quality kebabs and falafel too, with lots of Moroccan teas to entice you away from the wine. These are served in authentic Moroccan tea glasses and food comes on intricate, beautiful crockery.

C/ Villarroel, 99
Eixample
🚇 **Urgell**
Map p.392 C4 **55**

Yasmin

93 451 69 52

Bastela (a puff pastry pie stuffed with chicken, almonds and dried fruit with cinnamon and sugar drizzled on top) is a Moroccan classic and nowhere in town does it better than Yasmin. This haven of perfectly cooked couscous has an authentic atmosphere, with hanging Moroccan tapestries, mirrors, coloured tiles and occasional live belly-dancing shows. This is Morocco without the dust and haggling – just the gorgeous food in a tranquil environment.

Pizzerias

Other options **Italian** p.329

Spain isn't well known for its pizza production, and Barcelona is not overrun with delicious pizza places. But, there are a few establishments where you can get a decent fix if tapas is getting a little monotonous. Most places will allow you to take your order home, even if they don't advertise themselves as a takeaway. Some, such as La Veronica, offer a wonderful variation of pizza ingredients, such as roquefort cheese and apple, or salmon and mint. Other restaurants, like Pizza Cuatro offer a wide range of foods, although for a good selection with views of the harbour, Al Passatore has 24 pizza varieties on its menu.

Pizzerias	
Al Passatore	93 319 78 51
The Chicago Pizza Pie Factory	93 215 94 15
Fratelli La Bufala	93 481 49 63
Il Commendatore	93 322 55 53
La Bella Napoli	93 442 50 56
La Locanda	93 317 46 09
La Pizza del Born	93 310 62 46
La Veronica	93 412 11 22
Made in Italy	93 319 85 54
Pizzeria Cuatro	93 330 68 60
Pizzeria San Marino	93 302 01 82
Vitali Pizza	93 444 47 37

Portuguese

Pg d'Isabel II, 14
Barceloneta
🚇 **Barceloneta**
Map p.409 F1 **56**

7 Portes

93 319 30 33 | www.7portes.com

Located in fabulous Barceloneta, this is one of the city's oldest restaurants, having been open since 1836. Although the area and the restaurant's history can attract a touristy crowd, the authentic decor and wonderful cuisine encourages many local residents to frequent the place too, and with non-stop service from lunch through to dinner, 7 Portes is usually buzzing. Fish dishes are skinned and deboned in front of diners at their table, paella specials change daily, and regional dishes are always on the menu. Portions are enormous.

C/ Mercè, 28
Ciutat Vella
🚇 **Barceloneta**
Map p.409 D1 **57**

Bodega La Plata

93 315 10 09

Bodega La Plata is one of three very famous restaurants on the medieval street of Carrer Mercè. Open since the 20s, it has retained many original features. The menu consists mainly of raciones and is a blend of Spanish and Portuguese food. The tables can get quite crowded, but its popularity is representative of its quality. The cascading barrels of wine that perch above the bar are typical of Spanish and Portuguese restaurants. Breakfast is served, as well as lunch and dinner, and they'll even let you take your own food in, as long as you order a glass of wine to accompany it. Bodega La Plata has a very strong family feel to it and, with doors almost permanently open, it's easy to see why.

C/ Quintana, 5
Barri Gòtic
🚇 Via Júlia
Map p.402 C3 58

Can Culleretes

93 317 64 85

Probably the longest running restaurant in Barcelona, Can Culleretes was established in 1786 as a pastry shop and has been serving food of one kind or another ever since. Many of its original architectural features are still in place, and it does attract a great deal of tourist attention because of its heritage. Traditional game dishes like partridge dot the menu, along with fresh seafood. It has three dining rooms but you should book if possible as it does get busy, especially in the summer months. Memorabilia of famous Spanish matadors, flamenco dancers and some of Hollywood's glitterati line the walls.

Seafood

C/ Fusina, 5
Born
🚇 Arc de Triomf
Map p.404 A4 59

Arrel del Born

93 319 92 99 | www.arreldelborn.com

Chef Manuel Diaz is known locally for his sensational seafood. Heavily influenced by Catalan recipes and flavours, he does basic dishes, like sauteed langoustine with onions, but does them very well. The decor is minimalist and quite modern, considering the old town location, but this really works and creates an inviting atmosphere. Diaz's menu and ingredients change every season, so he's permanently working on new creations, and drawing loyal crowds back to sample his latest flourish of inspiration

C/ El Gran de
Gràcia, 81
Gràcia
🚇 Fontana
Map p.393 E1 60

Botafumerio Moncho

93 218 42 30 | www.botafumerio.es

An established leader in Galician seafood for more than thirty years, this place shows why the region has such a fine reputation for its fish. The decor is classic: wooden walls, crisp fresh linen and a gallery of gently lit tables. A huge range of Galician white wine is available to accompany the food, as are an array of meat dishes. Tapas and raciones can be eaten at the bar and torpedo sandwiches are available. Apparently a popular choice for Bill Clinton and Woody Allen when they're gracing Catalan shores, this is also a firm favourite among local residents.

Pl de les Olles, 8
Ciutat Vella
🚇 Barceloneta
Map p.409 F1 61

Cal Pep

93 310 79 61 | www.calpep.net

Although Cal Pep could be classified as a tapas restaurant, it is better known for its seafood, and for Pep himself. The vibrant, smiling Pep Manubens is usually hovering behind the long bar of this gem near the Picasso Museum, smiling brightly and greeting everyone who walks through the door. He's a delight and always happy to give drink recommendations, which is helpful, because the selection is lengthy and varied. After choosing your fish, it will be cooked before your eyes, and if seafood isn't what you fancy, there are plenty of meat dishes, such as beef stew.

C/ Sant Carles, 4
Barceloneta
🚇 Barceloneta
Map p.409 F3 62

Can Sole

93 221 50 12

Once a favourite of artist Joan Miro, Can Sole has been serving up fresh catches for more than a century. Located in Barceloneta, it is one of the few restaurants that has remained untouched and authentic. Serving up simple fresh fish, you can expect anything you order, from mussels to langoustine, lobster to cod, to be heavily doused in garlic and butter, perfectly cooked and extremely generous in size. It is a celebration of Barcelona's ancient fishing tradition, rather than a modern eatery.

Pl Prim, 1
Poblenou
🚇 **Poblenou**
Map p.412 B3 63

Els Pescadores

93 225 20 18 | *www.elspescadors.com*

Much of the original tavern that now houses Els Pescadores has been beautifully preserved. Original wooden rafters, the marble bar and a lot of the wooden tables have been in place since long before the present owners were born. Old fashioned and charming, fresh fish is delivered here daily, and meat dishes are also available. There are more than 150 wines and cavas in the cellar and a large stock of spirits behind the bar. Your order will come fresh from Catalan waters, whether it's shellfish or cod, the local favourite.

C/ Fusina, 5
Port Vell
🚇 **Arc de Triomf**
Map p.404 A4 64

Salamanca

93 221 50 33 | *www.gruposilvestre.com*

With the smell of the sea wafting across the terrace from Port Vell, few locations are as perfect for eating seafood. Unlike many waterfront restaurants, which serve soggy paella and frozen prawns, everything at Salamanca is fresh. Enormous langoustine, succulent lobster and fresh, crisp platters of paella can be ordered. There are lots of quality local cheeses and cold meats available as platters, so you need not limit yourself to one selection. With seating for 250 on the outside terrace, you should get a decent table.

Spanish

Other options **Mediterranean** p.330

Hotel Arts,
C/ Marina, 19-21
Port Olímpic
🚇 **Ciutadella/Vila Olímpica**
Map p.411 D2 65

Arola

93 483 80 90 | *www.arola-arts.com*

Owned by the Michelin-starred Sergi Arola, this seriously hip restaurant is right on the seafront, in Port Olímpic. Arola wanted a well-respected place with a relaxed atmosphere. and he seems to have managed, with top class food served among sofas and throw cushions. The outside area, often livened up by a DJ, is a great place for a cocktail, and the inside has none of the stuffiness usually associated with Michelin stars. The menu offers pica-pica dishes, minuscule tapas that are served for both lunch and dinner. Closed through January, Arola is particularly wonderful in summer months when the warm weather and glistening sea view can be enjoyed.

Pl de Palau, 13
Born
🚇 **Barceloneta**
Map p.409 F1 66

Bossborn Tapes

93 295 58 66

A stone's throw from the marina, Bossborn Tapes, with its long wooden bar, looks like a classic tapas spot. It has a youthful atmosphere, in part because it was recently opened by a young Catalan called Albert Bosser, a man with bright ideas and boundless energy. It is on the site of the famous Estrella de Plata, which meant he was stepping into some super-sized boots. But rather than trying to outdo a legend, he opened the doors with new, fresh tapas ideas (such as bull meat) mixed with classics like tortilla. The result is a delightful restaurant in a prime location.

Take your pick...

C/ Lledo, 1
Barri Gòtic
🚇 *Jaume I*
Map p.403 E4 **67**

Cafe l'Academie

93 419 82 53

On the edge of the very pretty Plaça Sant, sits Cafe l'Academie. Reservations are recommended. This place is so famous (and profitable) that it can afford to close every Saturday and Sunday. The outside seating is especially delightful at night, beneath the little church. Dishes are hearty, which can make a nice change after too much tapas. Its popularity among locals and tourists is testimony to its quality, and the fact that the staff speak English encourages non-Catalans through the door. Iberian ham and eggs is a house fixture and is delicious. Open for breakfast, Cafe l'Academie is a wonderful place to start the day, or to finish it in candlelight over some wine.

C/ Valencia, 181
Eixample
🚇 *Hospital Clínic*
Map p.393 D3 **68**

Cata 181

93 323 68 18 | www.cata181.com

Cata 181 is a rare gem. Unknown to tourists and loved by Barcelonins, it is another fantastic example of modern Spanish cuisine. Offering larger tapas (known as raciones), and hearty fish, meat and pasta dishes, it combines flavours beautifully and offers unique food. The decor, though, is a bit reminiscent of an airport lounge - the designers opted for a strict blend of grey and orange. For private parties, try and book the back room, a lovely transformed wine-cellar where privacy reigns and anything goes. Run by the delightful Santi, Cata 181 is a hidden jewel in the heart of the city.

C/ Comerç, 24
Born
🚇 *Arc de Triomf*
Map p.404 A3 **69**

Comerç 24

93 319 21 02 | www.comerc24.com

Comerç 24 is not for the fainthearted. It's a top choice for serious foodies, and a lot of the dishes are of an acquired taste but, if theatrical modern Spanish cuisine is your thing, Comerç 24 will blow you away. Run by Carles Abellan, a disciple of El Bulli (p.316), Comerç 24 is fast becoming a top restaurant in its own right. The food is often unique - egg shells filled with egg foam and truffles are popular starters – and a good example of where Spanish cuisine is headed. The decor is an eclectic mix of yellow and grey hues, which results in a very intimate atmosphere. It's one of the few restaurants that sticks to the smoking ban, leaving everyone focused on the sights and smells of the food.

Rla de Catalunya, 100
Eixample
🚇 *Diagonal*
Map p.393 E3 **70**

La Bodegueta

93 215 48 66

You may not find better tapas in Barcelona than at La Bodegueta. The decor is old-fashioned, the atmosphere is smokey, it's always manically busy, and the waiters are classically grumpy. But despite all that, La Bodegueta will bring you back time and again. The padrones peppers are great, the steak tartare is mouthwatering and the fresh anchovies are tangy. There is nothing greasy or oily about the tapas here. Unpretentious and totally traditional, La Bodegueta serves classic tapa as it should be.

C/ Escudellers, 14
Barri Gòtic
🚇 *Drassanes*
Map p.402 C4 **210**

Los Caracoles

93 319 82 53

A plate of snails certainly makes for an interesting experience in this tavern-turned-restaurant; as long as you don't mind tourist-inflated prices. Los Caracoles (literally 'the snails') is a firm fixture on Barcelona's visitor trail due to its authentic old interior; hams hang from the ceiling, wine barrels pile up around the room, and chickens roast on spits in the open kitchen. It can get pretty full, but it's worth muscling your way in at least once. If munching on molluscs doesn't whet your appetite, suckling pig, steak and seafood should satisfy the hungry. And if the volume of dining traffic has slowed the service to a snail's pace, you can always occupy yourself by studying the pictures of celebrity diners on the walls. Reward yourself with a large glass of red if you can spot John Wayne.

Los Caracoles

C/ Comerç, 17
Born
🚇 **Arc de Triomf**
Map p.404 A3 **71**

Santa Maria

93 315 12 27 | *www.santamania.biz*

The tapas dishes here are delectable. The menu doesn't change often but, with eager eaters packed in every night, there seems little need. Paco Guzman has created a unique place. The quirky interior with bare light bulbs and a smokey atmosphere may not sound appealing, but the overall effect is a restaurant with a fabulous atmosphere and lots of well-fed, happy diners. Guzman doesn't take bookings for parties of less than six, so if there are fewer of you, get in early and perch at the bar with a drink.

Pl Sant Josep
Oriol, 9
Born
🚇 **Liceu**
Map p.402 C3 **72**

Taller de Tapas

93 268 85 59 | *www.tallerdetapas.com*

Although part of a growing chain, this particular location offers up the very best of what Taller de Tapas has to offer. With seating that spills onto the adjacent square, the interior of warm woods and sleek, glass seafood cabinets creates a very cosy atmosphere. The langoustine, clams and hunks of tuna meat that entice visitors inside look almost unreal in their perfection. Farmhouse fresh meats are also on offer for those who don't want fish and, though the wine list isn't enormous, it's very carefully chosen.

337

Steakhouses

Other options **Argentinian** p.319

While Barcelona does meat with a viciously carnivorous passion, it doesn't really do steakhouses. The places listed here are particularly popular for their meat dishes, but could be as well known for their pork or roast beef as for slabs of sirloin. Other meat-eater friendly spots include those listed in the Argentinian restaurants section (p.319).

> ### Hidden Charges
> You won't be hit with hidden service charges, but they'll get you with the bread time and again. After handing it out freely at the start of meals, bread is then placed on the bill at a surprising rate per head. Free tapas appetisers are often given out though, compliments of the kitchen. Water usually comes bottled, and tap water should be avoided.

Av Tibidabo, 31
Sarrià-Sant Gervasi
🚇 **Vallcarca**
Map p.385 E1 **73**

Asador de Aranda

93 417 01 15 | *www.asadordearanda.com*

There are four branches of Asador de Aranda in Barcelona but, if you have the privilege of choice, head directly to this one. Located in the modernist house, Casa Rivoralta, the stunning location and architecture will take your breath away. Intricate stained glass ceilings, vaulted archways and a quaint terrace have all been perfectly preserved. Several dining rooms and an incredible array of carvery meats set the scene, with suckling pig, black pudding and roast lamb just a few of the delights on offer. Takeaway is available, but when you've a setting like this and a parking service to go with it, why eat in your living room?

C/ Casp, 19
Eixample
🚇 **Universitat**
Map p.393 F4 **74**

El Mussol

93 301 76 10

El Mussol is a chain of restaurants that specialise in grilled dishes. The real focal point is the excellent selection of perfectly cut Iberian ham, served bright red and paper thin. There are dishes that don't contain meat, although few vegetarians would want to eat in a place so heavily focused on grilled carcass. The scrambled eggs and mushrooms, though simple, are delicious. The decor is very rustic and, as with many chain restaurants in Barcelona, it looks like a unique, family-run establishment.

C/ Ramon Turro, 13
Sant Martí
🚇 **Bogatell**
Map p.405 D4 **75**

Els Pollos de Llull

93 221 32 06 | *www.elspollos.com*

Els Pollos de Llull specialises in roast chicken, known on the menu as Chicken a l'ast. For succulent rotisserie style poultry, this is the very best place to dine. It is child friendly and even has a special space for kids to draw and play games, giving parents a chance to eat in relative peace. A large attic is available for private bookings and takeaway can be ordered. The chicken is cooked in a special spice, herb and apple sauce. There are plenty of desserts to choose from, and this is a good family option.

C/ Carme, 28
Born
🚇 **Catalunya**
Map p.402 B2 **76**

Rincon de Aragon

93 302 67 89 | *www.rincon-de-aragon.com*

The regional cuisines of northern Spain can get confusing and difficult to distinguish. The Aragonese food of Rincon de Aragon refers to food specifically from the Zaragoza region. What is clear, is the amazing quality of the meat served in this tiny, 64 capacity restaurant in the Born. A giant roaster cooks up meat to perfection and if you are booking a group meal there, the owner is happy to organise a special menu. Unchanged since it opened in 1971, Rincon de Aragon offers all porks and beefs in a manner that makes most non-vegetarians drool. There is a very impressive wine menu to accompany the food.

La Rambla, 35
Ciutat Vella
 Drassanes
Map p.402 C4 **77**

Tablao Cordobes
93 317 57 11 | www.tablaocorbes.com
This is a very famous Flamenco joint that serves dinner while shows take place. Since 1970, Tablao Cordobes has been presenting Barcelona with some of Spain's finest, most beautiful and dramatic Flamenco artists. Every 90 minutes, new dinner sittings begin, with fantastic hot or cold meat selections available. Around 45 minutes into your meal, the show begins. This is an impressive culinary experience and a wonderful way to enjoy quality Spanish cuisine while viewing this stunning art form.

Thai

Pl Regomirr, 1
Barri Gòtic
Drassanes
Map p.409 D1 **78**

Matsuri
93 219 66 00 | www.matsuri-restaurante.com
Matsuri is actually two restaurants joined by a large kitchen. One side serves fresh sushi, and the other side serves delicious, traditional Thai food, not an easy thing to find in a Catalan city. Opened by the delightful Edo Komori, a Brazilian who gathered skills cooking in New York, Miami, Thailand and Japan, Matsuri offers first class south east Asian cooking at very reasonable prices. Favourites such as pad Thai and green curry are on the menu, as well as some interesting creations of Edo's own. Matsuri can seem a little out of place tucked away in Barri Gòtic, but it's well worth seeking out.

C/ Comerç, 27
Born
Arc de Triomf
Map p.404 A4 **79**

Thai Cafe
93 268 39 59 | www.grupoisbl.com
Thai Cafe offers a modern interpretation of the cuisine in hip surroundings. Although the food isn't absolutely traditional, you can still get all the favourites, like pad Thai and fish cakes. A large Buddha looks ominously down on diners but, otherwise the decor is fairly modern. Ingredients are fresh and blend the salty, spicy, sour and sweet notes traditionally found in Thai food. Described as a restaurant lounge, the vibe is very relaxed.

C/ Diputacio, 273
Eixample
Passeig de Gràcia
Map p.393 E4 **80**

Thai Gardens
93 487 98 98 | www.thai-gardens.com
This is part of a chain with restaurants in Madrid, Casablanca, Mexico and Sao Paulo and claims to create cuisine based on ancient Siamese recipes. All ingredients are imported weekly from Thailand and the restaurant proudly notes the lack of monosodium glutamate in its food. The interior is stunning – frosted glass doors act as a partition between rooms, while bamboo chairs and silk cushions offer comfortable seating. Thai orchids add colour to each table and tranquil music helps the ambiance.

C/ Valencia, 205
Eixample
Passeig de Gràcia
Map p.393 D3 **81**

Thai Lounge
93 454 90 32 | www.thailounge.com
This is a sophisticated haven of all things Thai, with a popular takeaway menu that is 20% cheaper than dining in. Beige walls and soft lighting create a very intimate atmosphere, and service is impeccable. Despite its generic name, the gentle nature of Thailand and its people is present and everything is executed as if you were eating in Bangkok.

Gran Via de les Corts Catalanes, 674
Eixample
Passeig de Gràcia
Map p.393 F4 **82**

Thai Sabai Sabai
93 301 53 65
Thai Sabai Sabai has many loyal followers because it produces delicious, unfussy Thai food. If bowing waitresses and gold gilt leaves you cold, this is a relaxed restaurant where the focus is all on the food. Takeaway is available until late and, although filled with flowers and the requisite Thai fountain, this is a comfortable and relaxed dining experience. The chu-chi pla (red curry and coconut milk fish fillets) is particularly popular.

339

Vegetarian

C/ Diputacio, 164
Eixample
🚇 **Rocafort**
Map p.392 C4 83

Amaltea
93 454 86 13 | *www.restaurantamaltea.com*

As well as delicious meat-free dishes, such as vegetable moussaka, set lunches or *plato combinados* for around €6, there are many events held here. There is a dance school in the building, where tai chi lessons, yoga, Pilates and meditation classes take place weekly. A separate cafe is next to the impressive ecology bookshop. Amaltea's website is updated regularly to display the latest events.

Via Laietana, 28
Ciutat Vella
🚇 **Jaume I**
Map p.403 E3 84

Comme-bio
93 319 89 68

Vegetables are very much the focal point of Comme-bio. This may sound obvious, but the focus here is on greenery, with rice, tofu and pasta a secondary concern. There is a good choice of what are described as 'environmentally friendly' sandwiches. Combination platters are available for those with raging appetites and there's also a shop that sells organic produce. Many of the items sold are rarely found in Barcelona.

C/ Mercaders, 10
Port Vell
🚇 **Jaume I**
Map p.403 E3 85

El Arcano
93 310 21 79

El Arcano is quite unique. Aside from serving up top vegetarian food, it also offers a tarot reading service. This is taken very seriously and is not gimmicky, costume-style stuff. The real centerpiece is the bar, originally built in an 18th century stable, complete with ornate detailing. A fantastic sample menu is available for those who fancy a bit of everything.

C/ Carme, 16
Eixample
🚇 **Liceu**
Map p.402 C2 86

Fresc Co
93 301 68 37 | *www.frescco.com*

For €8.30 on weekdays and €9.95 on evenings and weekends, Fresc Co serves up fast, healthy, vegetarian food. A vast salad bar lines one side of the restaurant and main courses include pasta and omelettes. The homemade soups are extremely popular and Fresc Co has recently spread to Madrid, Valencia and Girona.

C/ Sant Eusebi, 64
Sarrià-Sant Gervasi
🚇 **Fontana**
Map p.393 D1 87

La Granja
93 201 57 50

Lots of care is used in the cooking here, and although takeaway is available, this is a restaurant in which to dine, rather than a place to grab a quick bite. Gorgeous, homemade vegetable lasagna and tofu stew are just two of the choices. Relaxed and inviting, La Granja is popular among both meat lovers and vegetarians.

C/ Pintor Fortuny, 25
Ciutat Vella
🚇 **Urgell**
Map p.402 B2 88

Restaurante Biocenter
93 301 45 83

The buffet-style salad bar serves food made only to strict, eco-friendly standards. The opening hours are not ideal, as doors don't unlatch for dinner until 20:00, but if you're desperate for a healthy fix, Biocenter has opened a food market across the street, where you can buy ingredients used in the restaurant.

C/ Sant Antoni Abat, 52
Gràcia
🚇 **Sant Antoni**
Map p.401 F2 89

Sesamo
93 441 64 11 | *www.sesamo-bcn.com*

Sesamo offers simple set menus that change daily. Rice, pasta, salad and other dishes are created around whatever is in season, and chefs aim for what they term a 'global menu' so, hopefully, there is something for everyone. Sesamo has a real community of visitors. Rarely do people eat here once and fail to return.

Great things can come in small packages…

Perfectly proportioned to fit in your pocket,
this marvellous mini guidebook makes sure
you don't just get the holiday you paid for,
but rather the one that you dreamed of.

Singapore Mini Visitors' Guide
Maximising your holiday, minimising your hand luggage

Cafes & Coffee Shops

Barcelona's celebrated cafe culture is similar to that of Paris or Milan. Part of every self-respecting resident's day is spent sipping on a strong cafe cortado in the shade of an umbrella on a sidewalk. Most cafes are independent and family run, and many become restaurants or bars at night. Open from the crack of dawn often until well past midnight, a cup of coffee is never far from reach. Tapas, hot food, homemade pastries and croissants are served all day. With such fantastic, old-fashioned coffee and tea available, spending time in a chain store seems a waste, especially as they're usually more expensive. All cafes are family-friendly, even when they switch into bar mode at night, but not all have facilities for mothers.

Pl Nova, 3
Barri Gòtic
🚇 *Jaume I*
Map p.403 D3 90

Bilbao Beria

93 317 01 24

Directly below the steps of the Cathedral de la Santa i Santa Eulalia sits this whirring tapas cafe and bar. It's perfect for a lunchtime beer or coffee and has more than 100 tapas dishes to choose from. This range changes daily, and each is of a high standard. Open from first thing in the morning until last thing at night, this cafe is a well known haven in the city. Fruit kebabs, mini hamburgers and wonderfully fresh crab meat are just some of the delicious snacks on offer.

Pl Bonsucces, 6
Raval
🚇 *Catalunya*
Map p.402 C2 91

Buenas Migas Focacceria

93 481 51 38 | www.buenasmigas.com

Buenas Migas specialises in foccacia bread. Delectable slices covered in local delicacies such as Iberico ham and Manchego cheese, or tomato and mozzarella, fill this cafe with a heavenly aroma, making it a fantastic spot for a light bite. It is also a stone's throw from MACBA (p.164). Warm, surprisingly comfortable wooden seating welcomes you as you enter and the coffee is very good. Those needing some respite from traditional Spanish cafe con leche should also head here for a mocha latte or frothy cappuccino.

Catalan treats

Melon soup, anyone...?

Cafe Fiorino

Pg de Gràcia, 58
Eixample
🚇 *Passeig de Gràcia*
Map p.393 E3 92

93 487 11 92

Cafe Fiorino is well located, on Passeig de Gràcia, just outside the epic ring of Plaça de Catalunya's noise and crowds. Although frequented by tourists and very near the center, Cafe Fiorino is big enough to make finding a seat easy (ish), which is understandably rare in this area. If you've spent hours wandering the streets and need a break, or want a fast hit of caffeine between meetings, this is the best place to head. Super fast, super efficient and super cheap, it also offers top quality bocadillos and sweet treats.

Cafe Zurich

Pl de Catalunya, 1
Ciutat Vella
🚇 *Catalunya*
Map p.402 C1 93

93 317 91 53

Although you may pay a tad more than in other cafes, this is an institution of sorts and most residents will end up arranging to meet someone here eventually. Located directly in the centre of the city, on a heaving, traffic heavy corner of Plaça de Catalunya, Cafe Zurich has been whipping up cortados for decades. Even in bad weather, you'll be lucky to get a seat outside, despite the fact that the tables and chairs take up most of the pavement. Fortunately, the waiters are very efficient.

Farga

Gran Via de les Corts
Catalanes, 630
Eixample
🚇 *Passeig de Gràcia*
Map p.393 E4 94

93 342 60 40

One of several Fargas in the city, this branch is the flagship. Split into two separate areas, one side offers tapas and the other raciones (larger tapas). Go through to the next section and a real treat awaits; you'll find a delicatessen/patisserie/coffee shop combo that's a delight to the eye. The delicatessen offers a fine array of meats and cheeses, while the patisserie boasts gateaux, pastries and cakes. The decor is very minimalist, but it's classy, with low lighting, dark wooden tables and the aroma of strong, ground coffee beans.

Farggi

Pl de Catalunya, 19
Eixample
🚇 *Catalunya*
Map p.403 D1 95

93 486 04 22

On the corner of Plaça de Catalunya is a prominent and popular Farggi cafe. There are several around the city, but this is the best one. Known for both its coffee and ice cream, savoury food is also available. But, what really brings the crowds in is the gelateria that runs almost the entire length of the interior. An outside area exists, but the calm, air conditioned indoor seats are more appealing for enjoying an ice cream, escaping the swirling traffic and the often torturous heat.

Forn de Sant Jaume

Rla de Catalunya, 50
Eixample
🚇 *Passeig de Gràcia*
Map p.393 E4 96

93 216 09 42

Specialising in both croissants and sweets, Forn de Sant Jaume is heavenly. Like many other cafes in the city, it has split itself in two. One side is a tapas restaurant that serves beer and wine, while the other is the cafe and patisserie, where cakes and pastries can be enjoyed with a cup of coffee. There are pavement tables and a takeaway. It's good for birthday cakes too.

Il Caffe di Francesco

Pg de Gràcia, 66
Eixample
🚇 *Passeig de Gràcia*
Map p.393 E3 97

93 488 25 90 | www.ilcaffedifrancesco.com

Part of the Spanish coffee trade since 1907 and open in this location since 1992, Il Caffe di Francesco prides itself on being one of Barcelona's premier Spanish coffee houses. A far cry from the latte-mocha-decaf creations of some franchised places, simple, top grade coffee of every variety is available in this well located caffeine emporium. Next to the beautiful Casa Maria and across the street from the very impressive Hotel Majestic, Il Caffe di Francesco offers a quiet, shaded haven despite its manic surroundings. Snacks are available, but essentially, this is the place to stop if you simply want a darn good cup of joe.

C/ Joaquin Costa, 43
Ciutat Vella
🚇 **Sant Antoni**
Map p.402 A1 98

Lletrafait

Although quite a bustling cocktail bar at night, Lletrafait is much more enjoyable as a cafe during the day (although it does serve up a respectable mojito). With a back wall lined with couches, you find students reading books, chatting and skimming the daily papers. If you forget your own reading material, lovely dog-eared editions of Spanish and English books are piled on the tables. Otherwise, you can buy something new in the adjacent bookshop. Anything hanging on the walls will be for sale, as this is also an art gallery.

C/ Avinyo, 25
Barri Gòtic
🚇 **Drassanes**
Map p.409 D1 99

Venus
93 301 15 85

As well as offering up a top cafe cortado, Venus is a delicatessen with Mediterranean and vegetarian dishes, wines and pastries. Flooded with light, it is also an aesthetic pleasure. Giant cake stands fill glass cabinets, and paper-mache ornaments adorn every window. There is also varied artwork on the walls. And, while you may not leave having purchased a purple, paper-mache octopus, you'll love the food and drinks on offer.

Internet Cafes

Internet cafes are dotted nicely around the city but they aren't always easy to stumble across. Wi-Fi is available in many bars which is a useful option and often means you can get online free with your cocktail or coffee. Internet cafes charge from anywhere between €1 and €4 an hour. Some will give you 24 hour or monthly packages, which are much better value if the local internet joint becomes a second home. Most good cafes also offer international calling, microphones, scanners, webcams and other computer software. One of the most notable listed here is Net-movil, as it's conveniently located on La Rambla. It is one of the largest venues in the city with 70 computers and uses fiber optic internet connection. It offers internet classes for those in need. The Easyinternetcafe is here too.

Internet Cafes

Bornet	Barri Gòtic	93 268 15 07
BZCnet	Sant Andreu	93 311 06 72
Cibermarchando	Eixample	93 510 26 55
Communicat	Eixample	93 412 50 53
Easyeverything	Ciutat Vella	www.easyinternetcafe.com
Net Gaming	Sarrià-Sant Gervasi	93 414 30 24
Net-movil	Ciutat Vella	93 342 42 04

Bakeries

Bakeries are dotted throughout Barcelona and nearly every barrio has a few top quality places for pastries, sweets, cakes and bread. Residents learn to make use of these places for their daily loaf, as store bought bread isn't of great quality. As well as the usual delights, you'll find local favourites such as bisbalenc, a barrel shaped puff pastry filled with sugared zucchini and sprinkled with pine nuts or assorted dried local fruits. Sometimes you get both, which is known as grana de capella. Flaona, a popular snack of pastry stuffed with cheese or whipped cream will line the shelves of most bakeries, along with homemade sandwiches, excellent coffee and often a selection of local wines. The sweet delights and home made cakes on offer in Barcelona's bakeries are epic in scope and size, but the decor and (often original) 50s design makes them even more of a treat.

C/ Palla, 8
Barri Gòtic
🚇 *Jaume I*
Map p.403 D3 `103`

Caelum

93 302 69 33

This exquisite cafe and bakery is tucked away in a very tranquil and peaceful corner of the Barri Gòtic. Old-fashioned pie stands and traditional fairy cakes adorn the beautifully weathered cabinets. Cakes, tarts and pastries are available to eat with an excellent cup of coffee, or to takeaway. The atmosphere and friendly staff are unfamiliar in this Catalan heartland, but the freshly baked delights and coffee are impressive. You'll find it very easy to pile on the pounds over a newspaper.

Pl de la Virreina
Gràcia
🚇 *Fontana*
Map p.393 F1 `104`

L'Art Del Pa La Fleca De Tots

93 865 26 06

Close to the Aladdin's den that is Gràcia market, is a patisserie and coffee house that serves up an array of sweets, cakes, pastries and delicious hot drinks. A wonderful way to while away a morning is with one of their delectable cappuccinos, ordered as takeaway and enjoyed while browsing the clothes, jewellery, bags and hand made goods on sale under the tiled roof of the market. Pink and white meringues swirl in the windows and, along with the other homemade goods, are available to order for large parties. The apple tarts are a rare treat.

Fruit Juices

Other options **Cafes & Coffee Shops** p.342

Barcelona is bustling with independent fruit juice sellers and little juice bars. Vendors walk along the beach with their goods, and set up stalls along the pavement, so you're never far from a good apple-pomegranate-papaya concoction. Fruit stalls in markets often sell their own mixes alongside the raw ingredients, and Gràcia has lots of health food shops. Less common are juices packed with an extra punch of protein, vitamin C or fiber. Those available in Barcelona tend to be simple but delicious, straight up and untouched.

Pg de Gràcia, 46
Eixample
🚇 *Passeig de Gràcia*
Map p.393 E4 `100`

Fresh & Ready

93 216 03 39

Despite being part of a chain (this is the largest and most centrally located), the Fresh & Ready franchise is a useful place to know. Firstly, you don't feel as though you're in a chain. Secondly, it is exclusive to Barcelona. Thirdly, it sells really great fruit juices. Excellent for a healthy snack too, sandwiches and salads are on offer all day long. It has become popular among tourists, but don't let that put you off. It's well worth trying and you're likely to head back time and again for a truly delicious boost of vitamin C.

C/ Cardenal Casanas, 7
Raval
🚇 *Liceu*
Map p.402 C3 `101`

Juicy Jones

93 302 43 30

Like most juice bars, Juicy Jones has other things on offer besides fruit drinks. A haven of all things good for you, it has vegan food and an array of tofu. Closed on Mondays, it serves fresh food and juices during lunch and dinner hours through the rest of the week, and with its eclectic, funky decor, has a really vibrant ambiance.

C/ Xiquetsde Valls, 9
Gràcia
🚇 *Diagonal*
Map p.393 F1 `102`

La Botiga del Sol

93 415 55 30

The main focus of La Botiga del Sol, a little place near the lovely Plaça del Sol, is its juice bar. Offering a big choice of combinations, it's also popular for its fresh organic produce and vitamins. Located in the heart of Gràcia, the locals are huge fans. You can drop in and stock up on your ginseng and herbal teas, and grab a juice to go while you're at it.

345

On the Town

Barcelona comes alive at night. The city is non-stop from dusk till dawn and, unless you're a high energy sort, you'll need to get used to siestas. Dinner is served late and some clubs don't open their doors until 03:00. The weekend starts on Thursday and Sundays are often the biggest night of the week. Monday is the only time you might have trouble finding clubs open. Drinks are relatively inexpensive and special offers serve up cocktails for as little as €3. Opening hours are vague and nights out can last until the early morning, simply because bars keep serving until the last customer falls out the door. Some stay open almost 24 hours a day. Violence is pretty rare, and generally you won't get into trouble for being a little bit vocal, unless you're acting in a threatening manner. Be aware though, that this is a city that attracts lots of hen and stag parties so police (and locals) may be less sympathetic if they think you're just in town for a weekend of raucous boozing. Women should be aware that drinks can get spiked here as easily as in other cities.

Drink Driving

Spain is one of the last European countries to seriously crack down on drink drivers. The government pledged back in 2004 to cut the number of road deaths in Spain and, as a result, if you get busted driving under the influence you face a six or 12 month ban. See p.133 for more. Bars and clubs are always happy to find you a taxi if you don't fancy wandering off alone, and public transport if very reliable.

Door Policy

The only spots with strict door policies are large nightclubs and expensive hotel bars. Apart from a few gay bars that have men-only nights, there is little prejudice against large groups, gender or age. The only thing that may cause problems is being too drunk. Although this is a city that never sleeps, door staff don't welcome the inebriated and if you're drunk you may have trouble gaining access to anywhere with a bouncer. Smaller, local places may keep serving you. Those in large groups may want to call ahead; especially large groups of men. Women don't usually have as much trouble. If nothing else, it may enable you to book a table or seating area.

Dress Code

Barcelona has no real dress code. It's a relaxed city where anything goes. Head out for a night and you'll see men in drag, women in bikinis and a lot of people without shoes on. Open minds and easy going attitudes reign, so wear what feels good, unless you're heading somewhere smart. Buda Bar (p.349), for example, would expect a shirt and smart shoes. The hotel bars would also expect smart casual gear, although even the five star hotel bars are more relaxed than those in many other cities.

Omm Session (p.366)

Bars

Other options **Nightclubs** p.364, **Pubs** p.360

Barcelona has a vast selection of bars. Many are quintessential old Spanish joints, with long wooden serving areas and bright lighting, tapas served from glass cabinets and barrels of wine overhead. A lot of modern, very trendy bars are springing up as well, and most cater to the city's love of live music. Cocktail bars are hugely popular due to the local adoration of mojitos, while *cevercerias* (the Spanish equivalent of an English pub) are on almost every street corner.

There is no minimum drinking age in Spain, but the minimum age for buying alcohol is 16 and that's fairly well enforced. The beautiful hotels, especially along Passeig de Gràcia, have some gorgeous bars that are open to non-guests and few franchises exist. Generally, bars tend to be family-run, passed on through generations and very welcoming.

C/ Pau Claris, 155
Eixample
🚇 **Passeig de Gràcia**
Map p.393 F3 **105**

Amatller
93 215 44 05

Recently opened on the old site of El Deva Cevezeria, Amatller is a tranquil and welcoming respite from the mayhem of its surroundings. Named in honour of the stunning Casa Amatller by Gaudi, this bar does not have the same impressive facade, but it offers up fine beer and is open almost all hours of the day. Just try and ignore the garish lime green walls with orchids hand-painted across them, and think of the Gaudi version instead.

C/ Correo Viejo, 3
Born
🚇 **Barceloneta**
Map p.403 E4 **106**

Andu
646 553 930

Andu offers perfect escapism from the high-end bars in Barcelona. What makes this special is its authenticity and simplicity, despite being opened by an Austrian and an Australian. If you didn't know better, you'd think it had been part of a Catalan family for generations. Typical of many establishments in the city, it is narrow but very long and cosy. Home cooked tapas and suitably strong drinks are always on offer. This is a real Catalan 'locals' bar, unknown to tourists, and so a perfect break from the mainstream. Be warned about the drinks though; they are lethally loaded, so one or two should be all you'll need.

C/ Aurora, 7
Raval
🚇 **Sant Antoni**
Map p.402 A3 **107**

Aurora
93 422 30 44

The deep red walls strike you immediately when entering Aurora for the first time. Eclectic electronic beats pump through the bar, which an equally eclectic crowd jive along to. Open until dawn at the weekend, it's the type of place where you'll find yourself stuck. Once you arrive, order a cocktail and get yourself comfortable; you'll find it hard to move again for the rest of the evening. People-watching is a great sport as the local crowd are truly fascinating - lots of mohawks and dreadlocks. You'll find yourself surrounded in no time as everyone is so friendly, and with no bouncer to kick you out at closing time, it's easy to stay until the sun comes up.

C/ Pintor Fortuny, 3
Raval
🚇 **Catalunya**
Map p.402 C2 **108**

Bar Lobo
93 481 53 46 | www.grupotragaluz.com

From the people who brought us the fabulous Cuines Santa Caterina (see p.328) and Hotel Omm, comes Bar Lobo. Located right next to H1891, a hip new example of hotel modernity in Raval, Bar Lobo is trendy, inspiring, exciting and very cool. Margaret Mead quotes rather questionably adorn the walls of this black and white

347

establishment, but a very large bar welcomes you as soon as you cross the threshold, and it's replete with every type of spirit, wine or beer, all served up by very attractive staff. Outdoor seating is available for the balmier summer evenings, and decent food is served too. New and somewhat unique, Bar Lobo seems to be a sign of things to come in Barcelona.

Sangria jugs

C/ Sant Pau, 65
Raval
🚇 *Liceu*
Map p.402 A4 **109**

Bar Marsella

93 442 72 63

Many a bar across Spain claims to have supplied drinks to Hemingway, and to be fair, he liked his alcohol and travelled the length and breadth of the country. Bar Marsella, however, is able to boast serving not only Hemingway, but Picasso, Miro and Gaudi too. Having kept its doors open since 1820 (with little inclination to modernise the decor) this is the place to drink absinthe. Order a reasonably priced cocktail or beer and you'll quickly have absinthe and a sugar cube rammed into your free hand. The rustic, historic vibe is infectious, so you're unlikely to pop in for just the one.

C/ Santa Monica, 4
Raval
🚇 *Drassanes*
Map p.408 B1 **110**

Bar Pastis

93 318 79 80

A love of Edith Piaf and Paris inspired Valencianos Carme Pericas and Quime Ballester to open Bar Pastis back in the 40s. In homage to the great French singer, her music still plays long into the night and only Pastis is served, although they've four different types to choose from. The decor and regular crowd are fairly bohemian, and the walls are decorated with the paintings of bar founder and part-time artist, Ballester.

C/ Marina, 16
Port Olímpic
🚇 *Ciutadella/Vila Olímpica*
Map p.411 D2 **111**

Barnabier

93 221 02 12

Barnabier is a huge beer hall, located in one of the 'twin towers' of Barcelona that were built in time for the 1992 Olympics. The views of the Mediterranean are spectacular and you can enjoy a beer in this *cerveceria* while looking right out across the port. With the city's big casino near-by and the gorgeous Hotel Arts next door, this is a good place to start an evening. Designed to cater to the thirsty during the hot Olympic summer months, Barnabier still holds a vast selection of beers from around the world.

C/ Ramon Trias Fargas, 2-4
Port Olímpic
🚇 *Ciutadella/Vila Olímpica*
Map p.411 D3 **112**

Bestial

93 224 04 07

Bestial initially opened to wide arms and huge smiles. This was mainly because it replaced Planet Hollywood, a horrendously tacky building from the US chain that was extremely unpopular among locals. Although it now advertises itself as a bar/restaurant, and offers an epic array of Italian/Catalan fusion food, it is best as a spot for drinks. With a waterfront terrace, it makes a welcome break from the wonderful, but sometimes claustrophobic, haunts of the inner city. Located across from the Hotel Arts, it has also become a popular watering hole among media and fashion types. The interior is minimalist but still manages to be welcoming, airy and extremely relaxed. Neon-lit walkways curve around the bar and the overload of wood somehow absorbs the noise so, even on a packed weekend night, you won't find yourself shouting to be heard.

Boadas

C/ Tallers, 1
Ciutat Vella
Catalunya
Map p.402 C2 **113**

93 318 95 92

Miguel Boadas opened this fabulous little bar back in the 40s, having grown up in Cuba and trained at Havana's la Floridita, another haunt of Hemingway. He moved to Barcelona with a relaxed, happy Cuban attitude and poured all of that into Boadas. Now run by his daughter, Maria Dolores, Boadas serves a huge array of cocktails, some of which Miguel designed himself and named after figures like Joan Miro and some of his favourite places in Barcelona. The vibe is totally chilled, but not physically very relaxing (there are no tables, so you have stand all evening). The bar is long and tiny and full of Cuban and Spanish memorabilia.

Buda Bar

C/ Pau Claris, 92
Eixample
Passeig de Gràcia
Map p.393 F1 **114**

93 318 42 52 | *www.budarestaurante.com*

Although part of a global chain, this is a great spot for drinks if you want to add a little glam and opulence to an evening. The gothic-oriental interior is the backdrop for very scantily-clad waiting staff in slinky cocktail dresses. The atmosphere is buzzing, the acoustics loud and unless you get there unfashionably early, you'll need to ring ahead and reserve a table. Seeing and being seen is the order of the night, but you'll meet some interesting characters and enjoy a fine cocktail while you're at it.

Cafe Barroc

C/ Rec, 67
Born
Barceloneta
Map p.393 F4 **115**

93 268 46 23 | *www.riberbar.com*

A trendy cafe by day, this is in fact a very hip nocturnal spot. Home to some of the beautiful people of Barcelona, Cafe Barroc offers an eclectic mix with its Gothic, historic building and modern music spun by regular in-house DJ, Sebi. Faux candelabra lighting adorns the ceilings, gold gilt and deep red velvet seating lines the walls and darkness pervades, but at night it really comes alive and, located next door to the Karma bar (see p.353 for review) this is an area to target at weekends for a night out.

Cafe de l'Opera

La Rambla, 74
Barri Gòtic
Liceu
Map p.402 C3 **117**

93 317 75 85 | *www.cafeoperabcn.com*

Although many find the bars, cafes and restaurants of La Rambla overpriced tourist traps, it is an interesting strip. When you're gasping for a cocktail, Cafe de l'Opera is one of the best places to stop. The decor alone is worth the visit. Located near to the beautiful and newly-renovated Liceu Theatre, this cafe/bar, a real throwback, has been untouched since it opened its doors decades ago. The first floor looks like a theater balcony, tobacco stained walls are dimly lit with antique chandeliers and the old feel of the place makes it extremely cosy.

Cafe de la Ribera

Pl de les Olles, 6
Born
Barceloneta
Map p.409 F1 **116**

93 319 50 72

With cascading ivy flowing down over its canopy from the apartments above, partially exposed original brickwork and a rustic doorway, Cafe de la Ribera is a throwback to the Barcelona of the 30s. Conveniently located next to Carrer Rec, home to some of the city's most gorgeous clothing boutiques, this is a good spot for a daytime drink. But it's also lovely at night, and there are two very tiny floors with original Spanish tiles framing the brickwork. The atmosphere in Cafe de la Ribera is both romantic and delightfully retro.

349

Cocktail Bars
Pla (p.356) in the Barri Gòtic
has particularly good
cocktail lists. Everything
from a kir royal to a
caipirinha, a mojito to a
Martini is available, and they
are served very strong. Smoll
Bar (p.359) and Kynoto
(p.353) are also excellent
choices, providing great
music and comfortable
seating as well as a top
drink. Gimlet (p.352) in El
Born is also excellent and
feels a lot more special
because it is a little hidden.

C/ Ferran, 23
Barri Gòtic
🚇 *Liceu*
Map p.402 C4 **118**

Cafe Schilling
93 317 67 87

Although fantastic for a cafe con hielo (iced coffee) on hot
summer days, Schilling really comes alive at night. Known
by many as a gay bar, it's actually gay friendly, with a
vibrant mix of genders, nationalities and ages filling it up
every night of the week. Technically open until 03:00, it's
often swinging into the early hours of the next day, as
cocktail juggling waiters keep the party going behind the
warm wooden bar. It is more reminiscent of 20s New York
than 21st century Barcelona but that only adds to its
charm. A beautiful, marble floor welcomes you as you
walk in the door and excellent nibbles are available, but
the service can be very slow.

C/ Vallespir, 65
Sants
🚇 *Plaça del Centre*
Map p.391 F2 **119**

Celler de Gelida
93 339 26 41 | www.cellerdegelida.net

Wine connoisseurs are flocking from across the city to
Celler de Gelida. With hundreds of different varieties to choose from and home delivery
for when you've selected your favourite, Celler de Gelida has established itself as a very
serious wine merchant. The bar within is becoming a popular and sophisticated
hangout. Their knowledge is excellent and their opinion seems to be that the finest
bottles are not necessarily the most expensive. Their huge selection is very broad and
changes several times a year. The popularity and reputation of Celler de Gelida earned
it a Mayor's Award in 2006.

Pg del Born, 12
Born
🚇 *Jaume I*
Map p.403 F4 **120**

Creps al Born
93 269 03 25

Advertising itself as a bar that specialises in 'crepes and cocktails', it's easy to get the gist
of what this little establishment has on offer. In the middle of the very hip Passeig del
Born, you can expect to see jugglers, live bands, bongo drums or jewellery sellers, on the
pavement outside, making this a good spot for being nosey. Although it has no outside
seating, the action inside the bar tends to spill onto the street. An array of sweet and
savory crepes are on offer to soak up the powerful effects of the extremely strong
cocktails. Black and red in decor, it's not great during the day as it can feel dark, but from
the early part of the evening until dawn, it's a very cool place to see and be seen.

C/ Carme, 40
Raval
🚇 *Liceu*
Map p.402 B2 **121**

Dostrece
93 301 73 06 | www.dostrece.net

The crowd at Dostrece tends to be a mix of
youthful visiting business types and young
professional residents. The cocktail
combinations are pretty original, with
variations on classics like cosmopolitans
and Martinis. Lunch and dinner are also
available. If it's a hot summer night and
you're after outdoor seating, it is available
in the park across the street, where you'll
still get table service. The dining room is
transformed into an extension of the bar
after midnight, allowing more room for the
growing, grinding dance crowd.

Ubiquitous Moritz

C/ Llacuna, 142-144
Sant Martí
🚇 *Llacuna*
Map p.412 B1 122

Drunken Duck

93 356 88 47

Drunken Duck is a classic pub, bar and restaurant rolled into one. Dark wood lines the bar, English-speaking waiters take your food order and you've got Guinness, Heineken and Paulaner on tap. There are 29 other types of bottled beer available and, besides the tapas, English pub food is served hot for breakfast, lunch and dinner. This is not a bar trying to replicate a British pub for Catalan customers – it's a bar opened by two Brits with a pub influence that came from growing up on English shores. It attracts a mixed crowd, but has become a favourite expat hangout for both the top nosh and the quality draught beer.

Pg d'Isabel II, 4
Barceloneta
🚇 *Barceloneta*
Map p.409 E1 123

El Monasterio

www.salamonasterio.com

With its underground maze of drinking holes, it is easy to forget in El Monasterio that you're anywhere near the ocean. You are, in fact, a stone's throw from the lapping tide. The upstairs cafeteria remains open from early morning until late at night and is a good pit stop for snacks and tapas, while the underground bar has become a magnet for late night revellers. The outdoor terrace is very popular, but you'll need to get there early for seating. Live music shows and film screenings are organised on a regular basis, attracting quite an artistic crowd.

C/ Montcada, 22
Barri Gòtic
🚇 *Jaume I*
Map p.403 F4 124

El Xampanyet

93 319 70 03

This 30s champagne bar lies on an ancient, Gothic backstreet near the Picasso Museum. It is old meets new, with its blue, Spanish-tiled walls, zinc bar and marble tables decorated with a muddle of antiques. The crowd is totally mixed, not in background, but in age. Old, fairly slow-moving locals who have been hanging out here for years sit at the bar from the late afternoon onwards, while the evening introduces lots of young men and women who want good, fresh tapas and a drink before heading to the local clubs. But it works, making El Xampanyet a welcoming place for everyone.

C/ Argenteria, 6
Born
🚇 *Jaume I*
Map p.403 E4 125

El Rovell del Born

93 269 04 58 | *www.elrovelldelborn.com*

Although this classifies itself as a restaurant, it is far better enjoyed as a bar and snack joint. El Rovell del Born is definitely sleeker and more modern than the majority of tapas holes in Barcelona. El Rovell, literally translated from Catalan, refers to the yolk of an egg. So, it'll come as little surprise that the egg dishes on their menu are promoted the most heavily and a source of great pride to the owners. For excellent tapas and raciones, good beer or an excellent selection of Albarino wines, you can't miss this place; just look for the guy on the outdoor step handing out cards.

C/ Riera de Sant
Miguel, 55
Gràcia
🚇 *Fontana*
Map p.393 E2 126

Esbaskah

93 218 24 71 | *www.esbaskah.com*

Esbaskah is absolutely tiny, but it's got big personality and a loyal following. The focus is on music, so while you may spot the odd couple having a private drink at the bar, it's a prime destination for young music lovers in Gràcia. Primarily focused on house and techno tracks, it also plays old-school classics, remixed nightly by some seriously talented Catalan DJs. Dancing is what Esbaskah is all about and those who love it make impressively good use of its teeny dancefloor.

351

Fonfone

C/ Escudellers, 24
Barri Gòtic
🚇 Liceu
Map p.402 C4 127

93 317 14 24 | www.fonfone.com

The decor of Fonfone is some of the funkiest in town. Orange, pink, yellow and green bubble lights illuminate the serving area and create a classic club atmosphere in this bar environment. Music is pumped out by top DJs seven nights a week. Classic 80s, funk, electronica, house, and what they like to call 'future funk' reverberate throughout this popular bar, making it a good venue for pre-clubbing dancing and drinking.

Fritz Mar

Pg Maritim de
Barceloneta, 34
Port Olímpic
🚇 Ciutadella/Vila
Olímpica
Map p.410 C3 128

93 221 77 65 | www.fritzgroup.com

Although Fritz Mar boasts a superb Italian kitchen, it actually promotes itself as a beach bar with great music. It is situated right on the edge of the sand, with a terrace area that has comfortable seating, low lighting and better yet, views of the sea. There is an inside bar, but it's quite little and wasting such a view seems a shame. It tends to be busy even in the winter months and attracts quite a trendy crew of young people. The food is good, but the ambiance and music are the main reasons why Fritz Mar remains to be so popular.

Gimlet

C/ Rec, 24
Born
🚇 Jaume I
Map p.403 F4 129

There is no website, email address or even a telephone number for this place, and net curtains ensure you can't see what's happening inside, yet it's always packed. PR, promotions and happy hours don't factor here. This is a bar that has grown through word of mouth, and is known across the city as producing some of the finest cocktails available. It now has a sister bar on Calle Santalo that operates under the same name, but this small original den in El Born is legendary. The bar staff are experts at their trade. Whatever you want, they can make it. And if you don't know what you want, they'll whip up something spectacular anyway. The interior is elegantly simple and retro and the crowd that squeezes into the tiny space is friendly. We highly recommend it.

Hivernacle

Pg de Picasso
Parc de la Ciutadella
🚇 Arc de Triomf
Map p.404 A4 130

93 295 40 17

Even after Parc de la Ciutadella closes at night, crowds are drawn to its side entrance on Paseo Picasso for access to the wonderful Hivernacle bar and restaurant. Housed inside a 19th century greenhouse, Hivernacle has live jazz and classical music concerts playing during summer months. The interior decor, unsurprisingly, focuses on greenery and a little outside terrace has seating for those wanting a view across the park. The setting of Hivernacle is wonderfully romantic and you feel transported back to 1884, when the greenhouse was built.

Indian Lounge

C/ Sant Ramon, 23
Raval
🚇 Liceu
Map p.402 A4 131

620 530 903

By day, Indian Lounge is a good spot for enjoying Indian teas or smoking a shisha (water pipe) with flavored tobacco. By night, cocktails are poured in the bar area and can be enjoyed on comfortable sofas in the downstairs lounge, an area with lots of cool seating and authentic, Indian decor. The first Friday of each month is a great time to go, as Bollywood party nights are organised, and on Fridays and Saturdays, the bar is opened up to serve breakfast between 06:00 and 08.30 - perfect if you're an early riser, or simply needing some food before heading home at the end of a long night.

Just In Bar

C/ Tusset, 28
Sarrià-Sant Gervasi
🚇 *Gràcia*
Map p.393 D2 **132**

93 415 70 32 | www.justinbar.com

Grinding bodies on the dancefloor, pumping tunes and flowing cocktails are the general vibe here after 23:00 every night. Before that, this is quite a relaxed and tranquil place for a drink. It's like two venues under one roof, with an atmosphere which reflects the fact that VIP members get a free caipirinha, sex on the beach or mojito on entry; and then €5 drinks all night. The music gets loud and the crowds thicken but if you're in need of something funky, this hip, popular and very atmospheric bar is a good bet.

Karma

Pl Reial, 10
Barri Gòtic
🚇 *Liceu*
Map p.402 C4 **133**

93 302 56 80

Located in the heart of the Ciutat Vella quarter, on the edge of one of Barcelona's most stunning squares, Karma is a pulsating bar offering cocktails and live music late into the night. While most other premises on the square are restaurants, Karma is the one place where you can sit outside and see spectacular architecture and the central fountain, without having to order food. The downstairs area is described by the owners as a *discoteca* but that's the commonly used word for a club in Barcelona. It's not a club by most people's standards due its tiny size, but it offers funky tunes and attracts a very hip crowd.

Kasparo

Pl Vicens Martorell, 4
Raval
🚇 *Catalunya*
Map p.402 C1 **134**

93 302 20 72

This bar/cafe is in a very peaceful little square in often-hectic Raval. Food is available and the menu is quite an eclectic mix, offering tapas and Thai curry, and the two Australians who run it never close the kitchen. This, and the fact that drinks are served day and night, makes Kasparo a good place for lazing away hours. A children's playground is opposite, so it's quite popular with parents during the day, and the outdoor terrace (there is no inside seating) makes it a delightful early evening watering hole.

Kynoto Sushi Lounge

C/ Ciutat, 5
Barri Gòtic
🚇 *Jaume I*
Map p.403 D4 **135**

93 304 23 76 | www.kynoto.com

With a small upstairs area that is packed on weekend nights, Kynoto serves some of the finest sushi in the city. And, with giant, orange plastic light shades, an orange-tiled floor and orange leather lounge seats throughout, it is loyal to the Barcelonin trend of embracing startling interior colours. This is tempered by the sleek, dark wooden bar, and brown leather seating cubes. During the day, a free Wi-Fi service is available with your jasmine tea, and at night, the lights are lowered, the cocktails are shaken and the music starts. You can order sushi until late in the evening, should the drinks stir your hunger.

La Cova del Drac

C/ Vallmajor, 33
Sarrià-Sant Gervasi
🚇 *Lesseps*
Map p.385 D4 **136**

93 319 17 89 | www.masimas.com

The focus of La Cova del Drac is music. It's known as a jazz bar because of the frequent live shows and association with Barcelona's Jazz Radio, but other live concerts focus on flamenco, piano and at times, R&B. The interior is set up well for seeing a live show. Exposed brickwork winds around part of the bar, comfortable high stools give a good view of the stage and lighting is low and seductive. Private parties are often found enjoying a night here and San Miguel is now sponsoring La Cova del Drac's annual jazz festival.

353

La Fira

C/ Provença, 171
Gràcia
Diagonal
Map p.393 D3 **137**

93 978 10 96

If looking pretty with a mojito in hand is getting dull and you're looking for entertainment as well as refreshment, La Fira will keep you occupied. Designed around the theme of a circus; real-life dodgems, carnival masks and fortune tellers can all be found within this large, intriguing bar. Calling itself a 'bar museum', and dedicated to all things carnival, it is truly unlike anywhere else. You can wind through halls of distorted mirrors, buy food and drinks from bar areas designed to look like funfair stalls or sit on a swing. La Fira is as wacky and surreal as Barcelona's master of idiosyncrasy, Salvador Dali. Only in Barcelona could such a place work so well and it also offers damn good drinks.

La Tramoia

Rla de Catalunya, 15
Eixample
Universitat
Map p.393 E4 **138**

93 412 36 34

Designed to seat large numbers but not to feel overcrowded, La Tramoia is more reminiscent of wine bars found in London or Paris. Despite being adjacent to hectic Plaça de Catalunya, the roomy layout makes it feel peaceful. Both tapas and raciones are available. Chefs can be viewed behind glass windows, so it can feel more like a restaurant, but with a bar tucked neatly along one curved wall and small dishes available, La Tramoia is excellent for lunchtime coffee or evening cocktails.

La Vinya del Senyor

Pl Santa Maria, 5
Born
Jaume I
Map p.403 E4 **139**

93 310 33 79

Beyond its extensive wine and cava list, La Vinya del Senyor offers an excellent location for spending an evening. Set opposite the spectacular Santa Maria Church, which is floodlit at night, it's a charming spot. A small but delectable tapas menu is on offer to compliment whatever wine you choose, and friendly staff are on hand to advise you of what works with what. Follow the thin, spiral staircase upstairs and you may be lucky enough to get the tiny top room to yourself, with a table in the window and a stunning view of this Gothic plaza.

Luz de Gas

Davant de Palau
de Mar
Port Velll
Barceloneta
Map p.409 E2 **140**

93 484 23 26

We may all be familiar with the idea of house boats, but Luiz de Gas offers up the wonderful concept of a 'bar boat'. Floating elegantly on the edge of Barcelona's Port Vell, among stunning yachts and sun worshippers is this spectacular boat. Characterised by very smart navy and white, typically nautical trimmings, and well-treated mahogany, this is a good place to enjoy a glass of wine, and the available list is extensive. Large white, canvas umbrellas offer protection from the pounding sun in the summer and food is available with your drinks. If you start to feel queasy from the lapping water, simply step off onto the adjacent dock with its own, fixed bar.

Lupino

C/ Carme, 33
Ciutat Vella
Liceu
Map p.402 B2 **141**

93 412 36 97 | www.lupinorestaurante.com

A magnet for the young, fun and laid back crowd of the city center, Lupino has been widely popular since it opened its doors a few years ago. Interior designer and architect, Ellen Rapelius, has created a modern and sleek bar area, designed around a brightly lit, blue catwalk. The catwalk leads onto an outdoor terrace that overlooks the back of the vibrant Boqueria Market (p.310). The relaxed sounds of mambo and jazz are played by live DJs. You can get food in the open-plan kitchen area, snacks and coffee in the cafe or drinks in the bar.

C/ Rec, 59
Born
🚇 *Jaume I*
Map p.403 F4 **142**

Mamaine

Mamaine might be more appropriate on a beach in Aruba rather than in the heart of European city. Self-promoted as a *tropical cockteleria*, Mamaine offers drinks of every colour, size and variety. Served against a backdrop of fluorescent, lime green walls and bamboo; the tiki-bar touches feel like they transport you to the Caribbean; especially after a few of their super-charged Martinis. Loved by locals and well-known by tourists, it has a mixed feel that works. The atmosphere naturally encourages everyone to relax and party over a caipirinha or two. Mamaine is also a delightful daytime spot, with outside seating.

Rla de Catalunya, 91
Eixample
🚇 *Diagonal*
Map p.393 E3 **143**

Meson Cinco Jotas

93 487 89 42

Although the inside of Meson Cinco Jotas is fairly average, the outside seating area makes it worth a stop if you're strolling down Rambla de Catalunya. Located on what is, by far, one of Barcelona's most beautiful streets, the magnificent views of Tibidabo mountain are spectacular, while the Parisian feel and the top quality beers are desirable at any time of day. Locals gather around the small cluster of outdoor tables, so seating isn't always guaranteed.

C/ Gignas, 21
Barri Gòtic
🚇 *Barceloneta*
Map p.409 E1 **144**

Milk

93 268 09 22 | *www.milkbarcelona.com*

Only open since 2005, Milk is still relatively unknown, but it can't be long before word spreads about this fantastic little bar. Opened by an Irish couple who moved to Barcelona from San Francisco, Milk is chic, plush and sophisticated, without being intimidating or overpriced. The website claims the bar is decorated like 'a millionaire's living room' which is a bit of an exaggeration, although its original 50s Florence Broadhurst wallpaper and hand made sofas are decadent. The food is fantastic, but most noteworthy is the 'recovery brunch' they serve on Saturdays and Sundays, which includes favourites such as eggs Benedict, alongside a selection of the day's foreign and local papers. One of the very few bars in Barcelona to offer happy hour, patrons can enjoy a large selection of cocktails every night from 19:00-21:00 for only €3.50.

Final Av Tibidabo
Tibidabo

Mirablau

93 418 58 79

Heading towards the top of the Tibidabo mountain sits Mirablau. With gigantic windows overlooking the city, you simply won't get better views. On a clear night, you can see the city's lights all the way to the ocean, and on a clear day, the spires of the Sagrada Familia poke teasingly out from among the rooftops. For views this sensational you can expect to pay a little more, but it's worth it. The music is a bit too commercial, but with sights this incredible, it's unlikely you'll be paying attention.

C/ Riera Alta, 4-6
Raval
🚇 *Liceu*
Map p.402 A2 **146**

Muebles Navarro

93 442 39 66

You may get the sense when quenching your thirst in this former furniture shop that the new owners forgot to remove the old stock before opening. There is plenty of seating and, because of the sheer enormity of this building in the cramped quarters of Raval, it doesn't feel overcrowded. Mismatched sofas, tables and shelving units fill this space and due to its unique shape and size, it is often the location for book-club meetings and discussion groups. Rather than becoming a warehouse style club, Muebles Navarro is a spacious, relaxed and fairly gentle place to enjoy a cocktail. There are tapas-esque dishes to help you through the evening, such as large cheese plates.

355

Pg de Gràcia, 4
Eixample
🚇 *Passeig de Gràcia*
Map p.393 E4 **147**

Navarra

93 318 58 95

A favourite among residents since 1939, what makes Navarra so appealing is how unchanged it has remained since. The original, stained-glass dome ceiling still sits proudly above the authentic wrought-iron railings around the bar. A real high-society joint in the 50s, Navarra is now a much more relaxed bar, though it does have a full menu. It is very fast-paced and very large, so not for those wanting a peaceful beer with the newspaper.

C/ Arai, 5
Ciutat Vella
🚇 *Jaume I*
Map p.403 D4 **148**

Oviso

Planted on the corner of the bohemian Plaça de George Orwell, Oviso is a center for the more grungy side of Barcelona. With peacocks, lions and tigers painted across the inside walls, it is a central hub in the Gòtic district for excellent sweet and savoury crepes and all things artistic. Foreign films are projected on the back wall once a week with big, sloppy beanbags on the floor in front. However, the rest of the bar serves as normal so the sound quality may not be quite up to par. Outside seating is available in the square for those balmy summer evenings or a quick daytime coffee. Oviso is a fantastic venue for really getting to know the hippy heart of the city.

C/ Santa Anna, 10
Ciutat Vella
🚇 *Catalunya*
Map p.402 C2 **149**

Pa Pastes Cafe

If the hustle and bustle of hagglers, street performers and tourists on La Rambla becomes grating, take a quick turn onto the tranquil Carrer de Santa Anna and pop into Pa Pastes Cafe. Untouched since opening and very unglamorous, it's a dream Spanish cafe. Empanadillas, quiches, flantas and bocadillos are available alongside the cold beer. Daily specials are advertised on chalk boards, offering a decent pit stop between La Rambla and the shopping heaven of Avinguda del Portar de L'Angel. You may be welcomed with a bit of a Catalan scowl but the cold brew makes it worthwhile and it's a great place to spot characterful locals and daily patrons, enjoying a daytime San Miguel.

C/ Agla, 4
Ciutat Vella
🚇 *Liceu*
Map p.402 C4 **150**

Pile 43

93 317 39 02

Pile 43 could only really be found in a city as surreal and quirky as Barcelona. Not only does it serve amazing cocktails, but it's also a furniture shop. This is not a common combination, but somehow it works and people keep coming back to check out the latest shipments. Antique, one-off pieces from the 50s, 60s and 70s seem to fill this tiny bar, and the decor changes according to what pieces have been delivered. Everything in here is for sale and, not only is it a great place to enjoy a mojito while buying a chest of drawers, it also plays excellent, well-chosen 60s and 70s pop music.

C/ Bella Filla, 5
Barri Gòtic
🚇 *Catalunya*
Map p.402 B2 **151**

Pla

93 412 65 52

If you can move your eyes away from the arty images projected on the wall of Pla, you'll find yourself in a really cosy bar/restaurant, lit mainly by candles, in keeping with the Gothic location. An excellent Mediterranean menu is available but the bar area is great for cocktails and simple snack food. It's one of the few places in the city that adheres to the smoking ban and the friendly staff and superior drinks meet most tastes. It has a unique atmosphere within an area overwhelmed with dark, edgy watering holes.

Sports Bars
The best places for watching foreign sports in Barcelona are in the British and Irish pubs (see p.321). There are no sport-themed bars per se, but most local bars will show Spanish Primera Liga games.

C/ Princesa, 23
Born
Jaume I
Map p.403 F4 152

Princesa 23

93 268 86 19 | *info@princesa23.com*

If you've loaded up on culture in the Picasso Museum and need to rest your feet and enjoy a drink, Princesa 23 is seconds from the great master's permanent exhibition. However, despite its location, this is not a touristy bar. If anything, it has a predominantly local, female clientele. The kitchen serves up delicious tapas and bocadillos throughout the day, giving it a cafe feel until about 22:00, when it becomes a lively bar with easy-listening music and a gentle, amiable crowd. Almost Moroccan in decor, there are lots of lounge seats and throw cushions. On the 23rd of every month, the owners throw a party for regulars and offer cheap deals on drinks. Live sporting events are shown on the television, making this a good alternative to the British and Irish pubs that normally show foreign sports.

C/ Rossello, 277
Eixample
Diagonal
Map p.393 F3 153

Public

Tucked away off the Rambla de Catalunya is this haven of trendiness and culture. With its purple-hued backdrop, impressive collection of artwork (all for sale of course) and outside seating, Public is a great pit stop. Heaving bar and arty hang-out by night, quiet, relaxed cafe by day, the atmosphere remains chilled. Adored by local patrons, and loved by all who work there, it's a really sweet place to have a coffee or cold beer.

C/ Quintana, 6
Barri Gòtic
Liceu
Map p.402 C4 154

Q Bar

93 270 18 52

With its luxurious sofa seating, chandelier lighting and delicate archways, Q Bar seems more like someone's very smart home. There are gorgeous views over the adjacent garden and terrace, and the atmosphere is chic, chilled and sophisticated. They have what they call an international gastrobar, which serves bar food from around the world. Staple dishes from Mexico, Japan and Peru can be ordered, and are a good accompaniment to drinks. This is a very cosy spot and a good place for gathering friends for some relaxed chat over cocktails.

Pl Sant Augusti, 3
Raval
Liceu
Map p.402 B3 155

Rita Blue

93 342 40 86 | *www.ritablue.com*

For some serious mambo action, Friday and Saturday nights at Rita Blue are the place to be. If you aren't a trained mambo dancer, you'll learn a lot from the pros on the dancefloor. If live DJ techno sets are more your thing, local acts hit the decks every Wednesday and Thursday evening. Part of Rita Blue is a restaurant but, with slightly average Mexican and Mediterranean food, it's a far better venue as a bar and nightclub. The decor consists of funky, 50s lamps, illuminating the scene for some brilliant mambo dancing.

C/ Argenteria, 62
Born
Jaume I
Map p.403 E4 156

Sagardi Euskal Taberna

93 319 99 93 | *www.sagardi.com*

Plaça de Jacint Reventos, a square on the edge of El Born, is encircled with a vast array of tapas restaurants, wine bars and patisseries. If a good beer is what you want though, Sagardi Euskal Taberna is a great option. Offering a range of brews from around the world, it's fantastic if you've overdosed on San Miguel and you're pining for a good Czech or Australian beer. With a large menu to choose from, food is always available, but it's got much more of a bar feel than a restaurant ambiance. Outside seating is hard to come by, especially in the summer.

357

C/ Rec, 60 *Born* 🚇 *Jaume I* *Map p.403 F4* **157**	## Salero *93 319 80 22* Although part of this establishment is a restaurant, it's best known as a fantastic place for drinking cocktails. White-washed walls, white lilies, candlelight and comfortable Moroccan furniture create the most wonderful atmosphere and, if you get peckish, there is tapas and sushi available until late. A very cosy private room in the back of the bar is available for intimate parties but, whether en mass or on your own, the mojitos are worth the visit. Located opposite Abac (p.327) restaurant, this is a great place to stop off on the way home from supper, for a pre-dinner daiquiri, or for an evening of supping.
C/ Nou de la *Rambla, 22* *Sants-Montjuïc* 🚇 *Liceu* *Map p.402 B4* **158**	## Salsitas *93 318 08 40* | *www.gruposalsitas.com* The fresh tropical fruit cocktails served at Salsitas mirror the rather questionable pineapple and palm décor, but don't let that put you off. The drinks taste great, the bar is massive and there is a beautiful, all white dining room to enjoy a delicious dinner as well. Salsitas is known as a haven for the young and glam but attracts quite a mixed crowd, due to the excellent music. A chill out bar with comfortable sofas greets guests in the entrance and aside from the restaurant, there is also a large dance area.
C/ Sant Pau, 68 *Raval* 🚇 *Liceu* *Map p.402 A4* **159**	## Sant Pau 68 Sant Pau 68 is another establishment in Barcelona which metamorphoses from a restaurant into a full bar at midnight. Sant Pau's restaurant is cleared away in record time as the clock strikes twelve and opens out into a dancefloor. It has quickly become a hot spot in the Raval area, popular among those turned off by swanky, pretentious new bars. The focus here is on good music, strong cocktails and ensuring everyone has enough room to dance. Its unpretentious nature is the reason it's so loved.
C/ Avinyo, 26 *Barri Gòtic* 🚇 *Jaume I* *Map p.403 D4* **160**	## Siddartha *93 301 04 22* Hermann Hesse's novel of the same name is the story of a young man's journey of self-discovery and enlightenment; but the bar Siddhartha in Barri Gòtic can lead you on a journey of carnage and debauchery. Perfect for a drink or two, anything more will lead to a headache as dark as the interior itself. The drinks are ridiculously powerful but the low lit, Gothic setting of this tiny delight is a great stop. Long and very narrow tables are draped in deep red velvet, the lighting is little more than candlelight and funky, bohemian bar staff pour killer cocktails until the wee hours. Maybe buy the novel to escape from the day that follows.
C/ Angels, 8 *Raval* 🚇 *Catalunya* *Map p.402 B2* **161**	## Silenus *93 302 26 80* Another hybrid Barcelonin venue, Silenus advertises itself as a restaurant but is delightful as a cafe and bar during the day or in the early evening. Outside seating is available in a quiet backstreet, and there's an extensive wine list. Staff in this eclectic joint are extremely knowledgeable, and are always on hand to recommend a good bottle, either enjoyed alone or as an accompaniment to food. The setting is good too; beautiful stained-glass doors open to reveal a place lit delicately with handmade paper-mache light shades, and filled with lovely, dark, chunky old wooden tables.

Bars & Pubs

C/ Comtesa de
Sobradiel, 9
Barri Gòtic
🚇 *Jaume I*
Map p.403 D4 **162**

Smoll

With a tiny little doorway that opens onto an extremely small alley, Smoll is not an easy place to stumble across. Loyal locals take up the 60s pop art seating of this tiny Gothic treat and many argue it serves the best mojito in town. Everything from the ashtrays to the light fixtures is for sale (although not cheap) and the array of colours is overwhelming. Neon pinks, yellows, and greens characterise everything from the glasses to the sofas, but set against a simple white backdrop, the effect is far from gaudy. Delightful Ecuadorian bar staff pick their own tunes while mixing cocktails and will happily serve you until the early hours of the next day.

Av Catedral, 6-8
La Ribera
🚇 *Jaume I*
Map p.403 E3 **163**

Taverna del Bisbe

93 319 18 19 | www.comybe.com

You can get a good gazpacho or hot bocadillo here, but the sights are the main draw. At night, lit up and twinkly, the towering cathedral is impressive and during the day this is a good spot to enjoy a beer on the terrace and the sounds of local musicians playing for change. The menu has passable Mediterranean food, but this is also just a quiet spot to watch the crowds pass by.

Pl Verreina, 5
Gràcia
🚇 *Fontana*
Map p.393 F1 **164**

Terra

Gràcia is an area that warrants exploration. Home to the city's bohemians, it boasts some of the most delightful cafes, restaurants, wine bars and shops. Plaça de la Verreina is one of the prettier squares and located below its old, white-stucco church sits Terra. Children are permanently heard playing outside, visitors wander in after a service across the square or a walk in the nearby Jardins Mestre Balcells, and locals laze for hours on the outdoor patio seats. Although not that different to most bars in the city, Terra's very relaxed ambiance and delightful location make it stand out.

**C/ Consell
de Cent, 329**
Eixample
🚇 *Universitat*
Map p.393 E4 **165**

Txestatu

93 487 53 98

Txestatu, located in the heart of the city, is one of the most famous of Barcelona's Basque bars. Serving a huge selection of tapas and montaditos (similar to canapes), the food is unchanging but ever-popular and there are lots of txakoli (Basque wines) to choose from, as well as beer, cider and wines from other regions. The decor is very simple and very traditional and you can drink and snack at either the bar, the tables or outside on the terrace.

C/ Numancia, 179
Les Corts
🚇 *Maria Cristina*
Map p.384 A4 **166**

Up & Down

93 205 51 94

Split onto two levels, the upstairs of Up & Down usually attracts the dapper, post-theater crowd and businessmen, while the downstairs area contains the dancefloor and hosts parties for a slightly younger crowd. Technically, Up & Down is a private club, but it doesn't operate as one anymore. If you aren't dressed quite smartly, however, you can get turned away at the door. There is a cover charge, so this is an evening's destination rather than a bar to pop into for one drink, but if you eat in the upstairs restaurant you won't be expected to pay on the door. Up & Down was immensely popular in the 80s (the decor has remained unchanged) and is still considered one of the most cosmopolitan places to drink in the city.

Dress

People-watching in Barcelona is excellent for the very eclectic, bohemian and often wonderfully grungy nature of people's dress. Mohawk hair styles and tattoos reign, although there is a smarter, preppier side to the city as well. Only very smart bars and clubs will have a dress code – otherwise, wear what takes your fancy. Just remember how hot it gets in summer months. Overheating in bars and clubs is very common.

359

C/ Ferran, 38
Ciutat Vella
🚇 Jaume I
Map p.403 D4 167

Vildsvin

93 317 94 07

The sleek, fresh oyster bar in the entrance of Vildsvin gives it an air of decadence but, in truth, this is a very relaxed hangout. After battling the crowds on La Rambla, turn off onto Ferran, walk towards the light that floods down the street from Plaça Saint Jaume and turn into Vildsvin for coffee and a snack, or cocktails and oysters. As in all self-respecting Barcelona bars, you can have either at any time of day or night. The decor is modern and fresh and the cocktail menu is impressive, the atmosphere is very chilled and you'll feel very welcome to wile away hours in peace and quiet.

C/ Bonavista, 6
Gràcia
🚇 Diagonal
Map p.393 F2 168

Xampanyeria Casablanca

93 237 63 99

Xampanyeria, translated literally, means champagne bar and there are plenty of these in Barcelona. But be warned: there are many that serve cheap cava, even cheaper champagne, and charge ridiculous prices for the privilege of the hangover that inevitably cripples victims the next morning. Xampanyeria Casablanca, however, is an excellent exception to this rule and has become popular among locals and tourists for this reason. Apart from the amazing range of champagnes and cavas, delicious, fresh tapas dishes are available too. There are four types of cava that can be ordered by the glass and many more that can be quaffed by the bottle.

Ladies Nights

Ladies nights and happy hour specials are not that common in Barcelona, simply because few people in the city need any incentive to drink and have a good time. However, there are organised ladies nights for the increasingly frequent groups of (mostly British) hen weekends. Many companies will organise private entertainment and restaurant bookings. A quick internet search turns up hundreds, but two companies in particular are renowned. Check out www.lastnightoffreedom.co.uk (+44 (0)870 751 4433) or www.redsevenleisure.co.uk (+44 (0)800 970 2744).

Pubs

Other options **Bars** p.347

There are many pubs in Barcelona. Some have loutish holiday makers that may make new residents cringe a little about the country folk they have left behind, but most just offer a good dose of north European pub culture. Irish pubs are particularly prevalent, and British pubs, often owned by genuine expats, are pretty easy to find too. Carrer Ferran (map p.402 C4) is a good place to start.

Sports bars don't really exist, but pubs take up the slack. All offer live sport on TV and will typically show British football, Gaelic games, and international cricket and rugby. Fans of American sports may struggle to see a game, but southern hemisphere rugby fans can normally catch big tri-nations and super league games.

Foreign tipples will cost more than they do in your local, but there is usually a good choice of north European, American and Antipodean beer and lager. Most pubs look just as they might in their home country and don't attract a large Catalan crowd. Some bar staff may even look a little confused if you try to order in Spanish.

Moll de Mestral, 40
Vila Olímpica
🚇 Ciutadella/Vila
Olímpica
Map p.411 E3 169

Australian's Tavern

93 221 11 77

While many may argue that Australian's Tavern is a vestibule of all things gimmicky, it does guarantee a simple, fun night out. Replete with a giant, plastic great white shark, and a few plastic kangaroos and crocs, it is a temple to all things Aussie, and while it may not be for everyone, it serves both Australian and international beers, which can be sipped on the covered terrace in the hot summer months.

Flann O'Brien

C/ Casanova, 24
Eixample
🚇 *Fontana*
Map p.393 D1 **170**

93 201 16 06
A very popular Irish bar among the settled expat population of Barcelona, Flann O'Brien is the perfect destination for Celts needing a taste of home. Classic Irish whiskeys and beers are available and, no matter what sporting event you want to watch, you'll find it beaming down from one of the television screens. This isn't a bar seeking to replicate an authentic Irish brew house, it simply offers a familiar haven to the British and Irish residents of Barcelona looking for familiar banter over a pint of Guinness.

The George and Dragon

C/ Diputacio, 269
Eixample
🚇 *Passeig de Gràcia*
Map p.393 E4 **171**

93 488 17 65 | www.georgeanddragon-bcn.com
One of the larger English pubs in Barcelona, the George and Dragon is on a corner of Passeig de Gràcia, and a firm favourite among British tourists and expats. If you've a hankering for toad-in-the-hole or a decent Sunday roast, the George and Dragon offers a food menu that would give any pub on English soil a serious run for its money. Beers on tap include Guinness, Boddingtons and Bass and all British live sporting events are broadcast on multiple screens, including games from the English Premiership.

P. Flaherty's Irish Pub

Pl Joaquim Xirau
Barri Gòtic
🚇 *Drassanes*
Map p.408 C1 **172**

93 412 62 63 | www.pflaherty.com
One of several P. Flaherty pubs in Spain (the others being in Serville, Zaragoza and Sotogrande), the Barcelona brewery is the newest; its doors swung open in 2001. The large menu includes Irish classics like stew, chicken doused in Irish whiskey sauce and full breakfasts using only Irish sausages and bacon. Sports events permanently flash across the numerous television screens in the bar, and there are a plethora of draught beers available. Prices are reasonable, and the drinks flow until late into the night.

The Quiet Man

C/ Marques de
Barbera, 11
Eixample
🚇 *Liceu*
Map p.402 B4 **173**

93 412 12 19
With a 03:00 closing time at weekends, this is not a pub that stays quiet for very long. Tranquil and peaceful during the day, it can get busy and rowdy at night, as Irish beers and sprits flow freely. Celtic music floats from the surrounding sound system, the ambience is quintessential Irish jollity, and the walls are lined with the standard tacky memorabilia. Stouts, ambers and red beers are all readily available and the bar staff offer a lovely smile while serving; a rare treat after so much Catalan scowling.

Scotch Tavern and Museo del Whisky

C/ Sitges, 3
Ciutat Vella
🚇 *Catalunya*
Map p.402 C2 **174**

Heralding itself as a whisky museum, the Scotch Tavern offers the finest choice of drams in Catalonia, with over 600 different carefully chosen malt whiskys. A tiny doorway leads visitors into a dark bar that looks very serious, but usually guarantees a fun evening out. The decor is comfortable and the waitresses are extremely knowledgeable. It's proud of its Scottish heritage and loyally promotes the real beauty of Scottish whisky. Of course, beer is available if the ambiance is all you're after.

Gay & Lesbian

Gay marriage and adoption are both legal in Spain, and Barcelona residents tend to be free-thinking and liberal. The gay social scene is huge and all straight bars and clubs are very 'gay friendly'. Gay bars and clubs are also popular with straight party goers. Whether you want some serious clubbing or a drag show, there is something for everyone. The 'Gayxample' part of the Eixample area is a real hub for gay and lesbian bars and clubs, but these are dotted all over the city and growing in number every day.

C/ Josep Anselm Clave, 6
Port Vell
Drassanes
Map p.408 C1 175

Antinous

93 301 90 70 | www.antinouslibros.com

If the bar and club scene gets a little exhausting, then Antinous is a fantastic place to hang out and immerse yourself in the gay scene. Both a bookshop and a coffee shop for gay men and women, you can browse gay literature, enjoy a great cup of coffee and learn more about community events. New clubs, shows and meeting groups are advertised, so if you're fresh to the area and want to meet people, this is one to remember.

C/ Balmes, 32
Eixample
Passeig de Gràcia
Map p.393 E4 176

Arena Sala Madre

93 487 83 42 | www.arenadisco.com

Arena Sala Madre (the first in the chain to open) plays up-to-date house music to a bustling and energetic crowd. It has a dark room for those wanting some intimacy without having to head home, and wild erotic shows are on every day during the week, except Mondays when it's closed. Like the other Arena clubs, Arena Sala Madre is very popular among straight clubbers as well, with a mixed crowd.

C/ Consell de Cent, 257
Eixample
Universitat
Map p.393 D4 177

Atame

93 454 19 01

The young, camp crowd here is drawn to the classic pop and Spanish music. Sunday evenings are particularly large from 23:00 onwards, when live acts hit the stage. Drags and cabaret acts heat the place up and a risque time is had by all. Atame translates into 'tie me up' and that pretty much sets the tone. The ambience early on is extremely relaxed, but the latter part of night tends to get pretty raucous.

C/ Casanova, 30
Eixample
Universitat
Map p.393 D4 178

Cafe Miranda

93 453 52 49 | www.mirandabarcelona.com

While some argue that Cafe Miranda has become gimmicky, the first gay cabaret restaurant and bar in Barcelona still draws huge crowds. To avoid queuing, call and make reservations. Drag queens entertain with live shows, music is sensationally kitsch and the interior is like a Hans Christian Andersen tale. While weekends can be popular with British hen parties, week nights offer quality cuisine, strong drinks, and a spectacular time.

Rda Sant Pere, 19-21
Eixample
Urquinaona
Map p.403 F1 179

Cafe Ole

93 453 05 10 | www.matineegroup.com

Brought to Barcelona in 2003 from Ibiza, Cafe Ole kicked off the Sunday tradition of a 'tea dance party'. It has become a very popular weekly tradition in Barcelona, with local resident DJs J. Louis and Rafa Ariza spinning their discs till the early hours of Monday. Once inside, you'll be welcomed by hordes of young, buzzing dancers and find yourself forgetting that work beckons the next day. The general attitude is that there is simply no other place to see out the weekend.

Dietrich

93 451 77 07 | *www.dietrichcafe.com*

You'll find leather, chains, whips and drag aplenty here. Dietrich is a serious club environment with a live show on its epic stage every night. Top DJs play all the newest sounds in house, dance and R&B to get the mixed crowd on the dancefloor. While this sensational nightclub is popular among the straight community, the clientele are predominantly gay men. No matter what your taste in music, gender or cocktail, Dietrich should appeal to anyone looking for a wild night and lots of loud music.

Gay Day at Space

93 467 59 71 | *www.spacebarcelona.com*

A franchise of the world famous Space Ibiza, Space in Barcelona has an exclusive 'gay day' every Sunday when doors are open to men only. Sexist maybe, but it results in a fantastic night of uninhibited clubbing, top music and spectacular dance shows. The club itself is worth seeing. Around 1000 glasses of water are lit against one wall, and the entire place has been refurbished with bright colours. Other nights attract a mixed crowd, but are still immensely popular among the local gay community.

Metro

93 323 52 27 | *www.metrodiscobcn.com*

Metro is considered the pioneer of Barcelona's gay club scene, and its popularity has not faded since its doors first flung open. It is enormous, with two separate main areas, five bars, a video lounge and a dark room. One area plays contemporary sounds, while the other (complete with removable roof) plays more old-school anthems. Daily drag acts, pop acts and sex shows guarantee that this 100% gay club is permanently heaving. Cameras have been placed in rather surreptitious parts of the bathrooms, so be warned, but the atmosphere at Metro is generally warm and open. Thursday night, rather randomly, is Bingo night, but it's very popular and sets the tone for the vibrant, energetic weekend that is to follow.

Sweet Cafe

www.sweetcafebcn.blogspot.com

There really isn't much cafe-like about this swinging new player on the Barcelona gay scene. Open only until 03:00 it's a great pre-clubbing venue for those who want cocktails and good music. DJ Lluis' mantra is that 'anyone with an open mind is welcome', but the clientele are predominantly gay men. However, it's also a haven of local art: festivals of short films, paintings and sculptures, video installations and private readings all take place. It's easy to keep up with what is going on as they advertise themselves on flyers all over the city - just look out for their cherry logo.

Z:eltas

93 451 84 69 | *www.zeltas.net*

In the same location as Sweet Cafe, above, Z:eltas is an excellent pre-club cocktail bar. It is open to all but has a predominantly gay crowd. The interior consists of a deep, glowing orange decor, with chilled music. It will certainly get you in the mood to head on to one of the many excellent nightclubs in the city, and it's not uncommon for drags and gorgeous waiters to get up on the long bar and start the party early. Diversity is the reigning characteristic of Z:eltas and it's a great place to meet up with old friends, make new ones, or grab a few quick cocktails before the clubs open.

Nightclubs

Whether it is 14:00 on a Monday or 02:00 on a Saturday, there is always somewhere pumping out tunes, pouring strong cocktails and with its doors wide open. Live music is very popular and shows take place every night across the city, performed by both local artists and big names. Music festivals frequently take place and attract top name DJs and musicians. Late night clubs are open to all and are local in nature, with most being independents. The young residents of the city love to party and don't feel the need to travel to do so. New sounds, new people and late finishes are the order the night here.

Pg Maritim de
Barceloneta, 34
Port Olímpic
🚇 *Ciutadella/Vila*
Olímpica
Map p.410 C3 185

Baja Beach Club

93 225 91 00 | www.bajabeach.es

At 2,500sqm, Baja Beach has the largest dance space in Barcelona, including an outdoor terrace that can seat 400. Despite the presence of a restaurant, this is very much a club. Live DJs spin fabulous samba, salsa and Brazilian music between R&B classics, to fill the large dancefloor. Designed to look like a tropical beach with murals of sand, sea and surfers, the decor is Miami Beach circa 1980. Live entertainment runs throughout the night and shots are distributed without reservation.

Pg Maritim de
Barceloneta, 32
Port Olímpic
🚇 *Ciutadella/Vila*
Olímpica
Map p.410 C3 186

Carpe Diem

93 224 04 70 | www.cdlcbarcelona.com

In terms of pricing and fashion consciousness, Carpe Diem gives the clubs of New York, London and Paris a run for their money. It has great DJs, luxurious interiors and highly trained mixologists. It's a place that has to be seen to be believed. From the outside it looks like two giant tents, but the inside is utterly lavish. Before midnight it's a wonderful place to wine and dine, after midnight it pumps until dawn, and draws the rich and famous. With its sea-front views, Carpe Diem is a place to try at least once.

Pl Reial, 13
Ciutat Vella
🚇 *Liceu*
Map p.402 C4 187

Club 13

93 317 23 52 | www.club13bcn.com

Club 13 offers a more chic evening than some of the larger house clubs. Part wine bar, part club, this underground den of debauchery has an upstairs restaurant that offers excellent food and views across Plaça Reial. Downstairs, Club 13 is a series of small, intimate seating areas surrounding a large dancefloor and elegant bar. The red velvet and black leather seating can be booked in advance. Club 13 is great for those wanting the music and late nights without the long queues, cover charges and teenagers.

C/ Nou de la
Rambla, 113
Raval
🚇 *Paral·lel*
Map p.401 F4 188

Club Apolo/Nitsaclub

93 301 00 90 | www.sala-apolo.com

This is essentially two different events in one venue. Club Apolo is an old converted ballroom that has remained popular through changing ownerships, and can hold 1,000 people. During the week, it hosts live concerts, shows and visual events. On Fridays and Saturdays, it becomes Nitsaclub, a hardcore marathon of techno, electronica and house that attracts a young and dedicated clan of dancers. The serious crowds (and queues) start at 04:00. A large dancefloor encircles a stage, which is reminiscent of the original ballroom format. Three bars ensure easily accessible drinks.

C/ Ramon Trias
Fargas, 24
Port Olímpic
🚇 *Ciutadella/Vila*
Olímpica
Map p.411 D1 189

Club Catwalk

93 221 61 61 | www.clubcatwalk.net

When DJs fly from as far away as New York to play a venue, it should be a winner. This is a clubber's paradise, but not as intense as some other venues. There are gorgeous white, canopy couches to offer respite when it all gets a bit much. Split over two levels, one dancefloor is dedicated to dance tunes, while the other blends

R&B with hip-hop. Club Catwalk has a tinge of Miami glitz to it, but with few traces of pretentiousness.

Club Zac

Av Diagonal, 477
Eixample
Fontana
Map p.392 C1 190

93 319 17 89 | www.masimas.com

Owned by the genius behind Moog, Club Zac is a welcome alternative to the repetitive trend of dance and techno music. Offering up funk, soul, jazz, Motown and even flamenco, live shows reign until 02:00, after which, the dancefloor opens and the all-night clubbing begins. Some dance tracks slip into the line up so a slightly younger crowd has started to attend, but overall, it's a welcome break from dance clubs and with its elegant, winding bar around the curved walls, it's also a good spot for an after-dinner mojito. Until 2006, Club Zac was home to La Boite.

Jamboree

Pl Reial, 17
Ciutat Vella
Liceu
Map p.402 C4 191

93 319 17 89 | www.masimas.com

While Jamboree had its heyday in the 60s, it's still an immensely popular jazz and blues club. It seems like two different venues under one roof; the upstairs dancefloor is a magnet for young R&B and hip-hop fans, while a narrow, dark staircase leads into the original live act area, still used today by jazz and blues artists. Brick archways, low lighting and wooden benches give a suitably historic feel. There's no charge before 01:00, and afterwards it'll only cost a few euros to enter.

La Paloma

C/ Tigre, 27
Eixample
Universitat
Map p.402 A1 192

93 301 68 97 | www.lapaloma-bcn.com

A veritable institution, La Paloma must be seen to be believed. This ornate old ballroom caters to everyone. Closed from Monday to Wednesday, Thursday nights kick off the weekend with a live band for a mixed and largely middle-aged crowd. The atmosphere is buzzing and the music contagious, yet the place transforms at about 02:00 when the slightly younger crew arrive for the mix of funk and Latino music. Plush red sofas fill cubby holes for those seeking privacy, but the vibrancy of the crowd is contagious. Break-dancing shows begin at about 03:00 on Friday nights and the party continues until 05:00. With its very ornate setting, mixed crowd and wacky mix of music (you'll even hear cha cha) La Paloma is a truly one-off experience.

Macarena

C/ Nou de Sant
Francesc, 5
Ciutat Vella
Drassanes
Map p.408 C1 193

93 302 45 93 | www.macarenaclub.com

Forget the cheesy dance fad of the early noughties. This is a club for those that want to push the weekend on until 05:00 on a Monday morning. Crowds head here for the mixed sounds of techno and house, but be warned; bouncers respect the locals and refuse entry to those making noise outside. Reggae and hip-hop are big on weekend nights but Monday is the most popular evening to attend. The dancefloor isn't large, but strong cocktails, excellent tunes and a loyal fan base make it something of an institution.

Moog

C/ Arc del Teatre, 3
Port Vell
Liceu
Map p.402 B4 194

93 301 49 91 | www.masimas.com

While a 05:00 finish is unfashionably early to many committed clubbers, Moog still has an incredibly loyal following. Open every night of the week, and staunchly committed to offering the best sounds in techno and house, Moog is extremely popular. International DJs play on most Wednesday nights, but the owners stay loyal to local talent too, allowing Catalan DJs to regularly showcase their abilities. The dancefloor can get a little squeezed, especially on weekends, but the 70s dance lounge upstairs offers space to breathe and relax.

Moll de la Fusta, 4
Port Vell
🚇 *Drassanes*
Map p.408 C1 **195**

Octopussy

93 221 40 31

Clubbing is always more fun when you're doing it with a waterfront view. This is why Octopussy is currently one of the hippest clubs in Barcelona. Its outdoor terrace remains popular whatever the season due to the glass cover and central heating in the cooler months. The music is spot on, the atmosphere is electric and, although only open until 03:00 (obscenely early to most Catalans), it's a great clubbing experience. Unlike most other clubs there is no cover charge, but there is a smarter dress code; jacket and tie aren't necessary, but swimming trunks are out.

C/ Rosselló, 265
Eixample
🚇 *Diagonal*
Map p.393 E2 **196**

Omm Session

93 445 40 00 | *www.hotelomm.es*

Attached to the new and uber modern Hotel Omm is Omm Session. It's good for a post-dinner cocktail before the crowds arrive, or as a spot for some all-night dancing. The sleek furnishings, infectious tunes, resident DJs and well crafted cocktails bring people back. If you're not afraid to get there unfashionably early, you're more likely to get one of the sofas that align the edges of this small, one room club. It's a place that attracts a lot of the young and gorgeous upper class, but it's unpretentious and promises a knockout drink.

C/ Lincoln, 15
Gràcia
🚇 *Fontana*
Map p.393 E1 **197**

Otto Zutz

93 238 07 22 | *www.grupo-ottozutz.com*

Fabulously popular in the 80s, Otto Zutz still attracts a local and loyal crowd. It has eight different bars spread over three floors. The first floor pumps out loud, heavy house. The second is all funk and hip-hop, while the third plays soul. Wednesday nights are hugely popular, as banquet-style feasts are served up before live music shows (you need to book in advance), while Thursday nights see organised parties and entertainment provided by DJs from around the country. Occasional live jazz concerts occur and are always a sell out, but any night guarantees great tunes and cocktails.

Av Tibidabo, 61
Tibidabo

Partycular

93 211 62 61

This club, which enforces a dress code, is hidden behind an unmarked doorway on the hills of the Tibidabo Mountain. But don't let any of this put you off. Donning a smart pair of shoes and shedding your favourite T-shirt is well worth it. Partycular is home to the elite of Barcelona. It welcomes all however, serves up a killer cocktail, offers breathtaking views across the city, and is set in a majestic old mansion. There's a large dancefloor and intimate little corners dotted around. It's a rare treat if you fancy some quality music, good drinks and a spacious environment with views.

C/ Almogavers, 122
Poblenou
🚇 *Bogatell*
Map p.405 F3 **199**

Razzmatazz

93 320 82 00 | *www.salarazzmatazz.com*

This is not a club for the fainthearted. If you are after hardcore sounds and a seriously late night then this is the place for you. Away from the more cramped quarters of the city, in the direction of Port Olímpic, a small entrance fee gives access to five rooms. The Loft and Lolita serve up electronica and dance while Pop bar offers the latest in pop and disco. Temple is for the more gothic clientele but, wherever you plant yourself, you'll be served music by top DJs. The music is loud and the crowd is always heaving but for those seeking a real adrenaline rush, Razzmatazz should please.

Parties at Home

Mi Casa es Su Casa
If you'd prefer to do the
cooking yourself, the
fresh food market La
Boqueria (p.310) is a
good place to start.
And for cooking
lessons, turn to p.208.

Dinner parties and cocktails at home are very popular, often preempting a night on the town. Food, music and flowing wine at home are common on Sundays for lunch, when markets and restaurants are usually closed.

While the Spanish pride themselves on doing everything personally, help is readily available, from catering and music to decorations. Whether you're looking for salsa dancers, tapas caterers or wine glasses to hire, many companies exist to take the hard work out of a party and they're relatively inexpensive. While it's common to don a feather boa and dress up for a club night, parties at home are rarely themed, unless they involve a group of people enjoying supper before heading out. Dinner parties start late and end late, however, so they're not always a quiet alternative to a large night out.

Parties at Home

Adhoc	93 487 17 14	Party venues, catering and flowers
Citron Productions	97 769 02 48	Flamenco dancers and live music
Parties and Dinners	657 939 256	Catalan food by Catalan chefs
Parties Catering	93 266 47 95	Catered food for parties at home
Totalismo Events	95 841 90 66	Parties anywhere in the country

Party Organisers

Other options **Party Accessories** p.299

Party organisers are abundant, catering for the most intimate of dinners and the largest of weddings. Simply do a search on the internet and thousands pop up. We have listed a few here that we found to

Party Organisers

Actor's Gallery	93 268 76 00	www.actorsgallery.com
Adhoc	93 487 17 14	www.adhocevents.com
D'Elite Spain Wedding	93 254 67 50	www.spain-wedding.com
Fersa	95 351 11 10	na
Fox Events BCN	639 030 701	na

be particularly professional, good value for money and well connected. In a country where *manana* is a common response to the simplest of requests, hiring a company to handle the hard work is definitely worthwhile.

Caterers

Most Catalans argue that their food is on a par with France and Italy and, whether you agree or not, they throw their heart and soul into what they're doing. Catering is big business in Barcelona, so you can easily get a firm to help. Mediterranean, Catalan and traditional Spanish cuisine are the most commonly catered foods, and prices can vary massively. Private caterers tend to be more costly than restaurants that deliver

Caterers

Azulius	93 237 31 86
Catering Matas Arnalot	93 894 03 20
Dinner Party Solutions	654 585 929
Food & Mambo	90 210 29 66
Imperium Events	93 455 89 08
Kat's Kitchen	687 818 318
Miracle	93 759 03 46
Parties and Dinners	657 939 256
Parties Catering	93 266 47 95
Prats Fatjo	93 263 45 24

to your home. As with other services, it's normally worth getting three quotes before making a decision.

367

Cabaret & Strip Shows

The cabaret scene in Barcelona is epic. It is a city that's unapologetically flamboyant and encourages even the meekest of folk to let their hair down. There are some amazing, quality acts to be found. There are, of course, a lot of seedy versions too. The infamous Cafe Miranda is a gay cabaret restaurant that has hordes of loyal followers (see p.362) but there are a lot of straight cabarets too. Bars and clubs dotted throughout the city's dark little streets can offer some seriously good clean fun, or outrageously camp filth, depending on what you're after. Strip joints often advertise themselves as having cabaret acts, but offer little more than naked grinding on a stage.

Av Paral·lel, 60
Raval
🚇 *Paral·lel*
Map p.401 F4 **200**

Arnau

93 441 48 81

Arnau had its heyday back in the 70s, but it's still considered an institution among cabaret lovers. The glittering red sign and the black and white images of Fred Astaire make it feel like a Broadway venue. But despite its endearingly dusty exterior, the acts at Arnau have kept up with the times. It's a mixture of Catalan tradition with lots of glitter and buckets of melodrama. From Wednesday to Sunday, two acts hit the stage at 22:00 and midnight. Get there early for a seat.

C/ Riereta, 7
Raval
🚇 *Paral·lel*
Map p.402 A3 **201**

Cafe Concert Llantiol

93 329 90 09 | www.comedyinspain.com

As well as offering top cabaret, Cafe Concert Llantiol also serves up magic, mime, live music, dance and clown shows. It's a haven of all things theatrical, and a very popular venue for big shows and fund raisers. Its in-house cabaret performances have been going for years and are considered to be of the very highest quality.

C/ Sant Pau, 58
Raval
🚇 *Liceu*
Map p.402 A4 **202**

Conservas

93 302 06 30

Conservas is hugely popular for cabaret but also hosts a fair amount of fringe theater, with monthly music and experimental poetry readings as well. It's more underground and artistic than the music hall venues listed here but that only adds to the vibe of dark glamour and certainly doesn't lessen the quality of the performances.

C/ Montserrat, 9
Ciutat Vella
🚇 *Drassanes*
Map p.408 B1 **203**

El Congrejo

93 301 29 78

As well as offering cabaret performances throughout the week, El Congrejo has a mixed crowd of loyal fans because of its transvestite shows on Friday and Saturday nights. Located not far from Port Vell, El Congrejo is a popular spot. Although entry for shows is free, you'll pay a higher than normal rate for a cocktail. Even if drag shows aren't your thing, the performances have to be seen to be believed, and the atmosphere created by the rowdy crowd ensures a very lively night.

Casinos

Many bars host their own poker nights in quiet back rooms, but there is a proper casino in Port Olímpic, known as Gran Casino de Barcelona. It is the largest in Spain and one of only 33 legal gambling facilities in the entire country. Spread over 33,000 square feet, with four restaurants, 206 machines and 54 tables, it is next to the Hotel Arts. Gambling is not legal in any other form in Spain, so you won't easily find details on poker nights or blackjack tables in bars. Dress codes are strict, the legal gambling age of 18 is enforced, and either a passport or photographic driving licence will be required upon entry, no matter how legal you might look.

C/ de la Marina, 19
Port Olímpic
🎫 Ciutadella/
Vila Olímpica
Map p.411 D3 204

Gran Casino de Barcelona
93 225 78 78 | www.casino-barcelona.com

The Gran Casino de Barcelona should please anyone looking for a flutter on the Blackjack table, a few whirls on the slot machines or dinner in glistening surroundings. Tables offer everything from American and French roulette to slot machines. Besides the gambling and fine restaurants, there is a fantastic bar, waterfront views, open air cabaret and a disco. Regular gaming tournaments are also held. Torn jeans, tracksuits, and swimwear are not allowed. The dress code is strict and you'll have to pay €4.50 as an entrance charge.

Cinemas

Barcelona doesn't have a huge number of cinemas, but there are some excellent little independent movie houses that specialise in low-budget local productions, and independent works from the rest of Spain. Film festivals are very common, the largest being the Gay and Lesbian film festival in October, held at the Mercats de la Flors, and L'Alternativa, the annual independent film festival of Barcelona, held every November (see annual event listings in General Information, p.40, for more on these).

Otherwise, *cinaplexes* are often found in shopping centres and always offer English-speaking films. Non-Spanish films are rarely dubbed, and are instead played in their original language, with Spanish subtitles. There isn't much of a selection of foreign films beyond British or American releases. Release dates are around the same time as in other countries and prices are reasonable, ranging from €4 - €9, depending on viewing time and location.

Finding details on films is frustrating, as few places have websites and recorded timings are, unbelievably, often wrong. You're better off going to the cinema and finding out the time, so you can plan your evening accordingly.

Cinemas

Alexis	Eixample	93 210 50 50	www.cinesa.es
Cines Icaria-Yelmo	Port Olímpic	93 221 75 85	www.yelmocineplex.com
Filmoteca de la Generalitat	Les Corts	93 410 75 90	www.cultura.gencat.net/filmo
Imax	Port Vell	93 268 33 00	www.imaxintegral.com
Renoir-Les Corts	Les Corts	93 490 55 10	www.cinesrenoir.com
Verdi	Gràcia	93 237 05 16	www.cines-verdi.com

Comedy

The English-speaking comedy scene was, until recently, almost non-existent. It's still not booming, but two new venues have opened up, attracting UK and Ireland based stand-ups. These shows often also include north American and Antipodean talents. The best known is the Giggling Guiri Comedy club in Raval. Performing monthly in both Madrid and Barcelona, some big acts have been frequenting the Catalan capital recently. Located in the Teatro Llantiol, names such as Danny Bhoy, Russell Kane and the New Zealander Al Pitcher have had the expat crowds roaring.

Another venue worth checking out is the Guinness Laughter Lounge on La Rambla, which has started its own annual stand-up festival. It may not be big on quantity, but the large number of fans are testimony to its quality.

Comedy

The Giggling Giuri Comedy Club ▶ p.315	C/ Riereta, 7	93 329 90 09	www.comedyinspain.com
The Guinness Laughter Lounge	C/ Reina Amalia	93 442 98 44	www.gloungebcn.com

369

Concerts

Live music is big in Barcelona, and some of the biggest names in music play the city's large stadiums and auditoriums. The Rolling Stones, Beyonce, and The Police have all played Barcelona in 2007, at impressive venues like the Olympic Stadium, L'Auditori, Palau de la Musica and Gran Teatre del Liceu. Whether it's jazz and blues, techno and pop or classical music you want, you'll find it almost every night of the year.

Aside from the large venues listed below, hundreds of bars host live music nights and there are a number of music festivals. Summercase is an annual event in July, with upcoming acts including Lily Allen, Scissor Sisters and The Chemical Brothers. Sonar Music Festival in June takes place in clubs across the city and is a pretty hardcore, three-day dance, techno and house music festival. See Annual Events, p.40, for more on these.

La Rambla, 51-59
Ciutat Vella
🚇 *Liceu*
Map p.402 C4 **205**

Gran Teatre del Liceu
93 485 99 98 | www.liceubarcelona.com

Located on La Rambla, and stunning in all its 1840s glory, the Gran Teatre del Liceu is a premier spot for live music. Dominated by classical and opera sounds, it hosts these acts throughout the year, as well as dance shows. Split into two areas, the Liceu has both an auditorium and a main stage. After surviving two fires and a bombing over the past century, it remains both a top musical arena and an architectural must-see.

C/ Lepant, 150
Eixample
🚇 *Glòries*
Map p.405 E1 **209**

l'Auditori
93 247 93 00 | www.auditori.com

L'Auditori has been open since 1999 and is now one of the cultural epicenters of Barcelona, l'Auditori is home to the city's symphony orchestra. It has a modern symphonic room that hosts big names such as Bertrand Chamayou, Orlando Furioso and Ivo Pogorelich as part of the Barcelona International Piano festival. As a mark of its popularity as a venue, there are already 10,000 residents who subscribe to the seasonal shows each year.

l'Auditori

Teatre Lliure

Pg Olímpic ◀
Montjuïc
🚇**Hostafrancs**
Map p.399 F2 207

Olympic Stadium

93 426 20 89 | www.bsmsa.es

A redesign of an original 1929 building on the same site, the Olympic stadium was revamped in 1992 for the games. It is a building of epic proportions that has a capacity for up to 77,000 people, hosting both athletic and social events. Musical shows are played by top artists, but it's also impressive to just wander around, with free entry when there are no events on. Its state-of-the-art infrastructure and top quality sound system make it a first class concert venue. Tickets are available through a variety of websites and agencies, one of the best being www.coasttocoasttickets.com.

C/ Sant Francesc de Paula, 2
Barri Gòtic
🚇**Barceloneta**
Map p.409 F1 208

Palau de la Musica

93 295 72 00 | www.home.palaumusica.org

The Palau de la Musica is a wonderful venue and is worth a visit for its interior alone. Whether it's Christmas carols from the Mississippi Gospel Choir or a performance of a Beethoven symphony, the stained glass central dome, gilt seats and ornate window trimmings give a spectacular view. Constructed between 1905 and 1908 by Spanish Modernist architect Lluis Domenech, it is one of the main architectural features of the city. In 1997, it was tagged as a World Heritage Site by UNESCO.

Fashion Shows

With so many independent clothes and jewellery designers, showcases occur on a regular basis. There are, however, two events each year that really put the city on the map internationally. Barcelona is home to Bread and Butter (www.breadandbutter.com), a large display of individual exhibits every July. Designers from across Europe, are given several days to show off their wares to buyers and fashion writers from around the world. Similarly, the Barcelona International Jewellery Fair, also at the city's International Convention and Exhibition Center, displays jewellery designers from as far away as Asia, every November.

Theatre

Other options **Drama Groups** p.213

The people of Barcelona are not shy about venting their inner thespian, as evidenced by the extravagant street performers found on La Rambla. As with other arts in this most creative of cities, the theatre is respected and encouraged.
There are few English-language plays performed in Barcelona but theaters are often architecturally spectacular, and watching plays in Spanish is an excellent way of polishing up on your communication skills. The Teatre Lliure in Sants Montjuïc is renowned for its fringe productions, while the Teatre Tivoli and Teatre Poliorama on La Rambla are centrally located and visually stunning. For music, dance and dramatic art, the Teatre Nacional de Catalunya is known across Spain and attracts some big names in dramatic and performance arts. The Grec Festival (p.42), which takes place in Barcelona every summer, is dedicated to theatre, art and music and usually has some wonderful performances by actors from around the world in plays both old and new. The Liceu is listed on the facing page.

Theatre

Teatre Lliure	Pl Margarida Xirgú, 1	Sants-Montjuïc	93 289 27 70	www.teatrelliure.com
Teatre Nacional de Catalunya	Pl Arts, 1	Eixample	93 306 57 00	www.tnc.es
Teatre Poliorama	La Rambla, 115	Ciutat Vella	93 317 75 99	na
Teatre Tivoli	C/ Casp, 8-10	Eixample	93 412 20 63	www.serviticket.com

DIGITALGLOBE™

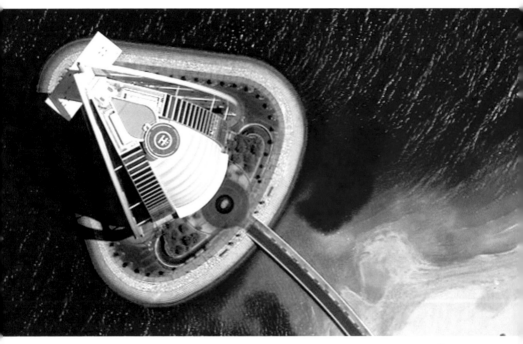

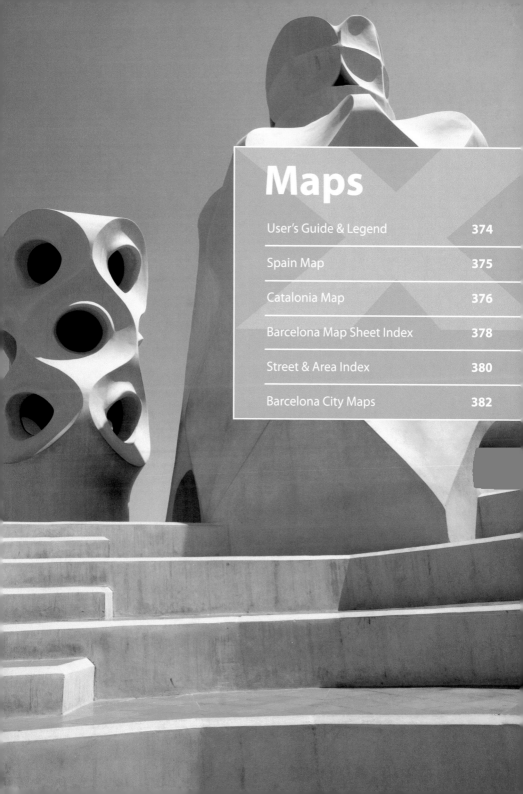

Maps

Maps

User's Guide

This section is intended to help you get your bearings when you first arrive in Barcelona, and give a clear idea about all the areas outlined in the guide. Provided is an overview of Spain, a map of Catalonia, a map index and detailed street maps of both central and outer Barcelona. Central areas are blown up to a scale of 1:6,000 (so, 1cm = 60m) and include hotels, places of education, shopping centres, heritages sites, beaches and parks. Outlying areas are shown on a scale of 1:12,000 (so, 1cm = 120m) and show the same type of information. The map legend below illustrates what the different colours and symbols mean.

You may have noticed that some of the places we mention in the guide have map references, like this: *Map p.000 A1* 10. The page number (*p.000*) refers to the page that the map is on. The grid reference (*A1*) goes horizontally, then vertically, and the annotation 10 shows exactly where to go.

Our annotations are in six different colours, which identify the chapter each item is from. Green annotations are hotels from the General Information chapter, red annotations are bars, cafes, restaurants and other spots from the Going Out chapter. The central margin on each map page gives a full key. And, to help you work out how to get to these places, we've included a metro map on the inside back cover of the book.

More Maps
Beyond these pages
and our very own
Barcelona Mini Map
(see right for details)
there are a number of
other useful resources.
One of the most
common maps available
is the orange, A5 sized
Michelin Barcelona.
You'll see it at any
news stand.

Need More?

We understand that this residents' guide is a pretty big book. With this in mind, we've created the *Barcelona Mini Map* as a more manageable alternative. This packs the whole city into your pocket and once unfolded is an excellent navigational tool. It's part of a series of Mini Maps that includes London, Dubai, Sydney and New York. Visit our website, www.explorerpublishing.com for details of how to pick up these little gems.

Map Legend

Online Maps

There are a few websites which have concise and searchable maps of Barcelona. The most obvious example is Google maps (http://maps.google.com) which gives detailed street directories of almost anywhere you could want. A very up to date and useful option is Barcelona's own city hall website (www.bcn.es/guia/welcome.htm) and www.euroave.com. Try Google Earth (downloaded from http://earth.google.com) if you want to see a satellite image of what you are looking for.

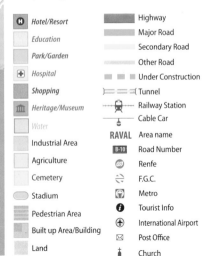

Ⓗ Hotel/Resort		Highway
Education		Major Road
Park/Garden		Secondary Road
✚ Hospital		Other Road
Shopping		Under Construction
🏛 Heritage/Museum		Tunnel
Water		Railway Station
Industrial Area		Cable Car
Agriculture	RAVAL	Area name
Cemetery	B-10	Road Number
Stadium	Ⓡ	Renfe
Pedestrian Area		F.G.C.
Built up Area/Building		Metro
Land	❶	Tourist Info
	✈	International Airport
	✉	Post Office
	♀	Church

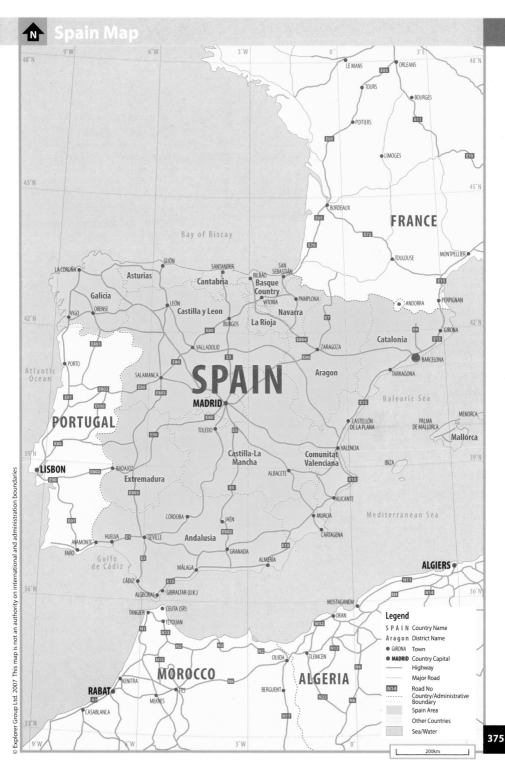

FRANCE

LE MANS • ORLEANS
TOURS •
POITIERS •
LIMOGES •
BORDEAUX •
MONTPELLIER •
TOULOUSE •
ANDORRA •
PERPIGNAN •

Bay of Biscay

LA CORUÑA •
GIJÓN • SANTANDER SAN SEBASTIÁN
BILBAO •
Asturias **Cantabria** **Basque Country**
VITORIA • PAMPLONA •
Galicia
ORENSE • LEÓN • **Navarra**
VIGO •
Castilla y Leon **La Rioja** GIRONA •
BURGOS • ZARAGOZA • **Catalonia**
VALLADOLID • BARCELONA •
SPAIN **Aragon** TARRAGONA •
SALAMANCA •
PORTUGAL Balearic Sea
PORTO • **MADRID**
Atlantic Ocean MENORCA
TOLEDO • CASTELLÓN DE LA PLANA PALMA DE MALLORCA
BADAJOZ • VALENCIA • **Mallorca**
LISBON **Castilla-La Mancha** **Comunitat Valenciana**
Extremadura ALBACETE • IBIZA •
ALICANTE •
CÓRDOBA • Mediterranean Sea
JAÉN • MURCIA •
HUELVA • CARTAGENA •
AVAMONTE • SEVILLE • **Andalusia**
FARO • GRANADA • ALMERÍA •
Gulfo de Cádiz MÁLAGA •
CÁDIZ • **ALGIERS** •
ALGECIRAS • GIBRALTAR (U.K.)
TANGIER • CEUTA (SP.) MOSTAGANEM •
TÉTOUAN • ORAN •

MOROCCO OUJDA • TLEMCEN •
KENITRA • **ALGERIA**
RABAT • FES • BERGUENT •
CASABLANCA MEKNES

Legend

S P A I N Country Name
A r a g o n District Name
● GIRONA Town
● **MADRID** Country Capital
—— Highway
—— Major Road
N14 Road No
····· Country/Administrative Boundary
 Spain Area
 Other Countries
 Sea/Water

200km

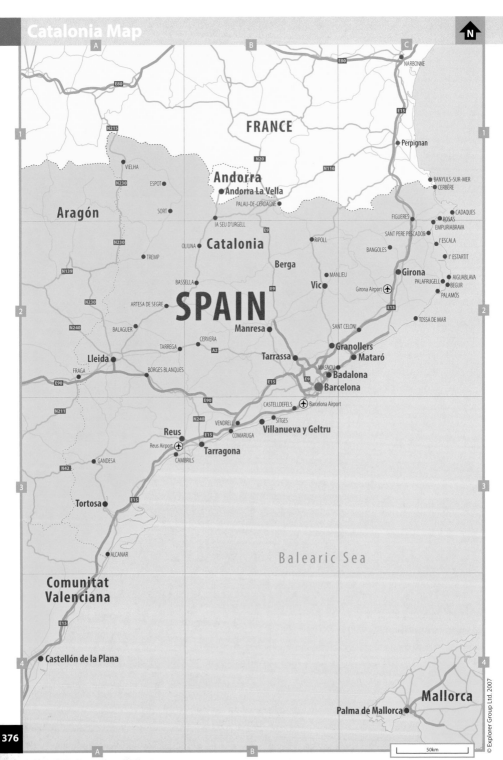

© Explorer Group Ltd. 2007

Barcelona Explorer 1st Edition

Babywear p.98
Bank Loans p.22

Written by residents, the London Explorer
is packed with insider info, from arriving
in the city to making it your home and
everything in between.

London Explorer Residents' Guide
We Know Where You Live

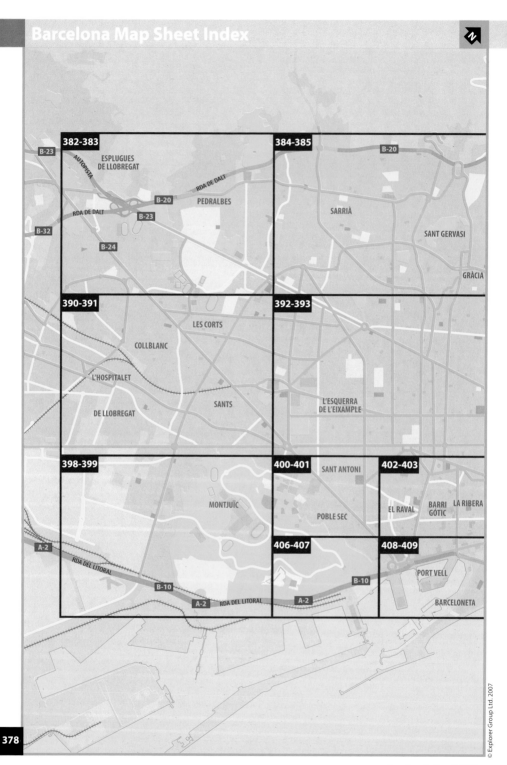

382-383

B-23

AUTOPISTA

ESPLUGUES
DE LLOBREGAT

RDA DE DALT

B-20

PEDRALBES

RDA DE DALT

B-23

B-32

B-24

384-385

B-20

SARRIÀ

SANT GERVASI

GRÀCIA

390-391

LES CORTS

COLLBLANC

L'HOSPITALET

SANTS

DE LLOBREGAT

392-393

L'ESQUERRA
DE L'EIXAMPLE

398-399

MONTJUÏC

A-2

RDA DEL LITORAL

B-10

A-2   RDA DEL LITORAL

400-401

SANT ANTONI

POBLE SEC

402-403

EL RAVAL

BARRI
GÒTIC

LA RIBERA

406-407

B-10

A-2

408-409

PORT VELL

BARCELONETA

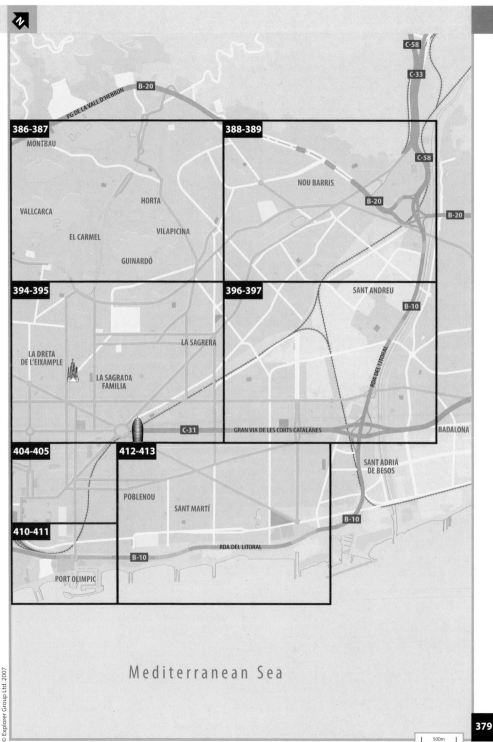

Main Streets	Map Ref
Rda del Guinardó	395 D1
Rda del Litoral	397 E3
Rla de Guipúscoa	395 F3
Rla de Prim	396 C4
Rla del Brasil	391 E2
Rla del Poblenou	412 B3
Travessera de Dalt	386 A4
Travessera de Gràcia	393 D1
Travessera de Les Corts	392 A1
Túnel de la Rovira	386 C3
Via Augusta	393 E1

Main Areas	Map Ref
Barceloneta	409 F3
Barri Gòtic	403 D3
Born	403 E4
Clot	395 E3
Eixample	392 C4
Gràcia	385 F4
Horta	387 E3
L'Hospitalet de Llobregat	390 A3
La Ribera	403 E3
La Sagrera	395 F2
Les Corts	383 E4
Montjuïc	399 E2
Nou Barris	389 D1
Parc de la Ciutadella	404 B4
Pedralbes	383 E2
Poble Sec	401 D3
Poblenou	412 B2
Port Olímpic	411 E3
Port Vell	408 C2
Raval	402 B3
Sant Andreu	397 D1
Sant Antoni	401 D1
Sant Gervasi	385 E3
Sant Martí	412 C1
Sants	391 E3
Sarrià	384 A1

Main Plaças	Map Ref
Plaça de Catalunya	403 D1
Plaça de Francesc Macià	392 C1
Plaça de la Reina Maria Cristina	383 F4
Plaça de la Universitat	393 D4
Plaça de l'Angel	403 E4
Plaça de les Glòries Catalanes	395 D4
Plaça de Sant Jaume	403 D4
Plaça de Tetuan	394 A4
Plaça del Pi	402 C3
Plaça d'Espanya	392 A4
Plaça d'Urquinaona	403 E1
Plaça Nova	403 D3

Main Stations	
Arc de Triomf	404 A2
Barceloneta	409 F2
Canyelles	388 A1
Catalunya	403 D1
Ciutadella / Vila Olímpica	411 D2
Clot	395 E3
Collblanc	391 D1
Diagonal	393 E2
Drassanes	408 B1
Espanya	392 A4
Fabra i Puig	388 A4
Fontana	393 F1
Girona	394 A4
Glòries	395 D4
Horta	387 E2
Hospital de Sant Pau	394 C2
Jaume I	403 E3
Lesseps	385 F4
Liceu	402 C3
Maragall	387 F4
Marina	405 D2
Paral·lel	401 F4
Passeig de Gràcia	393 E4
Plaça de Sants	391 E3
Poble Sec	401 D2
Poblenou	412 C2
Sagrada Família	394 B3
Sant Andreu	388 C4
Sant Antoni	401 F1
Sants Estació	392 A3
Tarragona	392 A3
Trinitat Nova	389 D1
Trinitat Vella	389 E4
Universitat	392 D4
Urquinaona	403 E1
Zona Universitària	383 D3

Plaça de la
Constitució

D'AUGUST FONT I CARRERAS

AV DE JACINT ESTEVA FONTANET

AV DE LLUÍS COMPANYS

C/ DA LA VIA AUGUSTA

AUTOPISTA

C/ JULI CULEBRAS I BARBA

C/ DE L'ESGLÉSIA

C/ DA LA VIA AUGUSTA

B-23

St. Magdalena

C/ MANUEL FLORENTIN PEREZ

Plaça de
Doña Carolina

C/ DEL DOCTOR POUPLANA

C/ D'ANEL LES MISTRES

C/ DELS LLEONS

C/ DE FERRER I BASSA

**ESPLUGUES
DE LLOBREGAT**

C/ DE JOAN MIRÓ

AV DE JACINT ESTEVA FONTANET

I SALA

C/ ANGUERA

Plaça de
Pau Vila

Parc de
Pompeu
i Fabra

C/ DEL PROF.
BARRAQUER

C/ DE JOAN MIRÓ

C/ DE FINESTRELLES

C/ DE SANTA ROSA

C/ DE TENERIFE

Plaça del Coll
Finestrelles

Parc Torrent
d'en Farre

C/ DELS SOMETENTS

C/ DE MELCIOR LLAVINES

C/ DE GAIETÀ FRIERA

AV DELS PAÏSOS CATALANS

C/ CASAL SANT JORDI

Hospital Sant
Joan de Déu

C/ DE SANT JOAN DE DÉU

Plaça de
la Dona

C/ DE LAUREÀ MIRÓ

DE SANT MATEU

AV DELS PAÏSOS CATALANS

AUTOPISTA

Plaça de
l'Alcade
Baró de Viver

Institut Nacional
d'Educacio
Fisica

Institut de Batxillerat
Joanot Martorell

RDA DE DALT

RDA DE DALT

C/ DEL MOLÍ

Parc de
Can Vidalet

B-24

C/ DE SANT MATEU

B-23

Parc de
Cervantes

AV DIAGONAL

186

96

115

C/ DE VIDAL I RIBAS

C/ DEL CAQUIS

C/ DE LES MAGNOLIES

Plaça de
Jacint
Benavente

Pavello del
Hospitalet
Nord

C/ D'ALBERT BASTARDAS

AV CAMÍ DE LA TORRE
MELINA

Real Club
de Tennis
Turo

Plaça Blas
Infante

C/ DE L'EUCALIPTUS

C/ VERGE DE LA MERCÈ

Plaça de la
Bóvila

Parc de
les Bobiles

AV DEL TORRENT

C/ DE GRAVINA

C/ DE FLORIDABLANCA

C/ D'AMADEU VIVES

CTA DE COLLBLANC

AV DE MANUEL AZAÑA

C/ DEL GENERAL BATET

Real Club
de Polo

Can Vidalet

C/ DE LA MINA

AV DE SEVERO OCHOA

Plaça de
l'Alzina

C/ D'ANTIGA

TOMÁS GIMÉNEZ

Plaça de
la Pubilla
Cases

C/ DELS NARANJOS

C/ DE VINARÓS

AV DEL BOSC

C/ D'EMPURIES

AV DE JOSEP MOLINS

AV DE MANUEL AZAÑA

AV DE MANUEL AZAÑA

CAMÍ DE LA XILE

C/ DE LES AMAPOLAS

Pubilla Cases

Hospital
Cruz Roja

C/ DEL PSUERGA

C/ DE LA HIERBABUENA

Plaça Mare
de Déu
del Pilar

C/ DE DR. RAMON SOLANICH

CTA DE COLLBLANC

Senator
Barcelona

Pl
d'Elvissa

AV D'ISABEL LA CATÓLICA

C/ DE LA RECLUSA

C/ DE LA PRIMAVERA

AV DE MIRAFLORS

C/ L'ESTEVE GRAU

Plaça de la
Llibertat

C/ DE LLEVANT

C/ DE FINESTRELLES

C/ DE COLLSEROLA

Cementiri
de Sants

C/ DEL CARDENAL REIG

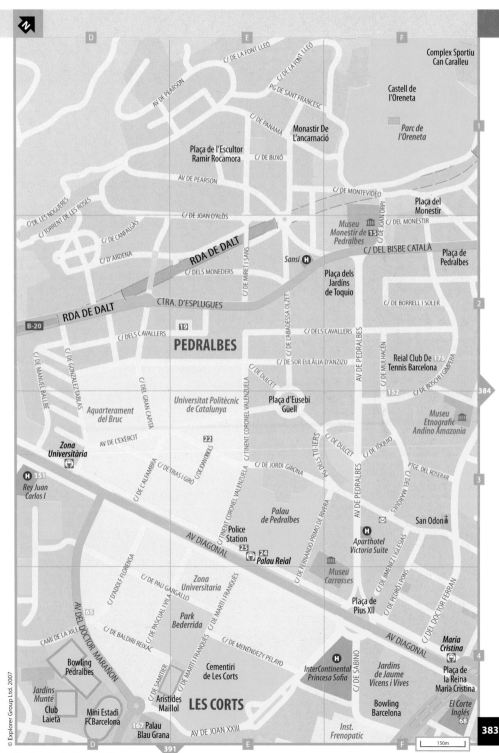

Complex Sportiu
Can Caralleu

Castell de
l'Oreneta

AV DE PEARSON

C/ DE LA FONT LLEÓ

C/ DE LA FONT LLEÓ

PG DE SANT FRANCESC

C/ DE PANAMÀ

Parc de
l'Oreneta

Monastir De
L'ancarnació

Plaça de l'Escultor
Ramir Rocamora

C/ DE BUXÓ

C/ DE MONTEVIDEO

AV DE PEARSON

Plaça del
Monestir

C/ DE JOAN ORPI

C/ DEL MONESTIR

C/ DE LES NOGUERS

C/ DE JOAN D'ALÒS

Museu
Monestir de
Pedralbes 15

Plaça de
Pedralbes

C/ TORRENT DE LES ROSES

C/ DE CANFALGAS

C/ DEL BISBE CATALÀ

C/ D'ARDENA

Sansi H

RDA DE DALT

C/ DELS MONEDERS

C/ DE MIRET I SANS

Plaça dels
Jardíns
de Toquio

C/ DE BORRELL I SOLER

B-20

RDA DE DALT

CTRA. D'ESPLUGUES

C/ DELS CAVALLERS

C/ DELS CAVALLERS

AV DE PEDRALBES

C/ DE MULHACÉN

Reial Club De 175
Tennis Barcelona

C/ DE L'ABADESSA OLZET

C/ DE MANUEL BALLBÉ

C/ DE GONZALEZ TABLAS

PEDRALBES 19

C/ DE SOR EULÀLIA D'ANZIZU

C/ DE BOSCH I GIMPERA

152

384

C/ DEL GRAN CAPITÀ

Universitat Politècnic
de Catalunya

C/ DE DULCET

Plaça d'Eusebi
Güell

Museu
Etnografic
Andino Amazonia

Aquarterament
del Bruc

AV DE L'EXÈRCIT

22

C/ TINENT CORONEL VALENZUELA

C/ DE DULCET

C/ DE TÒQUIO

PTGE. DEL ROSERAR

Zona
Universitària

C/ DE L'ALAMBRA

C/ DE TRIAS I GIRÓ

C/ DE JORDI GIRONA

PG DELS TILLERS

C/ DEL MARQ

H 151

Rey Juan
Carlos I

AV DE PEDRALBES

San Odon

Palau
de Pedralbes

AV DIAGONAL

Police
Station
25

Palau Reial
24

Aparthotel
Victoria Suite

C/ DE JIMENEZ I IGLESIAS

C/ DE PEDRO PONS

C/ DEL DOCTOR FERRAN

C/ D'ADOLF FLORENSA

C/ DE PAU GARGALLO

Zona
Universitaria

Museu
Carrosses

C/ DE FERNANDO PRIMO DE RIVERA

Park
Bederrida

C/ DE PASCUAL I VILA

C/ DE MARTÍ FRANQUÉS

Plaça de
Pius XII

AV DIAGONAL

Maria
Cristina

65

C/ DE BALDIRI REIXAC

C/ DE MENENDEZY PELAYO

Plaça de
la Reina
Maria Cristina

Bowling
Pedralbes

CAMÍ DE LA XILE

AV DEL DOCTOR MARAÑON

C/ DE SABINO

InterContinental
Princesa Sofia H

Jardíns
de Jaume
Vicens i Vives

El Corte
Inglés
68

Jardíns
Munté

C/ DE SAMITIER

Arístides
Maillol

Cementiri
de Les Corts

LES CORTS

Bowling
Barcelona

Club
Laietà

Mini Estadi
FCBarcelona

167 Palau
Blau Grana

AV DE JOAN XXIII

Inst.
Frenopatic

383

© Explorer Group Ltd. 2007

150m

391

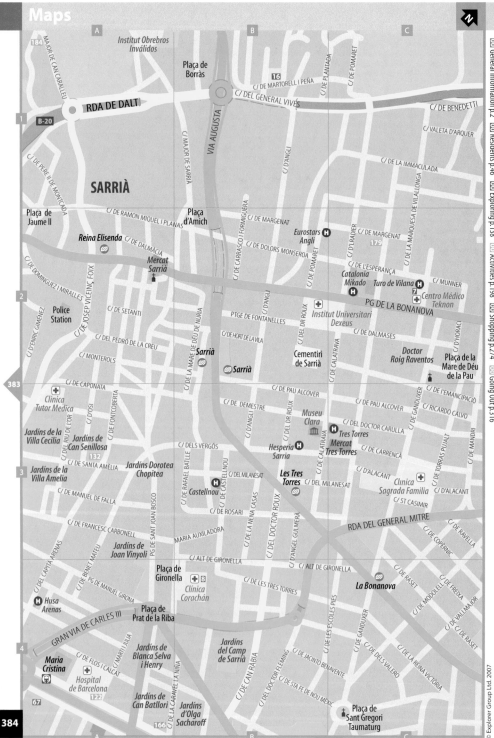

Barcelona Explorer 1st Edition

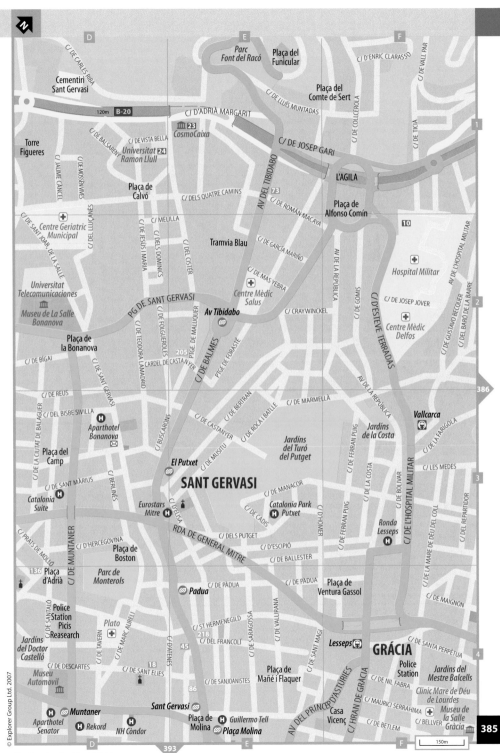

N

A **B** **C**

C/ DE JERICO

Carles
Riba

B-20

Vall d'Hebron

Mercat
Vall d'Hebron

C/ DE BASSES D'HORTA

AV DE MARTI I CODOLAR

PG DE LA VALL D'HEBRON

Plaça de la
Vall d'Hebron

C/ DE SEGUR

Tir Amb Arc

La
Taixonera

AV DE LA GRANJA VELLA

Parc Vall
d'Hebron

1

AV DE L'HOSPITAL MILITAR

C/ DE PALOU

C/ DE SAMANIEGO

C/ DE COLL I ALENTORN

La Clota

C/ DE CAPCIR

C/ DE LA PURISSIMA

C/ DE MEDIONA

94

C/ D'ARENYS DE JOSEP SANGENIS

C/ DE PLUTO

C/ DELS CORTADA

Plaça de
la Clota

C/ D'ALARCÓN

C/ DE VECIANA

C/ DE SANTA ROSALIA

C/ DE FASTENRATH

C/ DE ROSSEL

DE JOSEP SANGENIS

MONTBAU

Penitents

Plaça
d'Olèrdola

C/ DE SANT CRISPI

C/ DE SANTA ROSALIA

C/ DE SANTA ALBINA

C/ DE FARNÉS

PTGE MANLLEU

C/ DE LA MARE DE DÉU DELS ANGELS

C/ DE DANTE ALIGHIERI

C/ DE MONTORNÈS

PASSATGE DE CARDEDEU

C/ DE CARDEDEU

Parc la Creueta
del Coll

C/ DE LORDA

C/ DE MORATIN

C/ DE SIGUENZA

C/ DEL PANTÁ DE TREMP

2

C/ DE CASTELLTERÇOL

MARE DE DÉU DEL COLL

C/ DE L'HORTAL

Jardíns
Jaume
Planas
Alemany

C/ DEL LLOBREGÓS

Mercat
Carmel

C/ DE MÓRA D'EBRE

C/ FONT DEL COLL

Plaça
Grau Miró

C/ DE RAMON ROCAFULL

C/ DE LA CONCA DE TREMP

385

C/ DE RUBENS

C/ DEL TORRENT DEL REMEI

C/ FONT DEL REMEI

C/ DE TIRSO

C/ DE LA MURTRA

C/ DE LLUIS MARIA VIDAL

Plta. de
Montserrat

C/ DEL PORTELL

RAMBLA DEL CARMEL

C/ DE CEUTA

VALLCARCA

50 Parc
Güell

Monte
Carmel

C/ DE CAN XIROT DEL CARMEL

TÚNEL DE LA ROVIRA

C/ DEL DOCTOR BOLE

C/ DE LA GRAN VISTA

3

C/ DE VERDI

C/ DE SOSTRES

Casa Museu
Gaudi
22

C/ D'OLOT

C/ DE MUHLBERG

TÚNEL DE LA ROVIRA

C/ DE MERCEDES

Complex
Pau Negre-Can Toda

C/ DE PASTEUR

EL CARMEL

C/ DE MOLIST

AV DE POMPEU FABRA

C/ DE RAMIRO DE MAEZTU

C/ D'ALBERT LLANÀS

C/ DE SANT

C/ DE LARRARD

C/ DE SANT JOSEP DE LA MUNTANYA

La Salut

C/ DE JAUME PUIGVERT

C/ DE JOSEP SERRANO

Mercat
Lesseps

Hospital
de l'Esperança

C/ D'ALEXANDRE DE TORRELLES

AV DE CAN BARO

C/ DEL BARÓ DE SANT LLUIS

C/ DE LA MARE DE DÉU DE LA SALUT

C/ DE MIQUEL DELS STS. OLIVER

C/ DE BISMARCK

C/ DE TENERIFE

4

TRAVESSERA DE DALT

Plaça de
Sanllehy

C/ DE POTOSI

C/ DEL CARDENER

Hospital
Evangèlic

C/ DE LA GRANJA

C/ DE RABASSA

C/ DE MASSENS

40

C/ DE BALCELLS

Nou
Sardenya

C/ DE LES CAMÉLIES

C/ DE FRANCA

Plaça de
la Font
Castellana

C/ DE MARTI

PG. D'AMUNT

386

A **B** **C**

394

Explorer Group Ltd. 2007

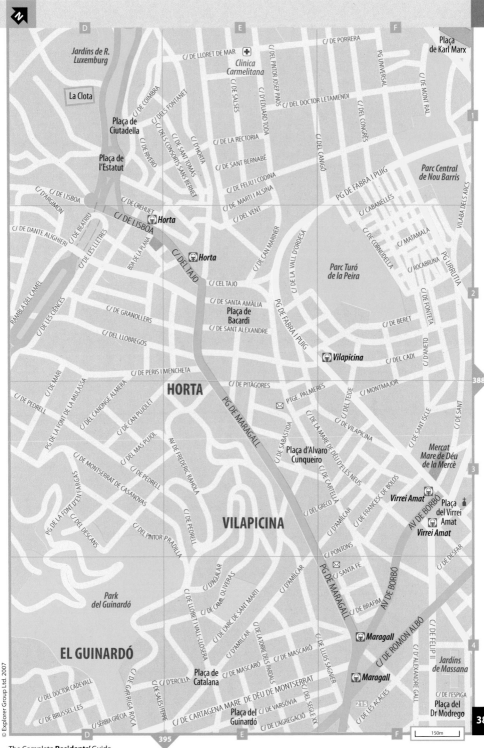

Jardíns de R. Luxemburg

La Clota

Plaça de Ciutadella

Plaça de l'Estatut

C/ DE LISBOA
C/ D'ARGIMON
C/ DE DANTE ALIGHIERI
RAMBLA DEL CARMEL
C/ DE LES CIÈNCES
C/ DE MARI
C/ DE PEDRELL
PG DE LA FONT DE LA MULASSA
C/ DE MONTSERRAT DE CASANOVAS
PG DE LA FONT D'EN FARGAS
C/ DEL DESCANS

C/ DE COIMBRA
C/ DELS FONTANET
C/ DELS CONSORTS SANS BERNET
C/ DE RIVERO
C/ DE SANT TOMÀS
C/ D'HORTA
C/ DE CREHUET
C/ DE BEATRIU
C/ DE LES LLETRES
BDA DE LA PLANA
C/ DE LISBOA
C/ DEL TAJO
C/ CEL TAJO
C/ DE GRANOLLERS
C/ DEL LLOBREGOS
C/ DE PERIS I MENCHETA
C/ DEL CANONGE ALMERA
C/ DEL MAS PUJOL
C/ DE CAN PUJOLET
C/ DE PEDRELL
AV DE FREDERIC RAHOLA
C/ DE PEDRELL
C/ DEL PINTOR PRADILLA

C/ DE LLORET DE MAR
C/ DE SALSES
C/ DEL PINTOR JOSEP PINÓS
C/ D'EDUARD TODA
C/ DE LA RECTORIA
C/ DE SANT BERNABÉ
C/ DE FELIU I CODINA
C/ DE MARTÍ I ALSINA
C/ DEL VENT
C/ DEL DOCTOR LETAMENDI
C/ DEL CANIGÓ
C/ DEL CONGRÉS

Clínica Carmelitana

Horta

Horta

Plaça de Bacardi
C/ DE SANTA AMÀLIA
C/ DE SANT ALEXANDRE

HORTA

PG DE MARAGALL

C/ DE PITÀGORES
PTGE. PALMERES
C/ DE SABASTIDA

C/ DE CAN MARINER
C/ DE LA VALL D'ORDESA
PG DE FABRA I PUIG

Vilapicina

Plaça d'Alvaro Cunqueiro

C/ DE LA MARE DE DÉU DE LES NEUS
C/ DE VILAPICINA
C/ DEL TEIDE
C/ DE CARTELLÀ
C/ DEL GRECO
C/ D'AMÍLCAR
C/ DEL GRECO
C/ DE FRANCESC DE BOLÒS

VILAPICINA

Park del Guinardó

EL GUINARDÓ

C/ DEL DOCTOR CADEVALL
C/ DE BRUSSEL·LES
C/ DE GARRIGA ROCA
C/ DE SÈRBIA GRÈCIA
C/ DE SALES FERRÉ
C/ D'ERCILLA
C/ DAGUILAR
C/ DE CAMIL OLIVERAS
C/ DE L'ARC DE SANT MARTÍ
C/ DE LLOBET I VALL-LLOSERA
C/ D'AMÍLCAR
C/ DE LA TORRE DELS PARDALS
C/ DE MASCARÓ
C/ DE MASCARÓ
C/ DE CARTAGENA
C/ DE MASCARÓ

Plaça de Catalana

Plaça del Guinardó
C/ DE VARSÒVIA
C/ DE L'AGREGACIÓ
MARE DE DÉU DE MONTSERRAT
C/ DEL SEGLE XX
C/ DE LLUÍS SAGNIER

C/ DAMÍLCAR
PG DE MARAGALL
C/ SANTA FE
C/ PONTONS
C/ DE BRAFIM
AV DE BORBÓ
C/ DE DESFAR
C/ DE FELIP II
C/ D'ALEXANDRE GALÍ
C/ DE ROMON ALBÓ
C/ DE L'ESPIGA
C/ DE LES ACÀCIES

Maragall

Maragall

Virrei Amat
AV DE BORBÓ
Plaça del Virrei Amat
Virrei Amat

Mercat Mare de Déu de la Mercè

Parc Turó de la Peira

Plaça de Karl Marx

Parc Central de Nou Barris

C/ DE PORRERA
PG UNIVERSAL
C/ DE MONT RAL
PG DE FABRA I PUIG
C/ CABANELLES
C/ MATAMALÀ
C/ DE CORNUDELLA
C/ ROCABRUNA
C/ DE BERET
C/ DE FONTEIA
C/ DEL CADI
C/ D'ANETO
C/ DE MONTMAJOR
C/ DE SANT ISCLE
C/ DE SANT
VILABA DELS ARCS
PG URRUTIA

Jardíns de Massana

Plaça del Dr Modrego

150m

A

Parc de Josep Maria Serra Martí · **Canyelles**

C/ DE ANTONIO MACHADO

PG DE C/ DE LA GUINEUETA

RAMBLA DEL CAÇADOR

PG DE VALLDAURA

C/ DEL MARNE

C/ DE LA GASELA

Parc de la Guineueta

C/ DE L'ARTESANIA

C/ DE MARÍN

Plaça de Can Ensenya
Parc Central de Nou Barris

Mercat la Guineueta

C/ D'ALSÀCIA

C/ DE LLORENA

Plaça de Llucmajor

PG DE VERDUM · **Llucmajor**

Plaça de Jardins Alfabia

C/ DEL NIL

C/ DE DEIÀ

C/ D'ALÚDIA

C/ DE LA SELVA

C/ DE VALLDEROSSA

PG DE VALLDAURA

C/ DE SANTA ENGRÀCIA

C/ DE BOADA

C/ DE L'ESCULTOR ORDÓÑEZ

Plaça de Sóller

C/ DEL PINTOR ALSAMORA

C/ DE CASAS I AMIGÓ

Cementiri de Sant Andreu

C/ HORITZONTAL

PTGE. PORTA

C/ NOU DE PORTA

C/ D'ALLOZA

C/ DE LA MALADETA

C/ DE L'ESTUDANT

AV DE RIO DE JANEIRO

El Corte Inglés

C/ DE ROSSELLÓ I PÒRCEL

C/ DE DESFAR

C/ DE ARNAU D'OMS

C/ DE PIFERRER

C/ D'ALELLA

Centre comercial Heron City

PG D'ANDREU NIN

Parc Esportiu de Can Dragó

AV DE RIO DE JANEIRO

Plaça de Garrigó

PG DE FABRA I PUIG

83

C/ DE VELIA

C/ D'ANTONI COSTA

C/ DE LA JOTA

Sant Andreu Arenal

Bus Station

Fabra i Puig

C/ DE PARDO

C/ DE LA RIERA D'HORTA

C/ D'IGNASI DE ROS

388

B

Antoni Gelabert

C/ DE L'ARTESANIA

C/ D'ALCÀNTARA

C/ DE LA MINA DE LA CIUTAT

C/ DE LES TORRES

C/ DE VIDAL I GUASCH

C/ DEL QUARTER DE SIMANCAS

C/ DE JAUME PINENT

C/ DE FORNELLS

C/ B·ALLOT

B-20

C/ DE CAMPRECIÓS

C/ D'ALMANSA

Plaça del Verdum

C/ DE VILADROSA

C/ DE JOAN RIERA

C/ DE CASALS I CUBERÓ

Plaça F. Layret

Via Julia

VIA JULIA

C/ DE CANYAMERES

Plaça Sta Engracia

C/ DEL POU

C/ DE PABLO IGLESIAS

Plaça Angel Pestaña

C/ DE NOU PINS

C/ DELS ARITJOLS

C/ DEL CONVENI

Valldaura

C/ BALTASAR GRACIAN

C/ D'ARGULLÓS

C/ DEL VINYAR

Plaça de Harry Walker

Plaça Verda de la Prosperitat

AV DE RIO DE JANEIRO

Parc Esportiu de Can Dragó

AVINGUDA MERIDIANA

C/ DE BARTRINA

Plaça Miquel Casablancas i Joanico

Plaça de Can Galta Cremat

Plaça d'en Xandri

C/ D'AGUSTÍ MILA

C/ DE GRAU

C/ DE BALIARDA

C/ DE SANT HIPÒLIT

C/ LA TRAMUNTANA

C/ GRAN DE SANT ANDREU

C/ DE MALATS

C/ DE PONS GALLARZA

123

CARRER DE BASCÒNIA

Plaça de Maria Brossa

C/ DE LANZAROTE

C/ DE RENART

C/ DE CASTELLBELL

C/ DE RENART

C/ DE COROLEU

C/ DE D'IGNASI

C/ D'OTGER

Mer. St. Andreu

Plaça Sot Paletes

Sant Andreu

C/ DE JOAN TORRAS

Plaça del Mercadal

Plaça del Comerç

C/ DE MALATS

Plaça de l'Estació

C/ DE CINCA

C/ DE SÒCRATES

C/ DEL VALLÈS

C/ DE CONCEPCIÓ ARENAL

C/ DEL LLENGUADOC

C/ DE LES MONGES

C/ DE GRAN DE SANT ANDREU

Plaça de Can Fabra

Plaça de Ramón Riera

Sant Andreu Comtal

141

C

C/ DE JAUME PINENT

384

396

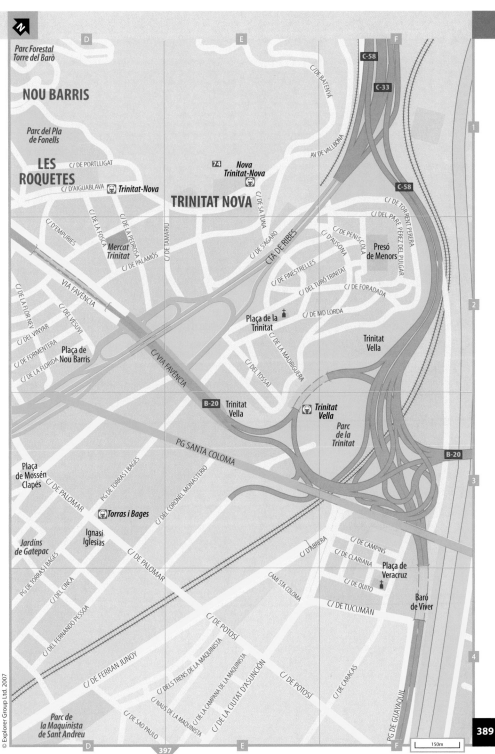

© Explorer Group Ltd. 2007

Parc de les Planes

Mercat De La Florida

C/ DE LA PRIMAVERA
AV DE MIRAFLORS
C/ DE PIERA
C/ D'ALACANT
C/ L'ENGINYER MONCUNILL

382

TRAVESSERA DE COLLBLANC
C/ DE RIUS I CARRIÓ
Poliesportiu Fum D'estampa
Sant Ramón Nonat

C/ DE SORT
CTA DE COLLBLANC

C/ DEL TEIDE
C/ DE CERAVALLS
C/ DE MENORCA
C/ DE CATALUNYA
C/ DE LA FLORÍDA
C/ DEL JARDÍ
C/ DE FONT
C/ DE COTONAT
C/ DEL MONT
C/ DE VALLPARDA
Parc de la Marquesa
C/ DE FARNÉS
C/ DE LA CREU ROJA

C/ DEL TEIDE
C/ DELS PINS
Florida
C/ DE LES MUSES
C/ DE L'ALEGRIA
C/ DE MARTÍ I BLASI
C/ DE LA M. DE DÉU DE NÚRIA
AV DEL TORRENT GORNAL
C/ DE GRANER
C/ DE PUJÓS
C/ D'ESTRUCH
C/ DE BESA
C/ D'OCCIDENT

C/ DE L'ABEDUL
C/ DE LA LIBEL LULA
C/ DE LES MIMOSES
C/ DELS GARROFERS
Parc dels Ocellets
C/ DE VINYATA
C/ D'ORIENT
C/ DE PROGRÉS

C/ DE L'EBRE
AV DE PONENT
C/ DE TORNS
Mercat de Torrent Gornal

C/ DE LA LLIBERTAT
C/ DEL NORD
C/ DEL TEIDE
AV DE VILAFRANCA
C/ DE GRANADA
C/ DE MARTORELL
C/ DE LLANÇA
C/ DE PARRS

Plaça de Blas Infante
C/ DE MAS
COLLBLANC

C/ DE LA MUNTANYA
AV DE JOSEP TARRADELLAS JOAN
C/ DE TERRA BAIXA
Torrassa
C/ DEL MONTSENY
C/ DE LA JOVENTUT
C/ DEL PROGRÉS
C/ DE CLARET

C/ DE LEONARDO DA VINCI
AV DE VENTURA GASSOL
C/ DE PAU SANS
C/ DEL CANIGÓ
C/ PINTOR SOROLLA
PASSATGE D'OLIVERAS
Plaça Espanyola
C/ DE RAFAEL CAMPALANS

C/ DE LA CIUTAT COMTAL
C/ DE SANT PIUS X
C/ DE TREBALL
Club Natació L'hospitalet
C/ DE LA MARE DE DÉU DELS DESEMPARATS

Parc de la Cabana
C/ DE FISOLA DE LA CREU
C/ DE SALAMINA
C/ DE PUJADA
C/ DE JANSANA
Sta. Eulália de Provençana
C/ DE LA CULTURA
C/ D'ALBEREDA
Mare de Déu dels Desemparats
RBLA CATALANA

AV DEL CARRILET
C/ DE CORIOMINAS
PTGA. DE SALVADORS
C/ DE SANTIAGO APÓSTOL

L'HOSPITALET DE LLOBREGAT
C/ DE LAVINIA
C/ DE ISAAC PERAL
Sta Eulalia
AV DEL METRO

C/ DE JUAN RAMÓN JIMÉNEZ
C/ FERRERÍU GUARDIA
C/ DE LA FORTUNA
C/ DEL CLOTET
C/ DE CASTELAO
C/ DE GASOMETRE
C/ DE SANTA EULÀLIA

MIG C/ NARCIS DE MONTURIOL
C/ DE BELLOCCI PRIMA
C/ DE PI I MARGALL
Plaça Camilo Jose Cela

SANTA EULÀLIA
C/ DEL BADALONA
C/ DE ROSELL
C/ DEL MESTRE CARBO
C/ D'ANGEL GUIMERÁ
C/ DE MUNS
C/ DE L'ANSELM CLAVÉ
C/ DE PARETO

C/ DE L'APRESTADORA
C/ UVA
C/ DEL GENERAL PRIM
Mercat de Sta. Eulália

Plaça de Monturiol
C/ DE BUENOS AIRES

C/ DELS JONCS
C/ D'HERRERO
C/ D'AMADEU TORNER
C/ DE LA INDEPENDÈNCIA
C/ DE LA IGUALTAT
Plaça Francesc Macià i Llussà
AV DEL CARRILET
C/ DE L'APRESTADORA

GORNAL
C/ DE CAN TRIES
C/ DE JERUSALEM
C/ DE NATZARETH
C/ DE CASTELAO
C/ DEL PRAT DE LA MANTA
C/ DE BLAS FERNÁNDEZ LIROLA
C/ D'ENRIC MORERA
C/ MODERN
C/ DE BACARDÍ
C/ DE L'ALHAMBRA
C/ DE L'APRESTADORA
C/ DE L'APRESTADORA

C/ TRANSVERSAL
Parc de l'Alhambra
Ildefons Cerda

AV DE LA GRAN VIA DE LES CORTS CATALANES

Ildefons Cerda
398
63 Grav Via2

Barcelona Explorer 1st Edition

General Information p.2 — Residents p.46 — Exploring p.138 — Activities p.198 — Shopping p.274 — Going Out p.316

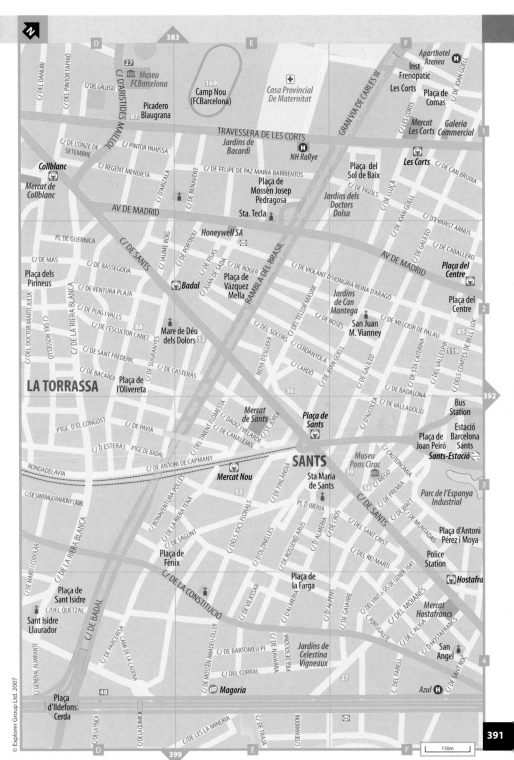

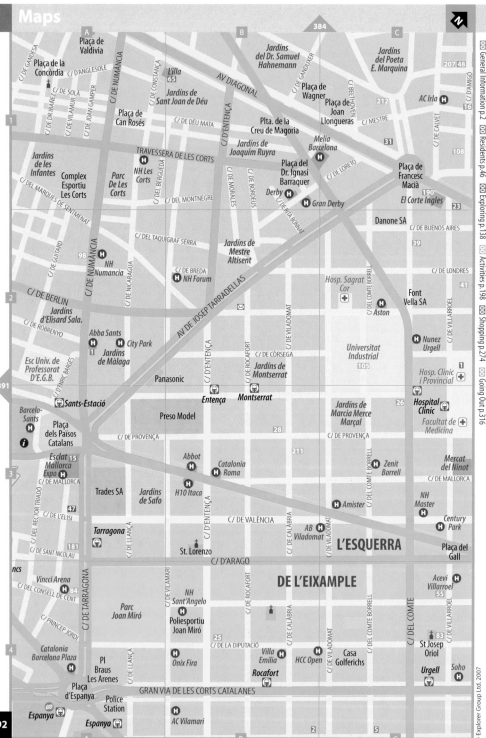

Plaça de Valdivia

Plaça de la Concòrdia

C/ D'ANGLESOLE

C/ GANDESA

C/ DE IBANEZ

C/ DE SOLÀ

C/ DE VILAMUR

C/ DE JOAN GAMPER

C/ DE NUMANCIA

C/ CONSTANCIA

L'illa 65

AV DIAGONAL

Jardíns de Sant Joan de Déu

Plaça de Can Rosés

C/ DE DÉU MATA

C/ D'ENTENÇA

Jardíns del Dr. Samuel Hahnemann

C/ DE GANDUXER

Plaça de Wagner

Plaça de Joan Llongueras

Jardíns del Poeta E. Marquina

C/ BEETHOVEN

C/ MESTRE

AC Irla

207 48

C/ D'AMIGO

212

16

TRAVESSERA DE LES CORTS

Plta. de la Creu de Magoria

Jardíns de Joaquím Ruyra

Melia Barcelona

31

C/ DE CALVET

Jardíns de les Infantes

Complex Esportiu Les Corts

C/ DEL MARQUES DE SENTMENAT

Parc De Les Corts

NH Les Corts

C/ DEL BERGUEDA

C/ DEL MONTNEGRE

C/ DE MORALES

C/ DE BORDEUS

Plaça del Dr. Ignasi Barraquer

Derby

Gran Derby

C/ DE RITA BONNAT

C/ DE LORETO

Plaça de Francesc Macià

190

El Corte Ingles

23

108

Danone SA

C/ DE BUENOS AIRES

C/ DEL TAQUIGRAF SERRA

Jardíns de Mestre Altisent

C/ DE BREDA

NH Forum

AV DE JOSEP TARRADELLAS

C/ DE GUITARD

93

NH Numancia

C/ DE NUMANCIA

C/ DE NICARAGUA

39

C/ DE LONDRES

Hosp. Sagrat Cor

C/ DEL COMTE BORRELL

Aston

Font Vella SA

41

C/ DE VILLARROEL

C/ DE BERLIN

Jardíns d'Elisard Sala.

C/ DE ROBRENYO

Abba Sants

City Park

Jardíns de Màlaga

C/ D'ENRIC BARGES

C/ D'ENTENÇA

C/ DE ROCAFORT

C/ DE CÒRSEGA

Jardíns de Montserrat

C/ DE VILADOMAT

Universitat Industrial

105

Nunez Urgell

Hosp. Clinic i Provincial

Esc Univ. de Professorat D'E.G.B.

Sants-Estació

Panasonic

Entença

Montserrat

Marcia Merce Marçal

Jardíns de Marcia Merce Marçal

26

Hospital Clinic

391

Barcelo-Sants

Plaça dels Països Catalans

Preso Model

C/ DE PROVENÇA

28

C/ DE PROVENÇA

Facultat de Medicina

Esclat Mallorca Expo

15

C/ DE MALLORCA

Abbot

Catalonia Roma

211

Zenit Borrell

Mercat del Ninot

C/ DE MALLORCA

Trades SA

Jardíns de Safo

H10 Itaca

C/ DE CALABRIA

Amister

NH Master

Century Park

47

C/ DE L'ELISI

C/ DE RECTOR TRIADO

Tarragona

C/ DE LLANÇA

C/ D'ENTENÇA

C/ DE VALÈNCIA

AB Viladomat

L'ESQUERRA

Plaça del Gall

181

C/ DE SANT NICOLAU

St. Lorenzo

C/ D'ARAGO

Acevi Villaroel

55

Vincci Arena

84

C/ DEL CONSELL DE CENT

C/ DE TARRAGONA

C/ DE VILAMARI

NH Sant'Angelo

C/ DE ROCAFORT

DE L'EIXAMPLE

C/ DEL COMTE BORRELL

C/ DEL COMTE

C/ DE VILLARROEL

St Josep Oriol

83

C/ PRINCEP JORDI

Parc Joan Miró

Poliesportiu Joan Miró

25

C/ DE LA DIPUTACIÓ

Villa Emilia

Casa Golferichs

Urgell

Soho

Catalonia Barcelona Plaza

Pl Braus Les Arenes

Onix Fira

Rocafort

HCC Open

C/ DE VILADOMAT

Plaça d'Espanya

Police Station

Espanya

Espanya

AC Vilamari

GRAN VIA DE LES CORTS CATALANES

2

5

Barcelona Explorer 1st Edition

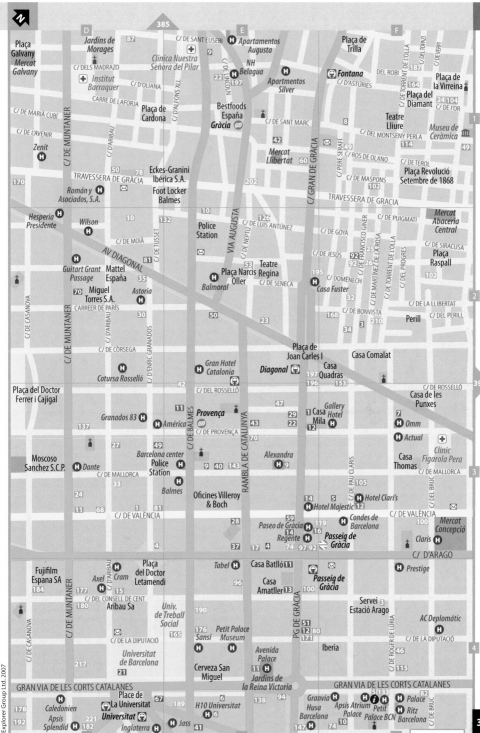

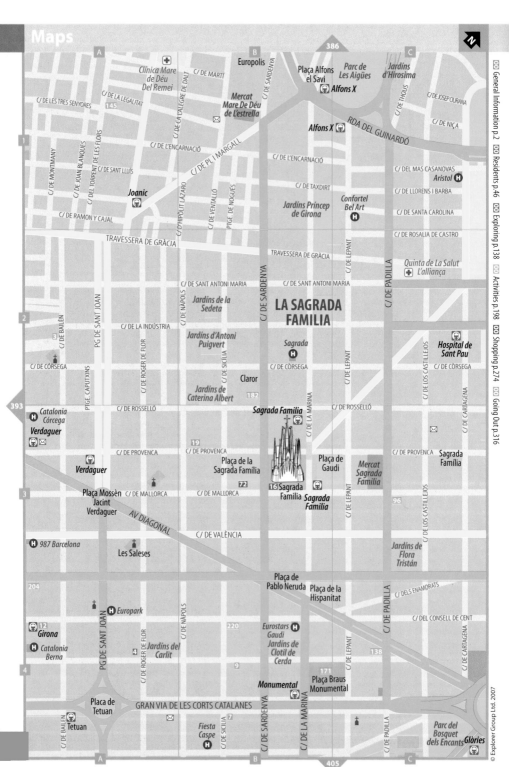

386

A · B · C

Clínica Mare de Déu Del Remei
Europolis
Plaça Alfons el Savi
Parc de Les Aigües
Jardíns d'Hirosima

C/ DE MARTÍ
C/ DE LA LEGALITAT
C/ DE CATALEGRE DE DALT
145
Alfons X
C/ DE THOUS
C/ DE JOSEP QURANA

Mercat Mare De Déu de L'estrella
C/ DE LES TRES SENYORES
C/ DE SARDENYA
C/ DE NIÇA

Alfons X
RDA DEL GUINARDÓ

C/ DE MONTMANY
C/ DE JOAN BLANQUES
C/ DE TORRENT DE LES FLORS
C/ DE SANT LLUÍS
C/ DE L'ENCARNACIÓ
C/ DE L'ENCARNACIÓ
C/ DEL MAS CASANOVAS
Aristol

C/ DE TAXDIRT
C/ DE LLORENS I BARBA

Joanic
C/ DE PL I MARGALL
Jardíns Príncep de Girona
Confortel Bel Art
C/ DE SANTA CAROLINA

C/ DE RAMON Y CAJAL
C/ D'HIPOLIT LAZARO
C/ DE VENTALLÓ
PTGE DE NOGUES
C/ DE ROSALIA DE CASTRO

TRAVESSERA DE GRÀCIA
TRAVESSERA DE GRÀCIA
C/ DE LEPANT
C/ DE PADILLA
Quinta de La Salut L'alliança

1

C/ DE SANT ANTONI MARIA
C/ DE SANT ANTONI MARIA

C/ DE NÀPOLS
Jardíns de la Sedeta
LA SAGRADA FAMÍLIA
Hospital de Sant Pau

PG DE SANT JOAN
C/ DE LA INDÚSTRIA
Jardíns d'Antoni Puigvert
Sagrada
C/ DE LOS CASTILLEJOS
C/ DE CÒRSEGA

C/ DE BAILEN
C/ DE SICILIA
C/ DE CÒRSEGA
C/ DE LEPANT

2

C/ DE CÒRSEGA
Claror
Jardíns de Caterina Albert
182
Sagrada Família
C/ DE LA MARINA

PTGE. CAPUTXINS
C/ DE ROGER DE FLOR
C/ DE ROSSELLÓ
Sagrada Família
C/ DE ROSSELLÓ

393
Catalonia Córcega
Verdaguer
19
C/ DE PROVENÇA
Plaça de la Sagrada Família
72
Plaça de Gaudi
Mercat Sagrada Família
C/ DE PROVENÇA
Sagrada Família

Verdaguer
C/ DE MALLORCA
16 Sagrada Família Sagrada Família
C/ DE CARTAGENA

Plaça Mossèn Jacint Verdaguer
C/ DE MALLORCA
C/ DE LEPANT
96

3

AV DIAGONAL
C/ DE VALÈNCIA

987 Barcelona
Les Saleses
Jardíns de Flora Tristán

Plaça de Pablo Neruda
Plaça de la Hispanitat
C/ DELS ENAMORATS

204
C/ DE PADILLA
C/ DEL CONSELL DE CENT

12
Girona
Europark
Eurostars Gaudi
Jardíns de Clotil de Cerda

Catalonia Berna
C/ DE NÀPOLS
220
171
138

PG DE SANT JOAN
C/ DE ROGER DE FLOR
Jardíns del Carlit
4
9
Plaça Braus Monumental
C/ DE CARTAGENA

4

Monumental

Plaça de Tetuan
GRAN VIA DE LES CORTS CATALANES

C/ DE BAILEN
Tetuan
Fiesta Caspe
C/ DE SICILIA
C/ DE SARDENYA
C/ DE LA MARINA
C/ DE PADILLA
Parc del Bosquet dels Encants
Glòries

7
405

A · B · C

© Explorer Group Ltd. p.1 2007

Barcelona Explorer 1st Edition

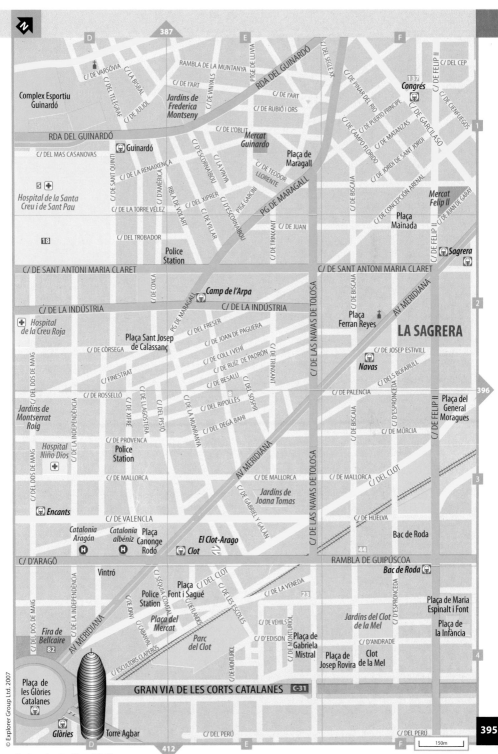

Complex Esportiu
Guinardó

C/ DE VARSÓVIA
C/ LA BISBAL
C/ DEL TELÈGRAF
C/ DE JULIOL

RAMBLA DE LA MUNTANYA
C/ DE L'ART
PTGE DE LLÍVIA
C/ DE VINYALS

RDA DEL GUINARDÓ

Jardíns de
Frederica
Montseny

C/ DE L'ART
C/ DE RUBIÓ I ORS

C/ DEL SEGLE XX

C/ DE PINAR DEL RÍO
C/ DE FELIP II
C/ DEL CEP

137
Congrés

C/ DE GARCILASO
C/ DE CIENFUEGOS

RDA DEL GUINARDÓ

Guinardó

C/ DEL MAS CASANOVAS

C/ DE L'OBLIT

Mercat
Guinardo

Plaça de
Maragall

C/ DE CAMPO FLORIDO
C/ DE PUERTO PRÍNCIPE
C/ DE MATANZAS

C/ DE JORDI DE SANT JORDI

C/ DE SANT QUINTÍ
C/ DE LA RENAIXENÇA
C/ D'AMÈRICA
C/ D'ESCORNALBOU
C/ LA VINYA

C/ DE TEODOR
LLORENTE

PG DE MARAGALL

C/ DE BISCAIA
C/ DE CONCEPCIÓN ARENAL

Mercat
Felip II

5 ✚
Hospital de la Santa
Creu i de Sant Pau

RBLA DE VOLART
C/ DEL XIPRER
C/ D'ESCORNALBOU
C/ DE VILLAR

PTGE GARCINI

Plaça
Mainada

C/ DE LA TORRE VÉLEZ

C/ DE JUAN

C/ DE FELIP II
C/ DE JUAN DE GARAY

18

C/ DEL TROBADOR

C/ DE TRINXANT

Sagrera

Police
Station

C/ DE SANT ANTONI MARIA CLARET

C/ DE CONCA

Camp de l'Arpa

C/ DE SANT ANTONI MARIA CLARET

C/ DE BISCAIA

C/ DE LA INDÚSTRIA

PG DE MARAGALL

C/ DE LA INDÚSTRIA

C/ DE LAS NAVAS DE TOLOSA

AV MERIDIANA

LA SAGRERA

✚ Hospital
de la Creu Roja

C/ DEL FRESER

Plaça
Ferran Reyes

Plaça Sant Josep
de Calassanç

C/ DE JOAN DE PAGUERA

C/ DE CÒRSEGA

C/ DE COLL I VEHÍ

C/ DE JOSEP ESTIVILL

C/ DE RUÍZ DE PADRÓN

Navas

C/ DE FINESTRAT

C/ DE BESÚU

C/ DE TRINXANT

C/ DELS BOFARULL

C/ DEL DOS DE MAIG

C/ DE ROSSELLÓ

C/ DE PALENCIA

Plaça del
General
Moragues

Jardíns de
Montserrat
Roig

C/ DE LLAGOSTERA
C/ DE XIFRE
C/ DEL PISTÓ

C/ DE LA MUNTANYA
C/ DE RIPOLLÈS
C/ DEL SOSPIR

C/ DE DEGÀ BAHÍ

C/ DE BISCAIA
C/ D'ESPRONCEDA
C/ DE MÚRCIA
C/ DE FELIP II

Hospital
Niño Dios
✚

C/ DE LA INDEPENDÈNCIA

C/ DE PROVENÇA

Police
Station

C/ DE MALLORCA

AV MERIDIANA

C/ DE MALLORCA

C/ DE MALLORCA
C/ DEL CLOT

C/ DEL DOS DE MAIG

Encants

C/ DE VALÈNCIA

Jardíns de
Joana Tomàs

C/ DE GABRIEL Y GALÁN

C/ DE LAS NAVAS DE TOLOSA

C/ DE HUELVA

Bac de Roda

Catalonia
Aragón
Ⓗ

Catalonia
albéniz
Ⓗ

Plaça
Canonge
Rodó

El Clot-Arago

Clot

44

C/ D'ARAGÓ

RAMBLA DE GUIPÚSCOA

Bac de Roda

Vintró

Plaça
Font i Sagué

Plaça de Maria
Espinalt i Font

C/ DE LA INDEPENDÈNCIA

Police
Station

C/ SÈQUIA COMTAL
C/ DEL CLOT
C/ DE LES ESCOLES
C/ DE LA VENEDA
23

C/ D'ESPRONCEDA

Plaça de
la Infància

AV MERIDIANA

Plaça del
Mercat

C/ DE FERRANDIS

Parc
del Clot

C/ DE VEHÍLS
C/ D'EDISON

Jardíns del Clot
de la Mel

C/ D'ANDRADE

Fira de
Bellcaire
82

C/ DE COMBANAL
C/ D'OSONA

C/ DELS ESCULTORS CLAPERÓS

C/ DE MONTURIOL

Plaça de
Gabriela
Mistral

Plaça de
Josep Rovira

Clot
de la Mel

Plaça de
les Glòries
Catalanes

GRAN VIA DE LES CORTS CATALANES C-31

C/ DEL PERÚ

C/ DEL PERÚ

Glòries

Torre Agbar

150m

© Explorer Group Ltd. 2007

395

The Complete **Residents'** Guide

CONGRES

C/ DE CONCEPCIÓN ARENAL

AV. MERIDIANA

C/ DE DUBLIN

Fabra i Coats

C/ DE NADAL

C/ DE RAMON BATLLE

C/ DE PARELLADA

C/ SEGRE

C/ DE PORTUGAL DOMÈNECH

C/ DE ROVIRA I VIRGILI

C/ DECUBA

C/ DEL DOCTOR SANTPONC

C/ DE VIRGILI

C/ DE JOSEP SOLDEVILA

C/ DELS PAGÀS

C/ DE PACÍFIC

C/ DE NEOPÀTRIA

C/ DE SANT ANDREU

C/ GRAN DE SANT ANDREU

C/ DE LLIUVA

Plaça de l'Abat Escarré

Plaça de Montserrat Roca i Balta

C/ DE LES ANTILLES

Parc Pègaso

C/ DE SANT SEBASTIÀ

C/ DE BORRIANA

PG DE L'ONZE DE SETEMBRE

C/ DE BORRIANA

C/ DE COLL

C/ DE MARTÍ MOLINS

C/ DE MOSSÈN JULIANA

Plaça del Doctor Carach Mauri

C/ DE SANTA COLOMA

Sant Andreu

Narcís Sala

C/ DE VIRGILI

C/ SEGRE

Plaça de Pere Falqués

Jardíns d'Elx

Sagrera

C/ DE NOBEL D'OLIVA

C/ DE MONLAU

C/ DE LA SAGRERA

C/ DEL CAMP DEL FERRO

Plaça d'Albert Badia i Mur

Pare Manyanet

C/ DE LA RIERA D'HORTA

Plaça de Pere Falqués

PG DE COELLO

C/ DE GARCILASO

C/ DE BERENGUER DE PALOU

C/ DE FERRAN TURNÉ

Plaça de Koba

C/ DE JOSEP SOLDEVILA

C/ DE JAUME BROSSA

PG DE LA VERNEDA

C/ DEL'INDÚSTRIA

Circuit Mpal. Aeromodelisme Rec Comtal

C/ PONT DEL TREBALL

RDA DE SANT MARTÍ

RAMBLA DE PRIM

PTGE. VIA TRAJANA A

PTGE. VIA TRAJANA B

Sagrera

RDA DE SANT MARTÍ

C/ DE SANTANDER

VIA TRAJANA

C/ DE SANTANDER

C/ DE CANTÀBRIA

C/ DE PUIGCERDÀ

C/ DEL CAMP ARRIASSA

Plaça Ignasi Juliol

Parc de Sant Martí

C/ DEL FONDAL DE SANT MARTÍ

C/ D'ALMACELLES

Plaça de la Verneda

C/ DEL MARESME

C/ DE CA N'OLIVA

CAMÍ LA VERNEDA

Menorca

Mercat Provençals

C/ DE MENORCA

C/ DE CANTÀBRIA

C/ DE MENORCA

C/ DE BINEFAR

C/ DE MENORCA

RAMBLA DE PRIM

C/ DE PROVENÇALS

Parc de Sant Martí

C/ DEL TREBALL

C/ DE L'AGRICULTURA

C/ DE CANTÀBRIA

C/ DE PUIGCERDÀ

C/ DEL MARESME

C/ DE HUELVA

C/ DE HUELVA

C/ DE HUELVA

RAMBLA DE PRIM

C/ DE L'ESTARTIT

RAMBLA DE GUIPÚSCOA

RAMBLA DE GUIPÚSCOA

La Pau

Plde Mercè Capsir

Plaça de Soledad Gustavo

Sant Martí

Sant Martí

Plaça del Repòs

C/ DEL MARESME

Plaça de Conxita Badia

C/ DE CA N'OLIVA

C/ DE L'EMPORDÀ

Plaça de Fernando de los Ríos

C/ D'EXTREMADURA

Jardíns Joaquima Raspall

Plaça d'Eduard Torroja

Jupiter

CONCILI DE TRENTO

La Verneda

Plaça de la Palmera de Sant Martí

Plaça de la Cultura

Plaça de la Pau

C/ DEL CONCILI DE TRENTO

C/ D'ANDRADE

Plaça dels Porxos

Andrade-Sant Martí

C/ D'ANDRADE

C/ DE PUIGCERDÀ

Mercat Sant Martí

C/ D'ANDRADE

Plaça d'Artur Martorell

Plaça de Manuel Ainaud

Besòs

GRAN VIA DE LES CORTS CATALANES

C-31

GRAN VIA DE LES CORTS CATALANES

Besòs

CTRA. DE MATARÓ

Centre Olímpia

C/ DEL PERÚ

C/ DE CANTÀBRIA

Plaça de Puigcerdà

C/ DEL PARAGUAI

Plaça de Zenòbia Camprubí

C/ DEL PERÚ

C/ DE BERNAT METGE

General Information p.2 Residents p.46 Exploring p.138 Activities p.198 Shopping p.274 Going Out p.316

© Explorer Group Ltd. 2007

Barcelona Explorer 1st Edition

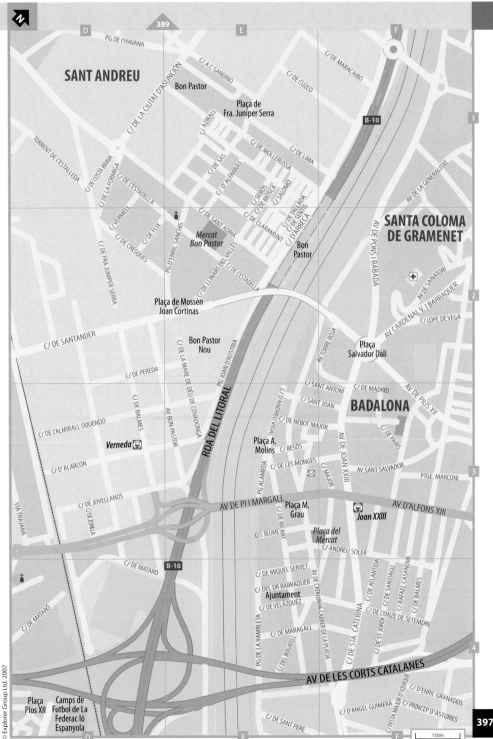

SANT ANDREU

PG DE L'HAVANA

C/ A.C. SANDINO

Bon Pastor

Plaça de
Fra. Juniper Serra

C/ DE CUZCO

C/ DE MARACAIBO

C/ DE LA CIUTAT D'ASUNCIÓN

C/ A DRALL

C/ DE LIMA

C/ DE MOLLERUSSA

B-10

AV DE LA GENERALITAT

SANTA COLOMA
DE GRAMENET

C/ DE COSTA BRAVA

C/ DE SÁS

C/ DE ALFARRÁS

C/ DE LA FORMIGA

C/ DE L'ESTADELLA

TORRENT DE L'ESTALLEDA

C/ VERMELL

C/ DE ELIX

C/ DE SANT ADRIÀ

C/ SEROS

C/ DE BIOSCA

C/ DE SENYS

C/ SALOMÓ

C/ DE FALLADA

C/ DE CLARAMUNT

C/ D'ARBECA

AV DE PONS I RABADA

AV DE LA GENERALITAT

C/ DE SANATORI

C/ DE CRESQUES

Mercat
Bon Pastor

PG D'ENRIC SANCHIS

Bon
Pastor

C/ DE FRA JUNIPER SERRA

C/ DE LINARES DEL VALLÈS

C/ DE L'ESTADELLA

Plaça de Mossèn
Joan Cortinas

AV CARDENAL V. I BARRAQUER

AV CARDENAL V. I BARRAQUER

AV/ LOPE DE VEGA

C/ DE SANTANDER

Bon Pastor
Nou

AV TORRE ROJA

Plaça
Salvador Dali

RDA DEL LITORAL

C/ DE LA MARE DE DÉU DE COVADONGA

C/ DE PEREDA

PG JOAN D'AUSTRIA

C/ SANT ANTONI

C/ DE MADRID

AV DE PIUS XII

C/ DE BALMES

C/ SANT JOAN

C/ DE PARIS

C/ D'ANDROMEDA VIGAL

C/ DE NEBOT MAJOR

BADALONA

C/ DE L'ALMIRALL OQUENDO

AV BON PASTOR

Verneda

Plaça A.
Molins

C/ BESÓS

AV DE JOAN XXIII

AV SANT SALVADOR

PTGE. MARCONI

C/ D'ALARCON

PG ALAMEDA

C/ DE LES MONGES

C/ MAJOR

C/ DE JOVELLANOS

C/ DE ZORILLA

VIA TRAJANA

AV DE PI I MARGALL

Plaça M.
Grau

Joan XXIII

AV D'ALFONS XIII

C/ J. BLUME

C/ DE RICART

Plaça del
Mercat

C/ DE MATARO

B-10

C/ ANDREU SOLER

C/ DE MIQUEL SERVET

C/ DEL DR BARRAQUER

Ajuntament

C/ DE VELÁZQUEZ

AV DE CATALUNYA CARRER DE LA PLATJA

C/ DE STA. CATERINA

C/ DE ATLANTIDA

C/ DE SANTIAGU

C/ DE RAFAEL CASANOVA

C/ DE BALMES

C/ DE MATARO

PG DE LA RAMBLETA

C/ DEL ROCAFELL

C/ DE MARAGALL

C/ DE ST JORDI

C/ DE L'ONZE DE SETEMDRE

Plaça
Pius XII

Camps de
Futbol de La
Federac ló
Espanyola

C/ DE SANT PERE

AV DE LES CORTS CATALANES

C/ FESTA MAJOR D'IQUIQUE

C/ D'ENRIC GRANADOS

C/ D'ANGEL GUIMERÀ

C/ D'PRINCEP D'ASTURIES

150m

The Complete **Residents'** Guide

390

N

General Information p.2 • Residents p.46 • Exploring p.138 • Activities p.198 • Shopping p.274 • Going Out p.316

A

B

C

C/ DE LES CIÈNCIES

C/ DE LES CIÈNCIES

C/ DE L' ARQUITECTURA

C/ DE F. BOIX I CAMPO

C/ DE SOWETO

Jardíns dels Drets Humans

C/ DE L'ACER

C/ DE L'ALUMINI

C/ DE L'ENERGIA

C/ DE GERNIKA

C/ DE PEDROSA B

C/ DE LA PEDROSA

C/ DE LA FONERIA

Mare de Déu del Port

C/ DE PEDROSA C

Fira de Mostres Montjuic-II

C/ DE LA MECÀNICA

Jardíns de L'Arboreda

C/ DE LA BOTÀNICA

C/ DEL ALTS FORNS

C/ DE LA BOTÀNICA

Police Station

PG DE LA ZONA FRANCA

C/ DE LA PEDROSA

C/ DEL FOC

C/ DE LA METAL-LÚRGIA

Bauhaus 'Pg Zona Franca

C/ DE LA INDÚSTRIA

C/ DE L'ACER

C/ DEL FERRO

C/ DEL FOC

C/ DEL PLOM

C/ DE LA INDÚSTRIA

C/ DE SANT ELOI

C/ DEL COBALT

C/ DE LA PEDROSA

C/ DE L'ESTANY

C/ DE LA METAL-LÚRGIA

C/ DE L'ACER

C/ DEL FERRO

C/ DEL PLOM

C/ DELS MOTORS

Plaça del Nou

C/ DELS MOTORS

C/ D'ASCO

C/ D ARNES

C/ ROJALS

C/ DEL PINETELL

C/ DE FORES

C/ DE RIUDOMS

C/ DE SOVELLES

C/ DEL CISELL

C/ D'ALBARCA

C/ DEL SERRAT

Estació De Cantunis

C/ D'ULLADECONA

C/ DE L'ENCUNY

PG DE LA ZONA FRANCA

C/ DELS MOTORS

RDA DEL LITORAL

AVENIGA DEL PARC LOGISTIQUE

C/ DELS MOTORS

B-10

Consorci Zona Franca

C/ NÚMERO 61 DE LA ZONA FRANCA

C/ NÚMERO 1 DE LA ZONA FRANCA

C/ NÚMERO 60 DE LA ZONA FRANCA

RDA DEL LITORAL

C/ NÚMERO 2 DE LA ZONA FRANCA

© Explorer Group Ltd. 2007

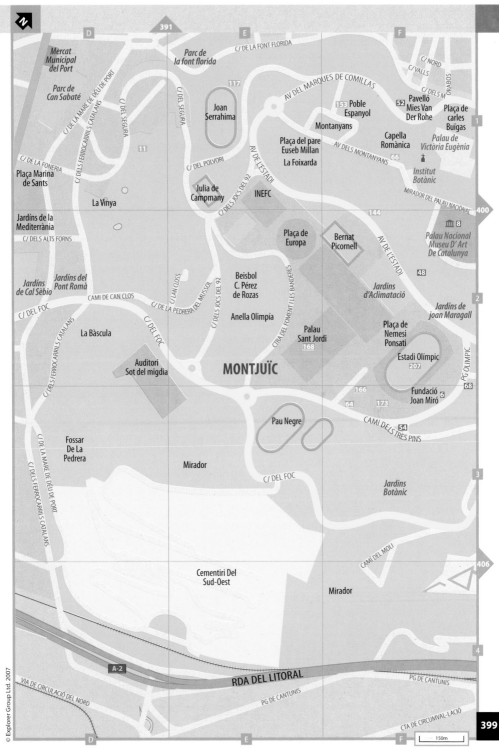

The Complete **Residents'** Guide

150m

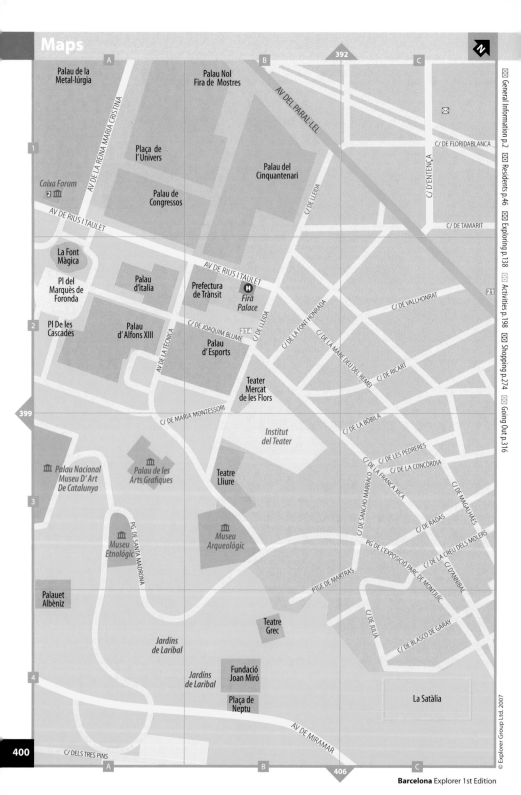

Palau de la
Metal·lúrgia

Palau Nol
Fira de Mostres

AV DEL PARAL·LEL

C/ DE FLORIDABLANCA

Plaça de
l'Univers

Palau del
Cinquantenari

Caixa Forum
2 🏛

Palau de
Congressos

AV DE RIUS I TAULET

La Font
Màgica

AV DE RIUS I TAULET

Pl del
Marquès de
Foronda

Palau
d'Italia

Prefectura
de Trànsit

🅗
Fira
Palace

C/ DE VALLHONRAT

Pl De les
Cascades

Palau
d' Alfons XIII

C/ DE JOAQUIM BLUME
214

Palau
d'Esports

C/ DE LA FONT HONRADA

C/ DE LA MARE DEU DEL REMEI

C/ DE RICART

Teater
Mercat
de les Flors

C/ DE MARIA MONTESSORI

Institut
del Teater

C/ DE LA BÒBILA

C/ DE LES PEDRERES

C/ DE LA CONCÒRDIA

🏛 Palau Nacional
Museu D'Art
De Catalunya

🏛
Palau de les
Arts Grafiques

Teatre
Lliure

C/ DE SANCHO MARRACO

C/ DE LA FRANÇA XICA

C/ DE MAGALHÃES

C/ DE RADAS

🏛
Museu
Etnológic

PG. DE SANTA MADRONA

🏛
Museu
Arqueológic

PG DE L'EXPOSICIÓ PARC DE MONTJUIC

C/ DE LA CREU DELS MOLERS

C/ D'ANNIBAL

Palauet
Albèniz

PTGE DE MARTRAS

C/ DE JULIA

C/ DE BLASCO DE GARAY

Teatre
Grec

Jardíns
de Laribal

Jardíns
de Laribal

Fundació
Joan Miró

La Satàlia

Plaça de
Neptu

AV DE MIRAMAR

C/ DELS TRES PINS

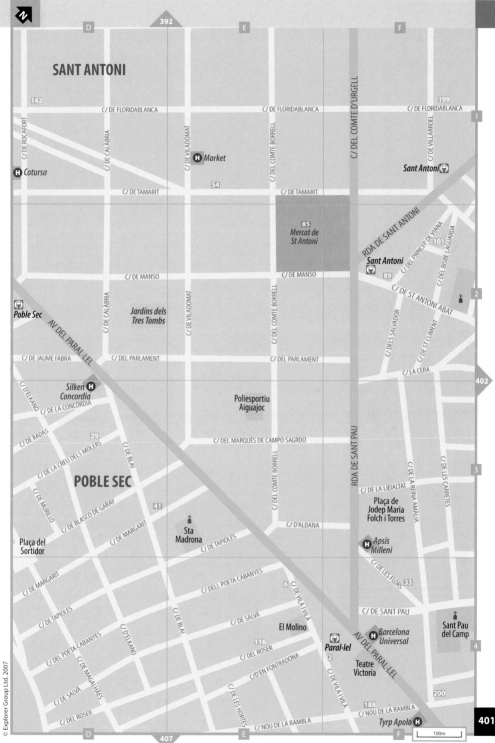

SANT ANTONI

C/ DE FLORIDABLANCA
C/ DE FLORIDABLANCA
C/ DE FLORIDABLANCA

C/ DE ROCAFORT
C/ DE CALABRIA
C/ DE VILADOMAT
C/ DEL COMTE BORRELL
C/ DEL COMTE D'URGELL
C/ DE VILLARROEL

142
199

H Cotursa
H Market
Sant Antoni H

C/ DE TAMARIT
C/ DE TAMARIT
54

85
Mercat de
St Antoni

RDA DE SANT ANTONI
101
C/ DEL PRINCEP DE VIANA
C/ DEL BISBE LAGUARDA

C/ DE MANSO
C/ DE MANSO
Sant Antoni
89
C/ DE ST ANTONI ABAT

Poble Sec

C/ DE CALABRIA
C/ DE VILADOMAT
C/ DEL COMTE BORRELL
C/ DELS SALVADOR
C/ DE ST CLIMENT

Jardíns dels
Tres Tombs

AV DEL PARAL·LEL

C/ LA CERA

C/ DE JAUME FABRA
C/ DEL PARLAMENT
C/ DEL PARLAMENT

402

Silken H
Concordia

C/ DEL KANO
C/ DE LA CONCORDIA

Poliesportiu
Aiguajoc

RDA DE SANT PAU

C/ DE RADAS
29

C/ DE LA CREU DELS MOLERS
C/ DE BLAI

C/ DEL MARQUÈS DE CAMPO SAGRDO

C/ DE LA LIEIALTAT
C/ DE LA REINA AMALIA
C/ DE LES CARRETES

3

POBLE SEC

C/ DE MURILLO
C/ DE BLASCO DE GARAY
41

Plaça de
Jodep Maria
Folch i Torres

Plaça del
Sortidor
C/ DE MARGARIT

Sta
Madrona

C/ DE TAPIOLES
C/ DEL COMTE BORRELL
C/ D'ALDANA

Apsis H
Milleni

C/ DE LES FLORS 33

C/ DE MARGARIT
C/ DELL POETA CABANYES
6 C/ DE VILA I VILA

C/ DE TAPIOLES
C/ DE BLAI
C/ DE SALVA
El Molino
C/ DE SANT PAU

C/ DE POETA CABANYES
C/ D'EL KANO
116
Sant Pau
del Camp

C/ DE MAGALHAES
C/ DEL ROSER
AV DEL PARAL·LEL
Barcelona H
Universal

4

C/ DE SALVA
C/ D'EN FONTRADONA
Paral·lel
2
Teatre
Victoria

C/ DEL ROSER
C/ DE LES HORTES
C/ DE VILA I VILA
188
C/ NOU DE LA RAMBLA
200

C/ NOU DE LA RAMBLA
Tyrp Apolo H

© Explorer Group Ltd 2007

100m

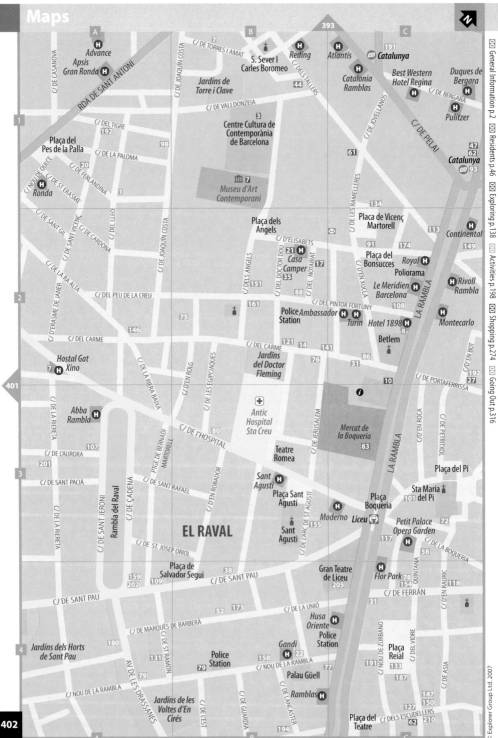

A

B

C

Advance
Apsis
Gran Ronda

S. Sever I
Carles Boromeo

Reding

Atlantis

Catalunya

C/ DE CASANOVA

RDA DE SANT ANTONI

C/ DE JOAQUIN COSTA

C/ DE TORRES I AMAT

7

C/ DELS TALLERS

Catalonia
Ramblas

Best Western
Hotel Regina

191

Duques de
Bergara

C/ DE BERGARA

Jardíns de
Torre i Clave

44

C/ DE JOVELLANOS

Pulitzer

Plaça del
Pes de la Palla

C/ DEL TIGRE

192

C/ DE LA PALOMA

98

3

Centre Cultura de
Contemporània
de Barcelona

C/ DE PELAI

61

C/ DE VALLDONZEIA

47
62

Catalunya

93

1

C/ DEL NOU DE DULCE

20

C/ DE ST ERASME

C/ DE FERLANDINA

1

Ronda

🏛 7

Museu d'Art
Contemporani

C/ DE LES RAMELLERES

134

Plaça de Vicenç
Martorell

Continental

113

149

C/ DE SANT GIL

C/ DE SANT VICENÇ

C/ DE CARDONA

C/ DE JOAQUIN COSTA

Plaça dels
Angels

C/ D'ELISABETS

✉

91

174

Royal
Poliorama

Rivoli
Rambla

C/ DE LA RA ALTA

C/ DELS ANGELS

C/ DEL DOCTOR DOU

21

Casa
Camper

C/ DEL NOTARIAT

17

Plaça del
Bonsucces

Le Meridien
Barcelona

2

C/ D'ERASME DE JANER

35

151

88

108

LA RAMBLA

Montecarlo

C/ DEL PEU DE LA CREU

161

C/ DEL PINTOR FORTUNY

Police
Station

Ambassador

Turin

Hotel 1898

8

C/ DEL CARME

146

75

121

14

141

76

Jardíns
del Doctor
Fleming

31

Betlem

86

10

192
27

Hostal Gat
Xino

7

C/ EN ROLG

C/ DE LES EGIPCIAQUES

C/ DEL CARME

C/ DE PORTAFERRISSA

C/ D'EN BOT

401

C/ DE LA RIERETA

C/ DE LA RIERA BAIXA

Antic
Hospital
Sta Creu

C/ DE JERUSALEM

Mercat de
la Boqueria

83

C/ D'EN ROCA

C/ D'EN PETRITXOL

Abba
Rambla

107

C/ DE L'AURORA

80

C/ DE L'HOSPITAL

Teatre
Romea

Plaça del Pi

201

C/ DE SANT PACIÀ

PTGE DE BERNAD I
MARTORELL

Sant
Agustí

Plaça Sant
Agustí

Plaça
Boqueria

Sta Maria
del Pi

101

72

3

Rambla del Raval

C/ DE SANT JERONI

C/ DE ÇADENA

C/ DE SANT RAFAEL

C/ D'EN ROBADOR

Moderno

Liceu

Petit Palace
Opera Garden

C/ DE LA BOQUERIA

C/ DE LA RIERETA

EL RAVAL

Sant
Agustí

155

117

58

Plaça de
Salvador Seguí

38

C/ DE SANT PAU

Gran Teatre
de Liceu

205

Flor Park

76
154

QUINTANA

118

C/ D'EN RAURIC

159
202

109

LA RAMBLA

31

C/ DE FERRAN

C/ DE SANT PAU

52

173

C/ DE LA UNIÓ

AV DE LES DRASSANES

C/ DE MARQUÉS DE BARBERÀ

Husa
Oriente
Police
Station

C/ DE ST RAMON

C/ NOU DE ZURBANO

C/ DEL VIDRE

C/ DE ASIA

Jardíns dels Horts
de Sant Pau

180

131

79

Police
Station

79

Gandi

158

22

C/ NOU DE LA RAMBLA

77

Palau Güell

Plaça
Reial

191

133

187

4

C/ DE NOU DE LA RAMBLA

Ramblas

147
150

127
210

C/ DE LEST

C/ DE GUARDIA

C/ DE LANCASTER

Jardíns de les
Voltes d'En
Cirés

194

Plaça del
Teatre

C/ DELS ESCUDELLERS

62

A

B

C

© Explorer Group Ltd. 2007

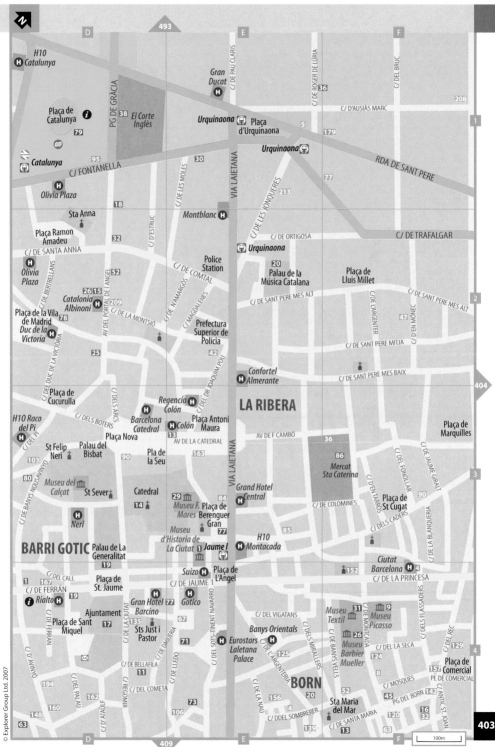

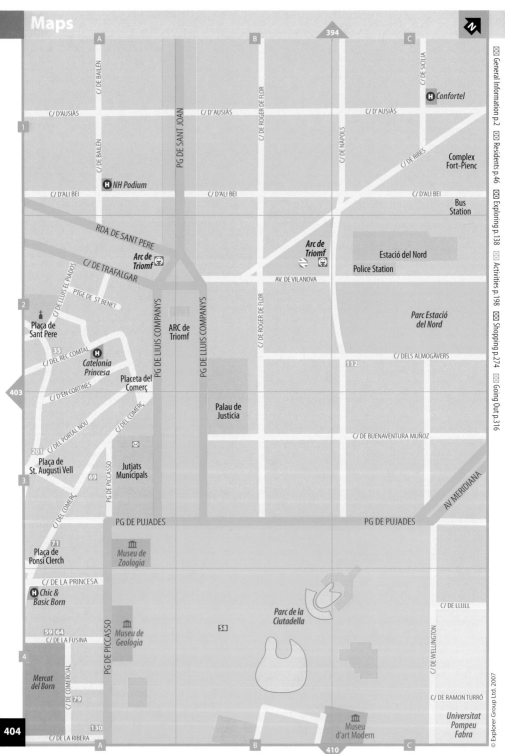

394

A

B

C

C/ DE SICILIA

H *Confortel*

C/ DE BAILÉN

C/ D'AUSIÀS

C/ D'AUSIÀS

C/ D'AUSIÀS

PG DE SANT JOAN

C/ DE ROGER DE FLOR

C/ DE NÀPOLS

C/ DE RIBES

Complex
Fort-Pienc

1

C/ DE BAILÉN

H NH Podium

C/ D'ALI BEI

C/ D'ALI BEI

C/ D'ALI BEI

Bus
Station

RDA DE SANT PERE

Arc de
Triomf

Arc de
Triomf

Estació del Nord

Police Station

C/ DE TRAFALGAR

Arc de
Triomf

AV. DE VILANOVA

2

PTGE DE ST BENET

C/ DE LLUIS EL PIADOS

Plaça de
Sant Pere

PG DE LLUIS COMPANYS

ARC de
Triomf

PG DE LLUIS COMPANYS

C/ DE ROGER DE FLOR

Parc Estació
del Nord

35

C/ DEL REC COMTAL

H Catelonia
Princesa

C/ DELS ALMOGÀVERS

403

C/ D'EN CORTINES

Placeta del
Comerç

112

C/ DEL PORTAL NOU

C/ DEL COMERÇ

Palau de
Justicia

C/ DE BUENAVENTURA MUÑOZ

201

3

Plaça de
St. Augusti Vell

PG DE PICASSO

Jutjats
Municipals

69

C/ DEL COMERÇ

PG DE PUJADES

PG DE PUJADES

AV MERIDIANA

71

Plaça de
Ponsi Clerch

🏛 Museu de
Zoologia

58

Parc de la
Ciutadella

C/ DE LLULL

C/ DE LA PRINCESA

H Chic &
Basic Born

C/ DE WELLINGTON

59 64

C/ DE LA FUSINA

PG DE PICASSO

🏛 Museu de
Geologia

4

Mercat
del Born

C/ DE COMERCIAL

79

C/ DE RAMON TURRÓ

Universitat
Pompeu
Fabra

130

C/ DE LA RIBERA

🏛 Museu
d'art Modern

410

A

B

C

General Information p.2 · Residents p.46 · Exploring p.138 · Activities p.198 · Shopping p.274 · Going Out p.316

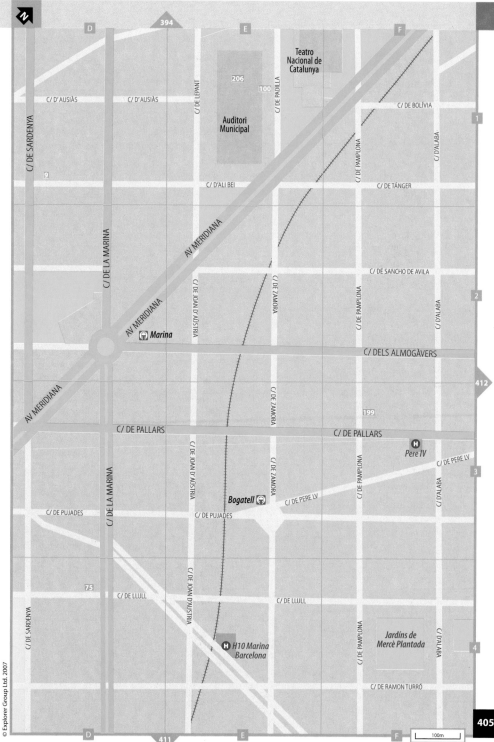

© Explorer Group Ltd. 2007

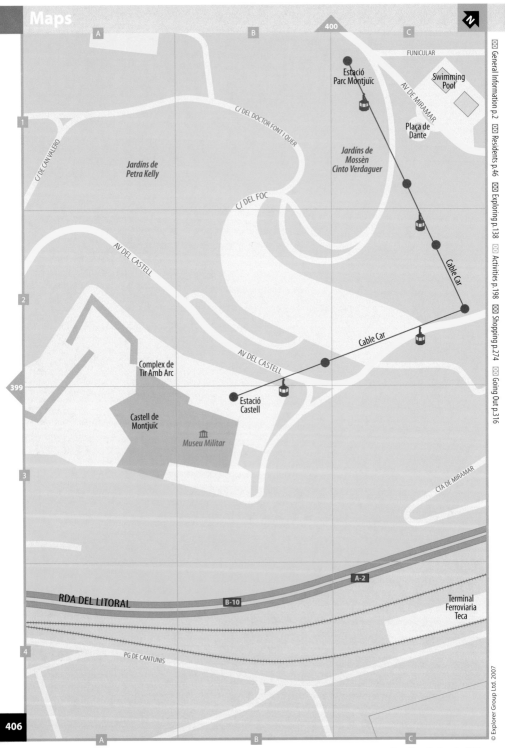

FUNICULAR

Swimming Pool

Estació
Parc Montjuïc

AV DE MIRAMAR

Plaça de
Dante

Jardíns de
Mossèn
Cinto Verdaguer

C/ DEL DOCTOR FONT I QUER

C/ DE CAN VALERO

Jardíns de
Petra Kelly

C/ DEL FOC

Cable Car

AV DEL CASTELL

Cable Car

AV DEL CASTELL

Complex de
Tir Amb Arc

Estació
Castell

Castell de
Montjuïc

🏛 Museu Militar

CTA DE MIRAMAR

A-2

RDA DEL LITORAL

B-10

Terminal
Ferroviaria
Teca

PG DE CANTUNIS

General Information p.2 | Residents p.46 | Exploring p.138 | Activities p.198 | Shopping p.274 | Going Out p.316

© Explorer Group Ltd 2007

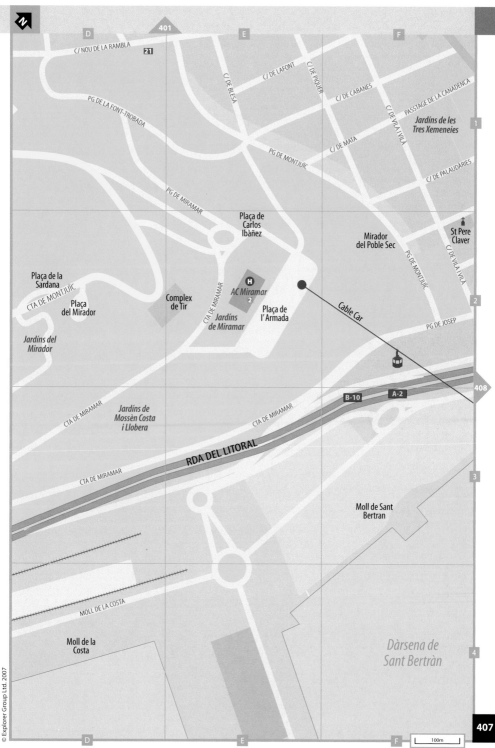

100m

A
B
402
C
193

C/ DE STA MADRONA

Hosperia
del Port
H

Mercat
Mere de Deu
del Carme

C/ DE CID

C/ DE PERACAMPS

AV DE LES DRASSANES

203
C/ DE STA MÓNICA

81

79

Centre d'Art

Frontó
Colom

PG DE LA PAU

172

C/ NOU SANT FRANCESC

C/ SANT FRANCESC

C/ D'EN RULL

Drassanes
110

195
C/ DE SILS

29

AV DEL PARAL·LEL

C/ DE PORTAL

Jardíns del
Baluard

82

STA MADRONA

Camandància
de Marina

LA RAMBLA

Museu
de Cera

175
51

C/ DE JOSEP ANSELM CLAVÉ

Medinacell
40

Plaça del Duc
de Medinaceli
H

1

C/ DE PUIGXURIGER

Museu
Marítim
30

Drassanes

Govern
Militar

37

C/ DE CARRERA

Jardíns de Walter
Benjamin

PG DE COLOM

RDA DEL LITORAL

B-10

Plaça
Portal
de La Pau
64

Monument
a Colóm

Port de
Barcelona

2

PG DE JOSEP CARNER

Plaça de les
Drassanes

Duanes

Moll de les
Drassanes

Golondrinas
65

Rambla
de Mar

PORT VELL

407

Estació Marítima

Real Club
Maritim

Cable Car

Moll de
Barcelona

Dàrsena
Nacional

Maremàgnum
66

3

Torre de
Jaume I

World Trade
Center

Eurostars
Grand Marina
H

Dàrsena de
Sant Bertràn

Moll dels
Balears

4

A
B
C

408

Barcelona Explorer 1st Edition

© Explorer Group Ltd. 2007

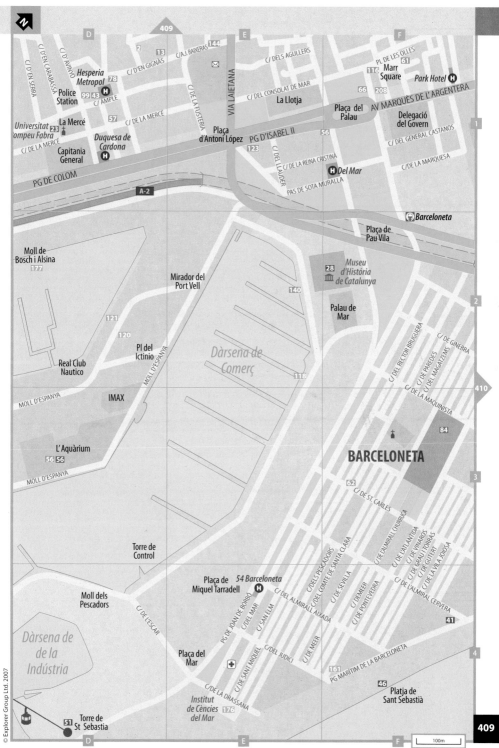

N

C/ D'EN CARBASSA
C/ D'AVINYO
C/ D'EN SERRA
C/ D'EN GIGNAS
2
13
C/A.J. BAIXERAS
144
VIA LAIETANA
C/ DELS AGULLERS

Hesperia
Metropol 78
Police
Station 99 43
C/ AMPLE
C/ D'EN GIGNAS
C/ DEL CONSOLAT DE MAR
La Llotja
PL DE LES OLLES 61
Marr 116 Square
66 208 Park Hotel

Universitat
ompeu Fabra 23
La Mercé
57
C/ DE LA MERCE
C/ DE LA FUSTERIA
Plaça
d'Antoní López
Plaça del
Palau
AV MARQUÈS DE L'ARGENTERA
Delegació
del Govern

Duquesa de
Cardona
Capitania
General
C/ DE LA MERCE
123
PG D'ISABEL II
56
C/ DEL LLAUDER
C/ DE LA REINA CRISTINA
C/ DEL GENERAL CASTANOS
C/ DE LA MARQUESA

1

PG DE COLOM
A-2
Del Mar
PAS DE SOTA MURALLA

Barceloneta

Plaça de
Pau Vila

Moll de
Bosch i Alsina
177
Mirador del
Port Vell
140
28 Museu
d'Història
de Catalunya

2

121
120
Pl del
Ictinio
Dàrsena de
Comerç
Palau de
Mar
C/ DEL RECTOR BRUGUERA
C/ DE PAREDIS
C/ DE GINEBRA
C/ DEL MAGATZEMS
C/ DE LA MAQUINISTA

Real Club
Nautico
MOLL D'ESPANYA
MOLL D'ESPANYA
118
410

IMAX
84

L'Aquàrium
56 56
MOLL D'ESPANYA
BARCELONETA
62
C/ DE ST. CARLES

3

Torre de
Control
Moll dels
Pescadors
C/ DE L'ESCAR
Plaça de
Miquel Tarradell
54 Barceloneta
PG DE JOAN DE BORBÓ
C/ DEL MAR
C/ SAN ELM
C/ DEL ALMIRALL AIXADA
C/ DELS PESCADORS
C/ DEL COMTE DE SANTA CLARA
C/ DE SANTA CLARA
C/ DE SEVILLA
C/ D'AMER
C/ DE PONTEVEDRA
C/ D'ALMIRALL CHURRUCA
C/ DE L'ATLANTIDA
C/ DE VINARÓS
C/ DE GRAU I TORRAS
C/ DE GUITERT
C/ DE L'ALMIRAL CERVERA
C/ DE LA VILA JOIOSA
41

Dàrsena de
de la
Indústria
Plaça del
Mar
Institut
de Cències
del Mar
176
C/ DE SANT MIQUEL
C/ DEL JUDICI
C/ DE LA DRASSANA
C/ DE MEER
161
PG MARÍTIM DE LA BARCELONETA
46
Platja de
Sant Sebastià

4

© Explorer Group Ltd. 2007

51 Torre de
St Sebastia

D
E
F
100m

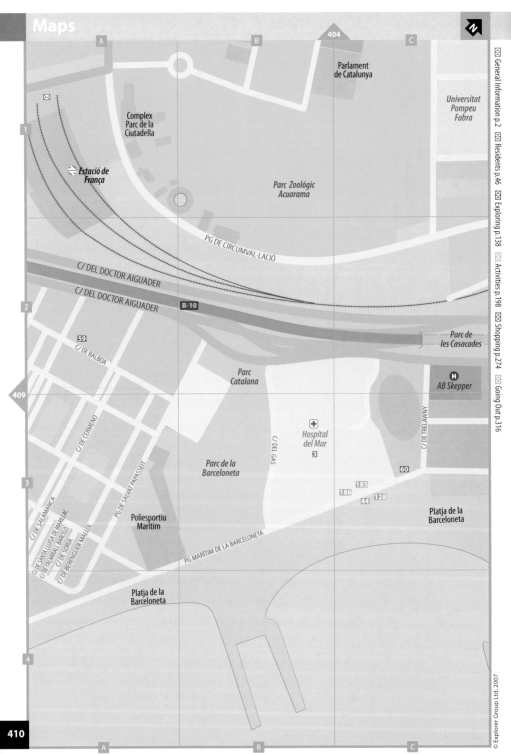

A B 404 C

Parlament
de Catalunya

Universitat
Pompeu
Fabra

1

Complex
Parc de la
Ciutadella

⇄ Estació de
França

Parc Zoológic
Acuarama

PG DE CIRCUMVAL·LACIÓ

C/ DEL DOCTOR AIGUADER

C/ DEL DOCTOR AIGUADER B-10

2

Parc de
les Casacades

59

C/ DE BALBOA

409

Parc
Catalana

H
AB Skepper

C/ DE CERMEÑO

Hospital
del Mar
3

C/ DEL GAS

C/ DE TRELAWNY

3

Parc de la
Barceloneta

PG DE SALVAT PAPASSEIT

60

185
186
44 128

Platja de la
Barceloneta

Poliesportiu
Marítim

C/ DE SALAMANCA

C/ DE SANTA LLUISA DE MARILLAC

C/ D'ALMIRALL BARCELÓ

C/ DE SÒRIA

C/ DE BERENGUER MALLOL

PG MARÍTIM DE LA BARCELONETA

Platja de la
Barceloneta

4

© Explorer Group Ltd. 2007

A B C

Barcelona Explorer 1st Edition

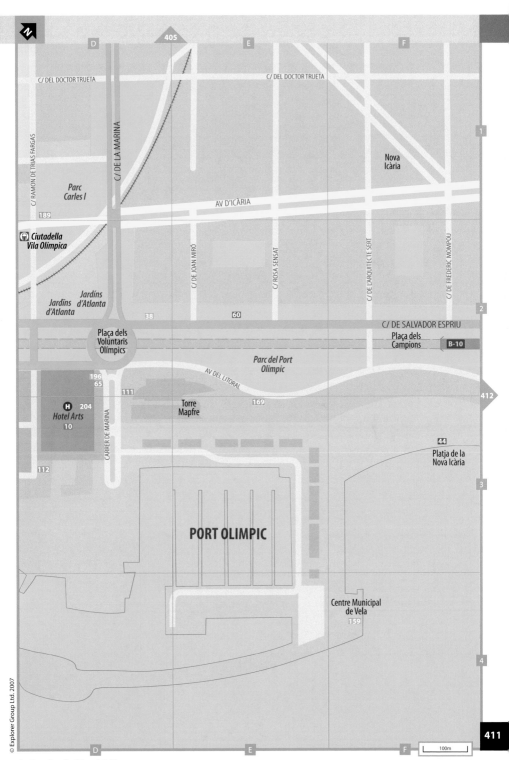

© Explorer Group Ltd. 2007

405

D   E   F

C/ DEL DOCTOR TRUETA

C/ DEL DOCTOR TRUETA

1

Nova
Icària

C/ RAMON DE TRIAS FARGAS

C/ DE LA MARINA

Parc
Carles I

189

AV D'ICÀRIA

Ciutadella
Vila Olímpica

C/ DE JOAN MIRÓ

C/ ROSA SENSAT

C/ DE L'ARQUITECTE SERT

C/ DE FREDERIC MOMPOU

2

Jardíns
d'Atlanta
Jardíns
d'Atlanta

38

60

C/ DE SALVADOR ESPRIU

Plaça dels
Voluntaris
Olímpics

Plaça dels
Campions

B-10

Parc del Port
Olímpic

196
65

111

AV DEL LITORAL

169

412

CARRER DE MARINA

204

Hotel Arts
10

Torre
Mapfre

44

Platja de la
Nova Icària

112

3

PORT OLIMPIC

Centre Municipal
de Vela

159

4

100m

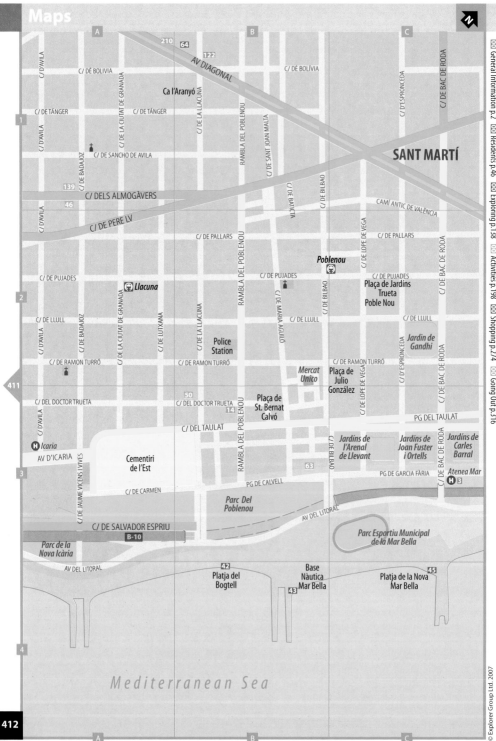

SANT MARTÍ

Mediterranean Sea

© Explorer Group Ltd. 2007

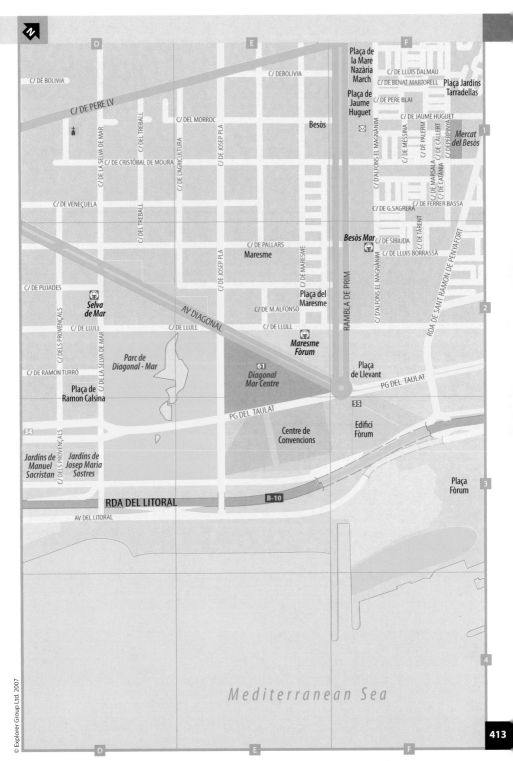

Not big, but very clever...

Perfectly proportioned to fit in your pocket, this marvellous mini guidebook makes sure you don't just get the holiday you paid for but rather the one that you dreamed of.

Sydney Mini Visitors' Guide
Maximising your holiday, minimising your hand luggage

Index

Index

The Complete **Residents'** Guide

Residents' Guides

All you need to know about living, working and enjoying life in these exciting destinations

Abu Dhabi

Amsterdam

Bahrain

Barcelona

Beijing *

Berlin

Dubai

Dublin

Geneva

Hong Kong

Kuala Lumpur *

Kuwait

London

Los Angeles

New York

New Zealand

Oman

Paris

Qatar

Shanghai

Singapore

Sydney

Tokyo *

Vancouver

Mini Guides
The perfect pocket-sized
Visitors' Guides

Mini Maps
Wherever you are,
never get lost again

Photography Books
Beautiful cities caught through the lens

Calendars
The time, the place, and the date

Maps
Wherever you are, never get lost again

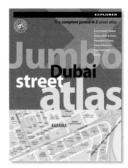

Activity and Lifestyle Guides
Drive, trek, dive and swim... life will never be boring again

Retail sales

Our books are available in most good bookshops around the world, and are also available online at Amazon.co.uk and Amazon.com. If you would like to enquire about any of our international distributors, please contact retail@explorerpublishing.com

Bulk sales and customisation

All our products are available for bulk sales with customisation options. For discount rates and further information, please contact corporatesales@explorerpublishing.com

Licensing and digital sales

All our content, maps and photography are available for print or digital use. For licensing enquiries please contact licensing@explorerpublishing.com

429

Ahmed Mainodin
AKA: Mystery Man
We can never recognise Ahmed because of his constantly changing facial hair. He waltzes in with big lambchop sideburns one day, a handlebar moustache the next, and a neatly trimmed goatee after that. So far we've had no objections to his hirsute chameleonisms, but we'll definitely draw the line at a monobrow.

Bahrudeen Abdul
AKA: The Stallion
Having tired of creating abstract sculptures out of papier maché and candy canes, Bahrudeen turned to the art of computer programming. After honing his skills in the southern Andes for three years he grew bored of Patagonian winters, and landed a job here, 'The Home of 01010101 Creative Freedom'.

Ajay Krishnan R
AKA: Web Wonder
Ajay's mum and dad knew he was going to be an IT genius when they found him reconfiguring his Commodore 64 at the tender age of 2. He went on to become the technology consultant on all three Matrix films, and counts Keanu as a close personal friend.

Ben Merrett
AKA: Big Ben
After a short (or tall as the case may have been) career as a human statue, Ben tired of the pigeons choosing him, rather than his namesake, as a public convenience and decided to fly the nest to seek his fortune in foreign lands. Not only is he big on personality but he brings in the big bucks with his bulk!

Alex Jeffries
AKA: Easy Rider
Alex is happiest when dressed in leather from head to toe with a humming machine between his thighs – just like any other motorbike enthusiast. Whenever he's not speeding along the Hatta Road at full throttle, he can be found at his beloved Mac, still dressed in leather.

Cherry Enriquez
AKA: Bean Counter
With the team's penchant for sweets and pastries, it's good to know we have Cherry on top of our accounting cake. The local confectioner is always paid on time, so we're guaranteed great gateaux for every special occasion.

Alistair MacKenzie
AKA: Media Mogul
If only Alistair could take the paperless office one step further and achieve the officeless office he would be the happiest publisher alive. Wireless access from a remote spot somewhere in the Hajar Mountains would suit this intrepid explorer – less traffic, lots of fresh air, and wearing sandals all day - the perfect work environment!

Claire England
AKA: Whip Cracker
No longer able to freeload off the fact that she once appeared in a Robbie Williams video, Claire now puts her creative skills to better use – looking up rude words in the dictionary! A child of English nobility, Claire is quite the lady – unless she's down at Jimmy Dix.

Andrea Fust
AKA: Mother Superior
By day Andrea is the most efficient manager in the world and by night she replaces the boardroom for her board and wows the pants off the dudes in Ski-Dubai. Literally. Back in the office she definitely wears the trousers!

David Quinn
AKA: Sharp Shooter
After a short stint as a children's TV presenter was robbed from David because he developed an allergy to sticky back plastic, he made his way to sandier pastures. Now that he's thinking outside the box, nothing gets past the man with the sharpest pencil in town.

Derrick Pereira
AKA: The Returnimator

After leaving Explorer in 2003, Derrick's life took a dramatic downturn – his dog ran away, his prized bonsai tree died and he got kicked out of his thrash metal band. Since rejoining us, things are looking up and he just found out he's won $10 million in a Nigerian sweepstakes competition. And he's got the desk by the window!

Iain Young
AKA: 'The Cat'

Iain follows in the fine tradition of Scots with safe hands – Alan Rough, Andy Goram, Jim Leighton on a good day – but breaking into the Explorer XI has proved frustrating. There's no match on a Mac, but that Al Huzaifa ringer doesn't half make himself big.

Enrico Maullon
AKA: The Crooner

Frequently mistaken for his near-namesake Enrique Iglesias, Enrico decided to capitalise and is now a regular stand-in for the Latin heartthrob. If he's ever missing from the office, it usually means he's off performing for millions of adoring fans on another stadium tour of America.

Ieyad Charaf
AKA: Fashion Designer

When we hired Ieyad as a top designer, we didn't realise we'd be getting his designer tops too! By far the snappiest dresser in the office, you'd be hard-pressed to beat his impeccably ironed shirts.

Firos Khan
AKA: Big Smiler

Previously a body double in kung fu movies, including several appearances in close up scenes for Steven Seagal's moustache. He also once tore down a restaurant with his bare hands after they served him a mild curry by mistake.

Ingrid Cupido
AKA: The Karaoke Queen

Ingrid has a voice to match her starlet name. She'll put any Pop Idols to shame once behind the mike, and she's pretty nifty on a keyboard too. She certainly gets our vote if she decides to go pro; just remember you saw her here first.

Hashim MM
AKA: Speedy Gonzales

They don't come much faster than Hashim – he's so speedy with his mouse that scientists are struggling to create a computer that can keep up with him. His nimble fingers leave his keyboard smouldering (he gets through three a week), and his go-faster stripes make him almost invisible to the naked eye when he moves.

Ivan Rodrigues
AKA: The Aviator

After making a mint in the airline market, Ivan came to Explorer where he works for pleasure, not money. That's his story, anyway. We know that he is actually a corporate spy from a rival company and that his multi-level spreadsheets are really elaborate codes designed to confuse us.

Helen Spearman
AKA: Little Miss Sunshine

With her bubbly laugh and permanent smile, Helen is a much-needed ray of sunshine in the office when we're all grumpy and facing harrowing deadlines. It's almost impossible to think that she ever loses her temper or shows a dark side... although put her behind the wheel of a car, and you've got instant road rage.

Jake Marsico
AKA: Don Calzone

Jake spent the last 10 years on the tiny triangular Mediterranean island of Samoza, honing his traditional cooking techniques and perfecting his Italian. Now, whenever he returns to his native America, he impresses his buddies by effortlessly zapping a hot dog to perfection in any microwave, anywhere, anytime.

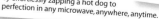

Henry Hilos
AKA: The Quiet Man

Henry can rarely be seen from behind his large obstructive screen but when you do catch a glimpse you'll be sure to get a smile. Lighthearted Henry keeps all those glossy pages filled with pretty pictures for something to look at when you can't be bothered to read.

Jane Roberts
AKA: The Oracle

After working in an undisclosed role in the government, Jane brought her super sleuth skills to Explorer. Whatever the question, she knows what, where, who, how and when, but her encyclopaedic knowledge is only impressive until you realise she just makes things up randomly.

Jayde Fernandes
AKA: Pop Idol
Jayde's idol is Britney Spears, and he recently shaved his head to show solidarity with the troubled star. When he's not checking his dome for stubble, or practising the dance moves to 'Baby One More Time' in front of the bathroom mirror, he actually manages to get some designing done.

Johny Mathew
AKA: The Hawker
Caring Johny used to nurse wounded eagles back to health and teach them how to fly again before trying his luck in merchandising. Fortunately his skills in the field have come in handy at Explorer, where his efforts to improve our book sales have been a soaring success.

Kate Fox
AKA: Contacts Collector
Kate swooped into the office like the UK equivalent of Wonderwoman, minus the tights of course (it's much too hot for that), but armed with a superhuman marketing brain. Even though she 's just arrived, she is already a regular on the Dubai social scene – she is helping to blast Explorer into the stratosphere, one champagne-soaked networking party at a time.

Katie Drynan
AKA: The Irish Deputy
Katie is a Jumeira Jane in training, and has 35 sisters who take it in turns to work in the Explorer office while she enjoys testing all the beauty treatments available on the Beach Road. This Irish charmer met an oil tycoon in Paris, and they now spend the weekends digging very deep holes in their new garden.

Kiran Melwani
AKA: Bow Selector
Like a modern-day Robin Hood (right down to the green tights and band of merry men), Kiran's mission in life is to distribute Explorer's wealth of knowledge to the fact-hungry readers of the world. Just make sure you never do anything to upset her – rumour has it she's a pretty mean shot with that bow and arrow.

Lennie Mangalino
AKA: Shaker Maker
With a giant spring in her step and music in her heart it's hard to not to swing to the beat when Lennie passes by in the office. She loves her Lambada… and Samba… and Salsa and anything else she can get the sales team shaking their hips to.

Mannie Lugtu
AKA: Distribution Demon
When the travelling circus rode into town, their master juggler Mannie decided to leave the Big Top and explore Dubai instead. He may have swapped his balls for our books but his juggling skills still come in handy.

Maricar Ong
AKA: Pocket Docket
A pint-sized dynamo of ruthless efficiency, Maricar gets the job done before anyone else notices it needed doing. If this most able assistant is absent for a moment, it sends a surge of blind panic through the Explorer ranks.

Grace Carnay
AKA: Manila Ice
It's just as well the office is so close to a movie theatre, because Grace is always keen to catch the latest Hollywood offering from Brad Pitt, who she admires purely for his acting ability, of course. Her ice cool exterior conceals a tempestuous passion for jazz, which fuels her frenzied typing speed.

Matt Farquharson
AKA: Hack Hunter
A career of tuppence-a-word hackery ended when Matt arrived in Dubai to cover a maggot wranglers' convention. He misguidedly thinks he's clever because he once wrote for some grown-up English papers.

Matthew Samuel
AKA: Mr Modest
Matt's penchant for the entrepreneurial life began with a pair of red braces and a filofax when still a child. That yearning for the cut and thrust of commerce has brought him to Dubai, where he made a fortune in the sand-selling business before semi-retiring at Explorer.

Michael Samuel
AKA: Gordon Gekko
We have a feeling this mild mannered master of mathematics has a wild side. He hasn't witnessed an Explorer party yet but the office agrees that once the karaoke machine is out, Michael will be the maestro. Watch out Dubai!

Pamela Grist
AKA: Happy Snapper
If a picture can speak a thousand words then Pam's photos say a lot about her - through her lens she manages to find the beauty in everything – even this motley crew. And when the camera never lies, thankfully Photoshop can.

Mimi Stankova
AKA: Mind Controller
A master of mind control, Mimi's siren-like voice lulls people into doing whatever she asks. Her steely reserve and endless patience mean recalcitrant reporters and persistent PR people are putty in her hands, delivering whatever she wants, whenever she wants it.

Pete Maloney
AKA: Graphic Guru
Image conscious he may be, but when Pete has his designs on something you can bet he's gonna get it! He's the king of chat up lines, ladies – if he ever opens a conversation with 'D'you come here often?' then brace yourself for the Maloney magic.

Rafi Jamal
AKA: Soap Star
After a walk on part in The Bold and the Beautiful, Rafi swapped the Hollywood Hills for the Hajar Mountains. Although he left the glitz behind, he still mingles with high society, moonlighting as a male gigolo and impressing Dubai's ladies with his fancy footwork.

Mohammed Sameer
AKA: Man in the Van
Known as MS, short for Microsoft, Sameer can pick apart a PC like a thief with a lock, which is why we keep him out of finance and pounding Dubai's roads in the unmissable Explorer van – so we can always spot him coming.

Mohammed T
AKA: King of the Castle
T is Explorer's very own Bedouin warehouse dweller; under his caring charge all Explorer stock is kept in masterful order. Arrive uninvited and you'll find T, meditating on a pile of maps, amid an almost eerie sense of calm.

Rafi VP
AKA: Party Trickster
After developing a rare allergy to sunlight in his teens, Rafi started to lose a few centimeters of height every year. He now stands just 30cm tall, and does his best work in our dingy basement wearing a pair of infrared goggles. His favourite party trick is to fold himself into a briefcase, and he was once sick in his hat.

Noushad Madathil
AKA: Map Daddy
Where would Explorer be without the mercurial Madathil brothers? Lost in the Empty Quarter, that's where. Quieter than a mute dormouse, Noushad prefers to let his Photoshop layers, and brother Zain, do all the talking. A true Map Daddy.

Richard Greig
AKA: Sir Lancelot
Chivalrous to the last, Richard's dream of being a mediaeval knight suffered a setback after being born several centuries too late. His stellar parliamentary career remains intact, and he is in the process of creating a new party with the aim of abolishing all onions and onion-related produce.

Roshni Ahuja
AKA: Bright Spark
Never failing to brighten up the office with her colourful get-up, Roshni definitely puts the 'it' in the IT department. She's a perennially pleasant, profound programmer with peerless panache, and she does her job with plenty of pep and piles of pizzazz.

Sunita Lakhiani
AKA: Designlass
Initially suspicious of having a female in their midst, the boys in Designlab now treat Sunita like one of their own. A big shame for her, because they treat each other pretty damn bad!

Sean Kearns
AKA: The Tall Guy
Big Sean, as he's affectionately known, is so laid back he actually spends most of his time lying down (unless he's on a camping trip, when his ridiculously small tent forces him to sleep on his hands and knees). Despite the rest of us constantly tripping over his lanky frame, when the job requires someone who will work flat out, he always rises to the editorial occasion.

Steve Jones
AKA: Golden Boy
Our resident Kiwi lives in a nine-bedroom mansion and is already planning an extension. His winning smile has caused many a knee to weaken in Bur Dubai but sadly for the ladies, he's hopelessly devoted to his clients.

Shabsir M
AKA: Sticky Wicket
Shabsir is a valuable player on the Indian national cricket team, so instead of working you'll usually find him autographing cricket balls for crazed fans around the world. We don't mind though – if ever a retailer is stumped because they run out of stock, he knocks them for six with his speedy delivery.

Tim Binks
AKA: Class Clown
El Binksmeisterooney is such a sharp wit, he often has fellow Explorers gushing tea from their noses in convulsions of mirth. Years spent hiking across the Middle East have given him an encyclopaedic knowledge of rock formations and elaborate hair.

Shawn Jackson Zuzarte
AKA: Paper Plumber
If you thought rocket science was hard, try rearranging the chaotic babble that flows from the editorial team! If it weren't for Shawn, most of our books would require a kaleidoscope to read correctly so we're keeping him and his jazz hands under wraps.

Tom Jordan
AKA: The True Professional
Explorer's resident thesp, Tom delivers lines almost as well as he cuts them. His early promise on the pantomime circuit was rewarded with an all-action role in hit UK drama Heartbeat. He's still living off the royalties – and the fact he shared a sandwich with Kenneth Branagh.

Shefeeq M
AKA: Rapper in Disguise
So new he's still got the wrapper on, Shefeeq was dragged into the Explorer office, and put to work in the design department. The poor chap only stopped by to ask for directions to Wadi Bih, but since we realised how efficient he is, we keep him chained to his desk.

Tracy Fitzgerald
AKA: 'La Dona'
Tracy is a queenpin Catalan mafiosa and ringleader for the 'pescadora' clan, a nefarious group that runs a sushi smuggling operation between the Costa Brava and Ras Al Khaimah. She is not to be crossed. Rival clans will find themselves fed fish, and then fed to the fishes.

Shyrell Tamayo
AKA: Fashion Princess
We've never seen Shyrell wearing the same thing twice – her clothes collection is so large that her husband has to keep all his things in a shoebox. She runs Designlab like clockwork, because being late for deadlines is SO last season.

Zainudheen Madathil
AKA: Map Master
Often confused with retired footballer Zinedine Zidane because of his dexterous displays and a bad head-butting habit, Zain tackles design with the mouse skills of a star striker. Maps are his goal and despite getting red-penned a few times, when he shoots, he scores.

The *Barcelona Explorer* Team
Lead Editor Matt Farquharson
Deputy Editor Tracy Fitzgerald
Editorial Assistant Grace Carnay
Designer Jayde Fernandes
Cartographers Noushad Madathil, Ashiq Babu,
Ramlath Kambravan
Photographers Victor Romero, Matt Farquharson
Proof Readers Joanna Holden-MacDonald, Kaye Holland

Publisher
Alistair MacKenzie

Editorial
Managing Editor Claire England
Lead Editors David Quinn, Jane Roberts, Matt Farquharson,
Sean Kearns, Tim Binks, Tom Jordan
Deputy Editors Helen Spearman, Jakob Marsico,
Katie Drynan, Pamela Afram, Richard Greig, Tracy Fitzgerald
Editorial Assistants Grace Carnay, Ingrid Cupido, Mimi Stankova

Design
Creative Director Pete Maloney
Art Director Ieyad Charaf
Senior Designers Alex Jeffries, Iain Young
Layout Manager Jayde Fernandes
Layouters Hashim Moideen, Rafi Pullat,
Shefeeq Marakkatepurath
Junior Layouter Shawn Jackson Zuzarte
Cartography Manager Zainudheen Madathil
Cartographers Noushad Madathil, Sunita Lakhiani
Design Admin Manager Shyrell Tamayo
Production Coordinator Maricar Ong

Photography
Photography Manager Pamela Grist
Photographer Victor Romero
Image Editor Henry Hilos

Sales & Marketing
Area Sales Managers Laura Zuffa, Stephen Jones
Corporate Sales Executive Ben Merrett
Marketing Manager Kate Fox
Marketing Executive Annabel Clough
Retail Sales Manager Ivan Rodrigues
Retail Sales Coordinator Kiran Melwani
Retail Sales Supervisor Matthew Samuel
Merchandiser Johny Mathew
Sales & Marketing Coordinator Lennie Mangalino
Distribution Executives Ahmed Mainodin, Firos Khan, Mannie Lugtu
Warehouse Assistants Mohammed Kunjaymo, Najumudeen K.I.
Drivers Mohammed Sameer, Shabsir Madathil

Finance & Administration
Finance Manager Michael Samuel
HR & Administration Manager Andrea Fust
Accounts Assistant Cherry Enriquez
Administrators Enrico Maullon, Kelly Tesoro
Driver Rafi Jamal

IT
IT Administrator Ajay Krishnan R.
Software Engineers Bahrudeen Abdul, Roshni Ahuja
Digital Content Manager Derrick Pereira

Contact Us

Reader Response
If you have any comments and suggestions, fill out
our online reader response form and you could win prizes.
Log on to **www.explorerpublishing.com**

General Enquiries
We'd love to hear your thoughts and answer any questions
you have about this book or any other Explorer product.
Contact us at **info@explorerpublishing.com**

Careers
If you fancy yourself as an Explorer, send your CV
(stating the position you're interested in) to
jobs@explorerpublishing.com

Designlab & Contract Publishing
For enquiries about Explorer's Contract Publishing arm
and design services contact
designlab@explorerpublishing.com

PR & Marketing
For PR and marketing enquiries contact
marketing@explorerpublishing.com
pr@explorerpublishing.com

Corporate Sales
For bulk sales and customisation options, for this book or
any Explorer product, contact
sales@explorerpublishing.com

Advertising & Sponsorship
For advertising and sponsorship, contact
media@explorerpublishing.com

Explorer Publishing & Distribution
PO Box 34275, Dubai
United Arab Emirates
Phone: +971 (0)4 340 88 05
Fax: +971 (0)4 340 88 06
www.explorerpublishing.com

Emergency Services

24 Hour Pharmacy Information	93 481 00 60
Bomberos (Fire Services)	80
General Emergencies	112
Guardia Urbana (City Police)	92
Medical Emergencies	61
Mossos d'Esquadra (Catalan Police)	88
Policía Nacional (State Police)	91

Airport Information

Emergencies	93 297 12 19
General Information	902 404 704

Lost Luggage

Air France	902 190 947
Flightcare	93 298 33 30
Groundforce	93 298 48 49
Iberia	93 401 31 29
Newco Spanair	93 298 34 39

Helplines

Addiction Counselling	93 291 91 31
Alcoholics Anonymous	616 684 338
Barcelona NEST	93 586 35 30
Centre Medic Terapeutic	93 490 66 66
Centre Medicina Esportiva	93 487 43 74
Centre Rehabilitació	93 221 37 22
Connie Capdevila (family therapy)	93 217 98 41
Jill Jenkins (child psychologist)	93 586 35 30
Narcóticos Anónimos	902 114 147
Servimèdic Rehabilitació i Traumatologia	93 490 62 33

Money Exchange Centers

Chequepoint	900 354 538
Inter Change	93 481 49 15
Maccorp Exact Change	93 342 51 60
Money Exchange	93 324 82 59

City Information Online

City Government Services	www.bcn.cat
City Transport Network	www.tmb.net
Interactive City Map	www.bcncat/guia/welcomec.htm
Local Weather	www.meteocat.com
Online Maps	www.euroave.com
Online Maps	www.maps.google.es
Tourism Department	www.turismedebarcelona.com
Transport Links	www.atm.cat

Motorbike & Scooter Hire

BarcelonaMoto.com	600 370 343
Motissimo	93 490 84 01
Quads & Mopeds to Rent	97 234 13 10
Vanguard	93 439 38 80

Main Government Hospitals

Hospital Clínic i Provincial	93 227 54 00
Hospital de l'Esperança	93 367 41 00
Hospital del Mar	93 248 30 00
Hospital Santa Creu i Sant Pau	93 291 90 00
Hospital Vall d´Hebrón	93 274 60 00

Transport

Acciona Trasmediterrànea (Ferries)	93 295 91 00
Barna Bikes	93 269 02 04
Bicing	902 315 531
Budget Bikes	93 304 18 85
EMT (Buses)	93 223 51 51
FGC (Trains)	93 205 15 15
General Information	10
Iscomar (Ferries)	902 119 128
Metro	93 318 70 74
Renfe (Trains)	90 224 02 02
Trams	902 193 275

Taxi Companies

Barcelona Taxi Van	670 531 619
Fonotaxi	93 300 11 00
Radio Taxi 033	93 303 30 33
Servitaxi	93 330 03 00
Taxi Amic	93 420 80 88

Embassies & Consulates

Australia	93 490 90 13
Austria	91 556 53 15
Belgium	93 467 70 80
Brazil	93 488 22 88
Canada	93 412 72 36
China	93 254 11 96
Denmark	93 488 02 22
France	93 317 81 50
Germany	93 292 10 00
Greece	93 321 28 28
Holland	93 363 54 20
Hungary	93 405 19 50
India	90 290 10 10
Ireland	93 491 50 21
Italy	93 467 73 05
Japan	93 280 34 33
Mexico	93 201 18 22
New Zealand	93 209 03 99
Norway	93 218 49 83
Poland	93 322 72 34
Portugal	93 318 81 50
Russian Federation	93 204 02 46
South Africa	91 436 37 80
Sweden	93 488 25 01
Switzerland	93 409 06 50
United Kingdom	93 366 62 00
United States	93 280 22 27